A Leonard Bloomfield Anthology

Leonard Bloomfield
April 6, 1944.

# A
# Leonard Bloomfield
# Anthology

EDITED BY

CHARLES F. HOCKETT

INDIANA UNIVERSITY PRESS

BLOOMINGTON · LONDON

# Contents

# Editor's Preface

In 1961, when plans for the present work were still tenuous, I wrote to Bernard Bloch soliciting his suggestions as to which of Bloomfield's articles should be included. He responded with a list of 49 titles (which he thought was perhaps too many for practicality), and commented as follows:

> I put in everything that seemed for some reason particularly interesting or revealing of Bloomfield's way of working, his personality, his pet ideas, and his chief lines of work; I included working articles, general statements of principles, reviews good and bad [i.e., favorable and unfavorable], obituaries, because each in its way struck me as typical and important. Some articles that I have left out have almost as good a reason for being in as these, but for one reason or another they interest me less.

This is as clear a statement as one could ask for of the aims that should be served by a volume of reprints of Bloomfield's writings. I would add only that the selections ought to show how Bloomfield's interests and attitudes changed with the passing years.

Lesser scholars than Bloomfield have been honored after death by the republication of everything they ever wrote. In Bloomfield's case that would amount to something like twelve volumes of the size of his 1933 *Language*, if my rough computation is correct—or, if only pieces in journals were included, to four or five volumes of that size. But no purpose would be served. Even among the journal articles, there are some that are readily available for the specialized scholars who need them, and of no great interest to others—a fact which in no way reflects on their quality, which is almost uniformly of the highest. In deciding what *not* to include here, I have been guided by the following principles:

First: language-teaching materials are excluded. Bloomfield's abiding interest in this aspect of applied linguistics is represented by our items B4 and B63.

Second: books still in print and available to those who want them have not been drawn on. This applies especially to the 1933 *Language*.

Third: technical material of primary interest to specialists in a particular branch or area of linguistics has been set aside except for representative samples. Bloomfield's research in Germanic was much more extensive than our few items (B1, B20, B34, B48) would suggest: see Moulton's discussion in item 69. The balance is in the journals, in libraries all over the world, where it belongs.

Fourth: items superseded by later articles from Bloomfield's own pen are excluded, except for some early writings included to show how his views changed in the course of his career, and except, in a few instances, for brief passages of general interest that are not repeated or paraphrased in the later reworking. On the second score, his 1925 'On the Sound System of Central Algonquian' was unquestionably a masterpiece, but was entirely reworked and updated in the 1944 'Algonquian' (B65)— except for the single footnote of the former, which we reprint (B19). This fourth principle has been violated in one case: 'Menomini Morphophonemics' (1939; our B50). Some of those who have counseled me have suggested that it might have been violated also in order to include some excerpts from the 1914 *Introduction to the Study of Language*, now long out of print. I have not done so, feeling that the early articles reprinted here do his early approach justice, that it would be difficult to know what passages to choose from the book, and that Bloomfield himself replaced the whole book in 1933.

Finally: Bloomfield treated some topics in different ways for different audiences, and only the best version (as I judge the matter) is reprinted here. The chief example is the 1939 monograph *Linguistic Aspects of Science*, from which we draw only one unusually penetrating and characteristic passage (B51). Otherwise, this work largely duplicates the 1935 article 'Linguistic Aspects of Science' (B44), enlarging on it mainly by way of material designed to tell the linguistically untrained reader about language.

Perhaps a sixth principle played some part in my decisions: I suspect that an item originally printed in a relatively obscure place tended to appeal to me more than one I had known about for a long time.

After a complete selection had been worked out on the principles described above, practical exigencies forced certain modifications. It had been my plan to include the entire section on sound system and grammar from the *Tagalog Texts* of 1917, which runs to nearly 200 pages. It is true that the Malayo-Polynesian specialist has access to this work when he needs it; but it seemed to me desirable that the *Anthology* include one extended example of Bloomfield's way of organizing and presenting the enormously complicated details of a single language. But this 'excerpt' would have been a heavy enough straw to break the camel's back, and it had to be deleted. In part by way of compensation, but in part also at the urging of the members of the Editorial Advisory Committee of the Indiana University Studies in the History and Theory of Linguistics, item B50 now reprints the 'Menomini Morphophonemics' in its entirety (against principle number four), for its historical importance, instead of as an abbreviated excerpt. I think I should emphasize that I have no objections to this inclusion; the original abbreviated form of B50 had been proposed only to save space.

It turns out, then, that all but five of the 49 articles recommended by Bloch are included. Two of those five (B19, B54) are represented by excerpts. One of the others is the 1941 'Proto-Algonquian –*i·t*– "Fellow"'', excluded on the third principle and to save space. Another is the 1942 'Outline of Ilocano Syntax'—unfortunately, with the consequence that Bloomfield's work on Malayo-Polynesian is sadly underrepresented. The last is the 1929 'Notes on the Preverb *ge*- in Alfredian English', taken out late in the editing process to make room for the 1925 'Einiges vom germanischen Wortschatz' (B20) on a suggestion from W. G. Moulton. The 'Notes' is more interesting to those Germanicists whose concentration is on Old English, the 'Einiges' more interesting to those who are specialists in German or in Germanic as a whole; either serves very well to demonstrate Bloomfield's understanding of Germanic, and the one we have chosen also shows—if any evidence be needed—that he could write excellent German as well as excellent English.

Bloch did not list the following items of those that appear here: B1, B3, B5, B10, B12, B14, B20, B22, part of B29, B46, B47, B51, B53, B55, B62, and B66.

To round things out I have added material that is about Bloomfield rather than by him: items 7, 11, 15, 41, 68, 69, and 70. Item 69 was prepared by W. G. Moulton especially for this volume, for which I tender him my sincerest thanks.

The ordering is essentially chronological; the few departures will be self-explanatory. Comments in square brackets, initialled whenever there could be any question, are mine. Bloomfield's wording and punctuation (or that of the other writers involved) are never altered—unless quite unwittingly, for in a few cases I have tried to undo what I suspect was imposed on the original manuscript by an editor or typesetter. The numbering of footnotes in the originals has not been regarded as important: I have renumbered whenever there was reason to do so.

In many of the interpolated notes the reader will detect the personality of the editor. I believe it would be dishonest to pretend that it is not there, and I have not hesitated to speak in a personal vein whenever I have felt that that could reveal more of the character of Leonard Bloomfield than would otherwise be possible. However, my own current opinions on matters of substance are not expressed.

No one will be entirely satisfied with the exact choice of materials for this *Anthology*. I am not completely satisfied myself, but have been unable to find any feasible alternative that suits me better. But this admission implies no abrogation of responsibility: criticisms of my choices should be directed at me, not at any of those who have kindly given me the benefit of their counsel.

Bloomfield's voice of wisdom has been stilled for two decades. The mantle of leadership which he wore so gracefully, obvious to all others but invisible to his own perception, has fallen to the ground, for none of us has had the wisdom or power to bear it. We cannot know what would have been his considered opinion of the many new or renovated proposals that have been the topics of our discussions in these twenty years; if we could, we might not agree, but our own views would be the better for the exchange. We can still know, if we will but heed, his reaction to the pettishness, the prima-donnaism, the neglect of already accumulated experience, and the antiscientific bias that have all too often characterized our discussions; for these things are not new, and he spoke critically and cogently of them in his day. That is an important reason for the publication of this volume.

CHARLES F. HOCKETT

Ithaca, N.Y.
March, 1968

# Acknowledgments

All royalties earned by this book, beyond minimal clerical expenses, are payable to the Bernard and Julia Bloch Memorial Fund of the Linguistic Society of America.

Permission to prepare and publish the volume was kindly granted to the editor and publisher by The Northern Trust Company of Chicago, Illinois, in its capacity as cotrustee of the Bloomfield Estate.

A number of the editor's colleagues have been extremely helpful; they and other individuals are named at appropriate places in what follows, particularly in section 70 (2).

Permission to reprint articles, excerpts, and other writings has been granted by the individuals and agencies listed below. Most of the sources are nonprofit scholarly journals. It is gratifying to be able to report that none of these have required more than a nominal reprint fee, and that most requested no fee at all. In this way, they become genuine cosponsors of the book. The editor is deeply grateful.

The sections of the present book are here listed in order, each followed either by the agency which has granted permission to reprint or by a cross-reference to an earlier entry in which the agency has already been named.

B1, B24, B28. The University of Chicago Press, the journal *Modern Philology*, and its current editor Prof. Donald F. Bond.

B2, 7 (Aron's review), 11, B14, 15, B16. The Johns Hopkins Press, *The American Journal of Philology*, and its current editor Prof. Henry T. Rowell.

B3, B5, 7 (Diekhoff's review), B23, 41 (Kroesch's review). The University of Illinois Press and *The Journal of English and Germanic Philology*.

B4, B58, B64. The Regents of the University of Wisconsin (copyright owners), The University of Wisconsin Press, and *Monatshefte für deutschen Unterricht* (the earlier *Monatshefte für deutsche Sprache und Pädagogik*).

B5: see B3.

B6. *The American Journal of Psychology* and its current editor, Prof. Karl M. Dallenbach.

7, 41 (excerpts from Bloomfield's *Introduction* and *Language*). Both books were originally published and copyrighted by Henry Holt and Co., to which, in 1959, Holt, Rinehart and Winston, Inc., became the successors. In granting permission for the inclusion of brief excerpts in the present book, Holt, Rinehart and Winston, Inc. have specified an exact format and location for the acknowledgements. Formal acknowledgment is therefore given as a footnote at each relevant place. The reader should note that these acknowledgments do not reflect the actual publication and copyright history of the two books; that is given in full at the beginnings of 7 and 41.

7 (Diekhoff's review): see B3.

7 (Bolling's review), B13, 41 (Sturtevant's review). *The Classical World* (formerly *The Classical Weekly*) and its current editor-in-chief, Prof. Edward A. Robinson.

7 (Aron's review): see B2.

B8, B9. The American Philological Association and its current Secretary-Treasurer, Prof. William M. Minton.

B10. The University of Illinois Press and the editors of *University of Illinois Publications in Language and Literature*.

11: see B2.

B12. The recipient of this letter very kindly gave me permission to print it when I was editing Bloomfield's *The Menomini Language* (Yale University Press, 1962) for publication.

B13: see 7 (Bolling's review).

B14: see B2.

15: see B2.

B16: see B2.

B17. *The Modern Language Journal* and its current managing editor, Prof. Robert F. Roeming.

B18, B19, B21, B27, B30, B33, B34, B35, B37, B38, B39, 41 (Kent and Bolling reviews), B42, B43, B45, B46, B48, B49, B59, B60, B62, B67, 68, 70 (Bloch's obituary). The Linguistic Society of America and its current Secretary-Treasurer, Prof. Archibald A. Hill.

B19: see B18.

B20. Max Niemeyer Verlag, Tübingen (successor to Max Niemeyer Verlag, Halle).

B21: see B18.

B22. Carm, de Ruyter and Co., Hamburg (successor to M. L. Friedrichsen and Co.).

B23: see B3. George Allen and Unwin Ltd., London, for the paragraph cited from Jespersen's *Philosophy of Grammar*.

B24: see B1.

B25, B61. Columbia University Press and *American Speech*.

B26, 41 (Edgerton review). The American Oriental Society and Prof. Ernest Bender, current editor of its *Journal*.

B27: see B18.

B28: see B1.

B29. The International Phonetic Association and A. C. Gimsen, Hon. Secretary and Editor of *Le Maître Phonétique.*

B30: see B18.

B31. The *Atti del XXII Congresso Internazionale degli Americanisti* were not copyrighted. Correspondence with a colleague in Rome (Dr. Mario Saltarelli) revealed that both its publisher and its printer have vanished without legal successors. The International Congresses of Americanists maintain no permanent secretariat or continuing committee. Dr. Sol Tax was the editor for the most recent International Congress of Americanists to be held in the United States (1949); in that capacity he has granted the permission.

B32. The University of Washington Press and Dr. June Helm, current editor of the American Ethnological Society.

B33: see B18.

B34. see B18.

B35: see B18.

B36. *Studies in Philology* and its current editor, Prof. O. B. Hardison, Jr.

B37: see B18.

B38: see B18.

B39: see B18.

B40. The Institute for Research in Language Teaching (formerly The Institute for Research in English Teaching), Tokyo, and its secretary, the Hon. Y. Hiyane.

41 (excerpts from Bloomfield): see 7

41 (Edgerton's review): see B26.

41 (Kroesch's review): see B3.

41 (Meillet's review). The Société de Linguistique de Paris and its current Secrétaire-générale, Prof. E. Benveniste.

41 (Sturtevant's review): see 7.

41 (Kent and Bolling reviews): see B18.

41 (Debrunner's review): Walter de Gruyter and Co., and Prof. Dr. W. P. Schmidt, current coeditor of *Indogermanische Forschungen.*

B42: see B18.

B43: see B18.

B44. The Williams and Wilkins Publishing Company.

B45: see B18.

B46: see B18.

B47. (Never before published.)

B48: see B18.

B49: see B18.

B50. The Académie Tchécoslovaque des Sciences, and J. Vachek, its Rédacteur Scientifique.

B51. The University of Chicago Press.

B52. The Modern Language Association of Southern California, and Mrs. Betty Benson, its President.

B53. After Bernard Bloch's death, Walter Bloch kindly gave me access to the file of correspondence between his father and Leonard Bloomfield, and granted permission for the printing of these letters.

B55. Clarence L. Barnhart. A revised form of this story appears in *Let's Read: A Linguistic Approach* by Leonard Bloomfield and Clarence L. Barnhart; copyright 1961 by Clarence L. Barnhart; all rights reserved.

B56. The National Council of Teachers of English and their current director of publications, Mrs. Enid M. Olson.

B57. The American Council of Learned Societies.

B58: see B4.

B59: see B18.

B60: see B18.

B60 (excerpt in footnote), B65. The Wenner-Gren Foundation for Anthropological Research, and its Director of Research, Mrs. Lita Osmundsen.

B61: see B25.

B62: see B18.

B63. *The Yale Review*.

B64: see B4.

B65: see B60.

B66. The Yale University Press.

B67: see B18.

68: see B18.

70 (Bloch's obituary): see B18.

70 (Sturtevant's obituary). The American Philosophical Society and its Executive Officer, Mr. George W. Corner.

70 (Hall's obituary). J. H. Gottmer, Publisher, and Prof. A. Reichling, Editor of *Lingua*.

# Bibliography

This is as complete as possible, based mainly on the listing given in *Language* 25.94–98 (1949) at the end of Bernard Bloch's obituary notice. The dates of works published (or to be published) posthumously are marked here and elsewhere with a dagger.

1909.   *Before Dawn: A Social Drama* (translation of Gerhart Hauptmann's *Vor Sonnenaufgang*, 1889). *Poet Lore* 20.241–315. Also published as a separately bound book, with unchanged pagination; Boston: The Gorham Press.

'A Semasiologic Differentiation in Germanic Secondary Ablaut' (University of Chicago Dissertation), Part I. *Modern Philology* 7.245–288.     B1. (excerpts)

1910.   (ditto), Part II. *Modern Philology* 7.345–382.

1911.   'The Indo-European Palatals in Sanskrit' *American Journal of Philology* 32.36–57.     B2.

Review: Richard Loewe, *Deutsches Wörterbuch* (Sammlung Göschen No. 64, 1910). *Journal of English and Germanic Philology* 10.122–129.

Review: Heinrich Schröder, *Ablautstudien* (Heidelberg, 1910). *Journal of English and Germanic Philology* 10.131–135.

Review: Francis A. Wood, *Indo-European $a^x : a^x i : a^x u$. A Study in Ablaut and in Word-Formation* (Strassburg, 1905). *Journal of English and Germanic Philology* 10.628–631.     B3.

1912.   'The *E*-Sounds in the Language of Hans Sachs.' *Modern Philology* 9.489–509. Dated Cincinnati, 30 December 1909.

'A Type of Scandinavian Word-Formation.' *Publications of the Society for the Advancement of Scandinavian Studies* 1.45–53.

'Etymologisches.' *Beiträge zur Geschichte der deutschen Sprache und Literatur* [*Paul und Braunes Beiträge*] 37.245–261.

Review: Wilhelm Braune, *Althochdeutsche Grammatik*, 3. u. 4. Aufl. (Halle a/S, 1911). *Journal of English and Germanic Philology* 11.269–274.

Review: Alfred Dwight Sheffield, *Grammar and Thinking: A Study in the Working Concepts in Syntax* (New York and London, 1912). *Journal of English and Germanic Philology* 11.619–624.          B5.

Review: Eduard Prokosch, *An Introduction to German* (New York, 1911). *Monatshefte für deutsche Sprache und Pädagogik* 13.92.          B4.

1913.  Review: Wilhelm Wundt, *Elemente der Völkerpsychologie: Grundlinien einer psychologischen Entwicklungsgeschichte der Menschheit*, 2. Aufl. (Leipzig 1913). *American Journal of Psychology* 24.449–453.          B6.

1914.  *An Introduction to the Study of Language.* New York: Henry Holt and Company; London: G. Bell.

Reviewed by:

Tobias Diekhoff (University of Michigan), *Journal of English and Germanic Philology* 14.593–597 (1915).          7(1).

George M. Bolling (Ohio State University), *The Classical Weekly* 10.166–168 (1917).          7(2).

Albert W. Aron (University of Wisconsin), *American Journal of Philology* 39.86–92 (1918); and *Monatshefte für deutsche Sprache und Pädagogik* 19.55 (1918).          7 (3).

'Sentence and Word.' *Transactions of the American Philological Association* (for 1914: published 1915) 45.65–75. Abstracted, with brief comment, in *Jahrbuch für Germanische Philologie* 38.62 (1916).          B8.

Review: Sigmund Feist, *Kultur, Ausbreitung und Herkunft der Indogermanen* (Berlin, 1913). *Journal of English and Germanic Philology* 13.472–475.

1916.  'Subject and Predicate.' *Transactions of the American Philological Association* (for 1916: published 1917) 47.13–22.          B9.

Review of: Francis A. Wood, *Some Parallel Formations in English* (Göttingen and Baltimore, 1913); Elias Wessén, *Zur Geschichte der germanischen N-Deklination* (Uppsala, 1914); Karl Kärre,

*Nomina agentis in Old English* (Uppsala, 1915);
H. O. Schwabe, *The Semantic Development of
Words for Eating and Drinking in Germanic*
(Chicago, 1915). *Journal of English and Germanic
Philology* 15.140–144.

Review: Leo Wiener, *Commentary to the Germanic
Laws and Mediaeval Documents* (Cambridge,
Mass., 1915). *Journal of English and Germanic
Philology* 15.299–304; added to Alexander
Green's review of the same work, 15.293–299.

1917. *Tagalog Texts with Grammatical Analysis. University
of Illinois Studies in Language and Literature* Vol.    B10.
3, Nos. 2–4.                                             (excerpts)

Reviewed by: Frank R. Blake (Johns Hopkins University), *American Journal of Philology* 40.86–93
(1919).                                                 11.

1918. 'Physigunkus.' *Modern Philology* 15.577–602.

1922. Review: Edward Sapir, *Language: An Introduction
to the Study of Speech* (New York, 1921). *The
Classical Weekly* 15.142–143.                          B13.

Review: Truman Michelson, *The Owl Sacred Pack
of the Fox Indians* (Washington, D. C., 1921).
*American Journal of Philology* 43.276–281.            B14.
Rejoinder by Michelson, *American Journal of
Philology* 44.285–286 (1923).                          15.

Review: Otto Jespersen, *Language: Its Nature,
Development, and Origin* (New York, 1922).
*American Journal of Philology* 43.370–373.            B16.

1923. *First German Book*. Columbus, Ohio: R. G. Adams
and Co. (copyright by Leonard Bloomfield).

1924. 'The Menomini Language.' *Proceedings of the
Twenty-First International Congress of Americanists* (First part, held at The Hague, 12–16 August
1924) 336–343; The Hague. Actually printed later
than October 1925.

Review: Ferdinand de Saussure, *Cours de Linguistique Générale*, 2d ed. (Paris, 1922). *Modern Language Journal* 8.317–319.                             B17.

1925. 'Call for the Organization Meeting' [for the formation of the Linguistic Society of America; written
by Leonard Bloomfield for the organizing committee that included also George M. Bolling and
Edgar H. Sturtevant]. *Language* 1.6–7.

'Why a Linguistic Society?' *Language* 1.1–5.          B18.

'Notes on the Fox Language' (Sections I–III). *International Journal of American Linguistics* 3.219–232.

'Einiges vom germanischen Wortschatz.' *Germanica: Eduard Sievers zum 75. Geburtstage* 90–106; Leipzig.          B20.

'On the Sound-System of Central Algonquian.'          B19. *Language* 1.130–156.          (excerpt)

1926.   'A Set of Postulates for the Science of Language.' *Language* 2.153–164. Summarized, with brief comment, in *Jahresbericht für germanische Philologie* 7.29 (1926). Reprinted in *International Journal of American Linguistics* 15.195–202 (1949); in Martin Joos, ed., *Readings in Linguistics* (Washington, D. C.: American Council of Learned Societies, 1957) 19–25.          B21.

1927.   'On Some Rules of Panini.' *Journal of the American Oriental Society* 47.61–70.          B26.

'On Recent Work in General Linguistics.' *Modern Philology* 25.211–230.          B28.

'Literate and Illiterate Speech.' *American Speech* 2.432–439. Reprinted in Dell Hymes, ed., *Language in Culture and Society* (New York: 1964), 391–396.          B25.

'American English.' *Le Maître Phonétique* III 5.40–42.          B29.

'Notes on the Fox Language' (Sections IV–XI). *International Journal of American Linguistics* 4.181–219.

'The Word-Stems of Central Algonquian.' *Festschrift Meinhof: Beiträge zur afrikanischen Sprachwissenschaft* 393–402; Hamburg. Submitted (or          B22. received) 20 May 1926.          (excerpt)

(with George M. Bolling) 'What Symbols Shall We Use?' *Language* 3.123–129.          B27.

Review: P. W. Schmidt, *Die Sprachfamilien und Sprachenkreise der Erde* (Heidelberg, 1926). *Language* 3.130–131.          B30.

Review: Otto Dempwolff, *Die L-, R-, und D-Laute in austronesischen Sprachen* (Berlin, 1925). *Language* 3.199.

Review: G. W. S. Friedrichsen, *The Gothic Version*

*of the Gospels: A Study in Style and Textual History* (Oxford, 1926). *Journal of English and Germanic Philology* 26.401–406.

Review: Otto Jespersen, *The Philosophy of Grammar* (New York, 1924). *Journal of English and Germanic Philology* 26.444–446.  B23.

Review: Karl Lokotsch, *Etymologisches Wörterbuch der amerikanischen (indianischen) Wörter im Deutschen* (Heidelberg, 1926). *Modern Philology* 24.489–491.  B24.

Review: Friedrich Maurer, *Untersuchungen über die deutsche Verbstellung in ihrer geschichtlichen Entwicklung* (Heidelberg, 1926), *Modern Philology* 24.491–493.

Note on: Eric Rooth, *Altgermanische Wortstudien* (Halle a/S, 1926). *Modern Philology* 24.500.

1928.  *Menomini Texts*. (*Publications of the American Ethnological Society* 12); New York: G. E. Stechert & Co., Agents. Bulk of manuscript completed, and probably submitted, before mid-1925.  B32. (excerpts)

Reviewed by: Truman Michelson, *Language* 5.189–190 (1929).

*First German Book*. 2d ed. New York: The Century Company.

Reviewed by: Hans Kurath, *Modern Language Journal* 13.661–663 (May 1929).

'The Story of Bad-Owl.' *Atti del XXII Congresso Internazionale degli Americanisti* (Roma, Settembre 1926) 2.23–34; Roma.  B31.

'The Plains Cree Language.' *Atti del XXII Congresso Internazionale degli Americanisti* (Roma, Settembre 1926) 2.427–431; Roma.

'A Note on Sound Change.' *Language* 4.99–100.  B33.

Review: G. G. Kloeke, *De Hollandsche expansie in de zestiende en zeventiende eeuw en haar weerspiegeling in de hedendaagsche Nederlandsche dialecten* ('s Gravenhage, 1927). *Language* 4.284–288.  B34.

Review: Adolf Stender-Petersen, *Slavisch-germanische Lehnwortkunde: Eine Studie über die ältesten germanischen Lehnwörter im Slavischen in sprach- und kulturgeschichtlicher Beleuchtung* (Göteborg, 1927). *Journal of English and Germanic Philology* 27.396–398.

Review: M. J. van der Meer, *Historische Grammatik der niederlandschen Sprache*, 1. Band (Heidelberg, 1927). *Journal of English and Germanic Philology* 27.550–551.

Note on: L. Grootaers and G. G. Kloeke, *Handleiding bij het Nord- en Zuid-Nederlandsch Dialectonderzoek* ('s Gravenhage, 1926). *Modern Philology* 25.376.

Note on: Erich Maschke, *Studien zu Waffennamed der althochdeutschen Glossen* (Greifswald, 1926). *Modern Philology* 25.504–505.

Note on: Werner Salow, *Die deutsche Sprachwissenschaft in der Allgemeinen Deutschen Bibliothek: Ein Beitrag zur deutschen Philologie im Zeitalter der Aufklärung* (Greifswald, 1926). *Modern Philology* 25.507.

1929.   'Notes on the Preverb *ge-* in Alfredian English.' *Studies in Philology: A Miscellany in Honor of Frederick Klaeber* 79–102; Minneapolis.

'Otfridiana.' *Journal of English and Germanic Philology* 28.489–502.

Review: Bruno Liebich, *Konkordanz Pāṇini-Candra* (Breslau, 1928). *Language* 5.267–276.          B35.

(With Archer Taylor) Review: *Festschrift til Hjalmar Falk* (Oslo, 1927). *Modern Philology* 26.367–369.

Review: H. de Boor, *Untersuchungen zur Sprachbehandlung Otfrids: Hiatus und Synaloephe* (Breslau, 1928). *Modern Philology* 27.221–224.

Note on: Eduard Hartl, *Die Textgeschichte des Wolframschen Parzival*, 1. Teil (Berlin and Leipzig, 1928). *Modern Philology* 26.373.

1930.   *Sacred Stories of the Sweet Grass Cree.* (Canada, Department of Mines: National Museum of Canada, Bulletin No. 60; Anthropological Series, No. 11); Ottawa: F. A. Acland.

'Salic *litus*.' *Studies in Honor of Hermann Collitz* 83–94; Baltimore.

'OHG *eino*, OE *ana* "solus".' *Curme Volume of Linguistic Studies* 50–59 (Language Monograph No. 7); Baltimore.

'Old English Plural Subjunctives in -*e*.' *Journal of English and Germanic Philology* 29.100–113.

'German ç and x.' *Le Maître Phonétique* III 20.27–
28.                                                                    B29.

'Linguistics as a Science.' *Studies in Philology*
27.553–557.                                                            B36.

1931. Obituary of Albert Paul Weiss. *Language* 7.219–221.  B38.
Review: John Ries, *Was ist ein Satz?* (Prag, 1931).
*Language* 7.204–209.                                                  B37.
Review: Virgil Moser, *Frühneuhochdeutsche Gram-
matik*, 1. Band (Heidelberg, 1929). *Journal of
English and Germanic Philology* 30.407–408.

1932. 'The Word.' *Le Maître Phonétique* III 38.41.        B29.
Review: Eduard Hermann, *Lautgesetz und Analogie*
(Berlin, 1931). *Language* 8.220–233.                                  B39.

1933. *Language*. New York: Henry Holt and Company
Reviewed by:
Franklin Edgerton (Yale University), *Journal of
the American Oriental Society* 53.295–297
(1933).                                                               41 (1)
Samuel Kroesch (University of Minnesota), *Jour-
nal of English and Germanic Philology* 32.594–
597 (1933).                                                           41 (2)
Carl F. Voegelin (Depauw University), brief
notice, *Le Maître Phonétique* III 43.53 (1933)
with added note by Daniel Jones.
Antoine Meillet (Paris), *Bulletin de la Société de
Linguistique de Paris* 34:3.1–2 (1933).                                41 (3)
Edgar H. Sturtevant (Yale University), *The Clas-
sical Weekly* 27.159–160 (26 March 1934).                              41 (4)
Roland G. Kent (University of Pennsylvania),
*Language* 10.40–48 (1934) (with an added note
by George M. Bolling, pp 48–51).                                       41 (5)
George M. Bolling (Ohio State University), *Lan-
guage* 11.251–252 (1935).                                              41 (6)
A. Debrunner (Bern), *Indogermanische Forschun-
gen* 54.148–149 (1936).                                                41 (7)
'The Structure of Learned Words.' *A Commemora-
tive Volume Issued by the Institute for Research
in English Teaching on the Occasion of the Tenth
Annual Conference of English Teachers* 17–23;
Tokyo.                                                                 B40.

1934. *Plains Cree Texts.* (*Publications of the American
Ethnological Society*, 16); New York: G. E.
Stechert and Co., Agents.

Reviewed by: David Mandelbaum, *American An-thropologist* 38.114–115 (1936).

Review: William Havers, *Handbuch der erklärenden Syntax: Ein Versuch zur Erforschung der Bedingungen und Triebkräfte in Syntax und Stilistik* (Heidelberg, 1931). *Language* 10.32–40.                    B42.

Review: G. Pilhofer, *Grammatik der Kâte-Sprache in Neuginea* (Berlin, 1933). *Language* 10.63–64.

'A Note on Transcription.' *Le Maître Phonétique* III 46.54.                    B29.

1935. *Language*. (British edition); London: G. Allen & Unwin, Ltd.

'The Stressed Vowels of American English.' *Language* 11.97–115.                    B43.

'Linguistic Aspects of Science.' *Philosophy of Science* 2.499–517.                    B44.

1936. 'On Laves' review of Dempwolff.' *Language* 12.52–53.

'Language or Ideas?' *Language* 12.89–95.                    B45.

Review: Arthur F. Bentley, *Linguistic Analysis of Mathematics* (Bloomington, Indiana, 1932) and *Behavior, Knowledge, Fact* (Bloomington, Indiana, 1935). *Language* 12.137–141.

1937. 'Notes on Germanic Compounds.' *Mélanges linguistiques offerts à M. Holger Pedersen* (*Acta Jutlandica* 9:1) 303–307; København.

*The Language of Science* (unpublished mss).                    B47.

1938. 'Initial [k-] in German.' *Language* 14.178–186.                    B48.

Obituary of Eduard Prokosch. *Language* 14.310–313.                    B49.

Review: Roger Williams, *A Key into the Language of America*, 5th ed. (Providence, 1936). *New England Quarterly* 11.416–418.

1939. *Linguistic Aspects of Science*. (*International Encyclopedia of Unified Science* 1:4). Chicago: University of Chicago Press.                    B51. (excerpt)

Reviewed by:

E. N. (=Ernest Nagel?), *Journal of Philosophy* 36.613–614 (1939).

Frederick B. Fitch, *Philosophical Review* 49.678–680 (1940).

James W. Wilson, *Language* 16.347–351 (1940).

'Menomini Morphophonemics.' *Études phonolo-*

*giques dédiées à la mémoire de N. S. Trubetzkoy*
(*Travaux du Cercle Linguistique de Prague* 8);     B50.
Prague.                                              (excerpt)
Review: Louis H. Gray, *Foundations of Language*
(New York, 1939). *The Modern Language Forum*
24.198–199.                                          B52.

1940.  *Teaching Children to Read.* In dittographed form
       from typescript; Copyright by Leonard Bloom-
       field.                                        B55.

1941.  'Ideals and Idealists.' (Rejoinder to Wilson's review
       of *Linguistic Aspects of Science.*) *Language* 17.59.
       'Proto-Algonquian  –*i·t*–  "Fellow".' *Language*
       17.292–297.
       Review: Morice Vanoverbergh, *Some Undescribed
       Languages of Luzon* (Nijmegen, 1937). *Acta Lin-
       guistica* 2.129.

1942.  *Outline Guide for the Practical Study of Foreign
       Languages.* Baltimore: Special Publication of the
       Linguistic Society of America.
       (First draft of §4.8 and of all but the first section of
       Chapter V of:) Bernard Bloch and George L.
       Trager, *Outline of Linguistic Analysis.* Baltimore:
       Special Publication of the Linguistic Society of
       America.
       'Philosophical Aspects of Language.' *Studies in the
       History of Culture: The Disciplines of the Human-
       ities* (*presented to Waldo Gifford Leland*) 173–177.
       Menasha, Wisconsin.                           B57.
       'Linguistics and Reading.' *The Elementary English
       Review* 19.125–130, 183–186                   B56.
       'Outline of Ilocano Syntax.' *Language* 18.193–200.

1943.  'Meaning.' *Monatshefte für deutschen Unterricht*
       35.101–106.                                   B58.
       Obituary of Franz Boas. *Language* 19.198.    B60.
       Review: Mauricio Swadesh, *La Nueva Filología*
       (México, 1941). *Language* 19 168–170.        B59.

1944.  *Colloquial Dutch.* (War Department Education
       Manual EM 550); Madison, Wisconsin: Pub-
       lished for the United States Armed Forces Insti-
       tute by the Linguistic Society of America and the
       Intensive Language Program, American Council
       of Learned Societies. Also in a civilian edition,
       New York: Henry Holt and Company.

*Spoken Dutch: Basic Course*. Vol. 1, Units 1–12.
(War Department Education Manual EM 529);
imprint as above. Also (1945) a civilian edition,
New York: Henry Holt and Company.

'Secondary and Tertiary Responses to Language.'
*Language* 20.45–55. Reprinted (in part) in Harold
B. Allen, ed., *Readings in Applied English Lin-
guistics* (New York: Appleton-Century-Crofts,
Inc., 1958) pp 195–202; 2d ed. (1964) pp 274–281.　B62.

Review: Frederick Bodmer, *The Loom of Language*
(New York, 1944). *American Speech* 19.211–213.　B61.

1945.　*Spoken Dutch: Basic Course*. Vol. 2, Units 13–30.
(War Department Education Manual EM 530);
imprint as above. Also a civilian edition, New
York: Henry Holt and Company.

*Handleiding voor de gids* (for *Spoken Dutch: Basic
Course*) (War Department Education Manual
EM 531); imprint as above.

(With Luba Petrova) *Spoken Russian: Basic Course*,
Vol. 2, Units 13–30 (War Department Education
Manual EM 525); imprint as above. Also a civilian edition, New York: Henry Holt and Company.

[*Spoken Russian: Basic Course*, Vol. 1, Units 1–12
(War Department Education Manual EM 524)
was worked and reworked by so many partici-
pants that Bloomfield, who had done much of the
original work with Luba Petrova, refused to allow
his name to appear on it. The co-author of record,
'I. M. Lesnin', was his invention.]

Grammatical introduction (unsigned) to Part II,
Russian-English, *Dictionary of Spoken Russian*
(War Department Technical Manual TM 30–
944); Washington, D. C.: War Department.

'About Foreign Language Teaching.' *The Yale Review* 34.625–641.　　　　　　　　　　　　　B63.

'On Describing Inflection.' *Festschrift für M. Blakemore Evans* (*Monatshefte für deutschen Unterricht*　B64.
Vol. 37, No. 4/5) 8–13; Madison, Wisconsin.　　(excerpt)

1946.　*Spravočnik Rukovoditelä dlä Spoken Russian* (War
Department Education Manual EM 526); imprint as above.

'Algonquian.' In Harry Hoijer and others, *Linguistic*

          *Structures of Native America* (*Viking Fund Publi-
          cations in Anthropology* 6: New York) 85–129.      B65.
          'Twenty-one Years of the Linguistic Society.' *Lan-
          guage* 22.1–3.                                      B67.
†1958.   *Eastern Ojibwa: Grammatical Sketch, Texts, and
          Word List*. Ann Arbor: University of Michigan
          Press.
†1961.   (With Clarence L. Barnhart) *Let's Read: A Linguis-
          tic Approach*. Detroit: Wayne State University
          Press. (An updating, by Barnhart, of the 1940
          *Teaching Children to Read*.)
†1962.   *The Menomini Language*. New Haven and London:   B66.
          Yale University Press.                            (excerpt)
†1965.   (Edited by Harry Hoijer:) *Language History; from
          'Language'* (*1933 edition*). New York: Holt, Rine-
          hart and Winston. (Chapters 17–27, with notes
          brought up to date by the editor.)
†In mss. *Menomini-English Lexicon*. (About 11,000 entries.)
          *Cree-English Lexicon*. (About 6,000 entries.)
          *Fox-English Lexicon*. (Smaller; based on excerpting
          of the published texts of Jones and Michelson.)

# A Leonard Bloomfield Anthology

# B1. *From* A Semasiological Differentiation in Germanic Secondary Ablaut

1909–1910. *Modern Philology* 7.245–288, 345–382.

[This was Bloomfield's doctoral dissertation at the University of Chicago, written 1908–1909 under the direction of Francis A. Wood.

We reprint the introductory discussion, except for the initial two pages of critical apparatus and acknowledgments. In the original, this is followed by 75 pages of examples drawn from all the Germanic languages, systematically grouped into 250-odd paragraphs. Of these, we include the first and the last two, as illustrative of the rest.

The kinds of forms dealt with here are discussed in §4.7 of the 1914 *Introduction*, and in §§14.8,9 of the 1933 *Language*.]

I

A striking characteristic of the Germanic family of languages is its feeling for vowel grades and vowel variations. A few inherited vowel variations become, in the "strong" verbs, models for the expression of tense differences. Derivative nouns and verbs also stand—at least in the older dialects —in a definite ablaut relation to their primitives: one need only cite the old causative verbs or nouns such as NHG. *Schnitt, Schuss, Fang*. In short, the vocalism of Germanic is characterized by a vivid sensibility to a few ablaut variations, such as $a$–$\bar{o}$, $e$–$a$–$\bar{e}$, $i$–$a$–$u$, and for these ablaut variations as bearers of meaning.

Though this predisposition has remained, the last fifteen hundred years have changed the well-defined system of the old Germanic. The systematic parallelism of the strong verbs is still felt—we inflect one strong verb by the analogy of another—but in the nouns and weak verbs the change has been thoroughgoing. Formations have multiplied, new methods of formation have arisen, new stems or "bases" have been created.

No phonetic process could derive, for instance, NHG. (Pruss.) *knibbern, knabbern, knubbern*—which are felt as connected—from a single Germanic ablaut base: such sets of forms are the result of analogy—in some cases of centuries of analogic formation and re-formation. In some cases, among which we may probably include the above example, the sensitiveness to onomatopoetic vowel variations (as in *bim* : *bam* : *bum*, *piff* : *paff* : *puff*) has created part of the parallel forms from the nucleus of a single Germanic base; in other instances the approach of two somewhat similar bases might give the appearance of relationship and then cause new forms to be made in imitation. Thus the approach of two IE. roots in Dutch dial. *nippen* 'pinch' (< G. *hnīpan*, cf. E. *nip*, ON. *hnippa* 'stossen') and Dutch *noppen* 'nop, pick cloth' (< G. *hneupan*, cf. E. *nop*, ON. *hnupla* 'wegraffen') may have caused like parallel-forms to arise from a single root of either type. Cf. Wood, *Indo-European* $a^x$ : $a^x i$ : $a^x u$, especially §408.[1]

Thus the MHG. has *knabbern* : *knubbern* 'nagen,' *kittern* 'kichern,' : *kuttern* 'girren, lachen;' the Waldeck dialect *ferlatsken* 'Schuhe breit treten' : *ferlutsken* 'durch unordentlichen Gebrauch verderben,' *sprikel* n. 'Reiser; dürres Kind' : *sprokel* n. 'kleines, dürres Holz'; the East Frisian has *nibbe nib* f. 'Schnabel, Mund' : *nubbe nub* f. 'Knuff, Stoss, Schlag;' the E. forms like *flip* : *flap* : *flop*, *tip* : *tap* : *tup*, dialectic *tip* 'a ram' : *tup* 'a ram', or *dab* : *daub* : dial. *dub* 'bungler, idiot.'

The relation in such sets of words is as much an ablaut relation as that in E. *lie* : *lay*, *sing* : *sang* : *sung* or Greek λείπω : λέλοιπα : ἔλιπον. In the above-cited cases the ablaut is "secondary" or later, that is all—and it may be that a study of the cases nearer to us, where origins are often more apparent, may give us some help in penetrating into the mystery of the "original" or IE. ablaut. With this ultimate end in view a number of examples are here given of secondary Germanic ablaut forms exhibiting a certain more or less well-known feature of semasiologic differentiation, a development such as must have had part in the formation of the IE. vowel system.

## II

The commonest form of the Germanic secondary ablaut is that of the vowels *i–a–u*.[2] The origin of this ablaut is apparent, though not in every case traceable. Parallel roots of the types IE. *kneb*, *kneib*, and *kneub* might give the Germanic forms *hnapan*, *hnipan*, *hnupan*; and if these became associated in the feeling of the speaker they might lead him to form sets like NHG. *knabbern* : *knibbern* : *knubbern*. Or else a root of the nasal and liquid series would give derivatives like E. *slink* : dial. *slank* : dial. *slunk*,

---

[1] Phonetic changes, such as umlaut or the E., Dutch, and HG. change of Germanic $\bar{o} > \bar{u}\,(u)$ have also created sets of forms that have been analogically imitated. Some of the examples that follow are due to this.

[2] Examples below. Cf. Wilmanns, *Deutsche Grammatik*, II, 22; Paul, *Prinzipien der Sprachgeschichte*[2], 144 ff.; Wood, *op. cit.*; Goettsch, *Mod. Phil.*, VI, 253 ff.

and the German words could have been modeled after such a set of forms.[3]
The part that umlaut and other phonetic developments may have played
has been mentioned; also the independent feeling we have today for ono-
matopoetic variants like *bim* : *bam* : *bum*—this feeling may have been
developed by the other factors.

There is a good reason why the vowels *i* : *a* : *u* are common in sets of
connected words. Of all the vowels these three are farthest separated in
the scale of natural pitch—they differ most, from one another, in acoustic
effect and in anatomic production; so that if several distinct forms (out
of a possible greater number) are to be created or are to survive, these
forms with their clearly marked character will be the most favored—especially if a differentiation of meaning is at the same time developing. Thus
it is natural, if words with distinct meanings were to survive, that we have,
for instance, MHG. *kittern* 'kichern' : *kuttern* 'girren, lachen,' rather
than, say, *\*kettern* : *\*köttern*.

Although there are many cases of secondary ablaut with less extreme
vowels than *i* : *a* : *u*, the principle just stated has been an important factor
in the development of the modern Germanic vocabularies. We have seen
how an old ablaut base—a strong verb IE. *\*sleng-* Germanic *\*slinkan*
E. *slink*, let us say—has given rise to a number of words—as E. *slink*
(strong verb) : dial. *slank* (weak verb) : dial. *slunk* (weak verb). Such words
are perhaps often identical in meaning, cf. NHG. (Pruss.) *knibbern* :
*knabbern* : *knubbern* 'hastig und mit Geräusch nagen,' but it is natural
if not inevitable that such words should become semasiologically differentiated. E. *slink* 'sneak' : dial. *slank* 'go about in listless fashion' : dial.
*slunk* 'wade through a mire' are examples.

What has determined the direction of this differentiation of meaning?
In many cases the old laws of derivation must have been decisive. Germanic *\*prangjan* is the causative of *\*pringan* : hence NHG. *drängen* :
*dringen*; this explains the difference in meaning of the two words, the
transitive use of the former while the latter, at least in its literal sense, is
intransitive. The meaning of NHG. *würfeln* is explained by its being a
regular denominative from the noun *Würfel*, which in turn is regularly
derived from the base in *werfen*. But one cannot so explain the meanings
of *slink* : *slank* : *slunk*, nor indeed the great majority of such modern
Germanic word groups: another force has been at work.

This force is the old inherent Germanic sense for vowel pitch. It is by
the pitch of the stem vowel that sets of words like *slink* : *slank* : *slunk* have
become differentiated.

If a word designating some sound or noise contains a high pitched vowel

[3] In Scandinavian, especially, the nasal or liquid could not have been felt as a necessary
adjunct of *i* : *a* : *u* ablaut, since the nasal early disappeared in verbs like ON. *drekka* : *drakk* :
*drukken*, Dan *drikke* : *drak* : *drukken*.

like *ǐ* it strikes us as implying a high pitch in the sound or noise spoken of; a word with a low vowel like *ŭ* implies low pitch in what it stands for. For Germanic we need only think of NHG. *bim!* : *bam!* : *bum!* or E. *screech* : *boom.* Who would apply *Bim!* to the roar of a cannon, *Bum!* to the tinkling of a bell? And *Bam!* would better fit the bang of a fist on the *Biertisch* than either of the above noises.[4] Church Slavic *krikŭ* 'Geschrei,' *kričati* 'schreien' : *krakati* 'krächzen'; Greek κρίζω 'knarre' : κράζω 'schreie' : κρώζω 'krächze;' κνίζω 'ritze, kratze, reize' : κνύζω 'kratze,' κνυζάω 'knurre, winsele;' βάζω 'rede' : βύζω 'schreie wie der Uhu' (Wood, *op. cit.*) and similar words illustrate this general principle, but so far as I know no full material illustrating its operation has ever been collected. Its far-reaching effects on our vocabulary are surprising. It has affected not only words descriptive of sound like E. *screech, boom,* or the doublet MHG. *kittern* : *kuttern*; for not only the direct imitative values of the vowels have come into play, but also their more remote connotative effects. A high tone implies not only shrillness but also fineness, sharpness, keenness; a low tone not only rumbling noise, but also bluntness, dulness, clumsiness; a full open sound like *ā* not only loudness, but largeness, openness, fulness. Nor must the subjective importance of the various mouth positions that create the different vowel sounds be forgotten: the narrow contraction of *ǐ*, the wide opening of *ā*, the back-in-the-mouth tongue position of *ū* are as important as the effect of these vowels on the ear of the hearer.[5] Though there are many exceptions, due for the most part to the older rules of derivation above illustrated—such words belong to an older stratum— yet the development in question is a very common and characteristic one for Germanic wherever a number of words standing to each other in a relation of secondary ablaut have become differentiated as to meaning.

An impetus to this development was surely given by such purely ono-matopoetic words as *bim* : *bam* : *bum*; and another impetus may have been accidental models. Thus NHG. *dringen* implies the penetration of some small, usually sharp object into a larger one; *drängen* meant origi-nally to cause such penetration, and neither the subject nor the action of the verb *drängen* needed to be fine, small, or penetrant: in this case the relative vowel qualities of the words happened to accord with the mean-ings: and on such an accidental model the forms in question would multiply.

The following is a list of modern Germanic secondary ablaut sets that show this differentiation. The etymologist will find some sets of words in

---

[4] This general fact has been remarked by many observers, not only by linguists but also by critics of style—especially of poetic style where vowel tones play an important role. Cf. most fully perhaps A. H. Tolman in the *Andover Review* for March, 1887, the *Atlantic Monthly*, April, 1895, and in his *The Views about Hamlet and Other Essays* (Boston, 1904).

[5] Cf., most recently, Thomson, *IF.*, XXIV, 1ff.

which several old ablaut bases are involved, others in which one base has by regular phonetic derivation given rise to all the forms, still others whose existence is due to analogy after more or less definite models, and finally words directly due to the sharpened sense for parallelism of vowel sound and meaning—the etymological character of the material does not, however, here concern us.

The practical linguist, the "Kenner" of a given dialect will no doubt find sets of words that are not sets at all, sets of words which no speaker of the dialect ever associates with one another. Where such "sets" of words are not even the result of differentiation from a single origin, our plea must be lack of first-hand acquaintance with the dialect, though it may be remarked that a varying subjective element often enters into one's connecting certain words as related in meaning: thus the writer's judgment as to some words in the dialects familiar to him varied from time to time. There is nevertheless amply enough of indisputable material to illustrate the importance of vowel pitch in semasiologic differentiation of secondary ablaut sets in the modern Germanic dialects.

If we possessed sufficient records of the Germanic tongues in their historic development, each set of words could be traced to its origin from one or several roots, many analogies could be recognized, and the semasiologic development could be observed; but unfortunately the meagerness of our records and their uncolloquial character frustrate such an attempt. Even where parallel forms are met with, our lexicographers have usually been unable to see any divergence in use, though this may often have existed in actual speech. In fact, where a modern lexicon sets up, as equivalent, forms like NHG. (Pruss.) *knibbern* : *knabbern* : *knubbern*, the actual consciousness of the speaker differentiates: thus *knibbern* is a more audible gnawing than *knubbern*, and the object gnawed is harder; *knabbern* refers to a louder but less crisp sound than *knibbern*.

A few words from mediaeval sources are: MDan. *baldre* 'beat, strike': *buldre* 'quarrel, make uproar' (Kalkar); MLG. *nipen* 'kneifen': *nopen napen* 'antasten, anstossen' (Lübben); MHG. *snarren snerren* 'schwatzen, plappern': *snurren* 'rauschen, sausen.'

To repeat: the forms with high-pitched vowel—the scale, running downward, is *i* (*y*), *e* (*ö*), *a*, *o*, *u*—represent high-pitched, clear, shrill sounds, fine, small, bright, flashing, quick, sharp, clear cut objects or actions; the forms with low-pitched vowel express low, muffled, rumbling, bubbling, sounds and dull, loose, swaying, hobbling, slovenly, muddy, underhand, clumsy actions or objects. The *a* vowel will often express the large, the loud, the rattling, the open. A diphthong is likely to express a wide swing or scope.

The differences between words, not the similarities are, of course, in question.

**1**. N. *pipla* 'pipe gently (of young birds)' : *pupla* 'bubble, prattle.'

E. *peep* : dial. *pip* 'crack the eggshell in hatching,' dial. *pipple* 'cry, whimper' : *pop* 'shoot,' *pop out* 'blab' : *poop*, dial. *pup* 'cacare' : *pipe*.

Dutch *piepen* 'chirp, squeak' : *poepen* 'pedere, cacare' : *pijpen* 'pipe, whistle.'

OF. *pipen* 'piepen, wimmern, pfeifen' : *pupen* 'leise furzen: seine Notdurft verrichten.'

Westf. *pīpen* 'piepen, wimmern, pfeifen, winselnd ausstehen; küssen' : *pupen* 'küssen,' *puppen* 'pedere,' *puppern* 'schlagen (vom Herzen).'

Pr. *pīpen* 'pfeifen, piepen, winseln' : *peppeln* 'sprechen, pappeln' : *pappeln* 'viel, unverständlich sprechen,' *pāpern* 'plappern' : *pūpen* 'pedere,' *puppern* 'schnell klopfen (vom Herzen), schnell u. mit dumpfem Laut bewegt werden.'

Lux. *pīpen* 'weinen,' *pipsen* 'leise sprechen' : *pūpen* 'pedere.'

Siebenb. *pīpsn* 'pfeifen, kränkeln' : *pū mache* 'cacare.'

. . .

**248**. OF. *winken* (st. u. sw.) 'winken, nicken, sich neigen, abnehmen' : *wenken* 'winken, nicken, schläfrig werden' : *wanken*, 'wanken, schwanken, sich hin u. her bewegen.'

Pr. *winken* (sw. doch fehlerhaft auch st.) 'ein Zeichen geben, mit Hand oder Auge; sich die Auge zuhalten' : *wanken* 'schwanken; herumwandeln' : *wunk* m. 'scherzhafte Umbildung von *wink* in *einem einen Wunk mit dem Zaunpfahl geben*.'

NHD. *winken* : *wanken*.

**249**. E. dial. *whinge* 'whine, cry, whimper' *whang* 'beat, thrash, bang,' dial. 'eat voraciously, chop, wrench.'

# B2. The Indo-European Palatals in Sanskrit[1]

1911. *American Journal of Philology* 32.36–57.

[Bloomfield in 1940 told me of a time his uncle, Maurice Bloomfield, had over-heard him worrying about how a certain sound could have changed into a certain other sound, and had said 'Don't worry about that. *Any* sound can turn into *any* other sound.' The episode was not dated, but it must have been later than the writing of the present paper. In this connection it is instructive to compare Bloom-field's approach here with that in his 1938 'Initial [k-] in German' (our B48).]

1. The Indic and the Iranian languages differ greatly in their treatment of the IE. stopped consonants. We are struck by the frequent change of stops to spirants in Iranian, as opposed to the "conservative" history, in this respect, of the Sanskrit. The former is a spirantizing language, like the old Germanic.

Thus the Iranian shows us spirants for the IE. aspirated voiceless stops, as in Av. *paθ-a* O. P. *paθi-m* (Sk. *path- pathi-*), and for the IE. voiceless stops before consonants, as in Av. *āfš* (Sk. *áp*), *suxra-* O P *θuxra-* (Sk. *š'ukrá-s*), Av. *θwąm* O.P. *θ(u)wam* (Sk. *tvám*).[1]

The Younger Avestan, moreover, shows us spirants for the IE. aspirated and simple voiced stops, as in *a'wi* (Sk. *abhi*) *and γ°nā* (Sk. *gnā́*). We may note also such YAv. double spirants as in *uxδa-* (Sk. *ukthá-m*) and *vax°δra-* (Sk. *vaktrá-m*).

2. To recall these well-known facts would be, strictly speaking, sufficient for our purposes in the present discussion: it may, however, be instructive to consider briefly what physiological causes probably brought about these changes of pronunciation in Iranian and Younger Avestan.

The spirantizing of voiceless aspirates in Iranian is parallel to that in Germanic, and may like the latter be attributed to a pronunciation with

---

[1] As constant reference to an often divergent set of views might prove confusing, we may here refer once for all to the treatment of the IE. palatals in Aryan in Brugmann's Grundriss I², §§610–618, 714–720. 1007, 12, which has been looked upon as the standard view of the subject. All examples are taken from the Grundriss and from Whitney's Sanskrit Grammar³, §§142, 145–147, 214–224, c. 612, d. 617, b. 832, a. 833, a. 890, a.

*increased stress of breath.* Cf. especially H. Meyer, Z. f. d. Alt. 45, 101 ff. The agreement of Iranian and Germanic in not spirantizing these sounds after a spirant, as in Av. *spara-ṯ* (Sk. *sphurá-ti*) is significant not only of a like cause for the Iranian and the Germanic phenomena, but also of this particular cause: for the utterance of a preceding spirant, in requiring a comparatively great volume of breath, lessens the breath stress for the following stop and so prevents spirantization. Similarly in E. *ten* we pronounce an aspirated fortis, *ten* or *then*, but in E. *step* a simple fortis or voiceless lenis, *step* or *sḍep*. So also G. *tut* vs. *Stute*, Dan. *Time* vs. *Stime*; and it is conceivable that the very great breath stress of Dan. *Time* may in time produce *θime* while the *t* in *Stime* would be retained as a stop.

The similar retention of the stop after nasals in Iranian, as in Av. *pantå* (Sk. *pánthā-s*) is an indication that breath stress was weaker here than in Germanic, where spirantization took place in spite of the escape of breath in a preceding nasal. Another indication of such a difference between Iranian and Germanic is the retention in Iranian of voiceless unaspirated stops. The general increase of breath stress in Iranian was sufficient to make spirants of voiceless stops followed by aspiration (with open glottis), but not of voiceless stops immediately followed by closing of the vocal cords for a vowel, as in Av. *pita* O. P. *pitā* (Sk. *pitå*). Before a consonant, however, where the closing of the vocal cords was not so immediate, spirantization took place, as in the examples above given. This is an illustration of the familiar fact that the utterance of a voiceless sound, i. e., of one with open position of the glottis, involves the passing through the mouth of far more breath than the utterance of a voiced sound, during which the vocal cords are closed and allow breath to pass only in the interstices of their vibration,—compare the well-known experiment of trying to blow out a candle first with a voiced, then with a voiceless sound.

Thus we may perhaps also explain the fact that the voiced stops became voiceless in Germanic, but in Iranian, where the breath stress was weaker, remained sonant. This is for various reasons a most doubtful matter, as is also the spirantizing of the voiced aspirates in Germanic; suffice it therefore to note that in Germanic both these classes of sounds were changed to sounds requiring more breath for utterance, whereas in Iranian this was not the case, aspirate and simple sonant stops here coinciding, most probably as simple sonant stops.

A different explanation is necessary for the phenomena of Younger Avestan. Here the Iranian voiced stops became voiced spirants. Increased breath stress alone would probably have turned these sounds into voiceless stops, as in Germanic and later in High German and Danish; it seems rather as if in the Younger Avestan *looseness of articulation* were involved. This is surely the case where Younger Avestan changed Iran. *ft χt* to *fδ xδ*, as in *uxδa-* and *vaxᵊδra-*. Such groups as *ft χt* can be conveniently pronounced with any degree or increase of breath stress; they are stable in such highly stressed languages as English, German, and Danish. The YAv. change to double spirants is a decided sign of loose articulation of stops.

3. It is probable, then, that the Iranian dialects diverged from the Sanskrit in being spoken with increased breath stress, and that the Younger Avestan further differed in loosely articulating its stops. However this may be, it is certain that the Iranian languages differed from the Sanskrit in *tending toward spirant pronunciation of stopped consonants*, and that this is especially true of the Younger Avestan. In the following pages, whenever mention is made of the "stronger breath stress of the Iranian" or "looser articulation of the Avestan", the empirical reader will always be able to substitute the words "more spirant pronunciation" without in any way affecting the argument. To what extent the greater conservatism of Sanskrit is due to the greater antiquity of the language in our records need not here concern us: the nature of the divergence between early Iranian and Sanskrit as we know them is all that will affect our present considerations.[2]

4. This difference between the phonetic character of Iranian and Sanskrit may help us to understand the differing development of the IE. palatals in the two languages. We should first have to form a hypothesis, however, as to the character of these sounds in Indo-European, were it not that the opinion of Brugmann (Gr. I[2], §543 and K. Vgl. Gr. §157) has found general acceptance. Brugmann's view is that the stop-articulation of these sounds is the more original; that they were in Indo-European slightly palatalized $k$-sounds ($k'$ $k'h$ $g'$ $g'h$) which in the development of the so-called *centum* languages were not distinguished from simple velar consonants, but in the eastern (*satəm*) languages became sibilants. Phonetic parallels are of course in favor of this view, for the gradual change of slightly palatalized velars to sibilants is a familiar phenomenon. A palatalized velar $k'$ $g'$ is pronounced as a simple stop articulated somewhat farther forward in the mouth than a plain velar (French dialects, Norwegian dialects, Lithuanian, modern Slavic languages, Magyar).[3] Articulation of the middle tongue against the higher parts of the palate is not so rapid or precise as in other parts of the mouth. Especially as the removal of the tongue after the stop is not so quick as after a velar or dental, the resulting acoustic effect resembles an affricate,—the stop being followed by the sound of the breath passing between the palate and the tongue

---

[2] In the above and following paragraphs theorizing as to the nature of the IE. voiced aspirate stops has been avoided,—or rather, it has been relegated from here to a note at the end of these remarks.

[3] An early stage is heard in the German pronunciation, e.g., of *Kind* as opposed to *Kalb* and *Kuchen*.

$(k' > k'h > k'\chi')$. Cf. Brugmann Gr. I², §47, 1. Meanwhile the point of articulation passes forward, approaching that of dental consonants $(k'\chi' > t'š')$, as in Old French (*ch, g*), English, Norwegian, Swedish, Slavic languages. In some languages, which tend to articulate either with the back or with the tip of the tongue and not with intermediate points, the palatal character of *t'š', d'ž'* may be nearly or wholly given up, the result resembling *tš, dž*, as in Italian and English. Where the palatal character is retained the stop grows less and less close and is finally assimilated to the spirant: the result is a more or less palatal *š', s*, or *š* sound, as in modern French (*c, ch, g*), Italian dialects (*š', ž'*, cf. Passy, Petite Phonétique Comparée, p. 85), Portuguese (*c, g*), and modern Slavic languages. As the reverse of this process is very rare—if indeed it be not inconceivable,— we must assume for the IE. palatals a pronunciation *k' k'h g' g'h*. From this developed the sibilants of the *satəm* languages.

5. The standard view then supposes that in all the so-called *satəm* languages—and therefore in all Aryan and long before any distinction between Iranian and Indic—this development had uniformly taken place; in other words, that any and all Iranian and Sanskrit representations of the IE. palatals are later forms of Ar. sibilants *š' š'h ž' ž'h* (before stops *š ž*, before sibilants *χ γ*).

This hypothesis does very well for the facts of Iranian, where the IE. palatals are everywhere pronounced as sibilants, e.g., Av. *vasō* O. P. *vasiy* (Gr. ἑκών), Av. *zī-zanāṯ* O. P. *vispa- z(a)na-* (Gr. γένος), Av. *hazah-* (Gr. ἔχω Goth. *sigis*),—as sibilants even in the combinations IE. *k̂s ĝzh*, e.g., Av. *aša-* (Gr. ἄξων), Av. *uz-važaṯ* (Lat. *vexit*). We know, moreover, that these sibilants were well on in their development in the Aryan period, for the new palatals which in Aryan times developed from IE. velars and labiovelars before IE. front vowels did not coincide with the old IE. palatals, but remained as palatal stops or affricates *č ǰ*, as in Av. *čiṯ* O. P. *čiy* (Sk. *cid*), Av. *jva^i ti* O. P. *jīvāhy* (Sk. *jīva-ti*). In other words: before the palatalization in Aryan times (earlier than IE. *ĕ ŏ > ă*) of IE. velars and labiovelars, the IE. palatals had developed so far that the new palatals never coincided with them—never "caught up" with them:—the IE. palatals had, we may safely say, developed into sibilants.

This, the standard view, is further supported when we consider the characteristics of Iranian mentioned in §§1–3. Strong breath stress (or at any rate spirant tendency) in pronouncing *k' g'* makes the spirant glide more noticeable than otherwise, so that the affricate stage is more quickly reached than where the breath stress is weaker. Strong breath stress (especially if combined with loose tongue articulation) hastens the weakening of the stop element and its assimilation to the spirant element. Iran. *s z* were somewhat palatal sibilants, cf. such spellings (or dialectic forms) as O. P. *a-θaha^h* (Av. *saṇha te* Sk. *š'ąsa-ti*), *ā-yadana-* (Av. *yaza^i te* Sk.

*yája-tē*). The development of IE. *k̂s ĝzh* from *k'š g'žh* through more and more relaxed and spirant articulations to *š ž* is also natural; it is of little moment whether or not we assume an intermediate stage *χš γž*: some such thing there must have been.

6. When we come to the Sanskrit, however, we find the conditions—as indeed we might expect them—quite different. IE. *k̂* before vowels, semivowels, nasals, and *r* has, to be sure, gone through the development to the palatal sibilant *š'* as in *vaš'mi* (Gr. ἐκών); note especially the conversion of *s* before Sk. palatals to the same sound as in *tátaš' ca*.

Aside from this case (and one other), however, the facts differ greatly from those of Iranian. To begin with IE. *ĝ* before vowels, semivowels, etc., has in early Sanskrit times the pronunciation of a simple voiced palatal *stop g'* or better *d'* (written *j* as in *jánas-*), coinciding with the *d'* developed in Aryan from IE. velars and labiovelars before IE. front vowels (as in *jīva-ti*). As to the character of this sound in early times, cf. Whitney, l. c., §44, a and especially Brugmann, K. Vgl. Gr., §22, 4, with references. As was inevitable, this sound came to assume a spirant glide (cf. §4), but in classical times it never acquired the metrical value of a double consonant and was never considered otherwise than as a simple voiced *stop*. According to the standard view, now, this palatal stop is a development from an Ar. sibilant *ž'*—a reversion, as it were, to an older state: IE. *ĝ* (=*g'*)> Ar. *ž'* > Sk. *j* (=*d'*),—cf. for instance Brugmann, Gr. I², §62, Anm. 2. Phonetically this is of course most unlikely,—just as it is unlikely that the *k*-sounds of the *centum* languages are derived from sibilants like those of the *satəm* languages, cf. §4.

The same holds true of the IE. palatal voiced aspirate: in Sanskrit IE. *ĝh* and Ar. *g'h* (< IE. *gh gᵘh* before front vowels) are represented alike as *h*, e.g. *sáhas-* (Av. *hazah-* Goth. *sigis*) and *hán-ti* (Av. *jaⁱnti* Gr. θείνω). Here, indeed, it might be urged that the representation in Sanskrit of IE. *ĝh*> Ar. *ž'h* had not "reverted" so as to coincide with that of Ar. *g'h*, but that the two sounds never had coincided until they both became *h*;— in other words, that IE. *ĝh*> Ar. *ž'h*> Sk. *h* and that Ar. *g'h*> Sk. *h*. Unfortunately for the current view of this matter there is an obstacle to this assumption: the Sanskrit law of deaspiration, when operating on IE. *ĝh* leaves the usual representation of IE. *g*, namely *j* (=*d'*) as in *jánghā* (<IE. *ĝhcⁿghā*, Goth. *gaggs*). Hence the current view of this subject is forced to assume that here too the Ar. sibilant *ž'h* acquired stop value in Sanskrit, that IE. *ĝh* (=*g'h*)> Ar. *ž'h*> Sk. **jh* (=*d'h*)> Sk. *h* or *j* (=*d'*). Moreover this return of the sibilant to stop value must have been very early, since Sanskrit deaspiration took place before the change of *zh* to *s*, *š*, cf. Brugmann, Gr. I², §827.

Finally there are a few cases of IE. *sk̂(h)*, where we find these sounds represented by Sk. (*c*)*ch*, as in *chinát-ti* (Gr. σχίζω), *ducchúnā* (*duš*+*š'unā*).

This (c)ch makes the preceding vowel "long by position" (Whitney, l. c., §§44, a. 227); it is also produced by the combination of -t š'- as in *tac chakyam* (*tat* + *š'akyam*): hence its character as a double sound, namely as a palatal affricate (*t'š'*) is plain. Note also the phonetic spelling *cš'*. Here again the standard view is forced to suppose that IE. *sk̂(h)* ( = *sk'(h)*) > Ar. *š'š'(h)* > Sk. (*c*)*ch* ( = *t'š'*)—again a development contrary to the usual course of such sounds and to the course which such sounds had previously taken in the same language.

7. The current supposition, in short, is that the IE. palatals developed uniformly over the entire Aryan territory: that their spirantization and stop-loosening was as fast in the otherwise "conservative" Sanskrit territory as in the Iranian with its spirant tendency; that when Sanskrit and Iranian grew to be separate languages the former as well as the latter pronounced the IE. palatals as sibilants *š' š'h ž' ž'h*. The Sanskrit, however,— repenting the precipitate course it had taken in company with the Iranian, —changed *š'š'(h)* ( < IE. *sk̂(h)*) back to (*c*)*ch* ( = *t'š'*), *ž'* back to *j* ( = *d'*), and *ž'h* back to *jh* ( = *d'h*, later *d'* or *h*), leaving only *š'* at the end of the alphabet as a spirant,—a last trace of the bad company and profligate habits of the past.

If we examine the actual forms of the Sanskrit language, however, we find nothing anomalous; and if, in tracing the origin of these forms and in comparing them to Iranian forms, we keep in mind the physiologic aspect of the process of palatization (outlined in §4) and apply what we know about the difference between Iranian and Sanskrit treatment of consonants (cf. §§1–3), we shall probably find in the history of the IE. palatals in Sanskrit nothing unusual or surprising. Beginning with the Indo-European, we shall now try to reconstruct this history.

8. The IE. palatals *k̂ k̂h ĝ ĝh* (probably pronounced *k' k'h g' g'h*, cf. §4) seem to have gone rapidly along the course of palatalization in one part of the Aryan territory (in which otherwise also spirant tendency later appears), namely in that dialect which later became the Iranian language; for, when the Ar. velars ( < IE. velars and labiovelars) became palatal before front vowels, these new palatals were in this dialect distinct from the old palatals.[4] At the end of the Aryan period then, the Iranian started out with one set of more or less purely spirant palatal sounds, say *š' š'h ž' ž'h*, and one set of (new) palatal stops *k' k'h g' g'h*.

The further history of the palatals in Iranian is clear (cf. §5). The old palatals, if not already pronounced as sibilants soon reached this pronunciation. Examples are:

  (a) Av. *s* ( < IE. *k̂*): *vasō* O. P. *vasiy* (Gr. ἑκών).
        ( < IE. *sk̂*): *jasa*ⁱ*ti* (Gr. βάσκε).

---

[4] This is much like the state of things in the Slavic languages, e.g. modern Russian, where several degrees of palatalization coexist.

   ( < IE. *sk̂h*): *hi-siδyāṯ* (Gr. σχίζω).
   ( < IE. *k̂sk̂*): *pərˀsaⁱti* ( < IE.* *pr̥k̂-sk̂e-ti*).
(b) Av. *z* ( < IE. *ĝ*): *zī-zanaṯ* O. P. *vispa-z(a)na-*
     (Gr. γένος).
   ( < IE. *ĝh*): *hazah-* (Gr. ἔχω Goth. *sigis*).
   ( < IE. *zĝh*): GAv. *zaē-mā* (Gr. σχοῖμεν).
(c) Av. *š* ( < IE. *k̂s*): *aša-* (Gr. ἄξων).
   ( < IE. *k̂p*): *šiti-š* (Gr. κτίσις).
   ( < IE. *k̂ph*): *rašō* (Gr. ἐρέχθω).
   ( < IE. *k̂-t*): *vašti* (Gr. ἑκών).
   ( < IE. *k̂-q*): *saškuš-təmō* ( < IE.* *k̂e- k̂q-*)
(d) Av. *ž* ( < IE. *ĝzh*): *uz-važaṯ* (Lat. *vexit*).
   ( < IE. *ĝ-d*): *mərˀždikəm* ( < IE.* *mr̥ĝ-d-*).
   ( < IE. *ĝ-dh*): *važdri-š* (IE.* *u̯eĝh-*).
   ( < IE. *ĝ-bh*): GAv. *vīžⁱbyō* (dat. abl. pl. of *vīs-*).

The new palatals became *č* and *ǰ*, probably palatal affricates, except in positions where stops became spirant (cf. §2). In such positions *š* and *ž* were spoken: the coincidence under these conditions with certain representations of the old palatals, (c) and (d) above, affords the best possible example of the connection between spirantizing tendencies and tendencies which accelerate palatalization. Examples:

(e) Av. *č* ( < Ar. *k′*). *čit* O. P. *čiy* (Gr. τὶ).
(f) Av. *ǰ* ( < Ar. *g′*): *ǰvaⁱti* O. P. *ǰīvāhy* (Gr. δίαιτα).
   ( < Ar. *g′h*): *ǰaⁱnti* O. P. *a-ǰanam* (Gr. θείνω).
(c) Av. *š* ( < Ar. *k′*): GAv. *vašyetē* (Gr. ἔπος).
(d) Av. *ž* ( < Ar. *g′*): *dažaⁱti* (Goth. *dags*, Lith. *degù*).
   ( < Ar. *g′h*): *snaēžaⁱti* (Gr. νίφ-α).

**9.** In that dialect of Aryan which later became the Indic language the spirantizing tendency of usual speech was less than in the sister dialect. Consequently palatalization proceeded much less rapidly.

In the utterance of unvoiced sounds, where the glottis is open, more breath is passed through the mouth than in the utterance of voiced sounds.[5] Unvoiced palatal stops, therefore, are more susceptible to affrication and spirantization than voiced stops. In a language where the breath stress is at all strong—strong enough to develop even a voiced palatal with some rapidity—this difference does not show itself; in the early history of Sanskrit, however, we must ascribe to it the more rapid development of IE. *k̂* (*k̂h*) as compared to *ĝ ĝh*.[6]

---

[5] Cf. the candle experiment cited in §2.
[6] Similarly perhaps F. *ciel* ( < Lat. *caelum*), but *gendre* ( < Lat. *gener*), with *s* and *ž*. French breath stress is decidedly weak.

As a consequence of this more rapid development of IE. $\hat{k}$ it came about that when the new Aryan palatals developed from velars before front vowels, the IE. *unvoiced* $\hat{k}$ was already well along toward spirantization, but the IE. *voiced* palatals $\hat{g}$ $\hat{g}h$ were still stops and accordingly coincided with the new voiced palatal stops Ar. g' g'h.

In the combinations IE. $s\hat{k}$ and $s\hat{k}h$ the IE. palatal did not develop so rapidly as in independent $\hat{k}$ because the preceding s here lessened the breath stress for the following $\hat{k}$ $\hat{k}h$, cf. §2. The s was assimilated to the following palatal, becoming a palatal sibilant,—cf. the similar change later in Sanskrit, as in *tataš' ca* from *tatas + ca*. Thus IE. $s\hat{k}(h)$ ($= sk'(h)$) became $š\hat{k}'h > š'k'\chi' > š't'š'$ which was then simplified to $t'š'$[7]—written (c)ch and pronounced as a prolonged t' plus decided spirant glide, cf. *tac chakyam* in later times from *tat + š'akyam* (§6), but *tac ca* pronounced *tat'-t'a* (with much slighter glide) and written without the h, from *tat + ca*—the c in ca being t' with a slight glide. IE. $s\hat{k}$ also occurs in the compounds *ducchúnā* (*duš + š'unā*) and *párucchēpa* (*paruš + š'ēpa*).—IE. $\hat{k}s\hat{k}$ either became $s\hat{k}$ as in Latin *posco* (Brugmann, Gr. I², §707, Anm.); or, if this change is not to be assumed for Aryan, it became $\hat{k}\hat{k}$ where the lengthened tongue pressure incident to articulation of a double stop preserved the stop value, giving Sk. t'š', ((c)ch), cf. below.

What has been said in the last three paragraphs applies to the IE. palatals before vowels, semivowels, nasals, and r. In these positions, then, Sanskrit possessed at the end of the Aryan period the following sounds: unvoiced: š', t'š', k' (Ar. palatal); voiced: g' (IE. palatal and Ar. palatal), g'h (IE. palatal and Ar. palatal), g'g' (Ar. palatal, from older zg').

These sounds suffered little change in Sanskrit. In historic times š' had reached palatal sibilant pronunciation. t'š' written (c)ch was a palatal affricate: both t'š' as well as k' g' g'h g'g' were spoken with the front rather than the middle of the tongue; the latter set of sounds early added a spirant glide, and were later different from the dentals scarcely in any respect but this. We write t' (Sk. c), d' (Sk. j), d'h (Sk. *jh>j, h), d'd' (Sk. jj). As for this last sound: it in no case represents an IE. palatal, but always Ar. zg', which developed like IE. $s\hat{k}$, except that in the voiced sound the final spirant glide was less noticeable. Hence the parallelism of Ar. zg' > Sk. d'd' with Sk. cc rather than (c)ch. Cf. also *taj jalam* for *tad + jalam*. Where d'h was not deaspirated the voiced stop element was lost, leaving voiced h.[8] Thus, in the positions named, the Sanskrit spoke:

    (a)  Sk. š'( <IE. $\hat{k}$): *váš'mi* (Gr. ἐκών).
    (b)  Sk. (c)ch (pr. t'š', <IE. $s\hat{k}$): *gáccha-ti* (Gr. βάσκε).
         ( <IE. $s\hat{k}h$): *chinát-ti* (Gr. σχίζω).

---

[7] For an analogous simplification, cf. prim. Slavic *štš'* > Slov. and Russ. t'š' (as in *sveča*), Brugmann, Gr. I², §316, Anm. 2. Cf. also Sk. *vṛkši < *vṛ̥škši, š'ikša-ti < *š'iškša-ti*.

[8] This pronunciation will be spoken of in the note on the IE. sonant aspirates.

($<$ IE. $\hat{k}s\hat{k}$): $p\underset{.}{r}cchá\text{-}ti$ ($<$ IE. $*pr\hat{k}\text{-}s\hat{k}e\text{-}ti$).
(c) Sk. $j$ (pr. $d'$, $<$ IE. $\hat{g}$): $jánas\text{-}$ (Gr. $\gamma\acute{\epsilon}\nu o s$).
($<$ IE. $\hat{g}h$): $ján\underset{}{g}h\bar{a}$ (Goth. $gaggs$).
($<$ Ar. $g'$): $jíva\text{-}ti$ (Gr. $\delta\acute{\iota}\alpha\iota\tau\alpha$).
($<$ Ar. $g'h$): $ja\text{-}gh\breve{a}na$ (Gr. $\theta\epsilon\acute{\iota}\nu\omega$, $\acute{\epsilon}\text{-}\pi\epsilon\phi\nu o\nu$).
(d) Sk. $h$ (voiced sound, $<$ IE. $\hat{g}h$): $sáhas\text{-}$ (Gr. $\acute{\epsilon}\chi\omega$,
Goth. $sigis$).
($<$ Ar. $g'h$): $hán\text{-}ti$ (Gr. $\theta\epsilon\acute{\iota}\nu\omega$).
(e) Sk. $c$ (pr. $t'$, $<$ Ar. $k'$): $ci\text{-}d$ (Gr. $\tau\acute{\iota}$).
(f) Sk. $jj$ (pr. $d'd'$, $<$ Ar. $zg'$): $májja\text{-}ti$ (Lith. $mazgóti$).

**10.** Before sibilants the IE. palatals $\hat{k}$ $\hat{g}$ appear in Sanskrit as $k$. Even here IE. $\hat{k}$ $\hat{g}$ must in Aryan times have possessed some palatalization, though much less than in the same combination in the Iranian part of the territory. We may suppose that IE. $\hat{k}s$ was in pre-Indic $k'\check{s}$. Whatever spirant glide may have followed $k'$ was of course lost in the sound of the $\check{s}$: as the palatalization of the $k'$ was thus scarcely noticeable, the combination was finally pronounced $k\check{s}$, coinciding with $k\check{s}<$ IE. $qs$, $q^us$.

The combination IE. $\hat{g}zh$ is also found in Sanskrit as $k\check{s}$. Now voiced sibilants (except for the sibilant glide of $d'$ or $d'd'$) were not pronounced in Sanskrit, but were lost. We may suppose that the Sanskrit breath stress was too weak to enounce a sibilant with closed glottis—of this more below. In Sanskrit pronunciation, then, $zh$ would have been lost. We must therefore ascribe the change of IE. $zh$ to $\check{s}$ to a pre-Sanskrit stage—perhaps to a dialectic change in the Aryan period. In this, Sanskrit resembles Celtic and Germanic, in which also the normal processes of the language acted on a basis of pre-Celt. and pre-Germ. $ks$ $ts$ $ps$ and not $gzh$ $dzh$ $bzh$ (cf. Brugmann, Gr. $I^2$, §§766, 2. 796, b. 827). It is worth noting also that the Iranian alone has preserved the combinations in question as voiced sounds. In Sanskrit, then, IE. $\hat{g}zh>k'\check{s}$ (for "aspiration" attached to a voiceless $\check{s}$ sound means nothing) $>k\check{s}$. Examples:

(g) Sk. $k\check{s}$ ($<$ IE. $\hat{k}s$): $ák\check{s}a\text{-}s$ (Gr. $\ddot{\alpha}\xi\omega\nu$).
($<$ IE. $\hat{k}p$): $k\check{s}iti\text{-}\check{s}$ (Gr. $\kappa\tau\acute{\iota}\sigma\iota s$).
($<$ IE. $\hat{k}ph$): $rák\check{s}as\text{-}$ Gr. $\acute{\epsilon}\rho\acute{\epsilon}\chi\theta\omega$).
($<$ IE. $\hat{g}zh$): $a\text{-}v\bar{a}k\check{s}\bar{\imath}t$ (Lat. $vexít$).
($<$ IE. $\hat{g}dh$): $k\check{s}am\text{-}$ (Gr. $\chi\theta\acute{\omega}\nu$).

**11.** The statements in the preceding § do not apply to IE. $\hat{k}$ $\hat{g}$ + sibilant *before stops* (i.e. before $t$ $d$, as no other case seems to occur). In this position IE. $\hat{k}s$ $\hat{g}z$ did not become Sk. $k\check{s}$ because the $\check{s}$ $\check{z}$ dropped out before the preceding IE. palatals had lost their palatal value. Thus IE. $\hat{k}st>$ Ar. $k'\check{s}t>k't$ and IE. $\hat{g}zd>$ Ar. $g'\check{z}d>g'd$. Cf., for the law of dropping sibilants between stops in Sanskrit, Brugmann, Gr. $I^2$, §828 (who, however, does not draw the necessary conclusions about the cases involving IE. palatals). This process is decidedly natural for a language with weak breath stress, where a sibilant between stops is at best weakly pronounced. In the case of the voiced combination we need only remember that the Sanskrit nowhere pronounced a voiced sibilant. The early date of this law appears in the treatment of *rapš′á-tē* < *\*ra^xp-sk̂e-*: here the *s* dropped out before the general pronunciation of *k̂* and its pronunciation in the combination *sk̂* had diverged: i.e. before the former had lost its stop value.

The word *pr̥cchá-ti* (§9) may also be an illustration of this law, unless, like Lat. *posco*, we suppose it earlier to have dropped the first *k̂*.

**12.** To return to Sk. *kṣ̌*. When Sanskrit reduced its final consonant groups to simple consonants, final *-kṣ̌* had to become *-k*.

It is natural, however, that during the operation of the law spoken of in §11 even final IE. *-k̂s* was affected when it came before stops. Thus *\*rāk′š tatra* was spoken *\*rāk′ tatra*. Such forms as *\*rāk′* survived and were spoken alongside the forms in *-k* < *-kṣ̌*, competing with them, as we shall see, at some advantage.

In historic times forms with final *-k* < IE. palatal were used as follows, —*-k′* having everywhere else superseded *-k*:—exclusively in the roots and root-stems *diš′-*, *dr̥š′-*, *spr̥š′- ruj-*,[9] *dih-*;[10] in the stems *ū́rj-*,[11] *bhiṣ̌áj-*,[12] *r̥tvíj-*;[13] optionally in the root *naš′-* 'attain'.[14]

Sporadic instances of forms with final *-k*, where *-k′* has generally been adopted, are the following: (RV.:) *anák* (stem *anákṣ̌-*, cf. *náš′a-ti*), *ámyak* (root *myakṣ̌-*, cf. *miš′rá-s*); (Vedic:) *prāṇadhŕ̥k dadhŕ̥k* (root *dr̥ṅh-*, cf. Av. *dar^ezaye^iti*, Uhlenbeck, l. c., s. v. *dŕ̥hyati*), *puruspŕ̥k* (root *spr̥h-*, cf. Av. *spar^ez-*, Uhlenbeck, l. c., s. v. *spr̥hayati*); (*Māitrāyaṇī-Saṃhitā:*) *viš′vasrk* (root *sr̥j-*, cf. Av. *har^eza^iti*, Uhlenbeck, l. c., s. v. *sr̥játi*). Here belong finally the Vedic *s*-aorist forms *asrāk* (root *sr̥j-*) and *adrāk* (root *dr̥š′-*), when used as 2d person sg.

As for the competing forms with *-k′*, they will be spoken of below.

**13.** At the time of the simplification of final consonant groups final *-k′t* (either < IE. *-k̂t* or < IE. *-k̂st* by the law in §11) became *-k′*. Thus IE.

---

[9] The final of *ruj-* is not treated in Sanskrit as an IE. palatal, but, wherever the treatment of the two would necessarily differ, as an Ar. velar. Historically, however, the final of *ruj-* is probably an IE. palatal, cf. Lith. *lúszti*, *láužyti*, Russ. *luznut′*, mentioned by Uhlenbeck, Et. Wb. d. Ai. Spr., s.v. *rujáti*.

[10] The final of *dih-* is not treated in Sanskrit as an IE. palatal; but cf. Brugmann, Gr. I², §597, 1.

[11] The final of *ū́rj-* is not treated in Sanskrit as an IE. palatal; historically it is considered such by Brugmann, Gr. I², §608.

[12] The final of *bhiṣ̌áj-* is not treated in Sanskrit as an IE. palatal; historically it falls into this class, cf. Brugmann, Gr. I², §597, 1.

[13] The final of *r̥tvíj-* is not treated in Sanskrit as an IE. palatal; the derivation of the word from the root *yaj-* shows the Sanskrit treatment to be unhistoric.

[14] On the rationale of generalized *k*-forms, cf. Meillet, IF. 18, 418.

-$\hat{k}t$ and -$\hat{k}st$ always gave -$k'$ and IE. -$\hat{k}s$ sometimes gave -$k'$, sometimes -$k$.

**14.** At the time of the simplification of final consonant groups IE. $\hat{k}$ $\hat{g}$ before stops were still uniformly palatal stops $k'$ $g'$. Breath stress in Sanskrit, we may suppose, was too weak for the formation of a spirant or sibilant glide between stops—cf. the earlier dropping of $s$ between stops, §11.

After the time of the simplification of final consonant groups, however, IE. $\hat{k}$ $\hat{g}$ before $t$ $d$, $dh$ lost their stop articulation. Concretely expressed: the tongue, instead of passing from a vowel position (1) upward to form a palatal stop (2) and then (while loosening this) forming with the tip a dental stop (3), took, without change of breath or time used, a simpler course. We must remember in this connection that (as we had occasion to note in §9) later, in historic times Sanskrit had no strictly palatal stops corresponding to $k'$ or $g'$, but pronounced its "palatals" with the blade rather than the middle of the tongue. So here, the tongue, instead of forming (2) passed more directly from (1) to (3), only approximating (2) in a position (2a). This approximation (2a) produced in the voiceless group a sibilant sound, $\check{s}$ or $\d{\check{s}}$. In the utterance of the voiced group, however, there was not breath enough passing through the mouth to make (2a) audible as a spirant or sibilant—(the Sanskrit could not pronounce a voiced sibilant):—(2a) formed simply a prolongation of the vowel ("compensatory lengthening").[15] In these cases the dentals (3) were pronounced farther back in the mouth than usual, becoming (as the Sanskrit made this distinction) "linguals", not dentals. That is: -$ik'ta$-> -$i\d{s}\d{t}a$- but -$ig'da$-> -$i$ . . . [$\d{\check{z}}$] . . . $da$-> -$i\d{d}a$-. The change of $a > \bar{o}$ before dropped $\hat{g}$ is similar to that before dropped Ar. $h$ in sandhi, as in $y\acute{o}$ $d\acute{a}m\bar{e}$ < Ar. *$yah$ $dam$- (instead of phonetic *$yaz$ $d$-). In both cases the $\bar{o}$ is due to the quality of $ah$ and $a$ + spirant-position. The change to $\bar{e}$ instead of $\bar{o}$ in $\bar{a}$-$mr\bar{e}\d{d}ayati$ $tr\d{n}\bar{e}\d{d}hi$ is probably due to the preceding $r$ ($r\d{n}$) sound: here $a$ had a value nearer $e$, as also before Ar. $z$, cf. Sk. $s\bar{e}dy\acute{a}$-$t$ (Av. $hazdy\bar{a}$-$\d{t}$). Cf. Brugmann, Gr. I², §§830, 8, a. 1005, 5.

A possible case of IE. $\hat{k}q$ later $k'k$ shows the same treatment of $k'$ as before dental, namely $\check{s}'ik\d{s}a$-$ti$ < *$\check{s}'i\check{s}k\d{s}a$-$ti$ < *$\hat{k}i$-$\hat{k}q$-$se$-; cf. above, footnote; Brugmann, Gr. I², §§615, 2. 829, Anm. I; Whitney, l. c., §§1030, a. 1040.

Examples of the above change:

(h) Sk. $\d{\check{s}}\d{t}$ ( < IE. $\hat{k}t$): $v\acute{a}\d{s}\d{t}i$ (Gr. ἑκών).
( < IE. $\hat{k}st$): $c\acute{a}\d{s}\d{t}\bar{e}$ ( < IE. *$q^{u}e\hat{k}s$-).

---

[15] As to the inability of the Sanskrit to pronounce voiced sibilants, cf., aside from the historic state of the language, the treatment of IE. $z$ (about which some comment will be made below), and the retention of the sibilant in Ar. $sk'$ (Sk. $vr\d{s}'c\acute{a}ti$), but not in Ar. $zg'$ (Sk. $m\acute{a}jjati$).

(i)  Sk.—*ḍ* (<IE. *ĝd*): *mṛḍiká-m* (*ṛ* long in RV.,
                    <IE. \**mṛ-ĝd-*).
     (<IE. *ĝzd*): *śōḍaš'a* (<IE. -*ĝz-de-*).
(j)  Sk.—*ḍh* (<IE. *ĝdh*): *ūḍhá-s* (<IE. \**ueĝh+to-*).
     (<IE. *gzdh*): *śōḍhā́* (<IE. \*-*gz-dh-*).

**15.** In the position before dentals the IE. palatals have thus coincided in Sanskrit with Ar. *š ž* (<IE. *s z* after *ĭ, ŭ, ṛ, r*), as in *tíṣṭha-ti* and *mīḍhá-m* (Av. *mižḍə-m*).

**16.** We have now considered the development of the IE. palatals in the following positions:

(1) before vowels, semivowels, nasals, and *r*, to *š' j h* (*c*)*ch* (§9);
(2) before preserved sibilants, to *k*, giving *kṣ* (§10);
    (2a) final -*kṣ* becoming -*k* (§12),
    (2b) or, before initial stops, -*k'* (§§11, 12);
(3) before dental stops (or sibilants+dental stops), to *k' g'*, giving *k't g'd(h)* (§11);
    (3a) final -*k't* becoming -*k'* (§§11, 13),
    (3b) *k't* and *g'd(h)* otherwise becoming *ṣṭ* and —*ḍ(h)* (§14).
(4) before velars the treatment of palatals was probably the same as before dentals (§14).

**17.** Before labial stops, where palatals were followed by closure of the lips, inaction of the tongue, and stoppage of the breath current, these sounds suffered no change, but remained as *k' g'*, the former coinciding with the -*k'* of §12 and of §13. Hence we may say that in all these cases the Sanskrit retained the IE. palatals until a late prehistoric time at a stage which, so far, we have represented by *k' g'*—meaning thereby to indicate stopped consonants articulated with the "middle part" of the tongue (*Zungenrücken*) against a point of the palate forward of the *k g* point, and pronounced without spirant vanish.[16]

In historic Sanskrit these *k' g'* sounds are uniformly represented by the so-called "cerebrals" or "linguals" written *ṭ ḍ*. Whitney, l. c., §45, says: "The lingual mutes are by all native authorities defined as uttered with the tip of the tongue turned up and drawn back into the dome of the palate (somewhat as the usual English smooth *r* is pronounced"). They are (§46) "perhaps derived from the aboriginal languages of India".

We have here most probably a case of sound substitution. It is easy to see how a people unaccustomed to hearing correctly or articulating sounds formed with the middle tongue against the dome of the palate, would substitute "linguals" for these sounds. The difference in the place of

---

[16] By this time, needless to say, Sk. *c* and *j* from whatever source had become *t' d'*,—stops with a spirant glide, formed very near the "dental" points of tongue and palate.

articulation would be slight if any; the change would be only in the manner: instead of bringing the dorsal surface of the tongue against the palate, the Hindu articulated with the tip. Examples:

(k) Sk. $ṭ$ ($<$ IE. $\hat{k}$): *viṭ-páti-ṣ* (historic form, beside
  *viš'-páti-ṣ*).
  ($<$ IE. -$\hat{k}s$): *rā́ṭ tatra* ($<$ *rḗks t-*).
  ($<$ IE. -$\hat{k}st$): *avā́ṭ* ($=a$-*vākṣīt* Lat. *vexit*,
    formed without the connecting *ī*).
  ($<$ IE. $\hat{k}t$): *ánaṭ* (root *naš'-* $+ t$).
(l) Sk. $ḍ$ ($<$ IE. $\hat{g}$) *viḍbhyás* (dat. abl. pl. of *viš'-*, GAv.
    *vīz$^i$byō*).

**18.** The occurrence of $ṭ$ $ḍ$ for older $k'$ $g'$ ($<\hat{k}$ $\hat{g}$) is strictly phonetic, then, (1) before labials (2) finally where a following -$t$ or -*št* have been dropped, and (3) finally where a following -*š* has been dropped before initial stops. Accordingly we should inflect as follows, e.g., the noun stem *viš'-* (IE. *u̯iḱ-* Av. *vīs-*):

| | |
|---|---|
| Nom. sg. | *víṭ* (before stops, otherwise:) *vík*, |
| loc. pl. | *vikṣú*, |
| *bh*- cases | *viḍbhyā́m, viḍbhíṣ, viḍbhyás*, |
| other cases | *víš'am, viš'ā́, viš'í*, etc. |

Most noun stems ending in IE. palatals differ from *viš'-* in forming the loc. pl. with analogic $ṭ$ for $k$, e.g., -*liṭsu* from -*lih-*. In the later language *viṭsu* is the loc. pl. of *viš'-*: the long survival of the phonetic *vikṣu* being due probably to frequency of use. The complete victory of -$ṭ$ over -$k$ in the nom. sg. is due mostly to the analogy of the *bh*-cases, though the occurrence of -$ṭ$ before initial stops no doubt gave the start. A few isolated and rare -$k$ forms are quoted in §12, end: these sporadic survivals in the literature may well be the reflex of a usage common in the spoken language. The forms *ṣā́ṭ* and *ṣaṭsú* of the numeral *ṣa(k)ṣ-* also show victory of the -$ṭ$ form.

On the other hand, the nouns named in §12 as having -$k$ in the nom. sg. have extended this sound to exclusive use. They also have retained, like *viš'-*, the *k*-form in the loc. pl. On the basis of these two forms they have then substituted velar forms for the $ḍ$ of the *bh*-cases, e.g. *dṛgbhíṣ*. In the case of the radical noun from the root *ruj-* and of the other nouns in -$j$ ($<$ IE. $g$) mentioned in §12, this process left no distinction between these nouns and the nouns in -$j$ ($<$ IE. $g$, $g^{u̯}$)—whose influence of course came into play in all these cases.

In verb forms the peculiar combinations made by IE. palatals plus dental endings have helped to keep the roots in IE. palatals distinct. The roots *ruj-* and *dih-*, however, which are treated as if their finals represented IE. velars or labiovelars, are probably the victims of analogic transference, cf. the notes in §12. On the other hand the root *bhrajj-* is treated (in its few forms, e.g., pple. *bhṛṣṭá-s*) as if its final were an IE. palatal; its cognates however show plainly that its final is not of this class: e.g., CSl. *obrŭzgnǫti*, cf. Uhlenbeck, l. c., s. v. *bhṛjjáti*. Note also such formations as *mūḍhá-* for *mugdhá-* and finally the transference to palatal conjugation of the root *ruh-* with IE. *-dh*.

Single verb forms with *-ṭ* for *-k* or *vice versa* are also found. Thus the root aorist and *s*-aorist of roots in IE. palatals ought to form the 2d person sg. in *-k* or *-ṭ* ( <older *-kṣ* or *-k'ṣ* before stops) and the 3d person sg. in *-ṭ* ( <older *-k't* or *-k'ṣt*). As a matter of fact the *-k* forms quoted in §12, end, (*adrāk, asrāk*) with *nak* (from *naš'-* 'attain') and *rōk* (from *ruj-*) and the *-ṭ* forms *ánaṭ* (*naš'* 'attain'), *aprāṭ, abhrāṭ, ayāṭ, asrāṭ* are used indifferently for the two persons. The forms *ayās* and *srās* occur twice each for the 2d person sg.; the latter form is explained by Bartholomae as belonging to a 3d sg. \**srāt* with *-t* for *-ṭ* through dissimilation by the preceding *r*. *Ayās* is probably quite unphonetic: the analogic relationship is well explained by Whitney, l. c., §555, a.

Such forms as *uddhi* for \**ūḍhi* ( <\**uĝ-dhi*), imperative of *vaš'-*, are formed on the model of *dug-dhi* and the like, with the feeling that *-š'* before *-dh* as before *-bh* ought to give *-ḍ. ṣaḍ-ḍhá ṣaḍ-dhá* for *ṣōḍhá* ( <\**-eĝz-dh-*) are of course of similar origin.

**19.** To sum up, our theory of the IE. palatals in Sanskrit is as follows. IE. *k̂* etc. are, in accordance with the standard view, which is based on phonetic likelihood, supposed to have been slightly palatalized velar stops. —(1) In Aryan (i.e., before the palatalization of IE. velars and labiovelars and before the subsequent change of IE. *ĕ, ŏ > ă*) there were two dialects: the Iranian with strong spirant tendency, which developed IE. *k̂* etc. so rapidly that the new Ar. palatals could not coincide with them; and the Indic which spirantized *k̂* etc. less rapidly, so that, while IE. *k̂* never coincided with the new Ar. palatals, IE. *ĝ* and *ĝh* did. Before vowels, semivowels, nasals, and *r* IE. *k̂ ĝ ĝh* became Sanskrit *š' j h*.—Before stops and sibilants they at first remained *k' g'*. After the dropping of sibilants between stops, *k'š* became Sanskrit *kṣ*.—The simplification of final consonant groups reduced *-kṣ* to Sanskrit *-k* and *-k't* to *-k'*.—Now *k't* everywhere became *ṣṭ* and *g'd(h)* everywhere became—*ḍ(h)*.—(2) Finally *k'* and *g'* (which now remained only in final position and before labial stops) became *ṭ* and *ḍ*.

**20.** Having constructed our edifice we must now defend it. The two points most liable to objection from the viewpoint of the current theory are above marked as (1) and (2). We shall now consider these points.

**21.** As to point (1), we must observe that we have determined no anterior limit, chronologically, to the state of things there described. The "dialectic" difference between Iranian and Indic in the treatment of the IE. palatals may date back—and probably does date back—to the time when the IE. dialects first began to diverge in their pronunciation of these sounds.

The objection to (1) then will be: How is it possible that of the Aryan sister languages, which long formed a unit, making in common many changes of pronunciation, flexion, use of forms, vocabulary, etc., one should be a thorough-going *satəm* language, the other far from that and almost a *centum* language?

We may answer that this is not only possible, but that this our view is decidedly in accordance with the results of modern investigation. When we say that Iranian and Indic in common changed IE. *ĕ*, *ŏ* to *ă*, but even before that time—and indeed from the Indo-European time—diverged in the pronunciation of the IE. palatals, we are only implying that two successive sound changes, though in part coinciding as to territory, may be topographically of different extent. Iranian and Indic were mutually intelligible dialects in Aryan times, although the old *centum-satəm* sound change had left some difference between them. So the Italic, for instance, agrees in a number of developments with the Celtic and in a number with the Greek. *A priori* it is, in fact, much more likely that one of the so-called *satəm* languages should differ somewhat from the others in its treatment of the palatals, than that the eastern languages and the western languages should be cut apart like two halves of a cheese.

Such a division as that between *centum* and *satəm* languages has value only as a description or classification of actual facts. As the Sanskrit does not actually represent the IE. palatals by sibilants, but only partly so and mostly by palatal, velar, and lingual stops, the burden of proof rests entirely on those who wish to class Sanskrit with the sibilant languages and insist that the Sanskrit sibilants are hidden behind the historic Sanskrit stops.

**22.** This brings us to the second point of objection. We have supposed that in certain positions the IE. palatals remained palatalized velar stops in Indic until shortly before the historic time, when they were changed to the Sanskrit lingual stops. In other words, we assumed a sound substitution $k'$ $g' > ṭ$ $ḍ$ where the current view supposes a development of $k'$ $g' >$ $š'$ $ž' > ṭ$ $ḍ$. Aside from the methodic consideration that it is unnecessary to suppose such a roundabout development as the latter, our chief argument was that a development from $š'$ $ž'$ to $ṭ$ $ḍ$, or in general from sibilants to stops is improbable and unparalleled.

The objection may be urged, now, that this development is paralleled in Sanskrit, that the IE. sibilants in Sanskrit sometimes appear as lingual and as dental stops. Let us consider these phenomena and attempt to divine their meaning.[17]

We must note, first, that the actual representation of IE. sibilants and of IE. palatals does in one set of cases universally coincide: namely, the IE. palatals before dental stops coincide with Ar. *š ž* in the same position (cf. §15).

Secondly we must note that the following representations of IE. sibilants as stops are rare in the older language. If in some cases the analogies involved seem indirect, we must remember that they were not made any oftener than this would lead us to expect. The representations in question become regular only after the grammarians, who naturally were struck by what seemed to them decided and peculiar sound-changes, prescribed them as correct.

Thus when we find a few cases in the older language of *š* before *s* in inflection "becoming" *k*, so as to give *kš*, the explanation is obvious:— *vášṭi* : *vákši=vivēšṭi* : *vivēkši*. Similarly, Vedic 2d and 3d sg. *piṇak* as if from a palatal root.

So obvious is this explanation that even some advocates of the prevalent view have decided to adopt it, although giving up the change *š > k* forces the corollary that IE. *k̂ ĝ* before sibilants at least never quite became sibilants, but were "Ar. *χ γ*".

The second supposed change of sibilants to stops is that to linguals. Final -*š* (IE. -*s* + -*s* of nom. sg. or -*s*, -*t* as verb endings) appears in a few old cases as -*ṭ*. Later this is considered regular, and the final -*š* of radical noun stems appears as -*ṭ* -*ḍ* also before the endings -*su* and -*bh*-, e.g. *dvíṣam, dvíṭ, dviṭsú, dviḍbhíš*; imperfect tense: *ádvēṣam, ádvēṭ, ádvēṭ*.

The standard view wisely leaves *dvíṭ, ádvēṭ* out of play; *dviṭsú* is allowed to be unoriginal; but *dviḍbhíš* is considered the regular phonetic development of \**dviž-bhiš*. From this *dvíṭ*, etc., developed.

The facts of the language are decidedly against this view. The prefix *duš*- nowhere changes its final to a stop, lingual or other; similarly the adverb *sajús̄*. The change of -*š* to *ṭ ḍ* occurs "only once in RV. and once in AV. (-*dvíṭ* and -*pruṭ*), although those texts have more than 40 roots with final -*š*; in the Brāhmaṇas, moreover, have been noticed further only -*pruṭ* and *viṭ* (ShB.), and -*š'liṭ* (K.)". On the other hand we still meet in RV. *vivēš* and *á-vivēš* from *viš*- and perhaps a few other cases, cf. Whitney, l. c., §§225, a. 226, d. Even in the later language most cases of final -*š* fall into the class of *haviš*- (*havír ásti, havís tíṣṭhati*, etc., *havírbhiš, havíššu* or *havíḥṣu*). Our judgment has been too much under the spell of the traditional descriptive grammar, which naturally emphasizes the most striking

---

[17] To avoid constant reference to the divergent view we may here refer to Brugmann's Grundriss I², §§819–830. 1005, 5. 1007, 11. Examples are taken from Brugmann and from Whitney, l. c., §§164–168, b. 172. 172, a. 225–226, f. 612, b. 617, b. 620, b.

changes. It was the similarity of *váṣṭi* to *dvéṣṭi* (and later of *vákṣi* to *dvékṣi*) that caused *ádvēṭ* to be formed like *ávaṭ*. In the case of the nouns the necessity was felt that a root noun, in the nom. sg., before *-bh*, and before *-su*, had to have a stop. Owing to forms like *ádvēṭ* the stop thought of was the lingual. Otherwise expressed: as *š'* gave in various connections *šṭ, kš, ṭ, ṭs, ḍbh, š*, which also gave *šṭ* was made to give *kš*, and later *ṭ, ṭs, ḍbh*. Note further such parallels as *lékši* with the new *dvékši* and *alīḍhvam* with (*s*-aor.) *astōḍhvam*. When the feeling had arisen that the stop form of *š* was *ṭ ḍ*, forms like *dviḍḍhi* and forms and spellings like *dviḍḍhvam* arose, cf. *uḍḍhi*, §18, end, and Brugmann, Gr. I², §830, Anm. 2.

**23**. Parallel to forms with *kš* from roots in *-š* are a few forms with *ts* from roots with *-s*, as fut. *vatsyámi* from *vas-*, desid. *jíghatsa* from *ghas-*. The regular treatment would have given \**vassyámi*, etc., or \**vaḥsyámi*, etc. (similarly pronounced), which were not felt as *s*-forms; hence imitation of the nearest lying combination of stops + *s*, as in *patsyámi*. There is no need of any such far-fetched explanation as change of *s* to *t* before *s*, or development of a stop within *ss*.

Again, parallel to the supposed change of *-š* to *-ṭ -ḍ* a change of *-s* to *-d* is considered phonetic in the Vedic *mādbhiš*, etc., from *mās-* and *uṣádbhiš* from *uṣás-*; but there is no reason for abandoning Whitney's explanation of these forms as substitution of *t*-stem forms for *s*-stem forms. Whitney adduces the parallel case of the perf. act. pple.; and, in general, inflection from several stems is so characteristic of the older stages of IE. languages that these ancient and rare forms also are best looked upon as survivals. Cf. for the rest Goth. *mēnōps* and the relation Sk. *yákṛt, yakn-ás*: Lat. *jec-in-or-is*.

There is further one word stem in which IE. *z* is said to have given Sk. *d*: *madgúš-*, cf. Lat. *mergus*, which belong to Sk. *májja-ti*, Lith. *mazgóti*. First note that the *jj* in *májja-ti* is pronounced *d'd'* (with a slight glide), cf. *jj < d + j* in *taj jalam*. This *d'd'* is, as we have seen, parallel to (*c*)*ch* (the first *c* serves, of course, only to indicate that *ch* is a *double* consonant, not a mere aspirate), except that in this combination, pronounced *t'š'*, the *š'* corresponds to the second *d'* of the voiced combination, where sibilant could not be pronounced. Just as *sk'* (= *sk̂*) > *s'k'h* > *s'k'χ'* > *š't'š'* > *t'š'*, so in the voiced combination *zg'*, with slower development, *zg' > z'g'h >* (some such thing as) *d'y' > d'd'*. Now the noun \**mazgu-* regularly > \**mēgu-*, for which *madgú-* was formed from *májja-ti* just as *tád gácchati* corresponds to *taj jagáma* or, practically, as *tyāgá-s* corresponds to *tyájati*.

Thus it appears that the alleged developments of sibilants to Sanskrit stops are in no case instances of phonetic change.

**Note on the IE. "sonant aspirates".** In the above discussion the treatment of IE, *ĝh* was brought up as little as possible, owing to the uncertainty which surrounds the nature of the IE. "sonant aspirates". We shall here recall a few of the properties of these sounds as indicated by their development in the various IE. languages and then show that our view of the development of the IE. palatals in Sanskrit is consistent with the development of IE. *ĝh* to voiced *h*.

(1) The stop element in the IE. "voiced aspirates" was voiced, as a preceding voiceless stop is assimilated. The second element or "aspiration" cannot be pronounced before an immediately following stop, but is left until the stop or stops have been articulated, and is then uttered: in the meantime the glottis is not opened, i.e., the voice continues, as in "assimilation" of surds to sonants,—showing the "aspiration" to have been a voiced sound. In Sanskrit when the stop element is absent the sound uttered is a "voiced *h*" (*stimmhafter Hauch*). We may, then, provisionally ascribe to the "sonant aspirates" the value of a stop closely followed by a voiced breathing—a volume of breath being sent through the open mouth sufficient to be audible as an aspiration (*Hauch*), but not sufficient to necessitate greater opening of the glottis than is consistent with voicing.

(2) The inherent difficulty of pronouncing these sounds is due to the general fact that a delicately graded or "halfway" muscular movement is harder to make than a decided or "all the way" one. Hence the instability of these sounds. They are preserved only in the highly conservative and ancient Sanskrit. In Germanic they were preserved up to the time of the sound-shifting, when they were changed by the strong breath stress, which probably assimilated the stop element to the succeeding spirant element. Sanskrit and Germanic alone kept the "sonant aspirates" apart from other classes of stops.[18]

(3) In Greek and Italic a total opening of the glottis was substituted for the delicately graded opening with voice continuation. Thus the aspiration became voiceless and the stop was assimilated to it. Similar is the result when an English-speaking person first tries to pronounce a "sonant aspirate" as above described, or a Čechish voiced *h*.

(4) The other IE. languages substituted ordinary vibration of the vocal cords for the period of more open vibration: or, from another point of view, they assimilated the voiced aspiration to the following action of the vocal cords.[19]

(5) The difficulty of pronouncing these sounds affects even Sanskrit. In the passage from vowel to stop to "breathing" the (lip or) tongue had to make its stop articulation rapidly: and this rapid action had to be made

[18] This conservative phonetic character of Germanic among the IE. languages is general, cf. a forthcoming paper by Dr. E. Prokosch.

[19] [Throughout this paper, and typically in later publications (even in the 1933 *Language*), Bloomfield wrote '(vocal) chord' instead of customary 'cord'. Surely his usage was no more than the result of a trivial lapse in learning; on that assumption, I have in all cases 'corrected' the spelling. See Kent's review of the Book *Language*, our 41(5), near the end.—CFH]

most rapidly exactly where it is most difficult, in the back of the mouth. Hence we find *h* for *bh* less frequently than *h* for *dh*; and, could we distinguish the cases of *h* for *gh* from those of *h* for (historic or analogic) *g'h*, there is no doubt that we should find them more numerous than the preceding. In the case of *g'h* ( < IE. *ĝh* and Ar. *g'h*) the difficulty of pronunciation was by far greatest, as the middle tongue had to be raised to the highest part of the palate—an articulation nowhere retained in Sanskrit. Hence we find here universal loss of the stop and retention of voiced *h*.

# B3. Review of Wood

1911. *Journal of English and Germanic Philology* 10.628–631.

*Indo-European $a^x$ : $a^xi$ : $a^xu$. A Study in Ablaut and in Word-Formation.* By Francis A. Wood, Ph. D. Strassburg, 1905.

Though years have passed since the publication of Wood's book, its lesson has not been learned. Between 1905 and the present there has been printed much etymologizing that was discredited in advance by the volume before us. The reason for this lies partly in the quiet manner of Wood's work and partly in the fact that the observance of Wood's principles lessens one's chance of publishing new etymologies.

The chief etymological principle of Wood's work is stated in §1: "Synonymy alone is insufficient evidence of relationship." Of this principle the whole book is an illustration, its body being a collection of parallel words in different ablaut-rows, but otherwise alike in form and meaning, as e.g. (§535), E. *snap* "schnappen' and cognates (with plain *e/o*-vocalism): E. *snip* "schnippen", OSw. *snēpa* "kastrieren" and cognates (with *ei*-vocalism): and ON. *snoppa* "Schnauze" OSw. *snōpa* "kastrieren" and cognates (with *eu*-vocalism). These words are related in meaning but not for that reason of common origin. On the contrary, such similarity of sound as there is may be merely a result of the common meaning, i.e., the common meaning may have assimilated the words in form. Another and in this case more likely possibility is that accidental similarity of sound affected the meaning, or finally, that some of the words were formed on analogies in which others were involved.

Although no one would perhaps try to identify the different members of the above or of most of Wood's groups, it is apparent how the principle involved applies to much modern etymologizing. To quote (§6): "For example, we find Germ. *stauma-*; *þauma-*; *dauma-*; 'vapor' in OE, *stēam* 'exhalation, steam'; OHG. *thaum, doum* 'dunst'; *toum* 'dunst'. We might assume an IE. *\*dhoumo-* 'vapor', which with prefixed *s-* would give *\*s-dhoumo-*, *\*stoumo-*. From *\*stoumo-* might come in certain positions *\*toumo-*. There would then be three forms: *\*stoumo-*, *\*toumo-*, *\*dhoumo-*. This gives us a very simple phonetic explanation of these three words—but a very absurd one."

Let us mention no names![1]

Or again, the Greek γνόφος δνόφος ψέφος ψέφας κνέφας "darkness" are derived from various and independent sources: the common meaning has assimilated them in form (§5). Synonymous words might be collected to prove almost any desired sound-law—if synonymy were all that is necessary.

On the other hand, Wood points out (§4) that words of similar sound may influence one another's meaning, as in the case of E. *mash* (cf. G. *mischen*), many of whose meanings are due to the influence of E. *smash*, an entirely different word.

In short, the etymologist must take a concrete view of things. He is dealing with historic fact: if he wishes to show that two words are related he must show that their history has really been divergent, not convergent, —that their similarity is not the result of assimilation. Thus (§30), of synonymous Gic. *skrimp- hrimp- krimp-* "it is altogether more probable that some developed from others as rime-words than that all are derived phonetically from a common form. . . . Thus from original *skrimp-*, *hrint-*, *krink-*, etc., there might arise *skrint-*, *skrink-*; *hrimp-*, *hrink-*; *krimp-*, *krint-*.

"*The hypothesis that such forms are phonetically related would not be established by anything short of historical proof.*"[2]

In §6 Wood attributes such developments as the above especially to the "formative period of a language,"—a concept which we must oppose. A language is formed (i.e., a new speech-community is segregated) by definite changes in the outer surroundings of a group of people—by migrations or the arrival of new neighbors or changes in conditions of communication,—but this has nothing, primarily, to do with those inner processes which are here involved. Greek, and especially Germanic, passed through a period of rime-word formation and word-creation, and what we know of the parent language shows traces of a similar period in IE. times, but such things have nothing directly to do with changing language boundaries. At the time when High German and Dutch, or, say, Greek and Aryan, were first becoming mutually unintelligible, the processes of thought in any of these speech communities were not for that reason other than at other times. The only event which directly changes the inner analogic or phonetic conditions of language is a change in man. The rime-word formation of early Germanic was not a phenomenon of social or political history or geography, but of the human spirit.

We dwell so long on this minor point because our objection to the

---

[1] We might add to Wood's statement that the phonetics of such reim'-dich-oder-ich-hau'-dich etymologies are usually most shaky: the famous prefixal *s*, prefixed to *d*, *dh*, etc., would by all IE. parallels give not *st*, but *zd*, *zdh*.

[2] The italics are our own.

quoted expression involves exactly the principle taught by Wood's work. Namely, the vocabulary of the IE. languages as we have it is the product of countless analogic and "contaminative" developments, formations, and re-formations, the result of a myriad workings and changes of human language tendencies and habits. It exhibits numberless groups of rime-words, ablaut-parallels, and other traces of associational and emotional activity of the human mind. From this immense material it is easy to gather parallel-words galore to prove almost any desired "phonetic law", especially if the law, like the ciphers of the "Baconians", is formulated ad hoc; but such empty groupings of words and blatant assumptions have no claim to truth. We are dealing with history. The task of the etymologist is not to advertise himself by discovering as many such "sound-laws" as possible, but rather to study faithfully and carefully the actual material before him.

The best illustration possible of what the etymologist should do is Wood's book. It contains almost 500 groups of words illustrating the fact that the three ablaut series (plain-vowel, type *slex-*, vowel+*i*, type *sleix-*; vowel+*u*, type *sleux-*) occur in parallel roots, as in Gr. φληδάω "schwatze", φληδεῖν "platzen": φλιδάω "fliesze über, strotze": φλυιδάω "fliesze über, zerfliesze" (§268). A tenth of Wood's examples might have precipitated some scholars into a vortex of unfounded "phonetic developments"; in the book before us there is no random theorizing. The parallelism in question is exhibited as a fact. Certain processes which must have contributed to its existence are mentioned, and there is ample discussion, as we have above indicated, of the principles involved.

It is needless to add that the book contains many a suggestive grouping of material and many a new etymology,—a phase of the author's work which needs not here to be spoken of, as it is universally well recognized.

To our mind two questions come up which Wood leaves unanswered. The first is: where shall we consider the facts sufficient to indicate that a sound-change has taken place? Our own answer is to point to the "circulus" in which every science moves. Certain sound-changes are obvious, so are certain analogic modifications. Detailed study of what is known will usually guide us in new matters, which in turn will confirm or modify our basic assumptions. The phonetician offers much help, though the setters-up of sound-laws have been slow to accept his delimitations of the probable. Less useful has been the psychologist in matters of analogy. Nevertheless the linguists will in time study analogy and perhaps come to definite results.

The second question involved but not answered in Wood's book is that of semantic change. If "synonymy alone is insufficient evidence of relationship," to what extent is dissimilarity of meaning, in phonetically comparable words, evidence of non-relationship? Wood's answer is, that any meaning may develop from any word. A word meaning "fiddlestick" might in time come to mean "notwithstanding". It is here that we disagree with Wood, not in principle but in application. There seems, indeed, to be no bound to semantic development, but in a given case far more caution seems to us needed than Wood is wont to apply. The parent language must, for instance, have had some word for so concrete an idea as, say, "sneeze," but so far as we can see, Wood derives every word for this idea from some word of different meaning, such as "rub" or "grate" or "move quickly, snap",—in fact, the parent language, if Wood's semantic derivations were taken together, would appear to have had a rather colorless vocabulary. Though no one can question the commonness of semantic change, it must yet be remembered that on the whole the meaning of words is fairly tough, especially of every-day words. A great many differences in vocabulary must go back to primitive IE. times: indeed, the farther back we look into the history of any IE. language, the more diversified and concrete a word stock do we find.[3] However, any divergence of the reader's opinion from Wood's in this question will not lessen the value of this excellent book or of the sound linguistics embodied in its classically accurate form.

[3] Cf. Jespersen, *Progress in Language*, §272.

# B4. Review of Prokosch

1912. *Monatshefte für deutsche Sprache und Pädagogik* 13.92–94 [bears date of receipt by editor: 25 February 1912]

*An Introduction to German.* By Eduard Prokosch, Assistant Professor of German and Comparative Philology in the University of Wisconsin. New York: Henry Holt and Company, 1911.

It is perhaps a significant fact that America, more liberally supplied than any other country with normal schools, chairs of pedagogy, and other appliances of teaching aspiring teachers to teach, has had to wait until now for a modern language text book based on sound pedagogic principles. Although it is a good twenty years, for instance, since the theoretical grammar method has been banished from the Prussian schools, our publishers have been turning out, year after year, elementary language books that would not receive the slightest consideration in countries educationally more advanced. Needless to say, the sound book has at last come not from an expert on Methods of Teaching, but from a man who thoroughly knows his subject, in this case, language.

For it is obvious to any student of speech that even a concise and methodic exposition of the grammatical facts of a language is not necessarily a good instrument for introducing a learner to the use of that language. The simplest consideration as well as long-continued tests by experience show that in the case of German the discrepancy is most decided. Space forbids, and in view of previous discussions[1] it is unnecessary here to develop this point. Suffice it to say that the presentation of grammatical theory by the teacher and translation into the vernacular by the student have never taught anyone a language. We must therefore doubly welcome Prokosch's book in the hope that it will hasten the development in America of modern and effective teaching of living languages.

The basis of Prokosch's book is some thirty-five pages of German text, divided into thirty-two lessons, each a connected and sensible unit. As this text includes over a thousand different words and presents every usual

---

[1] See for instance O. Jespersen, *How to Teach a Foreign Language*, New York, 1908, and L. Bahlsen, *The Teaching of Modern Languages*, translated by M. B. Evans, Boston (1903, 1905).

inflection and construction, the material is ample for a year's work, provided, of course, that the student is expected genuinely to assimilate it, to recognize all the words, forms and constructions when he sees them, and to be able to use them, in a modest way, in speech and writing. There is a danger that teachers who are accustomed to the old style books may try to cover the ground too rapidly and find their classes getting little good out of the short but (when thus used) difficult texts; a fuller and more conciliatory preface addressed to teachers would lessen this danger. A good class can profitably be kept a week at each lesson, conversing on the new forms and words and reproducing the text orally and in writing. This distribution of the matter into large units has however one defect: it makes the first day's lesson on a new text rather difficult. If, as is proper, the teacher presents new vocabulary and forms by oral example and explanation in German rather than by the time-honored method of telling the students to "look up the words and translate," he will have to spend two whole hours, for instance before letting his class use lesson 9, the first narrative piece. It would be better—though it might increase the danger above alluded to—if the selections had been more numerous and shorter; say, in the beginning five to ten lines each,—a beautiful model of such a text is the anecdote about Frederick the Second and the eggs on p. 75 of Bahlsen.

Prokosch's use of longer texts is due, perhaps, to his principle of giving in connection with each text a uniform grammar lesson; the second part of the book (consisting of "Exercises," each to be used in connection with the corresponding text lesson) begins each exercise by giving appropriate references to the third part, which is a systematic grammar. Now, it is obvious that only a longer piece of text can in each case illustrate sufficiently the points of grammar involved,—in the 9th lesson, for instance, (1) the preterit of weak verbs, (2) of *sein* and *haben*, (3) the possessive pronouns, (4) the prepositions with the dative, and (5) the dependent word order. It is not necessary, however, that any one text should illustrate all these things or any one of them. Indeed, even as the book stands, many matters come up before they are covered by reference to the grammar, and no harm is done; so why not go farther, letting the texts be as they will, regardless of what grammar or how much grammar is involved in each, and, whenever enough instances of some one phenomenon (say, preterits of weak verbs) have occurred, give a summary with references to the occurrences in the texts, and then grammar assignment? As just remarked, this is to a certain extent done; thus, in lesson 7, where the grammar reference is to nouns of the first class, strong declension, fourteen such nouns are named as having already occurred in previous texts. This principle, carried out, would allow the texts to be of more convenient size and give infinitely greater freedom in their selection.

Another disadvantageous consequence of leaving too much influence to the grammar is that the references are too full: the grammar part of the book, being systematic, gives many a form and many a statement for which the student is not fully prepared when he gets the reference.

The second part of each "Exercise" is the vocabulary, the third consists of questions as a basis for conversation, and the fourth of "Drill." This "Drill" is the weakest point in the book. The student is requested, for instance, in lesson 7, to "decline (sing. and plur.)" *das Zimmer, ein* (!) *Fenster*, etc.,—it reminds one of the books hitherto in use. Although such exercises are a test of whether the student has learned his lesson or not (the plea for so many stupidities of the old method!) they will do him no good. When the time comes to use or recognize, say, a dative plural, the proper verse of the hurried rigmarole of "*das Zimmer, des Zimmers*," etc. will be in a very distant and inaccessible part of the student's mentality. Let him, instead, repeatedly use each form in a sentence.

At the end of each "Exercise" are English sentences for translation; these are useful for review, but inevitably difficult and disconcerting when the German expressions are still unsettled in the student's mind.

These first two parts of the book contain a few inconsistencies. Now and then words are used (usually with a translation) in the exercises which are not given in the vocabulary (*und, oder*, lesson 1; *dann, am Ende*, lesson 3; *steckt, stellt*, lesson 6; *täglich*, lesson 7): this impairs the student's sense of sureness. On the same principle a few words and forms bound to come up in conversation, even though they are not included in the text, should be given in certain vocabularies: for instance, in lesson 1: *blau* (the book is blue), *Lehrerinnen, Schülerinnen* (for conversation; the plurals *Lehrer, Schüler* are given); in lesson 2: *scharf, Türen*; in lesson 3: the plurals *wollen, sollen*; in lesson 4: *schliesst, in* with the accusative; in lesson 6: *stellt, steckt* (used in the exercise). In lesson 9 the farmer speaks to the thief, first as *Sie* (l. 11), then as *du* (l. 17), which is misleading to the English student. There are also a few misprints (lesson 4, l. 2; lesson 13, l. 8, l.10; p. 61, l. 1). In the first few lessons the meaning of the forms in the paradigms (*der, ein, ich, du*, etc.) is not explained. In lesson 3 the composition sentences give the un-English "The whip shall beat the poodle" (*soll*) and "The servant does not want to (=will not) mow the oats", where the bracketed expression is wrong. If students are taught that *er soll* means "he is to" and *er will* "he wants to," the less common uses of the German words will take care of themselves; the introduction of the difficult English "shall" and "will" is most undesirable.

The third part, "Grammar," is excellent, by far the best of its kind. The subjunctive, especially, is here at last described as it is, not on the basis of Latin grammar: *er sei*, "First Subjunctive"; *er wäre*, "Second Subjunctive," both *present* in tense. The only case of a tradition injudiciously clung to is the nomenclature in §77. The fact is that *Sie* has nothing "polite" about it: it is the regular word for "you," *du, ihr* having only their limited field (as part of which use to and by *children* should be mentioned). The present statement, in connection with the persistent use of *du* in the texts misleads the beginner, who in America is lamentably but universally too old for *du*. §127 does not sufficiently impress the necessity of using the pronoun *Sie* in the imperative. One drawback of the grammar has been mentioned: as it is systematic it presents to the student more than is appropriate for him at the time he gets many of the references. A good instance is the reference (lesson 2) to §§235–237, which confronts him with all the facts about "normal," "inverted," and "dependent" word-order. All that the student needs to be told at this stage is that *in a German statement the verb always stands second*; questions and commands as in English.

Beside the brief introduction on pronunciation on the first pages, the book contains an appendix on "The Sounds of German" and a few texts in phonetic transcription. As the publishers refused to print in transcription more of the book and in a more conspicuous place, the author cannot be blamed for neglect. It would, however, be possible to give a set of systematic transcribed exercises on pronunciation, introducing the sounds group by group, first the easier, then the more difficult. The open pronunciation of long *ä* should not be given: it is a spelling pronunciation rarely heard and prevents giving the simple rule that *ä* equals *e*. The reproduction of Viëtor's Sound-Chart on p. 279 lacks *s, z, i:, y:, u:*, and the : after *e*. It would have been wise, for the sake of simplicity, to omit the signs for the French *j*-sound, the spirant *g*, and the uvular *r*.

The trifling character of these emendations should be significant. Prokosch's book is head and shoulders above any that have been used in this country. If we had had such books twenty years ago the *Nation's* and many others' criticism of our modern-language teaching (to wit and namely: that it has been a complete failure) would never have been made. Nor may a modest hope be out of place, as this book has come from the pen of a linguist (or "philologist"), that the science of language may in time come to hold, in America also, its proper place among the sciences.

# B5. Review of Sheffield

1912. *Journal of English and Germanic Philology* 11.619–624.

*Grammar and Thinking. A Study of the Working Concepts in Syntax.*
By Alfred Dwight Sheffield. New York and London, 1912.

We must heartily welcome a sensible volume on the larger aspects of
language, especially as some of the American books on the subject have
been poor and provincial. Sheffield, though not so excellent as Whitney,
Morris, or Oertel, is fortunately a clear thinker and knows what he is
about.

The purpose of the book is, to use the author's words, a fresh appraisal
of the notions that our terms (in grammar; more specifically, in syntax)
presuppose. As such an appraisal of the notions and terminology of
scientific linguistics, if at all necessary, would have to be made on an
entirely different plan and scale from those of S.'s book, we infer that he
is speaking with reference to pedagogic language-work. In this inference
we are supported by the statement (p. 2): 'In fact, the grammar taught in
our schools lies under a stigma as unprogressive. It can hardly be said to
offer the elements of present linguistic science.'

Once granted that this is the field, the school study of English grammar
comes into focus, for anything more than the roughest nomenclature for
word-forms is utterly out of place in school modern-language study,—
and in the ancient-language study of schools terminology has only a relatively greater importance on account of the many unfamiliar forms and
constructions met by the pupil; anything like a theoretical-scientific treatment of the language studied can be attempted in school only at the price
that the pupil fails to learn the language itself. Here again our conclusion
is borne out by the author, who devotes his final paragraphs (p. 183 ff.)
to an estimate of the value of English-sentence-study in school, aptly saying (p. 188): 'Sentence-study . . . is high-school philosophy.' By the way he
adds that 'It can profitably keep in view the diverse speech-material that
the pupil meets in his work with foreign languages . . .' He should perhaps have added that such work must be strictly limited to the English
grammar class-room; in the foreign-language class there is at best only
enough time to give the pupil command over the forms of the foreign

language itself and to familiarize him with the foreign civilization (literature, history, geography, customs, general mental point-of-view, etc.).

It will be seen that I have tried to define the author's exact purpose by
eliminating those possible purposes which his book cannot serve. What
has forced me to this round-about method is the greatest fault of the book:
its construction is not sufficiently organized. S. develops his exposition
somewhat as a sculptor hews a stone gradually into more and more definite
shape. Each chapter brings the whole thought into more intelligible form,
but at no one time is any one articulate part of the subject systematically
chiselled into clearness. The complex nature of any scientific matter is a
strong temptation to such treatment, but to succumb, as does S., is to deny
the reader the clearness that is in one's own mind. A previously uninformed
person would have to study through S.'s book carefully two or three
times before he could understand it. If I have rightly defined the author's
purpose, he would have achieved it far better by a patient and graded
laying-out of his course along a straight ascending line, beginning at the
level of the high-school English teacher's presumable knowledge of conceptual and linguistic processes. When he got to the top of the hill he could
have allowed a survey of the whole field that would show the unessential,
if advantageous character of the particular road taken. S., however, is a
hard leader; even the transition from paragraph to paragraph and sentence to sentence is often insufficiently bridged, though a few words could
have done it, for S. himself always knows whither he is bound. As an extreme case a single sentence may be cited (p. 37): '. . . we shall probably
create no confusion by calling formatives, as well as affixes, prefixes, when
added before the kernel.' Only those who know something of the subject
will here know that S. means some such thing as '. . . by giving the name
formatives not only to suffixes, but also to prefixes.'

This difficult arrangement will cause regret to those who realize what
great harm is done by the barbarous ignorance of our whole school-
system about matters of language,—all the more regret when it is clear
that S. brings study and sound reasoning to bear on such questions as the
relation of sentence-structure to thought, the varying functions of words,
the relation of word-form to word-function, and so on. Especially commendable are the passages where such classifications, diagrams, or tables
are evolved as could be used in pedagogic treatment of grammar (e.g.
pp. 33 f., 40, 50 f., and nearly all of the long chapter on *Terms of Syntax
and Parts of Speech*): where S. is most concrete he is most successful.
S. knows enough about language to have helped teachers of grammar up
to a plane where their dogma and methods would not only correspond in
a decent degree to the facts of the English language, but also give the
pupils some light on the relation between speech and thought.

Possibly, if S. had definitely pictured to himself such an audience, he could have succeeded in better arranging his book. One is, in fact, tempted to think that he did not take care enough about formulating his general point of view. He passes without explicit warning from statements about language in general to statements that apply only to thc European languages usually studied or only to English. A moment's reflection, to be sure, or a look into earlier pages, always shows that S. is not making a mistake, but it does not show that he is not leading an uninformed reader —the very reader in whose hands the book would be useful—into false notions. A separate chapter on English syntax and perhaps a few on the appropriate foreign languages, would have made these transitions avoidable.

Similarly, S., who is thinking of schools, includes in his idea of grammar a normative element and makes such statements as (p. 10): "Where confusions of word-form defeat the ends of expression it is . . . right to call them ungrammatical' and (p. 11): 'Geographical and social differences . . . are bound to give dialectic and illiterate speech, and since differences of this kind are marked off from what is standard not by sharp lines but by a penumbra of doubtful forms, it seems legitimate to expect that *grammar* should make clear some norm of practice.' He then goes on to say that the older grammarians and stylists (videlicet: of literary languages) aimed at too rigid and narrow a standard of what was correct. All this, of course, is true and appropriate; one might expect, perhaps, for the benefit of the reader (on the principle of a certain German maxim), a passing comment on the fact that the scientific study of language has nothing to do with the normative (i.e. purely pedagogic) purpose of teaching people of ('fixing') the use or the better use of a literary language; that the scientific study of language cannot exclude from its observation dialectic speech or that of the illiterate, but may even find these the most suitable fields for certain observations,—especially as a vast preponderance of all human speaking and even of all English speaking has been dialectic and illiterate. Most surprising it is, therefore, when S., instead of making this precautionary remark, suddenly (p. 13) contrasts the scientific study of language with the setting up of normative rules, not as something entirely incommensurable, but as another attitude upon the same question,—as an attitude involving the fault opposite to that of the older grammarians and rhetoricians! He calls it 'the point of view now uppermost' and a 'reaction from pedantry,'[1] and labels as 'partisanship for the slip-shod' such statements as Sweet's in his *New English Grammar*, that the sub-

[1] No one would deny, of course, that there may be today among teachers and authors of school text-books such a reaction and such a partisanship for the slip-shod—but this has nothing to do with the point of view that 'looks especially to understanding speech as a development,' that 'values any fact, whether from classic writing, dialect, or slang,' whose 'interest is purely scientific, taking the facts as they are, without venturing theories as to what they ought to be,'—in short with the scientific study of language.

junctive is nearly extinct, implying that Sweet should have added some disapproving comment. This of course is a confusion of two entirely different activities.

This lack of a definite orientation is what to scholars in the field itself will appear the great fault of the book. Although it has decided scientific value, especially of a suggestive kind, its confusion of distinct and even unrelated concepts must arouse the caution of professional students. This is quite aside from any demands of depth, scope, and detail that the immense subject of the book might call forth from scientific readers, were it primarily intended for them: the faults I am referring to pertain to simple and well-established matters.

Thus, in continuing (p. 14) the discussion of scientific linguistics, S. confuses the factors—sound-change and analogy—that constitute change in language (or, more accurately change in the form of words) with the entirely unrelated question of the selection of words and constructions by good usage. 'Such a liberal tone . . . is apt . . . to foster a notion that sense-association and phonetic law *determine* usage. Of course they *influence* usage, but their working is wholly subject to men's need of conveying to one another distinctions of meaning.' Needless to state that sound-change and analogy are not, so far as we know, subject to our needs of expression, but are, respectively, psycho-physiologic and psychologic processes that occur involuntarily and cannot be directed by our needs and desires. They are the processes which constantly alter the form of our speech-material. The selection by the educated community of words and forms from this speech-material has nothing to do with sound-change and analogy, and these processes do not even remotely 'influence' the selection for literary and cultivated speech, which is a matter of collective taste,—of social form. What has misled S. is the consideration that literary speech should not be too ready to adopt innovations—whether of sound-change or of analogy—which the unfixed dialects have made. Farther on in the book (p. 83) a suggestion of 'concerted effort to shape usage' is again, though here without explicit connection, hitched on to a discussion of the universal unconscious processes of language-change.

A similar misconception probably underlies the statement (p. 55) that "the Chinese, . . . having a special regard for blood-relationships, use two names each for 'brother,' 'sister,' to distinguish elder and younger in each case", etc. The Chinese have inherited these words from the past just as we have ours, and the inheritance shows nothing about the degree of their regard for blood-relationships: either the terms or the regard may exist, arise, or die out quite independently of each other; for a possible example (Finnish) of the loss of the double terminology, see (Steinthal-) Misteli *Charakteristik*, p. 2.

Possibly derived from Jespersen's *Progress in Language*, (p. 55?), which

S. has otherwise read understandingly, is the erroneous notion that sound-change may in some way be controlled by the semantic value or lack of value of the sounds affected. Thus (p. 23 f.) 'Whenever in the history of such a sentence-word (L. *amavi*) slurring and contraction obscure the marks of these terms (tense, person, etc.), it is because a fresh ordering of speech-material has brought them otherwise into view. Thus *amavi*, 'love-did-I,' has given place to *j'ai aimé* (*ego habeo amatum*), 'I did love.'[2] Again (p. 70): 'After word-order had acquired functional value, and the more precise relating-words were current, relating endings lost their importance, and would become assimilated, slurred, and dropped, from the natural tendency of speakers to trouble themselves over no more speech-material than is needed to convey their thought.' Such views as this are quite natural, but as no facts in their favor have ever been ascertained, science has not adopted them; a concrete view of the circumstances, more-over, makes it very unlikely that such facts will ever turn up. The pheno-mena we designate as phonetic change are minutely gradual, unconscious changes of habit in the execution of certain extremely practised and there-fore very much mechanized movements, namely those of articulation. Psychologically viewed, these gradual changes of habit fall into an entirely different plane—one many degrees lower as to consciousness,—from any desire or need of expressing one's thought. Such a desire or need may influence my selection of words or whole expressions, their position, their emphasis and melody, and may even impel an analogic change, but it cannot influence that remote part of my psyche that is without my com-mand or knowledge leading me, as the decades go by, to hand on to posterity certain habits of tongue-position differing by a millimetre or a few sigmas from those which my elders taught me.

Space forbids entering farther into this complex question or at all into a few others of less primary importance. In spite of these errors of prin-ciple, we must hope that S. will continue his studies and publications in this field. Work that will contribute to improve the situation as to lan-guages, English or other, in our schools, is to be welcomed with open arms.

---

[2] Here the example is faulty, for the L. perfect has lived on in the Romance languages by the side of the new compound forms (Cf. e.g. Suchier, *Gr. d. rom. Phil.* I[2], 804): how the latter can be held responsible for sound-changes in the former is a mystery to me. That they are driving the old forms into disuse is another matter.

# B6. Review of Wundt

1913. *American Journal of Psychology* 24.449–453.

*Elemente der Völkerpsychologie, Grundlinien einer psychologischen Entwicklungsgeschichte der Menschheit.* Von Wilhelm Wundt. Zweite unveränderte Auflage. Leipzig: A. Kröner, 1913. pp xii, 523. M. 14.

The monumental volumes of Wundt's *Völkerpsychologie* find not only a summary but also a crowning supplement in the *Elemente der Völkerpsychologie*. Here the entire mental history of man is outlined in a continuous narrative; the various activities, such as custom, myth and religion, and art, are not separated but dealt with in conjunction. We pass from 'Primitive Man' to 'the Age of Totemism,' then to 'the Age of Heroes and Gods,' and finally into 'the Development toward Humanity.' It is safe to say that no other man could have told the story as Wundt has; his vast learning, powerful psychologic insight, vivid sense of history, and, not least, his stylistic ability to present states of flow and change have produced a work of tremendous and awing effect.

It is not necessary to recall here the justification of a social psychology as an inevitable consequence of the rejection, by empirical science, of the metaphysical postulate of an individual soul as the substratum or receiver of experience.[1] Familiar, also, are the general results of the social psychological method: the exclusion of reflective rationalizing explanations, in which logical processes are falsely projected by the explainer into the communal developments. In the *Elemente* one can see the larger results of this methodic precaution. Nowhere is a reflection about the consequences of a development assumed as the cause of that development. Hence the frequent reversal of the naïve view of things: the demon is not a causal explanation of natural happenings, but a creation of emotions, especially fear (p. 355), for the primitive knows only magic causality (pp. 90 ff.). Again, the god grows out of the demon, religion out of the beliefs in demons and spirits, and law out of custom. All this is too familiar to require comment.

---

[1] *Völkerpsychologie*[3], I, 1, p. 9; *Grundriss der Psychologie*[11]. §2, 1.

In one respect, however, the *Elemente* differs, even externally, from the *Völkerpsychologie*. In the latter the subject of language receives two volumes, placed at the beginning of the work,—naturally enough, for language is 'the universal substratum of mental culture' ('die allgemeine Trägerin der geistigen Kultur,' *Elemente*, p. 487). And it appears, at first, when one studies these volumes, that Wundt's social psychology has done for our knowledge of linguistic development exactly what it has done for the other spheres of social activity. Especially the processes of linguistic change had been interpreted only too much as if they were acts of logical reflection; by putting an end to such interpretation and showing the concrete psychological character of changes in language, Wundt has done an inestimable service to the science of linguistics. In the *Elemente*, however, we find but a few pages in the division on 'Primitive Man' (I, §§5 and 6) devoted to language. A sketch of gesture-language and one of a supposedly rather 'primitive' language, the Ewe of Togoland, is all we receive. Of the development from lower to higher forms, or even of any criteria of distinction between these, we learn nothing. This is due to the fact that minute analysis of the processes of change is excluded from the *Elemente*. Descriptions—and Wundt is a master of what may be called kinetic description—of typical stages of the social institutions suffice for the purposes of this book. Could they not have been given for language also? In the *Völkerpsychologie* Wundt has contributed much toward the detailed psychological interpretation of the processes of linguistic change, but toward a history of the development of language ('die generelle Entwicklung') he has given little. The origin of language is splendidly treated and there are valuable ideas and discussions which have bearing on the general further evolution of language; but an outline of this evolution or even a sufficient indication of the direction of development there is not. This, I believe, accounts for the scant treatment of language in the *Elemente*, where only such an outline, with portrayal of typical stages would have been in harmony. Toward this we find in the *Elemente* only a sketch of the origin of vocal language in the light of gesture (Wundt's greatest single linguistic contribution lies here), and then the description of a 'primitive' language.

To regard Ewe as such is, however, a mistake. Language, like the other communal activities, changes most rapidly where there is most contact of communities,—where there are wars, migrations, and, above all, transferences of language to new peoples; and Africa, everything indicates, has long been the scene of all these happenings (*Elemente*, pp. 136 ff.). Further, Ewe is spoken by several millions of people and even serves as a literary language.[2] It is a member, moreover, of the widespread West-Sudanese

[2] Finck, *Die Sprachstämme des Erdkreises*, p. 119; cf. also Cust, *The Modern Languages of Africa*, pp. 203 ff.

family of languages, which possibly may be related to the other great family of the Bantu languages. Plainly, then, this language has behind it a long history of spread, migration, and change. This becomes a certainty when we learn more of its forms. It is a nearly monosyllabic language: the languages of whose history we know anything show a constant shortening of the word toward monosyllabism. This is the direction in which the languages of Europe have developed, especially, of course, English. When, further, we learn that in Ewe the word-order is fixed, we must entirely refuse it the title of a 'primitive' language, for linguistic history everywhere shows us that the syntactic utilization of word-order is a gradual accomplishment. Wundt thinks it a primitive characteristic that in Ewe the modifying word follows its subject ('man big,' not 'big man'), as in gesture-language. It is obvious that fixed word-order allows of only two possibilities, the one realized in Ewe, as in modern French (where we can see it growing out of the free word-order of Latin), the other, for instance, in modern English and in Chinese. Of the Indo-Chinese family of languages,—divergent modern forms of a single older speech,— Chinese and Burmese let the modifier precede, Tibetan and Siamese let it follow. In other words, the correspondence of the Ewe word-order with the order of gesture is, for the question in hand, accidental. When Wundt further cites lack of inflection as a primitive characteristic, he runs directly counter to the evidence of all known linguistic history. Wundt further cites the prevalence of what is called sound-symbolism, but this, again, is a feature which we see growing in some highly developed languages, notably German and English,—as Wundt admits (*Elemente*, p. 67). The symbolic words,—such as, for instance, in English, *clash, crack, crunch, sputter, splutter*,—originate by the same processes as other words and can by no means be cited as traces of the birth-hour of language. No objection can be made to the statement that the method of expression in Ewe is highly concrete. It is an accepted doctrine, however,—and one supported by Wundt's own chapter on Semantic Change in the *Völkerpsychologie*,—that abstract expressions develop at need out of concrete, provided the individualization of concepts (cf. below) has once taken place. A language like Ewe has no highly abstract expressions because the people who speak it have no occasion to speak of abstract matters. Should the occasion arise, the words would soon find themselves.[3]

The source of Wundt's error lies in the fact that, to repeat, his social psychology does not contain in regard to language a view of the general development comparable to that of the other fields of social activity. It would be needless here to give a detailed statement of Wundt's views on points related to this question. Suffice it to say that the rationalizing interpretation, which here also reverses the true course of development, is not

[3] Cf. especially F. Boas, *Handbook of American Indian Languages*, I, 64 ff.

entirely overcome in the *Völkerpsychologie*. In its extreme form this interpretation sees 'primitive' language as a system of monosyllabic words,
each with a separate conceptual content; in the course of development
these gradually merge into an 'agglutinative' state, in which a number of
them lose their full conceptual value and become modifying affixes; finally
the syllables of such groups lose their formal and semantic identity still
more, until polysyllabic inflected words, like those of Latin and Greek,
result. As the historically observable course of events is always diametrically opposed to this, the auxiliary supposition becomes necessary that
development continues only until a language 'enters into history' (by
being recorded in writing), at which point there begins a period of 'decay.'
This theory, developed chiefly by August Schleicher, may be seen in its
application to the various languages of the world in A. Hovelacque's book,
*La linguistique* (fourth edition, Paris, 1888). The selection of Ewe as a
typical 'primitive' language,—even though Wundt is far beyond the gross-
ness of such theorizing as I have described,—is nevertheless a reflex of
such views. Actually,—that is, wherever the facts are accessible,—language is always seen to develop from longer words to shorter, from words
involving more experience-content to words of simpler conceptual value.
Or, more correctly, the sentence of imperfectly analyzable associative
structure, whose parts merely resemble parts of other sentences, gives
place to the sentence fully analyzable into separately apperceptible units
(words) which are felt to occur with unchanged identity in other sentences.
It is this contrast which really embodies the linguistic phase of Wundt's
statement (*Elemente*, p. 73): 'So ist das Denken des Primitiven fast rein
assoziativ. Noch ist die vollkommenere Form der Verknüpfung der
Begriffe, die apperzeptive, die den Gedanken in ein Ganzes zusammen-
fasst, nur spurweise in der Verbindung der einzelnen Erinnerungsbilder
vorhanden.' We must, accordingly, mark as most primitive those languages in which the sentence scarcely or not at all breaks up into words,
but is analyzable only as an associative complex, in the sense that parts of
it resemble parts of other sentences. Thus a language in which 'I-cut-
bear's-leg-at-the-joint-with-a-flint-now' is a single highly inflected word[4]
is a relatively primitive language. By the same token Latin *ambulo*, *ambulas*,
*ambulat*, *ambulabam* are as sentences more primitive than, say, the English
equivalents *I am walking, you are walking, he (she) is walking, I was walking*, because the English sentences consist of several independent symbols
each with conceptual value (words), while the Latin expression views each
occurrence as a whole, with only associative indication of resemblance to
other occurrences.

The importance of a proper understanding of these things for the mental
history of man is not only guaranteed by the function of speech as the

[4] R. A. Marrett, *Anthropology*, p. 139.

substratum of communal mental life, but follows immediately from the nature of our concepts of quality, action, and relation. These,—as no one has, to my knowledge, better described than Wundt (*Völkerpsychologie*[3], I, 2, p. 513 ff.),—depend for their existence upon a separately apperceived object of symbolic value which serves as dominant element in the complex forming the concept. This symbol-object is, of course, the word: without it no concept of action, quality, or relation can exist. Hence, without independent words for such ideas, no scientific thought is possible. The central thread of the mental history of man is a development whose most immediate external manifestation is the attainment of linguistic symbols for concepts other than those of objects. L. Lévy-Bruhl, in his *Fonctions mentales dans les sociétés inférieures* (Paris, 1910), has observed the connection between primitive habits of thought and non-isolating habits of speech. So much is certain: no people, so far as is known, has arrived at what may properly be called logical or scientific thought without speaking a language at least as far along toward conceptual expression as Sanskrit, Ancient Greek, or Latin. The 'magic causality' of the savage becomes fully intelligible only when we learn that his thought lacks the linguistic forms which make possible our logic. I shall quote a few passages from the *Elemente* which, now more or less parenthetic, could, by a juster and fuller treatment of the evolution of language, have become integral, and, I venture to think, central motifs of the discussion. Pp. 91 ff., especially p. 93: 'Kausalität in unserem Sinne existiert für den primitiven Menschen nicht. Will man auf seiner Bewusstseinsstufe überhaupt von dieser reden, so kann man nur sagen: ihn beherrscht die Zauberkausalität. Diese aber bindet sich nicht an Regeln der Verknüpfung der Vorstellungen, sondern an Motive des Affekts.' P. 463 f.: 'das Heldenzeitalter . . ., dessen Grundstimmung die Gebundenheit an die objektive Welt ist, in die zwar das Subjekt seine eigenen Gemütsbewegungen hinüberströmen lässt, die es aber niemals von den Objekten zu lösen vermag . . .'

# 7. Reviews of Bloomfield's *Introduction*

*An Introduction to the Study of Language.* By Leonard Bloomfield. New York: Henry Holt and Company, 1914. 12mo. Pp x + 335. $1.75. London: G. Bell; 6s. [Copyright renewed 1942 by Leonard Bloomfield, although the book was not reprinted at that time.]

[Dedicated to A(lice) S(ayers) B(loomfield). Surely written largely at The University of Illinois, and before Bloomfield's departure for Europe; thus mainly in 1913. Chapters:*

1. The Nature and Origin of Language.
2. The Physical Basis of Language.
3. The Mental Basis of Language.
4. The Forms of Language.
5. Morphology.
6. Syntax.
7. Internal Change in Language.
8. External Change of Languages.
9. The Teaching of Languages.
10. The Study of Language.

In the Preface to the 1933 *Language*, Bloomfield commented on one aspect of his 1914 book as follows:†

> The deep-rooted things about language, which mean most to all of us, are usually ignored in all but very advanced studies; this book tries to tell about them in simple terms and to show their bearing on human affairs. In 1914 I based this phase of the exposition on the psychologic system of Wilhelm Wundt, which was then widely accepted. Since that time there has been much upheaval in psychology; we have learned, at any rate, what one of our masters suspected thirty years ago, namely, that we can pursue the study of language without reference to any one psychological doctrine, and that to do so safeguards our results and makes them more significant to workers in related fields.

* From AN INTRODUCTION TO THE STUDY OF LANGUAGE by Leonard Bloomfield. Copyright 1914 by Holt, Rinehart and Winston, Inc. Copyright 1942 by Leonard Bloomfield. Reprinted by permission of Holt, Rinehart and Winston, Inc.

† From LANGUAGE by Leonard Bloomfield. Copyright 1933 by Holt, Rinehart and Winston, Inc. Copyright © 1961 by Leonard Bloomfield. Reprinted by permission of Holt, Rinehart and Winston, Inc.

Despite long 'psychologizing' passages in the 1914 book, it seems to me there are some grounds for suspecting that Bloomfield was uncertain about the psychology and would really have preferred to leave it out. §10.3 includes the following passage:*

> The relation of linguistics to psychology is, on the one hand, implied in the basic position of the latter among the mental sciences. These sciences, studying the various activities of man, demand in differing degrees but none the less universally, a constant psychologic interpretation. Perhaps this is but negatively true: perhaps the student of a mental science could and ideally should refrain from any running psychologic interpretation; in practice, however, such interpretation is unavoidable. In describing an analogic or semantic change, for instance, linguists most usually outline the conditions of mental predisposition which brought it about. If they do not do this in terms of scientific psychology, they will resort to rationalizing 'popular psychology', —to such explanations as that the new form was desired for greater 'clearness' or 'convenience'. As language is in its forms the least deliberate of human activities, the one in which rationalizing explanations are most grossly out of place, linguistics is, of all the mental sciences, most in need of guidance at every step by the best psychologic insight available.

Whether my reading of this passage is right or not, it is clear that Bloomfield was not insensitive to his critics. In particular, Diekhoff's remarks (the first review reprinted below) seem to point away from the psychologizing Bloomfield of 1914 towards the nonpsychologizing one of 1933.]

(1) Tobias Diekhoff (University of Michigan), *Journal of English and Germanic Philology* 14.593–597 (October 1915). [Submitted to the Editor 12 January 1915.]

Before offering any opinion on individual points of the book before me, I wish to state it as my judgment that, on the whole, it is decidedly a good piece of work, and I beg to regard the following remarks, largely confined to questions which as yet do not seem to me to have found a final answer, not as intended to point out weaknesses in the book, but rather as indications that it thoroughly interested me.

Throughout the author shows sound learning in the use of the vast material treated, and on the whole good pedagogic sense in the subject matter chosen and in the manner of presentation. Yet it is doubtful if "the general reader and the student who is entering upon linguistic work" will not often be bewildered by a mass of intricate detail, highly technical terminology, and not infrequently a style anything but popular and inviting to the general reader and the novice in matters linguistic; for example in the treatment of phonetics. But if not among the general readers and the novices, the book certainly should, and I sincerely hope it will, find its readers among students with some training in language study. The author disclaims any originality in the presentation of his subject. Though there may be little that is strikingly new to those initiated, yet it is to be considered no small service to the scholarly pursuit of language work in America to have made accessible to students investigations for most of them under lock and seal in articles of technical journals presupposing the knowledge which this book means to supply, or written in foreign languages with which our students are not sufficiently familiar.

That the author has at least thoroughly digested his material, and has formed wellfounded opinions on the questions he treats, is apparent on every page, not only in the subject matter itself, but also in the freedom with which the author supplies illustrative material, first from the English language, (as it should be, because with it all of his readers are familiar); and also from foreign languages, ancient and modern, with which at least many can reasonably be supposed to have some acquaintance. Less commendable, in my judgment, is the strange proneness of the author to bring in illustrative examples from languages of which not one out of a thousand readers can reasonably be expected to have even a most superficial knowledge; and I, for one, have the uncomfortable feeling that conclusions based upon the alleged phenomena of such languages fail to be convincing. Illustrations are to serve the purpose of demonstrating *ad oculos* statements supposedly based on them. They are the premises for an argument, and if I cannot verify the premises, the conclusion deduced from them falls to the ground, and the illustration becomes bewildering rather than illuminating. This is the more true, if at times the author fails to be wholly convincing in instances which the reader can control and in which he has every reason to suppose the author much more competent than in his use of obscure dialects. If, for example, in various places we are told that *flash, flame, flare, flimmer, flicker,* are derivatives, or perhaps more justly developments of a consonant combination *fl*, it is doubtful at least if popular consciousness is aware of any connection, and I, for one, who have been somewhat engaged with these matters should be inclined to see in the *fl*-element, common to the words mentioned as well as to a number of others of remoter meaning, very little more than a striking coincidence, though as a mere hypothesis, I might not be bold enough to deny the possibility of such word-formation. Certainly the *fl*-element ought not to be put in the same class with universally recognized morphological elements such as inflectional endings or suffixes of various kinds; which, after sinning in this direction, the author himself indicates. Again, the author might have some difficulty in convincing many readers of any difference between the Latin "puella cantat" and our "the girl sings"; the former being considered the equivalent of "the girl she-sings." And the less he is convinced here, the more staggering to the general reader and the beginner in linguistics it might be to comprehend and accept the Greenlandish "takuwa": "appearing-of-it-to-him," as the next approach in that language to our "he sees it"; or the Georgian "m-e-smi-s": "me-to-sounding-is" as the equivalent of our "I hear." It is quite true, as our author means to illustrate, "that the categoric and other distinctions of one's own language are not universal forms of expression or of experience"; yet the conclusion ought not to be pressed too hard that the idiomatic differences between various languages indicate a corresponding difference in the mental make-up of the peoples concerned. To come back to the Latin "puella cantat" it might be suggested that the early Germanic dialects furnish frequent examples of the same "inclusion" of the actor in the finite verb together with the action-meaning, as our author, of course, well enough knows. That is, in Gothic and the other older Germanic dialects the pronominal subject, now obligatory, is quite frequently left unexpressed. Even if it should have been the growing lack of distinctness of conjugational forms that induced, as seems probable, at first the more frequent, and finally the regular use of the pronoun as subject, yet I cannot convince myself that in this outward remedy of a growing indistinctness any corresponding psychological change should have been involved. At a time when the use of the pronominal subject is unsettled, "nimu" is no more and no less than "ih nimu," and when finally "ih nimu" prevails, the new form was in every way the equivalent of the old. Similarly, "puella cantat" is no more and no less than "the girl sings," or "a girl sings," as the context may decide. What I mean to say is, that there is some danger of being betrayed into seeing, back of differences in linguistic expressions, greater differences of psychologic habits than the facts warrant. Modes of utterance, or idiomatic turns are very often the result of the most curious historical development, and they no more adequately express psychological analyses, or complex psychological operations, than the sound of the individual word can be said to cover a single psychological concept. Both become conventional; and often enough the outward form finds not only its explanation but receives also its real present value from its historical development. I should not agree that the German: "Das Lied wurde gesungen," now is, or, for that matter, ever was equivalent to "The song became sung," and do not suppose that the author seriously means to propose this as its meaning, though he might easily be so understood (p. 173). Just how the compound passive with *sein*, in Gothic the rival of a simple form similar to that in Latin, though also of different origin, gradually displaced the simple form, and, in turn, was itself replaced by the new formation with *werden* need not be recounted here. But as the compound form was in Gothic evidently quite the equivalent of the contemporary simple form, so are also the later developments. If we agree now, that in languages whose history we can at least partly unravel, word combinations, syntactic groups, as well as single words have a conventional meaning rather than the one naturally derived from them by a logical analysis, it becomes apparent how great the danger of misapprehension in dialects so remote and so little known. I hasten to say, however, that I fear less for our author in this regard than for his readers, particularly the class for which this book was professedly written.

I fear some danger for these also from the first chapter of the book, on the "Nature and Origin of Language." It would be to no purpose to quarrel with the author and those with him who are convinced that the evolutionary theory finds its application in the most diverse fields, and so try to make a connection between the human speech as we know it and the surrogate found in the hypothetical *species homo* in an infinitely lower stage of development. Yet it seems to me that it is more a matter of faith than of demonstrable knowledge, that gesture-language is essentially the resultant of earlier purposeful movements, as the deictic movement of earlier grasping; and, particularly, that from expressive movements, incidentally accompanied by vocal utterances, language should have directly developed. His belief is as good as other opinions or hypotheses; it is no better, in my judgment, because it explains no more of the nature of real language than the others. I quarrel with the author only for his unduly dogmatic assertion, first, that "gesture-language is nothing but a higher development of the expressive movements common, in their basis, to many animals." And that, second, "Vocal language is not essentially different. It consists, at bottom, of expressive movements. In the case of gesture-language the expressive movements themselves remained the means of communication; consequently the connection between a gesture and the original expressive movement is nearly always apparent, as when the deictic gesture is plainly a weakened grasping movement and the depicting gestures scarcely differ from natural imitative movements. In the case of vocal speech, on the other hand, it was not the movement itself that attracted attention and became the starting point for further development, but the sound which the movement produced." (p. 14) "Expressive movements are the physical phase of mental processes: whatever the mental processes the expressive movements correspond to them. Man's mind and his expressive activity have developed in indissoluble connection." (p. 15) I wonder if even the term "expressive movement" is not implying too much in this connection. Are we not led to infer that behind an "expressive movement" there is the *purpose* to express? Are these movements more than merely accompanying, or parallel physical movements? It is not without significance that in the last sentence quoted the term "expressive activity" has taken the place of "expressive movement." When the spontaneous physical movement, *accompanying* mental processes becomes associated with or productive of the expressive activity consisting of sounds voluntarily uttered for the purpose of communication with others, we have the beginnings of language, in the widest sense, a language in which also the higher types of animals may have a share; in man only have these sounds become articulate speech: the man who explains how, solves the question as to the origin of speech. But to me it seems that expressive movements, so-called, have no connection with language. To make clear the problem let me compare the human prototype before he had *speech* with a singing bird. He produced his "speech sounds," incoherently, without articulate meaning, as the bird his song, and as a baby its prattle. It remains to explain, first, how *he* came to associate these sounds with definite psychic experiences of his own, and, second, how *others* came to comprehend this association. The answer to these questions can at best be a mere hypothesis, and should never be given with any great assurance.

I have somewhat singled out this one part of the book because the author has clearly spent most earnest thought and conscientious labor upon it and repeatedly finds occasion to refer to his assumptions or conclusions. From a man of his learning and logical incisiveness I should have expected an answer in a less certain tone, such as I appreciate in his treatment of "Internal Change in Language," Chap. VII, and "External Change in Language," Chap. VIII, two chapters which I consider to have been particularly well done. Chapter IX, "The Teaching of Languages," does not altogether seem to fit into the book. To be sure, it shows the author as a young teacher of high ideals and contains some valuable suggestions; but the tone irritates me. Or is, perchance, this tone justified by an all too common lack of understanding and appreciation of the ideals and strivings of the serious members of our profession, and the view lamentably common also in places of influence and authority, that any one with some glibness in a foreign tongue, though without serious linguistic or literary training, is amply equipped to impart language instruction even in schools of higher standing, so long as he can laboriously, with the aid of the grammar and dictionary, render a foreign text into English, and in case of urgent necessity by the same means transfer a simple English selection into the foreign idiom? I grant, actual conditions, prevalent views outside of our ranks, amply justify the tone, and I might express the wish that, of the two classes of readers for whom the book was written, this part particularly be seriously studied by the general reader who may be in position to influence the raising or lowering of the standards of language instruction, in our colleges and universities as well as in the high schools.

Chapter X, "The Study of Language," gives a very brief outline of the history of language study and contains a useful bibliography. A full index fittingly closes the book, enhancing its usefulness for reference after a first connected reading, and this it will surely, and deservedly, receive from many seriously interested in language study for its own sake.


(2) George M. Bolling (Ohio State University), *The Classical Weekly* 10.166–168 (26 March 1917)


The first point to be noted with regard to this book is that there is no work in the English language with which it should be compared. Naturally one thinks first of Oertel's Lectures on the Study of Language; but that is written for a different audience, and consequently on a different plan. For a parallel the author himself looks back to Whitney's Language and the Study of Language (1867); but the study of language, it is hardly necessary to say, has been revolutionized in the half century that intervenes. Midway, to be sure, lies Strong, Logeman and Wheeler, Introduction to the Study of the History of Language (1891), a book valuable in its day, but no longer adapted to modern needs. It deserves, however, to be mentioned here because of its relation to Paul's Prinzipien der Sprachgeschichte; which, though much closer, recalls that existing between Wundt's Völkerpsychologie, Volumes 1–2, Die Sprache, and the present work. The book thus aims at doing a service which is being done by no other work.

The importance of this service cannot be overestimated. The teaching of various languages bulks large in the education given to the youth of the country. An important part of our intellectual life consists of the study of the cultural tradition of various peoples, and in this philological work are involved many questions of a linguistic nature. Both teachers and philologians need a knowledge of the principles of linguistic science, for it would seem axiomatic that no one can reflect profitably upon the phenomena of any language, unless he first knows what language itself is.

Whitney found that pupils who had enjoyed "the ordinary training in the classical or the modern languages or in both" were still capable of forming "views respecting the nature of language and the relation of languages of a wholly crude and fantastic character". Professor Bloomfield writes somewhat differently:

> While questions of a linguistic nature are everywhere a frequent subject of discussion, it is surprising how little even educated people are in touch with the scientific study of language.

It is in Germany a subject of reproach

> dass der Philologe oft noch zu sehr an der altüberkommenen Betrachtung-
> sweise hängt, die von einem mehr naiven als wissenschaftlichen Nachdenken
> über das Wesen der Sprache hervorgerufen wurde.

The quotation is from the Preface of Brugmann's Griechische Grammatik[2] (1889), which was considered worth reprinting in 1899 and 1913, in spite of a certain improvement recognized in his Kurze Vergleichende Grammatik (1904), pages V and 30. This improvement was not sufficient to keep Hirt, Handbuch der Griechischen Laut- und Formenlehre[2] (1912), 57, from writing in the same strain, "die einfachsten Tatsachen sind unbekannt"; nor Kretschmer from speaking, Einleitung in die Altertumswissenschaft, I[2] (1912), 463, of "eine bedauerliche Entfremdung zwischen der Sprachwissenschaft und der klassischen Philologie".

Now I have no wish to enter upon the question whether there is a similar condition of affairs among our philologians; still less to seek to parallel Brugmann's citation of Meisterhans and Blass with American names. But I do wish to suggest that there are symptoms which should lead us to reflect upon this question. Why should the author of a Greek Grammar in 1915 feel put upon the defensive for "making use of the principle of Analogy"? That is a straw, but it may serve to show the direction in which the wind is blowing. More serious symptoms are the lack of books already noted; the fact that persons who have been taught from one to five languages are (to put it mildly) "surprisingly out of touch with the scientific study of language"; and that our classical philology is very largely inspired by German philology, which is itself infected with this neglect of linguistics.

Our first need is to base our teaching of the classical languages squarely and fairly upon the principles of linguistic science. To form crude and fantastic ideas about the nature of language ought to be made impossible for any one who has studied Latin. That result cannot be attained without making it a great deal easier for the student to acquire that power of reading Latin which is the key to the enjoyment of its literature and the appreciation of the relation between ancient and modern civilisation. Prerequisite to this is a truer understanding of the nature of language on the part of our philologians and of our teachers themselves.[1]

[1] The necessity of a knowledge of the principles of linguistic science is not to be confused with the desirability of a study of comparative grammar. I should strongly advise any student who desires to fit himself to be a teacher of Latin or of Greek to include comparative grammar in his preparation. I should not advise any one to 'adapt' Hirt's Handbuch for a textbook in our Schools. It seems worth while to say this because we have recently (American Journal of Philology 26.242 f.) been told that Hirt "modestly suggests that the gymnasia would do better by Greek, if they ceased to afflict students with a modicum of Xenophon and Homer and taught instead his handbook". This is a misrepresentation of Hirt's views upon a very important question. The problem confronting him at Leipzig may be restated

Under these circumstances it seems to the reviewer that one question alone is of prime importance: Can the work under review render the service it has undertaken to render? This question may be answered without hesitation in the affirmative. Among students of linguistics, there is a general consensus of opinion about the fundamental principles on which their work is based, and such agreement extends frequently even to matters of detail. Professor Bloomfield's book is limited avowedly to the presentation of this 'accepted doctrine', and the non-linguist may use it without fear of being misled upon such questions. To set forth this doctrine with sufficient wealth of illustration, in a form that is small in compass and yet such as may be read with ease and pleasure, was no light task; and the skill with which it has been accomplished is deserving of high praise.

On the other hand, the very nature of this task renders it inevitable that another should find points at which he might wish for a different treatment. The broadest criticism I should offer is the wish that more space had been given to the processes of linguistic change. Room for this in part might have been gained by the exclusion of the phonetics of the second chapter, the subject being one that is usually handled separately. I must add, however, that the section is in itself most admirable, and that I should be loath to lose it.

One idea that runs through the book is open to such serious objection as to require separate notice. At times reflective examination of a language may show that certain differences of sounds are distributed according to conditions which may readily be observed and stated. Our English vowels, for instance, are longer in final position and before voiced sounds than before unvoiced, longer in *bid* than in *bit*, in *bee, bead* than in *beat*. In such cases Professor Bloomfield speaks of "automatic sound-variation".[2] Now this term suggests very strongly an idea, which Professor Bloomfield would no doubt disclaim, that such changes have no sufficient causes but just happen of themselves—automatically. But even worse than this is another

in terms of American life: What shall we do with *graduate students* desirous of becoming teachers of Latin who come to the University ignorant of Greek? That problem is already not unheard of in America and there is danger that it may become acute. At present we seem to have three possibilities: (1) to treat the aspirations of such students as we do undesired kittens; (2) to allow these students to persist in their ignorance, and turn them out with Masters' degrees upon an unsuspecting public; (3) to put into their hands a Beginners' Book, written for School children, that they may get a modicum of Xenophon and Homer. Hirt believes that *for such students* a survey of the laws of the structure of the Greek language is better than this modicum of text, claims to have had the best results in so teaching them, and has made his Handbuch suited to their needs. In this he may be right or wrong—that is another question—, but the problem is apt to become pressing, and we really should be able to devise some solution better than any of the three mentioned above.

[2] [It is clear from this and the next few paragraphs of the review that Bolling and Bloomfield are actually in perfect accord, but that there are difficulties in mutual understanding stemming from the lack of any generally accepted terminology for the discussion of synchronic states of affairs, as over against language history.—CFH]

suggestion, that each speaker continually makes these variations (according to the conditions involved) in each production of the sound; that we, for instance, start always with the short vowels and automatically leave them unchanged when we say *bit, beat,* but automatically lengthen them when we say *bid, bee,* or *bead.* Such a position hardly requires refutation. A phonetic change is a historical event or a series of such events occupying a definite portion of time; the final result is then transmitted by tradition, and it is a mistake to suppose that the process is being continually repeated. Such changes are due to complexes of causes that in their totality are unknown. Sometimes one (or more) of the elements of the complex can be ascertained; we then speak of 'conditioned' phonetic changes. Now, after the change is an accomplished fact, it is obviously a matter of indifference whether such 'conditions' are perpetual or not. The new sound goes on its own path, and what happens to it is another chapter in its history. It is surprising to find that Professor Bloomfield (221) maintains on the contrary that the process is being repeated automatically as long as these 'conditions' are undisturbed.

> The pre-Germanic spirant-voicing after unaccented vowel, for instance, left such automatic variations as *\*wása* 'I was': *\*wēzumún* 'we were' . . .; when, however, the stress was later shifted everywhere to the first syllable, the variation was of course no longer automatic, but purely traditional, as still in the modern forms, *was*: *were.* So, by a pre-English vowel assimilation . . . *\*fōtiz*, the nominative plural of *\*fōt* 'foot', became *\*fētiz*, a variation whose automatism was destroyed by the phonetic change which dropped the second syllable of *\*fētiz*, giving Old English *fēt* . . . .

The examples really prove the contrary. Old English *fēt* shows that at the time of the loss of the final syllable *\*fētiz* was already established as the traditional pronunciation. Had the form still been *\*fōtiz* varying automatically to *\*fētiz* because of the following vowel, a form *\*fōt* should have resulted when that vowel was suppressed.

The whole concept of sound-automatism appears to me, I confess, as the introduction of some mystic power for which there is no place in our explanation of language. Here also it is entirely needless.

My opinion about the division of syllables and words differs also from that of Professor Bloomfield to some extent, as may be seen by a comparison of the American Journal of Philology, 33.403 f., 34. 157 f. On page 152 examples of Umlaut and Ablaut are given where we have been led to expect definitions. On page 154 it would be well to explain that in distinguishing between sound-variation and affixation there are two points of view, one historical, the other descriptive. From the former, the difference in vowel quantity between *amās, amat* (from *\*amāt*) is sound-variation; from the latter, we may either view it in this fashion, or analyse *am-ās,* *am-at.* The historical point of view is not always possible, but the descriptive must not be confused with it. The same applies to affixation and infixation (155) and the Indo-European nasal present would illustrate the impossibility of coming to a decision on historical grounds. On pages 204 f. the discussion of 'phonetic law' might be improved, in what direction can be seen from Wundt's article in Philologische Studien 3.196 ff.

Separate mention must be made of the last two chapters. Of these the first, The Teaching of Language, is written from the standpoint of modern languages; only *mutatis mutandis* can it be applied to the teaching of the Classics, but anyone who is teaching the latter can surely gain from reading and reflecting upon it. The second, The Study of Language, contains very sound and sane advice for the student who is planning to devote himself to the study of language. To the books mentioned in it I should like to add Otto Jespersen, Phonetische Grundfragen (Leipzig, 1904), and A Modern English Grammar on Historical Principles (Heidelberg, 1909–1914); P. Kretschmer, Sprache, in Einleitung in die Altertumswissenschaft herausgegeben von A. Gercke und E. Norden[2], 463–564 (Leipzig, 1912: especially valuable for the classicist); and L. Sütterlin, Das Wesen der Sprachlichen Gebilde. Kritische Bemerkungen zu Wilhelm Wundts Sprachpsychologie (Heidelberg, 1902).

Professor Bloomfield has put a valuable tool within the reach of teachers of language and philologians. It is to be hoped that the classicists will be among the first to make use of it.

(3) Albert W. Aron (University of Wisconsin), *American Journal of Philology* 39.86–92 (January–March 1918). [Aron also published a briefer version of this review, in German, in *Monatshefte für deutsche Sprache und Pädagogik* 19.55, January 1918.—CFH]

Leonard Bloomfield's book is intended to offer the general reader and the student who is entering upon linguistic work a summary of what is now known about language, such as Whitney's Language and the Study of Language and The Life and Growth of Language did a half-century ago. There is need of a book that sets up the goal which Bloomfield has set himself. We have no one book of the nature of Whitney's which embodies for us the results of the great progress of linguistic science in the last fifty years. Unlike most other writers on linguistics, but like Whitney, the author does not limit himself to the treatment of one language group, such as Indo-European, but takes up the various possible modes of human expression. There is probably no one other factor which is so conducive to the transforming of the ordinary uninteresting, meaningless details of phonology and morphology of a single language into living phenomena fraught with interest, as this comparative method of attack. In accordance with the general direction which progress in linguistic study has taken since Whitney, the author emphasizes the importance of phonetics and of the modern psychological interpretation of language. He treats in ten chapters the following topics . . . [here follow the chapter titles].

It is perhaps partly due to the necessity of using the technical terminology of scientific psychology and of constantly linking psychological doctrine with linguistic phenomena that Bloomfield's style does not always have the simplicity and clearness of Whitney's. Also in another related respect he has emulated neither his great predecessor nor that other master of linguistic science, Hermann Paul. Both these scholars choose their examples from their respective mother-tongues. Bloomfield does not avail himself, as he might, of this pedagogical advantage of proceeding from the known to the unknown. It is well known how intangible phonetics seems to the beginner and that here, if anywhere, the starting-place should be familiar sounds and articulations. It may reasonably be assumed that besides English a rather large percentage of the readers of this book will understand French, German, and Latin. Yet on p. 28 the bilabial spirant of Dutch and Spanish is discussed, that of South German is not mentioned; there follows a discussion of coronal articulation in Spanish, the modern languages of India, French, German, and finally English; on p. 29 the *r*-sound of Slavic, Italian, French, German is treated, then finally that of American English. Considerably more space is devoted to the Czech *r* than to the American. On p. 30 we find a description first of Slavic, then German and French, and finally of English *l*; on p. 32 the spirant pronunciation of *g* in modern Greek precedes that of German. Leaving the field of phonetics, we find (p. 132) examples chosen from Italian instead of from the more generally known Latin to illustrate how the ending of a word may show its gender. In exemplifying the use of the reflexive construction where we use the passive (p. 173), why place Russian before French? etc., etc.

As may be seen from these few examples, a more sparing use throughout the book of out-of-the-way illustrations would have been more conducive to clearness and would have added to the value of the book. It hardly seems necessary for the purposes of an "introduction" to discuss the dialectic differences in the use of numeratives in Chinese (p. 131), which have no essential bearing on the question at issue, or to discuss group-stress in French, Japanese, English, German, Russian, Czech, Icelandic, and Polish (p. 149), in short, to confuse the beginner by discussions of and illustrations from approximately *seventy* different languages and dialects.

The chapter on the Physical Basis of Language does not come up to the high standard of the rest of the book. A treatise on phonetics which lacks plates or diagrams of the vocal organs is, of course, handicapped to begin with. In his desire to give examples for every possible sound, an entirely unnecessary proceeding for the purpose of this book, the author often loses himself in a mass of intricate detail, as when he distinguishes between the manner of opening the glottis in some Armenian dialects and in Georgian, or tells that wide unrounded *u* "is said to be spoken also in Armenian and in Turkish", or recounts the occurrence of palatal stops in French dialects, Lithuanian, Hungarian, Spanish, Italian, and French. As above mentioned, the unknown regularly precedes the known.

The author's presentation of the positions of the glottis is at variance with the facts. "Both in whispering", says he, "and in ordinary speech the unvoiced sounds are pronounced with the glottis in its widest-open position, the muscles of the vocal cords being relaxed and the breath passing freely through the larynx: this, as we have seen, is also the position for regular breathing" (p. 26). As a matter of fact, with unvoiced sounds the vocal cords form an angle of about fifteen degrees, in ordinary breathing of about twenty-five degrees. The regular breathing position is not the "widest-open position". The latter, with a much greater angle than in normal breathing, is the position in violent breathing (after running, etc.) or in blowing.

The statement that the glottal stop "is used in German initially in the pronunciation of words that in writing begin with a vowel" (p. 24) is only partly true. The syllable beginning with a glottal stop must ordinarily be accented.

The author unnecessarily aggravates the difficulty encountered in trying to see the raising and lowering of the velum by directing the reader to breathe through both mouth and nose, and then pronounce 'ah'. It is much simpler to breathe through the nose alone and then to say 'ah'.

The discussion of the dentals is inexact. English and German *d* and *t* are coronal or dorsal, French *d* and *t* usually dorsal. The author gives all three as coronal (p. 28). It is doubtful whether *n* ever occurs as an entirely unvoiced sound in such words as *mint, snow*; certainly not "often" (p. 29).

Unsatisfactory, too, is the treatment of the blade sounds. For Bloomfield they are synonymous with what we call in Jespersen's terminology 'rill spirants', namely unvoiced *s*, voiced *z*, and the sibilants in *shall* and *azure*. But, as noted above, English, German, and French *d* and *t* are often or usually blade sounds. Why Bloomfield applies the name 'abnormal sibilants' to the sibilants in *shall* and *azure* I do not see.

The traditional division of sounds into 'consonants' and 'vowels' is given up (p. 33) in favor of the terms 'noise-articulations' and 'musical articulations'. I cannot see why the two conventional terms, which stand for something quite definite if they are understood, as they ordinarily are, as names for a manner of articulation, are "untenable for purposes of exact terminology", when the author admits that there is no definite boundary between the noise-articulations and the musical-articulations. Moreover, these latter terms belong properly to a treatment of phonetics emphasizing the acoustic side, while the author presents physiological phonetics.

The chapter on the Teaching of Languages seems out of place in this book. The author himself seems to have felt this, for he drops the objective scientific tone otherwise observed and adopts a polemical one. It is presumably to this fact that such over-statements may be ascribed as " Of the students who take up the study of foreign languages in our schools and colleges, not one in a hundred attains even a fair reading knowledge, and not one in a thousand ever learns to carry on a conversation in the foreign language." While not of the opinion that this chapter on technical modern language pedagogy belongs here, the reviewer is heartily in accord with most of the views expressed. Briefly but convincingly the author shows the essential fallacy of the grammar-translation method as a "process of logical reference to a conscious set of rules " and " as a method of study, . . . worthless, for it establishes associations in which the foreign words play but a small part as symbols (inexact symbols, of course) of English words ". He then sketches how the direct method grows out of "a conscious or unconscious accordance with the fundamental processes of language learning and, for that matter, of speech in general ". On a basis of sound psychology he explodes the myth that the power of learning languages wanes in adults.

In the following I shall take up some of the details in which the author seems to be in error or in which I disagree with him.

p. 4. The author speaks of the various systems of gesture-languages as "strikingly uniform ". While not saying so in so many words he seems to imply that they are mutually intelligible. Wundt, upon whom the author "depends for his psychology, general and linguistic" (cf. Preface), says of the gesture-language of the South Italians that it is closely akin to that of savages in that many gestures have only symbolical significance, "wenn sie auch infolge der sehr verschiedenen Kulturbedingungen in der Beschaffenheit der gebrauchten Symbole erheblich abweicht" (Wundt: Völkerpsychologie, I. Band, 1. Teil, 3. Auflage, p. 154). A Dakota Indian, for instance, would not understand a Neapolitan, even though he would sooner understand the gestures than the sound-language (Wundt, p. 157).

p. 8. The noise made by crickets is cited as a type of audible expressive movement; Wundt says, " die Geräusche vieler Insekten, die . . . durch das Aneinanderreiben horniger Teile des Hautskeletts entstehen, (gehören) weder nach ihren physiologischen Bedingungen noch wahrscheinlich nach ihrer psychologischen Funktion hierher" (p. 259).

p. 13. Even if the author follows Wundt in seeing the origin of language in audible expressive movements accompanying first pain and rage, then other intense emotions, he should not neglect to mention that Wundt says of recent investigations in this field, "dass sie durchweg eine wiederum wachsende Hinneigung der allgemeinen Meinung zur Nachahmungs-theorie bekunden" (2. Band, 2. Teil, p. 632).

p. 102. An instance of how language interpretation may go astray if it neglects historical method may be seen in the author's treatment of sound-variation in word-initial in Irish. He speaks of the semantic difference between the short forms of French *vous* and *a* and the longer ones employed in liaison, and then goes on to say, "An instance still farther along towards semantic differentiation occurs in Irish. This language has a sound-varia-tion in word-initial which, however, does not depend upon the phonetic character of the preceding word-final, but arbitrarily on the preceding word; that is, Irish words may be divided into a number of otherwise arbitrary classes, according to the effect they have on a closely following word-initial. . . . This variation has semantic value in that it does not de-pend automatically on the adjoining sounds but implies a division of words into classes, etc.". He gives as illustrations: *tá ba* 'there are cows' but *a va* 'his cows'; *uv* 'an egg', *an tuv* 'the egg', *na nuv* 'of the eggs', *a huv* 'her egg', on p. 128 *bó* 'cow', *an vó* 'the cow', *ar mó* 'our cow', etc.

From the standpoint of elementary Modern Irish grammar the author's statements might be allowed to pass. Seen from the historical point of view, however, these variations in word-initial do depend on the phonetic character of the original preceding word-final. Most of the examples come under the following three rules of Irish sandhi:

1. lenition or aspiration: an initial stop sound was changed to an aspi-rate or a spirant after a word originally ending in a vowel. Here belong such examples as *a va* 'his cows', etc.

2. nasalization or eclipsis: after all words originally ending in -*n*, the nasal was pronounced before an initial vowel and the mediae. (This is only part of the rule). This explains *na nuv* 'of the eggs', the *n* being the original ending of the genitive plural; likewise *ar mó* 'our cow', the hom-organic *m* appearing before *b*, and, in Irish, *mb* regularly becoming by assimilation *mm* or *m*.

3. gemination: after words which originally ended in -*s* or postvocalic *t* and *k* sounds. It is too complicated a phenomenon to be discussed fully here, but the result before an accented initial vowel was an *h* sound. This is the explanation of *a huv* 'her egg', *a* being an old feminine genitive.

*an tuv* is a parallel to English *an egg, a cow, ant* being used before vowels, *an* before consonants.

I do not wish to deny that these sandhi phenomena appear most con-sistently within semantically related groups; these, however, are not 'arbitrary classes' but depend automatically on the original adjoining sounds.

p. 109. When the author takes the three 'genders' of nouns as an illustration of "word classes which are not expressed by formational similarity at all, but seem to go back, none the less, to emotional associations of the speakers", I believe the uninitiated reader is still uninitiated.

p. 145. "The Slavic languages distinguish categorically between, on the one hand, durative and iterative (in Slavic grammar called, together, 'imperfective') action . . . and on the other hand, punctual and terminative action (in Slavic grammar, together, 'perfective')". The author quotes here only the view of one school of Slavic grammarians, such as, for instance, Vondrak in his Altkirchenslawische Grammatik; Leskien, on the other hand, divides into 1. imperfective, 2. perfective, 3. iterative, but states that the iterative may be imperfective or perfective.

"He burst out weeping" does not strike me as 'inceptive terminative' but rather as 'inceptive durative'.

p. 145. In the list of Sanskrit 'conjugations' the *denominative* is omitted. The fact that it is not formed from the verb from which the other examples are derived is no reason for not including it in the list.

p. 152. As an example of stress-variation used as a means of morphologic sound-variation the author cites *address* with accent on the first syllable as noun, on the second as verb. The reviewer has often heard the former pronunciation, but it is not considered "correct".

p. 158. I think it unfortunate that the author feels it necessary to use the term *kernel* in place of the now generally used name *root*. It is loose usage to make *stem* and *root* synonymous, as is done here.

p. 206. In primitive Germanic the nominative and accusative singular of 'stone' are not *stainoz, *stainon respectively, but *stainaz and *stainan.

p. 220. In the discussion of the influence of language mixture in producing change in articulation, the substitution of the Indian for the Spanish basis of articulation in Chile is an interesting parallel to the assumed mingling of peoples speaking Dravidian and Indo-European languages. (Cf. R. Lenz: Beiträge zur Kenntnis des Amerikanospanischen, Zeitschrift für romanische Philologie XVII, 158–214).

p. 224. The author prefers the name 'false analogy' to 'analogy', "because it conveys at least the idea of innovation, as opposed to the regular assimilative processes by which all speech is formed". The term 'false analogy' was given up in linguistics when the old belief, that analogical change like all language change indicated a deterioration of speech, was given up. Analogy is a regular process in all speech formation, so that there seems to be no ground for resuscitating the old expression.

p. 225. There is no basis for assuming that the numeral *four* in Primitive Indo-European may have begun with a uvular stop sound.

p. 229. Why the plural of Pre-Germanic *wasa is *wēzumé here but *wēzumún on p. 216 is not clear. However, either form is possible.

The author brings his task to a close by giving the reader good practical hints on how to begin the study of linguistics.

This "Introduction to the Study of Language" cannot help but be of great profit to the serious student. It is what the author intended it to be, "a summary of what is known about language". The whole book bears witness to the rare scholarship of the author. My regret is that he has not succeeded in making it in the best sense of the word "popular".

# B8. Sentence and Word

1914. *Transactions of the American Philological Association* 45.65–75.

[1914 was Bloomfield's first year of membership in the American Philological Association. The paper was delivered at the 46th Annual Meeting, held at Haverford, Pennsylvania, in December; thus actual publication was in 1915. Abstracted, with brief comment, in *Jahrbuch für Germanische Philologie* 38.62 (1916).]

The first task of the linguistic investigator is the analysis of a language into distinctive sounds, their variations, and the like. When he has completed this, he turns to the analysis of the semantic structure,—to what we call the morphology and syntax of the language, its grammatical system. The method generally pursued in this semantic analysis is admittedly a makeshift: we adhere to the process of synthetic description which has been developed out of the practice of the Alexandrine and Roman grammarians. Taking the single word as our unit, we name the big classes of words (parts of speech) and then describe the inflection of each; there follows a hasty survey of such matters as derivation and composition; finally we discuss the uses and interrelations of the various inflected words in the sentence (syntax).

This procedure is a makeshift, for it has long been recognized that the first and original datum of language is the sentence,—that the individual word is the product of a theoretical reflection which ought not to be taken for granted, and, further, that the grouping of derived and inflected words into paradigms, and the abstraction of roots, stems, affixes, or other formative processes, is again the result of an even more refined analysis. It needs but little scientific reflection to make us realize that the grammarian ought by no means to extract such products with magic suddenness, live and wriggling, out of the naïve speaker's hat. This has long been recognized. Wilhelm von Humboldt begins his discussion of polysynthetic languages (*Über die Verschiedenheit des menschlichen Sprachbaues*, I, paragraph 17) by saying: "Wenn man, wie es ursprünglich richtiger ist, da jede, noch so unvollständige Aussage in der Absicht des Sprechenden wirklich einen geschlossenen Gedanken ausmacht, vom Satze ausgeht, so zerschlagen Sprachen, welche sich dieses Mittels bedienen, die Einheit des Satzes gar nicht, . . . " Increased psychologic understanding has only confirmed this great scholar's intuition. Since we have learned to distinguish between an investigator's logical analysis after the fact and the actual psychic occurrence, and to observe the latter without confusing it with such logical analysis, we find it obvious and easily proved that in most of our speaking we are conscious of the whole sentence only, not of the words into which it may be divided. The experiment is easily made: one asks a speaker to tell how many words he has used in the casual sentence just spoken. The answer, if it comes at all, will be surprisingly long in preparing,—and this with our ceaseless training, throughout our reading and writing, in this form of linguistic analysis. I need hardly refer to the fact, so well illustrated by Brugmann (*Grundriss*, II², 1, 1 ff.) that in some cases we do not even upon reflection succeed in making a division into words: shall a German write *Es kommt zu Stande* in two, three, or four words? Shall we write *in stead of* as two or as three? *In as much as* in one, two, three, or four words? We have many instances of the writing of uneducated people (who lack the practice of copious reading) in which the word-division is entirely wrong. Hence we repeat to-day in more decided terms the quoted dictum of Humboldt, as when Brugmann says (*op. cit.* II², 1, 3): "In allem Übrigen (ausser der Semasiologie) hat eine streng wissenschaftliche d. h. auf die Natur des Objektes selbst gegründete Darstellung nicht vom Wort, sondern vom Satz auszugehen."

Brugmann adds, however, that, for practical reasons, he retains the traditional manner of exposition. In doing so he is following a practice which, I believe, is universal. It is generally taken for granted by students of language that the traditional procedure, even if theoretically wrong, need not draw us into any errors: we shall go safely if we never, in a weak moment, make deductions which rest not upon the facts of the language, but merely upon the peculiarity of our method. I believe that we have not succeeded in avoiding this pitfall,—that some of the current doctrine of linguistic science is a transference of our own process of analysis into our beliefs about the course of linguistic history, and, as our process of analysis is, admittedly, not in harmony with the facts of speech, but, in a sense, diametrically opposed to them, the transference may (and, I think, sometimes does) lead to false conclusions.

A bit of the older history of our science well illustrates what I mean. The personal verb-forms of the Indo-European languages were easily analyzed, as soon as people began to reflect upon such things, into personal endings attached to a stem (e.g. δίδω-μι δίδω-ς δίδω-σι, older and West Greek δίδω-τι). Proceeding from this analysis and taking for granted that it represented a historic synthesis, Bopp identified the personal endings with old forms of the personal pronouns. Similarly he saw in the *i*-suffix of the future and optative the root (itself, of course, the creature of a similar analysis) of the verb *īre*. These theories were given up not only because Bopp's specific explanations were in conflict with the ascertained sound-developments of the languages concerned, but also because we realize that Bopp was inspired chiefly by the feeling that our analysis of forms is necessarily in accord with their historic origin,—and we know now that this feeling was wrong. When scholars to-day speculate upon the origin of the personal verb-inflection they turn rather to an adaptation-theory and suppose that the endings of these forms have come more or less accidentally to their personal meaning; so, for instance, Hirt, *I.F.* XVII, 36. That is to say, the grammatical analysis of a given stage of a language must not lead us into thinking that the forms are the result of a corresponding conglutination.

Bopp's error is a thing of the past,[1] but if a genius like Bopp could fall into such an error, it is obvious that we, too, need the corrective of an occasional analysis in the psychologically justified direction, proceeding from the sentence, the concrete datum, to the less and less explicit articulations in the sequence of speech.

A serious error that has outlived the agglutination theory is our definition of the sentence. The ancients, for whom grammar was an ancillary discipline of logic, necessarily looked upon the sentence as a combination built up out of words. Dionysios Thrax[2] defined the sentence as πεζῆς λέξεως σύνθεσις, διάνοιαν αὐτοτελῆ δηλοῦσα, Priscian[3] translated this: Oratio est ordinatio dictionum congrua, sententiam perfectam demonstrans. It is Wilhelm Wundt who, in his *Völkerpsychologie*, I, 2, 234 ff., first showed that, when we understand the psychology of the thing, this definition is topsy-turvy: a sentence, says Wundt, is the linguistic expression of the voluntary analysis of a total experience into its parts, which then stand in logical relation to one another.

It has been objected that this definition does not distinguish a sentence from a word, such as τρίπους, which also involves an analysis of the total experience which it expresses. We are face to face, then, with the problem of distinguishing between the analysis made by a speaker who says τρεῖς πόδας ἔχον and that made by one who says τρίπους,—between sentence and word. Meanwhile we cannot retain even Wundt's definition of the sentence, for it implies an articulation of the sentence into parts which we have no right to look upon as essential or universal. The assumption that every sentence must break up into two or more independent—and logically articulated!—components is rightly characterized by Kretsch-

---

[1] The Editor reminds me of Professor Fay's articles; needless to say, I do not agree with their tendency. It is fair to add, however, that I know Fay's "Return to Bopp" only from the summary in *Idg. Jahrb.* II. [Neither the *Transactions* nor the *Proceedings of the American Philological Association* identify the Editor in question. Professor Fay was Edwin W., of the University of Texas.—CFH]

[2] *Τέχνη*, par. 11.

[3] *De Arte Gramm.* II, 15.

mer (in Gercke and Norden's *Einleitung in die Altertumswissenschaft*[2], I, 515 ff.) as a vestige of the old rationalizing view, according to which it was built up out of such components. Kretschmer defines the sentence as the linguistic expression of an affect,—that is, of an up-and-down of emotional volume and tension. Perhaps we should do better to say that the sentence is the linguistic expression of an affect involving a single total experience, for an affect of higher order may be accompanied by the utterance of a succession of sentences, each of which corresponds to a subordinate up-and-down movement of the emotional curve. What we most need is not, however, a definition of the sentence or of the word,—we have a very decided naïve feeling for these units,—but rather an understanding of the difference between a succession of words, such as τρεῖς πόδας ἔχον and what we feel to be a single inflected, derived, or compounded word, such as τρίπους.

The phonetician, first of all, tells us that physical difference there is none. His ear tells him, and the difficulties of orthographic separation above referred to prove to him, that there are in an utterance no pauses to indicate its structure. We have the proof in ourselves whenever we hear people speaking a language which we do not understand, for it is then beyond our power to find the word-divisions. What is it, then, that enables us to analyze utterances into words and morphologic elements?

To begin with, it is not any reflection of the speaker's. Even people who have studied language and may be to an abnormal extent conscious of the facts of speech, utter many sentences every day without the least reflection upon their analysis. As a writer on logic puts it, we ought to write all our sentences with hyphens between the words; a phonetician would say that we ought not to indicate the word-division at all. The division of the sentence is not a reflective one; it is a matter of implication, and is due to the associational connections of the parts of the sound-sequence which constitutes the sentence,—as it were, to their connotation. A Latin sentence such as *exībant* is, like every sentence, primarily and so far as any logical reflection on the part of speaker or hearer may be concerned, a unit. The various parts of this sound-sequence, however, have been heard and uttered by the speaker (or the hearer) in other sentences and have, in these other earlier occurrences, always corresponded to an element of meaning which is present also in this new experience accompanying the sentence *exībant*. All these past occurrences of parts of the present sound-sequence exercise upon the latter the subtle force known to psychologists as simultaneous association or fusion: they give them a tone of recognition which we, for our purposes, may speak of as their meaning. Thus the first part of the sound-sequence *exībant* owes its value to earlier utterances (heard and spoken from childhood on), such as *excessit, exēgit*, and the like; the next sound, to such as *abīrem, redīmus,* and the like; the next sound, -*b*-, has occurred also in numerous utterances, such as *regēbat, vidē-bit, conābitur,* in all of which it corresponded to a vague notion of continuity of action, past or future; the -*a*- has occurred also in *regēbat, eram, fuerat,* parallel with a semantic element of past time; the -*nt,* finally, is one of the most familiar sound-successions in the language, and has been heard and spoken innumerable times in sentences that expressed an event in which more than one actor, including neither speaker nor hearer, performed an action or was the goal (object) of an action, e.g. *dolent, conantur, dēlectantur, exeunt,* and so on. Now, though all this dissection is far too clumsy to do justice to the intangible implication-values that are immediately and automatically involved in the speaking or hearing of the sentence *exībant,* yet we can be sure that the meaning of this sentence to a Latin was due to these very associations, for we know that in language the sentences which a speaker may utter are not confined to those which he has actually heard before, but may consist of entirely new combinations of the habitual speech-elements. A speaker of Latin who happened never to have heard the form *exībat* could use it, and use it without the slightest consciousness of innovation, since he had many times heard *exībant, amābat, amābant,* and so on. In other words, we may, very clumsily, indicate the associational values in the sentence *exībant* by dividing it into *ex-ī-b-a-nt.*

If, now, we take the corresponding English sentence, *ðejwrgòwiŋáwt,* we find a similar associational habituation of the different parts of the sound-sequence. *ðej* has occurred in *ðejdənájdit, ðejsédsow,* and the like, where also there was a third person plural actor; *wr* in such expressions as *wijwrwéjtiŋ, juwwrðér,* and so on; *gow* in *letsgów, downtgów,* and the like; *iŋ,* expressive of continued action, in *hijzrájtiŋ, ajmwéjtiŋ,* and so on; *awt,* in value like the Latin *ex-,* in *komanáwt, hijrænáwt,* and many other utterances; and here, as in the Latin sentence, these parts are in ordinary speech by no means drawn into the focus of the attention or explicitly distinguished, but are rather, by the associative effect of their earlier occurrences,—one might almost say, mutely,—symbolic of the meaning. Their utterance in certain situations of experience, and the reproduction of a corresponding meaning whenever they are heard, is a matter of habit, not of explicit agreement or reflection.

There are, however, occasions when we utter such a sentence with a full and explicit insistence upon some one part of it, and thus show a consciousness of its division into parts and try, indeed, to arouse the same consciousness in the hearer. Suppose that an element of the situation is in doubt or in question, for instance, the identity of those who went out. Then we say *ðéj wrgowiŋawt.* Here it is no longer the mere implicit associational value of the sound-group *ðej* that lends it meaning; our attention, like a vivid spotlight, focuses this part of the utterance, singling it out from the rest; and the hearer's attention, by the loud tone and other phonetic features, is drawn to it. We may similarly, if the time of the occurrence be in question, accent the *wr* and say *ðej wŕ gowiŋawt*, and so on. One element, however, of those found by analysis to make up this sentence, we cannot so emphasize, namely the sound-group *iŋ*, expressive of continuity of action. Its associational value is clear, but apperceptive value it can never have: it never falls into the focus of the attention. Besides this habit of never clearly considering the element *iŋ*, we have another limiting its use: it is spoken after an element expressive of action, such as *gow* or *rajt*, to which it lends the meaning of continuity, and it never occurs in any other connections. This, moreover, is true of all the parts of the Latin sentence which we have examined, *exībant*.[4]

This is the difference between a formative element and a word, of course: both recur as the expression of a constant element of meaning, but the formative element is bound to certain positions with regard to the other elements, while the word may occur in all kinds of connections; and, above all: while both occur usually as associatively determined parts of a sentence, the word may be focused by the attention (clearly apperceived), while the formative element never rises to this explicit recognition.

It is a commonplace of psychology that, of these two forms of the structure of experience, the associative or passive, and the apperceptive or active, the former is the primary and usual one, the latter the more developed and rarer. The greater predominance of associational processes characterizes for us the mental habits of savages (sympathetic magic, and the like; cf., in connection with language, Lévy-Bruhl, *Les fonctions mentales dans les sociétés inférieures*, and Marrett, *Anthropology*; Jespersen's *Progress in Language* is, of course, familiar), the course of dreams, and morbid mental processes (Wundt, *Grundriss der Psychologie*). Opposed to all these, the higher phases of mental life, such as sane thinking or scientific reasoning, are characterized by the frequent and unhesitating resort, whenever the occasion demands, to apperceptive focusing of parts of an experience.

It would be strange if linguistic history, as the agglutination theory assumed, showed us a retrogressive development,—a development from forms of speech which allowed not only of associative but also of occasional apperceptive distinction, toward forms which moved only and always in the dim realm of associative reminiscence. As a matter of fact, linguistic history, wherever we know it, shows us progress in the direction from

---

[4] The sound-group *ex-*, to be sure, does occur in other connections, such as *ex urbe venit*, but it has then a different value, expressing spatial relation with regard to an object, not direction of movement; it is then a preposition, not an adverb.

associative toward apperceptive structure. Where in Old English one said *gáð út*, we express by a separate word both the actor and the tense: *ðej a:r gowiŋ awt*; where in Latin one said *Rōmam it* or *Rōmam vādit*, one uses in French a separate word for the direction and another for the actor: *il va à Rome*.

The differences, in this respect, between Latin or Old English and the modern languages are of interest because of the accessibility of the historic relation and all that it implies, but the structure of Latin or of Old English is not so widely different from that of our speech. If actor, action, and tense are there expressed in one word, we find in other languages not only these elements, but also objects, direct and indirect, and other features of the experience, all expressed without the possibility of a single apperceptive articulation, that is, in one word. Thus in the Fox language (Jones and Michelson, *Bulletin* 40, *U.S. Bureau of Ethnology*), *pyäte'kwäwäwa*, 'He brings home a wife' (*pyäte* 'hither, home,' '*kwäw* 'long hair, woman,' *ä* 'her,' *wa* 'he'), *nimāwinAtutAmawāwa*, 'I shall go and ask him for it' (*ni* 'I, in future action,' *māwi* 'go,' *nAtut* 'ask,' *Amaw* 'it, as secondary object,' *ā* and *wa*, both referring to animate third person).

It is interesting to notice that the first and most important division which logical reflection has always demanded of the sentence, namely, that into subject and predicate, is one of the rarest, and, where we know the history, one of the latest, to receive a corresponding word-division in the sentence: in Latin, Greek, and Sanskrit subject and predicate are usually both expressed in the verb-form: in Slavic and most of the Romance languages both possibilities are open (Italian *canta* or *ella canta*, Polish *śpiewa* or *ona śpiewa*).

In our languages we have in some cases the choice between the two methods of expression, one by a single word and one by a succession of several words. Thus, we may speak of a *horse-tamer* or a *tamer of horses*. The former kind of expression obviously analyzes itself into the elements *horse* and *tamer*, and linguistic scholars, taking for granted that our analysis corresponds to the historic occurrence, are wont to assume that such compound words are the product of a coalescence of independent words. This assumption meets with a very significant difficulty: the farther back we go in tracing the history of our languages, the less resemblance do the parts of such compounds bear to the individual words from which it is supposed that they were derived. Thus in Ancient Greek the parts of the word ἱππόδαμος differ from any independently occurring forms; ἵππο- differs from any actual form of ἵππος, and -δαμός 'tamer,' is a type of formation rarely found outside of compound words. Similarly, the τρι- of τρίπους does not occur as an independent word. Any one who reads Brugmann's section on noun-compounds (*Grundriss*, ii², 1, 49 ff.) or the second volume of Wackernagel's monumental Sanskrit Grammar will be impressed by the endless deviations, exceeding all possibilities of accidental or secondary development, of composition-stems from independent words, e.g. Greek κυδρός κυδιάνειρα, πατήρ ὄπατρος. The most widespread of these deviations, the type of ἵππος ἱππόδαμος, is so obtrusive that it has given rise to the supplementary theory that these compounds go back to a time (postulated *ad hoc*) when uninflected stems were used as words, and used, the compounds compel one further to assume, in the value of any and every case-relation. So Brugmann (*Grundriss*, II², 1, 78); upon this theory Jacobi has built his speculations in *Compositum und Nebensatz*. Needless to say that the whole assumption that compound words are historically the result of a coalescence has no other support than the circumstance that we analyze them into elements more or less closely resembling single words,—exactly as Bopp analyzed out of the personal verb-forms certain elements more or less closely resembling personal pronouns. In neither case does the analysis justify a historical assumption. Quite on the contrary, the farther back we go into history, the less do the elements of compounds resemble single words: we have every reason to believe that the compound words of the Indo-European languages represent an older type of formation in which meanings that are now usually expressed in several words were still merged into one word whose divisions had only an associative identity, —a word comparable to the formations of the American languages. The possibility of breaking up the sentence into those smaller units which we are accustomed to look upon as corresponding to simple words was of later development, exactly as the possibility of separating actor from action in Latin or Germanic speech has developed in historic times.

The compound word remained in use where its meaning had undergone transference or specialization and differed, accordingly, from that of the now more favored collocation of simple words. This accounts for the persistence of such types as the so-called exocentric compounds, ὠκύπτερος 'having quick wings,' English *long-nose* 'one who has a long nose,' and, in general, for our habit of using compounds where we mean something more specific than what would be expressed by a collocation, *e.g.* *blue-bird*, as opposed to *blue bird*.

To recite the evidence for this view would be to tell the entire story of compound words in the Indo-European languages.[5] So much, however, is certain, that, here as elsewhere, the course of linguistic history has been

[5] An interesting task, which I have undertaken and hope some day to finish. [Other activities interfered with this tentative plan. The interest in the nature of compounds was abiding, as shown by many passages in later articles and in the 1933 book; the specific concern with Indo-European compounds at least produced the 1937 article 'Notes on Germanic Compounds', *Mélanges linguistiques offerts à M. Holger Pedersen* 303–307 (København: Acta Jutlandica 9:1).—CFH].

from associational articulation of the utterance toward apperceptive structure; and that the grammarian's dissection of words, though of infinite practical value, must not mislead us into thinking that language is really a pasting together, by means of hyphens or a similar agency, of the elements which this dissection may reveal.

# B9. Subject and Predicate

1916. *Transactions of the American Philological Association* 47.13–22.

[Delivered at the 48th Annual Meeting of the APA, held in St. Louis, Missouri, December 1916; thus actually published during 1917.]

It is remarkable and perhaps characteristic of the progress of investigation into the more habitual and socialized of our mental processes, that linguistic theory is by no means clear as to the nature of subject and predicate in language, in spite of the fact that our speech-feeling seems to distinguish quite clearly between predicating and non-predicating utterances. The prevalent view, expressed in our practical handbooks (*e.g.* Goodwin's *Greek Grammar*, 1897, p. 196 f.) and many of our scientific manuals (such as Paul's *Prinzipien der Sprachgeschichte*[4], chap. 6), is that "every sentence contains two parts, a subject and a predicate."[1] With this view the speech-feeling often enough comes into conflict, and we then resort to auxiliary hypotheses and forced interpretations of various kinds, saying, for instance, that one or the other of two parts is left unexpressed in exclamations such as *ouch!* or *fire!*, or that the two are contained in one word in such Latin sentences as *cantat*[2] or *pluit*,[3] or, worst of all, we deny the name of sentence to such utterances as *yes* or to answers such as *yesterday*.[4]

There is a psychologic principle coming to be more clearly recognized by students of language, which shows the way to a better interpretation of the process of utterance and of the speech-feeling. This principle is to the effect that the mental phenomena must be viewed as they actually occur and not as their products or a record of their occurrence may be

---

[1] This notion arose in the seventeenth and eighteenth centuries; it appears in the Port-Royal *Grammaire générale et raisonnée* (1676), in Wolf, *Philosophia rationalis* (1732), in Hermann, *De emendanda ratione Graecae grammaticae* (1801), all quoted by Delbrück in the introduction to his *Syntax* (Brugmann and Delbrück, *Grundriss*, III), and in Bernhardi, *Anfangsgründe d. Sprachwissenschaft* (1805), quoted by Delbrück, *Einl. in d. Studium d. indogerm. Sprachen*[5], p. 34 ff.

[2] So even Delbrück, *Grundriss*, V. 10: "Bei der ersten und zweiten Person des Verbums steckt das Subjekt in der Verbalform."

[3] So even Wundt, *Völkerpsychologie*, II[3], 227 ("indefinite subject").

[4] Wundt, *op. cit.* 241. The standard view is presented in my *Introduction to the Study of Language*.

interpreted by an observer after the fact.[5] It is this principle which has led to Kretschmer's definition of the sentence as the linguistic expression of an affect—of a single rise and fall of the emotion prompting to speech.[6] It is this principle which makes it clear that a single word can express only one separately apperceived element: that it is wrong, for instance, to interpret a form like *cantat* as containing two such elements. A leisurely student may reinterpret such a form into a logical judgment predicating the act of singing of a certain person, but the logical judgment is not present in the speaker's mind when the sentence-word *cantat* is spoken; for what we mean by saying that *cantat* is felt as a single word (and not as two words) is exactly this, that it contains no opportunity for an apperceptive (and hence for a logical) act of division. The speaker's experience is simply that of a known and definite person's singing; his expressive reaction is a habitual unit, *cantat*, and such morphologic structure as we find in this word is merely associative; it exists only by virtue of the parallelism and contrast of other forms and is not explicit in the utterance itself. Finally, pursuing the same principle, I have suggested (*T.A.P.A.* XLV, 65 ff.) that even where there is a word-boundary, there is in most instances of utterance no apperceptive division; that, for instance, the English sentence, *she is singing*, is usually spoken in much the same way as the Latin, Italian, or Slavic one-word equivalent, and differs from the latter primarily only in being occasionally used for an attentively discriminating statement, *shé is singing*, which corresponds to Italian *ella canta*, not to Italian *canta*, Latin *cantat*.

If we keep this principle in view, it is not difficult, I believe, to reach a clearer understanding of the nature of predication in language.[7]

I. We may consider first a type of sentence about which there can be little question. If, in the course of a philosophical discussion, there occurs the statement, *homo mortalis est*, it is obvious that this sentence may well be the linguistic expression of a logical judgment. To the logical subject, that talked about and underlying the predication (τὸ ὑποκείμενον), corresponds the word *homo*, and to the logical predicate, that said about the subject (τὸ κατηγορούμενον), corresponds the phrase *mortalis est*. It is a natural transference of terms—but we must not forget that it is a transference of terms—to call the linguistic element corresponding to the

---

[5] See James, *Psychology*, 1890, I, 166 f., 274 f. (the "psychologist's fallacy") and Wundt, *Grundriss d. Psychologie*[11], 13 (the fallacy is "die eigenen Reflexionen des Psychologen über die Tatsachen in diese selbst zu verlegen") *Logik*[3], III, 150 f., and, generally, the works of the latter author.

[6] In Gercke and Norden, *Einl. in d. Altertumswissenschaft*[2], I, 516.

[7] In accordance with this principle the process of sentence-utterance has been most vividly and exactly described by James in his *Psychology*, I, 260–263; the consequences for linguistic theory were not in this connection (nor, so far as I know, in any other place) drawn by this great philosopher. See also Morris, *T.A.P.A.* XLVI, 103 ff., esp. 110.

logical subject a grammatical or linguistic 'subject' and to speak similarly of a grammatical or linguistic 'predicate.'

Another type of sentence differs from this by the absence of the verb: *beatus ille homo*; the division into subject and predicate is, however, no less clear. This type, entirely lacking in English, is in Russian, for instance, the only form for non-narrative statements of a certain kind: *mužík běden* 'peasant poor', *i.e.* 'the peasant is poor.'

Such examples as these have played an unduly important part in the development of syntactic theory. A student confronted by the task of analyzing his speech enters into a state of abnormally careful attention; this attention he exercises not only in the analysis, but also, inappropriately, in forming his examples, which, in consequence, are logically constructed statements of the type we have described, rather than casual phrases.

We may, however, take an utterance of this very type, such as *he is a lucky fellow*, and, with a different distribution of pause, duration, pitch, and stress, utter it not as the expression of a deliberate judgment, but as an enthusiastic exclamation, *he's a lucky fellow!*, or we may half plaintively, half enviously mutter, *he's a lucky fellow!* In these instances the speaker's frame of mind is far removed from that of logical predication. He is expressing primarily an emotion, and his speech comes forth without any apperceptive jointings. Though it is easy enough, once the words are spoken and remembered, to interpret the sentence, in cold blood, into a judgment, yet our task is not to interpret what the speaker may or should have meant to say, but to analyze the expression itself. It is an expression of emotion at a certain state of affairs, and lacks logical structure.

Yet there is a reservation. Although our ejaculation of wonder or envy differs in accentual features from the calm judgement, *he is a lucky fellow*, the two utterances are the same so far as distinctive word-form is concerned; and, what is more, the casual ejaculation is accompanied by a peculiar feeling-tone, a subtle and indescribable sense of completeness or roundedness, whose presence we are wont to signal by calling the statement a 'complete predication' or a 'complete sentence.' This appears clearly when we contrast *he's a lucky fellow!* with the otherwise equivalent *lucky fellow!* which lacks this tone of completeness.

This circumstance bears its explanation on the face of it: *the language from which our example is taken uses for many non-logical utterances the same distinctive word-forms as for the expression of a logical judgment.* If we ignore—as perhaps we have the right to ignore temporarily—certain features of duration, pitch, and stress, then we may say that the expression of a logical judgment (predicating, *e.g.*, a state of happiness of a known person) is often the same, in English, or Latin, and probably in most languages, as a rather explicit exclamation (*e.g.* of envy or surprise at the circumstance of his happiness). If we wish to keep the terms 'linguistic subject' and 'linguistic predicate,' we must therefore define them not straightway as the linguistic expressions of a logical subject and predicate, but rather as *linguistic elements which can be used in this function, but are used also in other utterances, as components of a habitual sentence-type.*

II. The type of sentence we have so far examined is in Latin and in Russian confined to non-narrative statements and therefore relatively often used as the expression of a logical thought-content. Of other types this is less true. When we say, *then Mary bought a hat,* we are usually in a narrative frame of mind; a concrete and colorful picture floats past the 'inner eye,' and from logical judgment we are far removed. To make a sentence of this type express a logical judgment we must postulate some rather strained situation, in which moreover the accentual features of the utterance will be entirely different. Outside of such unusual situations our sentence is by no means the utterance of a logical predicating-experience; yet it presents the characteristic structure which allows us to analyze it into a linguistic subject and predicate.

These linguistic predications of the narrative type differ in Latin and in Russian from those of equational type (*homo mortalis est, beatus ille*) because these latter in Russian always and in Latin optionally lack the finite verb. In English, German, and French the two types are merged.

Now, it is a fundamental principle of linguistic study that we have no right to inject into our analysis of a language distinctions not expressed in the language. If, therefore, we borrow the technical terms 'subject' and 'predicate' from logic for such a sentence as *man is mortal,* we are bound to keep them also for the structurally similar *Mary bought a hat,* and consequently to distinguish between the use of these terms in logic and their use in linguistics.

No doubt the extensive use in our languages of linguistic subject and predicate in non-logical utterances has contributed to the induration of the traditional rationalizing view, which tries to see in every sentence of language the expression of a logical judgment. We are now in a position to clear up some of the difficulties to which this view has led. For instance, Wundt, who strictly identifies linguistic subject and predicate with those of logic, is forced to make the following inconsistent statement (*Völkerps.* II³, 270): "If the speaker ever for the nonce grammatically chooses a subject different from that which logically he might intend to make his subject, then he has given his thought an inadequate form; in which case, to be sure, other than purely logical motives, such as euphony and the rhythm of speech, may at times excuse the deviation." Now, it is not for us to make excuses for a speaker or to heap humiliation and reproach upon him if he fails to accord with our theories of syntax. The situation Wundt describes is merely this,—and it is in our languages a very frequent one—that the linguistic subject and predicate would not, under a logical reinterpretation of the sentence, produce a correct logical judgment. Or, more exactly: if we write down the sentence and then read it with logical intonation, we may find the subject and predicate poorly chosen for the logical purposes of the situation. If I say, *The hat was priced at five dollars. A woman went in and bought it*, my second sentence, under logical interpretation, would present a poorly chosen subject, for it is the hat and not the unknown woman that ought, logically, to be the subject of the new statement; I should say: *The hat was priced at five dollars. It was bought by a woman who had entered the store in order to buy it*. This deviation of linguistic subject and predicate from a logical norm is, however, not, as Wundt's words suggest, a rare or occasional feature, but will be found extremely common in our languages.

III. While in modern English, German, or French the great majority of narrative sentences exhibits the structure of linguistic predication, this is not true of the older stages of these languages, of Latin, Italian, Greek and Slavic, or, in general, of the older type of Indo-European speech. These latter languages possess a kind of narrative sentence in which a linguistic subject and predicate cannot be found: the simplest instances are sentences of one word, such as *cantat*. Of whatever parts such an utterance may consist, they are not separated from each other by any apperceptive analysis, such as that of logical predication; if they were, we should speak of several words, not of one word. In English, for instance, a word such as *stones* contains two associatively joined elements; if we attentively separate these, we no longer use a single word, but speak of *several stones* or *some stones*, expressing the plurality by a separate word. So a Latin speaker, if he apperceptively analyzed the experience into an actor and an action, would no longer say *cantat*, but *illa cantat* (Italian *ella canta*, Russian *oná pojót*). The analysis into object and number in *stones*, into actor and action in *cantat* is never explicit; the word as a whole corresponds to the experience as a whole; this experience is associated with other partially unlike experiences, which are expressed by similar words, such as *stone*, *stony* (same material element) or *trees*, *rivers* (same element of number), *cantās*, *cantābat* (same element of action) or *saltat*, *dormit* (same element of actor); but the analysis involved in the existence and association of these parallel words is merely implicit and associative. We have therefore no right to speak of a linguistic subject and predicate in a sentence like *cantat*.

Two factors have led to the forced interpretation which sees in *cantat* a subject and a predicate. One is the obvious similarity between a one-word sentence and an English *she is singing*. The two might be used by a bilingual speaker of English and Italian of one and the same experience. To those who see in the English sentence the expression of a logical judgment, the obvious similarity of the English and the Latin-Italian sentences is a motive for seeking in the latter also a logical predication. For us, however, the similarity between the two types confirms the conclusion that normally the linguistic subject-and-predicate structure of the English sentence does not express any apperceptive analysis of the experience, but is merely a habitual formality.

The second factor is this: the duality of elements in *cantat* does correspond in a striking way to the duality in *she is singing* or *elle chante*. This correspondence has, however, in principle nothing to do with subject and predicate, and consists only in this, that Latin, like the modern languages, analyzes the situation into actor and action—though, to be sure, by a merely implicit analysis, whereas the English, French, or German sentence is at least capable of attentive separation. When an author is persuaded that the Latin word "contains a subject," he is mistaking an actor for a subject, a fallacy induced by the circumstance that in English, German, and French the subject is always viewed as an actor. To use the term 'subject' for 'acting person or object' would be an unwarrantable extension of the term which could only create confusion. Both the Latin *cantat* and the English *she is singing* are expressions of actor and action, but only the latter contains a (linguistic) subject and predicate.

One class of sentences of the ancient one-word type has received special attention from linguistic students, that of utterances about the weather, such as *pluit*. Both Paul (*op. cit.* 130 f.) and Wundt (*Völkerps.* II³, 227 f.) see in these a subject and predicate.[8] From our standpoint there are two reasons why this cannot be true. Psychologically it is not correct to attribute an act of logical judgment to a speaker who merely says *pluit* or *piove* or *it's raining*. His act of apperception is by no means an analytic one: he takes the experience as a whole without breaking it up into an underlying element and a predication about it. Linguistically, we mean, when we call *pluit* or *piove* a single word, that it is not capable of expressing more than one apperceptively grasped element of experience.

The ancients were able to make a logical extension of such a sentence as *pluit*; when they did so, they said Ζεὺς ὕει or *Iuppiter tonat*. Strepsiades asks, ἀλλὰ τίς ὕει; and his answer is, in burlesque form, the ancient view. As our analysis, today, when we devote attentive thought to meteorological phenomena, is rather akin to that of Socrates in the *Clouds*, we are forced, at such times, to diverge far from the usual utterance, *it's raining*.[9] The linguistic subject and predicate in the English *it's raining*

---

[8] Delbrück at first rejected this view, but later hesitates; cf. *Grundriss*, v, 37.

[9] This way of talking about the weather has come to us from of old, when the *it* still represented a concrete actor. Traces of the old state of affairs in Germanic in Grimm, *Deutsche Grammatik*, IV, 228.

thus give us an example of a linguistic predication which never represents a logical judgment.

If these examples have made clear to us the general nature of linguistic predication, especially in its divergence from logical predication or judgment, we may, in conclusion, briefly note a few of the features of linguistic subject and predicate that appear in our languages.

We have already had occasion to see that in English, German, and French the linguistic subject is looked upon as an actor and the linguistic predicate as an action performed by this actor: *Mary bought a hat, she is singing*, and even *it is raining*. This, indeed, is universal, no matter how inappropriate the identification may seem when we reflect upon it: *I hear a noise, Mont Blanc is high, the house was built, the house is being built*, and so on.

This is not true in Slavic or in Latin. Both of these forms of speech add a second type of linguistic predication, in which subject and predicate are viewed as equated terms: *beatus ille*.

Latin has a third type, in which the linguistic subject is not an actor, but an object fully affected or produced by the action-predicate: *domus struitur*. As this construction is known as the 'passive,' we may define this term in accordance with the conditions in Latin: in a language which employs a construction (morphologic or syntactic) of actor and action, a parallel construction in which some other feature is coupled with action, is a passive.

This somewhat obvious definition is worth formulating because there has been some uncertainty as to the application of the term. Most writers find in the Philippine languages three 'passives' (so the Spanish writers and with them H. C. von der Gabelentz, *Abh. Sächs. Gesell.* VIII, 481), but Wilhelm von Humboldt (*Kawi-Sprache* II = *Abh. Berl. Akad.* 1832, 3. Teil, 150) refused to apply this term to the Philippine constructions; he is followed in this by the best of our Philippine grammars, the late Dr. Seidenadel's description of the Bontoc Igorot language. Under our definition the Philippine constructions will receive the name of passives, as may be seen from a few examples taken from Tagalog. There is an actor-and-action construction, *e.g. sya y sumúlat naŋ líham*, 'he wrote a letter.' Beside this there is a sentence-type in which the (linguistic) subject is the object fully affected or produced, somewhat as in the Latin passive: *sinúlat nya aŋ líham*, 'was-written by-him the letter,' *i.e.* 'he wrote the letter'; this we may call the 'direct passive.' Secondly, there is a 'local passive,' in which the subject is the person, thing, or locality less fully affected by the action-predicate, as though an Indo-European dative or locative should become the subject of a passive construction: *sinulátan nya akó*, 'was-written-to by-him I,' *i.e.* 'he wrote to me.' Finally, there is a construction which we may call the 'instrumental passive,' in which the subject is the means or instrument or that given forth—in part somewhat as though an Indo-European instrumental could become the subject in a passive construction: *isinúlat nya aŋ kwénto*, 'was-written-down by-him the story,' *i.e.* 'he wrote down the story.' It may be worth mentioning that these languages have also the type of sentence in which the experience is not viewed as an action: *mabúti sya* or *sya y mabúte*, 'bonus ille.'

For the sake of completeness we may refer to another feature which has been confounded with subject and predicate. G. von der Gabelentz (*Die Sprachwissenschaft*[2], 369 ff.) invented the expression "psychological subject," which he used to name what we should call (with Wundt) the emotionally dominant element of the sentence: *e.g.*, in *today is mý birthday* the "psychological subject" is *my*. Wundt (*Völkerps.* II[3], 268 ff.) shows conclusively that the terms 'subject' and 'predicate' are here entirely inappropriate. Whatever the exact relation may be between an emotionally dominant element and the apperceptive processes, such as underlie logical judgment, a confusion of terms can have only bad results. It is interesting to see that in certain languages, namely Celtic and French, there is a tendency to identify the emotionally dominant element with a linguistic predicate: compare the Irish-English fondness for such constructions as *it's he that did it.*

# B10. The Preface to *Tagalog Texts*

1917. *Tagalog Texts with Grammatical Analysis.* 3 vols.: Part I.—*Texts and Translation*, pp xv + 107; Part II.—*Grammatical Analysis*, pp xi + 183; Part III.—*List of Formations and Glossary*, pp viii + 92. By Leonard Bloomfield, Assistant Professor of Comparative Philology and German, University of Illinois. (= *University of Illinois Studies in Language and Literature*, Vol. 3, Nos. 2, 3, 4; May, August, and November. Board of Editors: George T. Flom, William A Oldfather, Stuart P. Sherman. Copyright 1917, by the University of Illinois.)

[The editor's original plan was to reprint here Bloomfield's complete treatment of the sound system and grammar of Tagalog (as well as his Preface), as the only extended example in the *Anthology* of Bloomfield's way with a language. Reasons of space and expense have forced the deletion; it is nevertheless recommended that anyone seriously interested in understanding Bloomfield's views and methods study with great care either the *Grammatical Analysis*, or the 'Notes on the Fox Language' (*IJAL* 3.219–232, 1925, and 4.181–219, 1927), or some other of his writings in which he is minimally concerned with theory and maximally with accuracy and clarity of descriptive statement. The Preface, which we do reprint, is important in that it reveals his attitudes of the time, towards language, towards fellow scholars and predecessors, and towards other people.

In a letter dated 13 December 1965, Mr. Joe C. Sutton, editor of the *Illinois Alumni News*, answered a query of mine about Bloomfield's Tagalog informant as follows: 'I'm sorry, but our files yield no helpful information on Mr. Santiago. He attended here in 1914–17 and left without receiving a degree. For some years, he has been listed as "lost" in our records.' Thus, Bloomfield's work with Mr. Santiago must have been done during 1915 and 1916, after his return from the 1914 European trip.

This was Bloomfield's baptism of fire in 'field work'—the analysis of a language through data gathered directly from the lips of native speakers. The record itself speaks for the enormous patience and thoroughness with which the data were gathered, sifted, and classified. Less obvious are the following two points:

(1) The traditional 'philological' way to analyze a language was through the examination of inherited bodies of texts. This was the approach Bloomfield had been trained in. Since such texts were unavailable or unreliable for Tagalog, Bloomfield gathered his own—but then proceeded to treat them by just the methods he would have used (and, on occasion, did use) on inherited texts, such as those of Alfredian Old English or of Old or Middle High German. Of course, he

also sought to acquire some practical control of the language, and turned frequently to the informant to check on points about which he was uncertain. His subsequent field work with other languages, especially Algonquian, was organized in this same way. The texts themselves were treated as authoritative in a way in which many later field workers have not imitated him.

(2) Bloomfield's understanding of phonemics is virtually in its final form in the Tagalog treatment, except only for the term 'phoneme' itself. His later 'phoneme' is just what he here refers to by the term 'distinctive sound'.

In a note appended at the beginning of the corrigenda, Vol. III p. 406, Bloomfield wrote that the errors 'would have been far more numerous but for the accuracy and intelligence of the typesetter, Mr. Staley, and the unfailing kindness of the editor, Professor W. A. Oldfather.']

## Preface

This essay is purely linguistic in character and purpose.

In taking phonetic notes on Tagalog I noticed that the pronunciation of the speaker to whom I was listening, Mr. Alfredo Viola Santiago (at present a student of architectural engineering in the University of Illinois) presented certain features of accentuation not mentioned in the descriptions familiar to me. With the intention of briefly describing these features, I took down more extensive notes and asked Mr. Santiago to tell me in Tagalog the stories of "The Sun" and "The Northwind and the Sun," used as models by the International Phonetic Association.

The data so obtained showed that the features of accentuation I had observed were in part distinctive (expressive of word-meaning), and, further, that certain other features, which were but imperfectly described in the treatises I knew (so especially the use of the "ligatures"), appeared in Mr. Santiago's speech in a regular and intelligible manner. A more extensive study was thus indicated.

The results of this study were subject to two obvious limitations. The utterances I had transcribed were either translations or isolated sentences, and I could not determine to what extent the features of Mr. Santiago's speech which I had observed were general in Tagalog.

The former of these limitations was fully overcome when I asked Mr. Santiago to tell me connected stories. In addition to fortunate endowments of a more general kind Mr. Santiago possesses, as I found, that vivacity of intellect and freedom from irrelevant prepossessions which we seek and so rarely find in people whose language we try to study. This latter quality may be due in part to the fact that, as Mr. Santiago's education had been carried on entirely in Spanish and English, his speech-feeling for his mother-tongue has not been deflected by the linguistic, or rather pseudo-linguistic training of the schools, so familiar to us. However this may be, I cannot be grateful enough to Mr. Santiago (and I hope that the reader will join me in this feeling) for the intelligence, freshness, and imagination with which he has given us connected narratives in his native language,— stories he heard in childhood and experiences of his own and of his friends. It is to be hoped that some of these will be of interest to students of folk-lore (as, for instance, Nos. 9, 10, 11, the old Hindu fable in No. 4, and the Midas story, much changed, in No. 5); the texts are here given, however, only for their linguistic interest.

The second limitation could not be overcome. As there exists at present no adequate description of the dialectal differentiation of Tagalog, nor even an adequate description of any one form of the language, I can make no definite statement as to the relation of Mr. Santiago's speech to other forms of Tagalog.

What is here presented is, then, a specimen of the speech of an educated speaker from Mr. Santiago's home town, San Miguel na Matamés, Bulacán Province, Luzón. It would have been possible to include in the description the speech of at least one other educated Tagalog from a different region (uneducated speakers are unfortunately not within my reach), as well as such data as might be gathered from printed Tagalog books: I have refrained from this extension because, at the present state of our knowledge, a single clearly defined set of data is preferable to a necessarily incomplete attempt at describing the whole language in its local and literary variations. Comparison of literary Tagalog (chiefly the translation of José Rizal's "Noli me Tangere" by Patricio Mariano, Manila, Morales, 1913[1]) shows that Mr. Santiago's speech is not far removed from it. In most cases where my results deviate from the statements of the Spanish grammars, the evidence of printed books (and not infrequently the internal evidence of the grammars themselves) shows that the divergence is due not to dialectal differences but to the fact that the grammars are the product of linguistically untrained observers, who heard in terms of Spanish articulations and classified in those of Latin grammar.

This study presents, then, the first Tagalog texts in phonetic transcription and the first scientific analysis of the structure of the language[2]. Although the nature of the problem forbade the use of any material other than that obtained from Mr. Santiago, I have examined all the treatises on Tagalog accessible to me. No experience could show more clearly than the reading of these books the necessity of linguistic and especially phonetic training for anyone who wishes to describe a language. Not one of

---

[1] An English translation by Charles Derbyshire was published in 1912 by the Philippine Education Company in Manila and the World Book Company in New York, under the title "The Social Cancer".

[2] The entire syntax and much of the morphology, especially whatever relates to the accent-shifts in word-formation, will be found to be new. I have of course refrained from any and all historical surmises beyond the indication of unassimilated loan-words. The system of transcription used is, with a few deviations, that of the International Phonetic Association.

the works in the following list[3] contains an intelligible description of the pronunciation of Tagalog. The only general work of scientific value is the excellent second volume of P. Serrano Laktaw's dictionary. Much as one may admire the pioneer courage of Totanes and the originality of Minguella, these venerable men were as little able to describe a language as one untrained in botany is to describe a plant. Among the authors of monographs are several good names and one or two of the greatest in our science: nearly all of these authors mention the difficulty under which they labored for want of an adequate description of the language.

[3] They were accessible to me chiefly through the courtesy of the Newberry Library in Chicago. [Bloomfield's list runs to 34 titles. We give here the three whose author's names are mentioned in the Preface:—CFH]

Minguella, T., Ensayo de gramática Hispano-Tagala. Manila 1878. Método práctico para que los niños y niñas de las provincias tagalas aprendan á hablar Castellano. Manila 1886.
Serrano Laktaw, P., Diccionario Hispano-Tagalog. Primera parte. Manila 1889. Diccionario Tagalog-Hispano. Segunda parte. Manila 1914.
de Totanes, S., Arte de la lengua Tagala. Manila 1745. Sampaloc 1796. Manila 1850. Binondo 1865 (reimpreso).

# 11. Review of Bloomfield's *Tagalog*

1919. Frank R. Blake (Johns Hopkins University), *American Journal of Philology* 40.86–93 (January–March)

This work contains an extended treatment of Tagalog, the most important native language of the Philippine Islands, similar in general character and scope to Seidenadel's Bontoc Igorot Grammar with Vocabulary and Texts (cf. my review of the same in this Journal, Vol. XXXI, 3 [whole No. 123] 1910, pp. 339–342). It is the most elaborate and pretentious work yet published on any Philippine language, comprising in all 382 pages of text exclusive of title-pages, preface, table of contents, etc. It is based entirely, as the author tells us in the preface to Part I, p. 10 (166), on the spoken speech of a Mr. Santiago, an educated Tagalog of the town of San Miguel na Matamés, Bulacán Province, Luzon. Part I contains the Tagalog text in phonetic transcription, with accents indicated and the English translation on opposite pages, of thirty-four prose stories and selections illustrative of Tagalog life and ideas. Part II comprises what is practically a grammar of the Tagalog spoken by Mr. Santiago, divided into three parts, viz., Phonetics pp. 134–145 (290–301), Syntax pp. 146–209 (302–365), and Morphology, pp. 210–316 (366–472). Part III contains first a list of nominal and verbal formations, pp. 317–319 (473–475), arranged, with the exception of a few forms without affix, under the various formative elements, so that the list is at the same time a list of these elements; references are given in each case to the paragraphs of the grammar where the forms are discussed. The rest of the volume consists of the word index or vocabulary of the words occurring in the chrestomathy and grammar, the words being arranged according to roots, with the derivatives grouped under each root. Besides the translation of the words, at least one reference to a passage in which it occurs is given.

The texts in Part I offer an excellent body of linguistic material. The plan of furnishing each text with a translation on the opposite page is to be recommended, as it enables the student to test the correctness of his own translation of the text much better than would be possible on the basis of the vocabulary alone, and much more conveniently than would be possible if the translations were added in a body after all the texts.

The translation of several passages has been omitted thru oversight, viz., p. 68 (224), ll. 6, 7, 8; p. 90 (246), ll. 20, 21; p. 106 (262), l. 27; p. 114 (270), ll. 10, 11. On page 115 (271), ll. 29, 30, the translation "The cheapest thing is the blessing of the corpse at the door of the church and placed on the ground" is obscure; the meaning is—The cheapest form of blessing is that given to the corpse at the door of the church while lying on the ground. The translation of Tagalog *pitú-ng wíka'*, Spanish *siete palabras* ("seven words"), pp. 20, 21 (176, 177), by "Good Friday mass" is apparently incorrect. The service of the "seven last words of Christ" on Good Friday is a three-hour series of prayers and meditations and not a mass, and so far as I know, the term "Good Friday mass" is never applied to it. The only mass that is celebrated on Good Friday in the Roman Catholic Church is the so-called "Mass of the Presanctified" which is celebrated early in the day, and has no connection with the three-hour service, which is held from 12 to 3 p. m. in commemoration of the three hours that Christ hung on the Cross. In the Index, p. 387 (543), col. 2 near bottom, *siyéte-palábras* is translated "Easter Mass" (? !). The author makes the curious mistake of translating *kalabàw* ('water buffalo') by 'caribou' instead of 'carabao', p. 101 (257), ll. 18, 19 (as also in the Word-Index, p. 385 (511), col. 1); 'caribou' is of course the name of the American reindeer. A misprint which is not noticed in the Corrigenda is *pagisìgáwan* p. 48 (204), l. 37 for *pagsisìgáwan*.

An occasional note might have been added with advantage in order to facilitate the finding of a difficult or irregular form in the Index; e.g., to *pagsa-ulàn* p. 62 (218), l. 12—cf. *sa* in Index; or to *katuturán* p. 76 (232), l. 21—cf. *tuwìd* in Index. A table of contents giving a list of the selections would have been a convenience.

The Word-Index in Part III is excellent. So far as I know it is unique among Philippine vocabularies and lexicons in being furnished with references to a series of texts. In the explanation at the beginning of the index the statement "the forms are given with fullest accentuation and vocalism (*iy* for *y*, *uw* for *w* after consonant), regardless of actual occurrence" is obscure; the meaning is apparently that the forms are given with the fullest accentuation and vocalism that they can have under any condition, regardless of the fact that they may actually occur in the texts with different vocalization and accent. The reference *see Corrigenda* under article *-abála* is without meaning, as there is no mention of *abála* or its derivatives in the Corrigenda pp. 406–408 (562–564); similarly in the case of the reference *and Corrigenda* under *-álam*. Unnoticed misprints are *na-gáral* under article *áral*, so divided at the end of a line instead of *nag-áral*, and a superfluous *ŋ* at the end of article *-bitàw*. At the top of page 328 (484) the first and second lines of the first column are interchanged. The word *bakás* is defined as *mark, in*; what the *in* signifies does not appear. In the Corrigenda to Part II pp. 407, 408 (563, 564), several page references are incorrect, viz., p. 272, l. 2, which should be p. 277, l. 2; and p. 224, l. 25 (?). The Corrigenda to p. 297, l. 29 and to p. 313, l. 3, also apparently belong elsewhere.

The most important part of the work is the grammar contained in Part II, which gives an analysis of the speech of Mr. Santiago. This analysis, while containing a number of things that are new, and while characterized thruout by a wealth of example, is given under such unfamiliar forms, with such peculiar principles of arrangement, and in many cases with so much obscurity of statement (similar to that which has already been referred to in Parts I and III), that it is difficult at times even for one familiar with the grammatical structure of the Philippine languages in general to understand the author's meaning.

The most important contribution made by the author to the study of Philippine languages is his treatment of Tagalog Phonetics. Here he gives us the only really scientific treatment yet published of the phonetics of any Philippine language. His discussion of the relation between *i* and *e*, and between *o* and *u* is excellent, and his treatment of the syllable is one of the best things in his work. His discussion of the accent, however, while it contains a great amount of information on this important subject, is in many respects distinctly disappointing.

In the first place his system of accent marks is confusing; he uses the grave accent both for final primary accent and for secondary accent final and non-final. As all four kinds of accents that he mentions, viz., primary final and non-final, and secondary final and non-final differ in pitch and quantity of vowel, there is no more reason for using different marks for the two kinds of primary accent than for the two kinds of secondary. To be consistent all four should have been marked with different signs, or one sign should have been employed for all primary accents, and one for all secondary. According to the system actually used by the author, the words *gabi* (primary final), *bahay* (primary non-final), *aakyat* (primary non-final and secondary final), and *susulat* (primary non-final and secondary final), appear as *gabì, báhay, áakyàt, sùsúlat*. With a separate sign for each of the four accents they might be represented as *gabí, bâhay, âakyăt, sùsûlat*; or with acute accent mark for all primary, and grave for all secondary accents, as *gabí, báhay, áakyàt, sùsúlat*; either of which methods is certainly preferable to the one used by the author.

All former authorities agree that the primary accent falls on one of the last two syllables, but this is apparently not the case in the dialect of Mr. Santiago, for in any number of words thruout the work we find it marked on syllables before the penult. No statement, however, is anywhere made as to what syllables of a polysyllabic word are capable of bearing the non-final primary accent. No more satisfaction is given with regard to the secondary accent, nor is it stated under what conditions a word may have more than one secondary accent, as seems to be often the case.

It would have been a distinct advantage in the case of Tagalog words with both primary and secondary accents, to have compared them to words in some other language, English, French, German, etc., whose accent scheme approximates that of the Tagalog words, as otherwise it is practically impossible for a student to get any clear idea of how the Tagalog words sound.

The section on sentence accent is very good, and the grouping of words into the four accent classes, atonic, enclitic, pretonic, and orthotonic is especially to be commended, tho the statements with regard to them might be given with more clearness.

The development of a stress weaker than a secondary accent in a series of unstressed syllables, which is discussed in §50, should be more clearly and exhaustively treated. There is no way of knowing whether it refers exclusively to such cases as originally oxytone words which have become atonic (as, e.g., *ang mangà báhay* which becomes *ang manga báhay*, and then *ang mànga báhay*), or whether it has a wider application.

The Syntax is the most disappointing part of the whole grammar, being decidedly inferior to both the Phonetics and the Morphology. The chief defects are the great number of peculiar and unusual grammatical terms used without good reason for perfectly familiar and suitable designations, the lack of a clear and simple arrangement of the material, and the failure to give adequate treatment to many important categories.

It is divided into four chief divisions, viz., (1) Sentence and Word, (2) Subject and Predicate, (3) Attributes, (4) Serial Groups. In the first division the author enumerates what he considers the chief syntactic relations, viz., Attribution, Predication, and the Serial Relation; predication corresponding to the usual acceptation of that term; the serial relation being that between words connected by coordinating conjunctions like 'and', while attribution includes everything else, tho he does suggest that perhaps it would be well to set up one additional type to be known as "exocentric modification" (? !). He then takes up the parts of speech, of which he distinguishes two, viz., "full words" and "particles", but he states that "independent of this classification . . . are certain less important groupings of words and certain phrase types, some of which will appear in the course of the analysis" (what these are is not stated). "Others, however, demand mention at the outset". These last categories are the following, viz., (1) static and transient words, a transient being a word expressing "an element of experience viewed as impermanent, i.e., belonging to some limited portion of time" (or somewhat more simply, a verb—F. R. B.) while static words are all those that are not transient; (2) personal names; (3) the object construction (i.e., all nouns and words and expressions treated as nouns which are preceded by the definite article *ang*—F. R. B.); (4) expressions of indefinite quantity (i.e., expressions containing an indefinite noun after words denoting 'having' or 'not having'—F. R. B.).

The second division, Subject and Predicate, is clearly and logically arranged, sentences without subject and predicate structure, which he calls "non-predicative", the various kinds of subject, and the various kinds of predicate being discussed.

In the fourth division, Serial Groups, coordinating particles, paratactic sentences, parentheses, and anacoluthic sentences are briefly treated.

The bulk of the Syntax falls in the third division, Attribution, pp. 160–205 (316–365), about 44 pages, compared with about 20 pages for the other three parts. Throwing aside the older terminology of nominative, genitive, and prepositional or oblique cases, tho without good reason, the author distinguishes four attributive constructions (from the point of view of connective particle or case sign—F. R. B.), viz., (1) conjunctive attribution, all cases in which the attribute is joined to the modified word by the particle *ɳ* (=*ng*), *na* (usually called the ligature—F. R. B.); (2) disjunctive attribution (the attribute being in what is usually called the genitive case, tho its application is much wider than what is ordinarily understood by genitive, including case of the agent, instrumental, accusative, etc.— F. R. B.); (3) local attribution (the attribute being in what is usually called the oblique case—F. R. B.); (4) absolute attribution, in which the attribute merely precedes or follows. Conjunctive attribution comprises a treatment of the construction of descriptive, pronominal, and numeral adjectives, of adverbs of manner, and of relative, noun, and purpose clauses; disjunctive attribution covers the various uses of the genitive case forms; local, the various uses of the oblique case forms; absolute attribution includes the use of many of the chief adverbs and conjunctions.

Such a division of the material, while it groups together all the examples of these four types of construction, makes no provision for a connected treatment of material which is logically related, but which differs in grammatical construction, such categories as e.g., adverbs, comparison, various kinds of simple sentences, subordinate clauses, etc. The treatment of some of these categories, indeed, e.g., adverbs and subordinate clauses, will be found scattered in various places in all four of the sub-divisions mentioned above, and there is no way of finding and combining these scattered references except by reading thru the text.

This four-fold division is crossed by a very useful three-fold division from the point of view of the position of the attribute, viz., (1) loosely joined, i.e., at the beginning of a sentence, usually followed by the particle *ay*, or at the end of a sentence, (2) closely joined, immediately preceding or following the word modified, (3) enclitic, following immediately the first word of a modified expression, not counting loosely joined attributes.

The Morphology is devoted to an enumeration and discussion of the various forms of words, chiefly nouns and verbs. It is divided into three unequal divisions, viz., (1) Composition, in which are discussed certain combinations of words which somewhat resemble the compounds of other languages pp. 210, 211 (366, 367); (2) General features of word formation, in which are discussed roots, formative particles, reduplication, and accent shift, pp. 211–217 (367–373); and (3) Description of formations, pp. 218–316 (374–472), which are divided into three groups from the point of view of form, viz., (a) primary, those without formative particle or with *pag* or *pang*; (b) secondary, those made with the prefixes *si, paki, ka, pa, pati*; (c) irregular derivatives. From the point of view of meaning, each of these is divided into four groups, viz., simple static words, those that involve no idea of active or passive (i.e., ordinary concrete nouns—F. R. B.), e.g., *súlat* 'writing, document'; transients (i.e., verbs—F. R. B.), e.g., *sumúlat* 'wrote'; abstracts (i.e., verbal nouns of action), e.g., *pagsúlat* 'act of writing'; special static words, which tho nouns involve the idea of voice, e.g., *sulátan* 'writing-desk' (i.e., that upon which is written'). The three-fold formal division is neither logical nor convenient, but the fourfold semantic division is good, especially the distinction between simple and special static words.

The chief good points of this third division, which with the exception of eight pages makes up the whole of the Morphology, are: the great number and variety of the examples given, which consist of sentences containing the form in question; the lists of roots which are capable of taking the various formations; and the detailed account of the accent and accent-shift of the various forms. It suffers, however, from a number of defects. The explanations are often obscure, more unusual terms appear, e.g., a verb in the future tense is called a durative contingent transient, but there are no paradigms, and the discussion of both the verbal and the nominal systems loses in clearness and unity by the arrangement in which it is here presented.

The grammar as a whole is, from a mechanical point of view, not without a number of defects, some of them of a serious character. In the first place there are two peculiarities of writing which it has in common with Parts I and III. The sign for the glottal catch, which is apparently the upper part of a question mark, the dot at the bottom being omitted, is awkward, and until you become used to it gives a curious interrogative flavor to the word which contains it, which might be compared to the indefinite *f* or labial impression produced on modern readers by the old English *s* which resembles an *f*. Again the ligature *ɲ*, which really forms a part of the final syllable of a preceding word, is written alone. It would be better to connect it with a preceding word by a hyphen, e.g., *ito-ɲ*.

Other defects hinder the lucidity of presentation and ease of reference. The divisions and subdivisions of the material are not clearly enough indicated by difference in type, indenting, and the like, the same kind of numbers, e.g., (1), (2), etc., and the same kind of type being frequently used for the headings of sections of entirely different order or rank. There is no index, and the meagre table of contents, consisting of about a page and a half, is practically useless as a guide to the large amount of material here treated. The division of the whole text into short numbered paragraphs, and the numbering of the lines of the page (found also in Part I), however, are convenient devices, while the employment of a special notation (§339) to indicate the various peculiarities of word formation will be found useful.

Unnoticed misprints in the Grammar are '*interjectionss*' p. 151 (307), l. 21; 'reduplcated' p. 215 (371), l. 25; and the repetition of the word 'aspect' p. 217 (373), l. 26.

The dialect of Mr. Santiago, as the author states (Preface, p. 10 [166]), differs very little from ordinary written Tagalog. Examples of differences I have noticed, which may in some cases be differences between earlier and later stages of the language, are, e.g., the use of *namán* in the sense of 'however' instead of 'also'; *kanyá', kaniyá'* instead of *kayá'* 'therefore'; *ang táo-ng itó* 'this man' instead of *itó-ng táo* or *itó-ng táo-ng itó*; the use of forms like *sumúlat* and *sumusúlat* as preterite and present of the *um* class of verbs instead of *sungmúlat* and *sungmusúlat*; etc.

In a grammatical work like the one under discussion, in which the author follows an entirely new plan of arrangement, some attempt, at least, should be made to show where the new arrangement and the older and more familiar forms touch. The fact that practically no concessions to this natural demand are made by the author is responsible for much of the obscurity that mars his work. The least that could have been asked for in such a book would be a brief index of the familiar grammatical categories with references to the places in the grammar where they are treated, but not even this is furnished. Any grammarian is, of course, thoroly in sympathy with the invention of new terms and the setting up of new categories in the study of a new and peculiar form of speech, but familiar terms and categories should not be thrown overboard, as they are here, without good and sufficient reason, especially when the new terms and categories offer no special advantage over the old, or are in many cases decidedly inferior to them.[1]

[1] [Bloomfield remained unconvinced by this appeal or others like it. The Tagalog Grammatical Analysis demonstrates in detail his policy of working from form to meaning rather than the reverse; one may instructively compare Blake's treatment of the language (*A Grammar of the Tagalog Language; American Oriental Series* 1, New Haven: Yale University Press 1925). As to labels: in 1933 (the book *Language*), speaking of Tagalog, he retains the terms 'static word' and 'transient word', rather than Blake's 'noun' and 'verb'.

The grammatical analysis here given is probably not intended for practical use, and would certainly be almost useless as a handbook for beginners, but even as a scientific treatise it has failed to measure up to many of the chief requirements of such a piece of work. It can hardly be said to have filled the need, which certainly exists, of a *clear* presentation of the most important grammatical facts of the chief Philippine language. In spite of its evident and serious defects, however, the phonological material, the great number and variety of the examples, the word lists in the Morphology, and the number of novel points of view, will make the grammar a useful addition to the material at hand for the study of Tagalog.

To sum up briefly, Part I (Texts) and Part III (Vocabulary) are both first rate specimens of the class of linguistic writing which they exemplify. Part II (Grammar), however, representing an effort in the very field in which a man of the author's evident linguistic ability would be expected to shine, is disappointing; it is not in any sense a model Philippine grammar, and it will be useful to students of Tagalog chiefly for the new points of view it suggests, and as a store-house of linguistic raw material.

In the 1942 'Outline of Ilocano Syntax' (*Language* 18.193–200), dealing with a closely related Philippine language, the terms have become 'object expression' and 'open expression' —still not 'noun' and 'verb'. Clearly, Bloomfield believed that the differences between the Philippine languages and Indo-European are so profound that the difficulty of adjusting to new terms is less to be feared than the danger of being misled by a radical transfer of familiar ones.—CFH]

# B12. *From* a Letter to
# Mr. Carl Haessler

1920.

[The letter is dated 22 August 1920. The excerpt was quoted, with the permission of the recipient, in the Editor's Preface to Bloomfield's *The Menomini Language* (†1962).]

Have been writing down Menominee words and stories. They are a delightful people, of good culture: it must have been an elaborate and beautiful culture 200 years ago. The European-American takes it away and reduces them to the level of our yokelry, under pretext of civilizing,—but it is just the good things of civilization—bathtubs, telephones, freedom from bugs, good medical attendance, books, etc.—that they *don't* get. Determined effort to make them do the one kind of work of which the ordinary European yokel can conceive: farming,—the one thing the M., with artistic temperament and imagination and no sense of "thrift" can never learn. Lived 2 weeks with a medicine man and his wife, lovely old people, and learned the cooking terms etc. which have never been collected for any Algonquian language. They were very kind to me and patient teaching me, and it was hard, as they don't speak English.

# B13. Review of Sapir

1922. *The Classical Weekly* 15.142–143 (13 March).

[1920–1921 was Bloomfield's last year at the University of Illinois, 1921–1922 his first at the Ohio State University. It is clear, from the dates of publication of the works reviewed, that B13, B14, and B16 were all written at Ohio State, not at Illinois.

Until the 1920's, Bloomfield and Sapir moved largely in different circles. The earliest mention of Bloomfield by Sapir that I have found (in a rather hurried search) is in a letter to Robert H. Lowie, dated 28 November 1921, from Ottawa (Lowie edited Sapir's letters to him in the mid 1950's, and they were published finally, after Lowie's death, by his wife Luella Cole Lowie, in 1965). Sapir is at the Museum in Ottawa, not very happy with his job; he has just published his *Language* and is anxious to get reactions to it; officially, he is looking for candidates for field work tasks with some of the Indian languages of Canada. The relevant passage is brief and, in retrospect, somewhat amusing; it shows that Sapir could not have examined Bloomfield's Tagalog report in any detail: 'I have also written to inquire about L. Bloomfield, who has done work on Tagalog. Full-fledged philologists sometimes turn out disappointingly in the field.' In due time this worked out: Bloomfield's work with Cree in the summer of 1925 was under the auspices of the Museum in Ottawa, and must have been arranged for by Sapir shortly before he left the Museum for the University of Chicago.

The earliest mention of Sapir by Bloomfield seems to be this review.]

*Language: An Introduction to the Study of Speech.* By Edward Sapir. New York: Harcourt, Brace and Company, 1921. Pp vii+258.

This book is in every way to be commended to the general reader. The presentation is zestful; on the score of clearness no reader will complain who realizes that he must contribute some effort if he wants to learn things. In matters of human conduct, such as speech, we are so much under the spell of fetishes and tabus that no writer can spare us hard work, if we are to wrench ourselves away from these and acquire a scientific outlook. Although Dr. Sapir says in his Preface (iii) that his main purpose is to show "what I conceive language to be", the general reader may be assured that the book is dependable, for the author's conception is evidently the result of wide study and scientific experience.

For the specialist also Dr. Sapir's book is of interest, for it contains not only those general statements upon which all students of language are agreed, but also well-grounded expressions of opinion upon matters still under discussion. As regards these latter, Dr. Sapir in almost every instance favors those views which I, for one, believe to be in accord with our best knowledge of speech and of the ways of man. As Dr. Sapir gives no bibliography, one cannot say how much of his agreement with scholars who have expressed similar views is a matter of independent approach. For instance, on page 57 the author develops what he justly calls "an important conception",—the "inner" or "ideal" phonetic system of a language: it is exactly the concept of *distinctive features* developed by the school of Sweet, Passy, and Daniel Jones (see, for instance, the Principles of the International Phonetic Association [London, 1912], or, for the practical application, S. K. Chatterji's Brief Sketch of Bengali Phonetics [London, 1921], especially 3). The same concept was developed (independently, I think) by Franz Boas (Handbook of American Indian Languages, 16) and by de Saussure (Cours de Linguistique Générale [Paris, 1916]). It is a question of no scientific moment, to be sure, but of some external interest, whether Dr. Sapir had at hand, for instance, this last book, which gives a theoretic foundation to the newer trend of linguistic study.

This newer trend affects two critical points. We are coming to believe that restriction to historical work is unreasonable and, in the long run, methodically impossible. One is glad to see, therefore, that Dr. Sapir deals with synchronic matters (to use de Saussure's terminology) before he deals with diachronic, and gives to the former as much space as to the latter. The second point is that we are casting off our dependence on psychology, realizing that linguistics, like every science, must study its subject-matter in and for itself, working on fundamental assumptions of its own; that only on this condition will our results be of value to related sciences (especially, in our case, to psychology) and in the light of these related sciences in the outcome more deeply understandable. In other words, we must study people's habits of language—the way people talk—without bothering about the mental processes that we may conceive to underlie or accompany these habits. We must dodge this issue by a fundamental assumption, leaving it to a separate investigation, in which our results will figure as data alongside the results of the other social sciences. Dr. Sapir is here again in the modern trend; his whole presentation deals with the actualities of language rather than with hypothetical mental parallels. Especially well put is the following passage (9–10):

> From the physiologist's or psychologist's point of view we may seem to be making an unwarrantable abstraction in desiring to handle the subject of speech without constant and explicit reference to that basis. However, such

an abstraction is justifiable. We can profitably discuss the intention, the form, and the history of speech, precisely as we discuss the nature of any other phase of human culture—say art or religion—as an institutional or cultural entity, leaving the organic and psychological mechanisms back of it as something to be taken for granted. . . . Our study of language is not to be one of the genesis and operation of a concrete mechanism; it is, rather, to be an inquiry into the function and form of the arbitrary systems of symbolism that we term languages.

Where Dr. Sapir falls short in this respect, he does only what all the rest of us have done. His definition of the sentence, for example (36), goes right back to the irrelevant subject-and-predicate notion of logic[1], and is controverted by his own material, especially by his illuminating analysis of an English sentence (92–93), which is a good example of real linguistics. Had Dr. Sapir taken Meillet's definition (Introduction à l'Étude Comparée des Langues Indo-europécnnes[3], [Paris, 1912], 339), he would have had a definition in terms of linguistics—a definition, that is, in accord with the first thirty-five pages of his book, with the whole tendency of his exposition, and, in particular, with his description of the *word*, which he himself seems to distrust, saying (35), "In practice this unpretentious criterion does better service than might be supposed", an apology which is really a powerful proof of correctness. I wish to quote with approval in this connection this statement (13–14), "From the point of view of language, thought may be defined as the highest latent or potential content of speech, the content that is obtained by interpreting each of the elements in the flow of language as possessed of its very fullest conceptual value", and with approval to refer to such passages as that on the parts of speech (123–124). On the other hand, such questions as "What, then, are the absolutely essential concepts in speech. . . ?" (98), and such a passage as that on page 126 are out of accord with the author's own method in concrete problems. Such classifications as are attempted in the tables on pages 106–107 and 150–151 are similarly irrelevant, and are, indeed, invalidated by the author's own reservations. Like the rest of us, Dr. Sapir still pays tribute to aprioristic speculation which steals upon us in the guise of psychology; as his own approach is scientific, these false generalizations stand out from the rest of the discussion. Dr. Sapir has less of them than his predecessors; whoever is interested in the progress of our science will welcome his book as a forward step.

It is important, in the expansion of our science to its just province, that we should not commit the obvious fault of losing the historical accuracy of our predecessors; accordingly one regrets an error of principle in the historical part (190), where the author speaks as if the contrast of vowels

[1] Compare (98): "In every intelligible proposition at least two of these radical ideas must be expressed, though in exceptional cases . . .".

in *foot* : *boot* were a matter of sound-change now in progress. Of course sound-change while in progress does not show itself to us in this or any other way; the contrast in question is due to a sound-change dated about 1700, followed by varying distribution of the resultant forms in Standard English (see Wyld, History of Modern Colloquial English, 238 f.). The understanding of the process of sound-change—of immense "diagnostic value" for psychology, ethnology, and, indeed, all forms of human science —is our most valuable heritage from the purely historical linguistics of the nineteenth century. It represents the phase of work in which our predecessors refrained from premature psychologic interpretation, and it is probably premature psychologic interpretation which leads Dr. Sapir to ignore this result[2]. This is hardly worth mentioning, were it not that we who conceive of a science of human speech must not justify a criticism with which rule-of-thumb workers are only too ready.

The chapter on How Languages Influence Each Other (205–220) is especially suggestive and interesting. The last chapters, however, which discuss the relation of language to other phases of human conduct, yield scant results (221–235, 236–247), because these other phases are as yet little known to science. "Race", for instance, is not a scientific concept, but a popular notion developed in rationalization of certain inter-ethnic contacts. And, as to other such matters, what can be said in the way of science, when (242) the style of Mr. George Moore receives praise?

[2] Similarly, the statement about the umlaut-plural of German *Tag* (204) is wrong: it occurs in a number of dialects, and has parallels in Middle High German.

# B14. Review of Michelson

1922. *American Journal of Philology* 43.276–281 (July–September).

[Although Bloomfield mentions Algonquian—specifically, Fox—in his 1914 'Sentence and Word' (B8), and, very briefly, in the 1914 *Introduction*, I think we can infer that his extensive study of these languages began only after the Tagalog work was done; thus, perhaps in 1918. By the time of his first Algonquian field trip—to the Menomini, in the summer of 1920—he had probably excerpted and classified all the data in the earlier Jones and Michelson publications.]

*The Owl Sacred Pack of the Fox Indians.* By Truman Michelson. (Smithsonian Institution, Bureau of American Ethnology, Bulletin 72.) Washington: Government Printing Office, 1921.

The ethnological value of the text here presented by Michelson is evident: it gives the users' view of a Fox sacred bundle,—the story of its origin, a detailed statement of the ceremonies connected with it, and the text of the songs.

Linguistically this publication is not only the most accurate Algonquian text at our disposal, but is a model of text-presentation in general. What this means everyone will know who has worked outside of a few better-known Indo-European languages. There are many books about language, but very little of human speech is known to science. In the field of Algonquian, for instance, the books, with a few exceptions, such as the work of William Jones and this of Michelson, contain little beyond an array of inaccurate paradigms constructed on the Latin model and some pseudo-philosophizing on whatever grammatical categories happen to be foreign to the author's native speech. The phonetics are usually bad; of connected discourse or of word-formation nothing is told. Even Jones, who was part Fox and must have had good knowledge of the tongue, was unable, for want of linguistic training, to make an adequate description. Not only did he confuse his paradigms, but he arrived at no clear statement of such features as the "obviative" (the peculiar subsidiary third person of Algonquian grammar), and what little he gave of word-formation was full of errors. He was able, however, thanks to his native flair, to collect texts more accurate, more copious, and, above all, more intimate, than any before. It was his work[1] that really opened the field of Algonquian to science. Most inappropriately, Jones, invaluable for Algonquian, was sent to the Philippines, where he met his death. It is fortunate that Michelson, a scholar of the best Indo-European training, is carrying on the work.

One can imagine few more fascinating experiences in the study of mankind than to hear an Algonquian language spoken and to appreciate upon closer study the marvellous complexity of what one has heard. The scientific problem is correspondingly difficult. I believe that the solution, short of giving linguistic training to a native speaker, lies in the way of *sich einleben*—the notation of everyday speech and the attempt to become, to whatever extent is possible, a member of the speech-community. In the case of the Fox the external difficulties also are enormous; this people, treated with cruelty such as few have met, will scarcely admit one of the "Knife-People" to great familiarity; for the rest, trachoma is endemic, involving a price which Michelson has paid,—fortunately without permanent harm. As Fox is the most archaic of the Algonquian languages, its study cannot be replaced by that of the others.

The complexity of Fox appears in the circumstance that even Michelson finds in this text inflections hitherto unknown to him, and one or two features that he cannot understand; and indeed, one may know a good deal of an Algonquian language (as such things go) and yet hear a five-year-old child use an inflection or a stem that one has not heard before.

If one may judge from a comparison with the texts published by Jones, from the internal evidence furnished by grammatical analysis, and from comparison with the closely related Menomini, the present text is admirably reproduced. It will be invaluable for the future of Algonquian research—If, indeed, linguistic studies are to have any future. It is safe to presume that Michelson's phonetics are impeccable. One could wish that some of the phonetic finesses had been dealt with by a once-for-all statement rather than by diacritical marks and superposed[2] letters, so as not to clutter up the page (as some Greek said), and to keep it from being what Schopenhauer used to call *Augenpulver*. Thus, the inverted apostrophe is used instead of the letter *h*; the *h*-glide which precedes every sibilant is written every time; superposed *k*'s and *d*'s are used to indicate the acoustic effect of unvoiced solution-lenes; the lengthened sound of nasals in final

---

[1] *Algonquian (Fox)*, by William Jones, revised by Truman Michelson, in *Handbook of American Indian Languages*, by Franz Boas, Part I (Bulletin 40 of the Bureau of American Ethnology), Washington, 1911.

*Fox Texts*, by William Jones (Publications of the American Ethnological Society, volume 1), Leyden (Brill), 1907.

*Ojibwa Texts*, collected by William Jones, edited by Truman Michelson (same series, vol. 7), part 1, Leyden (Brill) 1917; part 2, New York (Stechert), 1919.

*Kickapoo Tales*, collected by William Jones, translated by Truman Michelson (same series, vol. 9), Leyden (Brill), 1915.

[2] [=superscript.—CFH]

syllables is marked by superposed letters; the peculiar twist of the diphthongal succession *ay* is uniformly rendered by writing *aiy*. A clearer page
will help the reader more than such constant reminders of phonetic details
which are uniform throughout the language; the more so, as no transcription, however painstaking, can reproduce the acoustic effect of a language
one has not heard. In the case of the open and closed sounds of *a*, tradition
is in favor of using two symbols, although the present text shows that the
variation is automatic. In one matter the meticulousness of the transcription is especially inconvenient; as the *h*-off-glide of final vowels is uniformly indicated, one cannot distinguish it, except by laborious comparison, from a significant *h* which has become final through loss of vowel in
sandhi: thus a word ending in *-a* is often indistinguishable from a word
ending in *-ahi* (with *i* lost in sandhi). The investigator, having learned which
features are significant, should give the reader the benefit of his knowledge; this I take to be the real value of phonetic transcription. The separation of words should be more fully carried out; especially successive
particles are run together in a troublesome way. As word-division is not a
phonetic matter, the reader will be helped if one writes, e.g. *kegimesi meg
ōn* rather than *kegimesimegōn* (14, 22).[3] Michelson's is the first Fox text
to be given with accentuation. It appears that while word-accent is not
significant, the sentence-accent is complex and interesting. The difficult
printing is practically faultless; I have noticed only 28, 36, end of line:
read hyphen instead of period.

The translation is careful and close. I venture, with due respect to the
difficulties of Fox, to suggest:

14, 20: ähwäpihatamähetīwātci[4] *they begin to cause each other to smoke*
(i.e. *to give each other a smoke*), rather than *they begin to be given a smoke
together*; to cause people to do something together is rather -etī- plus
instrumental -h-: änānuwasutīhānitci *they caused them to race with each
other*, Jones 208, 5.

16, 40: The text seems to say *By no means* (āgwi gäh māmahkātci) *the
women who belong to the gens*, (but rather) *the invited women are the ones
who join in the singing*; the translation given by Michelson makes more
plausible sense, but does not account for the negative in the text.

26, 3: nīyōnanākwiwīneyā sounds like *head* or *horns* rather than *ears*,
but Algonquian songs are desperate.

28, 33: *Not earlier or later* (nōta), *but by all means in the evening* (as
opposed to night), *that is when the burial is to be completed.* Construction
and verb-form do not admit of connecting the negative with the verb.

50, 39: *Verily, if their bodies get well, do not try to trouble them.* The

---

[3] For typographical reasons I quote in simplified transcription and without accent-marks.

[4] [Jones, Michelson, and Bloomfield conformed to the general practice among students
of American Indian languages at the time: c = later š; tc = later č.—CFH]

verb-form has animate object, hence cannot refer to the inanimate uwīya-wāwi, which, moreover, is preempted as subject of icigenig. Correspond-ingly emend the note, p. 69.

52, 40: *that there might thus be benefiting, that we might thus please the people.* For it is probable that the novel inflection -īnamegi is the im-personal passive of a transitive verb with animate object.

In view of the inadequacy of Jones' *Sketch,* one wishes that the lin-guistic notes on pp. 68 ff. were more extensive. Especially some syntactic comments would be helpful. The present text, being a direct statement, throws light on some points that are obscured in the narrative of Jones' *Texts,* with its persistent use of the aorist.[5] The Fox use of independent and conjunct verbs, it appears, is much like that of Ojibwa and Menomini.

To the note on §12 one may add the example in Jones' *Texts* 348, 1 (same verb as here). It is generally true that in Central Algonquian there are two types of derivatives from nouns and verbs ending in -*wa* and -*wi*: an older stratum, in which the *w* is not included, and a newer, in which the deriva-tion is made from the full stem in -*w*. The short stem before instrumental -*m*- appears also in täpesimäwa *he is happy with him,* cited by Michelson, *International Journal of American Linguistics,* 1, 6.

On §28: For treatment of the stem before -*tuge,* cf. nematcinägōtuge *he probably holds me in slight esteem, Texts* 60, 4; mehkamūtuge *he prob-ably found it,* ib. 122, 7.

§34: -tisō-, as reflexive stem from transitive verb with double object, occurs in Jones' *Texts*: panāpatamātisōwa *he ceases to see it for himself,* 382, 7; pītigatātisōwa *he carries it in for himself,* 250, 23, illustrating both types of double-object inflection. -tisō- reflexive from other stems at 284, 2. 286, 22.

§41(b): -asō-, reflexive-passive, occurs in Jones' *Texts* 220, 8. 12. 380, 8.

§41(c): -āgusi- (animate), -āgwat- (inanimate), reflexive-passive, in Jones' *Texts* 138, 20. 156, 22. 18. 204, 20. 340, 20. 380, 3; also nōtāgusiwa *he is heard,* Sketch, 744.

Page 71: I question whether the w of -wetci is an instrumental, and believe Jones' instrumental -w- to be altogether an error, except for a few irregular verbs, where it is rather part of the stem.

The list of sound-variations on page 72 is invaluable, the more so, as much of it applies also to other Central Algonquian; it is entirely the prod-uct of Michelson's researches. On the same page is given a table of the instrumental suffixes. The transitive verb in Algonquian is inflected not only for the actor, but also for the object; before the inflectional endings there is an element, called the instrumental, which indicates the nature of the action (by tool, by hand, by mouth, by heat, by cutting edge, etc.).

---

[5] ['Aorist' = simple conjunct with preverb *äh.*—CFH]

In most cases the instrumental differs according to the gender, animate or inanimate, of the object; accordingly, the author here arranges them in two parallel columns. The first pair, however, is a mistake: where the verb with animate object has instrumental -h-, that with inanimate object has -htō- (not -h- as here given). These stems are a living (freely formed) derivation in Menomini with transitive-causative meaning, and the examples in the published texts suggest that the same is true in Fox; they are:[6]

| animate object | inanimate object |
|---|---|
| kctemāgihäwa | ketemāgihtōwa *makes pitiful*, 56, 21. 204, 18. |
| tanwäwägihäwa | anwäwägihtōwa *makes resound*, 26, 18. 118, 1. |
| sōgihäwa | sōgihtōwa *binds*, 140, 7. 146, 1. |
| kaskihäwa | kaskihtōwa *controls*, 166, 21. 180, 11. |
| wanihäwa | wanihtōwa *loses*, 182, 11. Michelson, *American Anthropologist*, n. s., 15, 473. |
| acihäwa | acihtōwa *makes*, 32, 1. 254, 15. |
| kīcihäwa | kīcihtōwa *finishes*, 24, 26. 254, 15. |
| mōcihäwa | mōcihtōwa *dreams of*, 24, 7. *Owl Pack*, 34, 34. |
| panātcihäwa | panātcihtōwa *ruins*, 116, 18. 274, 21. |
| apwīhäwa | apwīhtōwa *awaits*, 212, 18. 214, 21. 262, 1. |

For the instrumental for action with a tool, which has -hw- for animate objects, Michelson leaves the inanimate-object form undetermined; it has the form -h-. It is freely made in Menomini, and here, too, the examples accessible to me indicate that the same is true in Fox:

| | |
|---|---|
| tcāgahwäwa | tcāgahamwa *finishes up*, 116, 15. 314, 8. |
| sīgahwäwa | sīgahamwa *pours*, 258, 19. 264, 10. |
| sahkahwäwa | sahkahamwa *burns*, 30, 2. 66, 11. |
| patahkahwäwa | patahkahamwa *pierces*, 104, 2. 176, 15. |
| kehkahwäwa | kehkahamwa *points out*, 18, 12. 20, 7. |
| kaskahwäwa | kaskahamwa *controls*, 46, 10. 176, 8. |
| kāskāskahwäwa | kāskāskahamwa *scrapes*, 178, 19. 21. |
| panahwäwa | panahamwa *misses*, *Sketch* 742. 807. |
| pīnahwäwa | pīnahamwa *puts in*, 96, 13. 116, 23. |
| āpinahwäwa | āpinahamwa *unties*, 78, 4. 290, 22. |
| pagisahwäwa | pagisahamwa *hurls*, 12, 20. 372, 7. |
| anwäwähwäwa | kukwätwäwähamwa *makes resound*, 270, 8. 348, 23. (kukwät- *try*). |
| pasigumähwäwa | kīnigumähamwa *acts on nose*, 104, 1. *Sketch*, 768. (pasi- *graze*, kīni- *sharpen*). |

---

[6] For simplicity's sake I give always the third person singular independent; numbers are page and line of Jones' Texts.

natunähwäwa          natunähamwa *seeks*, 58, 11. 278, 5. (instrumental
                     conventionalized).
āpihwäwa             āpihamwa *unties*, 28, 2. 172, 17.
nasāhkuhwäwa         nasāhkuhamwa *roasts on spit*, 92, 5. 174, 16.

In the case of the instrumental -t- (-ht-) with inanimate object distinction
should be made between the two types of inflection -t- (-ht-) and -tō-
(-htō); the matter is complex, but there seems to be some agreement between the different languages.

Some mention should have been made of irregular verbs, which Jones
did not take up in his *Sketch*. For one of them the form with animate
object is now quotable: āwäwa *he uses him*, present text, 14, 16; the form
with inanimate object ayōwa *he uses it*, Jones, *Texts* 30, 15; all the occurrences in Jones, *Texts*, are reduplicated; the simple form is used in Menomini: āw or uah *he uses it*; would be Fox *ōwa. The form with -t- instrumental mentioned in the list of stems does not seem to occur in the
published Fox material; in Menomini this is a different verb: ōnäw *he
affects him by using, uses on him*, ōtam same, with inanimate object; this
is a normal meaning for the instrumental -n-: -t-.

The book is completed by a very useful list of the stems that occur in the
text. It is to be hoped that Michelson will use his qualifications, so rare
in a field of this kind, to give us a grammar, as complete as may be, of this
beautiful but self-willed language of the Sauks and Foxes.

# 15. Rejoinder to B14

1923. Truman Michelson (Bureau of American Ethnology), *American Journal of Philology* 44.285–286 (July September).

Many years ago when I told Dr. Swanton of an error in Algonquian grammar I had unwittingly made, he replied, "Never mind! You and Dr. Boas will be the only persons who will ever know it." That time has happily gone by, and for perhaps the first time in American linguistics a specialist in a given field may be criticized by another specialist in the same field.— It may be ungracious to reply to Professor Leonard Bloomfield's very kindly review (AJP. XLIII 276 ff.) of my "Owl Sacred Pack of the Fox Indians," but there are a few points in which the reviewer is in error.

First the question of *a* and A. I think Professor Bloomfield is quite right in assuming that they are really fundamentally one, because *a* never occurs before 'k, 'p, 't, 'tc, 's, 'c, nor on the original penult, nor before medial *m*; but at the same time the two sounds are for the most part easily distinguished: the combination -a'igä- seems to vary according to speakers. Now if the sounds are really distinct phonetically, even if not etymologically, two symbols are in order.

The difficulty of knowing whether final -A' has lost a final vowel or not is not as great as Professor Bloomfield thinks. The only ambiguity will arise when the next word begins with a sibilant. Thus -A' s- may be (say) -a'i + s- or it may be -A + s-.

The translation at 26.3 follows the meaning given by the native (Indian) author as mentioned on p. 9. As Professor Bloomfield says, Algonquian songs are desperate. I myself should have thought "horns" more probable than "ears" but followed Kiyana's interpretation.

The instrumental -w- with animate object can not be denied, and is not a part of the stem, even though very rare. The stems nä- (see) and awi- (dwell) in the compound wī$^d$tcawi- (dwell with) show this conclusively.

I now hasten to add that remaining criticisms are nearly all well taken, especially those on the instrumentals -'- -'tō-, -'w- -'-; I had reached the same conclusions on these last as will be seen when some of my volumes (which have been held up for years) appear.

# B16. Review of Jespersen's *Language*

1922. *American Journal of Philology* 43.370–373 (October–December).

*Language: Its Nature, Development, and Origin.* By Otto Jespersen. New York: Henry Holt and Co., 1922. 448 pp.

In every science it is demanded that the investigator understand the *method* of science. He must see the reasons for its existence, be aware of its limitations, and be able to follow it, through all difficulties and seemingly endless amassments of material, consistently to a conclusion, good or bad. In all sciences there are many who can do this; it requires, at this day, no gift of genius. In the sciences that deal with man, however, there is a second demand, much harder to fulfil, to wit, that the scholar divest himself (for the time being, at least) of all the prejudices and preconceptions of his person, of his social group, or even of all mankind. So rare is this ability that it has grown commonplace to say that our social sciences are merely systematized expositions of tribal belief. Linguistics has fared best, owing to several peculiarities of the matter it studies. It was, for instance, a great step in advance, but also a most abrupt confrontation of human prejudice, when Leskien asserted, in effect, that the historical changes in human speech are not due to any desires of people and are not subject to any deflection for convenience or euphony or clearness. Even in linguistics there are few scholars able to take such a step; one of these very few is Otto Jespersen. In his *Progress in Language* (1894) he showed that historical change in language is progressive, a phase of the evolution of man; that linguistic change leads to simpler, more flexible, more accurately and delicately expressive and less troublesome forms of speech. Whatever we may take to be the relation between language and thought, Jespersen's teaching means that in the history of language we can see the growth and development, through time (and at a strange rate of speed— like some queer plant's—intermediate between biologic evolution and cultural progress), of human emotion and reason. It was the last of the great linguistic discoveries of the nineteenth century. That the man who made it stands above the common run, even of men of science; that he is able to oppose not only the prejudices of his social group—a comparatively easy task—but also those of his own preconception; that he must be a man of rare breadth of view and constructive imagination,—all this is evident. He is able to give us the big view of things; witness his *Growth and Structure of the English Language*—a panorama, without equal, of the history of a language.

It is not to cavil, therefore, at a man whom I honor as (with the restriction of our studies) few can honor him, but under the absolute duty of defending and holding every inch of ground hitherto conquered by our science, that I enter protest against very many parts indeed of the present book, *Language*. It is in the first and more general, if less noble, demand of our science, that Jespersen seems to me to fail. He repeatedly violates, or, if you will, ignores, those very principles of method to which his great discovery, like most of what we know, owes its existence. In *Progress in Language* there was a single passage (on page 176) which implied, ultimately, that the loss (by sound-change) of inflectional endings in English was conditioned upon the circumstance that these endings were no longer needed for the expression of meaning. I shall not follow this idea to its basic incompatibility with any definition of *meaning* that would today be tenable; it is enough to point out that, from the very beginning of linguistic study, just such ideas—referring phenomena of linguistic change to desires or needs—were tried and tried again—lying as they do in the direct path of our tribal common sense; but these ideas were found wanting and discarded because they would not work with the facts. In the present book the idea referred to is elevated to a constantly recurring motif of the discussion. There is no need of citing many examples; it is a leading theme of the book. On page 310 *hope* and *hop* are identified, and the difference between them (older *p* : *pp*) explained by the statement (page 405) that "the mere strengthening of the consonant . . . to express symbolically the strengthening of the action has nothing unnatural in it." Indeed, the notion that words of certain meanings are somehow changed or created by the meaning itself ("sound-symbolism"—Jespersen makes use of that monument of it, Hilmer's *Schallnachahmung*, 1914) is developed at some length (especially on pages 396 ff.). The only evidence for this notion is the meaning-value of the words in question,—the meaning-value for a speaker of the language concerned of such words as English *slush* or German *quatsch*. Now, what does the method of our science tell us of such words? First, descriptively, it tells us that the meaning of a word is due to no metaphysical or super-linguistic forces, but to its associations for speakers of the language. The word may be simple, like *chair*, or it may be composed of more or less vague formative elements,—that is to say, it may be partly like other words, as in the plural form *chairs* (*boys*, *tables*). If the partial likeness, as in this case, is very freely spread through the language, we speak of an explicit or clear-cut meaning; if the words of similar form are relatively few, then we have vaguer, less definable meanings, as in the case of *slush* (cf. *slum, slubber, sloven, slubby, slop, slattern*, etc., and *mush, trash, tosh, bosh*, etc.,—all quoted by Jespersen, page 401, with historical suggestion for *bosh*), or German *quatsch* (*quaken, quieken, quabbern, quetschen*, etc., and *patsch, tratsch, kitsch, klatsch, matsch, pfutsch, putsch*, etc.). The 'symbolism' here is no super-linguistic force, but merely a normal linguistic association. Every language has its own habits in this regard, which to the speaker seem inevitable; the sphere of vague associations may, of course, be different from what it is in modern Germanic; in Algonquian, for instance, it is rather parts of the body, tools, and states of matter that are thus referred to: a word with -*āhkw*- somewhere near the end of it refers to solids, especially of the consistency of wood, one with -*āpehk*- to harder solids, one with -*epy*- to liquids, one with -*āpy*- to stringy things, and so on, down to some elements that are very vague indeed. Historically, the method of our science tells us that word-forms are created by sound-change and by analogic change (including "contamination" and the like); the words under discussion bear on their face the mark of the latter process, which Jespersen deals with on pages 279 ff., 388 ff., only to ignore it a few pages later. It is of one piece with all this that Jespersen believes certain words to have "resisted the old Gothonic consonant-shift" (*cuckoo, pipe*, page 406).[1]

One asks for the theoretical justification: how are we to revise our ideas of linguistic change? just how, for instance, are we to imagine that the ancestral form of *pipe* staid unchanged when all the other *p*'s in the language were on the way toward *f* ? Jespersen's theoretical discussion rests upon material that offers no resistance to the current hypothesis of analogic change and resultant parallel forms (Gothic *azgo*: English *ash*, Sanskrit *hṛd*-: Latin *cord*-, etc.), and upon material that is totally irrelevant, namely dialect-mixture. Thus, when Wheeler (quoted on page 293) found himself pronouncing [juw] beside [uw] in an increasing number of words of the type *new, tune, due*, etc., this was by no means an example of some gradual or irregular spread of a phonetic change from word to word, but merely the speaker's transition from one class-dialect of American English to another. A scientific method (or hypothesis or assumption) can be invalidated only *by its own rigorous application*—never by the citation of isolated and uninterrupted facts or by the ministrations, however shrewd, of common sense.

In these matters no concession can be made. In all the rest, Jespersen's new book is valuable, and it is charming throughout. It is full of the most apt observation, of knowledge gathered far and wide, of interestingness and humor. The very headings and distribution of the material are both novel and appropriate. The historical survey is original and suggests new

---

[1] [See fn 19 of B28, where Bloomfield acknowledges that he had confused Jespersen's two examples (obviously without any effect on the argument).—CFH]

valuations. Grimm, to be sure, is underestimated. This, one may guess, is due to Jespersen's natural bent—not for a moment be it thought "patriotic," but rather a bent of interest. It was Grimm's merit (aside from the genius of the man) that, by the strength of a method, he conquered for science a body of facts so vast that the generations since have worked well within the bounds he reached and scarcely ever gone beyond. The notion suggests itself that if Jespersen appreciated Grimm, he would never have been tempted to resort to the use of his pocket-knife in the laboratory of science. However, we cannot have everything at once, nor can one man be all things: we should not care to get along without the brave spirit of Otto Jespersen, and indeed, without that spirit, the science of language would not be what it is.

# B17. Review of Saussure

1923. *Modern Language Journal* 8.317–319 (October 1923–May 1924).

*Cours de Linguistique Générale.* By Ferdinand de Saussure. Publié par Charles Bally et Albert Séchéhaye, avec la collaboration de Albert Riedlinger. Deuxième édition. Paris: Payot et Cie., 1922.

It is gratifying to see a second edition of de Saussure's posthumous work on language; the popularity of the book betokens not only an interest in language, but also a willingness of the scientific public to face linguistic theory, which at almost every step shocks our preconception of human affairs.

In de Saussure's lifetime[1] the history of the Indo-European languages was widely studied; he himself had made at least one great contribution to it, his *Mémoire sur le système primitif des voyelles dans les langues indo-européennes* (1878). But in lecturing on "general linguistics" he stood very nearly alone, for, strange as it may seem, the nineteenth century, which studied intensively the history of one family of languages, took little or no interest in the general aspects of human speech. After de Saussure's death the present book was put together, largely from lecture-notes.

The value of the *Cours* lies in its clear and rigorous demonstration of fundamental principles. Most of what the author says has long been "in the air" and has been here and there fragmentarily expressed; the systematization is his own. It is known that the historical change in language goes on in a surprisingly mechanical way, independent of any needs, desires, or fears of the speakers; we do not know, for instance, in what direction we, in our time, are changing the English language.[2] Outside of the field of historical grammar, linguistics has worked only in the way of a desperate attempt to give a psychologic interpretation to the facts of language, and in the way of phonetics, an endless and aimless listing of the

---

[1] A portrait of de Saussure and an outline of his life and work by W. Streitberg appeared in *Indogermanisches Jahrbuch*, vol. 2, Strassburg 1915. The first edition of the *Cours* appeared in 1916.

[2] That is, as actually spoken; the literary language is a thing apart.

various sound-articulations of speech. Now, de Saussure seems to have had no psychology beyond the crudest popular notions, and his phonetics are an abstraction from French and Swiss-German which will not stand even the test of an application to English. Thus he exemplifies, in his own person and perhaps unintentionally, what he proves intentionally and in all due form: that psychology and phonetics do not matter at all and are, in principle, irrelevant to the study of language. Needless to say, a person who goes out to write down an unknown language or one who undertakes to teach people a foreign language, must have a knowledge of phonetics, just as he must possess tact, patience, and many other virtues; in principle, however, these things are all on a par, and do not form part of linguistic theory.

De Saussure distinguishes sharply between "synchronic" and "dia-chronic" linguistics. At any given time ("synchronously"), the language of a community is to be viewed as a system of signals. Each signal is made up of one or more units; these units are the "sounds" of the language. Not only has each signal a definite meaning (e.g. *hat, put*), but the combina-tion of these signals proceeds by definite rules and itself adds definite elements of meaning; for instance, the signal *s* in English is not used alone; added to certain other signals it gives plural meaning (*hats*), added to certain others, it gives the third-person present-tense verb form (*puts*). All this is a complex and arbitrary system of social habit, imposed upon the individual, and not directly subject to psychologic interpretation: all psychology will ever be able to do is to provide the general background which makes the thing possible. Similarly, the physiology of the thing (phonetics) does not matter: instead of the thirty-five or so sounds of English, any thirty-five distinct symbols, of whatever nature, would suffice to reproduce the system of the English language.

This rigid system, the subject-matter of "descriptive linguistics," as we should say, is *la langue*, the language. But *le langage*, human speech, in-cludes something more, for the individuals who make up the community do not succeed in following the system with perfect uniformity. Actual speech-utterance, *la parole*, varies not only as to matters not fixed by the system (e.g., the exact phonetic character of each sound), but also as to the system itself: different speakers at times will violate almost any feature of the system. This brings us to "historical linguistics," *linguistique diachro-nique*; when such personal and temporary features of *la parole* become general and habitual in the community, they constitute a change in the system of *la langue*,—a sound-change or an analogic change, such as are recorded in our historical grammars.

In detail, I should differ from de Saussure chiefly in basing my analysis on the sentence rather than on the word; by following the latter custom de Saussure gets a rather complicated result in certain matters of word-composition and syntax. The essential point, however, is this, that de Saussure has here first mapped out the world in which historical Indo-European grammar (the great achievement of the past century) is merely a single province; he has given us the theoretical basis for a science of human speech.

# B18. Why a Linguistic Society?

1925. *Language* 1.1–5.

Students of language do not need to ask *Why a linguistic society*? but many laymen have asked this question. The answer, to be sure, lies really in our work and in its results; but, for this very reason, it is desirable that our motives be understood.

The immediate answer is simple: of course, we seek the possibility of meeting and knowing each other. In our country are scholars who for a generation or more have worked in linguistics and have never met; some of them saw each other for the first time at our initial meeting on December 28th. For ourselves this is answer enough, but for the layman it is no answer at all, and leads him only to restate his question: Why should So-and-so want to meet So-and-so? and What have you, after all, in common? and Why will not the existing societies, Philological, Oriental, Modern Language, Anthropological, Psychological, and what not, serve you as meeting-places? The layman—natural scientist, philologian, or man in the street—does not know that there is a science of language.

Such a science, however, exists; its aims are so well defined, its methods so well developed, and its past results so copious, that students of language feel as much need for a professional society as do adherents of any other science.

The science of language, dealing with the most basic and simplest of human social institutions, is a human (or mental or, as they used to say, moral) science. It is most closely related to ethnology, but precedes ethnology and all other human sciences in the order of growing complexity, for linguistics stands at their foot, immediately after psychology, the connecting link between the natural sciences and the human. The methods of linguistics resemble those of the natural sciences, and so do its results, both in their certainty and in their seeming by no means obvious, but rather, in many instances, paradoxical to the common sense of the time.

This position of linguistic science appears at the very outset in its methods of observation. The work of directly observing and recording human speech is much like the work of the ethnologist; indeed, in our country, where such field-work has been best done, it has been performed chiefly by the ethnologic-linguistic school. But, linguistics demands, to mention a difference, the recording of speech-movements or of the resultant sound-waves. For this purpose a kind of simplified physiology of speech has hitherto been used; as it is in many ways unsatisfactory, methods of mechanical observation, both physiologic and acoustic, are being developed.

The layman usually has no conception of this task; he believes that languages which possess no written literature are mere "dialects" or "jargons," of small extent and subject to no fixed rule. Quite by contrast, linguistics finds, on the one hand, a similarity, repugnant to the common-sense view, between the languages of highly civilized people and those of savages, a similarity which disregards the use or non-use of writing. In every speech-community, certain combinations (morphemes) of a very limited number of types of vocal sounds (phonemes) are socially fixed as reactions to certain stimuli and as stimuli to certain reactions coordinated with the former stimuli (meaning). These habits—the structure and vocabulary of the language—are as exactly and firmly maintained, and their number and variety are as great in ruder societies as in our own. On the other hand, the differences are equally striking: the categories of Latin grammar, such as its parts of speech, are by no means universal, but represent merely one type of structure; other languages arrange the morphemes—sentences, clauses, phrases, words, compound-members, stems, affixes, and the like—upon entirely different patterns. It remains for linguistics to determine what is widespread and what little is common to all human speech.

For the speech of the past we depend upon written documents. Here we have the problem of interpreting into terms of language the written characters which never consistently symbolize these terms, and sometimes, as in Chinese, scarcely indicate them at all.

Without dwelling upon the difficult and peculiar technique of deriving the structural system and the lexicon from the record of actual speech-utterances—a technique which in some respects resembles the mathematical—we may mention rather the significance of its results. The structural features and the lists of words, stems, affixes, and the like which we here derive are in reality records of mass phenomena. Each item represents a limitless sequence of individual concrete acts of speech. As the physicist need not follow the path of each particle, but observes their resultant action in the mass, and their individual actions only when these in turn group themselves into a deflection of the mass condition (as in radio-active substances), and rarely has occasion to watch the impingement of a single particle, so in linguistics we rarely attend to the single utterance or speaker, but attend to the deviations of utterances and speakers only when they mass themselves into a deflection of the total activity (linguistic change); and it is this total activity, resultant of un-numbered units, which we for the most part observe. Moreover, as in the natural sciences, this resultant is immediately subject to our observation; we are not in the position of seeing only the individual occurrence and having to reach the mass phenomenon by endless registration and statistics —a state of affairs which has prolonged the infancy of such studies as economics.

Linguistics differs from the natural sciences in that its object depends upon those small and constantly altering groups of individuals, the speech-communities. Thus linguistics introduces into the order of the sciences the peculiar rate of change known as history—a rate of change more rapid than the biologic, and therefore more subject to observation.

Linguistic change is studied primarily by comparison of speech-communities which have diverged from a single older community. It is in this comparison that the science of language has achieved its greatest success and has most refined its method. The results here extend over periods of time and reach a degree of accuracy as yet unknown to the other historical sciences. With minute detail, including even features (such as the accentual) that may not be recorded in the written documents, linguistics traces the history of a language far beyond the earliest times accessible to other aspects of history. Where written documents exist they guide us a distance on the way; but, here again, as we have suggested, a peculiar and often ingenious technique is required, for the habits of writing become fixed independently of speech, and conceal as much as they tell.

In this phase too, the results of linguistics, far from being truisms, tend to run counter to the common sense of our time. To mention only the most far-reaching: language changes always and everywhere; this change goes on without deflection by secondary ("subjective") factors such as desire for intelligibility or euphony; linguistic change leads from greater to lesser complexity of the word-unit, from highly inflected to "simpler" languages; the writing of a language is not a model on which speech is formed, but merely a rough notation whose existence has only a very slight effect upon the primary activity, speech; standard and literary languages are not original forms from which dialects faultily deviate ("mistakes of language," "bad grammar"), but are only secondary creations on the basis of dialects, which latter root far more deeply in the past.

One need go no further to see that students of our science, however ready for alliance and cooperation with workers in related fields, have none the less a unique and common task which requires a highly specialized equipment, and well warrants the bond of a common scientific association. Let it not be taken invidiously, if we say, in particular, that linguistics cannot be properly viewed as a subsidiary discipline to the study of literature, or paired with it as "the linguistic side" of philology,[1] or

---

[1] Needless to say that that noblest of sciences, philology, the study of national culture, is something much greater than a misfit combination of language plus literature. It may be

even placed in any close connection with the study of fine arts, of which literary history and criticism form a part.

It would be superfluous to speak also of external conditions which add to our justification, were it not that these conditions are working great injury to the progress of our science and to the welfare of the public at large. Not only in the general public, but also in the academic system, linguistics is not known as a science. The notion seems to prevail that a student of language is merely a kind of crow-baited student of literature. Even the more personal and at first glance petty ill-effects of this situation are not always to be lightly dismissed. Unfortunately an instance lies at hand in the recent death of Carlos Everett Conant, one of our founders, the foremost student of Philippine languages; he died tragically, and the circumstances of his death indicate that he might have been spared, to the great benefit of science, had not his professional career been one of desperate hardship.[2]

The more direct harm to science is too obvious to need exposition; one may mention the American Indian languages, which are disappearing forever, more rapidly than they can be recorded, what with the almost total lack of funds and organization; or the case of American English, of which we know only that, both as to dialects and as to distribution of standard forms, it would present a complex and instructive picture, had we but the means and the equipment to study it.

To speak, finally, of the public interest, it is evident that a great and important, indeed the fundamental phase of our social life consists of linguistic activities, and that, in particular, elementary education is largely linguistic. Yet such movements as that for English spelling-reform or for an international auxiliary language are carried on, in principle and to a great extent in practice, without the counsel of our science. Our schools are conducted by persons who, from professors of education down to teachers in the classroom, know nothing of the results of linguistic science, not even the relation of writing to speech or of standard language to dialect. In short, they do not know what language is, and yet must teach it, and in consequence waste years of every child's life and reach a poor result.[3]

Not only the furtherance of our science, but also the needs of society, make it the duty of students of language to work together systematically and with that sense of craftsmanship and of obligation which is called professional consciousness. For this they need a Linguistic Society.

well to add in passing that the British use of "philology" for linguistics leaves no name for the former subject and ought not be imitated in this country; rather, the English would do well to adopt our usage.

[2] See his biography in *Who's Who*.

[3] As to foreign-language teaching, there are few schoolmen who realize that there is a large linguistic literature on this subject.

# B19. *From* On the Sound System of Central Algonquian

1925. *Language* 1.130–156.

[This treatment of Algonquian historical phonology was superseded by B65 We reprint, however, the earlier article's sole footnote, appended by Bloomfield to the introductory section.]

I hope, also, to help dispose of the notion that the usual processes of linguistic change are suspended on the American continent (Meillet and Cohen, *Les langues du monde*, Paris 1924, p. 9). If there exists anywhere a language in which these processes do not occur (sound-change independent of meaning, analogic change, etc.), then they will not explain the history of Indo-European or of any other language. A principle such as the regularity of phonetic change is not part of the specific tradition handed on to each new speaker of a given language, but is either a universal trait of human speech or nothing at all, an error.

# B20. Einiges vom germanischen Wortschatz

1925. *Germanica: Eduard Sievers zum 75. Geburtstage* 90–106; Leipzig.

Die Hauptergebnisse der Sprachforschung des 19. Jahrhunderts sind einerseits unsere Kenntnis des indogermanischen Sprachstammes und seiner Geschichte, andrerseits die prinzipiellen Bestimmungen über den Verlauf der Sprachgeschichte im allgemeinen (Lautwandel, Analogie, Entlehnung).

Was erstere Errungenschaft anbelangt, ist nun zu bemerken, daß die sicheren Gleichungen zwischen indogermanischen Sprachen, wie etwa die Verwandtschaftsbezeichnungen, Zahlwörter, die gewöhnlichsten Verben und vereinzelte Schaustücke (wie dtsch. *Leumund*: ai. *śrṓmata-*) schon durchaus bekannt sind. Im Germanischen (und auch in den andern idg. Sprachen) bleibt nun ein großer Teil des Wortschatzes ohne Entsprechungen: alte Wörter (wie etwa *trinken*, *bringen*, *Haus*) und außerdem ein ungeheurer Reichtum an modernen Dialektwörtern. Das natürliche war nun, nicht etwa neue, dem andersartigen Material entsprechende Gesichtspunkte zu finden, sondern immer weiter uridg. Gleichungen zu suchen. So ergaben sich viele zwar mögliche, aber doch ganz unsichere Etymologien, und auch dann blieb noch vieles unerklärt. In dieser Sachlage ist man darauf gekommen, das oben genannte zweite Ergebnis der Sprachforschung aufzuopfern, um dann bei loserer Methode alles erklären zu können. So wird vor allem der aus vorwissenschaftlicher Zeit stammende Begriff der „Lautsymbolik" ohne weitere Kritik wieder aufgefrischt (Hilmer, Die Schallnachahmung 1914; Jespersen, Language 1923), oder es werden sonstige Theorien über Wortschöpfung erfunden, oder der germ. Wortschatz wird etwa aus weit entfernten und ganz unbekannten Sprachen abgeleitet.

Prinzipiell ist nun aber jenes zweite Ergebnis der Sprachwissenschaft nichts etwa Relatives, das man im gegebenen Falle ausschalten könnte. Wenn wir sagen, daß der Lautwandel ohne Rücksicht auf Bedeutungsverhältnisse vor sich geht (vom Standpunkte des Forschers praktisch ausgedrückt: Ausnahmslosigkeit der Lautgesetze), so bedeutet dies, daß die (uns unbekannten) andauernden Reize oder Zustände, welche in einer

Sprachgemeinschaft einen Lautwandel auslösen, ganz unabhängig sind von den jeweiligen Reizen, welche den einzelnen Sprechenden zu einem Sprechakt veranlassen. Die zwei Vorgänge spielen sich auf ganz verschiedenen Lagen ab. Das mag nun richtig sein oder nicht; das bis jetzt gesicherte Material spricht aber für Richtigkeit, z. B. darin, daß nach Jahrtausenden die Entsprechungen der Grimmschen und Vernerschen Gesetze so klar dastehen. Wenn nun etwa Jespersen das Wort *Pfeife*, engl. *pipe* von der germ. Lautverschiebung ausschließen will (Language 406), so müßte dies bedeuten, daß in vorgerm. Zeit der Reiz, welcher den jedesmal Sprechenden zur Äußerung dieses Wortes veranlaßte, zugleich diejenigen Reize oder sonstigen Zustände aufhob, welche damals in der Sprachgemeinschaft existierten und allmählich den Wandel von *p* zu *f* bedingten. So etwas ist aber nicht nur an sich unwahrscheinlich, sondern wir finden auch keine Sprachen, in denen einzelne Wörter besondere Laute aufwiesen, in denen also etwa neben allgemeinem *ph-* oder *pf-* einzelne Wörter eine ältere Schattierung *p-* beibehalten hätten.

Wie werden sich nun die Probleme lösen, welche der größte Teil des germ. Wortschatzes aufwirft? Zum Teil gar nicht. Man muß eben nicht alles wissen wollen. Zwischen dem uridg. Sprachzustande und den ältesten Urkunden der idg. Einzelsprachen sind Jahrtausende verflossen; die älteren Urkunden sind spärlich, selbst aus neuerer Zeit haben wir meist nur schriftsprachliches (das heißt: ziemlich eingeengtes) Material; nur die heutige Sprache steht uns ganz und gar und in aller Natürlichkeit zur Verfügung. Was diese Mängel bedeuten, sieht man, wenn man Sprachgruppen ins Auge faßt, wo die Trennung viel später liegt, wie etwa Slavisch oder Romanisch: wie vieles ist selbst hier unerklärt! Der Sprachwandel ist eben zu kompliziert, als daß man bei lückenhafter Tatsachenkenntnis alles wiederherstellen könnte. Nur dies wissen wir seit der Junggrammatikerbewegung: die Vorgänge, die wir nicht kennen, verliefen ebenso wie diejenigen, welche wir kennen.

Auf die Lautsymbolik hat man z. B. bei den germ. Wörtern mit Doppeltenuis, -media und -spirans (*zucken* zu *ziehen* u. dgl.) des öfteren sich berufen: R. Trautmann, Germanische Lautgesetze, Kirchhain 1906; Janko, IFA 19, 46; Braune, Ahd. Gr.[3] 81; mit Vorbehalt auch Wilmanns, D. Gr. 1[3], 181; Brugmann, Gr. 2[2], 3, 312; besonders über Doppelmedien· Kauffmann, ZfdPh 32, 255; Hellquist, AfnF 7, 56a; 14, 43a; Några anmärkningar om de nordiska verben med media-geminata (Göteborg Högskolas Årsskrift 1908, 2); Neckel, AfdA 35, 83. Dies alles bedeutet einen Rückschritt gegenüber dem wissenschaftlichen Erklärungsversuch von Bezzenberger, GGA 1876, 1374; Paul, PBB 7, 133; Osthoff, PBB 8, 297; und besonders Kluge, PBB 9, 162: Uridg. Verschlußlaute (oder deren Vertreter) mit unmittelbar nachfolgendem *n* ergaben bei folgendem Wortton historische germ. Doppeltenuis; also nach Durchführung des Vernerschen Wandels, aber noch unter der alten Betonung, ergaben *bṇ-* und *bṇ-* (letzteres aus uridg. *bhn* und *pn*) ein *bb*, das dann durch den letzten Verschiebungsakt zu *pp* wurde. So die bekannten Gleichungen:

ae. *læppa* 'Zipfel, Fetzen' : ab. *lono* 'Schoß' (vgl. norw. *lafa* 'schlaff niederhangen').

me. *lappen* 'auflecken' : lat. *lambere* mit infigiertem Nasal (ae. *lapian* 'auflecken').

an. *slappi* 'langer, verwachsener Mensch' : lit. *slabnùs* 'schwach' (an. *slāpr* 'träger Mensch').

ae. *doppettan* 'tauchen' : lit. *dumbù* 'sinke ein' (got. *diups*).

mhd. *gupfen* 'stoßen' (falls nicht denominativ): ab. *gŭnǫti* 'biegen'.

mhd. *rupfen* : lat. *rumpere* (an. *reyfa* 'brechen, reißen, plündern').

mnd. *witt* 'weiß' : ai. *śvítna-* (got. *hweits*).

an. *botn* 'Boden' : ai. *budhná-* (ahd. *bodam*).

mhd. *zacke* : gr. δάκνω (got. *tahjan* 'reißen, zerren").

an. *freknur* 'Sommersprossen' : gr. περκνός 'dunkel'.

ae. *friccea* 'Herold' : ai. *praśnín-* 'fragend' (got. *fraihnan*).

ahd. *stecchal* 'steil' : ai. *stighnóti* 'schreitet' (got. *steigan*).

ahd. *lecchōn* : gr. λιχνεύω (got. *bilaigon*).

mhd. *ric* 'Hals' : gr. ῥικνός 'gebogen'.

an. *bokkr, bukkr, bokki* 'Bock' : ai. *bhugná-* 'gebogen' (got. *biugan*).

an. *lokkr* 'Locke' : lit. *lugnas* 'biegsam' (an. *lykna* 'sich beugen').

mhd. *stocken* 'steif werden' (falls nicht denominativ) : russ. *stúgnut* 'gefrieren'.

mhd. *tucken* 'ducken' : lit. *dugnàs* 'Boden'.

mhd. *slucken* : gr. λύγξ 'der Schlucken' (mhd. *slūchen* 'schlingen').

mhd. *smucken* 'schmiegen, kleiden' : russ. *smyknút'* 'annähern, streichen' (mhd. *smiegen*).

Da dieser Gleichungen nur wenige sind, und nicht alle überzeugend, können wir nicht behaupten, daß das Bezzenberger-Klugesche Gesetz sicher wäre: es kann auch ein anderer Lautwandel gewesen sein, der germ. *pp*, *tt*, *kk* erzeugte; die Lautmalerei aber wäre dadurch noch lange nicht bewiesen. Auch nicht dadurch, daß seit jener vorgerm. Zeit die Analogie gewirkt hat: Trautmann (a. a. O. 64) hat also Unrecht, wenn er die Nasalassimilation unmöglich nennt wegen Beispielen wie an. *sofna* 'einschlafen' (neben *suefn* 'Schlaf') und an. *ogn* 'Ofen' (neben got. *auhns*); das an. Verb gehört ja zu einer lebendigen Inkhoativbildung. Wichtiger für uns ist jedoch die Analogiewirkung im anderen Sinn: die Lautgruppen *kk*, *tt*, *pp* haben sich in gewissen Bedeutungen ausgebreitet, es gibt eine Menge z. T. sicherlich moderner Wörter dieses Typus. Daher die Gefühlsschattierung, die solche Wörter wie *zucken* fürs naive Sprachgefühl besitzen, und daher auch der nicht minder naive Versuch, ebendieses Gefühl statt einer geschichtlichen Erklärung gelten zu lassen.

Das Germanische hat das alte Suffixsystem der Wortbildung nur spärlich weitergeführt; statt dessen hat es ein System entwickelt, in welchem bedeutungsvoll und übertragbar (d. h. morphologisch aktiv) sind: Anlaute, dtsch. *gleiten, glitschen, glabbrig* usw., engl. (Schriftsprache) *flame* (lat. Lehnwort), *flare, flash, flimmer, flicker* oder *fly, flutter, flitter, flit, flip, flap, flop*; Auslaute, dtsch. *murren, knurren, knarren, surren, schnarren* usw., engl. *bash, clash, dash, flash, gash, gnash, hash, lash, mash, plash, slash, splash, quash, squash* (die letzten beiden mit später gestörtem Vokal); Vokale (mit sekundär gestörtem Ablaut), dtsch. *zwicken, zwacken*, engl. (ma.) *nitter* 'kichern', *natter* 'klappernd arbeiten', *nutter* 'leise wiehern'. Ältere Beispiele des Anlautwechsels PBB 37, 245, Beispielsammlung zum sekundären Vokalwechsel, Modern Philology 7, 245. 345.

Was die späteren Neubildungen betrifft, muß man auch an unterstützende Faktoren denken, wie das Eintreten von neuen Doppeltenues im Westgerm. vor *j, w, r, l*, vielleicht auch vor *n* (Kauffmann PBB 12, 504) und im Nordischen durch Assimilation (*mp* zu *pp*, usw.). Wenn also neben der Gruppe von ae. *slīpan* und *slūpan* (starke Verba) ein ne. *slip* 'gleiten, ausgleiten' vorkommt, so ist es höchstwahrscheinlich eine Neubildung, welche an ältere *pp*-Bildungen anknüpft, also als germ. *\*slippōmi*, ae. *\*slippian* zu symbolisieren wäre: aber es ist auch transitiv 'schlüpfen, schnell anziehen', was wohl Neubildung nach einem Typus *\*slupjō*, ae. *\*slyppan*, dtsch. *schlüpfen* wäre. Diese beiden Typen sind eben zusammengefallen in einer Anlaut- und Vokalreihe wie engl. *dip* 'tauchen' (ae. *dyppan*), *drip* 'tröpfeln, triefen', *flip* 'schnell fallen, schnell umdrehen', *grip* 'fest und schnell greifen', *clip* 'schnippen', *chip* 'abspalten in kleine Stücke', *nip* 'in kleinen Zügen trinken, scharf beißen, abschnippen', *rip* 'schnell und laut reißen (trans. u. intrans.)', *sip* 'nippen, schlürfen', *slip* 'gleiten', *snip* 'abschnippen', *strip* 'streifen, abstreifen', *skip* 'hopfen, überspringen' (*sk-* ist skandinavischer Typ), *tip* 'leicht anstoßen, umkippen', *trip* 'hüpfen, stolpern, stolpern machen', *quip* 'witzeln, spötteln', *whip* 'peitschen'. Wenn neben an. *dropi*, ae. *dropa*, ahd. *troffo* 'Tropfen' auch ein ahd. *tropho* steht, kann das ein Beleg für wg. Dehnung vor *n* sein, mag aber auch einfach Anlehnung an den Auslauttypus *pp* sein, falls das Wort nicht etwa alt ist und sein *pp* im ursprünglichen Lautwandel (nach Bezzenberger-Kluge also vorgerm. *n*- Assimilation) erhalten hätte. Isl. *hitta* 'treffen, begegnen', schwed. *hitta*, dän. *hitte* könnte *tt* aus *nt* haben (ae. *hittan* wohl Lehnwort); Falk-Torp ziehen es vor, germ. *tt* anzunehmen (zu got. *hinþan*, also etwa *\*hittōmi* aus *\*hiðnōmi*, falls wirklich alt).

In folgender Liste seien einige Beispiele gegeben aus der ungeheuren Menge. Diejenigen, woneben noch einfacher Konsonant vorkommt, sind wohl die älteren. Die Liste hier zu vergrößern hätte um so weniger Zweck,

als man diese Wörter nur einschätzen könnte, wenn man jedesmal alle als
Muster in Betracht kommenden Wörter der betreffenden Mundart gegen-
wärtig hätte; es käme darauf hinaus, neben der (jetzt wohl ziemlich voll-
ständig ausgearbeiteten) indogermanisch-germanischen Stammbildungs-
lehre eine solche der verschiedenen germanischen Mundarten und dann
eine gemeingermanische herzustellen.

*flapp-* engl. *flap* 'lose schlappen, mit etwas Losem oder Flachem
schlagen', nd. *flappen.*

*happ-* dän. *happe* 'stottern', schwed. *happla* 'stammeln' (zu mnd.
*haperen* 'verfehlen, stottern').

*(h)rapp-* me. *rappe* 'Schlag', *rappien* 'schlagen', schwed. *rapp* 'Schlag,
Peitschenhieb', dän. *rap* (zu an. *hrapa* 'eilen').

*stapp-* ahd. *stapfōn* 'fest auftretend schreiten' (zu ae. *stæppan : stōp*).

*tapp-* me. *tappen* 'leise klopfen' (wohl denominativ zu ae. *tæppa*
'Zapfen' neben mhd. *zāfen* 'ziehen').

*flipp-* engl. *flip* 'schnell und plötzlich bewegen', nd. *flippen.*

*kwipp-* engl. *quip* 'Wortspiel, scharfer Ausspruch', im 16. Jahrhundert
gebildet zur Reihe von *quillet, quillity, quib, quibble, quiddity,* welche
anknüpft an *quid* 'sagen, sprechen' (ae. *cwiddian), quide* 'Spruch' (ae.
*cwide*), also im Grunde an das st. V. ae. *cwedan,* und an schullateinisch
*quiditas,* das wegen der heimischen Wörter komisch wirkte: *quiddity*
bedeutet 'Kleinigkeit, Schnörkel, Haarspalterei'.

*tipp-* me. *tip* 'Zipfel, Spitze', schwed. *tipp,* ahd. *zipf.* Verbal: engl. *tip*
'leise anrühren', nd. *tippen* 'leicht schlagen'.

*flopp-* engl. *flop* 'sich schwer und mit aufklappendem Geräusch wenden
oder fallen', auch transitiv.

*hopp-* an. *hoppa* 'hüpfen, hopfen', ae. *hoppian,* mhd. *hopfen.*

*hnopp-* ae. *hnoppian* 'pflücken' (zu *ā-hnēopan*).

*klopp-* ahd. *chlopfōn* (zu *clioban* 'spalten').

*knopp-* ahd. *knopf* (zu an. *knyfill* 'kurzes Horn').

*kopp-* ahd. *kopf* 'Becher, Kopf' (zu *kubil*).

*kropp-* an. *kroppr* 'Körper', ahd. *kropf* 'Kropf' (zu an. *krof* 'Körper
von geschlachteten Tieren').

*slopp-* ae. *cū-sloppe* 'primula' (eigentlich 'Kuhfladen' zu *slūpan*).

*snopp-* an. *snoppa* 'Schnauze'.

*topp-* an. *toppr* 'Haarzopf', ae. *topp* 'Gipfel', ahd. *zopf.*

*flupp-* nd. *fluppen* 'schnellen, springen'.

*gupp-* mhd. *gupf* 'Spitze, Giebel' (zu *guffe* 'Hinterbacke').

*snupp-* mhd. *snupfe* (zu *snūben*).

*tupp-* norw. (ma.) *tuppa,* nhd. *zupfen,* engl. *tup* 'stoßen, begatten', me.
*tuppe* 'Widder'.

*hatt-* ae. *hæt* 'Hut' (zu ahd. *huot*).

*knatt-* an. *knǫttr* 'Ball' (zu ahd. *knetan*).

*kitt-* ahd. *kizzīn* 'Zicklein' (zu an. *kið* 'Böckchen').

*knott-* ae. *cnotta* 'Knoten' (zu ahd. *chnodo*).

*hlakk-* an. *hlakka* 'lachen' (zu got. *hlahjan*).

*hnakk-* ahd. *hnach* 'Nacken' (zu me. *nōk* 'Winkel, Ecke').

*kwakk-* engl. *quack* 'kwaken'.

*smakk-* engl. *smack* 'klappen, küssen, schmatzen', mnd. *smakken*, älter dän. *smakke*, schwed. *smakka*, ma. auch 'schmeißen'.

*snakk-* mnd. *snakken* 'reden, schwatzen' (zu an. *snøkta* 'schnauben').

*blekk-* ahd. *blecchazzen* 'blitzen' (zu mhd. *blīchen* 'glänzen').

*flekk-* ahd. *flec, fleccho* (zu an. *flīk* 'Zipfel, Lappen', doch beurteilen Falk-Torp s. v. *Flek* den Vokalismus anders).

*hnekk-* ae. *hnecca* 'Hals', ablautend mit *hnakk-* oben.

*sikk-* ae. *siccettan* 'seufzen' (zu *sīcan*).

*slikk-* nd. *slikk* 'Straßenkot, Lehm', engl. *slick* 'glatt' (zu ahd. *slīhhan*).

*tikk-* ahd. *zikkīn* 'Zicklein' (zu *ziga*).

*bokk-* mhd. *bocken* 'zu Boden fallen' (zu *biegen*).

*brokk-* ahd. *brocchōn* 'bröckeln' (zu *brehhan*).

*flokk-* ac. *flocc* 'Schar' (zu *flēogan*).

*flokk-* nhd. (schweiz.) *flock* 'Felsenabhang' (zu ahd. *fluah* 'rupes').

*klokk-* ahd. *klockōn* 'klopfen'.

*klokk-* ae. *cloccian* 'klucken, glucken'.

*knokk-* me. *knocken* 'aufschlagen, anschlagen, stoßen' (zu *knokien* 'schlagen', an. *knoka*).

*stokk-* ahd. *stoc* (zu and. *stūkan* 'stoßen').

*ṭokk-* ahd. *zocchōn* 'zerren, zucken' (zu *ziohan*).

*klukk-* schwed. *klukka* 'klucken, glucken', mhd. *klucken*.

Über den Ursprung der Doppelmedien und -spiranten werden ziemlich komplizierte Vorgänge postuliert (von Friesen, Om de germanska mediageminatorna, Upsala Universitcts Årsskrift, 1897; van Helten, PBB 30, 313). Von Friesen betont mit Recht (s. S. 14, 17), daß an eine „generatio spontanea" der Lautungen nicht zu denken ist, macht aber leider den Fehler, alle Fälle auf nominalen Ursprung und zwar bis aufs Uridg. zurückzuführen, was dann Hellquist Gelegenheit gab, in seinem genannten Buch die Lautsymbolik doch aufrecht zu halten. Das wahrscheinlichste hat wohl Kluge (a. a. O.) vermutet; wenn es erlaubt ist, seine Erklärung ein wenig zu erweitern, wird man sich den Ursprung so vorstellen: die Sprache (vorgerm.) besaß Doppelkonsonanten und hatte folgende Paradigmentypen:

1.

Nom. *strutōn* (mhd. *stroʒʒe* 'Luftröhre', mnl. *strote*).
Gen. *struttes* (aus *strudnés*, dtsch. (ma.) *strotze*).

2.

Nom. *knuðōn* (ahd. *chnoto*).
Gen. *knuttes* (aus *knuðnés*, ae. *cnotta*).

3.

Nom. *laþōn* (mhd. *lade* 'Latte').
Gen. *lattes* (aus *laðnés*, and. *latta*).

Es wurden nun die Paradigmata 2. und 3. nach dem Muster von 1. ausgeglichen, indem entweder ein neuer Nominativ (also *knutōn*, *latōn*) oder, häufiger, ein neuer Oblikstamm, *knuðð*es > *knuddes* (ahd. *chnotto*), *laþþes* (me. *laththe*, engl. *lath*, ahd. *latta*) geschaffen wurde. Dann kam bekanntlich noch der gänzliche Ausgleich alles Lautwechsels innerhalb der Paradigmen, wobei irgendeine der obigen Formen sich verallgemeinern konnte und der Oblikstamm oft als starkes Substantiv aufgefaßt wurde.

Die sich so ergebenden Auslautstypen haben sich manchmal mit Bedeutungsinhalten verknüpft und dadurch ausgebreitet, so z. B. *bb* für schnellere Tätigkeiten und für klotzige Gegenstände. Dieser Umstand ist es, der ganz regelrecht dem naiven Sprecher das Gefühl einer Lautsymbolik gibt, welches der Sprachforscher bei der Wortbedeutung mitregistrieren soll, nicht aber anstatt einer historischen Erklärung annehmen darf.

Substantivische Beispiele:

*babb-* nl. (ma.) *babbe* 'Geschwür an der Backe', älter engl. *babbin* 'Bündel Reisig', *babber-lipped* 'mit schwulstigen Lippen', engl. (ma.) *babber* 'Unterlippe des Pferdes', nd. *babbert* 'Maul'. An diesen Typus knüpfen sich die Kinderstubenworte schwed. (ma.) *babbe* 'kleiner Bube, Kind', *babba* 'kleines Mädchen', älter engl. *bab*, *babbon*, engl. (ma.) *babby* 'infans'; nd. *babbe*, *bab* 'Vater, Papa', älter engl. *bab*, elsäss. *bappe*; nl. (ma.) *babbe*, *bab* 'Großvater' (daneben *bappe*), *bebbe*, *beb* 'Großmutter' (auch *beppe*, *bep*). Endlich der Name (ursprünglich wohl Kose oder Neckname) ae. *Babbae oppidum*, *Bæbban burh* 'Bamborough', engl. Familienname *Babb*. All dies zu mhd. *buobe*, ahd. *Buobo* (Eigenname), engl. *bavin* 'Reisigbündel', siehe Hirt-Weigand unter *Bube*.

*drabb-* me. *drabbe* 'Bodensatz, Dreck', nd. *drabbe* 'Spülicht, Schlamm, Schmutz', zu an. *draf* 'Abfall', ae. *dræf*, ahd. *trebir*, s. Falk-Torp s. v. *Draf*.

*flabb-* norw. (ma.) *flabb* 'Schnauze, großes Maul', schwed. *flabb* 'hängende Unterlippe bei Tieren', engl. (ma.) *flabs* 'große breite Schwämme', engl. *flabby* 'weich, schwach, schlapp', nd. *flabbe* 'loses Stirnband'.

*glabb-* schwed. (ma.) *glabb* 'schlecht bereitete, klebrige Speise', nd. *glabber* 'Schleim, Geifer, zäher, klebriger Schmutz'.

*kabb-* schwed. (ma.) *kabb* 'Holzklumpen, Klotz'.

*kabb-* schwed. (ma.) *kabba* 'Schote' (zu ahd. *cheba*, *cheua*).

*knabb-* schwed. (ma.) *knabb* 'Pflock', *knabbe* 'Knollen, Klumpen, untersetzter Bursche', ahd. *knappo*, zu ae. *cnafa*, ahd. *chnabo*; *pp* in ae. *cnæpp* 'Gipfel, Knopf', analogische Nom.-Form mit *p* in ae. *cnapa*, as. *knapo*.

*labb-* norw. schwed. (ma.) *labb* 'Pfote, Tatze, Fuß, Socke', ahd. *lappa* 'Lappen'.

*skabb-* ae. *sceabb*, an *skabb* 'Krätze' (zu ahd. *skaban* usw.).

*slabb-* me. *slabbe* 'dünnes, flaches Stück, besonders von Stein', engl. (ma.) auch 'Pfütze', mhd. *slappe* 'herunterhängender Teil der Kopfbedeckung'.

*stabb-* an. *stabbi* 'Stock', zu *stafr*.

*hibb-* engl. (ma.) *hibble* 'kleiner Haufen, Hügel'.

*kibb-* engl. (ma.) *kibble* 'Stock, Knüttel'; dieses Wort deutet auf Ursprung des *i*-Vokals dieser Reimwortgruppe aus *y*.

*þibb-* engl. (ma.) *thibble* 'Rührstock'.

*þwibb-* engl. (ma.) *thwibble* 'Rührstock', zu ae. *þwære*, *þwirel*.

*þribb-* engl. (ma.) *thribble* 'kleiner Rührstock'.

*bobb-* engl. *bob* 'kleiner rundlicher Körper, kleiner Klumpen', nhd. (bair.) *poppen* 'Kügelchen, Knoten, Bläschen', schwed. *bobba, bobb* auch 'kurze, dicke Person', dtsch. (ma.) *poppel, popper* 'Geschwür, Eiterbeule', *boppele* 'kugelförmige Blüte', *poppel* 'kleiner Mensch', usw. Als. Kinderwort und Kosename fries. *bobbe* 'infans; Puppe', engl. (ma.) *bobby* 'Großvater', ahd. *Boppo* (Eigenname), engl. *Bob* als Kosename für *Robert* (dergleichen Anknüpfungen sind sekundär), ebenso schwäb. *Bopp* für *Baptist*.

*brobb-* engl. *brob* 'Zapfen; Strohhalm'.

*dobb-* engl. (ma.) *dob* 'kleiner Klumpen, kleines Pferd', *dobbet* 'kleine Person', *Dob, Dobbin* als Kosenamen, auch für Pferde, mnd. *dobbel* 'Würfel beim Spiel', mhd. *toppel*, zu ahd. *gitubili*, s. Falk-Torp unter *Dobbel*.

*gobb-* norw. (ma.) *gobb* 'Rücken, Schulterpartie', me. *gobbe* 'Masse, Klumpen', *gobbet* 'Teil, Portion, Stück, Fragment', engl. *gob* 'Klumpen', Schleimklumpen', dtsch. *goppe* 'hölzerne Schüssel', auch *ff*- Formen, s. Falk-Torp unter *Gubbe*.

*hobb-* engl. *hob* 'Zapfen, Pflock, kleiner Heuhaufen u. dgl.', auch als Kosename für *Robin* und *Robert*, ferner 'Tölpel', mnl. *hobbe* 'caseus major', nd. *hobbe* 'höckerartiges Stück Erde'.

*knobb-* me. mnd. *knobbe* 'Klotz, Knorren, knorriger Mensch'.

*kobb-* engl. *cob* 'runder Klumpen, Knoten, Walze, Pferd', Geschlechtsname *Cobb*, bair. *koppen* 'Krone des Baumes', *fingerkoppen* 'der vorderste Teil des Fingers'.

*lobb-* schwed. (ma.) *lobba* 'Zweigwisch', nd. *lobbe, lob* 'hängende Masse, breiige Flüssigkeit; Hemdkragen zum Überschlagen', engl. (ma.) *lob* 'Herabhängendes, Klumpen, klebrige Speise'.

*(h)nobb-* me. *nobbe* 'Knoten am Faden', engl. (ma.) *nob* 'Klumpen, Kopf, reicher Mann, junges Pferd', nd. *nobbe* 'Knötchen am Zeuge', mhd. *nop, noppe,* nhd. (ma.) auch 'Hügelchen'.

*slobb-* engl. *slob* 'ekelhafter, unbeholfener, gemeiner Mensch'.

*bubb-* älter engl. *bub* 'Geschwür', engl. 'Knäuel im Zwirn', *bub, bubby* 'kleiner Bube', *bubby* 'weibliche Brust', dtsch. (ma.) *puppe* 'Bündel, Büschel, Wulst, Frucht, Zapfen der Kiefer; Wickelkind; Brust'.

*dubb-* schwed. norw. *dubb* 'Bolzen, Eisenpflock', dtsch. (tirol.) *tuppe* 'großes Stück Holz', (steir.) *duppel, tippel* 'Knauf, Beule, Kloß, grober Mensch'.

*gubb-* schwed. norw. *gubbe* 'alter Mann', das vielbesprochene Wort jedenfalls zu schwed. (ma.) *gubbe* 'Roggengarbe', *snorgubbe* 'Rotzklumpen', norw. (ma.) *gobb* 'Rücken, Schulterpartie'. Interessant ist schwed. (ma.) *gubbstol*; es bedeutet nach Rietz 'Stuhl aus einem ausgehöhlten Kiefernklotz, in dem *gubbar* (alte Männer) zu sitzen pflegen'. Die letztere Bestimmung ist offenbar sekundär, sonst wäre die erstere unerklärlich; vgl. das synonyme *kabbstol* zu *kabb,* oben. Nd. *gubbe* 'kleiner Heuhaufen', obd. *gupp* 'hölzerne Schüssel', *guppel* 'Buckel, Höcker'.

*hubb-* norw. (ma.) *hubb* 'Hügel', engl. *hubbe, hub* 'Teil des Herdes, der früher aus einem Lehmklumpen bestand; Mittelteil des Rades', *hubby* als Koseform für *husband,* nd. *hubbel* 'Unebenheit, Höcker, Erhöhung', hd. (ma.) *huppe* 'Hügel'; dies alles zur Gruppe von ahd. *hubil,* siehe Falk-Torp unter *Hob, Hovre.*

*klubb-* an. *klubba* 'Klotz, Kloben', engl *clubbe, club* 'Knüppel', dtch. (ma.) *kluppe* 'Büschel, Knäuel', *klüppel* 'Knüppel'.

*knubb-* norw. schwed. *knubb* 'Klotz', elsäss. *knuppe* 'Anschwellung, Knoten', dtsch. *knuppel, knüppel* (wenn aus *klüppel,* so hat unsere Gruppe *knubb-* die Dissimilation bestimmt, denn der gewöhnliche Lauf der Dissimilation wäre Ersetzung des *l*-Suffixes durch *r*-Suffix).

*kubb-* norw. (ma.) *kubbe, kubb* 'Klotz', und vieles mehr, engl. *cub,* dtsch. *kuppe.*

*lubb-* schwed. norw. (ma.) *lubb, lubba* 'dicke, runde Person, runder Fisch', engl. (ma.) *lub, lubber* 'Klumpen, klebrige Speise, unbeholfener Mensch', dtsch. (ma.) *luppe* 'große geschwollene Lippe'.

*(h)nubb-* nd. *nubbe* 'Knötchen am Zeuge'.

*skrubb-* norw. (ma.) *skrubb* 'Rute zum Putzen, magrer Mensch, magres Tier', ae. *scrybb* 'Busch, Gebüsch', engl. *shrub.*

*stubb-* an. *stubbi, stubbr* 'Stumpf', ae. *stubb,* mnd. *stubbe,* mhd. *stuppe,* zur Gruppe von an. *stūfr.*

*þrubb-* nd. *drubbel* 'Klumpen, Knäuel, Haufe', norw. (ma.) *trubb* 'kurze, dicke Figur', schwed. (ma.) 'klumpiger Gegenstand', zu dtsch. *Traube.*

Verbalbildungen, teilweise jedenfalls denominativ:

*babb-* nd. *babbern* 'beben, zittern'.

*babb-* schwed. *babbla*, engl. *babble*, nd. *babbeln*, dtsch. *pappeln* 'schwatzen'.

*blabb-* dän. *blabre*, engl. *blabber*, nd. *blabbern*, dtsch. *plappern*; älter dän. *blable* wird kaum Neubildung sein wegen der zwei *l*.

*brabb-* engl. *brabble* 'zanken, laut streiten', mnd. *brabbeln* 'schwatzen'. Ich vermute, daß alle drei Wörter, *babbeln*, *blabbern* und *brabbeln*, verschiedene Auswüchse einer alten reduplizierten Bildung mit zwei *l* sind, etwa *bla-blōmi* (mit anlautartiger Behandlung der zweiten Silbe), zu mhd. *blæjen* 'blöken' usw.; daneben *bla-blōmi* (Inlautbehandlung der zweiten Silbe), dän. *bavle*, *bravle*, schwed. (ma.) *bravla*. Die Dissimilationen, *babbeln* nach der Anlautgruppe von *bellen*; *brabbeln* nach der von an. *braka* 'lärmen', dtsch. (ma.) *brallen*; *blabbern* mit *r*- statt *l*-Suffix, nach der allgemeinen Regel.

*dabb-* norw. (ma.) *dabba* 'leicht mit Hand oder Fuß schlagen; platschen', me. *dabben*, dtsch. *tappen*; zu mhd. *tāpe* 'Pfote, Tatze'; mit *b* an. *dafla* 'platschen'; ai. *dabhnóti* 'versehrt, betrügt' kann sehr gut verwandt sein, 'trügen' (aus 'schlagen') bedeutete auch in älterer Zeit das engl. *dab*.

*drabb-* isl. *drabba* 'beschmutzen', engl. *drabble*, nd. *drabbeln*; wohl denominativ, s. oben.

*fabb-* norw. (ma.) *fabba* 'schlecht arbeiten', obd. *fapple* 'unruhig sein; unsicher tasten'.

*flabb-* älter engl. *flab* 'mit den Flügeln schlagen', (ma.) *flabber* 'lose hangen'.

*gabb-* an. *gabba* 'Spot oder Scherz treiben', me. *gabben* 'spaßen; verhöhnen; verklagen', engl. *gab*, *gabble* 'schwatzen', mnd. *gabben*, *gabbeln* 'Scherz treiben', schweiz. *gappe* 'spielen, gaukeln', zu ae. *gegaf*.

*glabb-* dän. (ma.) *glabber* 'maulfertiges Weib', engl. (ma.) *glabber*, *glub* 'schwatzen, plappern'.

*gnabb-* älter engl. *gnabble* 'beißen, nagen', nd. *gnabbeln*, *gnabben*.

*grabb-* schwed. norw. (ma.) *grabba* 'rasch greifen, raffen', engl. *grab*, mnd. *grabben*, nd. *grabbeln*, mhd. *grappeln*; zu ahd. *garba* und ai. *gr̥bhnáti*.

*kabb-* nd. *kabben*, *kabbeln* 'nagen, beißen, zanken, plappern'; zu elsäss. *kafle* 'nagen, kauen', engl. *chavvle*.

*labb-* schwed (ma.) *labba* 'anhangen, beschmutzen', norw. (ma.) 'plump aber rasch gehen, klapsen', mnd. *labben* 'lecken, schlürfen', nd. *labbern* 'saugen, gemein küssen'.

*sabb-* norw. *sabbe* 'langsam gehen, sudeln', mnd. *sabben* 'geifern', s. Falk-Torp s. v.

*skwabb-* norw. (ma.) *skvabba* 'schwatzen', schwed. (ma.) *skvabbel* 'Gezänk' (daher engl. *squabble*), angebildet an die Gruppe von an. *skvala* 'laut reden, rufen'.

*slabb-* norw. schwed. (ma.) *slabba* 'beschmutzen, unordentlich sein', me. *slabbeþ* 'wälzt sich im Schmutz', engl. *slabber* 'naß machen, beschmutzen', nd. *slabben, slabbern* 'schleckend trinken, essen, küssen; den Anzug beschmutzen'.

*stabb-* norw. (ma.) *stabba* 'langsam gehen, mit kurzen steifen Schritten gehen', engl. (ma.) *stabble* 'im Schmutz herumtreten'.

*swabb-* engl. *swabble* 'zänkeln, großschwatzen'.

*bibb-* norw. (ma.) *bibba, bibra* 'beben', engl. *bibber*, nd. *bibbern*, hd. (ma.) *bippere.*

*fibb-* norw. (ma.) *fible* 'schlecht arbeiten, herumtasten', obd. *fippern* 'sich schnell hin- und herbewegen', *fippe* 'beständig hin- und hergehen'.

*flibb-* nd. *flibbern* 'flimmern, schimmern'.

*gnibb-* nd. *gnibben* 'gnappend kratzen oder beißen, benagen', engl. *gnibble* mit *nibble* (aus *hn-*) zusammengefallen.

*gribb-* engl. *gribble* 'greifen, an etwas herumtasten', wohl zu jung als daß die Frage, ob *i* oder *y*, einen Sinn hätte.

*bobb-* obd. *poppern* 'beben; schnell und wiederholt leise klopfen, an einer Tür oder vom Herzen', *popple* 'beben', wohl Einfluß der Gruppe von *pochen.*

*gnobb-* schwed. *gnobba* 'nagen', nd. *gnobben.*

*grobb-* engl. *grob*, obd. *groppen* 'greifen, herumtasten'.

*lobb-* hd. (ma.) *loppern* 'lose, unbefestigt sein, lottern'.

*slobb-* engl. *slob, slobber* 'sich beschmutzen, besonders mit Nassem'.

*snobb-* me. *snobbin* 'seufzen'.

*sobb-* me. *sobben* 'seufzen, schluchzen', Anlaut nach ae. *sēofian, sīcan.*

*bubb-* nd. *bubbern*, obd. *puppere* 'beben'.

*fubb-* norw. (ma.) *fubba* 'mit dem Hintern wackeln, kleinlich arbeiten', *fubla* 'herumtasten'.

*glubb-* obd. *gluppen* 'heimliche Blicke tun, schielen'.

*grubb-* engl. *grubble*, nd. *grubbeln*, obd. *gruppen* 'greifen, tasten'.

*slubb-* norw. schwed. (ma.) *slubba, slubbra* 'beschmutzen, unordentlich sein', engl. *slub, slubber*, nd, *slubbern*, obd. *schluppen* 'schlürfend einhergehen'.

*snubb-* an. *snubba* 'zurechtweisen', schwed. (ma.) 'straucheln', mnd. *snubbelen.*

Zu den Anlauttypen, welche an der Wortbildung teilnehmen, haben sich in den nordischen Sprachen einige aus Konsonant plus *j* bestehende hinzugesellt. Diese Anlaute sind durch die bekannten Umlautserscheinungen in die Sprache gelangt und haben sich dann mit Bedeutungen verknüpft und analogisch ausgebreitet. Falk in einem Aufsatz über „Indskud av *j*", in Sproglig-historiske Studier tilegnede Prof. C. R. Unger, Kristiania 1896, 205 ff., geht auf eine m. E. ganz unhaltbare physiologisch-psychologische Ausdruckstheorie zurück, um diese Wörter lediglich nach seinem Sprachgefühl durch Infigierung eines *j* zu erklären; es wäre also Zufall, daß sie gerade in Sprachen vorkommen, welche durch normalen Lautwandel Anlaute von Konsonant plus *j* besitzen. Wenn er ferner meint, daß in Fällen, wie *flaksa* : *fjaksa* das *l* von dem *j* palatalisiert worden und mit ihm verschmolzen sei, können wir ihm um so weniger folgen, als er selbst Wörter anführt wie *fljota, fljuga, bljug*, wo *l* in derselben Stellung erhalten ist.

Bei den Schallwörtern mit *bj-* neben *b-* liegt schon an. vor *bjalla* 'Schelle' (zu ae. mnd. *belle*, mit *a*-Umlaut), neben *belja* 'brüllen'. Das Verb ahd. ae. *bellan* ist zwar an. nicht belegt, war aber urgerm. (vgl. ai. *bhāṣate* 'redet', lit. *balsas* 'Stimme, Laut') und kommt neunord. vor; es müßte wohl heißen *\*bella* und *\*bjalla*. Dem entsprechen nun schwed. (ma.) *bälla* 'schimpfen' und älter dän. *bjælde* 'schimpfen, rufen, bellen' (mit *æ* aus *a* nach *j*); erweitert, älter dän. *bjældre* und schwed. (ma.) *bjällra* 'schwatzen', norw. (ma.) *bjeldra* 'schreien'; Kompromiß- oder Dialektformen (mit erhaltenem *ja*) sind dän. (ma.) *bjaldre* 'bellen, rufen', norw. (ma.) 'schwatzen'. Daneben die *a*-Form norw. (ma.) *baldra* 'schwatzen', gebildet wie nd. *ballern* 'lärmen'.

Ähnlich oder aber diesem nachgebildet ist das Verhältnis von älter dän. *bæffe* 'bellen' (nach Falk aus dtsch. *bäffen*) gegenüber dem heutigen *bjæffe*, schwed. (ma.) *bjäffa*. Danach ist sicher Neubildung dän. *bjaffe* 'bellen', mit dem Vokalismus von *blaffe* (dies nach Falk aus dtsch. *blaffen*).

Sicher sekundär ist es, wenn danach neben älter dän. *bavle*, schwed. *babbla* 'schwatzen' mit *j* auftreten älter dän. *bjavle*, norw. (ma.) *bjabla*, schwed. (ma.) *bjäbbl, bjabba* 'klaffen', — denn eine e-Form von diesem Wort wird es kaum in alter Zeit gegeben haben.

Neben schwed. (ma.) *bäla* 'blöken' bestehen schwed. *bjäla* 'blöken' und dän. (ma.) *bjæle* 'brüllen, schreien'; Falk nennt beide onomatopoetische Bildungen; aber Wörter des Typus *\*bel-* in dieser Bedeutung sind im Germanischen häufig und zufällig gerade auch in den Schwestersprachen belegt; man darf sich nur nicht durch Abweichung vom Lautgesetzlichen (d. h. also durch Analogiebildungen) beirren lassen.

Dän. (ma.) *bolme* 'schreien, lärmen' : *bjålme*, wohl nach dem vorhergehenden.

Aschwed. *barma sik* : schwed. (ma.) *bjärmas* 'klagen, jammern', neben *bärmas*.

Norw. (ma.) *bugla, bugra* 'herumtappen, pfuschen' : *bjugla, bjugra*; vgl. *bjora* 'fleißig (wie ein Biber, *bjor*, an. *biōrr*) arbeiten', und die homonyme Gruppe *bugra* 'sich beigen' : *bjuga* 'sich beugen', an. *\*biūga* (zufällig ist diese Vokalstufe des st. Verbs nicht belegt), norw. (ma.) *bjugla* 'sich beugen oder nachgeben in den Knien'.

Norw. (ma.) *bokna* 'wühlen' : *bjåkna.*

Norw. (ma.) *fesa* 'flüstern, zischeln' (zu an. *fīsa* 'pedere'): norw. (ma.) *fjesa*; mit *ja, fjasa* 'verpuffen, auflodern, Geschwätz und dummes Zeug treiben'. Diese Gruppe ist nun in Parallelismus geraten mit der *fl*- Gruppe von norw. *flaas* 'unbedachte Person' (s. bei Falk-Torp s. v.), so *flas* 'leichtsinniges Wesen' : *fjas* 'Tändelei' (Falk-Torp s. v.).

Eine Menge Parallelformen der Gruppen *fatt* 'dumme Person' : *fjatt* bei Falk-Torp s. v. *fjott*, mit unannehmbarer Erklärung.

Ähnlich steht es mit den deutschen Wörtern, welche undeutsche Betonung haben. H. Schröder hat sie bekanntlich als Infixbildungen erklärt (Streckformen, Heidelberg 1906). Nach allem, was wir von der Sprache wissen, wären aber Bildungen z. B. mit einem Infix -*ar*- erst dann möglich, wenn Musterdoubletten wie *Schlaffe* : *Schlaraffe* schon bestanden: die Infixgewohnheit muß erst irgendwie zustande kommen. Die Erklärung wird gerade durch die Methodik unserer Wissenschaft leicht: undeutsche Betonung ist durch Lehnwörter in die Sprache gekommen. Es sei erlaubt, hier das Mod. Phil. 15. 577 eingehend besprochene schematisch wiederzugeben (vgl. Jsb. 43, 13!).

Ausbreitung betonter Suffixe von Fremdwörtern auf Heimisches ist bekannt (Paul, Prinzipien⁴ 399): *Bäckerei, Schweinerei, hofieren, Takelage, Lappalien, Schmieralien* (Wood, Mod. Phil. 9, 157 ff.), *Faselant.* Hierher gehören *in die Rabuse, Rapuse geben*, zu *rabben, rappen* 'raffen'; schweiz. *Flangguse* 'unordentliches Frauenzimmer; Ohrfeige', zu *Flangg, Flangge.*

Andererseits kann schon das Fremdwort selber wegen zufälliger Lautanklänge ungedeutet werden. So schon mhd. *fisiment* (*visamenta*) und frühnd. *fisepetenten* (*visae patentes*) umgedeutet als 'Dummheiten' wegen dtsch. *Fisel* 'Wisch, Rute usw.', *fiseln* 'kleinlich handeln usw.' Vermischung der beiden ist wohl das heutige *Fisimatenten.*

Nun kam es aber auch vor, daß der zweite Teil eines solchen Wortes an Einheimisches anklang. Ich glaube, daß dies bei frühnd. *Fisigunkus, Fisigunkel* (geschrieben auch *Physi*-) 'eingebildeter Narr' der Fall war: ein lateinischer Schulwitz wie etwa *\*physicunculus* wurde vielleicht durch dtsch. *Gunkel* 'Lump, schlaffer Mensch usw.' nahegelegt. Ist dies nun einmal geschehen, dann kann der zweite Teil des Wortes auf alle möglichen Weisen verdeutscht werden, oder, anders ausgedrückt, es entsteht ein unbetontes Präfix (etwa *fisi*-) für Scherzfremdwörter. So *Fisimagenken, Fisifatenten, Fislematantes* 'Flausen'; *Fisiguck* (zu *Gugger* 'Kukuk'), *Fisibutz* (zu *Butz* 'Narr'), schweiz. 'dummer, sonderbarer Mensch'; elsäss. *fisimikre* 'pfuschen' (zu *Micker* 'kleines Tier, kleines Ding'), *fisenickere* 'aufschneiden, schwindeln' (zu *nicke* 'feilschen, markten'); nd. *fisenülle* 'weibliche Scham' (zu *nüllen* 'futuere', mhd. *nol* 'mons veneris').

Andere Formen mit Verdeutschung des zweiten Teils:

*Laterne* wird verwandelt in *Latüchte* (wegen *Lüchte*), in *Latäusche* (wegen *Läusche*) und in *Latattere* (wegen *Lattere*), s. Hoffmann-Krayer, AfdA 32, 2 und Wood a. a. O.

*Bado* (d. h. franz. *badaud*) wird elsäss. zu *Badautle* (weil daselbst *Dautel, Flaute, Gautel, Hautle, Lautel, Mautle, Schaute, Tschaute* alles ebenfalls dumme Leute sind) und zu *Badutscherle* (wegen *Dutscherle, Butscher, Brutsch, Futsch, Hutscherle*, alles dumme Personen meist weiblichen Geschlechts), schweiz. zu *Baduntle* (wegen *Duntle, Buntle*; alle drei Wörter für dicke Weiber).

Endlich kann dann auch der erste, unbetonte Teil des Worts umgebildet werden, falls er, wie bei *fisi-*, an Einheimisches anklingt, so daß am Ende vom Fremdwort gerade eben nur noch die Betonung bleibt. So zu *Fisimatenten* auch noch *Fislematantes* (engere Anlehnung an dtsch. *fiseln*), *Fitzematenterle* (schwäb., zu *fitze* 'leicht mit der Peitsche schlagen, betrügen, hoffärtig tun'), *Fisperementli* (schweiz., zu *fispere* 'sich hin und her bewegen'). Zum *Fisigunk* auch noch *Fiselgunkes* (nähere Anlehnung an *fiseln*), *Filigunkes* (lat. *filiolus?*), *Fidigugger* (*fideren* 'lügen, aufschneiden'), *Spirigunkes* (*spirig* 'unruhig, mutwillig'), *Britschigunkel* 'weibliche Scham' (wegen *Britsche* 'ds.').

So erklären sich Gruppen wie *Kabine, Kajüte, Kabuse* (diese drei vorerst aus dem Romanischen, obwohl z. T. ursprünglich germ.), mit den Neubildungen *Kabacke* (nach *Baracke*; nicht etwa, nach Hirt-Weigand, aus dem morphologisch isolierten russ. *kabák*, sondern, nach Berneker Slav. Et. Wb., umgekehrt das russ. Wort aus dem dtsch.), *Kabutte, Kabuffe, Kamuff, Kaficke, Kaweiche*.

Jedenfalls dürfte es sicher stehen, daß man das neugerm. Wortmaterial nicht unmittelbar aus dem Jahrtausende weit entfernten uridg. zu erklären hat, und vor allem nicht durch phantastische Erfindungen, sondern daß es unter Beachtung der bisher gewonnenen sprachwissenschaftlichen Prinzipien aus den neugerm. Sprachverhältnissen als normale Entwicklung verständlich ist.

# B21. A Set of Postulates for the Science of Language

1926. *Language* 2. 153–164.

[Delivered at the 1925 Annual Meeting of the Linguistic Society, Chicago. Reprinted in *International Journal of American Linguistics* 15:4.195–202 (October 1949), and in Martin Joos, ed., *Readings in Linguistics* (Washington, D.C.: American Council of Learned Societies, 1957), pp. 19–25.]

## *I. Introductory*

The method of postulates (that is, assumptions or axioms) and definitions[1] is fully adequate to mathematics; as for other sciences, the more complex their subject-matter, the less amenable are they to this method, since, under it, every descriptive or historical fact becomes the subject of a new postulate.

Nevertheless, the postulational method can further the study of language, because it forces us to state explicitly whatever we assume, to define our terms, and to decide what things may exist independently and what things are interdependent.[2]

Certain errors can be avoided or corrected by examining and formulating our (at present tacit) assumptions and defining our (often undefined) terms.[3]

Also, the postulational method saves discussion, because it limits our

---

[1] For a clear exposition of this method, see J. W. Young, *Lectures on the Fundamental Concepts of Algebra and Geometry*, New York 1911.

[2] Cf. A. P. Weiss's set of postulates for psychology, *Psychological Review*. 32. 83.

[3] Examples are many. Bopp took for granted that the formative elements of Indo-European were once independent words; this is a needless and unwarranted assumption. The last descendant of his error is the assumption that IE compound words are historically derived from phrases (Jacobi, *Compositum und Nebensatz*, Bonn 1897; this even in Brugmann, *Grundrisz* II[2], 1, pp. 37. 78; cf. TAPA 45. 73 ff.). The notion is gaining ground that some forms have less meaning than others and are therefore more subject to phonetic change (Horn, *Sprachkörper und Sprachfunktion*, Palaestra 135, Berlin 1921); I, for one, can discover no workable definition of the terms 'meaning' and 'phonetic change' under which this notion can be upheld. The whole dispute, perhaps today as unstilled as fifty years ago, about the regularity of phonetic change, is at bottom a question of terminology.

statements to a defined terminology; in particular, it cuts us off from psychological dispute.[4] Discussion of the fundamentals of our science seems to consist one half of obvious truisms, and one half of metaphysics; this is characteristic of matters which form no real part of a subject: they should properly be disposed of by merely naming certain concepts as belonging to the domain of other sciences.

Thus, the physiologic and acoustic description of acts of speech belongs to other sciences than ours. The existence and interaction of social groups held together by language is granted by psychology and anthropology.[5]

Psychology, in particular, gives us this series: to certain stimuli (A) a person reacts by speaking; his speech (B) in turn stimulates his hearers to certain reactions (C).[6] By a social habit which every person acquires in infancy from his elders, A–B–C are closely correlated. Within this correlation, the stimuli (A) which cause an act of speech and the reactions (C) which result from it, are very closely linked, because every person acts indifferently as speaker or as hearer. We are free, therefore, without further discussion, to speak of *vocal features* or *sounds* (B) and of *stimulus-reaction features* (A–C) of speech.

## II. Form and Meaning

**1. Definition.** An act of speech is an *utterance*.

**2. Assumption 1.** Within certain communities successive utterances are alike or partly alike.

A needy stranger at the door says *I'm hungry.* A child who has eaten and merely wants to put off going to bed says *I'm hungry.* Linguistics considers only those vocal features which are alike in the two utterances, and only those stimulus-reaction features which are alike in the two utterances.

Similarly, *The book is interesting* and *Put the book away*, are partly alike (*the book*). Outside of our science these similarities are only relative; within

---

[4] Recall the difficulties and obscurities in the writings of Humboldt and Steinthal, and the psychological dispute of Paul, Wundt, Delbrueck. From our point of view, the last-named was wrong in denying the value of descriptive data, but right in saying that it is indifferent what system of psychology a linguist believes in (*Grundfragen der Sprachforschung*, Strassburg 1901). The trouble over the nature of the sentence is largely nonlinguistic; contrast the simplicity and usefulness of Meillet's definition (adopted below), *Introduction à l'étude comparative des langues indo-européennes*,[3] Paris 1912, p. 339. I am indebted also to Sapir's book on *Language*, New York 1921, and to de Saussure's *Cours de linguistique générale*,[2] Paris 1922; both authors take steps toward a delimitation of linguistics.

[5] Cf. Weiss, l. c., p. 86: 'The language responses establish the . . . social type of organization . . . .'

[6] Cf. Weiss, *Journal of Philosophy, Psychology and Scientific Methods* 15. 636: 'The significant thing about the speech reaction is that it may be either the adequate *reaction* to a situation, or it may be the adequate *stimulus* for either another speech reaction or some bodily reaction.'

it they are absolute. This fiction is only in part suspended in historical linguistics.

**3. Def.** Any such community is a *speech-community*.

**4. Def.** The totality of utterances that can be made in a speech-community is the *language* of that speech-community.

We are obliged to predict; hence the words 'can be made'. We say that under certain stimuli a Frenchman (or Zulu, etc.) will say so-and-so and other Frenchmen (or Zulus, etc.) will react appropriately to his speech. Where good informants are available, or for the investigator's own language, the prediction is easy; elsewhere it constitutes the greatest difficulty of descriptive linguistics.

**5. Def.** That which is alike will be called *same*. That which is not same is *different*.

This enables us to use these words without reference to non-linguistic shades of sound and meaning.

**6. Def.** The vocal features common to same or partly same utterances are *forms*; the corresponding stimulus-reaction features are *meanings*.

Thus a form is a recurrent vocal feature which has meaning, and a meaning is a recurrent stimulus-reaction feature which corresponds to a form.

**7. Assumption 2.** Every utterance is made up wholly of forms.


### III. Morpheme, Word, Phrase

**8. Def.** A *minimum* X is an X which does not consist entirely of lesser X's.

Thus, if $X_1$ consists of $X_2 X_3 X_4$, then $X_1$ is not a minimum X. But if $X_1$ consists of $X_2 X_3 A$, or of $X_2 A$, or of $A_1 A_2$, or is unanalyzable, then $X_1$ is a minimum X.

**9. Def.** A minimum form is a *morpheme*; its meaning a *sememe*.

Thus a morpheme is a recurrent (meaningful) form which cannot in turn be analyzed into smaller recurrent (meaningful) forms. Hence any unanalyzable word or formative is a morpheme.

**10. Def.** A form which may be an utterance is *free*. A form which is not free is *bound*.

Thus, *book*, *the man* are free forms; *-ing* (as in writing), *-er* (as in *writer*) are bound forms, the last-named differing in meaning from the free form *err*.

**11. Def.** A minimum free form is a *word*.

A word is thus a form which may be uttered alone (with meaning) but cannot be analyzed into parts that may (all of them) be uttered alone (with meaning). Thus the word *quick* cannot be analyzed; the word *quickly* can be analyzed into *quick* and *-ly*, but the latter part cannot be uttered alone; the word *writer* can be analyzed into *write* and *-er*, but the latter cannot be uttered alone (the word *err* being, by virtue of different meaning, a different form); the word *blackbird* can be analyzed into the words *black* and *bird* and the word-stress — —, which last cannot be uttered alone (i.e., it differs in form and meaning from the phrase *black bird*).

**12. Def.** A non-minimum free form is a *phrase*.

E.g., *the book*, or *The man beat the dog*; but not, e.g., *book on* (as in *Lay the book on the table*), for this is meaningless, hence not a form; and not *blackbird*, which is a minimum free form.

**13. Def.** A bound form which is part of a word is a *formative*.

A formative may be complex, as, Latin verb-endings -*abat*, -*abant*, -*abit*, -*abunt*, etc., or minimum (and hence a morpheme), as Latin -*t* of third person.

**14. Assumption 3.** The forms of a language are finite in number.

## IV. Example of a Special Assumption

The phenomena of specific languages will no doubt necessitate further assumptions of form; and these will sometimes modify the general assumptions. The following is an example of such a special assumption.

**Assumption S1.** A phrase may contain a bound form which is not part of a word.

For example, the possessive [z] in *the man I saw yesterday's daughter*.

**Def.** Such a bound form is a *phrase-formative*.

This assumption disturbs the definition of *phrase* above given. Strictly speaking, our assumptions and definitions would demand that we take *the-man-I-saw-yesterday's daughter* as two words. Convenience of analysis makes an assumption like the present one preferable for English. A similar assumption might be convenient for the Philippine 'ligatures'.

## V. Phonemes

**15. Assumption 4.** Different morphemes may be alike or partly alike as to vocal features.

Thus *book* : *table* [b]; *stay* : *west* [st]; -*er* (agent) : -*er* (comparative). The assumption implies that the meanings are different.

**16. Def.** A minimum same of vocal feature is a *phoneme* or *distinctive sound*.

As, for instance, English [b, s, t], the English normal word-stress, the Chinese tones.

**17. Assumption 5.** The number of different phonemes in a language is a small sub-multiple of the number of forms.

**18. Assumption 6.** Every form is made up wholly of phonemes.

These two assumptions are empiric facts for every language that has been observed, and outside of our science are theoretical necessities (Boas, *Handbook of American Indian Languages*, Bureau of American Ethnology, Bulletin 40, vol. 1, pp. 24 ff.) Such a thing as a 'small difference of sound' does not exist in a language. Linguists who believe that certain forms resist phonetic change, implicitly reject these assumptions, though, so far as I can see, we could not work without them.

The morphemes of a language can thus be analyzed into a small number of meaningless phonemes. The sememes, on the other hand, which stand in one-to-one correspondence with the morphemes, cannot be further analyzed by linguistic methods. This is no doubt why linguists, confronted with the parallelism of form and meaning, choose form as the basis of classification.

**19. Assumption 7.** The number of orders of phonemes in the morphemes and words of a language is a sub-multiple of the number of possible orders.

**20. Def.** The orders which occur are the *sound-patterns* of the language.

As, English word-initial [st-] but never [ts-].

**21. Def.** Different forms which are alike as to phonemes are *homonymous*.

## VI. Construction, Categories, Parts of Speech

**22. Assumption 8.** Different non-minimum forms may be alike or partly alike as to the order of the constituent forms and as to stimulus-reaction features corresponding to this order.

The order may be successive, simultaneous (stress and pitch with other phonemes), substitutive (French *au* [o] for *à le*), and so on.

**23. Def.** Such recurrent sames of order are *constructions*; the corresponding stimulus-reaction features are *constructional meanings*.

This expands the use of the term *meaning*.

**24. Def.** The construction of formatives in a word is a *morphologic construction*.

Thus, *book-s*, *ox-en* have the construction of formative plus formative and the meaning 'object in number'.

**25. Def.** The construction of free forms (and phrase formatives) in a phrase is a *syntactic construction*.

Thus, *Richard saw John, The man is beating the dog* show the construction of free form plus free form meaning 'actor acting on goal'.

**26. Def.** A *maximum* X is an X which is not part of a larger X.

**27. Def.** A maximum construction in any utterance is a *sentence*.[7]

---

[7] [See fn 6 in B37, where Bloomfield acknowledges an error in this English wording of Meillet's definition (fn 4 above). The correct reading is: A maximum form in any utterance is a *sentence*. Thus, a sentence is a form which, in the given utterance, is not in construction with any other form.—CFH]

Thus, a sentence is a construction which, in the given utterance, is not part of any larger construction. Every utterance therefore consists of one or more sentences, and even such utterances as Latin *pluit*, English *Fire!* or *Ouch!* are sentences.

**28. Assumption 9.** The number of constructions in a language is a small sub-multiple of the number of forms.

**29. Def.** Each of the ordered units in a construction is a *position*.

Thus the English construction of formative plus formative meaning 'object in number' has two positions; and that of free form plus free form plus free form meaning 'actor acting on goal' has three positions.

**30. Assumption 10.** Each position in a construction can be filled only by certain forms.

Thus, in the English construction of formative plus formative meaning 'object in number' the first position can be filled only by certain formatives (noun-stems), and the second only by certain other formatives (affixes of number, such as the plural-sign -*s*). And in the English construction of free form plus free form plus free form meaning 'actor acting on goal' the first and third positions can be filled only by certain free forms (object expressions) and the second only by certain other free forms (finite verb expressions). This assumption implies the converse, namely, that a given form will appear only in certain positions of certain constructions. Thus, an English noun-stem will appear only in the first position of the construction 'object in number', in the second position of the construction formative plus formative meaning 'object having such an object' (*long-nose*), and in certain positions of a certain few other constructions. Similarly, an object expression, such as *John, the man* will appear in the first position of the construction 'actor acting on goal', or in the third, or in certain positions of a certain few other constructions.

**31. Def.** The meaning of a position is a *functional meaning*.

That is, the constructional meaning of a construction may be divided into parts, one for each position; these parts are functional meanings. It would be more concrete, but perhaps less useful, if we said: the meaning common to all forms that can fill a given position, when they are in that position, is a functional meaning. Thus, in the English construction of 'object in number' the first position has the functional meaning 'object', or, more concretely, all the formatives (noun-stems) which can occur in this position, have in common, when they so appear, the functional meaning 'object'. And in the English construction of 'actor acting on goal' the first position has the functional meaning 'actor', or, more concretely, all the free forms (object-expressions, such as nouns, noun-phrases, pronouns, etc.) which can occur in this position, have in common, when they so appear, the functional meaning 'actor'. And in this same construction, the third position has the meaning 'goal', or, more concretely, all the free forms (largely the same as those just mentioned) which can appear in this position, have in common, when they so appear, the meaning 'goal'.

**32. Def.** The positions in which a form occurs are its *functions*.

Thus, the word *John* and the phrase *the man* have the functions of 'actor', 'goal', 'predicate noun', 'goal of preposition', and so on.

**33. Def.** All forms having the same functions constitute a *form-class*.

Examples of English form-classes are: noun-stems, number-affixes, object expressions, finite verb expressions.

**34. Def.** The functional meanings in which the forms of a form-class appear constitute the *class-meaning*.

Thus, the meanings found in all the functions of the form-class of English object expressions, namely 'actor', 'goal', etc. (§32) together constitute the class-meaning of these forms, which may be summed up as 'numbered object' or in the name 'object expression'.

**35. Def.** The functional meanings and class-meanings of a language are the *categories* of the language.

Thus, the above examples enable us to determine the following categories of the English language: from functional meanings: object, number, actor, action, goal; from class-meanings: object, number, numbered object (object expression), predicative action (finite verb expression).

**36. Def.** If a form-class contains relatively few forms, the meanings of these forms may be called *sub-categories*.

Thus, the English category of number contains only two meanings, singular-indefinite (*egg*) and plural (*eggs*). Hence one may speak of the sub-categories of singular and plural; it is convenient to do so when, as in this case, the sub-categories play a part in the alternation of other forms (see VII).

**37. Def.** A form-class of words is a *word-class*.

**38. Def.** The maximum word-classes of a language are the *parts of speech* of that language.


### VII. Alternation

**39. Assumption 11.** In a construction a phoneme may alternate with another phoneme according to accompanying phonemes.

As in Sanskrit sandhi: *tat pacati, tad bharati*.

**40. Def.** Such alternation is *phonetic alternation*.

**41. Assumption 12.** In a construction a form may alternate with another form according to accompanying forms.

As, in English, the plural affixes *book-s* [s], *boy-s* [z], *ox-en, f-ee-t*. Or, verbs: *He skates, They skate*, according to number of actor.

**42. Def.** Such alternation is *formal alternation*.

**43. Assumption 13.** Absence of sound may be a phonetic or formal alternant.

**44. Def.** Such an alternant is a *zero element*.

The postulation of zero elements is necessary for Sanskrit (Pāṇini 1, 1, 61), for Primitive Indo-European (Meillet, *Introduction à l'étude comparative des langues indo-européennes*[3], Paris 1912, p. 127 f.), and probably economical for English (singular *book* with affix zero, as opposed to *book-s*, cf. *f-oo-t* : *f-ee-t*).

**45. Def.** If a formal alternation is determined by the phonemes of the accompanying forms, it is an *automatic alternation*.

Thus, the alternation of [-s, -z, -ez] in the regular English plural suffix of nouns is automatic, being determined by the final phoneme of the noun-stem. This differs from phonetic alternation since not every [s] in English is subject to this alternation, but only the (four) morphemes of this form. Similarly, Sanskrit *tat pacati*: *tan nayati*, since the alternation takes place only in wordfinal (contrast, e.g. *ratnam*).

The phonetic alternations and the automatic formal alternations of a language allow of a classification of the phonemes, to which the sound-patterns (§20) may contribute. Thus, the regular English plural suffix implies a classification of those English phonemes (the great majority) which may occur at the end of a noun-stem into the classes (1) sibilant, (2) non-sibilant (*a*, unvoiced, *b*, voiced). Ordinary phonetics can go no farther than this; phonetics which goes farther is either a personal skill or a science for the laboratory.

**46. Def.** The classification of phonemes implied in the sound-patterns, phonetic alternations, and automatic formal alternations of a language is the *phonetic pattern*.

For the sound-patterns and phonetic pattern see Sapir, *Language*, 1. 37, and cf. Baudouin de Courtenay, *Versuch einer Theorie Phonetischer Alternationen*, Strassburg 1895.

**47. Def.** If formal alternation is otherwise determined, it is *grammatical alternation*.

As, English plural suffix -*en* in *ox-en* alternating with the regular suffix above described; the verb-forms in *he skates* : *they skate*.

**48. Def.** If the accompanying forms which determine one grammatical variant predominate as to number, this variant is said to be *regular*; the others are irregular.

Thus -*en* is an irregular plural suffix.

**49. Def.** If in a construction all the component forms are irregular, the whole form is *suppletive*.

If *go* be taken as the stem of the verb, then the past *went* is suppletive. Under this definition *better* as comparative of *good* would not be suppletive, since the ending -*er* is regular; a definition that will include such forms

can be made only within English (or Indo-European) grammar, after
'stem' and 'affix' have been defined for this language.

**50. Def.** Whatever has meaning is a *glosseme*. The meaning of a glosseme is a *noeme*.

Thus the term glosseme includes (1) forms, (2) constructions, (3) zero
elements.

The assumptions and definitions so far made will probably make it
easy to define the grammatical phenomena of any language, both morphologic (affixation, reduplication, composition) and syntactic (cross-reference, concord, government, word-order), though I cannot say whether
any such further definitions would apply to all languages. Other notions,
such as subject, predicate, verb, noun, will apply only to some languages,
and may have to be defined differently for different ones,—unless, indeed,
we prefer to invent new terms for divergent phenomena.

## VIII. Historical Linguistics

The following assumptions and definitions for historical linguistics are
added for the sake of completeness. Insofar as they are correctly formulated, they will merely restate the working method of the great majority of
linguists.

**51. Assumption H1.** Every language changes at a rate which leaves
contemporary persons free to communicate without disturbance.

The ways in which it changes are described in Assumptions H3 and
following.

**52. Assumption H2.** Among persons, linguistic change is uniform in
ratio with the amount of communication between them.

These two assumptions and the assumptions and definitions based on
them are necessarily loose, not because the process is too slow for any
methods of direct observation that have been used—assumptions could
ignore this—but because in historical linguistics it is our purpose to en-
visage the phenomena as relative. Ultimately no two speakers, and indeed
no two utterances, have the same dialect: our assumptions must leave us
free to examine the historical process with any desired degree of detail.

**53. Def.** If linguistic change results in groups of persons between which
communication is disturbed, these groups speak *dialects* of the language.

**54. Def.** A relatively uniform auxiliary dialect used by such groups is
a *standard language*.

**55. Def.** If linguistic change results in groups of persons between which
communication is impossible, these groups speak *related languages*.

**56. Assumption H3.** Phonemes or classes of phonemes may gradually
change.

For 'classes of phonemes' see §§45, 46.

**57. Def.** Such change is *sound-change*.

This assumption, by naming phonemes, implies that meaning is not involved. Owing to the assumptions that limit the number of phonemes (Assumptions 5 and 6), the change must affect the phonemes at every occurrence and do away with the older form of any phoneme that is changed.

**58. Assumption H4.** Sound-change may affect phonemes or classes of phonemes in the environment of certain other phonemes or classes of phonemes.

**59. Def.** This change is *conditioned sound-change*.

**60. Assumption H5.** Sound-change preponderantly favors shorter forms.[8]

**61. Assumption H6.** Linguistic change may substitute sames for differents.

**62. Def.** This change is *analogic change*.

**63. Def.** Analogic change which creates or enlarges a glosseme is *contamination*

For example, creation (of a morpheme), pre-Germanic *\*hweðwōrez* 'four', *\*fimfe* 'five' > *\*f-eðwōrez*, *\*f-imfe*. Increase in size (of a morpheme), late Latin *gra-ve, le-ve* > *gr-eve, l-eve* (Italian).

**64. Def.** Analogic change which extends the use of a glosseme is *adaptation*.

Late Latin *reddere* > *rendere*, extending to a new word the morpheme *-end-* of *pr-endere, p-endere, att-endere* (*v-endere*?).

**65. Def.** Adaptation which replaces one alternant by another is *proportional analogy*.

English *bēc* > *book-s*; the plural affixes vary according to the accompanying noun-stem (grammatical alternation, §41), and now one alternant replaces another. The diagram showing the proportional character is familiar.

**66. Def.** Analogic change of formatives is *formal analogy*.

It may of course be contamination, adaptation, or proportional analogy. In a language in which stems and affixes are definable, it is customary to distinguish between 'material' formal analogy (affecting stems) and 'grammatical' formal analogy (affecting affixes).

**67. Def.** Analogic change of words is *semantic change*.

It may of course be contaminative, adaptive, or proportional. E.g., English *meat* 'pabulum' > 'caro'; or *home* 'Heim' > 'Haus'. Probably proportional:

He left the bones and took   :   He left the bones and took   ::
    the flesh                     the meat

[8] Assumptions H5 and H7 try to embody the results of Jespersen's *Progress in Language*, New York 1894.

She cooked the beans with   :   She cooked the beans with
    the flesh                      the meat.

They have a lovely house   :   They have a lovely home (intensive)   ::
A fine new house for sale   :   A fine new home for sale (intensive).[9]

**68. Assumption H7.** Analogic change predominantly disfavors irregular glossemes and those which diverge from their fellows; it tends to disfavor them in inverse ratio to their frequency of occurrence.

This is necessarily vague, because we know little about replacement and obsolescence through such factors as unusual homonymy, word-tabu, and other deviations of glossemes, that is, about inadequacy of glossemes and its effects. Cf. Gilliéron, *Pathologie et thérapeutique verbales*, Collection linguistique, vol.11, Paris 1921.

**69. Assumption H8.** Whoever speaks a foreign language or dialect may in it substitute resemblant features of his native speech.

**70. Def.** This is *linguistic substitution*.

**71. Def.** Linguistic substitution of phonemes is *sound-substitution*.

**72. Assumption H9.** Whoever hears a foreign language or dialect may adopt features of it into his own speech.

**73. Def.** Such adoption is *linguistic borrowing*.

**74. Def.** Borrowed words are *loan-words*.

**75. Assumption H10.** The phonemes of analogic forms and loan-words may be changed so as to fit the sound patterns of the language.

Western European *peregrinus* > *pilgrim*; German *klüppel* > *knüppel*.

**76. Def.** Such change is *sudden sound-change*.

**77. Assumption H11.** Glossemes may go out of use.

Compare the comment on Assumption H7, §68.

[9] The word 'intensive' is meant merely to describe the meaning of *home* in its new use (intensive of *house*), and is not meant as a technical term. Cf. also Kroesch, LANGUAGE 2. 35–45 (1926).

# B22. *From* The Word-Stems of Central Algonquian

1927. *Festschrift Meinhof: Beiträge zur afrikanischen Sprachwissenschaft* (Hamburg) 393-402 (received by Editor 20 May 1926).

[This, like B19, was superseded by B65. The last section, however, makes some points in a way not exactly duplicated in any of Bloomfield's other writings. The first seven sections of the paper describe, in outline, the extremely complicated derivational system of Central Algonquian. The paper then concludes:]

It is evident that so complex a system as this cannot be perfectly rigid. One can sometimes observe THE DYING OUT OF ELEMENTS. A Menomini, telling a story which he had heard long ago from his father, used the expression *säkāwikanähsimew*, where the initial *\*säk-* 'fright', and the final *\*-hcim-* 'lay, throw an animate object', are clear, but the medial, so far as I could ascertain, was not understood. My best English speaking informant insisted that the record was wrong, that it should have been *säkā-kunähsimew* (*\*-ākunä-* medial 'snow'). But the medial *-āwikanä-* is common in Cree: *nāwikan* 'my back', *kaskāwikanähwäw* 'he wounds his back by tool or gunshot'. Similarly, some Cree use the incomprehensible initial *nisiwanāt-*, as in *nisiwanātisiw* 'he is ruined, destroyed', but most Cree employ instead the more intelligible combination of initial *wanāt-* 'loss' with prefixed *misi-* 'big': *misi-wanātisiw*. The obscure form is archaic: Fox *neciwanātcihäwa* 'he ruins him'; Menomini *neʔswanātesiw* 'he is in a mess', *neʔswanātcihew* 'he makes a mess of him, confuses him'; the initial is connected with Fox *nesäwa*, Menomini *neʔnew* 'he kills him', a stem no longer used in Cree.

There are occasional innovations. In a Menomini legend the Bear, a dangerous but comical character, receives the predicate *nenāwātsinenɩwakesiw* 'he is a smashing crashing fellow'. This word is highly comical, as even my speech-feeling could sense; the reason becomes clear upon analysis: *-nenɩwak-* is an impossible medial, formed by adding post-medial *-ak-* (before *-esi-*) to the final *-nenɩw-* 'man'.

Cree differs from the sister languages by forming medials with *-ä-* from almost any word. Thus Cree *ayōwinis* 'garment' is by history the diminutive of a noun, Fox *ayōweni* 'thing used', abstract of a verb, Fox *ayōwa* 'he uses it', reduplicated form of *ōwa, Menomini *uah* 'he uses it'; yet Cree has formed a medial from this late and secondary word: *pustayō-winisäw* 'he dresses', *katayōwinisäw* 'he undresses'. Similarly, Cree *astutin* 'hat', *pustastutinäw* 'he puts on a hat', and many others. Even the dependent noun of relationship *nikusis* 'my son' gives *-kusisä-* in *āpihta-wikusisān* 'halfbreed'; it could not, at first, have been a very respectful word, for treating the final as a medial implies a lower kind of son,—just as there is a medial for *ixkwäwa* 'woman' and for *nāpäwa* 'male', but none for *ilenιwa* 'man', a nobler word.

Actual confusion between the types of elements is rare. When Cree mixes up *atim* 'dog' and *-astim* saying, instead of *mistastim* 'horse' (initial *meʔθ-* 'big'), *mistatim*, *misatim*, this is due to a phonetic change (dissimilation) which interfered with the normal distribution of the two forms.

Evidently, the system here described is not very remote from that of noun-incorporation, clear-cut though the differences are. It suggests how object-incorporation may develop, or how it may break down into mere word-formation. It would be idle, however, to speculate, with only the present data, upon whether the Central Algonquian state of affairs represents the beginnings of a system of object-incorporation, or the vestiges of such a system. It may be either, or both, or neither, for in language there are really no transitional stages, or rather, everything is transition. Each linguistic system, as it is at a given time and place, is a self-sufficient entity. It is the product of a development, and it will develop in the future; but it need not, at the moment, tell us the direction of either past or future change.

# B23. Review of Jespersen's *Philosophy of Grammar*

1927. *Journal of English and Germanic Philology* 26.444–446.

*The Philosophy of Grammar*. By Otto Jespersen. New York: Henry Holt and Co., 1924. 359 pp. [And London: George Allen and Unwin Ltd.]

Under this title Jespersen increases his many gifts to the science of language by a discussion of the basic grammatical categories of English and kindred tongues. The 350 pages of the book are so full of matter that no review could exhibit its wealth. The author's keen yet sensitive observation and his combinatory skill are known to all students of English. It would be futile to voice differences of opinion on specific points without a more detailed exposition than is here warranted. Instead, I shall state the difference of general outlook which in my case probably underlies most such differences.

For Jespersen language is a mode of expression; its forms express the thoughts and feelings of speakers, and communicate them to hearers, and this process goes on as an immediate part of human life and is, to a great extent, subject to the requirements and vicissitudes of human life. For me, as for de Saussure (*Cours de linguistique générale*[2], Paris, 1922) and, in a sense, for Sapir (*Language*, New York, 1921), all this, de Saussure's *la parole*, lies beyond the power of our science. We cannot predict whether a certain person will speak at a given moment, or what he will say, or in what words and other linguistic forms he will say it. Our science can deal only with those features of language, de Saussure's *la langue*, which are common to all the speakers of a community,—the phonemes, grammatical categories, lexicon, and so on. These are abstractions, for they are only (recurrent) partial features of speech-utterances. The infant is trained to these features so thoroughly that after earliest childhood the variabilities of the human individual and the vicissitudes of human life no longer affect them. They form a rigid system,—so rigid that without any adequate physiologic information and with psychology in a state of chaos, we are nevertheless able to subject it to scientific treatment. A grammatical or lexical statement is at bottom an abstraction.

It may be urged that change in language is due ultimately to the deviations of individuals from the rigid system. But it appears that even here individual deviations are ineffective; whole groups of speakers must, for some reason unknown to us, coincide in a deviation, if it is to result in a linguistic change. Change in language does not reflect individual variability, but seems to be a massive, uniform, and gradual alteration, at every moment of which the system is just as rigid as at any other moment. This would be impossible, of course, if what we studied were the living realities, the actual utterances. These, however, involve, in each case, an overpowering majority of features which the linguist cannot study, features which, to speak optimistically, the other social sciences and physiology or psychology will someday describe, even as we today abstract and describe the features of the linguistic pattern.

In the study of linguistic forms, therefore, I should not appeal, as Jespersen sometimes does, to meaning as if it were separable from form, or to the actual human necessities and conveniences of communication. On the one hand, we flatter ourselves when we think that we (as linguists, at any rate) can estimate these; on the other hand, they do not affect the somewhat meagre abstraction which we can and do study. In setting up the grammatical categories, such as the part-of-speech system, I should not appeal beyond the actual forms of the language under consideration. Under forms we must of course include substitutive and syntactic features. Thus, in Chapter XIII, I agree with Jespersen in distinguishing for English a nominative and an oblique case, for when we say *Jack hit Tom*, both the word-order and the substitutive pronoun forms distinguish the two. But I disagree when Jespersen refuses to subdivide the oblique case. In *I gave the boy a book*; *I asked the boy a question*; *I called the boy bad names*, the fixed order of the two oblique elements is part of the linguistic form; these examples would justify us in setting up at least two types of oblique. And such substitute forms as *I gave it to the boy*, *I asked it of the boy*, *I called the boy by them*, distinguish the three examples; instead of the half-dozen morphologic distinctions of the old language, English has a wealth of syntactic variety.

When, in Chapter VII, Jespersen develops for syntax the concepts of *nexus* and *junction*, each of which exists in several ranks, he makes clear something which hitherto has been badly confused. But one should be careful not to universalize. One should except, for instance, (as I believe Jespersen does) the relation of preposition to object in English, *with John*; the relation between these two words is neither nexus (as in *John sang*) nor junction (as in *big John*), but a third and peculiar one, like the others a historical product and like them possessed of all the philosophical validity in the world, or, better, of none at all. In this connection one fully agrees with the note on p. 187.[1] One should except also languages whose structure makes these terms unsuitable. In Algonquian our adnominal and adverbial qualifications (adjuncts) are morphologic features, and our actor, objects, and possessor appear as mere repetitions, appositional, as it were, of an anaphoric morphological mention; as, in Menomini: wākihkumān *crooked-knife*, kīhki'taw *he-runs-fast*, anämun pakāmäw inäniw *the-subsidiary-dog he-hit-the-subsidiary-one the-man* (i.e., the man hit the dog), anämun sakēpuk inäniw *the-subsidiary-dog the-subsidiary-one-bit-him the-man* (i.e., the dog bit the man), tsān utā'sikan *John his-knife*. (The word order is variable; the commonest is that here given.) From these forms an entirely different system from that of nexus and junction will be derived. We have yet to learn what features, if any, are common to all of those arbitrary systems of requirement which we call languages. The real content and use of speech-utterances is the same the world over, but their linguistically fixed features vary enormously.

Similarly, the logical definition, say, of proper nouns, might serve as a device for stating the meaning of this category after it has been defined by formal linguistic features, as, in English, by lack of article in the singular plus some other peculiarities, in Tagalog by article *si* instead of *aŋ*.

While such differences of theory will often cause a change of wording and sometimes lead to a different result, yet for the most part the statement of facts will be the same: and it is in the statement of fact, in the wealth and delicacy of observation, that one finds the merit of Jespersen's book, by which English grammar will be forever enriched. One can only hope that Jespersen's teachings will find their way into our schools.

[1] [The note in question in Jespersen's book reads as follows: 'I may perhaps take this opportunity of entering a protest against a certain kind of "national psychology" which is becoming the fashion in some German university circles, but which seems to me fundamentally unsound and unnatural. It affects case-syntax in the following passage: "Wenn nun der sächs. gen. bei zeitbestimmungen im lebendigen gebrauch ist, so deutet dies darauf hin, dass der zeit im englischen sprachbewusstsein eine bevorzugte rolle eingeräumt wird, was namentlich in gewissen berufskreisen wie bei verlegern herausgebern, zeitungsschreibern der fall sein wird" (Deutschbein SNS 289). In the same work, p. 269, the dative in G. *ich helfe meinen freunden* is taken as a sign of "ein persönliches vertrauensverhältnis statischen charakters zwischen mir und meinen freunden," but "wenn im ne. *to help* (*I help my friend*) mit dem akk. konstruiert wird, so verzichtet es darauf, das persönliche verhältnis von mir zu meinen freunde auszudrücken . . . das ne. besitzt demnach einen dynamischen grundcharakter, der auch in anderen zahlreichen erscheinungen der sprache bemerkbar ist." What does *dynamic* mean in that connexion? And how does Deutschbein know that the case after *help* is not a dative still? In *give my friend a book* he acknowledges *friend* as a dative, why not here? The form is the same. The function is exactly the same as in the corresponding OE. sentence *ic helpe minum freonde*, of which it forms an uninterrupted continuation, and which in its turn corresponds in every respect to G. *ich helfe meinem freunde*. Why not simply say that in Modern English it is neither accusative nor dative, and then leave out all conclusions about "personal," "dynamic," and "static" national characters?'—CFH]

# B24. Review of Lokotsch

1927. *Modern Philology* 24.489–491.

*Etymologisches Wörterbuch der amerikanischen (indianischen) Wörter im Deutschen, mit steter Berücksichtigung der englischen, spanischen und französischen Formen.* By KARL LOKOTSCH. (*Germanische Bibliothek* begründet von Wilhelm Streitberg†. *I. Sammlung germanischer Elementar- und Handbücher. IV. Reihe Wörterbücher:* sechster Band.) Heidelberg: Carl Winters Universitätsbuchhandlung, 1926.

After a brief Introduction, which lists the chief families of American languages, the author gives a hundred and fifty-odd German words of American origin with their meanings and the presumable American source words. As the author says (p. 7), the German words are, with few exceptions, not loan words, but unassimilated foreign words. The interesting things about them would be their pronunciation and graphic variants, and above all their history: through what languages they passed, when and whence (certainly not from American languages) they came into German, and, finally, their fortunes in German, e.g., where they occur and to what degree they have been assimilated. Except for the classical example of *Hängematte*, and a few fragmentary and amateurish indications, this information is absent. For instance, as to pronunciation: "SQUAW . . . das . . . mit einem offenen *o* wie in *fall* zu sprechen wäre, wird deutsch fälschlich wie *skwau* gesprochen"—that is, the Germans should speak a sound which does not exist in their language and are mistaken in not doing so. About the initial *sk* not a word. The author seems to be interested only in the one thing he could not possibly do, in identifying the American source. Even the authors of the *Handbook of American Indians North of Mexico* (Bureau of American Ethnology, *Bull. 30*), specialists who used not only printed but also manuscript material, were often unable to identify with precision the language and form of American source words. Lokotsch, by the way, does not seem to have used this book; compare, perhaps, his general view of things American, impertinently expressed on page 24.

In short, one fails to see what purpose this compilation can serve. Sound popularizing tries to lead the layman toward an understanding and appreciation of science, not to encourage his taste for the bizarre, irrelevant, and inaccurate. The thing that could be done (to tell the history of these words) the author does not attempt; the thing that could not be done he insists upon trying.

In the case of some of the Algonquian words, I can check the statements.

CHICAGO.—"Diese amerikanische Riesenstadt im Staate Illinois liegt am Flusse Chicago, der hier in den Michigansee mündet, und hat nach ihm ihren Namen." (The author has a weakness for this kind of thing.) "Der Flusz bildete früher übelriechende Sümpfe" (Is that so?) "und hiesz danach bei den umwohnenden Indianern *tschikagong*, d. h. 'bei dem Stinktiere,' aus *tschikak* 'Skunks' [Why plural?], wozu der Lokativ *tschikak-ong* oder *tschika-gong* [Punctilious distinction, when not even the name of the language is mentioned] lautet." The name is from some Central Algonquian dialect. The initial *t* given by Lokotsch has never existed, even in German usage; he got it by mistaking the English spelling of *Chicago*. On page 59 he transcribes the same word as Abnaki *segankw*. The real source of our name is probably a word something like Fox *cegāgōha* (*c* is English *sh*), "wild onion," in formation a diminutive of the word for "skunk," Fox *cegāgwa*; the Chicago River is named after this plant, common hereabouts. The Menomini (in whose language the word for "wild onion" is a longer derivative, *sikākŭhsyah*) misinterpreted the name as *sikākuh*, "skunk-place," and explain it by the story that a skunk was once seen swimming the Chicago River. Other tribes of cognate speech may have had the same folk-etymology, for it was familiar to William Jones (*Handbook*, s.v. "Chicago"). The name went through French, of course, whence its spelling.

MANITU.—The explanation cited of the Algonquian *manetōwa* is antiquated. The *ū*-sound of the European languages is the real problem; i.e., why did the French hear *ū* and write *ou*? If we knew more, this feature would probably identify the lending dialect. The older English records, which got the word without the intervention of French, have final *o* (see *Handbook*, s.v. "Manito").

MISSISSIPPI.—Why "delawarischen Ursprungs"? And why *mitsche*, "grosz," when *misi* does the work?

MOKASSIN.—German has the word from English, but Lokotsch quotes only the irrelevant French and Spanish forms. For the exact provenience, see *Handbook*, s.v. "Moccasin."

MONDAMIN.—Lokotsch translates *Maisstärke* by "Eng. cornflower," to which gratuitous bit of misinformation he adds a poetic reference to *Hiawatha*.

PEMIKAN.—The essential thing is not mentioned: preservation in grease. For this, as well as the correct form and derivation of the Cree word, see *Handbook*, s.v. 'Pemmican," to which may be added that Cree *pimihkēw*, "he makes grease," is in its turn a regular derivative from *pimiy*, "grease."

TOBOGGAN.—". . . musz indianischen Ursprungs sein, doch kann das Grundwort nicht genau angegeben werden: etwa *odabagan* 'Schlitten'" (language not named). This sudden diffidence is unnecessary, as the type *utāpākana*, "sled, travoie," is common in Algonquian. For a history of the European loan, see *Handbook*, *s.v.* "Toboggan."

TOTEM.—"indianischen Ursprungs"; of course Algonquian, e.g., Fox *netōtāma*, "my brother or sister,"[1] Menomini *nitōtäm*, "my totemic animal ancestor"; information in *Handbook*, *s.v.*

WIGWAM.—Eliot's erroneous form is repeated, in spite of *Handbook*, *s.v.* The type *wēkiwami* (Menomini *wēkiwam*, Eastern probably *wīgwām*) is widespread.

ESKIMOS (p. 65).—If the etymology here and in *Handbook*, *s.v.*, is correct, the source word was not of the type of Abnaki *esquimantsik* (which Lokotsch quotes without naming language or family), but of the type *ackimōwa* (*c* means Eng. *sh*), "raw-eater," as Cree *askimōw*; but the white man may have taught the Cree this word. If I have rightly understood a remark of W. Thalbitzer's, the Algonquian word for Eskimo is due to a folk-etymology.

---

[1] Ritual word, used, e.g., of the deceased, or of the kin of a deceased person.

# B25. Literate and Illiterate Speech

1927. *American Speech* 2:10.432–439 (July).

[Reprinted in Dell Hymes, *Language in Culture and Society* (New York, 1964), pp. 391–396.]

## I

Literate and illiterate speech in a language like English are plainly different. We find it easy, aside from occasional points of detail, to judge of "incorrect" or "faulty" locutions, "bad grammar," "mispronunciation," and the like. This, in fact, is the layman's chief interest in linguistics.

When we try, however, to define what we mean by these judgments, to state the causes of "mistakes," or to set up a standard, we run into great difficulties. The popular explanation of these matters is certainly wrong; scientific students of language have dealt little with them explicitly, somewhat more by implication, and never in a satisfactory way. In this paper I shall give some facts from a speech-community where conditions differ from ours to so great an extent as to provide a kind of check, and shall try to draw conclusions; I may say at the outset that these conclusions are neither decisive nor complete enough to be satisfactory.

## II

The popular explanation of "correct" and "incorrect" speech reduces the matter to one of knowledge versus ignorance. There is such a thing as correct English. An ignorant person does not know the correct forms; therefore he cannot help using incorrect ones. In the process of education one learns the correct forms and, by practice and an effort of will ("careful speaking"), acquires the habit of using them. If one associates with ignorant speakers, or relaxes the effort of will ("careless speaking"), one will lapse into the incorrect forms.

It would be easy, but would require much space, to show that these notions do not correspond to the facts. There is no fixed standard of "correct" English; one need only recall that no two persons speak alike, and that, take it as a whole, every language is constantly changing. At the time when we learn to speak we are all ignorant babies, yet many children of five or six years speak "correct" English. Even some ignorant adults speak "good" English; on the other hand, there are highly educated people, even teachers and professors, who speak "bad" English. All speaking, good or bad, is careless; only for a few minutes at a time can one speak "carefully," and when one does so, the result is by no means pleasing. In fatiguing effect and in ungracefulness, "careful" speaking is like walking a chalk-line or a tight-rope.

If we leave aside all this, there is one error in the popular view which is of special interest. The incorrect forms cannot be the result of ignorance or carelessness, for they are by no means haphazard, but, on the contrary, very stable. For instance, if a person is so ignorant as not to know how to say *I see it* in past time, we might expect him to use all kinds of chance forms, and, especially, to resort to easily formed locutions, such as *I did see it*, or to the addition of the regular past-time suffix: *I seed it*. But instead, these ignorant people quite consistently say *I seen it*. Now, it is evident that one fixed and consistent form will be no more difficult than another: a person who has learned *I seen* as the past of *I see* has learned just as much as one who says *I saw*. He has simply learned something different. Although most of the people who say *I seen* are ignorant, their ignorance does not account for this form of speech. On the other hand, I once knew a school-teacher who, when she spoke carefully, sometimes said *I have saw it*; in normal speech she said *I have seen it*. In short, what we find is not well-informed and regulated activity opposed to ignorant and careless, but rather a conflict of definite, fixed locutions, one of which, for some reason, is "good," while the others are "bad."

Mistaken as are the popular notions on this subject, they are interesting because they throw some light on our attitude to language. The popular explanation of incorrect language is simply the explanation of incorrect *writing*, taken over, part and parcel, to serve as an explanation of incorrect speech. It is the writing of every word for which a single form is fixed and all others are obviously wrong. It is the spelling of words that ignorant people, or better, unlettered people, do not know. It is writing that may be done carefully or carelessly, with evident results as to correctness. With all this it accords that popular comment on a wrong form of speech is often given in terms that properly apply to writing, not to speech; for instance, he who says *git* instead of *get*, or *ketch* instead of *catch*, is popularly said to be substituting one *letter* for another, to be mistaking the *spelling* of the word. In sum, the popular ideas about language apply very well to writing, but are irrelevant to speech.

Now, writing, of course, is merely a record of speech. Making this record is an activity very different from the activity of speaking. This is especially striking among us, since our writing is not entirely parallel with speech, but contains numbers of such spellings as *go* : *throw* : *sew* : *beau* : *though*, where different spellings represent one sound-type, and such as *though* : *through* : *bough* : *cough* : *rough*, where one spelling represents different sound-types. Writing, like telegraphy or shorthand, is an activity that deals with language, but it is quite different, far less practised and ingrained, far more superficial in our make-up, than speech. Until quite recently only very few people knew how to read and write; even today many peoples do not write their language. Writing is based on speech, not speech on writing.

The fact that almost anyone except a professed student of language explains matters of speech by statements which really apply only to writing, is of great psychologic interest. In infancy, when we learned to speak, we necessarily had no words with which to describe what we were doing. After we had learned to speak, we had no occasion to acquire such words or to make such a description. Consequently, as adults, we cannot state what we do when we talk: we are unconscious of the movements we make with our tongue or vocal cords, of the sound-pattern or the grammatical structure of our speech.[1] Writing, on the other hand, we learned after we knew how to speak; in fact, we learned it through the medium of speech. The teacher told us, in words, what to do, and trained us to state it; we learned the names of the letters, and to spell words, that is, to state which letters we use for a given word. Consequently, ever after, we are able to describe what we do when we write: we are conscious of our movements in writing, and of the forms and succession of the letters. It is on the basis of such contrasts that some psychologists make out a very good case for the view that a "conscious" action is simply one which we are able to describe in words. Whether one accepts this view or not, it is easy to see why a normal person, when asked to explain something about language, really talks about writing; to see why it took generations of students to develop a set of technical terms about speech, and why it now takes a long time to learn the use of these terms, in case one wants to enter upon the scientific study of language.

### III

The popular view of "good" and "bad" English has led us a good way round and has shown us some interesting outlooks, but it has brought us back to where we started. The scientific view, though not satisfactory, will bring us farther. It has the advantage of being based on a more extensive

[1] This appears in the difficulty with which schoolchildren learn the few and fairly superficial facts of English grammar that have found a place in the school curriculum. To give anything like a full description of even his native language is a difficult undertaking for any linguist.

survey of various languages and of their history than any one person could make; also it has the advantage of a methodical approach. This last means that we shall not operate with the terms "good" and "bad" language, or their equivalents, since it is precisely these which we are trying to define.

We observe, to begin with, that in every group of people, savage or civilized, ignorant or educated, the infants learn, by imitation, the speech-habits of the older people round them. Even the child learning to speak does not use haphazard forms: he approaches more and more closely the forms used by his elders, and finally talks just like them. Speech defects after early childhood are individual abnormalities; aside from these, the individual's peculiarities of speech are minute. Through the rest of his life he seems to speak uniformly, so far as an observer could note.

History, however, shows that there is a constant and gradual, imperceptibly slow, change in the language of every community. This change is uniform within a group of people who are constantly talking with one another, say, within a single village. But where communication is less frequent, the changes are sure to be different. For instance, if people of the same speech settle so as to form two mountain villages, with a big valley between, then, in a few generations, different changes will have taken place in the two groups. In time they may find it hard to understand each other when they meet; if they stay apart long enough, they may finally be speaking mutually unintelligible languages. When some of the Angles and Saxons left the Continent in the fifth century A.D., they spoke the same language as the less enterprising members of their tribes who stayed at home. Since then, however, both the language of the emigrants and that of the stay-at-homes have changed, and, since there has necessarily been little communication across the North Sea, they have changed in different ways, until today an Englishman and a Dutchman or a North German do not understand each other's speech. In this way, wherever there are lines across which communication is hampered,—water, mountains, deserts, political boundaries, and the like,—we find differences of speech, even though history may tell us that once upon a time, say, at the original settlement, there was uniformity.

Now, as civilization progresses, the population grows denser, means of communication improve, and petty political boundaries lose their importance. More and more often people from different parts of the country, speaking different local dialects, have occasion to converse with each other. They soon learn, on these occasions, to avoid forms of speech that are misleading or unintelligible to the other fellow. Usually, too, there is some city which serves as a center for the larger activities of the nation. The contact of persons from different regions occurs more in this city than elsewhere; the provincial has more occasion to speak with natives of this city than with speakers of any one other dialect. In the history of

English, London played this part. Thus there arises a *Standard Language* of more or less definite form. Finally, civilization leads to the widespread use of writing. Since writing is a very deliberate activity, it is easy to adapt one's writing to the requirements of wider communication: one avoids provincialisms and, if there is a metropolis, imitates the writing of the city. Thus it happens that the *Standard Language* is most definite and best observed in its written form, the *Literary Language*. The next step is popular education: children are taught in schools to write and, if possible, to speak in the forms of the Standard Language.

It is at this point that the science of language gives its explanation, if I understand it aright, of "good" and "bad" language. The child, growing up in the province, say, in some mountain village, learns to speak in the local dialect. In time, to be sure, this local dialect will take in more and more forms from the standard language, but so far in the history of mankind complete standardization seems nowhere to have taken place. The child, then, does not speak the standard language as his native tongue. It is only when he reaches school, long after his speech-habits are formed, that he is taught the standard language. No language is like the native speech that one learned at one's mother's knee; no one is ever perfectly sure in a language afterward acquired. "Mistakes" in language are simply dialect forms carried into the standard language. The "bad" English for *I saw it* is not any haphazard error, but the perfectly fixed and definite form, *I seen it*, the form used in most American dialects of English. So far as age is concerned, *Do you want out?* is more respectable than *Do you want to go out?*—but the latter happens to be the form of Standard English: questions of age, of logical or esthetic value, or even of consistency within the system of the language are irrelevant. Dialect forms in the standard language are "bad."

Since only part of the population lives in the metropolis (when there is one, as in England), and since, even there, different social classes communicate little, and since the standard language, closely tied up with the literary language, tends to become archaic (that is, to ignore the changes of the last generations), it results that only relatively few children speak Standard Language as their real mother tongue. Almost everybody's standard speech will show dialect coloring and occasional lapses into dialect.

Sometimes a large dialect group will re-assert itself; thus, an Englishman will say that all Americans speak bad Standard English (that is, dialectally colored Standard), but we, finding the British standard too unlike our native forms, have developed a standard of our own, which deviates decidedly in pronunciation and to some extent in word-forms and constructions. The situation is all the more complicated in that we have no one center, like London. But, with the literary language in its usual function as a kind of guide to the standard speech, we have worked out in practice a fairly definite American standard, and are able, except for small details, to agree on what is and what is not " good,"—that is, Standard,— American English.

Beside mixing dialect into standard speech, we are likely to distort the latter in some other ways. Native speakers of dialect are prone, once in a while, to speak carefully, that is, to worry about their speech, and go too far in substituting school forms for native forms. A person whose native speech says *I see* : *I seen* : *I have seen*, after learning in school to say *I saw*, may occasionally go too far in substituting *saw*'s for *seen*'s and say *I have saw it*,—a "hyper-urban" form. Knowing that the standard language is close to the written form, we are likely to go too far in guiding ourselves by the latter, for instance, to pronounce a *t*-sound in *often*,—"spelling-pronunciation." Or again, many words common in writing are rare in speech; when, for once, we speak them, we may violate the habit of those who know the spoken form. Sometimes the spoken tradition of a fairly rare word in this way dies out: *author*, *Gothic* used to be pronounced *autor*, *Gotic*; the *th*-sound is due to lapse of the oral tradition.

These details could be elaborated, but in the main the scientific diagnosis of "bad" language seems to be: standard language with dialect features. In the local dialect one native speaker would thus be as good as another, and "mistakes" or "bad" forms impossible.

## IV

According to the scientists' view of the matter, then, a small community of people speaking a uniform language, and above all, a community without schools or writing, would not distinguish "good" and "bad" language. When I first studied such a community, I found, to my great surprise, that these distinctions were made, if perhaps less frequently than among us.

The Menomini Indians of Wisconsin, a compact tribe of some 1700 people, speak a language without dialectal differences and have no writing. Yet the Menomini will say that one person speaks well and another badly, that such-and-such a form of speech is incorrect and sounds bad, and another too much like a shaman's preaching or archaic ("the way the old, old people talked").

To a surprisingly large extent, considering how slight my acquaintance with their language, I was able to share in these judgments of the Menomini. A foreigner who recorded English as though it were an unwritten language, might obtain several forms of a locution, as, for instance,

> You'd better do that;
> You had better do that;

You would better do that;
You ought better do that.

His written record would probably fail to give him any distinction between the value of these forms. But if he listened to us long enough, and if fortune favored him, he might learn that the normal good form is the first; that the second is more deliberate and elevated; that the other two strike us as unidiomatic, vulgar, pedantic, or what you will,—in short, as incorrect. So in Menomini we have, for "What are you laughing at?"

> wä´ki' wä´h-ayä´niyan?
> wä´ki' ayāyō´sinaman?
> tā´ni' wähtā´hpiyan?

The first form is illiterate, childish, stupid; the second is normal; the third elevated, poetic, archaizing.

Some people say tsī´hpin instead of kī´spin for "if"; this sounds as bad as *git* and *ketch* in English.

Here is a sketch of the linguistic position of some of the speakers whom I knew best:[2]

Red-Cloud-Woman, a woman in the sixties, speaks a beautiful and highly idiomatic Menomini. She knows only a few words of English, but speaks Ojibwa and Potawatomi fluently, and, I believe, a little Winnebago. Linguistically, she would correspond to a highly educated American woman who spoke, say, French and Italian in addition to the very best type of cultivated, idiomatic English.

Her husband, Storms-At-It, a shaman, is half Potawatomi, and speaks both languages. Of English he knows not even the cuss-words. In Menomini he often uses unapproved,—let us say, ungrammatical,—forms which are current among bad speakers; on the other hand, slight provocation sets him off into elevated speech, in which he uses what I shall describe as spelling-pronunciations, together with long ritualistic compound words and occasional archaisms. He corresponds, perhaps, to a minister who does not put on much "dog," speaks very colloquially in ordinary life, but is at the same time very intelligent and able to preach or exhort in the most approved semi-biblical language.

Stands-Close, a man in the fifties, speaks only Menomini. His speech, though less supple and perfect than Red-Cloud-Woman's, is well up to standard. It is interlarded with words and constructions that are felt to be archaic, and are doubtless in part really so, for his father was known as an oracle of old traditions.

Bird-Hawk, a very old man, who has since died, spoke only Menomini,

---

[2] As some of these persons are living, I give only an English translation of their Indian names.

possibly also a little Ojibwa. As soon as he departed from ordinary conversation, he spoke with bad syntax and meagre, often inept vocabulary, yet with occasional archaisms.

White-Thunder, a man round forty, speaks less English than Menomini, and that is a strong indictment, for his Menomini is atrocious. His vocabulary is small; his inflections are often barbarous; he constructs sentences on a few threadbare models. He may be said to speak no language tolerably. His case is not uncommon among younger men, even when they speak but little English. Perhaps it is due, in some indirect way, to the impact of the conquering language.

Little-Doctor, a half-breed, who died recently in his sixties, spoke English with some Menomini faults, but with a huge vocabulary and a passion for piling up synonyms. In Menomini, too, his vocabulary was vast; often he would explain rare words to his fellow-speakers. In both languages his love of words sometimes upset his syntax, and in both languages he was given to over-emphatic diction, of the type of spelling pronunciation.

Little-Jerome, a half-breed, now in the fifties, is a true bilingual. He speaks both English (the dialectal type of the region) and Menomini with racy idiom, which he does not lose even when translating in either direction. He contrasts strikingly with the men (usually somewhat younger) who speak little English and yet bad Menomini.

To recite the features of good and bad Menomini would be to annotate almost every item of the grammar, and many of the lexicon.

In the pronunciation of good speakers, Menomini has, of course, its typical cadence and glide-sounds. Young people who speak English often diverge in Anglicizing the pronunciation. Older bad speakers exaggerate certain glide-sounds and miss some of the cadences, confusing short and long vowels. Over-elegant speech, on the other hand,—as from the lips of shamans or of the well-educated Little-Doctor,—displaces the stress-accent toward the end of a word, and gives full long quantity to vowels which in good, idiomatic speech are not entitled to it. This last feature is a fairly close parallel to our "spelling-pronunciations," such as the full form *fore-head* for *forrid* and the now perhaps accepted *waist-coat* and *seam-stress*, for *weskit* and *semstress*. Only, there is no writing in Menomini, hence no spelling to explain "spelling-pronunciations." Sometimes there is a clear analogic basis. Thus the word ninā́tumik "he calls me" may be distorted to ninā́tōmik or even to ninātṓmik; the ō being the long vowel that corresponds in Menomini to the short ŭ. Now, these distorted forms are probably due to the influence of other inflectional forms which properly have the long ō, such as nina-natṓmik "he will call me".

But in other cases this explanation seems not to hold, as when atä́himin "strawberry" is in spelling-pronunciation atä́hēmḗ'n, where the long ē corresponds to short ĭ.

As a whole, this phenomenon is due to the fact that Menomini has a living morphologic alternation of long and short vowels; in emphatic or rhetorical speech the long vowels are carried into forms where normally they do not belong.

In inflection, Menomini, like the other Algonquian languages, has an *obviative* form for subsidiary third persons. Thus, if our story is of a man meeting another man and of the ensuing occurrences, our first man will be spoken of in the normal third person form, and the other man in the obviative form. The good Menomini speaker has no such difficulty as we have with our single pronoun *he*. But bad Menomini speakers profit not at all from this distinction, but get as tangled in their two forms as a bad speaker of English with his one ambiguous *he*.

Whatever is hearsay and not the speaker's own experience has the predicate verb or particle in a special *quotative* form. Hence in traditional narrative all predicates are in this form, unless they be actual thoughts or speeches of the actors in the story, or parenthetic insertions of the narrator; these exceptions, indeed, make possible some nice shadings of sense and style. In ordinary speech even the bad speaker will use his quotatives correctly, but as soon as he embarks on a longer story, he may lapse into nonquotatives for whole sentences at a time, which make the story sound as though he had been present when it took place.

Many archaisms of the medicine-man's language are pinchbeck,—distortions in the direction of Ojibwa, or of Triballian. Others are genuine, as comparison with related languages will show. Still others are circumlocutions. No doubt the starting-point for these was in cases where the normal word was tabu during ritual. The Algonquian word for "bear" is lost in Menomini, and is replaced by a word which used to mean "little animal; in ritual other terms are used, such as "ant-eater," "berry-gatherer," "Bruin." But the habit has been extended to words where there is no tabu; the shaman uses long compounds or derivatives, such as "extensive woman" or "grandmother-expanse" for "earth," and "standing-men" for "trees," or "eternal men" for "stones."

## V

It would be useless to seek the criterion of good and bad Menomini by gauging the alternative forms as to consistency with the general system of the language, for Menomini, like English, contains many irregularities. It is often the irregular form that is the proper one, just as in English *You had better do it* is preferred to *You ought better (to) do it*, although the latter accords with the general forms of our syntax. Similarly, *forrid* is preferred to the logically more explicable *fore-head*. On the other hand, the irregular form may be less acceptable than a regular one: *I dove* is not so good as *I dived, I ain't* not so good as *I'm not.* A good Menomini speaker will say for "medicine-man" maskīhkī′wineniw, a form which has the accent on a syllable that in almost any other word would be incapable of stress, and has vowel-shortening in the last element; yet only a bad speaker will use the logical combination of the words "medicine" and "man," and speak the horrid-sounding maskī′hkiw-inä′niw.

The nearest approach to an explanation of "good" and "bad" language seems to be this, then, that, by a cumulation of obvious superiorities, both of character and standing, as well as of language, some persons are felt to be better models of conduct and speech than others. Therefore, even in matters where the preference is not obvious, the forms which these same persons use are felt to have the better flavor. This may be a generally human state of affairs, true in every group and applicable to all languages, and the factor of Standard and Literary Language versus dialect may be a superadded secondary one.

# B26. On Some Rules of Panini

1927. *Journal of the American Oriental Society* 47.61–70.

## I

In the first chapter of the first book of his Grammar, Pāṇini sets up the term pronoun (*sarvanāman*) as a designation of certain words. He does this so that in other passages he may, without repeating the list of these words, describe their inflectional and other peculiarities (e.g., dative singular masculine and neuter, pronominal *sarvasmai*, as opposed to nominal *pade*, *devāya*, 7, 1, 14). These passages are of course listed in the Indices of Boehtlingk's second edition (Leipzig, 1887).[1]

The rules defining the term pronoun read as follows (1, 1):

| | |
|---|---|
| 27. *sarvādīni sarvanāmāni,* | 27. *sarva* etc. are pronouns, |
| 28. *vibhāṣā diksamāse bahuvrī-hau,* | 28. option in direction-compound exocentric, |
| 29. *na bahuvrīhau,* | 29. not in exocentric, |
| 30. *tṛtīyāsamāse,* | 30. instrumental-compound, |
| 31. *dvaṁdve ca,* | 31. and copulative, |
| 32. *vibhāṣā jasi,* | 32. option before nom. pl. *-as,* |
| 33. *prathamacaramatayālpār-dhakatipayanemāś ca,* | 33. and *prathama, carama, -taya, alpa, ardha, katipaya, nema.* |
| 34. *pūrvaparāvaradakṣiṇotta-rāparādharāṇi vyavasthāyām asaṁjñāyām,* | 34. *pūrva, para, avara, dakṣiṇa, uttara, apara, adhara* in spatial relation not name, |
| 35. *svam ajñātidhanākhyāyām,* | 35. *sva* not in kinsman or property appellative, |
| 36. *antaraṁ bahiryogopasaṁ-vyānayoḥ.* | 36. *antara* in conjunction with outside and undergarment. |

The List (*gaṇa*) Sarva Etc. that goes with Rule 27 reads, with Boehtlingk's numbering, as follows:

1. *sarva*; 2. *viśva*; 3. *ubha*; 4. *ubhaya*.

---

[1] Apart from Pāṇini himself and his commentators, my obligation is to Boehtlingk's indices and to the writings of B. Liebich: *Pāṇini* (Leipzig, 1891); *Zwei Kapitel der Kāśikā* (Breslau, 1892); *Candra-Vṛtti* (*AKM* 14, Leipzig, 1918); *Zur Einführung in die indische Sprachwissenschaft*, I–IV (Heidelberg *SB*, 1919 ff.).

5. *ḍ-atara*; 6. *ḍ-atama*; 7. *itara*; 8. *anya*; 9. *anyatara*.
10. *tvá*; 11. *tva*; 12. *nema*; 13. *sama*; 14. *sima*; 15. *pūrva-parā-'vara-dakṣiṇo-'ttarā-'parā-'dharāṇi vyavasthāyām asaṁjñāyām*; 16. *svam ajñātidhanākhyāyām*; 17. *antaraṁ bahiryo-gopasaṁvyānayoh*.
18. *tyad*; 19. *tad*; 20. *yad*; 21. *etad*; 22. *adas*; 23. *idam*; 24. *eka*. 25. *dvi*; 26. *yuṣmad*; 27. *asmad*; 28. *bhavat-u*; 29. *kim*.

Bhaṭṭojīdīkṣita, *Siddhāntakaumudī* (ed. Vasu, Allahabad, n. d.) places 7 after 9, 22 after 23, and reads *tvat* for 10. This last variant is mentioned by Jayāditya, *Kāśikā* (my copy is a reprint of the Benares 1876–8 edition), which otherwise agrees with Boehtlingk's reading.

The traditional interpretation of these rules, as given, e.g., in the two books just named, and, except for one detail, accepted by Boehtlingk, is as follows:

(*a*) Whatever word is designated as a pronoun will nevertheless not be a pronoun (i.e., lack pronominal characteristics) in an exocentric compound, in an instrumental determinative compound, and in a copulative compound; except that it may (optionally) have pronominal characteristics in an exocentric compound of points of the compass (e.g. *northeast*) and in the nominative plural masculine (in the other genders the nominal and pronominal inflections here coincide) of a copulative compound.

(*b*) Designated as pronouns are the words in the List *Sarva* Etc.; numbers 15, 16, 17 with the limitations there stated. To this constituency is to be *added* the fact that the first six words in Rule 33 (which are not otherwise treated as pronouns) optionally have pronoun character in the nominative plural masculine, e.g. *prathame* beside *prathamāḥ*. And from this constituency is to be *subtracted* the fact that (12) *nema* and the words under 15, 16, 17 (in the senses there stated; in other senses they are not pronouns) optionally lack pronoun character in the nominative plural masculine, e.g. *nemāḥ* beside *neme*, *pūrvāḥ* beside *pūrve*.

In the case of (17) *antara* the restriction means that this word is a pronoun when it is a synonym of *outside* and in the sense of *undergarment*.

## II

What first strikes one in this passage is the repetitious and clumsy treatment of the words in 15, 16, 17 of the List. They are there cited not in stem form, but as inflected neuters, and restrictions of meaning are added, contrary to the usual form of the Lists. The option for nom. pl. masc. is stated by repeating in Rules 34, 35, 36 not only the entire section of the List, but also the restrictions of meaning,—in contrast with Pāṇini's usual elegant brevity. No wonder that Kātyāyana's one comment on Rule 34 is, "And needlessness of repetitive citation in the Text of Rules of *avara* etc., owing to reading in the Text of Lists." (I cite from S. D. Kudāla's edition of Patañjali's *Mahābhāṣya*, vol. 1, Nirnaya Sagar Press, Bombay 1917, which contains also Kaiyaṭa's *Pradīpa*, Nāgeśa's *Uddyota*, and selections from a *Chāyā*, commentary.)

Patañjali tries to discover what Pāṇini meant to indicate by this unwonted repetition. Did he mean to set up the restrictions under which these words have pronoun character? No, for that has been attained by the List. Did he mean to show that these words are not to be included when he tells us (5, 3, 2) that (25) *dvi* etc. are in certain cases excepted from pronominal treatment? (We interrupt to ask why anyone could be tempted to include 15, 16, 17 in a statement about "25 and the following"; of this more, immediately.) No, says Patañjali, for Pāṇini permits himself exceptions in matters of sequence. Pāṇini's real intent, he concludes, was to show us, by a repetition which otherwise would be purposeless, that the words in 15, 16, 17 and Rules 34, 35, 36 belong with Rules 32 and 33, i.e., have option of nominal form in the nom. pl. masc.,— e.g., *pūrvāḥ* beside *pūrve*.

The second of the suppositions which Patañjali rejects would be intelligible only if in the List 15, 16, 17 came after (25) *dvi*, etc. Only if that were the order could anyone suppose, even for a moment, that they were included in the "*dvi* etc." of Rule 5, 3, 2, and only then could one suppose, be it mistakenly, that Pāṇini's repetition was meant to indicate that the words in 15, 16, 17 constitute a special group and are not to be involved when an exception is stated for (25) *dvi* etc. And, indeed, Kaiyaṭa tells us that by some scholars (18) *tyad* and the following (including therefore (25) *dvi* and its successors) are read before (15) *pūrva* and the following. This shows us that since Patañjali's time the order of the List has been changed.

Patañjali's reason for rejecting this second possible motive is of interest. The reason is that when Pāṇini at 5, 3, 2 makes a statement about "*dvi* etc." this need not include the subsequent *pūrva* and its followers, for Pāṇini permits himself exceptions in matters of sequence. The Master, says Patañjali, has given us a formal indication of this by making an obvious and otherwise inexplicable exception to the sequence announced in 8, 2, 1. This rule says that from there to the end of the Grammar each rule is to be taken as uneffected with regard to preceding rules. Yet, at 8, 3, 13 he gives a rule which can apply only if the subsequent rule 8, 4, 41 be taken as already effected, and apply within just limits only if 8, 4, 53 be taken as already effected. He points out that Kātyāyana recognizes this in his comment on 8, 3, 13.

The motive which Patañjali finally attributes to Pāṇini seems inadequate. If Pāṇini meant to tell us that the words in 15, 16, 17 allowed of nominal nom. pl. masc., he could have added the word "*pūrva*-etc." to Rule 33.

He would not even have had to specify the extent of "*pūrva*-etc.", since these words stood at the end of the List. Kātyāyana seems to have the better of the argument: his objection is valid.

It is noteworthy that Kātyāyana cites our words not as "*pūrva* etc.", but as "*avara* etc." Kaiyaṭa says that he (or rather, Patañjali in paraphrasing him) does this *prakārārtham* "for the sake of the special meaning" (i.e., to symbolize that Rules 34, 35, 36 are *avara* "posterior" to the reading of the same words in the List, which is *pūrva* "preceding"). Nāgeśa, however, says that in reality Kātyāyana says "*avara* etc." because *avara* ought properly to precede, since its syllables are short (Kātyāyana on Pāṇini 2, 2, 34) and because it begins in a vowel and ends in short *a* (Pāṇini 2, 2, 23: the edition reads *ajādyantatvāt*, for *ajādyadantatvāt*).

Patañjali touches upon the peculiar form of Kātyāyana's citation. He opens his discussion of Kātyāyana's critique by asking: How do we know that the Text of Lists comes first and that therefore the reading of 34 in the Text of Rules is a repetition? By the symbolism that in the former we have "*pūrva* etc.", that is, "preceding etc." and in the latter "*avara* etc.", that is, "following etc."? No, for in the latter, too, we have "*pūrva* etc." Yet it is true that the Lists come first, the Rules second. The Master indicates this to us by his later reference (7, 1, 16) to "the nine beginning with *pūrva*."—That is, the fact that Pāṇini says "nine" decides for Patañjali that the List is meant, since only there does *pūrva* head a group of nine words, and since the mention of "nine" could have no other motive than to refer us explicitly to the List: what with the final position of "*pūrva* etc." in the List, the word "nine" would otherwise be superfluous. The fact that Pāṇini's reference is to the List and not to the Rules apparently decides for Patañjali that the List is to be read first.

This shows that Patañjali, at any rate, read *pūrva* and not *avara* as the first word in Rule 34. We shall find reason to believe that this was Pāṇini's own reading. Accordingly, Kātyāyana's "*avara* etc." remains unintelligible except as a laconic indication of a flaw, namely that Pāṇini's wording disagrees with the rules of order in copulative compounds (as above cited from Nāgeśa). From Pāṇini's general practice it appears that he did not begin his rule with *avara* (or with one of the other words with initial vowel) because to do so would have added a syllable (though not a mora) to the length of his rule; he arranges his words so as to merge or elide as many vowels as possible. Beyond this, I cannot account for the order in which Pāṇini cites these stems.

### III

Beside the repetition, the strange form of numbers 15, 16, 17 in the List, their historic change of place, and the later reference with "nine," our rules contain several peculiarities which the commentators do not mention. Why does Rule 33 cite its words in the masculine, when the normal form of citation is neuter (Rules 34, 35, 36)? Why does the word *ca* "and" stand in Rule 33? The commentators ignore these points, probably because their discussion of Pāninean methods had worked out the principles that the gender in which Pānini cites words is not necessarily significant, and that the placing of *ca* "and" does not necessarily indicate the end of an enumeration. At least, these decisions are given by Nāgojī (Nāgeśa) in his *Paribhāṣenduśekhara*, Numbers 73 and 78 (Kielhorn's translation, Bombay Sanskrit Series, No. 2, 1868–74).

Finally,—a point which lay outside the view of the ancients,—in the light of historical linguistics the doctrine of the rules as they are traditionally interpreted is most surprising. In the first six words of Rule 33 we see the lapse, widespread in Indo-European languages, of nominal words into pronominal inflection, especially in the nom. pl. masc. In Latin and Greek this has, of course, involved all the *o*-stems (and gone on even to the *ā*-feminines); in Germanic it has involved the whole strong adjective declension. The pronominal form of the nom. pl. masc. is favored also in the copulative compounds, Rule 32. But in the case of *nema* in Rule 33 and of the words in Rules 34, 35, 36 we are taught the opposite: *nema* has pronominal forms throughout, but in the nom. pl. masc. may have nominal form, *nemāḥ* beside *neme*; and the other words have pronominal forms throughout (except for an option in the ablative and locative singular, masculine and neuter, 7, 1, 16), but in the nom. pl. masc. also nominal form, e.g., *pūrvāḥ* beside *pūrve*.

## IV

Pānini and Kātyāyana recorded the facts of a standard colloquial language spoken by them as their mother-tongue and as the medium of everyday life; if, like ours, it was archaic in comparison with the normal dialects of the time, it was, like ours, native to many speakers, who with a little training were able to decide what could and what could not be spoken. The later grammarians, including, I venture to say, Patañjali, were in no position to criticize the facts thus given by their predecessors; for them Sanskrit was a second language, spoken to be sure, but preserved and by them acquired through a literary tradition, much as was classical Latin for a learned Italian of, say, the fifth century A.D. They could judge only of the form of Pānini's presentation. What is more, the text of Pānini was canonical. If Patañjali found a repetition in our passage, it was his task to divine what the Master could have meant by this unusual proceeding. If he found a discrepancy in the order of the rules in the Eighth Book, he could at best take it as an intentional and formal indication on the part of the Master, to the effect that exceptions of order occur in the Text. He could not, like Boehtlingk, see in the order of 8, 3, 13 and 8, 4, 41 one of the slips inevitable in a human construction of such size and complexity. He could not, as would any modern linguist, conclude from the order of 8, 3, 13 and 8, 4, 53 that Pāṇini did not concern himself with such far-fetched theoretical possibilities as someone's taking it into his head to say *śvaliḍ ḍhaukate*. For later students, Pāṇini, Kātyāyana, and Patañjali were the Three Seers, and especially the ultimate interpretation of Patañjali was canonically binding. If Nāgojī found a single passage where, under Patañjali's interpretation, the gender in which a word is cited is indifferently chosen, or a single passage where, under Patañjali's interpretation, the word "and" has no particular bearing, then he was obliged to conclude that Pāṇini could not have intended these features to be generally significant.

V

Probably the peculiarities of our passage are to be explained as follows.

The citation of the words in Rule 33 is in masculine form because it is only the masculine nominative plural that is involved in the rule. This helps to set off these words from the following, and incidentally saves a short vowel.

The word *ca* "and" in Rule 33 has the same value as in Rule 31 and in many other passages of the Grammar: it is used in the last of a series of (two or more) rules that are additively coordinated. This habit, taken from ordinary speech, serves in the Grammar to show where such an enumerative series ends. Thus, in Rule 31 "and in a copulative," the word "and" shows that "in a copulative" is the last of the three places where *sarva* etc. are not pronouns. Technically, we may phrase this by saying that the word "and" shows the continued validity (*anuvṛtti*) up to this point, and the cessation of validity (*nivṛtti*) at this point of the word *na* "not" in Rule 29. Similarly in Rule 33: the word "and" concludes the series of rules (two in number) which tell where option in the nom. pl. masc. is given. In technical language: the word "and" in Rule 33 marks the continued validity in this rule of the words "option before nom.-pl. -*as*" of Rule 32 and the cessation of this validity at the end of Rule 33. This indication is reinforced by quoting the words in masculine form. Thus the subsequent rules, 34, 35, 36, have nothing to do with option in the nom. pl.

The words in these subsequent rules were not intended by Pāṇini to stand in the List. These three rules simply state that these words, with these restrictions of sense, are pronouns. These words are treated in the Text and not in the List because they require restriction: they are pronouns only in the meanings here given. After Pāṇini's time and before Kātyāyana's, some tinkerer added them bodily, without reducing them to stem form, and with the statements of restriction, to the end of the List *Sarva* Etc. There Kātyāyana and Patañjali, and, according to Kaiyaṭa, some later students found them. This corruption of the List involved not only the repetition which Kātyāyana criticized and Patañjali tried to explain, but also another discrepancy: Rule 5, 3, 2 excludes "*dvi* etc." from a characteristic of pronouns which almost any page of Sanskrit shows to hold good for *pūrva* and its group (adverbial forms like *pūrvatra*). Patañjali explains this, as we have seen, as an exception to order. A later arranger of the List solved this difficulty by moving these final numbers of the List back to a place before 18 *tyad*; here they no longer interfered with "*dvi* etc." of Rule 5, 3, 2 or with rules about "*tyad* etc."

Pāṇini's reference at 7, 1, 16 to "the nine beginning with *pūrva*" would have lacked the mention of "nine" and would have read simply "*pūrva* etc.", had he intended these words to stand, as Patañjali found them, at the end of the List *Sarva* Etc. We have seen how Patañjali tries to explain the mention of the number "nine." In reality, 7, 1, 16 refers to Pāṇini's Text at 1, 1, 34, 35, 36, and the number "nine" is necessary to secure inclusion of all the words. This reference shows, incidentally, that for Pāṇini *pūrva*, and not *avara*, actually stood first in Rule 34.

The word *nema* in Rule 33 repeats number 12 of the List. The traditional interpretation, then, has it that the first six words in Rule 33, not being in the List, are normally nouns, but are in the nom. pl. masc. capable of pronominal inflection; but that *nema*, being in the List, is normally a pronoun, but is in the nom. pl. masc. capable of nominal inflection. Not to repeat the other arguments, one may surmise that if Pāṇini had meant this, he would have put *nema* into a separate rule. Probably *nema* did not stand in Pāṇini's List; he treated it in Rule 33 on a par with the six other words there cited: in Pāṇini's language *nema* had nominal character except for the option of a pronominally formed nom. pl. masc. In Sanskrit literature the word *nema* is little used, certainly not enough to carry on a (literary) tradition of its Pāṇinean inflection. Later grammarians were dependent for information on this point upon their interpretation of Pāṇini's statements and upon whatever examples they could find in old books. Probably some scholar who knew pronominal forms of the word in Vedic texts (perhaps *nemasmin* RV 10, 48, 10) inserted it in the List.

Boehtlingk in his edition of Pāṇini and more fully in the Petersburg Dictionary, *s. v. antara*, suggests the correct interpretation of *bahiryoga-* in Rule 36: "in conjunction with 'outside'" means "in contrast with 'outside.'" The word *yoga* is used in the same way at 4, 1, 48; everywhere else in Pāṇini it means "in (actual) context with" so that the only possible alternative meaning of *bahiryoga-* would be "in connection with the word *bahiḥ*, 'outside.'" There is no parallel for Kaiyaṭa's interpretation, "as a synonym of 'outside,'" which was taken over by Bhaṭṭojī and Jayāditya.

This faulty interpretation does not go back to Kātyāyana and Patañjali. The former says: "The mention of 'undergarment' is purposeless, because this effect is attained by *bahiryoga.*—No, for, rather, it has the purpose of applying to a pair of petticoats and the like." Patañjali expands these remarks, rejecting the latter. The Chāyā points out that this discussion was necessitated by the absence of the word *ākhyā* "appellative" in the rule, which otherwise could have been interpreted like Rule 35, giving "in an appellative for *undergarment.*" Now, Kātyāyana's second sentence is obscure, and Patañjali's interpretation of it seems far-fetched,[2] but so much is clear, that these scholars did not know *antara* in a sense of "outer," but interpreted *bahiryoga* as "inner."

## VI

In our view, then, the List *Sarva* Etc. should be read without (12) *nema*, (15) *pūrva* etc., (16) *sva*, (17) *antara*; and the Rules would be interpreted thus:

(a)  As interpreted by the ancients.

(b)  Designated as pronouns are the words in the List. Also the words *pūrva, para, avara, dakṣiṇa, uttara, apara, adhara* in the sense of a spatial or temporal relation when not specialized appellatives; the word *sva* when not an appellative for "kinsman" or "property"; the word *antara* when meaning "inner" or "undergarment." (Later, at 7, 1, 16, we learn that these nine words have optionally nominal inflection in certain forms; the

---

[2] Kātyāyana's remarks may perhaps be interpreted thus: In his and Pāṇini's speech one could say "an inner" for "an undergarment." K. questions whether this need be specially stated, since this usage would seem to be included under the definition "in contrast with outside" (Vārtika 1), but decides that, after all, it needs to be stated, since "an inner" refers to either of two petticoats or the like, worn one over the other, while "in contrast with outside" might be taken as appropriate only to the inside one (Vārtika 2).

This, however, is not Patañjali's interpretation. He paraphrases the two Vārtika's and explains and refutes the second by saying: Where this is not known: which is the inside one (*antarīyam*) and which the outside one (*uttarīyam*), here, too, that person who has first made examination, for him it is decided: this is the inner and this the outer. (Kaiyaṭa's gloss: In the case of a pair of petticoats of equal size and not donned, it is not known whether a given one is the outer or inner.—"Here too"; as soon as the identity of the undergarment is determined by forethought, then, too, it is a case of "conjunction with outside"). Thus it appears that Patañjali's interpretation of Kātyāyana's second Vārtika is: An undergarment is still an undergarment even when not recognized as belonging inside. His refutation is that, as soon as one recognizes it as an undergarment, one also recognizes that it belongs inside. He has underestimated Kātyāyana's point, probably because the expression "an inner" for an undergarment was unfamiliar to him.

A different interpretation is quoted by Kaiyaṭa: But others say: The word "and so forth" is included in the Vārtika 2; this means that in the case of a set of three or four petticoats, since the third and fourth are not in "conjunction with outside," the word "undergarment" deserves separate mention.

nom. pl. masc., however, in the pronominal senses, is always *pūrve*, etc., never *pūrvāḥ*). The words *prathama*, *carama*, *-taya* (i.e., words formed with this suffix), *alpa*, *ardha*, *katipaya*, *nema* optionally have the pronominal form in the nom. pl. masc., but otherwise have only nominal forms.

# B27. [With George Melville Bolling] What Symbols Shall We Use?

1927. *Language* 3.123–129.

The material of Linguistic Science is human utterance, and for its work the ideal medium is *viva voce* communication. Rather, this would be the case, did not factors of time and space greatly restrict its applicability. Human utterance is so fleeting that even the field-worker placed most fortunately as he is in the immediate presence of his material, must seek to hold this transitory phenomenon—to make an artificial record of it for re-examination.

Now to make a record that will permit an absolutely perfect reproduction of the utterance is, of course, beyond his or any human power. There can at most be only question of an approximation. For it the best device is undoubtedly a phonograph; but both its cost and cumbersomeness render its use for many purposes inadvisable, and thus even the field-worker is forced to fall further back upon a much older device—upon a system of graphic symbols as substitute stimuli for speech reactions. What is true of the field-worker is obviously true in a still higher degree of his less fortunately situated colleagues. For all linguists, then, written symbols are a necessity, and our problem is to make of them the best possible use.

To show that we are at present far from attaining such a use needs no reference to old articles on *Transkriptionsmisère*[1] nor any account of the recent Copenhagen Conference.[2] The fact is all too evident, and in evidence too are its harmful consequences. Of these may be mentioned first, the fact that our science is too esoteric; that it repels instead of attracting many who should be its closest friends (practical teachers of languages, historians and critics of literature, students of ancient life, etc., etc.); and that its effect in wider circles is practically nil. Then too, modern methods of printing and the rising cost of printers' labor are making our present procedure a costly luxury. We are rapidly reaching the point where linguistic matter is so expensive to print that the claim of our science upon

[1] Brugmann, *Idg. Forsch* 7.167–77 (1897).
[2] O. Jespersen and H. Pedersen, *Phonetic Transcription and Transliteration, Proposals of the Copenhagen Conference April 1925*. Oxford, 1926.

the economic resources of society does not suffice. This will make itself felt in the concrete instance in various ways: publishers cannot afford to buy our manuscripts; we cannot afford to print at private expense; our journals must grow smaller and fewer. Now if the complication and costliness of our present methods are inherent in the nature of our science, we shall, of course, have to put up with their consequences as best we can. The present writers, however, are convinced that these habits of ours are not only unessential to our work, but positively harmful to it.

The first source of our difficulties is an unwillingness to draw the practical conclusions from a fact which we would admit in theory. As linguists we all know that symbols are symbols, matters of convention, without any mystic tie between themselves and the thing symbolized. The same series of sounds *çvetas* can (and does) mean either 'white' or 'black'; *water* might perfectly well mean 'milk' and *milk* mean 'water'. We laugh at the peasant who says: 'bread *is* bread everywhere, but they call it *pain* in France'. Yet we act as if the symbol p for instance, could not perfectly well symbolize, say, a voiced velar spirant, or any other sound, if we so willed it. No! p *is* p! And o with a tail under it *is* an open o-sound (does that mean a lower or a looser articulation?) or a nasalized *o* as the case may be; to substitute ɔ or õ were heresy. The cause is a blind clinging to tradition.

Now our tradition is made up of many items, and these vary in strength and serviceableness. The habit of symbolizing unvoiced labial stops by p (we ignore matters of interest to the palaeographer) has a history running back for some three thousand years. So far as we recall, the symbol has never been used for any other purpose; nor have such sounds been represented by any other symbol in systems based on the Greco-Roman alphabet. To tamper with a convention of that sort would be madness, and there is no likelihood that any scientist will propose to do so. The symbol j has a much shorter and more varied history (jest, jamais, ja). In dealing with it we have a freer hand and a more difficult problem. The special conventions of our science, the queer-shaped letters and the diacritic marks, are but creations of yesterday. They have sprung up almost before our eyes in a haphazard fashion, inventions to meet a momentary need, controlled largely by the native speech-habits of the inventor, or dictated perhaps by a passion for an illusory 'accuracy', combined with the conveniences of a particular printer. At best they are inspired by considerations which are palaeographic, rather than linguistic—as when, for instance, vowel-length is marked in OE, ON, OI by an acute accent, but in OHG by an apex, a procedure as irrelevant to our purposes as would be reproducing the shapes of the letters in which these languages were written. Sometimes even such a basis is surprisingly narrow, and still the convention—cf. σ and s—may become a shibboleth.

Yet these are probably the very conventions to which we cling the most tenaciously. Brugmann, indeed, laid it down as a principle that we must do so: that for each language we must adhere to the tradition as developed by students of that language. The result is that the reader of the *Grundriss* is accommodated in his own field, but has to form new habits for half a dozen or more unfamiliar languages; not to mention the fact that, as the 'traditions' are far from uniform—witness the transliteration of Sanskrit —further readjustments are required as soon as the student turns from Brugmann to another author. From such a principle the only possible outcome is a hodge-podge wherein one symbol represents divers phenomena, and the same phenomenon is symbolized in various ways. Hirt had the wisdom to protest against the principle;[3] and the American Anthropological Association decided against it in a similar case.[4] Only by following in the way these scholars have led can we ever attain to self-consistency— the first requirement to be made of any system of symbols.

However, one valuable lesson may be gained from our experience with the system of transcription in the *Grundriss*. It is that we can adapt ourselves to changes in our symbols with almost kaleidoscopic rapidity. A proposal therefore to break with some of our traditions, even with some that appear the most sacrosanct, need not be regarded as peculiarly appalling.

The other great source of our trouble is the habit of cluttering up our pages with queer-looking symbols in our efforts to attain an 'accuracy' that is an illusion. No series of human speech-sounds can be represented exactly and completely by any system of written symbols—not even by one so complicated as the Lepsius or the *Anthropos* alphabet. An approximation is always the best that can be done; always there is question only of more or less exactness.

That means the necessity always of choosing what we shall symbolize and what we shall leave unindicated; and in doing this we must be guided by the purposes we have in hand. For many of them (syntactic discussions, for instance) the traditional spelling even in a language written as unphonetically as English is the most serviceable form. When more is needed, we must ask ourselves how much; bearing in mind that there is no sacrifice of scientific accuracy—no compromising with our professional conscience —in choosing between a 'narrow' and a 'broad' transcription.[5] A superfluous complication of the symbols cannot reproduce the sounds for a

---

[3] *IF* 21. 145–61 (1907); *Idg. Gram.* 1. 112–19 (1927).

[4] *Smithsonian Misc. Coll.* 66.6.

[5] For this distinction, cf. *Princ. Int. Phon. Ass.* 14–5 where it is rather implied, perhaps unintentionally, that 'narrow' and 'scientific' transcription are always to be identified; also *Propos. of the Copenh. Conf.* 8–9 where the possibility of such an understanding is excluded explicitly. In the former passage the point of real interest was that 'broad' transcriptions suffice for most practical purposes; and (we may add) for many scientific ones.

reader unfamiliar with the language; all it can do, and it will do it, is to confuse him.

But the striving for an illusion of accuracy has done worse than clutter our pages; it has actually kept back our knowledge. For instance the fairly simple matter of the diphthongs and their variants before [r] in the Western ('General') American type of pronunciation has been confused by attempts to be 'phonetically accurate', until today nobody knows where he stands or what his neighbor's record may mean. Our seven diphthongs, as in *see, say, sigh, boy, do, go, how*, involve certain automatic variations of the vowels and of the semivowels. These variations cannot profitably be indicated by separate characters; the best we can do is to tell about them in our text. So far as symbolism goes, we cannot do better than [sij, sej, saj, boj, duw, gow, haw]. Before [r] these diphthongs suffer certain automatic changes, so that *near, hair, hire, poor, door, hour* differ rather strikingly from the preceding series. Nevertheless they can be most intelligibly and plainly recorded in the same symbols as [nijr, hejr, hajr, puwr, dowr, awr] with the differences which go hand in hand with the following [r] stated to a certain extent in words.

We have, however, tangled things to the point where phoneticians misunderstand and disbelieve each other; cf. D. Jones, commenting, *Maître Phonétique* 5 (Jan.–March 1927), on an article of Kenyon's: 'We find it difficult to believe that two kinds of [ɛ] and an [æ] can exist as three separate phonemes in any language . . . .' Yet every speaker of Western American will bear out Kenyon's point. The trouble is merely in the pedantic and irrelevant symbolism which we all use.

Our speech has, like French, Italian, and many another, two levels of mid vowels, as in *men, son* and *man, saw*. If we use the Latin letters [e] and [o] for the higher vowels, we shall need two extra symbols. For these, following the *Principles of the International Phonetic Association* (London 1912) we shall use [ɛ, ɔ] writing *men, man* [men, mɛn] and *son, saw* [son, sɔ]. This is all that is needed; for tenseness, length, and lip-rounding play no distinctive part in our simple vowels, and need not be symbolized. There is then nothing strange about our diphthongs and simple vowels:

|  |  |  |  |
|---|---|---|---|
| *may* | [mej] | *sow, sew, so* | [sow] |
| *men* | [men] | *son, sun* | [son] |
| *man* | [mɛn] | *saw* | [sɔ] |

nor about their, in part altered, appearance before [r]:[6]

|  |  |  |  |
|---|---|---|---|
| *Mary* | [mejrij] | *hoarse, wore* | [howrs, wowr] |
| *merry* | [merij] | *horse* | [hors] |
| *marry* | [mɛrij] | *war* | [wɔr] |

[6] In Western America; my own dialect (chiefly Southern) differs for the back series: *hoarse, horse* [hɔs]; *wore, war* [wɔr] before vowel. GMB.

Jones would not have been incredulous had the matter been presented in this way, i.e. without conformity to our bad habits of recording and in particular to our habits of recording other types of English.

To take a simpler case, 'accuracy' combined (let us confess it) with the influence of traditional writing,[7] leads us to attribute to Russian a six-vowel system. Here the attempt to be irrelevantly 'exact' has actually deceived us about the linguistic facts. Russian has a five-vowel system: the high-front vowel and the high-back or high-mixed vowel are merely variants of a single phoneme, the latter occurring only and always after non-palatalized consonants. Hence we should use a single symbol in ['igo] *yoke*, [b′it′] *beat*, (front vowel) and ('pod igo) *under the yoke*, [bit′] *be* (back vowel). By giving up a pedantic and irrelevant distinction we lose nothing in communicative value (for the preceding symbol for an unpalatalized consonant suffices to distinguish the back vowel) but we actually gain in the accuracy with which the phonetic system is reproduced.

We wish then to be easily intelligible and economical, ends that in part oppose, in part support each other. The need is to re-examine in the light of these purposes our traditions to see how far they may profitably be changed. At least they have trained us, by their very inconsistency, to adapt ourselves quickly.

We would suggest to our fellow-workers as general principles:

(1) That we abandon our present conventions in the use of Roman, italic, and bold-face type. They entail a duplication of equipment in special symbols and serve only purposes that are essentially ornamental. Linguistic forms can (as far as necessary) be set off from each other and from the surrounding text by brackets, dashes, or what not. Variations in these can be used to distinguish (where needed) 'broad' and 'narrow' transcription, transliteration, etc., etc. The equipment thus released becomes automatically available for real work: e.g. italics for 'emphatic' consonants, bold-face for stressed vowels, etc. Foreign words in Roman type stand out as well as in italics; the latter can then be used for translations. For a specimen of such printing, see LANGUAGE 1. 130–56; 3. 9–11.

(2) That we use to the utmost Latin letters, including capitals and small capitals together with italic and bold-face types. Only where these do not reach should we have recourse to other alphabets and to diacritic marks. This applies chiefly to new needs and to particular emergencies that may arise. Diacritic marks that are well-known and already in the printers' stock are not to be recklessly discarded. But even among these are many whose right to a continued existence should be scrutinized closely. In general the presumptions are against any symbol with two marks above

---

[7] The fact that this writing ultimately rests upon conditions of an earlier state of the language is here irrelevant.

or below the letter, and very strongly against any with more. In a system employing such symbols, the number of type required mounts rapidly,[8] and their cost becomes prohibitive. When all that these marks indicate must be indicated, the solution will often be to put the diacritics after or before the letter, or to avoid one set at least of diacritics: higher and lower vowel-types, for instance can be distinguished better by different letters (small capitals, ɛ, ɔ) than by tails or dots under one (and sometimes both!) letters.[9] In making such readjustments advantage should be taken of the opportunity to iron out inconsistencies like those that have arisen in IE grammar from the principle of adhering to various (and unstable) traditions. More frequently, however, the solution will be found by regarding the next two suggestions.

(3) That we recognize frankly the will-o'-the-wisp nature of the effort to assign a separate symbol to each variety of sound. In part we do recognize this, as when we employ the same symbol p for the surd labial stops of both French and English in spite of their easily noticeable differences. But at other times we become too rigid. If [oˑ] and [o] represent tense, rounded vowels in French; that is no reason why [o] may not represent a loose vowel in German or a loose, unrounded vowel in English. For those[10] who do not know these facts, a once-for-all statement will suffice; neither for them nor for other readers is anything gained by diacritics, inverted v, or similar devices of the grimoire.

(4) That normally we symbolize only phonemes (distinctive features) so far as we can determine them; and that always before we indicate more, we convince ourselves that more is demanded by the purpose in hand. The gain in elegance (in the mathematician's sense) will repay us for whatever nostalgia may result. We know today that no purpose was served by those who wrote the Irish symbol instead of g in OE, presumably because the sound was a spirant. Who would wish for different symbols for the l's in E *little*, or for the sibilants in Gr. πρέσβυς? If in German the long vowels are tense and the short vowels loose, the long-sign will suffice. If our diphthongs are much altered before [r] the [r] will symbolize this.

To the present writers it seems that these suggestions should be the more welcome, because they lie in the direction not of crippling our science, but of greatly enhancing its power by giving it a suppler and more abstract

---

[8] If only five vowel letters and only six diacritics be used, it can be calculated that the possible combinations of zero, one, two, or three of these six diacritics with the five vowels is 210, and will cost well over $1,000.00 for the equipment.

[9] To illustrate: symbols such as [oˑ] (high long oral) and [ɔ̬] (low short nasalized) will express as much as the troublesome combinations mentioned in the preceding note, and their cost is practically negligible.

[10] The existence of such persons is not to be assumed too lightly. Periodical articles are written for scholars, not for college students.

symbolism. We are all working with Roman numerals and deceiving our-selves by attaching costly flourishes; let us stop discussion of the flourishes and adopt the Arabic digits. The history of our science, by blind accident, has trained us to great flexibility in responding to symbols; let us take advantage of this flexibility, now that we need to free ourselves from the magic of symbolism. Once we take advantage of the purely external character of our symbols and learn to make them do what we want, the door will be open for uniformity—uniformity as between different lan-guages and as between different scholars.

# B28. On Recent Work in General Linguistics

1927. *Modern Philology* 25.211–230.

[1926–27 was Bloomfield's last year at the Ohio State University, 1927–28 his first at the University of Chicago. Of the articles reprinted in this volume originally published in 1927, only this one is overtly marked as coming from Chicago; B22, B26, and B27 are labelled as from Ohio State. Considering the normal interval between submission and publication, one is led to suspect that all were in fact written at Ohio State. The same must be true of B31 and B32, published in 1928.]

## I. THE UNDERLYING METHOD

The nineteenth century, beside establishing a scientific method for the study of linguistic change, produced also a few treatises which attempted to define the place of language in the universe.[1] At the opening of the present century stands Wundt's great work; it is followed by lesser ones at more frequent intervals, until, in the present decade, the average rises to more than one a year.[2]

[1] W. von Humboldt, *Ueber die Kawisprache*, Berlin Abh., 1836–40; the general linguistic part re-edited, with full comment, by A. F. Pott, Berlin, 1876.

H. H. Steinthal, *Charakteristik der hauptsächlichsten Typen des Sprachbaues*, Berlin 1860; re-edited by F. Misteli, Berlin, 1893; *Einleitung in die Psychologie und Sprachwissenschaft*, Berlin, 1871; 2d ed., 1881.

M. Müller, *Lectures on the Science of Language*, London, 1861.

W. D. Whitney, *Language and the Study of Language*, New York, 1867; *The Life and Growth of Language*, New York, 1875.

F. Müller, *Grundriss der Sprachwissenschaft*, Wien, 1876 ff.

A. Hovelacque, *La linguistique*, Paris, 1876; 4th ed., 1888.

H. Paul, *Prinzipien der Sprachgeschichte*, Halle, 1880; 4th ed., 1909.

J. Byrne, *General Principles of the Structure of Language*, London, 1885; 2d ed., 1892.

G. von der Gabelentz, *Die Sprachwissenschaft*, Leipzig, 1891; 2d ed., 1901.

O. Jespersen, *Progress in Language*, London, 1894.

H. Sweet, *The Practical Study of Languages*, London, 1899; *The History of Language*, London, 1900.

H. Oertel, *Lectures on the Study of Language*, New York, 1901.

[2] W. Wundt, *Völkerpsychologie, I. Die Sprache*, Leipzig, 1900; 3d ed., 1911.

J. van Ginneken, *Grondbeginselen der psychologische taalwetenschap*, Lier, 1904–6; *Principes de linguistique psychologique*, Paris, 1907.

F. N. Finck, *Aufgabe und Gliederung der Sprachwissenschaft*, Halle, 1905; *Die Haupttypen des menschlichen Sprachbaus*, Leipzig, 1910.

Linguists are today agreed upon the essentials of their method; their disagreements can be precisely stated and discussed upon common ground; they do not in their actual work use the troublesome introspective terminology; they are not disturbed by the impossibility, today, of reducing human conduct to physiologic (neurologic) terms; yet they employ no extra-material forces. As, in general, neither psychology nor the other human sciences have reached this point, the quickening of interest in linguistics may be in part due to its occupying a strategic position from which to attack the study of man.

Now, our writers do not make this attack. They accept the finalism and supernaturalism of individual psychology, with many variations, only to discard it, of course, as soon as they approach the actual subject matter of linguistics. Their introductory discussions would have been far more interesting and fruitful had they worked in the opposite direction: insisted upon the psychologist's recognizing the methods and formulas with which we study language, and perhaps even outlined a psychology that would harmonize with these methods and formulas.

To the linguist who is interested in the implications of his method, no psychology can be acceptable which tries to explain on an individual basis phenomena which he knows to be historically conditioned by the social group. For the linguist an act of speech is the result of factors which may be grouped as follows:

1. Circumstances of the particular instance
   (a) Physical stimulus
   (b) Purely personal condition of the individual at the time

2. Circumstances socially determined
   (a) Extra-linguistic group-habits (e.g., customs, such as taboo or courtesy)
   (b) Linguistic patterns (the language of the community)

V. Porzezinskij, *Vvedenie v jazykovedenie*, Moskva, 1907; 3d ed. 1913.

F. Boas, *Handbook of American Indian Languages; Introduction*, B.A.E. Bull. 30, Washington, 1911.

E. Richter, *Wie wir sprechen*, Leipzig, 1912.

L. Sütterlin, *Werden und Wessen der Sprache*, Leipzig, 1913.

L. Bloomfield, *Introduction to the Study of Language*, New York, 1914.

F. de Saussure, *Cours de linguistique générale*, Lausanne, 1916; 2d ed., Paris, 1922.

E. H. Sturtevant, *Linguistic Change*, Chicago, 1917.

E. Sapir, *Language*, New York, 1921.

J. Vendryes, *Le langage*, Paris, 1921.

W. Horn, *Sprachkörper und Sprachfunktion*, Leipzig (Palaestra 135), 1921; 2d ed., 1923.

A. Meillet et M. Cohen, *Les langues du monde*, Paris, 1924.

O. Jespersen, *Language*, New York, 1924; *The Philosophy of Grammar*, New York, 1924.

W. Schmidt, *Die Sprachfamilien und Sprachenkreise der Erde*, Heidelberg, 1926.

In linguistics we know that the factors under (2b) are not to be explained on an individual basis, be it in mentalistic or in any other terminology; the facts of historical (and even of descriptive) grammar here involved are entirely foreign to the individual. He talks as he has heard others talk. The facts under (2a) are similarly viewed by ethnology and the other social sciences.

Let me now state the hypothesis which, I believe, removes the dissonance between the linguistic's psychologic theory and his technical practice: If the other social sciences were developed, let us not say to an ideal point, but merely to the point which linguistics has reached, the socially determined factors (2a) would be seen to encroach upon the personal factors (1b) until these latter would be reduced to purely physiologic terms: the momentary condition of the speaker's body.

The social patterns, linguistic and other, are, of course, merely an abstraction. They are the features common to a vast number of individual actions, in each of which appear also individual features. If we do not make this abstraction, two courses are open to us. We may study the individual from earliest infancy, when his acts are entirely explicable by (1), and observe how successive actions of his group-mates (parents, etc.), act by act, "condition" him to the social habits (2). This is individual psychology. Had we a perfect equipment for the study of physiology, we could make these observations on a physical plane, observing the modifications in the protoplasm (nervous structure, etc.) from act to act. Or, we may study the group, observing every act of a given type (e.g., every utterance of the word *centum*), with a view to the manner of transmission and to the modifications in the course of time. This is social psychology.

Linguistics does neither of these things, but remains upon the plane of abstraction. We do not trace all the vocal utterances of an individual from birth, be it in physiologic terms or in linguistic. We do not trace the usage of a linguistic form in a community, act by act. Once the individual has acquired the habit of using a certain linguistic form, we assume that under certain constellations of (1a), (1b), and (2a) he will utter it. Given the existence of a certain linguistic form in a community, we assume that it is spoken under such constellations, and concern ourselves only with its place in the total linguistic pattern and with its gradual modifications.

All this, including our diagram, holds good also for the hearer of a speech utterance. Should it happen that a few whispered words stir him to violent activity, we do not study the precedent storing-up of physico-chemical energy in his body, or the manner of its touching-off by a slight change; we not study the precedent physiologic modifications (neurologic) of the individual, thanks to which just these slight sound stimuli act as the match to the gunpowder. Not even the psychologist does this.

Just as the biologist is interested in a certain correlation of certain physico-chemical units, which correlation may be greatly modified by a very slight chemical change, so here the psychologist is interested in a certain correlation of biologic individuals (society), which correlation may be greatly modified by a very slight physiologic change. A ranting tirade may strike the eardrums and cause but a smile, a few whispered words the tragedy of Othello. The linguist goes not even so far; he concerns himself with an abstraction: the features of ensuing conduct common to "all" hearers of a given form, and their historic modification—meaning and semantic change.

Given an ideal equipment, we could thus describe any human act: The physiologist gives an account which includes the individual's predisposition (channels of nervous discharge) due to earlier stimulations and responses; the psychologist traces the formation of this predisposition, act by act, from the individual's birth; the social psychologist identifies the persons who were concerned in these earlier stimulations and through them traces the ancestry of this type of act; the linguist defines those features of the act (grammatical) which are habitual in the group, places them in the habit system (language), and traces their history; other social scientists in their sphere parallel the linguist.

This hypothesis assumes for the other human sciences a development comparable to that of linguistics; for psychology it implies the postulates of behaviorism.

In this I follow A. P. Weiss, whose psychology takes account of linguistics. For Weiss, the social group is an organism of a higher order than the many-celled biologic individual. Just as the unity of the latter is conditioned upon the interaction of many cells, so the unity of the social group upon the interaction of many individuals, primarily through language.[3]

Since a psychology is not necessary in linguistics, this statement might stand merely as a sketch of what I take to be the implications of the actual practice, in purely linguistic problems, of all linguists, whatever be their views on psychology. It has been made here, however, for two further reasons. In discussing certain fundamental problems, such as that of meaning, which could be dealt with by postulates, linguists are accustomed to appeal directly to psychology. And second, every now and then, before some knotty problem, a linguist will lay down the long-tried tools of his trade, not to sharpen or improve them, but to resort instead, for the nonce,

---

[3] See A. P. Weiss, *A Theoretical Basis of Human Behavior*, Columbus, 1925; on language, also *Journal of Philosophy, Psychology and Scientific Method*, XV, 631. For the general system see *ibid.*, XVI, 626; *Psychological Review*, XXIV, 301, 353; XXVI, 327; XXXII, 83, 171.

to incantations about whose value no two even of the psychologic shamans will agree.

## II. THE PROBLEM OF MEANING

The meaning of a word is defined in dictionaries and in the practice of linguists as if the object were always present when the word is spoken, e.g. *apple*: "the well-known firm-fleshed, smooth-skinned, round or oblong pome fruit of trees of the genus *Malus*, varying greatly in size, shape, color, and degree of acidity."[4] That is, the sounds *apple* are our conventional reaction to the sight, feel, smell, and taste of this object. But in reality we utter the sounds *apple* very often when no apple is present. Many of our words, indeed, stand at some remove from any actual sense stimulus, e.g., *although, causality*. In what way does the word *apple* "mean" or "refer to" an apple, when none is present? Why is the dictionary definition nevertheless sufficient? This problem is psychologic rather than linguistic and is for our science best dealt with by some convenient postulate. It is, of course, solved with magic ease if we are satisfied with the answer that, when the physical apple is not present, a "mental image" or "concept" of an apple takes its place.

That is why C. K. Ogden and I. A. Richards[5] take us not one step ahead; on page 14 the authors give a triangular diagram with the apices "Referent" (in our illustration, the actual, physical apple), "Thought or Reference" (image, concept, or thought of an apple), and "Symbol" (the word *apple*). For psychology or linguistics the book might as well end at this point; it further contains, strangely enough, much warning and example of popular terms posing as things; also some good advice ("Canons of Symbolism") in the spirit of normative logic.

De Saussure's system is more complex: (1) actual object, (2) concept, (3) acoustic image, (4) speech utterance; the series to be reversed for a hearer (p. 28). The totality of this is *le langage*; the actual speech utterance is *la parole*; and the segment formed by the two purely mental terms (2) and (3) is *la langue*, the socially uniform language pattern. De Saussure's careful statement lays clear the point at issue: What he calls "mental" is exactly what he and all other linguists call "social"; there is no need for the popular finalistic terms. We shall do better to drop (2) and (3) and speak instead of a socially determined correspondence between certain features of (1) and (4).

In his actual practice, de Saussure strictly rules out the metaphysical terms. Thus he warns us (p. 30): "La langue n'est pas une fonction du sujet parlant, elle est le produit que l'individu enregistre passivement; elle

---

[4] *Webster's New International Dictionary*, 1920.
[5] *The Meaning of Meaning*, New York, 1923.

ne suppose jamais de préméditation, et la réflexion n'y intervient que pour
l'activité de classement dont il sera question p. 170 sv."[6] Or again,
Osthoff's explanation[7] of verbal first members of compounds arising in
several Indo-European languages, an explanation typical of the linguist's
avoidance of mentalism, is for de Saussure paradigmatic (p. 195); he
recalls it in his final summary (p. 311):

> Autre exemple: l'indo-européen primitif ne connaissait pas de composés à
> premier élément verbal. Si l'allemand en possède (cf. *Bethaus, Springbrunnen,*
> etc.) faut-il croire qu'à un moment donné les Germains ont modifié un mode
> de pensée hérité de leurs ancêtres? Nous avons vu que cette innovation est
> due à un hasard non seulement matériel, mais encore négatif: la suppression
> de l'*a* dans *betahŭs* (voir p. 195). Tout s'est passé hors de l'esprit. . . .

The solution of the problem of meaning will doubtless lie in the psychologist's study of substitute stimuli: Under what conditions does the
child, when learning to speak, first say *apple* in the absence of an apple?
But here again the study will be largely social, for we may suspect that to
a large extent the function of substitute stimuli is determined by social
tradition.


### III. THE PHONEME

Formulation of the fact that each language consists of a strictly limited
number of sound types, each of which is, for the language, absolutely uniform and absolutely distinct from the others, has often forced itself upon
linguists in the needs of practical work, and has often been forgotten. The
phoneme is an abstraction obtained from series of utterances, e.g., the
English phoneme [t] from [tin, win, pin], etc., and [tin, tuk, it], etc. An
ear trained to other languages will hear differences between the [t]'s of
[tik, stik, botr, bit] which are not distinctive, that is, in English non-
linguistic. The same ear may fail to hear the difference between [bit] and
[bid] which is, in English, distinctive. The notion has been developed by
Sweet,[8] Jones,[9] and, no doubt independently, by Boas (p. 16), de Saussure
(p. 63), and Sapir (p. 57).

The existence of phonemes is of course implied in even the roughest
syllabic or alphabetic writing and in all study of language. But its explicit
statement not only guards the linguist against occasional lapses ("The
articulation of the sound is slightly weaker . . ." or "The difference be-

---

[6] The exception is there not stated as such, but seems to be this, that the individual is free
to associate various related forms with any given form.

[7] *Das Verbum in der Nominalcomposition*, Jena, 1878.

[8] *Practical Study*.

[9] *Principles of the International Phonetic Association*, London, 1912; cf. S. K. Chatterji,
*A Brief Sketch of Bengali Phonetics*, London, 1921, reprinted from the *Bulletin of the School
of Oriental Studies*, Vol. II, Part I.

tween phoneme *a* and phoneme *b* is so slight that perhaps . . ."), but justifies the very existence of our science. The logical demand that a science speak in quantitative terms is met by linguistics because it speaks in terms of phonemes; for the phonemes of a language we could substitute an equal number of units of any kind (Sapir, p. 18). Without them we should be in the position of the Indian informant who told me, "This word has a kind of a cold sound"; he could not say, "This word consists of such and such of the basic phonemes of my language arranged in such and such sequence." No wonder that the earlier linguists spoke in terms of "letters"; the actual continuum of speech sound (*la parole*) was not what they meant, and they had no term for the abstraction of the socially determined features of this sound continuum.

## IV. DESCRIPTIVE LINGUISTICS

Paul (p. 20) maintained, against Wundt,[10] that there was no scientific use in the mere description of a language; history was the only object of linguistics. This fallacy was possible because most Indo-Europeanists spoke a Germanic language and knew Latin and Greek from school and Sanskrit from grammars ultimately based on Panini. They were inconsistent enough to accept descriptive grammars for other languages,[11] and, perhaps without realizing it, they incorporated a great deal of descriptive work into their historical research. Since then, the study of less-known speech families has made it clear that a historic or comparative research depends upon the existence of two or more sets of descriptive data. Practice shows that descriptive study involves the full measure of scientific generalization and classification; only by a scientific process can one abstract from a series of actual speech utterances the socially determined features and their systematic patterning. Today descriptive linguistics is thus recognized beside historical, or rather as precedent to it. The theoretical justification is given especially by Finck,[12] and by de Saussure, who outlines the relation of "synchronic" to "diachronic" linguistics (p. 114).

The practice of descriptive research reveals some problems which were obscured under preoccupation with historical problems in relatively well-known languages. Given a linguistic form, such as an inflection or a word, how can we state its meaning? We have seen that this will be done in the form of what we may call the "primary" or "dictionary" meaning; but, within this limitation, what terms are available? Wherever the meaning is an object defined by some science, the answer is simple. Thus, for a plant

[10] E.g., *Sprachgeschichte*, p. 32.

[11] E.g., Vendryes, *Grammaire du vieil irlandais*, Paris, 1908; A. Leskien, *Handbuch der altbulgarischen Sprache*, Weimar, 1871; 4th ed., 1905.

[12] *Die Sprachwissenschaft.*

name we need only give the botanical names of all the species for which the word is used. The same solution exists for a few abstract meanings, such as the numerals. In most instances, however, the stimulus components which lead to the utterance of a form and the relevant components of the hearers' responses are very hard to isolate. We must abstract them after observing a large number of utterances. The meanings so reached often bear a very complex relation to any objects that can be scientifically defined; thus, one term of relationship may mean, "my mother's brother, my paternal grandmother's brother, the son of either, the son's son of either," and so on, with some troublesome refinements. In the case of social situations, such as degrees of affection, respect, or friendship, the comparable terms of the investigator's own language are misleading. Here the solution may come if some science gives us a precise terminology for the relations involved. Thus, a mysterious word for "friend" may, under improved ethnologic information, turn out to mean, "person of my sex who has gone through such and such a rite together with me."

The case of grammatical categories is even worse, because here the meaning often does not correspond to anything scientifically delimitable outside of linguistics, or to any habitual pattern of tribal action other than the grammatical habit. The gender system of animate and inanimate in an Algonquian language, for instance, includes among the animates some things which we do not regard as living, e.g., "stone," "pipe," "raspberry" (but not "strawberry"), "knee" (but not "elbow"), and ethnologic observation shows that the speakers do not (except in the grammatical forms of their language) make any differential distinctions; they neither say, "A raspberry has life, a strawberry has not," nor make a corresponding difference in any other way, as, for instance, in food habits or in religious ceremony. Here, assuming that the category of noun has been defined, we can at any rate list the animate names of things which our own tribal habit (science) declares lifeless, or, better, of those which the speakers themselves in some decisive non-linguistic activity treat as lifeless. But in the case, say, of a verbal tense or aspect, we are in a worse position still. A list of typical locutions seems to be about the best we can do. The path of investigation lies, evidently, in the preparation and comparison of such lists. This is the object of Jespersen's *Philosophy of Grammar*, an examination of the grammatical categories of the better-known European languages, worked out with marvelous detail and sensitiveness.

This leads to the problem of general grammar. Which, if any, linguistic forms are universal, which widespread? Nearly every language (modern Chinese may be an exception) has two main types of break in the semantic nexus—words and formatives. Wundt attempted to deal with this; the word boundary was defined by an act of apperception (or rather, by its occasional occurrence),[13] that of formatives was associatively determined. This was mere verbal duplication of the terms "word" and "formative." Similarly, the various syntactic devices can be studied for all language: cross-reference (*puella cantat*, "the-girl she-sings"), congruence, government, connective particles ("red *and* blue"), word order. Such study presupposes data for as many languages as possible; in fact, very few have been adequately recorded or described. A survey and bibliography are attempted in the books of Meillet and Cohen and of Schmidt.

## V. ECOLOGY

A summary of work on the distribution of dialects is given by Roedder.[14] The boundaries of successive linguistic changes (isogloss lines) do not coincide. A linguistic change may cover territory that has been dialectally differentiated by earlier changes. Isoglosses may be bundled along barriers to communication; if the barrier (e.g., a political boundary) is removed, the isoglossic bundle may be overlaid by later linguistic development. The isoglosses may be obscured also by linguistic borrowing; especially if a standard language arises, gradual borrowing may entirely obscure the line, for instance, of a phonetic change.[15] As the schematic example of dialect differentiation never occurs, and all the complexities of linguistic change are involved, the need in this problem is for large-scale co-operation. Above all, descriptive records of local speech forms are needed. As training for a beginner in linguistics, the recording of texts and the descriptive analysis of a dialect would be better than most of our doctoral problems.

One of the points here mentioned deserves further precision, though, so far as I know, it has nowhere been worked out: the character of standard and literary languages. Let us assume that the dialect of a class in some center (e.g., the upper class of London) becomes a standard language for a large group of speakers to whom other dialects are native. The standard language becomes the native speech, as time goes on, of a larger and larger number of speakers. As such we must, no doubt, suppose that it is subject to ordinary linguistic change and eventually even to dialectal differentiation. But, meanwhile, it is subject to some additional vicissitudes.

At the time when it becomes native to a new group of speakers, these may yet preserve in it certain features of their former dialect.

---

[13] *TAPA*, XLV, 65.

[14] *Germanic Review*, I, 281.

[15] Cf. Sturtevant, p. 79: Vendryes, p. 53 (here clearly expressed, but on p. 52 confused with the phonetic change itself).

Or, the standard language may gain new ground by gradual infiltration: form by form and word by word the substance of a dialect may be gradually replaced by standard speech, until the result is describable only as "standard with dialect features" or as "one of the types of standard resulting from secondary dialectal differentiation of the standard itself"— although these descriptions belie the historical process. Thus, our central type of American standard, like all standard English, keeps the group [rs], as in *horse, nurse, worse*.[16] Like the other forms of standard, it jocularly uses *cuss, hoss* as dialectal foreign words, and has the word *bass* (OE *bærs, bears*) as an older loan from a dialect; but, beyond this, it has the taboo word [ɛs] OE *ærs, ears*, in which the other types of standard keep [rs]. This suggests that our type of standard may go back to a gradually and never quite completely standardized dialect which spoke [s] for [rs].

On the other hand, the standard borrows forms, in normal fashion, from the dialects, e.g., *vat, vixen*; it need not here concern us whether these were ever foreign words with the connotation of rusticity or jocularity.

A group of dialect speakers with imperfect command of the standard may become so powerful as to crowd out (archaize) some standard forms during the generation or two it takes them to become genuine speakers of standard. This, rather than normal linguistic change, is perhaps killing the form *whom*.[17]

A literary standard is influenced by the graphic form. The normal literate speaker believes, of course, that the written form is a model which determines or at least preserves the spoken. This belief may be due in part to certain real experiences; the literate and even the semi-literate speaker actually obtains some of his speech material by linguistic borrowing from written records. The frequency of this may be guessed at from the occurrence of exceptional cases in which he misinterprets the (often ambiguous) written form and "mispronounces" it. Successful and socialized, these oblique loans from written speech are, of course, spelling pronunciations (*author, Gothic, Lithuanian*). Communities which have preserved an old written standard divergent enough to make loans recognizable, e.g., India and the Latin countries, give us an indication, in their *tatsama's* and *mots savants*, of how copious this borrowing really is.

Taking all this into consideration, one may, to suggest an extreme possibility, ask: Do literate standards, like ours, ever make a normal linguistic change that is not being made at the same time by the underlying population of dialect and semi-dialect speakers? Are not most of their apparent changes really borrowings, be it of single forms or on a large scale (trans-

---

[16] The fact that our standard has inverted [r], while in other types the actual form of this phoneme is a mixed vowel or modification of a preceding vowel, need not here concern us.

[17] Sapir, p. 166.

fer, infiltration), from the dialects, and counter-borrowings from the written form?[18]

## VI. Do Phonemes Change?

If each language at any given time moves within a limited number of phonemes, and these phonemes are subject to change in the course of time, then no word can be excepted from such change. For a word excepted from such change would thereafter contain an otherwise not current sound. Primitive Indo-European [k] appears in English as [h] (*centum* : *hund*); had some words been excepted on the way, we should now be speaking them with intermediate sounds, such as [kx] or [x]. Since forms which contradict the general sound development never exhibit sounds intermediate between the normal phonemes, but only an unexpected grouping of these, we cannot explain them as due to deviations from sound change. Two types of explanation are used. The divergent form does not go back to the supposed ancestor, but is an analogic extension of another form, e.g., English *live* does not represent OE *libban*, but the stem of OE *lifað*, *lifede*, *lifodon*, etc., which was at some time generalized; *to lib* and *to live* competed; finally the latter conquered. Or, the divergent form was borrowed from a different dialect; for the phonemes of this dialect the nearest phonemes of the home dialect were substituted; these, of course, need not be the historically correspondent phonemes; e.g., my dialect says [rɛðɹ] *rather*; I now borrow the Englishman's [raðə]; for his trilled [r] I substitute my inverted [r], for his [ə] my inverted [ɹ] syllabic, and for his [a] the nearest vowel of my dialect, that of *bother*, *hot*, etc. Two of these substitutions reproduce the historical correspondence, but the third does not; I now speak *rather* with the vowel of *bother*, *hot*, where the historian would expect me to use that of *man*, *bad*.

The alternative would be to drop the theory of gradual change in phonemes and define sound change instead as a sudden replacement of one phoneme by another. History and dialectal fact forbid this. It is therefore hard to assign any concrete meaning to statements like that of Jespersen: "Sometimes, when all ordinary words are affected by a certain sound-change, some words prove refractory because in their case the old sound is found to be more expressive than the new one."[19] Thus, English *peep* (for cry of small bird) is supposed to have resisted the English vowel shift, and *cuckoo* (p. 406) the pre-Germanic consonant shift.[20]

The commonest fallacy in this matter is to confuse the conflict of

---

[18] In this domain the greatest contribution is doubtless that of H. C. Wyld, *History of Modern Colloquial English*, London, 1920.

[19] *Language*, p. 288.

[20] I confused these two examples (*AJP*, XL, 372) I hope without prejudice to the argument.

doublets due to analogy and to borrowing with the process of sound change. The speakers who hesitated between *lib* and *live* were not, and the American speakers who pass from [rɛðr̩] to [rɑðr̩] are not making a sound change. This fallacy is most frequent where the examples are taken from a standard language with a complex history of dialect mixture and borrowing from graphic records. A favorite instance is the modern representation of OE ō as [uw]: *do, moon, soot*; as [u]: *foot, book, soot*; and as [o]: *blood, flood, soot*. Methodically, the first step here must be the recognition of the fact that the divergent forms have phonemes otherwise current in the language (*wolf, pull*; *son, love*); they could not, except by a chain of most improbable coincidences, result from deviations at odd points of a phonetic change.

The forms with [o] diverge at least as early as the sixteenth century, those with [u] somewhat later. If we were dealing with an isolated one-dialect community, these forms would be surprising, but, even here, explicable:

1. In ME long vowels were shortened before certain final consonants, giving paradigms like [sut, su:tes].

2. On the analogy of nouns with one stem form, two paradigms are created: [sut, sutes] and [su:t, su:tes].

3. Sound change of [u] to [o]; we now have [sot, sotes] and [su:t, su:tes].

4. In early modern time long vowels were (again) shortened before certain final consonants, giving paradigms like [sut, su:tes].

5. This results by analogic change in two paradigms: [sut, sutes] and [su:t, su:tes], beside the older [sot, sotes].

Thus, today, we have three forms for *soot* [suwt, sut, sot]; in other instances one or two of the forms have become obsolete.

Now this diagram is doubtless incorrect; the vastly more complex conditions of standard English make it very hard, if not impossible, to find out what really did happen. But so far as theory is concerned, every added complication that we may suspect only lessens the value of such examples as an argument for sporadic sound change. Any of the standard forms may have had an eventful history of borrowing, conflict, restoration from the graphic model, and so on. To state an extreme possibility: It may be that changes (1, 2, 4, 5) never occurred in standard English or in its upper-class-of-London ancestry, that every single form with [u] or [o] is a borrowing from other dialects. On the other hand, some of the forms with [uw] may be borrowings from the written form replacing older forms with [o] or [u].[21]

The much-quoted example of [juw] and [uw], as in *tune, due*[22] does not illustrate sound change, but the passing of speakers from one class dialect

[21] Cf. Wyld, *op. cit.*, pp. 236–39.
[22] Jespersen, *Language*, p. 290.

to another. In 1787 Elphinston attributes the forms without [j] to "vulgar indolence or bluntness."[23] We could not ask for more explicit evidence; the present-day phenomenon is not a sound-change in progress, but a conflict between doublets which were dialectally differentiated as early as the eighteenth century. The actual sound changes here involved lie far in the past. They may never have taken place in standard English and the changed forms may have been borrowed from dialects. Or, they may have occurred in standard and the [juw] forms may be borrowings from the written record (spelling-pronunciation; cf. Wyld, p. 293). In the latter case, for instance, the history may have been:

1. Sound change: [sju:r] > [ʃu:r], *sure*
   [sju:] > [ʃu:], *sue*
   [tju:n] > [čuːn], *tune*
   [dju:] > [ju:] *dew, due*
2. Standard borrows from written form: [sjuw, tjuwn, djuw]
3. Sound change: [sjuw] > [suw]
   [tjuwn] > [tuwn]
   [djuw] > [duw]
4. Middle-class standard borrows from written form: [sjuw, tjuwn, djuw]

I have dealt at such length with these matters, which could be settled only by specialized research, coupled with lucky finds, because even on the basis of what little we know, it is clear that the waverings or final arrivals of speakers cannot be viewed as examples of sound change. The very fact of a speaker's using two forms is proof of precedent analogic change or borrowing. The alternative hypothesis is not a self-contradictory dilution of the postulate of phonetic change, but the total abandonment of this postulate.

Another attack upon the postulate of uniform change of phonemes is that of Horn: Some elements of speech, unnecessary for the sense, have a weaker meaning than others and, consequently, are more subject to loss by phonetic change. Inversely, an element whose meaning is essential resists sound change (p. 24). This theory is revolutionary in that it makes the hitherto otiose mentalistic factors play an actual part in linguistic change.

Horn seeks to fortify his position by saying that his theory is not in-validated even if some of his examples can be explained in some other way (p. iv). In this he is wrong; methodically, any example which can be explained by those methods which even for Horn cover the vast majority of linguistic changes must be subtracted from the evidence for his supple-mentary theory. It is more legitimate when Horn says (p. 25) that not

[23] Jespersen, *Modern English Grammar* (Heidelberg, 1909), 1, 382.

every overcharacterization necessarily leads to phonetic weakening of the superfluous elements, since every language carries on a mass of superfluous forms.

Strangely, Horn nowhere takes cognizance of the fact that practically all of his examples are taken from the unstressed syllables of languages which historically have suffered phonetic loss in this position: Germanic, early Latin, early French.[24] Obviously, a theory which attributes these weakenings, wholly or in part, to any other factor than the stress relations, could make good only on the strength of examples from languages where this factor is absent. Horn gives no clear ones. Some of Horn's examples have not, as to details, been explained under the standard theory. But the fact that we are not omniscient, that some of the history, what with our meager data, is obscure to us, is no warrant for a finalistic hypothesis which, by its very nature, is certain to "explain" anything: the weakened forms were weakened first in "meaning," then in "form."

If we turn to languages which we can observe, we find no signs of feebleness in forms whose meaning, from a logical point of view, is superfluous. Nothing could be (mathematically) more superfluous than the personal inflection of the verb in modern English, German, or French. It is lacking in English in some common verbs (*he can, shall, will, may, must*), and in all preterits except *was : were*. Yet the speakers are in no position to drop these endings. Linguistic forms are carried on by tradition; they are not subject to any logical test, under which few, indeed, could pass muster.

In a large group of the cases I cannot believe even Horn to mean that the shortening represents phonetic change, cases like *quad* for *quadrangle* (p. 12), *hand-to-mouth* for *from hand-to-mouth* (p. 97). Here analogy and borrowing are the only possible factors; e.g., *prof* after the graphic form *Prof.*, and then analogic *quad* for *quadrangle*, *stude* for *student*, etc.

Some of the examples really are phonetic developments; the longer forms are analogic restorations, e.g., MHG *vliesen* (p. 7) shows the phonetic development, as do *gleich, glauben*, etc.; NHG *verlieren* has analogic *ver-* ("destruction, loss, removal"). OE *a-* represents older *\*oz-* before consonant; OHG *za-* is the anteconsonantal form of *zar-*.

Horn says (p. 23) that OE *bindu* cannot have analogic *-u* after *beru*, because the corresponding transfer was not made in nouns, *ār: gifu; word: fatu*. This is asking a great deal, especially as in historic time the verb form and not the noun replaces *-u* by analogic *-e*. He says (p. 22) that OE *binde wē, binde gē* weakened the verb ending because it and the following pronoun expressed the same meaning, so that it was superfluous; but, as Horn sees (p. 121), the verb plural had the same ending for all three persons—

---

[24] See Luick, *E. Stud.*, LVI, 185.

the pronoun, whatever its position, gave no "overcharacterization." Wood's explanation[25] is far more credible, especially as in Alfredian English the ordinary optative plural often ends in -e.

Of the ON third person singular in -r, Horn says (p. 27) that the second person is common in everyday speech; when the pronouns had made the distinction unnecessary, the endings could drop off or the endings of one person be transferred to another. Let him try that in German!

Horn ascribes the non-inflection of the English article to the existence of circumlocutions (chiefly prepositional, no doubt) and fixed word order, and says that German, by contrast, has kept the inflections because these constructions are not used. This looks well on paper, but will not hold under observation of the facts. In reality the two languages are in this respect almost wholly alike; for instance, where German uses a dative without a preposition, English also often lacks the preposition, and the word order is here the same in both languages: even *Er gab es mir, Er gab mir es* is paralleled in *He gave it me, He gave me it*. After prepositions, says Horn, the article, being superfluous, is weakened in German; but, look you, it is just the "superfluous" part which remains (*ums Haus*)!

The only examples which are in principle unexplained are formulas of greeting and address, such as *goodbye* (cf. [hwaj] for *How are you?*), German *morjn* (for *guten Morgen*), Russian *s* (for *sudar*), Spanish *usted* (for *vuestra merced*).[26] To say that they were weakened because they were weak in the speaker's mind is at best a tautology; a real explanation may some day be found.

The analogy of atrophy of an organ (p. 137) is particularly inept, quite as bad as was the old-time one of an object being worn away by much handling.

The teleologic basis for the theory seems to be this (cf. p. 117): If the inflectional syllables, e.g., in Old English, had been lost before the analytic locutions (especially prepositional) had arisen, the language would have become unintelligible. The answer is, obviously, that this happens right along; new locutions (produced by the analogies of the language) constantly replace old ones, which, viewed *post factum*, would have been unintelligible, had they remained in use. If only phonetic change occurred, every language would in time become unintelligible. The methodic question would be: At what point do the new locutions arise, and at what point do the old ones go out of use? Instead of resorting to a hypothesis that would cause trouble even to a mentalistic theory of speech, Horn would have done better to raise the question of a pathology of language.

[25] *MP*, XIV, 122.
[26] Horn, p. 18.

## VII. The Pathology of Language

The fact that languages do not become unintelligible seems queer when one embarks upon reasoning such as underlies the views of Jespersen and Horn. If sound change works blindly, how is it that the loss of inflections, for instance, does not cause confusion? We have seen the teleologic answer.

The chief factor, from this angle, is homonymy due to sound change. J. Gilliéron[27] thus approaches it; E. Richter[28] summarizes past work.

Some homonyms are tolerated, witness the gradual syncretism of nominative and accusative in Germanic; modern German still distinguishes them in masculine singulars and a few pronouns, English only in a few pronouns. Note also English [pejr, bejr, hejr, red], etc. Others have been removed or are evidently disappearing: Latin *apis* and *avis* in certain French dialects; OE *bere*, "barley," and *bēor*, "beer," in English; English *might*, *mite* and *let*, "allow" and "hinder." Chinese has gone notably far; its homonymous words have been largely replaced by two-word phrases.[29]

Another factor is taboo.[30] English [konij], "rabbit," seems to have been lost because of homonymy with a taboo word.[31] American English [kak], "rooster"; [ɛs], "donkey," seem to be meeting a similar fate.

Grammatical irregularity is a well-known factor, as in the replacement of the morphologically divergent [hozif, semstris, farid] by [haus-waif, sijmstris, fowr-hed]; a form of one category that sounds like another seems to be endangered: English *pease* taken as plural; American dialect *link* "lynx."

Instead of asking, however, which forms of a language are "bad," we shall be more relevant if we ask which forms of a language go out of use. We understand the rise of analogic doublets, such as *hoofs* beside *hooves*; we have scarcely touched the question: Under what circumstances do such doublets arise, and which wins, which becomes obsolete? When the question is put in this form, we see that we are merely making a study of analogic change.[32]

---

[27] *Pathologie et thérapeutique verbales* (Paris, 1921), "Collection linguistique," Vol. XI.

[28] *Festschrift für Kretschmer* (Vienna, 1926), p. 167.

[29] C. Arendt, *Handbuch der nordchinesischen Umgangssprache* (Berlin, 1891), p. 165; cf. B. Karlgren, *Études sur la phonologie chinoise*, Leyden, 1915.
See also Singer, *PBB*, XLVIII, 132.

[30] Meillet, *Linguistique historique et linguistique générale* (Paris, 1921), "Collection linguistique," VIII, 281.

[31] Cf. *NED*, *s.v.* "coney."

[32] So far as psychology is concerned, it would be facile and barren to attribute the therapeutic to a prevision on the part of speaker or tribe. "Prevision" would be here only another name for the fact that the troublesome forms do obsolesce. We must seek, rather, the circumstances which make the obsolescent form a response to a more and more limited number of stimuli, e.g., *Don't let him!* only to the situation where we want to stop someone, and no longer to the situation where we want to aid him. But we shall do better to confine ourselves to the linguistic facts.

It appears that the factors which militate against a form are limited types of homonymy (probably differing for different languages), incongruity with the grammatical pattern (e.g., irregularities of inflection), and taboo or homonymy with taboo forms; the chief factor favoring a form seems to be frequency (i.e., the commoner forms preserve grammatical irregularities which in less common words are analogically removed).

Under analogic doublets we must understand not only the morphologic, but also lexical alternates (*cock, rooster*) and phrasal groups (*contribute my mite, make my small contribution*).

## VIII. APPLICATIONS

The application of the results of linguistics to psychology has been discussed. The application to other social sciences is a thing of the future. The mentalist will say that the other social activities move upon a higher plane, in which intelligent choice and conscious striving are effective, language upon a mechanical and unconscious level. Under the hypothesis above suggested (§ I), one will say, rather, that language is a simpler activity, and that linguistics, owing to its simpler subject matter, has reached a scientific form of discourse, while the other human sciences are still to a large extent troubled with the elusive spiritistic-teleologic words of our tribal speech.

Attempts at application are likely to consist of purely verbal concessions to the finalism of the other sciences. Thus, the essentially impeccable technique, illustrated by well-chosen examples, of Vendryes, is marred at every step by verbal concessions to the non-linguistic view of man and society.[33]

Another possibility is that of oversimplification. Thus, Father Schmidt (p. 381) assumes a universally valid concept of "genitive," examines all languages to see whether the genitive precedes or follows its governing word, assumes in ethnology a similar concept of "matriarchate" (*Mutterrecht*), and shows (p. 453) that postposition of the genitive runs parallel, as a resultant, with matriarchate.

The chief scientific application of linguistics that can today be made is the direct one to psychology. Indirectly, as a paradigmatic example and as a demonstration of the needlessness of finalism, our results will serve the other human sciences, but this service is limited because their subject matter is far more complex than ours.

[33] E.g., p. 45 (Grimm's law): "une tendance naturelle... l'aboutissement naturel"; p. 46: "les spirantes sonores, par une sorte de reprise du sujet parlant, réagissent contre l'affaiblissement qui les atteint et deviennent des occlusives sonores"; p. 71: "Deux tendances opposées peuvent agir... Ou bien par paresse le sujet parlant se dispensera d'effectuer l'articulation... Ou bien, dans le désir de maintenir l'articulation..." There is so much of this that the book would do more harm than good to any but a professional reader.

The practical application concerns many activities, such as teaching children to read, teaching foreign languages, stenography, etc. All these can be summed up in the demand that our knowledge about human speech be applied to the educational process and be included in the content of education. Unfortunately our educators are ignorant of the results of linguistic science, and seem in no hurry to inform themselves. Prescientific notions about language, with the silly and dismal study of pseudo-grammar, still prevail in our schools, cf. G. Willis, *The Philosophy of Speech*, New York, n.d. Willis' book, for the rest, shows how little linguistic science has affected society; the author, who must have spent years at the study of Greek, Latin, and the modern languages, develops a linguistic of his own, as though no one had studied the subject before him—with the natural grotesque results.[34]

What with the publications of the last decade, there is today no good reason for popular ignorance about language, no excuse for our failing to embody into our culture the results of linguistic science.

[34] E.g., p. 26: "'Luck,' German 'gluck,' English 'to click for,' an imitation of the sound of the tossed coin struck on the table."

# B29. Contributions to
## *Le Maître Phonétique*

1927. 'American English', *LMPh* III 5.40–42 (October–December).
1930. 'German ç and x', *LMPh* III 20.27–28 (April–June).
1932. 'The Word', *LMPh* III 38.41 (April–June).
1934. 'A Note on Transcription', *LMPh* III 46.54 (April–June).

[There is no trace of phonemic theory in the 1914 *Introduction*, and the scattered transcriptions of English are in terms of 'general phonetics' of the cross-language type. To the extent that Bloomfield's discovery of phonemics was partly independent of the similar discoveries of others, surely it was the work with Tagalog that brought it about.

Just when his phonemic analysis of Chicago English, and the corresponding transcription, began to take shape is not known. Erwin A. Esper conducted some experiments at Ohio State University in 1921–1922 requiring carefully designed nonsense syllables; Bloomfield devised them to specifications, constraining them to what can be pronounced in English, and using vowel symbols with the same values assigned them in the 1927 article done with Bolling (B27). Esper's report was published in 1925 as *A Technique for the Experimental Investigation of Associative Interference in Artificial Linguistic Material* (*Language Monograph* 1).

The transcription (and the analysis it reflects) appears thereafter in various works: 'The Structure of Learned Words' of 1933 (B40), the book *Language* of 1933, and, with extensive discussion, in 'The Stressed Vowels of American English' of 1935 (B43). But these four short pieces in *Le Maître Phonétique* are the only surviving examples of his transcription of extended passages. Especially instructive is his treatment of words unstressed in context: e.g., *the* before a consonant with [e], but *of* with [o]. On this, see especially the comments by Roland Kent in his review of the 1933 *Language* (our 41). I have wondered if Bloomfield's English did not have certain traces of German influence, so that his own pronunciation actually supported some of these interpretations that strike most of us as wrong; but my acoustic memory of his voice does not supply the requisite evidence for either confirming or disproving this notion.

The subject-matter of these four pieces is, of course, of some importance; but they would be included here even if it were not, for the reason given above.

Since none of our Bloomfield articles in this volume includes a complete list of the symbols he used in his mature transcription of English, it will be convenient here to supplement the first of the following pieces (which lists and illustrates the symbols for vowels and syllabic consonants) by the consonant list, taken from the 1933 *Language* §5.11 :]

| | | | | |
|---|---|---|---|---|
| [b] | *big* | [n] | *knot* |
| [č] | *chin* | [ŋ] | *sing* |
| [d] | *dig* | [p] | *pin* |
| [ð] | *then* | [r] | *rod* |
| [f] | *fan* | [s] | *sod* |
| [g] | *give* | [š] | *shove* |
| [h] | *hand* | [t] | *tin* |
| [j] | *yes* | [θ] | *thin* |
| [ǰ] | *gem* | [v] | *van* |
| [k] | *cat* | [w] | *wag* |
| [l] | *lamb* | [z] | *zip* |
| [m] | *miss* | [ž] | *rouge* |

## Contribution 1

### e'merikn̩ 'iŋgliʃ [1]

ðe 'midl̩ 'westr̩n ('ʤenr̩l̩ e'merikn̩) 'tajp ov 'spijʧ, 'ɛz 'hr̩d, for 'instn̩s, in *ʃi'kɔgow, 'difr̩z sow 'marktlij from *'soðr̩n *'britiʃ ðɛt it wud bij kon'fjuwziŋ tuw e'temt tr̩n̩skripʃn wið ðe 'simbl̩z ðet hev be'kom kon'venʃn̩l̩ for ðe 'lɛtr̩.[2] in'sted, aj 'fɑlow ðe " 'prinsipl̩z " ov ðij *'aj *'pij *'ej.

ðe 'simpl̩ 'strest 'vawl̩z ar 'najn, 'ɔl 'lɛks end 'on-'rawnded :—

i    'pin *pin*, 'spirit *spirit*.

e    'pen *pen*, 'merij *merry*, 'verij *very*.

ɛ    'pɛn *pan*, 'mɛrij *marry*, 'kɛrij *carry*.

a    'faðr̩ *father*, 'far *far*, 'bam *balm*.

---

[1] ɪn spaɪt əv ði ʌnfəmɪljər əpɪərəns əv ðə trænskrɪpʃn juːzd ɪn ðɪs aˑtɪkl, wi a pʌblɪʃɪŋ ɪt æz sɛnt tu ʌs baɪ ðə raɪtə, ɪksɛpt ðət wi həv prɪntɪd ʧ, ʤ wɛə hi həz juːzd č, ǰ, sɪmblz wɪʧ a nɒt rɛkəgnaɪzd baɪ ði a.f. wi a nɒt kwaɪt klɪər æz tə ðə væljuːz əv sʌm əv ðə sɪmblz, pətɪkjuləlɪ o ənd ʌnstrɛst e. prɪzjuˑməblɪ, ʌnstrɛst e rɛprɪzɛnts ə saund əprɒksɪmeɪtɪŋ tu ə, wɪʧ ðə raɪtə rɪgaˑdz əz bɪlɒŋɪŋ tə ðə seɪm founiˑm əz e ɪn hɪz spiˑtʃ. wi houp hi wɪl ɪkspleɪn ðə væljuːz əv hɪz vauəl sɪmblz məˑ fulɪ ɪn ə fjuˑtʃə nʌmbər əv m.f.

[2] kom'pejr ðij edi'towrijl̩ 'nowt, *'em *'ef, 'ʤɛnjuwr̩ij–'marʧ, 'najntijn-'twentij-'sevn̩, 'pejʤ 'fajv ; ðe 'difikl̩tij ðejr iz 'djuw 'ɔlsow tu kon'fjuwʒn̩ ov dis'tiŋktiv wið 'nan-dis'tiŋktiv 'fijʧr̩z.

ɑ  'gɑt *got*, 'bɑrow *borrow*, 'bɑm *bomb*.

ɔ  'sɔft *soft*, 'sɔ *saw*, 'wɔʃ *wash*, 'wɔr *war*.

o  'son *son, sun*, 'hors *horse*, 'korn *corn*, 'morniŋ, *morning*.

u  'fut *foot*, 'puʃ *push*.

ɹ̩  'ʃɹ̩t *shirt*, 'fɹ̩ *fur, fir*, 'hɹ̩ij *hurry*.


i, e, u, end 'prɑbeblij o ar 'lowɹ̩ ðen in *'britiʃ, end o iz 'farðɹ̩ 'bɛk.  ɹ̩ hɛz ðe 'tip ov ðe 'toŋ 'tɹ̩nd 'op, 'nɑt 'totʃiŋ.  ɛ, a, ɑ, ɔ ar 'loŋgɹ̩ ðn̩ ðij 'oðɹ̩z.  in 'fajnl̩ po'ziʃn̩ en be'fowr 'vɔjst 'sawndz 'vawl̩z n̩ 'difθoŋz ar 'loŋgɹ̩ ðn̩ befowr 'onvɔjst, end hɛv 'rajziŋ-'foliŋ 'stres.  in 'menij 'distrikts ('sentr̩l *ili'nɔj) a end ɑ kowin'sajd. som 'spijkɹ̩z dis'tiŋgwiʃ 'tuw 'kwɔnitijz ov a befowr r : 'faːr *far*, 'haːrd *hard*, 'haːrdn̩ *harden*, bot 'arm *arm*, 'ʃarp *sharp*, 'gardn̩ *garden*.

ðe 'difθoŋz hɛv ðe 'seknd 'elemn̩t 'rɛðɹ̩ 'tens, w wið 'lip-'rawndiŋ.  ðe 'seknd 'elemn̩t iz 'lowɹ̩d if ðe 'fɹ̩st iz 'low, bot ðis ɔltɹ̩'nejʃn̩ iz 'nɑt dis'tiŋktiv.  ðe di'vɹ̩ʤns betwijn ðij 'elemn̩ts iz 'les ðn̩ in *'soðɹ̩n *'britiʃ, bot ðe dif'θoŋgl̩ 'kɛrektɹ̩ iz 'wel 'markt, e'speʃl̩ij hwen e 'vawl̩ 'fɑlowz :—

| | |
|---|---|
| ij | 'sij *see*, 'sijiŋ *seeing*. |
| ej | 'sej *say*, 'sejiŋ *saying*. |
| aj | 'haj *high*, 'hajɹ̩ *higher*. |
| ɔj | 'bɔj *boy*, 'bɔjiʃ *boyish*. |
| uw | 'duw *do*, 'duwiŋ *doing*. |
| ow | 'gow *go*, 'gowiŋ *going*. |
| aw | 'baw *bow, bough*, 'bawiŋ *bawing*. |

befowr r ðe 'seknd 'elemn̩t ov 'difθoŋz iz ijvn̩ 'mowr e'simɪlejted tu ðe 'fɹ̩st, bot ðe 'tensnes 'ɛnd, in ðe 'kejs ov w, ðe 'lip-'rawndiŋ, ar 'kept.  hwajl ij, ej, uw, ow befowr r hɛv ðos 'ɛktʃuwl̩ij ðe 'kɛrektɹ̩ ov 'loŋ 'tens 'vawl̩z (iː, ɛː, uː ɔː, 'motʃ ez in *'frentʃ), jet ðej ar ðe 'sejm 'fownijmz, end o'kejʒn̩l̩ij (" 'kejrfl̩ 'spijtʃ ") en pɹ̩hɛps dajl̩'lektl̩ij, ar 'spowkn̩ wi'ðawt ðis esimi'lejʃn̩, ez 'rijl̩ 'difθoŋz.  'ɛcpɹ̩ct 'ɔimbl̩z for ðijz 'vejrjn̩ts ar nɑt 'ownl̩ij on-'nesesɹ̩ij bot kon'fjuwziŋ ; ðe 'fɑlowiŋ r so'fajsez tuw 'indikejt ðe 'mɑnofθoŋgajzd 'vɛljuw.

| | |
|---|---|
| ijr | 'stijr *steer*. |
| ejr | 'tʃejr *chair*, 'vejrij *vary*, 'mejrij *Mary*. |
| ajr | 'hajr *hire*. |
| uwr | 'puwr *poor*. |

owr  'powr *pore, pour,* 'howrs *hoarse,* 'mowrniŋ *mourning,*
       'wowr *wore.*

awr  'awr *our, hour.*

in 'nɛrow trn̩'skripʃn̩ :

| | |
|---|---|
| 'mᴛɛ̀ɹĭ *merry.* | kʽʜʌɹn *corn.* |
| 'mɛ̀ːɹĭ *Mary.* | wòːɹ *wore.* |
| 'mæ̀ːɹĭ *marry.* | wɔ̀ːɹ *war.* |

in 'menij 'onstrest si'lɛbiks ðe 'difθɔŋz re'tejn ðe 'sekn̩d 'elemn̩t :
'pitij *pity,* 'felow *fellow,* 'intuw *into.* ijvn̩ ðe 'wijkest 'sileblz
'prɑbeblij in 'norml̩ 'spijʧ ('nɑt e'legrow) dis'tiŋgwiʃ 'ejt 'difrn̩t
si'lɛbiks :—

i  'finiʃ *finish,* i'mr̩s *immerse.*
e  'fiʃez *fishes,* e'gow *ago.*
u  gud-'najt *good-night.*
o  on'til *until,* 'ɛno *Anna.*
r̩  'dɑktr̩ *doctor,* 'terr̩ *terror.*
l̩  'bɑtl̩ *bottle,* 'pikr̩l̩ *pickerel.*
n̩  'botn̩ *button,* 'onjn̩ *onion.*
m̩  'bɑtm̩ *bottom.*

e'moŋ ðe 'nɑn-si'lɛbiks, r iz ðe 'sejm 'sawnd ez r̩.  be'twijn
si'lɛbiks, e'speʃlij befowr r̩, t iz 'ɔfn̩ re'plejst baj e 'vɔjst 'flipiŋ
iv ðe 'toŋ e'genst ðe 'suwpro-ɛl'vijl̩r̩ 'ridʒ (ɾ) —'nɑt dis'tiŋktiv.

### 'tekst

ðe 'norθ-wind n̩ ðe 'son wr̩ dis'pjuwtiŋ ez tu 'hwiʧ woz ðe
'strɔŋgr̩, hwen e 'trɛvlr̩ kejm e'lɔŋ, 'rɛpt in e 'wɔrm 'klowk.  ðej
e'grijd ðet ðe 'won huw 'fr̩st mejd ðe 'trɛvlr̩ tejk 'of iz 'klowk ʃud
bij kn̩'sidr̩d 'strɔŋgr̩ ðn̩ ðij 'oðr̩.  ðen ðe 'norθ-wind 'bluw wið 'ɔl
iz 'majt, bot ðe 'mowr ij 'bluw, ðe mowr 'klowslij did ðe 'trɛvlr̩
'fowld iz 'klowk e'rawnd im ; n̩ et 'lɛst ðe 'norθ-wind gejv 'op ðij
e'temt.  ðen ðe 'son 'ʃown 'awt 'wɔrmlij, end i'mijdjetlij ðe 'trɛvlr̩
tuk 'of iz 'klowk ; n̩ 'sow ðe 'norθ-wind woz o'blajdʒd tu kn̩'fes
ðet ðe 'son woz ðe strɔŋgr̩ ov ðe 'tuw.

LEONARD BLOOMFIELD.

## Contribution 2

### ʤɹmn̩ ç ɛnd x

hwajl aj e'grij wið pro'fesɹ̩ Jones' 'eksl̩nt defi'niʃn̩ ɛnd dis'koʃn̩
ov ðe 'tɹm 'fownijm in **m.f.** 1929, 'pejʤ 43, aj be'lijv ðɛt ðij
e'gzɛmpl̩ ov 'ʤɹmn̩ ç ɛnd x ɛz 'sepɹet 'fownijmz wil nɑt 'howld
'gud.

ɔl'ðow ðe defi'niʃn̩ ov e 'fownijm iz 'prapɹ̩lij 'mejd in 'pjuwrlij
fo'netik 'tɹmz, ðe 'frejz " in ðe 'sejm siʧu'wejʃn̩ " most bij 'tejkn̩
tuw e'plaj tu po'ziʃn̩ in 'sentn̩s-i'niʃl̩, 'sentn̩s-'midl̩, or 'sentn̩s-'fajnl̩,
ɛnd 'difrn̩sez ov ðis 'kajnd ar in 'menij (or 'mowst) 'lɛŋgweʤez
eks'tended tu 'wɹd-i'niʃl̩, 'wɹd-'midl̩, or 'wɹd-'fajnl̩, — ɔl'ðow ðe
'wɹd iz 'nɑt in 'prinsipl̩ e fo'netik 'entitij. 'ðos, in e'merikn̩ 'iŋgliʃ,
ðe 'toŋ-'flip ɾ ɛz en 'intɹvo ̩kɛlik 'vejrjn̩t ov ðe 'fownijm t o'kɹz
wi'ðin 'wɹdz, ɛz in **wɔtɹ̩** (*water*), ɛnd in 'wɹd-'fajnl̩, ɛz in **e't ɔl**
(*at all*), bot 'nɑt in 'wɹd-i'niʃl̩, ɛz in e 'tip (*a tip*).

'naw, 'ʤɹmn̩ x o'kɹz 'ownlij ɛftɹ̩ a, o, u, aw ov ðe 'sejm 'wɹd,
ɛz in 'ax (*ach*), 'dox (*doch*), 'bu:x (*Buch*), awx (*auch*). 'ʤɹmn̩
'trijts 'kɑmpawnd-'membɹz ɛnd 'sofiksez wið i'niʃl̩ 'kansn̩t
fo'netikl̩ij ɛz 'sepɹet 'wɹdz wið 'sekn̩dejrij 'stres. ðos it en'forsez
its 'lɔ ov pɹ̩'mited 'wɹd-'fajnl̩z in 'kejsez lajk 'hant-bu:x (*Handbuch*),
'hɑnt-arbajt (*Handarbeit*), 'hent-çen (*Händchen*), 'hant-liç (*handlich*),
'ʤost ɛz it 'doz in 'hant (*Hand*), ɛz o'powzd tu 'hendə (*Hände*).
'hens ðe ç ov ðe 'sofiks -çen iz 'trijted ɛz 'if it wɹ̩ in 'wɹd-i'niʃl̩, ɛz
in çe'mi: (*Chemie*), ɛnd 'formz lajk 'fraw-çen (*Frauchen*), 'pfaw-çen
(*Pfauchen*), 'ku:-çen (*Kuhchen*) 'mijrlij i'lostrejt i'niʃl̩ ç. ðos x
(ɛftɹ̩ a, o, u, aw ov ðe 'sejm 'wɹd) iz 'mijrlij e 'vejrjn̩t ov ðe
'fownijm ç (in ɔl 'oðɹ̩ po'ziʃnz).

it iz 'intɹ̩estiŋ tuw ob'zɹ̩v ðɛt so'fiksez wið i'niʃl̩ 'kansn̩t 'nevɹ̩
hɛv ðe si'lɛbik ə ; in hwɔt aj 'tejk tu bij ðe 'best pronon'sjejʃn̩
-çen hɛz e. it iz 'intɹ̩estiŋ 'ɔlsow ðɛt hwen tuw 'sofiksez kowe'les,
θruw ðe 'regjɹ̩ 'lɔs ov ə, intu 'won 'silebl̩ wið i'niʃl̩ 'kansn̩t, ðis
iz 'juwʒwlij 'trijted lajk e 'wɹd-i'niʃl̩ if e 'ful 'vawl̩ 'falowz, ɛz in
'hant-luŋ (*Handlung*), bot 'nɑt if ə 'falowz, ɛz in 'hendlər (*Händler*),
're:gnən (*regnen*),—ðow in 'ðis ðer ar 'menij 'lowkl̩ 'difrn̩sez.

Leonard Bloomfield.

## CONTRIBUTION 3

### ðe 'wr̩d

in 'spijkiŋ ov 'ʤr̩mn̩ ç ɛnd **x** (em. ef. 1930, 27), aj 'menʃn̩d ðe
fo'netik 'markiŋ ov ðe 'wr̩d-,juwnit wi'ðawt dis'kosiŋ it, be,kɔz aj
'tuk it, ɛnd its ve'rajetijz in 'difrn̩t 'lɛŋgweʤez, tu bij e 'mɛtr̩ ov
'kamn̩ 'naleʤ. e 'brijf 'somr̩ij ov ðis 'mɛtr̩, 'bejst 'ʧijflij an
\*pa'sij, wil bij 'fawnd in maj \*intro'dokʃn̩ tu ðe 'stodij ov
'lɛŋgweʤ, \*njuw 'jork, 1914.

LEONARD BLOOMFIELD.

## CONTRIBUTION 4

### e nowt an trɛn'skripʃn

it be'komz iŋ'krijsiŋlij plejn ðɛt ðe prablemz ov fo'netik
trɛn'skripʃn de'mɛnd en ɔlmowst mɛθe'mɛtikl pre'siʒn ov stejt-
ment. aj ʃud lajk, ðerfowr, tu sej e fjuw wrdz in ko'nekʃn wið
**m.f.**, dʒu'laj–sep'tembr, 1933.

aj duw nat kon'sidr on'nesesejrij ðe juws ov " speʃl " simblz,
sotʃ ɛz ʌ ɛnd ə ; it iz truw ownlij ðɛt aj fajnd ðijz tuw on'nesesejrij
for ðe \*ʃi'kɔgow tajp ov stɛndrd \*iŋgliʃ, ɛnd so'spekt ðɛt ʌ iz
on'nesesejrij for \*soðrn britiʃ iŋgliʃ.

aj duw nat θiŋk ɛnd hɛv nevr sed ðɛt stres ɛnd pitʃ ar nan-
di'stiŋktiv in enij kajnd ov \*iŋgliʃ. ov kowrs ðej ar di'stiŋktiv ;
witnes *convict* **'kanvikt** vrsos **kon'vikt**, ɛnd *four o'clock?* **fowr o
klak ?** vrsos *four o'clock* (.) **fowr o klak** (.)

hwer'evr, in enij lɛŋgweʤ, stres ɛnd pitʃ or enij oðr fe'namena
ar ðos di'stiŋktiv (e'tɛtʃt tu liŋ'gwistik mijniŋz), aj ʃud klɛs ðem ɛz
fownijmz, ijðr prajmejrij (ɛz, wrd pitʃ in \*tʃaj'nijz) or sekndejrij
(ɛz, wrd stres ɛnd sentns pitʃ in \*iŋgliʃ).

ðe trm " intow'nejʃn ", haw'evr, ət, it sijmz tu mij, tu bij kept
for nan-di'stiŋktiv fijtʃrz, sotʃ ɛz stres in \*frentʃ.

LEONARD BLOOMFIELD.

[auə kɔliːg iz hiə juːziŋ ðə təːm " founiːm " in ə njuː sens—
witʃ wiː rigret. hiðətuː ðə təːm həz bin meid tu əplai ounli tə
saund-kwɔlitiz, ənd wiː siː nou adikwit riːzn fər ikstendiŋ it in ðə
manə sədʒestid. in rifəːriŋ tə laŋgwidʒiz in witʃ lenθ, stres, ɔː pitʃ
ə distiŋktiv it iz ʳuəli səfiʳnt tə kɔːl ðiːz fiːtʃəz " signifikənt
elimənts ".—D. J.]

# B30. Review of Schmidt

1927. *Language* 3.130–131.

*Die Sprachfamilien und Sprachenkreise der Erde.* By P. W. Schmidt S.V.D. (Kulturgeschichtliche Bibliothek herausgegeben von W. Foy; 1. Reihe: Ethnologische Bibliothek mit Einschluss des altorientalischen Kulturgebietes 5.) Heidelberg: Carl Winters Universitätsbuchhandlung, 1926. Pp xvi + 596 and Atlas of 14 maps.

The Indo-Europeanist who opens this book will find himself in a strange world, colorful, adventurous, even heroic,—the world of Humboldt. One journeys to the ends of the earth (pp. 7, 9); danger and hardship are not considered. Into this world the reader is guided by the strong, kind, and warmly human personality of Father Schmidt.

Then with a start one realizes that this strange and vast world of human language is only that larger land within which lies our own well-cultivated domain. Upon this realization follows a profound regret: why have not the methods of our field been carried to the ventures without?

Thus, 'older' and less old languages play a part in the discussion (p. 5); one suspects the criterion of this to be one which would make modern English 'older' than the language of King Alfred (cf. the note on Hottentot and Bushman, p. 11). The whole second part of the book, 'Die Sprachenkreise und ihr Verhältnis zu den Kulturkreisen', will fail to instruct or convince, for it ignores what Indo-European has taught us about the variety of linguistic structure (even within a single stock) and of its mutability in the course of time. No one would today set up the simple concept of a 'genitive case' for even all Indo-European (e.g., modern English, French, the German dialects); Father Schmidt does so for all languages, patiently observes whether the 'genitive' precedes or follows its headword, and compares his results with a similar ethnologic schedule of 'matriarchate', deciding that originally ('die älteste Stellung') the genitive preceded, and that postposition of the genitive goes hand in hand with the 'matriarchate'.

Yet, along with Meillet and Cohen's *Langues du monde*, Father Schmidt's book will be indispensable for the general study of language, since the first part, 'Die Sprachenfamilien der Erde und die Geschichte ihrer Erforschung' contains a list of the languages of the earth (too optimistic, to be sure, in the assumption of relationships) and a splendid bibliography. It seems incredible that one man can have read and can know so much. In a human and manly way Father Schmidt speaks (p. iv) of the devoted labor of his predecessors; for fear of seeming thankless, one scarcely dares express the wish that all these workers had used less of sentiment and philosophy and more of the simple methods of science.

# B31. The Story of Bad-Owl

1928. *Atti del XXII Congresso Internazionale degli Americanisti* (held in Rome, September 1926) 2.23–34.

[The Cree original of this story is printed in *Plains Cree Texts* (1934) 190–205; the English translation on facing pages is identical with that given in §3 below. The four footnotes in the *Texts* version are here added, with the relevant passages in Cree. Bloomfield constructed the account in §2, realistically, on the basis of his experience with the attitudes of the sorts of people involved.]

**1.** Bad-Owl was a Plains Cree Indian who died on Sweet Grass Reserve a number of years ago. By the custom of his people, the following story was his for having lived and told it. I have it at second hand: Bad-Owl's friend Sakewew gave it to me in the summer of 1925; it forms part of some material collected for the Victoria Memorial Museum of Ottawa.

Bad-Owl's story deals with the conflict of supernatural forces, and the main incidents can be understood only as results of these forces; yet the actual happenings, down to the words spoken by the characters, are, to all appearance, transmitted just as they took place. In consequence, the story is a good example of the difference between the viewpoints of two cultures, and an example of one of the ways in which strange conduct of members of a foreign culture is to be explained.

I shall give first the actual happenings, as a European observer would have seen them, then a literal translation of the story as told by Sakewew.

**2.** Our European observer is an agent of the Hudson's Bay Company. Let him speak:

No white man will ever understand the Cree. One day he will act with chivalry and speak wisely; the next day he will talk and act like a petulant child. One of the best Cree I ever knew was Bad-Owl; I shall tell you of his conduct on the first two river trips he made for me.

In the old days, you must know, the best part of our work was the annual voyage from our western trading post down the Saskatchewan River to Hudson's Bay. With the first warm weather our Indians would bring their furs to the post. If an Indian failed to come, the chances were that he and his family had had poor luck in the winter's hunting and had starved to death. When we had traded in the furs, we would hire some of the younger men to help us carry them down the river; I or one of my clerks would go with the fleet. Sometimes one or another of the young braves would stay down river, taking a wife from among the Swampy Cree or Mushkagos, who live in the woods southwest of Hudson's Bay; after a year or two he would come back with us, accompanied by his wife and one or two children.

At our camping places on the way we would be met by Indians who came to look on and beg. One of these, who figures in my story, was an old man who lived in the Swamp Country. He had about a dozen wives, mostly young and pretty. With them and a flock of children, and often with a crowd of relatives and hangers-on, he would meet us where we landed to camp. They would come from their birch-bark wigwams, ragged and half-starved, and we would give them food and scraps of clothing or trinkets. Miserable as he was, this old man lorded it over his people; it was clear that his word was law among them. As for our own Indians, in spite of their Plains Cree contempt for the Swampy Cree, they did not joke with the old man, but stood aside when he came, talking in low tones or silently handing over the alms which I indicated.

Bad-Owl was one of the young Plains Cree who hired out to us one spring to make the river voyage. On our return trip that season, when we reached the old Mushkago's camp, we met a young Plains Cree who had married in the east. My interpreter told me that this young man feared that the old Swampy Cree would take his wife away from him, because she was a Swampy Cree and handsome. I laughed at the idea of the half-starved, decrepit old man overpowering the young fellow, or even the wife. Nevertheless, I soon saw that the young couple's fear was intense. My own Indians, too, with the exception of Bad-Owl, seemed depressed, as though they foresaw evil; yet they did not stay near the couple, and indeed, even the young husband seemed rather to avoid his wife. Bad-Owl remained sullenly aside. As for the old man, he did not, as usual, bring his people to our camp to beg.

The next morning there was excitement in our camp. It seems that the old man had seen the woman, had watched in the evening till she was alone, walked up to her, told her she was now his wife, seized her, and dragged her unresisting away. But Bad-Owl had been watching, unseen, from the top of the steep riverbank. He rushed down, picked up the old man, tossed him like a puppy into the river, and brought the young woman, hysterical with fear, back to our camp, and returned her to her husband.

But, strangely there was no rejoicing. Instead of seeing how absurd had been their fear of the old man, my Indians now became even more gloomy; it was as though they had wanted the old man to take the woman, and were angry and frightened at Bad-Owl's interference. Bad-Owl himself was no better than the rest. I gave orders to launch the canoes at once, and told them that I was hurrying only because of their absurd fear of the old beggar.

Just as we were ready to start, the old Mushkago and his crowd came to the river's edge. The old fellow seemed none the worse for his ducking. He stood on the bank and made a long speech, gesticulating and pointing upriver. I could not get our men to start: they listened reverently to every word, and as the old man spoke, their fear plainly increased. Only Bad-Owl, at whom the sermon was directed, sat sullen and impassive; he was in the big canoe with me and the most valuable goods, for he was my best riverman. When the old man's sermon was done, we started.

Now, I was particularly well disposed towards Bad-Owl, for he had acted according to the dictates of our own code; he had shown himself a gentleman. But I was disappointed. From that point of the trip to the very end Bad-Owl was sullen and ugly. For instance, we had hardly got round the first bend in the river, when one of the beetles which we call "beaver-bugs" fell down Bad-Owl's back. Of course, he merely picked it up and threw it into the water, but he did this with an air of having been greatly injured, muttering and grumbling. And so it went on: every trifle seemed to irritate him; he was sullen and unobliging. The others were no better; it was as though I had done them some wrong. I never had a more lonesome journey.

Yet Bad-Owl even now acted well in an emergency. The Saskatchewan river is treacherous. We ran into a windstorm and a huge flood-wave came to meet us. I shouted to Bad-Owl the Cree words for red flannel and for whiskey; my interpreter, badly scared, filled out the sentence. Bad-Owl nodded and spoke a few words; as the wave bore down on us, he chanted a kind of apostrophe to it, exercising his oarsmanship as if it were mere by-play. All our canoes came safely through. When we camped I gave Bad-Owl the whiskey. He poured some of it into the river and shared the rest with his comrades. That night a light appeared in the woods close to our camp. It often happens: a wild beast's eyes, a rotten log, or a will-o'-the-wisp. But our gang was on edge; I saw that they would not sleep. I sent Bad-Owl to see what it was; it disappeared and he came back, brandishing a stick and muttering.

He was sullen through the rest of the trip. When we arrived at the fort he took his red flannel, threw it into the river, and went home to his camp.

A hard winter followed. In spring Bad-Owl came with furs. He told a long story of how he and his family had almost starved to death; yet his supply of pelts was exceptional. I asked him to make the trip as leader of the gang; I was staying west that year and sending a clerk. He accepted gladly.

The rest of the story I have from the clerk. Bad-Owl behaved well on the trip; his sullenness was gone. When the fleet came to the camping place where the old Mushkago met them. Bad-Owl stayed by the canoes. A young man of the Swampy Cree came down to the water, and Bad-Owl had a long talk with him. Our men's fear seemed to be gone; Bad-Owl had even stipulated that the old Mushkago's alms were to be cut down to almost nothing. In the evening the old man came down to the water with his wives, and made his usual begging speech. When the old man saw Bad-Owl, the clerk feared trouble. But no: the old man's greeting was effusive. More than that, the clerk saw what I have often heard of but never seen: the old Mushkago lined up his wives and Bad-Owl (who had a wife and child at home) scanned them one by one and chose one for himself. Strangely, again, he picked out the oldest and ugliest one, a hideous old squaw. The old Mushkago politely begged him to take one of the pretty ones, but Bad-Owl stuck to his choice.

In the morning he took her back to the Mushkago's camp. He made a long speech; there was laughter; and then, a strange thing: all the Mushkago's wives except the one Bad-Owl had borrowed, packed up their belongings, took their children, and without a word left the old man. Some of them joined young men of the camp,—in most cases former husbands, my clerk was told,—and the rest went off alone. The Mushkago kept his one old woman. Bad-Owl looked on, smiling.

For a few years after that the old man would come to our landing place, but always alone with the old woman or perhaps with a few kinsmen; his big family and crowd of followers were gone. Bad-Owl remained my best riverman until I left the post, but I never learned the reasons for what happened on his first trips with me.

**3.** And now the story, as Sakewew, who had it from Bad-Owl himself, told it to me:

At the time of which I shall tell, the white men[1] were going down the river for the Hudson's Bay Company. And when thus, long ago, they went down-stream, a certain young man joined the Indians who were going along. Then, when his companions went home again, he stayed in the east, for he had taken a woman to wife there. Three years later Bad-Owl hired himself out to the whites and went away from there. Down yonder, at a place where they always stopped to rest, a certain Swampy Cree was awaiting their arrival. That old man, that Mushkago, had ten wives, for he was of manitou nature. The Swamp People feared him because he was of manitou nature: whenever there was a pretty woman, at once he would take her for himself. If people resisted him, at once he would kill them. In time thus, he came to be feared.

---

[1] C *wämistikōsiwak*: really "Frenchmen", but the term is often used for "white man" in general; this is here the case, if my understanding of *wītsihōwin* as "Hudson's Bay Company" is correct.

Then that young man thought, "Surely, if he sees my wife, that manitou person will take her away from me. For my wife is beautiful".

By this time they had a child, a boy; he was still in the swaddling bag.

Then the young man thought, "This is the time when the people from the west always arrive. I had better try to see them. Surely some Plains Cree will be in the river-gang", he thought.

And really it turned out that he did see some of his Plains Cree kinsmen, for a number of Cree were working with the gang, and one of them was Bad-Owl. And those Swampy Cree were there too, and the old man who had manitou power was there, hoping to be given something, for always he was given gloves, and each and all of his wives were given clothing; the white people gave him these things, because they feared him, for an ugly customer was that Mushkago.

Then at one time that Mushkago came to seize her. Bad-Owl was there; on the steep bluff at the edge of the river, close by there he was staying.

Presently, when the old man saw that young woman, "Dear me, it must come in spite of anything! I have seen you, and now there is nothing but I must marry you!" he said to her.

He had not yet come to beg for things. He was too much intent on taking the woman for himself and taking her home with him. So he used force. Then on the way home, this far from them, they saw him (Bad-Owl). At that the woman began to wail.

"He will tear my child from me, this man who means to take me with him! My poor child he will tear away from me, O my brother", Bad-Owl was told.

When Bad-Owl was told, "Brother, he will tear my child from me!" being a young man and himself already married, at once he grew angry.

"You too were born of a woman! It seems that you do anything that comes into your head!"[2] he said to the other.

He rose to his feet and made for him. In those days Bad-Owl was strong. He took hold of the old man; he gripped him by the arms; he walked him over to the steep bluff. In vain the old man who was a manitou tried to stop; he threw him down; he threw him into the water; under he went. Bad-Owl picked up an axe.

When the other came to land, "Have I made you angry?" Bad-Owl asked him.

"Yah, fellow-tribesman, you have not made me angry! I brought it on myself!" the other told him.

---

[2] *piku wāh-tōtaman kā-tōtaman!*: The translation follows the text; probably, however, the last word is a slip of the tongue or an error of record for *ka-tōtän*, giving the meaning: "You will do whatever you want," i.e., "I shall have to take the consequences of interfering with you; I cannot do other than I am doing."

[In the *Atti* version the last word of the quoted speech is "mind"; in the *Texts* version this has been replaced, as here, by "head".—CFH]

"You see, I was going to kill you, if I had incurred your anger".

"Yes, fellow-tribesman; I brought it upon myself. So this woman is your sister! I do not mind what you have done to me", he told him.

Then of those people from the trading post, the one who was at the head became frightened, for he feared the man who had been thrown into the water.

So he said, "Now, go away from here! Like fools you will be fearing this greasy old scab", he said.[3]

Accordingly they set out.

"Let me sit in the rear of the canoe", said Bad-Owl.

"Very well", he was told.

Then, when they had embarked to go west on the river, that one who had manitou power spoke as follows: "Just the same, you will look out for me, fellow-tribesman, in view of what you have done to me", he said; "You are the first to treat me in this way. As now you go on your river voyage, you will continue to be on your guard as you go along. And if you pass the things that will be on your way, off yonder, also, you will be on your guard; you will see my servant. And if you pass this, there where you camp you will see my little pet beast. And if you pass him, then yonder you will look out for my servant; and this last one you will not pass", he was told by that Mushkago who was a manitou.

As soon as they had gone round the first sharp bend in the river, suddenly something fell on his back. When he did like this, it turned out to be a beaver-bug. He threw it away. Unceasingly, at short intervals things reached him, things which the Swampy Cree had sent. But, in time, when Bad-Owl was not pierced by the many things, by the various insects, by the metal things of every kind, or by all the things which the other took from trees, then at last that Swampy Cree had used all his weapons. Bad-Owl did not care to retaliate.

Presently, as they were canoeing along the river, there suddenly appeared an upright wall of water.

Then the trader said, "Bad-Owl, I dread this which is about to come upon us. If you can deal with it, I will give you enough red flannel for one dress and this whiskey", he told him.

"Very well! That is no beast; it is a whirlwind. I have seen the like of it".

"Very well. When we arrive, give him some red flannel", said the trader.

"Oh, do not come here in your course! Be still! I have seen you and can witness that you have obeyed the command which sent you here!" he told it; "Be quiet! Do not come back!" he told it.

---

[3] The white man's words are no doubt correctly quoted; but the Indians take them for mere bravado, and assume that the white man shares their fear of the old sorcerer. Else, why does he give him presents?

And truly there was no wind.

"Now, after this, nothing more will frighten us. Now there will be only our fellow-tribesman's serving beast", said Bad-Owl.

So then he was given the whiskey. He made a libation for him who had been sent there; and he told him that he would give him also all of the red flannel that he had been promised.

Then in the evening they landed and pitched camp. Presently something appeared; it seemed like a fire to the trader.

"Come, Bad-Owl, try to do something about this! Shall I give you clothing to wear?" the trader asked him.

So Bad-Owl went to meet it; as he went, he took up the stem of a spruce with which to strike it. When he came near, it fled. The great cat and the great wolf feared Bad-Owl.

So the members of the trading party reached their homes. Nothing more occurred to frighten them. Then Bad-Owl stayed with his father-in-law. In the early winter they began to hunt far and wide, meaning to kill moose and all kinds of fur-bearing game. Presently, as winter progressed, there came a time when he and his father-in-law could not kill anything. There came a time when they could barely get home, being starved nearly to death. To be sure, they would see game, but someone always scared it off. His father-in-law and he could kill nothing. At last they grew weak. They could scarcely reach home each time, hunt as they might, for they never had anything to eat. Now, Bad-Owl and his wife had at that time a child.

"Now then, son-in-law, as for me, I can do nothing. There must be some reason for my not killing anything. I have heard that you threw into the water a Mushkago who has manitou power. I daresay he is the cause of your not being able to kill anything!" he was told.

He did not say anything.

Then, the next night, again came his father-in-law, breathing with the sound of one who has no strength left.

"Come in!".

He came in, leaning on a cane. Bad-Owl, too, for that matter, was weak with hunger. Then the old man filled a pipe. When he had filled it, he gave it to his son-in-law.

"Take this! My son-in-law, smoke! If things go on this way, we shall starve to death! If thus it is to be, greatly overcome is this child of yours and doomed to misery, if you can do nothing. Close by here I have come upon the tracks of two moose. 'All I shall succeed in doing is to frighten them off', I thought, and left it at having found their tracks. Tomorrow perhaps you might follow the trail of them, I thought of you, and therefore took care not to frighten them off", he said to him.

Only then did Bad-Owl remember his dream guardian.[4]

[4] A pair of moose is the Bony Spectre's characteristic gift.

"Oho! Was not the last the Bony Spectre said to me, 'You shall hunt nothing in vain!'? Come, I shall hunt this very night!" he thought.

Then he said to his wife, "Some moccasins that have never yet been worn", he questioned her.

"There are these here", his wife answered him.

"Give them here".

He was given them. He took off the moccasins he was wearing, and put on the others; after blackening his feet with charred wood, he put them on.

"Give me my knife", he said to his wife.

She gave it him. He made ready to go.

"Son-in-law, is it like this you mean to hunt?" the old man asked him.

"Yes", he was told.

"Be careful, at any rate!" his father-in-law said to him; "The path by which I came here, you will follow. In time you will come upon their tracks. They cannot yet be far off", he told him.

Thereupon he went out of the lodge. He followed back his father-in-law's trail. Presently he came upon the tracks where two moose had gone by.

"Come now, you told me I should hunt nothing in vain! Let it be now that these moose do not perceive my approach! Shall I give you fat to eat?" he said to that Bony Spectre.

Thereupon he followed their trail. When he thought them near, he took off his snowshoes; he walked on the snow. Presently he saw a fallen tree lying across his path. When he came to it, from behind it one rose to its feet. He fired at it; he loaded again. When he looked, he saw the other one; he shot it too. So he killed both of those moose, in the night, hunting in the dark. He took the ribs; he skinned and cut up the carcasses. When he had piled up the cuts of meat, he went home.

When those others heard the two reports, the old man gave thanks.

"He has not gone on a fruitless hunt!" he thought of his son-in-law who hunted in the night.

When Bad-Owl arrived, he threw the ribs into the lodge.

His father-in-law gave thanks.

"Ho, not yet! Wait a bit, daughter! Prepare some warm water. We have been too long without food. Let us vomit first".

So they prepared the water. Then, when they had vomited, the woman cooked the food.

"Ho, it was right close by here that I killed them!".

As they ate, the sound of wailing went by, through the air; dying off toward the east, went the sound of wailing. That was the Mushkago who had given them ill luck, who went off wailing, now that Bad-Owl had defeated him.

After that it seemed as though it were an easy thing for them to kill things, fur-bearing game of every kind.

"Now when they again go down the river, I shall go along. Even if no one employs me, I shall follow the party", he thought.

When spring came, they moved their camp to the trading post, when the season had come for the usual down-river trip.

As soon as the trader saw him, "Well, Bad-Owl, so you are here!".

"Yes!".

"My men are about to go down the river. You may go along with them. There will be one clerk with the party. But you will be the head man until you arrive yonder. You shall not work", the trader told him, "but you shall be the master over the things that are to be carried and over those which are to be taken away. And as for these men, this one is only to count up the goods and the furs; not you; you are merely to tell them what to do as they work, and where to stop for the night", Bad-Owl was told.

He agreed at once. He went with the gang.

"Oh, yes! Now, you are to give that Swampy Cree only a little bit of the different things", that man was told, and it was Bad-Owl who spoke; "Less than you have been in the habit of giving him", he was told.

So then they started down stream, with their load of furs, and at every point Bad-Owl was asked to say how the river-gang was to work.

Then, when they got near, that Mushkago moved his camp thither. He came with all his kinsmen, a camp of many tents, for he thought they would all be given things, foodstuffs, and all manner of goods. So then, towards evening, what did they see but a whole camp of birch-bark tents standing by the river's edge?

Then, "Here you will go ashore, and we shall camp for the night. Do not tell that Mushkago who is such a dangerous person", he said; "I shall stay here in the canoe", said Bad-Owl; "We shall camp right here", he said.

They did as he said; they beached their canoes. He stayed right there. A Swampy Cree, a young man, came to where he was.

This man said to him, "Was it you threw our chief into the water?"

"Yes".

"Ha, he does not suspect you are here. "I daresay we shall never again see that Bad-Owl, as our fellow-tribesmen called him', he always says, and that is why I wanted to take a look at you", he told him.

Then Bad-Owl said, "How many wives has he?"

"Ten", the other told him.

"Very well! I shall take one of them", he told him.

"Ho, there is one short little one, an old woman; she is the only one of the whole lot that he cares for", the other told him; "The others are

all young women. From me too he took a wife, and I cannot get her away
from him, for I fear him; I fear that he will kill me by the aid of his dream
spirits, for he is a manitou person, and no one ever lives two days whom
he seeks to destroy. For this cause, I know not how many of us are here,
whose wives he has taken away. He is a dangerous and evil being", the
other told him.

"Ha, do not tell him, if he comes here", he told the man.

It happened,—the young Swampy Cree went back to his camp,—it
happened that as he reached the camp, the one who had manitou power
was coming out of his tent; it was well on towards nightfall. He was coming
with all his wives. They came to where Bad-Owl was.

"But which one, now, is the chief of your canoe party, of your party of
tribesmen? As always, you have come now to your fellow-tribesmen.
What little present will you give them, as many as you are, what will you
give my wives here to have as their own? Surely you will give them something. But that one fellow-tribesman of mine I do not see here! Whoever
is chief, he will give me some little things, and he will manage to scrape
up some trifle for my wives here. And the rest of you will take from your
stock some little thing at least for each of my men; in this way everyone
will be satisfied", said that Mushkago.

"Well, go call your chief", was said of Bad-Owl.

Then he came to shore from his canoe.

"Why! It is none other than my fellow-tribesman! What little gifts shall
I pick out for him, I wonder?"

"Why, is this Bad-Owl, as he was called, with whom I used to play here
at practical jokes?"

"Yes, he it is!" he told him.

"Oh, fellow-tribesman, I will do whatever you say".

"Well then, fellow-tribesman, I should like to take home with me one
woman from among your women".

"Yes, fellow-tribesman, I have only these ten who are sitting here. They
are all I have, but one of them you may take, whichever one you wish",
said the Swampy Cree to Bad-Owl.

Secretly the other man pointed out to him the old woman of whom he
had told him. He stepped up to one after the other, to see which one he
would take.

"Most of them are handsome indeed, fellow-tribesman", the Mushkago said to him.

The wife whom the other loved, that was the one he took.

"Dear me, fellow-tribesman! You are a young man, to be taking just
the one who is old, when these others are so handsome!".

"Well, it happens that this is my choice, and so I am taking this one.
There now, fellow-tribesman, go home with your women!" he told the

Swampy Cree; "You are not to go anywhere else tonight. Tomorrow I shall try to see you once more".

Then the woman he had taken slept somewhere or other. He did not sleep with her. In the morning he took her over there.

"Ha, come in, tribesman!" he said to him.

He entered. All the Mushkago's followers came there.

"Now then, fellow-tribesman, I have taken this woman and mean to take her home with me, unless you abandon the weapons which you use".

"Yes, I shall do that. Whatever you say, I shall do. I love her too much whom you have taken".

"Very well, fellow-tribesman, I will give her back to you, on condition that never again you do as you have done. I shall strike down your helpers to the very last one. 'I shall give him one more interview. If he is not willing to do as I shall tell him, then let him in turn see my familiar beasts and wrestle with them', is what I thought concerning you. But now you shall again have this wife of yours. In whatever way your followers may feel inclined to laugh at you, they will laugh at you. And these women are to go back from wherever you have taken them. If you do not so, I shall destroy you beyond redemption".

"Yes, fellow-tribesman, I will do so; I wish to live. I am fond only of the one you took. These others may go back to their relatives".

"You have altogether too many wives. I shall not fail to hear of it, if you do any more killing. And so now I forbid you to exercise any more evil arts".

"Yes, fellow-tribesman, I shall do this which you say; I want to live, and I love this wife of mine. You will see that they go home".

Then he took him at his word. They went out of the tipi, and those other women went to their several homes, and all because evidently the Mushkago feared Bad-Owl.

That is the end of the story.

# B32. From the Preface to
## *Menomini Texts*

1928. *Menomini Texts* (*Publications of the American Ethnological Society* 12, edited by Franz Boas). New York: G. E. Stechert & Co., Agents. [Reviewed by Truman Michelson, *Language* 5.189–190 (1929).]

[The bulk of the Preface, including all the passages we cite except possibly the last, must have been written before mid-1925, since there is an added footnote reporting the death of Alanson Skinner in August 1925. Another footnote reports the death, after writing but before publication, of Captain Satterlee.]

. . .

The following Menomini gave me texts; those whose names are starred are no longer living:

. . .

Captain [John V.] Satterlee, co-author of the book of Menomini folk-lore, a man of eminent charm and intellect, was for many years the mediator between his people and those who would study them. He helped me, with unfailing kindness, to take my first steps in Menomini.

Jerome Lawe is an ideal linguistic informant: his speech in both English and Menomini is idiomatic and highly flavored. He served me as dictionary and grammar and gave me some of the best companionship I have ever enjoyed.

Charles and Louise Dutchman, in whose home in the pagan settlement called Zoar or Three Rivers . . . I dwelt for a number of weeks, were my chief informants and became my close and parental friends. Nehtsiwihtuk [Charles Dutchman] is a shaman; a man of abounding vitality and humor, yet given to philosophic speculation. Red Cloud Woman [Louise Dutchman] became as a mother to me, guiding my speech as one does a child's, for she has little English.

Most of my texts are by informants who speak little or no English.

. . .

The distinction between ordinary and mystic narratives is made by the Menomini, in that they often mention to which class a given story belongs: a general definition lies outside their habit. It seems to me (in this I differ from Skinner) that *ā'tsimuʌn* is applied quite generally to any narrative, whether traditional or personal. When I told the story of Gulliver and the Lilliputians, Mrs. Dutchman asked me if the latter were not human souls (*mitä'ʔtsyʌkuk*), and when I explained that this was not the case, and that the story had merely been invented for pastime by a certain Englishman, her comment was, "So it is no more than a tale" .... Inventing stories is not a Menomini way. The word *ä'teʔnō'hkʌkʌn*, on the other hand, applies to stories dealing with a far-off time when the world as we know it was in process of formation. The spirit animals enter in human or semi-human form, and the powers of the sky still dwell on earth. These stories are considered as true; they are told to inform and instruct; they often explain the origin of things, especially of plants and animals, and of customs. Even the lovable ineptitudes of Me'napus indicate by contrast the correct human way of obtaining food and the like.

. . .

The Menomini are being rapidly made over into the cultural type of the uneducated white American; of that European-American culture which, with its art and science, is worthy to stand beside their own and perhaps above it, they know nothing. They are suffering, therefore, what can be regarded only as a cultural loss, and they are fully aware of this, bearing it with a wistful resignation. The older Menomini are eloquent in their native speech, a very rich language which lends itself to elevated style and to the expressive refinements of a sensitive people. In addition, many of them are fluent in Ojibwa or Potawatomi or both. Today many Menomini children speak only the feeble English dialect, a thousand times bastardized by the standard language, which they receive from ignorant school-teachers and from the inhabitants of the surrounding countryside. The contrast is even more tragic in other respects, which lie beyond the scope of this book.

# B33. A Note on Sound Change

1928. *Language* 4.99–100.

[Delivered as 'A Reconstruction Confirmed' at the Nashville section of the 1927 Annual Meeting of the Linguistic Society.]

On the basis of correspondence between Fox, Ojibwa, Plains Cree, and Menomini, the following correspondences were set up in LANGUAGE 1. 147 ff., as representing distinct phonemes of an ancestral speech, 'Primitive Central Algonquian':

| PCA | Fox | Ojibwa | Plains Cree | Menomini |
|-----|-----|--------|-------------|----------|
| tck | hk | ck | sk | tsk |
| ck | ck | ck | sk | sk |
| xk | hk | hk | sk | hk |
| hk | hk | hk | hk | hk |
| nk | g | ng | hk | hk |

This left a discrepant case, namely, the very common initial element for *red*, as in Fox meckusiwa *he is red*, O mickuzi (misprinted 1. c. 152), Plains Cree mihkusiw, cf. M. mehkōn. For, although the group ck is, as above indicated, common enough in F and O, and the group hk common enough in Plains Cree and M, this distribution of the groups between the languages is unique.

Since there appeared to be no point of contact for analogic substitution of hk for ck, or vice versa, in any of the languages, and since borrowing of the stem for *red* seemed unlikely, it was necessary to suppose that the parent speech had in this stem for *red* a different phonetic unit, which was symbolized by

PCA çk     F ck     O ck     Plains C hk     M hk.

This supposition was necessary (or, in fact, justifiable) only on the assumption that *phonemes change*,—i.e., that sound change goes on regardless of meaning and is therefore subject to phonetic conditions only (and is not affected by frequency, euphony, meaning, etc. of words and other forms).

For those students who reject this postulate or seek in some way to dilute it, a correspondence like the above would be meaningless, since the ck of F and O, or the hk of Plains C and M, might be due to 'sporadic sound-change' or to "perseveration' of an old sound, or the like.

After the above-cited essay was in the hands of the editor, I was able to hear, for a week, the Swampy Cree of The Pas, Manitoba (on a field trip for the Victoria Memorial Museum of Ottawa). There I heard the forms:

mihtku- *red*, particle prefixed to nouns: F meckwi-, Plains C mihku-.

mihtkusiw *he is red*, cf. above.

mihtkuspwākan *catlinite pipe*, animate: F meck-uhpwāgana, Plains C mihkuspwākan.

mihtkustikwānäwisip *red-headed duck*.

mihtkwāpämak *red-willow*: Plains C mihkwāpämak, (cf. O mickwābī-mij, Baraga 250) M mehkūpīmak.

mihtkwāw *it is red*: F meckwāwi, O mickwā (Jones, *Ojibwa Texts* 2.144. 16; Baraga 250); cf M mehkīw.

mihtkwäkin *red cloth*: F meckwägenwi, O mickwägin (Baraga 251), Plains C mihkwäkin; cf. M mehkīkan.

The consonant-group htk did not, apparently, occur in any other element.

The postulate of sound-change without exceptions will probably always remain a mere assumption, since the other types of linguistic change (analogic change, borrowing) are bound to affect all our data. As an assumption, however, this postulate yields, as a matter of mere routine, predictions which otherwise would be impossible. In other words, the statement that *phonemes change* (sound-changes have no exceptions) is a tested hypothesis: in so far as one may speak of such a thing, it is a proved truth.

[When the foregoing was first published, the Editor of *Language*, George Melville Bolling, appended the following note, marked by square brackets and his initials:]

The example is an instructive commentary on Oertel, *Lectures on the Study of Language* 260: 'the "phonetic law" . . . rests its claim to recognition not upon a *causal explanation* but upon its *relative universality*. That is to say: Because a certain sound change can be observed in a large mass of cases it is elevated to the rank of a "phonetic law".' Compare also his contention (261) that law 'is used in grammar with a peculiar and special signification. It stands for a formula by which a large mass of phonetic correspondences are summed up.' One may adduce in refutation the way in which Sommer, *Handb. d. lat. Laut- u. Formenlehre*[2] 33–4, argues to the existence in Latin of a phonetic law -*rwo*- becomes -*ro*- (later -*ru*-) not from 'a large mass of examples' but from the single form *parum*.

# B34. Review of Kloeke

1928. *Language* 4.284–288.

[Used paradigmatically in the 1933 *Language*, §19.4.]

*De Hollandsche expansie in de zestiende en zeventiende eeuw en haar weerspiegeling in de hedendaagsche Nederlandsche dialecten; Proeve eener historisch-dialectgeographische synthese.* By Dr. G. G. Kloeke. (Noord-en Zuid-Nederlandsche dialectbibliotheek, onder leiding van Dr. L. Grootaers en Dr. G. G. Kloeke, Deel II). s'Gravenhage: Martinus Nijhoff, 1927.

Kloeke has carried out the enormous task of ascertaining, chiefly by field-work, partly by correspondence, the Dutch reflexes of West Germanic [u:] in the word *mouse* and, secondarily, in the word *house*. His data are given on a large-scale map (uniform with that in Number I of the series, *Handleiding bij het Noord- en Zuid-Nederlandsche dialectonderzoek;* cf. *Modern Philology* 25.376). Very roughly, the distribution of the forms is as follows:

(1) The word *mouse* is pronounced [mu:s] in an eastern district adjoining Germany and extending westward to a line which varies between 23°10′ and 23°40′. Within this general [mu:s] district, the form [my:s] is spoken in the Frisian towns (e.g., Dokkum, Leeuwarden, Sneek), in the district known as Het Bil(d)t[1], in a coastal patch on the Zuider-Zee (Workum, Hindeloopen to Genemuiden), in a large district extending south from the southeast coast of the Zuider-Zee (including Nijmegen and, in Germany, Cleves), and in a few isolated spots to the south. Within the [mu:s] district the pronunciation of *house* is, of course, generally [hu:s], but the form [hy:s] is spoken not only in the above districts of [my:s], but in a solid block bounded on the north by the line 54°, on the east by a line which varies between 24° 10′ and 24° 20′, and on the south by 51° 30′, plus a few large patches to the north and east.

(2) Diphthongal forms, such as Standard Dutch [møys] are spoken in

---

[1] See te Winkel's map, Paul's *Grundriss* I[2] 924; apparently the district embraces in Kloeke's list (*Handleiding* 68) Sint-Jacobi-Parochie, Sint-Anna-Parochie, Oude-Biltzijl. Lieve-Frouwen-Parochie.

a great central district, which includes the urban centers of Holland and Belgium.

(3) The form [my:s] spoken on the West Frisian islands, on the Zeeland islands, along the coast south of these latter, and throughout the territory west of the line 21° (including, e.g., Bruges). The extreme west (Dunkirk) speaks [mø:s].

By means of documents and the statements of early grammars Kloeke traces the older conditions. He controls this linguistic evidence by an independent study of the records of migration, commerce, politics, and religion. He combines skilful minute research with imaginative but realistic deduction. Stripped of details (many of which are interesting) the story runs thus:

West Germanic [u:] is preserved in modern Dutch in a number of homely or coarse words, such as *poes*, 'pussy', *poezelig* 'chubby', *snoet* 'snout, snoot' (120). These are ordinarily taken to be loan-words from [u:] dialects, but their familiar character makes it far more probable that they represent the oldest stratum of Dutch.

At some ancient time a cultural influence from the south spread the pronunciation of [y:] for [u:] (perhaps connected with the same phenomenon in French; see 195). It worked northward and covered all of Holland proper. The [y:] pronunciation (together with its modern successors) was thus in Dutch a linguistic loan; the above-mentioned words with [u:] represent the underlying native speech-form: 'We moeten dus aannemen, dat de *uu*-laag[2] . . . niet autochthoon is, en dat . . . een oorspronkelijke *oe*-laag door een *uu*-laag is overstroomd. Een bewijs daarvoor zie ik in het feit, dat in Holland (en in de andere gebieden waar de *uu* geheerscht heeft of nog heerscht) relicten met oude *oe* zich gehandhaaft hebben' (119). In the 16th and 17th centuries [y:] was still (as opposed to the present-day diphthong) the prevalent sound in Holland proper. Thus, [y:] is attested for Rotterdam as late as 1683 (and probably lasted well into the 18th century), Delft 1635, Leiden 1626 (mentioned as old-fashioned, 1683); Ghent had [y:] in the 16th century. In the great period of Hollandish expansion, then, [y:] was spoken. Wherever the commercial and cultural influence of the Holland cities went, the Holland pronunciation of [y:] for [u:] became the style. Either, as in the Bilt, there was actual immigration of upper-class Hollanders, or, as in the Frisian cities, the local upper class adopted the higher-toned form of speech from their contacts with the Holland upper class. Well-to-do and highly respected refugees carried the style into the German towns along the lower Rhine. The islands and maritime towns along the Zuider-Zee adopted the [y:][3]. The Dutch loan-words in Java-

[2] Here and below, *uu* is Dutch orthography for [y:], *oe* for [u:].
[3] The old Hanseatic cities along the Ijsel (Kampen, Deventier, Zutphen), as well as Zwolle, are excepted; these stood under North German cultural influence.

nese, Low German, and Russian are from the [y:] period; Russian distinguishes between Dutch words with West Germanic [iu] and [u:]. The Creole Dutch of the Virgin Islands has the monophthong.

This [y:] was the general Dutch standard; it was affected by everyone that made any claim to urbanity; gradually it was copied by wider and wider strata of the population, until today it has become the dialect form in the [my:s] districts above outlined, districts that lie in larger and smaller patches about the periphery of the great modern diphthongizing tract.

It is to be noted that [hy:s] is of wider and more coherent extent than [my:s]. The reason is evidently that the latter word was less common in intercourse with outsiders or with social superiors. In the large areas where one says [mu:s] but [hy:s] the former is the indigenous type, the latter a loan. Hyper-urban forms occur, e.g., *foot* pronounced as [fy:t] instead of [fu:t]: 'het is wel opmerkelijk, dat de *uu* voor elken Boerenfries met heerige allures nog altijd een deftiger cachet heeft dan de *oe*. Dat de *uu* eens beschaafd Hollandsch geweest moet zijn, weet niemand meer, maar de oude traditie van deftigheid is gebleven' (85).

Thus the peripheries of the 16th and 17th century Holland culture preserve today a speech-form which at the center no longer exists; the center has since then changed the long high vowels to diphthongs. Kloeke hints that English, Dutch, and German, which all diphthongize, have in common not only their Germanic heritage, but also the long influence of Romanic culture. It was probably in Brabant and Antwerp that the diphthongizing pronunciation first appeared on Dutch territory. At the end of the 16th century we find a northerner mocking the diphthongizing pronunciation of Antwerp (103). At the beginning of the 16th century Antwerp, with some 88,000 inhabitants, was the greatest Dutch city; Amsterdam numbered some 13,500. By the first quarter of the 17th century Amsterdam had the lead, with a population of 100,000. Doubtless it was the well-to-do citizens who left the declining southern cities for the flourishing northern; the diphthongs came as an upper-class pronunciation. The native upper class took up the style; in time it was copied by ever wider strata. We may suppose that by the year 1600 the diphthongs had prevailed in Amsterdam. In the 17th century the poets (Breero, Vondel) already rhyme West Germanic [iu] with West Germanic [u:]. Today the diphthong, in one form or another, has conquered Holland. Hyper-forms exist, as *kluiven* 'peck, gnaw' for older *kluwen*[4].

Kloeke's discussion is illuminating and as pioneer work in the field of Standard Language will stand beside the English studies of H. C. Wyld. One wishes that Kloeke paid more attention to the coincidence of pho-

---

[4] Normally, West Germanic [u:w] is Dutch [y:w], e.g., *gruwen*: German *grauen*; see te Winkel, Paul's *Grundriss* I² 825.

nemes and its reverse. The fact that West Germanic [snu:t] and [fo:t] are in Dutch spoken with the same vowel, the coincidence of West Germanic [iu] and [u:] in modern Dutch, or the coincidence, in the dialect of Schermerhorn (112) of the correspondents of modern Dutch *ui* and *eu*,—such points deserve more stress. The exact shading of sounds is far less important than the distribution of phonemes among words. That is why the divergence of *mouse* and *house* in large eastern areas of Kloeke's territory is so decisive for his argument. In linguistic history, and especially in matters of borrowing, it is the displacement of the system which is important.

Kloeke's theoretical deductions regarding standard speech and dialects are valuable. Dialects are not, in principle, more archaic than standard languages. They do, however, often preserve the standard forms of an older time; these have taken generations to seep down into the dialect and may meanwhile have been superseded in the standard speech. The notion that a central language acts as a kind of police, retarding change in the dialects, is the reverse of the truth. Dialect speakers imitate the upper-class speech; they do so until the indigenous character of the dialect remains in only a few homely forms.

All this, of course, explains many of the irregularities which often are cited against the postulate of change in phonemes. Kloeke's study is not only a very skilful application of the linguistic methods that were developed in the last century, but also one more confirmation of the correctness of these methods. Thus, from the irregular distribution of the phonemes Kloeke is able to deduce, convincingly, that borrowing must have occurred: 'Bij de principieele aanvaarding van *oe*-relicten kunnen we m. i. niet ontkomen aan de conclusie, dat ook de *uu*-uitspraak van buitenaf is geimporteerd' (122). 'Zoo zal de lezer na bestudeering en vergelijking der *muus/moes*- en *huus/hoes*-lijnen er opnieuw van doordrongen worden, dat de *oe* > *uu*-ontwikkeling niet op langzame phonetische verandering maar op ontleening berust' (191). Such deductions are valid, of course, only so long as we adhere to the postulate that sound-change is change of phonemes as such, and therefore not subject to deflection by semantic factors (frequency, homonymy, etc.). If we gave up this postulate, deductions like these of Kloeke's would lose all cogency; we could then say that Dutch *snoet* was simply excepted (say, by 'sound-symbolism') from a general change of [u:] to [y:], and that eastern Dutch [hy:s] versus [mu:s] represented not a cultural irradiation but 'sporadic sound-change' or what not.

It is surprising, therefore, and, as to Kloeke's reasoning, most confusing,—I have had to extricate his deductions,—when one finds him engaged in a polemic against the very principles on which his work is based. Thus, opposite the last-quoted important deduction we read (190): 'Ten spijt van klankwetten en verdere geboden der Junggrammatiker is hier[5] een woord uit het geordend verband zijner klankgenooten getreden; immers men kan toch bezwaarlijk beweren, dat er ten aanzien van de phonetische praedispositie der woorden *hûs* en *mûs* eenig principieel verschil bestaat, en met verklaring volgens analogie is hier in 't geheel niets aan te vangen.' The answer is given by Kloeke himself on the next page. Similarly, in the introductory chapter, Kloeke confuses the whole issue by a polemic against the very men who taught us even to recognize linguistic borrowing. He recalls Paul's fumblings as to the degree of 'consciousness' of linguistic change.[6] Fortunately, these statements remain purely extraneous and do not affect the methods and conclusions of this excellent book, which greatly furthers our knowledge of standard speech and its effect upon dialects.

[5] He is referring to [hy:s] *house*, beside [mu:s] *mouse*.

[6] One hazards the guess that Kloeke has allowed himself to be imposed upon by the sensationalism of writers who, finding Brugmann and Meyer-Lubke hard reading and desperately complete, set out to produce a 'deeper' and more 'spiritual' version of linguistics, with all the bothersome details replaced by 'intuition'. Kloeke has no need of this. Schuchardt, through a historical accident, stood aside from the theoretical formulations of his contemporaries. Gilliéron, in spite of much vigorous and pleasing metaphor, insists upon 'l'implacable régime de la phonétique' (*Généalogie des mots qui désignent l'abeille*, Paris, 1918, *Bibliothèque de l'École des Hautes Études*, No. 225, p. 14; cf. also p. 261).

# B35. Review of Liebich

1929. *Language* 5.267–275.

*Konkordanz Pāṇini-Candra.* By Dr. Bruno Liebich. (Indische Forschungen, begründet von Alfred Hillenbrandt, in zwanglosen Heften herausgegeben von Bruno Liebich, 6. Heft.) Breslau: Verlag von M. & H. Marcus, 1928.

In this pamphlet Professor Liebich makes another contribution to our knowledge of the grammatical literature of India. The treatise of the Buddhist grammarian Candra (or Candragomin) was recovered for the modern world by patient search[1] and made accessible by the labors of Professor Liebich;[2] he has also determined[3] Candra's date (fl. 470 A.D.). The present pamphlet is a concordance showing which rules of Pāṇini were used by Candra: so far as they fell within the scope of his work, Candra used almost all of them. Of the exceptions a few were ruled out by the different mechanics of Candra's work, and a few are otherwise vouched for as ancient. On the whole, Liebich concludes (p. 49) that in the fifth century of our era the text of Pāṇini's *Rules* had the form which it has today.

The descriptive grammar of Sanskrit, which Pāṇini brought to its highest perfection, is one of the greatest monuments of human intelligence and (what concerns us more) an indispensable model for the description of languages. The only achievement in our field which can take rank with it is the historical linguistics of the nineteenth century, and this, indeed, owed its origin largely to Europe's acquaintance with the Indian grammar.

---

[1] See S. K. Belvalkar, *An account of the different existing systems of Sanskrit grammar*, Poona, 1915, p. 58.

[2] Text, Leipzig 1902 (*Abhandlungen fur die Kunde des Morgenlandes* 11, 4); text with Candra's own commentary, Leipzig 1918 (same, 14); analysis, *Sitzungsberichte der Heidelberger Akademie der Wissenschaften phil.-hist. Kl.*, 1920, 13.

[3] See *Jahresbericht der schlesischen Gesellschaft für vaterländische Kultur* 81 (1903), iv, 24. On p. 47 of the present pamphlet Liebich refers to this article with the words 'in meinem Aufsatz: Das Datum Candragomin's und Kalidasa's (1903)'. The same reference without even the date, Belvalkar 58. One needs at least *Orientalische Bibliographie* (Berlin 1888 ff.) to learn where the article appeared. Such references, not uncommon among writers on Sanskrit grammar, create an unnecessary hardship. I shall try in what follows to give an elementary bibliography of the subject.

Indian grammar has been undervalued and neglected by many linguists, especially in America. In part this neglect is due to a misconception of its historical place. European scholars naturally supposed that Sanskrit grammar bore the same relation to Sanskrit literature as Latin grammar bears to Roman literature. They assumed that the classical Sanskrit of literature represented a real development (or, perhaps, stagnation) and that the so-called 'native grammar' pictured, more or less accurately, some stage of this evolution. When they found in the grammar forms which they had not seen in the literature, they accused the grammarians of fraud. Bopp,[4] for instance, so judged of a form like *ati-nu-* '(gone) out of the ship' (*nau-* 'ship'), a form which (whatever its history[5]) would be questioned by no modern linguist. Consequently, the European saw in classical texts a primary document, in the grammar a secondary one and unreliable at that. This was Whitney's view, to which he gave unfortunate expression.[6] We now know that this view was the reverse of the truth. Far from inventing forms, Pāṇini was describing a colloquial speech, a conservative upper-class language, to be sure, but a language native to him and used in everyday life by the Brahmins in his part of northwestern India. It is much the same language as that of the oldest Brāhmaṇas and Sūtras.[7] After Pāṇini's time Sanskrit spread over India as an ecclesiastical, literary, and official language. From the first century B.C. to the fourth century A.D. it superseded the Prākrits as the language of inscriptions.[8] The first step in upper-class education from that time on and largely to the present day was the acquisition of Sanskrit. It began, somewhat harshly and with bad linguistic pedagogy, by the child's memorizing Pāṇini's grammar or one of the grammars derived from it. Classical Sanskrit literature was written by men who had learned Sanskrit composition from grammar and dictionary and used these books as their guides and authorities for correct usage. Commentators on works of this literature hasten to justify unusual forms by a reference to the grammar. Deviations from the forms prescribed by Pāṇini are merely errors in Sanskrit composition.

[4] *Ausführliches Lehrgebäude der Sanskrita Sprache*, Berlin 1827, p. 325; cf. Liebich, *Panini*, Leipzig 1891, p. 42.

[5] Brugmann, *Grundrisz der vergleichenden Grammatik der indogermanischen Sprachen*[2] 2. 1. 137, Strassburg 1906.

[6] AJP 5.279 (1884). The crucial point is Whitney's belief that 'Sanskrit, even that of the most modern authors, even that of the pandits of the present day, is the successor, by natural processes of tradition, of the older dialects' (p. 294). The successors, in this sense, are of course the modern Indo-Aryan vernaculars; the tradition of Sanskrit is a learned one, based on phonetics, grammar, and dictionary. Whitney's article was reprinted with acknowledgment of the source but no word of comment, in the *Indian Antiquary* 14.33 (1885)—a quiet and overwhelming reproof, since in those days the *Indian Antiquary* was publishing the masterly articles of R. G. Bhandarkar and F. Kielhorn. See also G. Bühler, *Indian Antiquary* 23.141 (1894); 250, and Liebich, *Panini* 51.

[7] Liebich, *Panini* 50.

[8] Otto Franke, *Pāli und Sanskrit*, Leipzig 1893.

A second cause of our neglect of Indian grammar was a sense of superiority: because the Indians had not discovered the history of language, their work was supposed to be negligible. One forgot that the comparative grammar of the Indo-European languages got its start only when the Pāṇinean analysis of an Indo-European language became known in Europe. Historical linguistics depends upon a comparison of two or more languages or stages of the same language. Any gap in our knowledge of the languages or stages that are to be compared, sets an absolute limitation upon our results. If the accentuation of Sanskrit and Greek, for instance, had been unknown, Verner could not have discovered the pre-Germanic sound-change that goes by his name. Indo-European comparative grammar had (and has) at its service only one complete description of a language, the grammar of Pāṇini. For all other Indo-European languages it had only the traditional grammars of Greek and Latin, wofully incomplete and unsystematic. In the main, comparative and historical Indo-European grammar gathered its descriptive data as it went along. If one had had a complete and scientifically organized descriptive grammar, such as we have for classical Sanskrit, for a representative older stage of every Indo-European language (say, for Platonic Greek, Plautine Latin, Alfredian English, and so on), Indo-European comparative grammar would have developed with a speed and accuracy beyond our conception.

The third factor which led to the neglect of Indian grammar was its form. Pāṇini's treatise is intelligible only with a commentary; even with the many commentaries that we possess—and they contain a vast amount of intelligent and even brilliant scholarship—several lifetimes of work will have to be spent upon Pāṇini before we have a conveniently usable exposition of the language which he recorded for all time. The source of the difficulty is Pāṇini's brevity 'which a student of grammar is often likely to regard as the curse of his lot'.[9] Pāṇini's grammar consists of less than four thousand *Rules* (Sūtras, many of them only a few syllables long, few covering more than a line, in all some 80 pages of print), a *List of Roots* (Dhātupāṭha, some 25 pages of print), and a *List of Groups* (Gaṇapāṭha, 50 pages with liberal spacing).

One means by which Pāṇini attained this condensation is altogether commendable and, indeed, of great scientific importance, and is due to the thorough working up of the data. Whenever two or more forms have any feature in common, that feature is stated once and once only for all of them. If the common feature is present in an indefinite number of forms or in all forms showing a certain characteristic, then a general statement suffices: the forms are regular; if the common feature is present in only a limited number of forms and is not a function of any definable characteristic, then the forms are irregular and are listed by citation in the *Rules*

[9] Belvalkar, *Account* 23.

or as a group in the Gaṇapāṭha. In such a grammar the Latin nominative singular in -*s*, for instance, would not be mentioned over and over again (*servus, urbs, manus, facies*), but only once, and there would be a definition in the briefest possible unambiguous terms of the nouns whose nominative singular lacks this ending.

A second means of compression is not so directly implicit in the scientific form of presentation, but nevertheless greatly furthers it, much as a brief and accurate notation furthers mathematical reasoning. This second means is the use of abbreviations, silent letters, and arbitrary designations. Abbreviations are formed by writing the first member of any series with a silent letter which is placed arbitrarily at the end of the series. For instance, as a kind of preface to the grammar, the alphabet is arranged (in the so-called Çivasūtras) in a carefully planned order, with silent letters scattered through at certain points. By naming a single letter and one of the subsequent silent letters Pāṇini forms an abbreviation for all the letters (sounds) that intervene, including the letter named. This enables Pāṇini to say, for example, *jhal* for 'stop, sibilant, or *h*'. Silent letters and short arbitrary names for certain features—the meaning of all these is of course explained in special rules—further shorten the discussion. Thus, *kañ* denotes the suffix -*a*- by which *tā'dṛça*- 'such' is derived from *tad*- 'that' and *dṛç*- 'see'; the *k* and the *ñ* are silent letters which inform us as to the vowel-grade, accent, and other features of the derivative. This shorthand notation gives Hindu grammatical discussion a sweep and power which makes our terminology seem halting in comparison.

A third method of abbreviation is less happy. Although the basic arrangement of Pāṇini's treatise was relevant to the subject-matter, he subordinated this logical order to a requirement of conciseness: every rule is so placed that as many as possible of its words can be replaced by ditto marks because they repeat words of the preceding rule. For this purpose so many rules are torn from their natural place that the basic structure of the grammar is to a large extent obscured. Worst of all, the ditto marks (*anuvṛtti*) and their cessation (*nivṛtti*) at the end of a series of rules are not actually written in the treatise as we have it.

A fourth and even more unfortunate means of compression prevents our rearranging the rules. Even if one restores the words that have been replaced by imaginary ditto marks, one cannot rearrange the rules in natural order, because the position of a rule is one of the features which determines its validity (with relation to apparently conflicting rules) and its order of application (with relation to other rules that apply to the same form). Other features also, such as the more or less specific character of its wording, have to be considered in deciding whether a rule is applicable and in what relative order. For instance, an English grammar of the same kind might contain the following rules about nouns: (1) The plural adds [z];

(2) after unvoiced sounds [s]; (3) after sibilants and affricates [ez], and it might then be the order of these three rules which told us which one to apply in any given case, the later rule (3) outweighing (1) and (2). For certain irregular noun-plurals we should have the rule (4) *calf* etc. (the list would appear in the Gaṇapāṭha) voice the final spirant; here it might be the more specific nature of this rule which told us that it was to be applied *before* we made the choice between rules (1) and (2), or it might be the fact that this rule dealt with a sound farther from the end of the finished word, *calves*.[10]

The first great ancillary work to Pāṇini's grammar is the *Mahābhāṣya* of Patañjali.[11] In this treatise Patañjali discusses the *Supplementary Aphorisms* (vārtikas) of his predecessor Kātyāyana, which correct, supplement, eliminate as unnecessary, or justify the rules of Pāṇini; Patañjali gives a critique of Kātyāyana's vārtikas, deciding for or against each one, and adds vārtikas of his own. Already in this treatise much effort goes toward determining the real intent of Pāṇini's rules; since then many a life-work has gone into the task of elucidation. The chief later commentary is the *Kāçikā* of Jayāditya and Vāmana.[12] A great step forward was the thorough indexing of Pāṇini, a task performed by Otto Böhtlingk.[13] An English exposition of the *Rules*, based on the *Kāçikā*, is given by S. C. Vasu, *The Ashṭādhyāyī of Pāṇini*, Allahabad, 1891 ff.

The natural idea of rearranging Pāṇini's rules and supplying the dittoed words are carried out by Bhaṭṭoji Dīkṣita in his *Siddhāntakaumudī*.[14] For the reasons above stated the attempt was foredoomed to failure: the *Siddhāntakaumudī*, a splendid and brilliant piece of work, is as hard to deal with as Pāṇini. It has given rise to a large ancillary literature of its own.[15]

[10] While some such principles of interpretation (*Paribhāṣā's*) are given by Pāṇini in the form of rules, others are merely implicit in his treatise; these latter are discussed by Nāgojībhaṭṭa in his *Paribhāṣenduçekhara*, ed. and translated into English by F. Kielhorn, Bombay 1868–74 (*Bombay Sanskrit Series*, nos. 2; 7; 9; 12).

[11] The *Mahābhāṣya* was edited by F. Kielhorn, Bombay 1880–90 (*Bombay Sanskrit Series*, nos. 18; 20; 21; 22; 26; 28; 30), second edition, 1892–1909. The commentary of Kaiyaṭa and the sub-commentary of Nāgojī are included in an edition by several pandits, Benares, samvat 1943 (A. D. 1887), which is not accessible to me; also in a model edition by S. D. Kudāla, Bombay 1917 ff., of which only two volumes (one third of the work) have so far appeared. Belvalkar's account (pp. 28 ff.) of the Mahābhāṣya is to be corrected in one regard by F. Kielhorn's essay, *Kātyāyana and Patañjali: their relation to each other and to Pāṇini*, Bombay 1876, in another by the citation on p. 2 of the pamphlet here under review.

[12] Ed. by B. Sastri, Benares 1876–8, second ed. 1898; an excellent introduction is B. Liebich's *Zwei Kapitel der Kāçikā*, Breslau 1892; commentaries on the Kāçikā are Jinendrabuddhi's *Kāçikāvivaraṇapañjikā* (known also as the *Nyāsa*), ed S. C. Chakravarti, Rajshahi (Bengal) 1913 ff., and Haradatta's *Padamañjarī*, printed in *The Pandit*, vols. 10–21 (1888–99).

[13] *Pāṇini's Grammatik*, Leipzig 1887; Böhtlingk's first edition, Bonn 1839–40, had not the indices.

[14] Ed. with an English translation by S. C. Vasu and V. D. Vasu, Allahabad, n.d.

[15] An abridgment and simplification is Varadarāja's *Laghukaumudī*; in J. R. Ballantyne's edition (with English translation, fourth ed., Bombay 1896) it serves as an excellent introduction to Indian grammar.

An attempt to expand Pāṇini's doctrine into the form of a modern grammar was Theodor Benfey's *Vollständige Grammatik der Sanskrit-sprache.*[16] If one did not know of Benfey's many other achievements, one would take this grammar for the work of a lifetime. In the course of it he must have caught Pāṇini's hatred of repetition, for, after all, Benfey's treatise is too compact to serve the general linguist.

Franz Kielhorn, the foremost European student of Indian grammar, gave a greatly abridged summary of the Pāṇinean doctrine in his *Grammar of the Sanskrit Language*[17]

The non-Pāṇinean systems of Sanskrit grammar, such as Candra's, are in reality little else than rearrangements and simplifications of Pāṇini's doctrine.

A brief survey of both the Pāṇinean and the later systems is given by Belvalkar in his above-cited book. A good introduction to the Indian systems is a series of articles by Liebich, *Zur Einführung in die indische einheimische Sprachwissenschaft.*[18]

The extreme conciseness of Pāṇini and of his imitators impresses the modern reader in several ways: in part it merely obscures the content, in part it rests upon a useful and elegant notation, and in part it inheres in the scientific treatment and, once appreciated, will impose itself upon every treatise whose aim is description of a set of linguistic habits. This scientific condensation, which places every feature into its proper setting, is one of the two virtues which make Indian grammar a model for us. The other is completeness. Pāṇini gives the formation of every inflected, compounded, or derived word, with an exact statement of the sound-variations (including accent) and of the meaning. An English grammar on the same lines would provide accurately and completely for all such sets as the regular *kind : kindness* and the irregular *broad : breadth* (*long : length,* etc.), *high : height, young : youth, hot : heat, cold : cold*; it would provide for all the formal and semantic features of sets like *nation : national : nationality, hospital : hospitable : hospitality*; it would register the semantic peculiarities and the possibilities of formation of compounds like *red-bird* (a kind of bird), *red-head* (not a kind of head, but a person who has a red head), *blackhead, deadhead, bulkhead,* and so on; it would provide for the formation of adverbs like *along, away, ahead, aloft,* etc. For no language of the past have we a record comparable to Pāṇini's record of his mother-tongue, nor is it likely that any language spoken today will be so perfectly recorded.

Although Pāṇini's work has a history behind it, it is the achievement

---

[16] Leipzig 1852, the *Erste Abtheilung* of his *Handbuch der Sanskritsprache.*
[17] Fourth ed., Bombay 1896.
[18] *Sitzungsberichte der Heidelberger Akademie der Wissenschaften, phil.-hist. Kl.* 1919, 4; 15; 1920, 10; 13; cf. also his *Materialien zum Dhātupāṭha,* ibid., 1921, 7.

of one man. Indian grammar originated in unsystematic rules concerning the language of the Vedas, doubtless also in chance aphorisms which served as guides to correct upper-class speech (e.g.: *Does not* contracts to *doesn't*, *do not* to *don't*). Pāṇini's guiding principles of completeness, relevance, and brevity, and his methods of carrying out these principles, were the product of generations of scholarship. His one great fault, the extreme complication of the mechanism which determines the scope and order in which the rules are to be applied—this flaw, to whose mending lifetimes of labor have been devoted without final success—has at least the value of proving that the treatise is a unit, that Pāṇini (defined as the creator of this ingenious unity) was a man who really lived. His wording has been admirably preserved, doubtless because the text is a sacred one. Its nature is such that any additions by later hands will appear as foreign bodies. To recognize them is important not only because Pāṇini's grammar is one of the greatest monuments of man's intelligence, and not only because of the value of an accurate description of an early Indo-European colloquial language, but also because the great literature which uses classical Sanskrit as its medium was written by men who learned this language from whatever version and interpretation of Pāṇini's text was current in their time and place. Some accretions are very early. Both Patañjali and his predecessor Kātyāyana read at the very beginning of the grammar (1. 1. 6) a rule which does not fit into the Pāninean system and is probably marked as spurious by the completing word 'and' of the preceding rule, which closes a set of ditto marks. The rules 1. 2. 53–7, whose spuriousness is evident,[19] do not appear in Candra's grammar (though he has a sentence which approximates the first of them), but they are commented in the *Kāçikā* (seventh century)—as Liebich points out in the pamphlet under review (p. 48). In the introduction of our pamphlet Liebich shows the necessity, for this problem, of collecting the citations in Patañjali, whose work, again, is safeguarded by its very complication.[20]

The date of Pāṇini is one of the major problems of Indic chronology. Among the discussions are Th. Goldstücker's moody and fascinating book, *Pāṇini; his place in Sanskrit literature*,[21] Liebich's *Pāṇini* (with summary of older discussions), and Belvalkar's *Account*, pp. 13 ff. Pāṇini tells us (4. 1. 49) that the word *yavana* 'Greek' forms the irregular feminine *yavanānī*; Kātyāyana adds that this latter has also a semantic irregularity: it means Greek writing. Was this an oversight of Pāṇini's, or had the meaning changed after his time? Relatively, Pāṇini is contemporary with

---

[19] Cf. Böhtlingk's ed., pp. 18 and 477.

[20] See also Böhtlingk's ed, p. xix. On an accretion and transposition in the Gaṇapāṭha, see JAOS 47. 61.

[21] Published first as the introduction to a (never completed) photolithographic ed. of a MS of the *Mahābhāṣya*, London 1860; separately, London 1861; reprint, Allahabad 1914.

the old Sūtras and Brāhmaṇas (cf. above) or but little later than these earliest records of Indo-European prose. He is certainly some generations earlier than Patañjali, whose treatise is one of the few datable works of older Sanskrit literature. Patañjali gives as illustration of an event that occurred during his lifetime the sentences 'The Greek besieged Sāketa' and 'The Greek besieged the Mādhyamikas', which can refer only to Menandros, as Goldstücker saw,[22] and he refers to certain kings and dynasties in ways which enabled R. K. Bhandarkar to say with certainty that Patañjali wrote part of his book between 144 and 142 B.C.[23] Accounts of Chinese Buddhist pilgrims are used to date some of the later texts.

Indian grammar is not historical. It does not compete with such a work as the great historical Sanskrit grammar which Jakob Wackernagel is writing.[24] Three Europeans take rank beside the great Hindu authorities on Pāṇinean descriptive Sanskrit grammar: Franz Kielhorn, Otto Böhtlingk (through his indices), and, among the living, Bruno Liebich.

[22] *Panini*, pp. 176 ff.

[23] *Indian Antiquary* 1. 299 (1872); other references in Belvalkar's *Account* 32.

[24] *Altindische Grammatik*, 1, Göttingen 1896; 2. 1, 1905; 3. 1, 1929; Wackernagel throughout makes use of the Indian doctrine.

# B36. Linguistics as a Science

1930. *Studies in Philology* 27.553–557 (October).

[Note at bottom of first page: 'Address delivered before the Modern Language Association of America, Dec. 30, 1929.' The MLA and LSA meetings were held jointly in Cleveland, Ohio, that year. Bloomfield's address was the second of two on the evening program (apart from several delivered 'by title only'); the other was 'Literature as an Art', by Roberto Brenez-Mesén of Northwestern University.]

In speaking of linguistics as a science, I shall not deal with technical matters, but, presuming upon your patience, I shall speculate upon the service which the study of language may render to the sciences that deal with man, to humanistic studies, and to our view of the world. If in any sense I here represent linguists in general, I must add that very few of them share the beliefs to which I shall give voice. Even the methods of linguistic science which I take to confirm these beliefs are now being assailed,— mistakenly, in my opinion—by some students of language.

Linguistics is today a point of growth in science. On this, at least, there is agreement. Edward Sapir, an excellent scholar who would probably agree with very little of what I am saying tonight, writes, in the latest number of *Language* (5 [1929], 213): "... it is clear that the interest in language has in recent years been transcending the strictly linguistic circles. This is inevitable, for an understanding of language mechanisms is necessary for the study of both historical problems and problems of human behavior."

The question is how we are to interpret the spread of interest in language. Let me state my interpretation plainly at the outset: I believe that in the near future—in the next few generations, let us say—linguistics will be one of the main sectors of scientific advance, and that in this sector science will then win through to the understanding and control of human conduct.

In the domains of physics and biology science has for some time been working with success and has given us great power. In the domain of anthropology—that is, in the study of man's super-biological activities— science has been unsuccessful. In our universe man himself is the one factor of which we have no scientific understanding and over which we have no scientific control.

The truth of this contrast and its tragic import appear plainly in the fact that our achievements in non-human science do us little good, because we cannot understand or control their human consequences. We make powerful engines, but we have no way of deciding who is to use them, and we have seen them used for our destruction. We can prevent suffering and widen the scope of life, but the fruition of these our powers is distributed by such means as the hazards of gambling.

If we examine, now, the formulae which science uses in the area where it has been successful and compare them with the formulae that we use in the discussion of human affairs, we find a significant contrast. The physicist and the biologist do not content themselves with teleologic formulae. Teleology is a form of wording which says that things happen because there is a tendency for them to happen. Water seeks its own level; nature abhors a vacuum; trees strive towards the light. Physicists and biologists have long ago ceased to accept such teleologic pseudo-explanations, having recognized them as mere roundabout statements of the event. It is only when we deal with man that we are satisfied with teleologic formulae: men do things because they "want" or "choose" or "have a tendency" to do them. We speak this spell, without difficulty, over any and every human event, and remain as ignorant and helpless as we were before.

We keep ourselves in this dream by taking the primeval drug of animism. We look down upon animism when less fortunate groups of mankind resort to it in the face of lifeless things, as when the savage explains a thunderstorm by saying that an invisible manlike being directs the tempest. The Thunderer or Thunderbird is unseen, but his presence is convincingly manifest in the thunder and lightning. The savage is only doubling this absurdity when he applies his explanation to the acts of animals and persons by saying that inside the palpable and visible animal or person there lurks an impalpable and invisible double which somehow controls the former's actions. On this point Albert Paul Weiss published a beautiful little essay in the *Psychological Review* in 1919 (26, 327). Where we deal with man we have not yet progressed beyond the animistic view. In spite of the fact that the measured outcome of human activity (as, say, in lifting weights or in a metabolism test) never conflicts with the physical conditions, we insist that within each man and yet not as a part of his body there exists an invisible, supra-physical double, a "soul," "spirit," "mind," "will," "consciousness," or what not, which determines the actions of the man. Conveniently, of course, this invisible double is not subject to the regular sequences of events which science has found in the rest of the universe. Accounting with magic ease for anything and everything that may happen, animism obscures every problem and drugs us into accepting our ignorance and helplessness in the face of human conduct.

If it were possible to transfer the methods of physical or of biological science directly to the study of man, the transfer would long ago have been made. The monistic view of things—it matters not whether we call it materialism or idealism—which is implicit in all scientific endeavor, is as old as our civilization. We have failed not for lack of hypotheses which equate man with the rest of the universe, but for lack of a hypothesis (short of animism) which provides for the peculiar divergence of man. It is certain that the actions of man involve some factor which is not present in the actions of plants and animals, just as these involve a factor which is not present in the actions of inanimate matter. It used to be thought that in plants and animals there was a "vital principle" which is wanting in lifeless things. That was animism; today we know that the peculiar factor in living organisms is a highly specialized, unstable chemical combination, the protoplasm. Let me now state my belief that the peculiar factor in man which forbids our explaining his actions upon the ordinary plane of biology, is a highly specialized and unstable biological complex, and that this factor is none other than language.

This hypothesis is not original with me; it is very carefully worked out in Weiss's *Theoretical Foundations of Human Behavior* (second edition, Columbus, Adams, 1929). I need speak only of the perspective in which this view appears to a student of language.

It is a striking circumstance, perhaps a coincidence, that for more than half a century linguists have been studying a fundamental phase of human activity without taking recourse to teleologic or animistic formulae. To be sure, linguists, like other people, are finalists and mentalists in their explicit opinions about human affairs. It is only in their working methods that they have abandoned these forms of discourse. You may strip the teleologic and animistic verbiage from any linguistic treatise, and the effect is only an improvement in style, with all the technical procedures and all the results unchanged. Linguists do not pretend to explain conditions or changes by saying that the speakers strove toward an end, such as euphony or clearness, and when linguists speak of a soul or a mind, the term is otiose, for they suppose this soul or mind to act only along a single biologically explicable pattern—that of substitute stimuli—in what to linguists is known as analogic change. It is true that in the last years some students of language have tried to galvanize the finalistic and animistic factors into some effect upon linguistic forms, but these scholars have in this way produced nothing but less useful restatements of results that were gained by the ordinary methods of linguistic study. In short, the prescientific approach to human things has long been abandoned—and this in spite of theory—in the study of language, the very activity of man which, as some of us now hope, will account for the super-biological features of man's conduct.

How this account is to be made is a technical problem. Upon the success of this accounting depends the verification of the hypothesis which I have stated. It is a step in advance, at any rate, that we now confront a series of definite problems instead of the dreary routine of affixing a magic formula, without result, to any and every event that shows its head. To account for the infinite variety and poignancy of human experience, to explain the growth and coherence of the vast complexes of action which we call cultures, or even to tell in reasonable sequence the tale of a single human life. —the least of these things is today beyond our power, certainly beyond the power of any one science, and most certainly beyond the competence of linguistics. One can only indicate a few dark places into which the study of language may someday throw light.

Before a man performs an action, he often describes it in words. Now, man is not equipped to observe the physiologic sequences that lead to his actions, but he is very well equipped to observe the preliminary verbal statement. Accordingly he mistakes the verbal statement for the cause of his action; it is the one relatively constant antecedent; when it is absent, one can at least say that it took place "in the mind." It is this error which underlies such notions as "will," "wish," "desire," or "conscious striving." It is the source of the teleologic concept. The fact that man can describe in words some action that he may later perform, may turn out to be largely a matter of linguistics; a better understanding of the nature and function of language may teach us no longer to look upon the preliminary wording (disguised under some animistic term) as the cause of human actions.

By speech man reproduces the universe in symbolic sound-waves or in the secondary but more permanent symbols of writing, ineffectively, it would seem at first blush, yet with an ominous annihilation of space and time. This may be the source of man's power and the reality which we adumbrate when we speak of his intelligence or of his depth of feeling. By their common habits of speech, the individuals of a human speech-community influence each other and work together with an accuracy of adjustment that makes of the speech-community something like a single, super-biological organism,—Weiss's "compound multicellular" type of organization. It may be, now, the social value, the tremendous impact of his speech-forms when they are overtly uttered, that makes it possible for a man, even in the absence of significant outer events, to live most intensely and sometimes to bring forth from such an hour an enduring expression, which we call a work of art.

Whether at these points or at others, I believe that the study of language will be the ground where science gains its first foothold in the understanding and control of human affairs.

# B37. Review of Ries

1931. *Language* 7.204–209.

*Was ist ein Satz?* By John Ries. (Beiträge zur Grundlegung der Syntax. Heft 3.) Prag: Taussig & Taussig, 1931. (Gedruckt mit Unterstützung der Strassburger Wissenschaftlichen Gesellschaft zu Frankfurt a.M.) Pp viii + 236.

The author of Was ist Syntax? (Marburg 1894; a revised edition appeared as Number I of the present series, in 1927) and of the Wortstellung im Beowulf (Halle 1907) will always be heard with respect; it is to be hoped that we shall hear more from him including a syntax of modern standard German (see Number II of this series). In the present volume, Ries discusses the term *sentence*; on pages 208 ff. he quotes some 150 earlier definitions of this term; in the body of the book he comments on these, sets up a definition of his own, and discusses its applicability. More searching than his predecessors, Ries improves upon them and does perhaps as well as can be done with the traditional mentalistic approach to this question. I believe, however, that this approach leads nowhere.

Like earlier students, Ries commands the linguist (in particular, himself) to give a scientific definition of the semi-popular (in origin, philosophic-scholastic) term, *sentence*. This is a pseudo-problem;[1] we have no guarantee that the popular usage is consistent, and, even if it is consistent, we have no guarantee that it makes a classification that will be useful to science. We are under no obligation to adopt or redefine popular terms, or to bother with them at all. If a scientist, having discovered some useful classification, needs a name for one of his classes, he may invent one (e.g., *gas, ampere, ultra-violet*), or he may adopt and re-define some popular term that lies not too far away, and attach it to his class. The choice is a matter of taste.

For instance, the semi-popular term *syntax* is used, with some fluctuation, for a hodge-podge of things which present no scientifically useful common feature; in 1894, having discovered a relevant classification of certain grammatical phenomena, Ries adopted and re-defined this term

[1] Cf. Weiss, Psychological Review 32. 176 (1925).

(instead of inventing a name) for one of his classes; ever since then *syntax* has borne, for the linguist, not the vague meaning of the old, semi-popular term, but the precise (in this instance, much narrower) meaning which Ries gave to it. In the present case, however, Ries insists (1) that we define scientifically the things to which the term *sentence* is popularly applied (see, especially, 21–23), and (2) that we use *sentence* as a scientific term only in this way. I insist that (1) may be impossible or inept and, in any case, involves an unscientific approach, and that (2) is merely a question of taste. We do not ask a zoologist to define the term *fish* so as to include whales, or insist that if he will not include whales in a class with fish, he must not use the term *fish*.

Since Ries starts with a scholastic-popular term and with a critique of largely philosophic-psychologic earlier definitions, he does not reach the ground of linguistics. His definition reads: 'A sentence is a grammatically constructed minimum unit of speech which expresses its content with respect to the latter's relation to reality'.[2] These are not linguistic terms; however clear this definition may be to philosophers, it has no meaning in the linguistic world of discourse. We need either the rest of Ries's text or his demonstration by means of examples before we can guess that he means the finite-verb-and-subject 'sentence' of Indo-European, and along with it, doubtless, similar constructions (but what are the limits?) in other languages.

The group of phenomena with which we are here concerned may be described as follows.[3]

Some linguistic forms bear no partial phonetic-semantic resemblance to other forms; that is, they do not consist of lesser meaningful forms. Examples are *ouch*; *yes*; *boy*; the suffix *-ish*. Let us call these 'simple forms'.

Some linguistic forms bear partial phonetic-semantic resemblances to other forms; that is, they consist of two or more smaller meaningful forms. Examples are *boy-ish*; *a good boy*; *John ran away*. Let us call these 'complex forms', and let us say that they 'contain' two or more 'included forms'.

---

[2] Page 99: Ein Satz ist eine grammatisch geformte kleinste Redeeinheit, die ihren Inhalt im Hinblick auf sein Verhältnis zur Wirklichkeit zum Ausdruck bringt.

[3] I cannot here simply refer to *Language* 2.153 (1926) [the reference is to B21—CFH] because the term *sentence*, here to be avoided, is there employed. Lest I be accused of taking things easy (cf. Jahresbericht für germ. Phil. 1926–7.29), let me suggest that clearness and simplicity of statement is in this field by no means a sign of naïvety.

[The unsigned brief remarks in the Jahresbericht, on Bloomfield's 'Set of Postulates', are as follows: 'Empfiehlt die Methoden der Mathematik, von gewissen klar formulierten Definitionen und Axiomen aus schrittweise vorzugehen, auf die Sprachwissenschaft zu übertragen. Das wird die Linguisten zu grösserer Klarheit und Strenge im Denken erziehen, manches Missverständnis würde beseitigt und manche stillweigend gemachte Voraussetzung erst geprüft werden. Als Beispiel gibt B. eine Reihe von solchen Satzen, die durchweg einfach und klar sind, aber sich doch manchmal die Sache zu leicht machen.'—CFH]

The complex forms of any language present only a limited number of patterns. These patterns consist of features such as the selection of the included forms (we say *doggish* but not *\*horse-ish*; *manly* but not *\*boy-ly*; here belong also features of congruence, government, etc.), the order of the included forms (never *\*ish-boy* or *\*boy good a*), and phonetic modification (sandhi). Let us call these patterns 'constructions'.

The entire stretch of an actual speech-utterance may make up a single linguistic form. This form may be a simple form, as when one says *Ouch!* or *Yes!* or it may be a complex form, as when one says *Quickly!* or *John ran away*. In either case, the linguistic form which is coextensive with the whole speech, is the 'largest-form' in the utterance. If simple, it is the only form; if complex, it is larger than the included forms.

What is in one utterance the largest-form, may in another utterance figure as an included form; the largest-forms of the preceding utterances appear as included forms in the utterances *Ouch, damn it! Yes, sir! Come quickly! Then John ran away. When John ran away we went home.*

Many languages have special markers which appear in forms when they are used as largest-forms. We are told that in classical Chinese certain particles were used at the end of such forms. The modern languages of Europe similarly use certain pitch-phonemes at the end of largest-forms: our falling pitch at the end of statements and our rising pitches for the two kinds of questions.

Some utterances consist of more than one linguistic form. For instance, someone meets an acquaintance and says: *How are you? That's a pretty tie you've got on. Are you playing tennis this afternoon?* This utterance contains three largest-forms—that is, three forms none of which is in this utterance included, by virtue of some constructional pattern, in a larger form. In the modern languages of Europe each largest-form has, in this case too, its own pitch-marker. Indeed, English and some other languages, notably German, use a construction whose chief characteristic is the use of only one pitch-marker in what would otherwise be two largest-forms, as: *Ouch, damn it!* or *Yes, sir!* or *It's ten o'clock, I have to go home* (in contrast with: *It's ten o'clock. I have to go home*, with falling pitch on *o'clock*). German examples are: *Es war einmal ein Mann, der hatte drei Söhne*, or *Es ist ein Wetter, man tät keinen Hund aus der Stube jagen*. In part this placing of final-pitch is supplemented by a contrasting (rising) pitch-phoneme at the end of the first component, and in part by the use of special word-forms, such as *der* for *er* in German. Let us call this type of construction 'parataxis'.

In most languages, perhaps in all, certain forms never serve as largest-forms, e.g. *-ish* or *-ly* in English. Let us call these 'bound forms', and all others, 'free forms'.

Most or all languages favor certain ones among their free forms for use as largest-forms. These 'favorite largest-forms' are distinguished by lexical and grammatical features; in English, for instance, they consist of a verb (*Come!*) or contain one (*He came*). The favorite types, when used as largest-forms, have a meaning which may be roughly defined as 'complete and novel' (observation, instruction, etc.), while the non-favorite types have such meanings as 'intense stimulus' (*Ouch!*), 'decision on earlier speech' (*Yes! No!*), or 'supplementation of earlier speech' (*Tomorrow*). Needless to say, these meanings cannot be defined in terms of our science and cannot enter into our definitions; for every language the definition of the favorite largest-form types (and of everything else) is to be made in terms of forms, constructions, phonemes, or other linguistically determinable features.

The favorite largest-form types in English are two. One consists of forms that have the construction of actor plus finite verb (*John ran away; Did John run away?* etc.); the other consists of an infinitive verb-form with or without modifiers (*Come!* or *Come here!*).

When a language has several favorite largest-form types, some or all of them may show a common feature. In Latin, for instance, there were three favorite types:

(1) a finite verb containing a personal-anaphoric actor: *amat; pluit; ama! amate!* The finite verb could be accompanied by a more specific actor-form (in cross-reference with the personal-anaphoric actor-element that was morphologically present in the verb-form), and by other accompaniments: *Pater filium amat;*

(2) a finite verb containing a goal element: *amatur; pugnatur; amare! amamini!* with similar supplements: *domus struitur;*

(3) two substantive (noun, pronoun, or adjective) forms: *Beati possidentes; Usus tyrannus;* the meaning was that A 'is equated to or subsumed under' B.[4]

Here (1) and (2), having in common the finite-verb structure, together form a group which we may call the 'narrative' type of favorite largest-form, as opposed to (3) the 'equational' type. All three types have in common a binary structure: each consists of two (morphologically or syntactically distinct) component forms, one of which (A) is of substantival character. In type (3) the second form (B) also is substantival (in Latin; in Russian not always), but differs formally, for it is either an adjective or else is spoken after the first component. We may call these binary types of

---

[4] Ries 158 ff. (my examples from 164) views this type in Greek and Latin as a literary product and denies its existence in PIE. Even if true, these historical considerations should not affect our definition, even for these languages, not to mention general linguistics. In Russian, for that matter, this type is part of the normal colloquial language: *on dóma* 'he is at home'; *soldát xrábr* 'the soldier is brave'; see, e.g. Berneker, Russische Grammatik[2] 129, Leipzig 1911.

favorite largest-forms 'predications'; the A component is the 'subject', and the B component the 'predicate'.[5]

Almost any new language might add to the above material. What I have said may be all amiss. This cannot affect the point at issue: the method of scientific definition. We have, rightly or wrongly, delimited certain classes of phenomena, and may now proceed to give them names, for the purpose of shortening further discourse. I have suggested the following terms (LANGUAGE 2.153 [1926]):

> simple form: *morpheme*;
> largest-form: *sentence*;
> minimum free form: *word*;
> non-minimum free form: *phrase*.

This definition of the term *sentence* is due to A. Meillet (Introduction à l'étude comparative des langues indo-européennes[3] 339, Paris 1912): (Au point de vue linguistique, et abstraction faite de toute considération de logique ou de psychologie, la phrase peut être définie:) un ensemble d'articulations liées entre elles par des rapports grammaticaux et qui, ne dépendant grammaticalement d'aucun autre ensemble, se suffisent à elles-mêmes.

Ries does not see that of all the definitions he quotes, this one alone fulfils the essential condition of speaking in terms of linguistics, delimiting a recognizable class of linguistic phenomena. In particular, he condemns it for several faults of wording: superfluities, and the use of 'dépendant', since some included forms also do not 'depend' on other forms (e.g. *boy* in *good boy*). If we avail ourselves of Ries's criticisms, this definition will be re-worded: une forme qui ne fait partie d'aucune autre forme—where the word 'forme' implies, by virtue of our subject-matter, 'linguistique' and 'grammaticalement une', and 'fait partie' similarly implies 'grammaticalement'. For strictly scientific discourse this wording may be better, but one questions whether it would have served as well in Meillet's Introduction.[6]

---

[5] It is conceivable that in a language with a binary equational type, the two components might be quite alike, so that we could not distinguish an A ('subject') from a B ('predicate'). These terms are useful for the description of a language like Latin, which has more than one binary type; for languages like modern French, German, or English, which have only one binary type (our actor-and-action phrase), they are superfluous. In meaning, the subject in Latin and Greek is the thing talked about and the predicate an action, quality, equal, or classification assigned to it; meanings, however, cannot be stated in terms of our science and cannot be used for our definitions. The historical accident that the linguistic phenomena which here concern us, were first observed by philosophers and by them (wisely or unwisely) incorporated into their discipline of 'logic', concerns us not at all.

[6] E. A. Esper calls my attention to an error in my English wording of Meillet's definition, LANGUAGE 2. 158: 'A maximum construction in any utterance is a *sentence*'. For 'construction' one must, of course, read 'form', since otherwise, the definition, if it meant anything

Ries's own definition, interpreted by his text and his examples, covers only the narrative types of Latin and their close cognates in other Indo-European languages—what I should label as 'the PIE (or Latin, etc., as the case may be) narrative predicational sentence', or by some briefer made-to-order tag. As a matter of convenience, I would suggest that the term *sentence* be not defined to cover any specifically Latin or even Indo-European phenomenon; this would make it disputable (or force re-definition or rule it out) for descriptions of other languages. The term *sentence* is so handy that we had better apply it to some universal phenomenon of language. This is what Meillet has done.

at all, would exclude largest-forms that happened to contain only a single morpheme; e.g. *Come! Ouch! Yes.*

# B38. Obituary of Weiss

1931. *Language* 7.219–221.

Albert Paul Weiss was born September 15th, 1879, and died April 3d, 1931. These dates will be recorded, it is safe to say, near the beginning of a not unimportant chapter in the history of science: the study of man.

Weiss was not a student of language, but he was probably the first man to see its significance. He saw that language supplied the key to those phenomena of human conduct and achievement which hitherto had been attributed to non-physical forces. There had always been students who refused to believe in the spectres of our tribal animism (*mind, consciousness, will*, and the like) but these students had never given a clear-cut and satisfactory explanation for the super-biological actions of man—the actions which transcend the possibilities of the animal world. In our time these students are the behaviorists,—an ugly name, said Weiss, but accepted it for want of better. Weiss was a devoted pupil of Max Meyer; the latter's system, most thorough in eliminating animism and finalism, formed the basis of Weiss's work. The pupil's enormous advance was due to his evaluation of language.

In addition to 'handling' responses, man has developed a system of vocal responses, language. These vocal responses serve as stimuli to the speaker's fellows: the members of a speech-community co-operate, by means of language, in spite of the discontinuity of their individual nervous systems. The effects of this mediation between the nervous systems of separate individuals are so far-reaching that anyone who tries to explain human behavior and leaves language out of account, is sure to lapse into popular animistic pseudo-explanations, or else to give an incomplete picture. Our animistic terms (*mind, consciousness, sensation, perception, emotion, volition*, and so on) were produced, among the folk or by philosophers, in pre-scientific times, when language was taken for granted. Sequences of events in which human beings participate, can be understood only when one knows that the members of a speech-community have been trained to produce conventional speech-sounds in certain types of situations and to behave accordingly in response to these sounds. Viewed without its antecedents and consequences, *biophysically*, the speech-sound is a slight displacement of matter; it is effective *biosocially*, as a trigger-mechanism, thanks to the training (structural modification) of the speakers' nervous systems. By virtue of this common attunement the members of a speech-community cooperate; the space between their nervous systems is bridged, from moment to moment, by the sound-waves which they utter and hear. Beyond the other types of organization—atomic, molecular, crystalline, protoplasmic-unicellular, multicellular—language brings into the universe the *compound multicellular* or *social* type of organization.

'From a mere consideration of man's position in the scale of *biological* development, his libraries, museums, telephones, cinema, microscopes, telescopes, and sky-scrapers seem incomprehensible.'

'The great gap between the achievements of the modern man and the anthropoid apes or some of the highly socialized bees, wasps, ants, can best be understood as due to the absence of language in the animals.'

'Human achievement, as compared with animal achievement, differentiates itself particularly through its greater variety and through its coöperative character. The essential condition for producing these effects is a high degree of sensorimotor interchangeability between individuals. . . . Specific types of external stimuli, in addition to releasing specific manual responses, also release verbal responses, and these become, for other individuals, substitute stimuli for the original stimuli. . . . In the evolutionary development of language we approach, as a limit, a condition in which a greater and greater number of the objects and events in the universe (past, present, and future) are represented by substitute language stimuli and their more permanent substitutes, exhibiting a wider range of interrelationships than the original objects and events themselves. In this sense language as a form of behavior is the reduction of all the objects and processes of the universe to library dimensions.'

'The language mechanism forms the characteristic factor in human behavior.'[1]

It is significant that, having found this key, Weiss devoted his last years

---

[1] 'Linguistics and Psychology,' LANGUAGE 1.52 (1925); the last sentence is from 'One Set of Postulates for a Behavioristic Psychology,' Psychological Review 32. 83 (1925); cf. Theoretical Basis[2] 425 ff. (see below).

Of special interest to the linguist are:

'The Relation between Structural and Behavior Psychology,' Psychological Review 24. 301 (1917);

'The Relation between Functional and Behavior Psychology,' ibid. 353;

'The Mind and the Man-Within', ibid. 26. 327 (1919);

'Conscious Behavior', Journal of Philosophy, Psychology and Scientific Methods 15. 631 (1918);

'The Relation between Physiological Psychology and Behavior Psychology,' ibid. 16. 626 (1919);

and, above all, A Theoretical Basis of Human Behavior, Columbus (R. G. Adams & Co.) 1925; second edition, revised (and much enlarged), 1929.

to phenomena such as the esthetic and ethical, which until now had been least accessible to materialistic interpretation.

Weiss's style is direct. He says big things so simply that the reader, unforewarned, fails sometimes to grasp the full import. His plainness of speech sometimes goes beyond the conventional; a rhetorician would blue-pencil more than one of his sentences. Unhampered by ornament or mannerism, this Spartan style speaks powerfully and at times with great beauty.[2]

In word and deed, as in his writings, Weiss was completely the man of science. He was an excellent mathematician: in everyday converse he spoke accurately and without prejudgment, so that his hearers sometimes found depth or wit in what for him was only straightforward speech. He was an inventive and skilful technician: in daily life his helpful competence, his utter divorcement from the simian and the rapacious traits of our species, led one to see a high grace or a saintly unselfishness in what for him must have been merely plain, sensible conduct. He attributed importance to no person, least of all to himself. As he had been in good fortune, with the prospect of unbounded ventures, so he remained through years of sickness, when for long periods he was denied even the slightest activity. The transition was sudden, an afternoon of outdoor play broken off by the apparition of heart-disease. He had been a leader of his time, as a scientist may, guiding into the unknown a band of younger bold explorers; now he depended, no less manfully, upon the devotion of his wife. What the world owes to her cannot be measured; the debt includes all Weiss's work of these last years.

Every step in the advance of human knowledge meets with a resistance which has grown feebler as the centuries have passed. The time may be near when Albert Paul Weiss will be counted a heroic figure in the progress of science.

[2] See, for an instance, the closing pages of the Theoretical Basis, in the second edition.

# B39. Review of Hermann

1932. *Language* 8.220–232.

*Lautgesetz und Analogie.* By Eduard Hermann. (Abhandlungen der Gesellschaft der Wissenschaften zu Göttingen. Philologisch-historische Klasse, Neue Folge 23.3.) Berlin: Weidmann, 1931.

This treatise is an example of the theoretical fugues of many present-day European linguists, who temporarily abrogate both the general inhibitions of science and their fidelity to linguistics, in order to enjoy ein Schäfer-stündchen with the common notions of the street. These excesses embar-rass the communion of linguistics with the sister sciences and endanger the supply of sound linguists in the coming generation.

The rise of modern technology and science did not at first affect people's view of human institutions; linguistic study, in particular, remained for a time true to its philosophical and literary origin. However, language, the most fundamental of human activities, is also the simplest. Whoever observes or records forms of speech, is sure to find facts that invite the kind of grouping and presentation which we call science. Alphabetic writ-ing implies phonemic structure; the Greek tradition reveals the structure of the phrase; the resemblances among the Latin languages and among the Germanic show an alluring but incomplete order; at the end of the eighteenth century, the Hindu grammar taught Europeans to see the structure of words. In an epoch when the scientific method was revolution-izing, at great speed, all the conditions of life, this method was bound, no matter how indirectly, to affect even the student of language. Slowly, and not without dispute and misunderstanding (such as appeared in Schleicher's pseudo-evolutionary theory), the linguist adopted the essen-tial habits of the scientific method. The result was so favorable as to carry linguistics far ahead of the other human sciences. The methods developed by the linguists of the nineteenth century are still today the working methods of every competent linguist, including Hermann. They have been refined and supplemented, but not replaced, by later acquisitions, notably the phonemic principle and the mapping of dialect differences. Under these methods the phenomena of linguistic change, which baffled the scholars of the seventeenth and eighteenth centuries, can be compactly recorded and classified, and even subjected, within methodically defined limits, to inference and prediction. Like all scientific methods, they are justified by their performance and only by this.

The method of linguistic history classifies linguistic change into three great empirical types. One type is the change of phonemes or combinations of phonemes, such as [þ] > [d] in older German, or, more recently, [st-] > [št-] in part of the German area. The second type is the extension of significant elements into new combinations, which we call analogic change (E cow-s beside older kine) or semantic change (E bread and meat beside older bread and flesh or bread and flesh-meat). The third type is the adoption of features and forms from foreign speech, as in E rouge from French, or Central-Western American E ['raðr] rather from New England, beside native ['rɛðr]. This classification and all the technique that goes with it, is the common equipment and, up to the present day, the only methodical equipment, of all linguists, from Eduard Hermann down to the greenest student.

In order to transmit his method to new persons, and in order to make possible a synthesis with the results of other sciences, the scientist formulates his method in theoretical terms. This formulation takes the shape of a set of consistent assumptions (that is, hypotheses, postulates, axioms), stated in terms of the particular science, excepting only that a minimum number of basic terms is necessarily taken over, undefined, from other sciences. The nineteenth-century masters fulfilled this demand of formulation only so far as was required by the need for transmission. The present-day student who looks forward to a wider synthesis, will seek a more complete and formally unified statement; in LANGUAGE 2.153 (1926) [our B21—CFH] the reader will find an attempt at such a statement. It is customary to speak of methods in terms of assumptions. Our critique of the ancient Greek etymologists, for instance, takes the form of saying that they made no consistent assumptions about phonetic change.

It is possible that a set of assumptions entirely different from ours would lead to better results. It is possible, also, that inconsistencies lurk somewhere in our assumptions. It is probable that our assumptions will be refined, and certain that our application of them (that is, the skill with which our methods are applied to our data by each one of us and by our craft as a whole) will improve as we gain in practice and in accumulated results. Any particular formulation of our methods may fail to represent them correctly and will surely be antiquated, if in no other way, then at least by the progressive refinement of our technical vocabulary. At this moment I am not concerned with defending our assumptions, and least of all with defending my formulation of them; what concerns me is the fact that even some of the ablest men in our craft do not seem to understand the nature of a scientific assumption.

One can invalidate a set of assumptions only by presenting an alternative set which fits more inclusively or more snugly over the data of observation. One can invalidate single assumptions by showing that they are inconsistent with the rest of the set, and one can add single assumptions, by way of replacement or otherwise, provided that these new assumptions are consistent with the assumptions which one proposes to retain. Facts of observation which are not covered by our assumptions are kept in the foreground as an unexplained residuum. Indeed, this setting off of problems is one of the advantages of scientific procedure; as the discrepant facts accumulate, they may reveal a common characteristic which either betrays their true place within our assumptions or leads to a revision of the assumptions themselves. Above all: any change in the assumptions necessitates a complete weeding out of all earlier conclusions that depend upon the rejected assumptions, and a re-working of all data embodied in those conclusions. This re-working, if the change in the assumptions is justified, will lead to a more inclusive classification of the data, or to a classification that fits more accurately and simply into the total result of science.

All this is so elementary that I did not say it in LANGUAGE 2.153 and say it now with fear of the editorial waste-basket. Yet a scholar of the very highest rank, A. Sommerfelt, NTS 1.22 (1928), agrees with my formulation of our assumptions, including the definition of the phoneme as a 'minimum same of vocal feature', but at the same time insists that these phonemes are to have 'psychic values', which differ in different significant forms (e.g., in different words) and enable some of these forms to resist phonetic change. Sommerfelt actually quotes the sentence, 'Linguists who believe that certain forms resist phonetic change, implicitly reject these assumptions', a sentence whose only possible raison d'être is to raise the question of consistency in anticipation of just such objections as Sommerfelt's; the same question, with the same intent, is raised page 153, fn.3, in connection with the term *meaning*. Needless to say, any effective change in the assumptions and definitions which establish the terms *meaning* and *phoneme*, necessitates a radical revision of the whole of any system of linguistic assumptions. Yet Sommerfelt does not even touch upon the question of consistency.

In fact, Sommerfelt does not enable his readers to make any such test, for he does not state what place the term *psychic value* is to occupy in our system, or even tell us whether it is to figure among the undefined initial terms or is to be introduced by assumptions and definitions within the system. Apparently the psychic values are features of meaning, for Sommerfelt objects to the phonemes' being meaningless—though they get this quality from the definition ('minimum sames of vocal feature') which Sommerfelt accepts. Sommerfelt implies that his psychic values will account for the different fortunes of phonemes in different linguistic forms;

that is, the psychic-valued phonemes will improve our power of generalization by enabling us to include in one class and yet to differentiate (1) the ordinary changes of phonemes like E [s] or [z], which under the present assumptions we class as *sound-change*, and (2) their special adventures as constituents of significant forms like the E morphemes (e.g., the noun-plural suffix) of the shape [-ez, -z, -s], which under the present assumptions we class as *analogic change*. Apparently the latter example is chosen because two of the alternants consist of one phoneme each, but Sommerfelt does not explain the bearing of his example either in terms of the current assumptions or in terms of his unstated assumptions. He suggests that phonemes will have meaning if one defines them as contrast-phenomena: like everyone else, I had defined them in precisely this way (§§5; 15), yet Sommerfelt does not show how this definition is inconsistent with meaningless phonemes or why it necessitates his psychic-valued ones. Further, Sommerfelt suggests that the system in which phonemes have psychic values will recognize (require?) different 'degrees of consciousness', including several 'subconscious states'; thus, the speakers may, by subconscious action, forestall a threatening sound-change in any significant form.

Since these latter terms are foreign to the immediate subject-matter of linguistics, it is perhaps safe to infer that they figure among the undefined terms which Sommerfelt would take over, at the outset, from another science, and that *psychic value*, too, figures among these fundamental terms. Since different schools of psychology employ terms of this sort in entirely different ways, and some psychologists do not use them at all, I took care not to admit any of them to my set of undefined terms (154); to take them in would have conflicted with the fact that linguists of different psychologic persuasions use the same linguistic methods. Sommerfelt does not tell us which psychologist's *consciousness*, *degrees of consciousness*, *subconscious states*, and *psychic values* enter into his system of linguistics.

In view of all this and of the exigencies of our common task, I feel compelled to state frankly my conclusion, namely that Sommerfelt's objection —which would have the approval today of most European and some American linguists—is due neither to their having formulated a new linguistic method (and, indeed, only the present method appears in their work), nor to faults in the formulation of the present method, but rather to their underestimating the value of formulating one's assumptions and to their desire to employ in linguistics a few terms of popular psychology whose vagueness will give us a teleologic lift across rough places without abrogating (at least, not for keeps) the assumptions implicit in the great mass of our past results.

Our assumptions (that is, to repeat, our working methods) leave a great many facts unexplained. The phenomena of dissimilation and assimilation of non-successive phonemes (G *dörper > dörpel > Tölpel*) and of the so-called contamination of significant forms (L *gravis > grevis*, beside *levis*), do not seem to fit into the ordinary categories of change, and necessitate special assumptions. Many forms and groups of forms deviate from the shape which the great mass of similar forms leads us to expect: witness, the treatment of PIE [e, i] in Germanic, the occasional labial development of PIE labiovelars in PGic, as in *wolf* (but ON *ylgr* 'she-wolf'), and single forms, such as the Greek nominative singular [ˈpous] 'foot', where we expect [oː]. The historical antecedents of some forms are entirely obscure: witness, the third-person-singular present-tense ending in ON (*safnar*) and in English (*loves*), or words like E *boy, girl, bad*. We do not know why a given change occurs when and where it does—a fact which Hermann forgets on page 73 of the present treatise. In this, linguistics is no better off than the other branches of human study: we are forced to embody every descriptive or historical fact in a separate little assumption. Finally, we can co-ordinate our basic assumptions about linguistic change with our knowledge of non-linguistic processes only in the matter of linguistic borrowing, which is obviously a phase of cultural borrowing in general. While analogic change resembles the phenomena studied by Pavlov,[1] the type of sound-change seems confined to language. However, the study of the non-linguistic phases of human activity has not developed methods comparable to ours in effectiveness; where it has reached results beyond those of common-sense observation, as in the use of large-scale statistics, these results bear at least a family resemblance to the generalizations of linguistics.[2] The great nineteenth-century linguists tried to effect a synthesis by interpreting their methods in terms of Herbartian or Wundtian psychology, but the breakdown of these psychologies has made it plain that the interpretation was merely tautological, because the psychologic terms were at bottom derived from linguistic phenomena.[3]

Of course, we can alter our assumptions to fit the unexplained facts, provided that we thrust into the unexplained residuum a sufficient number of the facts which are explained by our present assumptions. If we assume, for instance, that PIE [oː] > Attic Gk [ou], we shall account for Gk [ˈpous] 'foot', but leave unexplained a great body of forms with Gk [oː], such as

---

[1] I. P. Pavlov, Conditioned Reflexes, translated by G. V. Anrep, Oxford, 1927; Lectures on Conditioned Reflexes, translated by W. H. Gantt and G. Volborth, New York, 1928; the application to human activities was begun by Max F. Meyer and A. P. Weiss; see the latter's Theoretical Basis of Human Behavior[2], Columbus, 1929.

[2] Recall the famous first chapter of Buckle's History of Civilization. Statisticians, so far as I know, do not mention the resemblance, which the linguist will espy, for example, in P. Sargant Florence, The Statistical Method, New York, 1929, 4 ff.; 46 ff.; H. Forcher, Die statistische Methode, Leipzig, 1913, 315 ff.; N. Reichesberg, Die Statistik und die Gesellschaftswissenschaft, Stuttgart, 1893.

[3] Delbrück's remarks, Grundfragen 43 f. (1901), implied really a forewarning of this.

[ˈdoːtoːr] 'giver', [ploːˈtos] 'afloat', the verb-suffix [-oː] 'I', and so on. This, of course, is why Hermann (52), like all other linguists, sticks to the present assumption. In the extreme case, if we sufficiently loosen our assumptions, we can 'explain' all facts, at the cost of abandoning all the classifications which we have made since the year 1816 or thereabouts. For instance, if we devise a consistent set of assumptions which allow of sporadic sound-change—the difficulty of doing this need not now concern us—we can 'explain' any and all changes of linguistic forms, but we must then abandon all results that were gained by an implicit or explicit use of the present assumption of sound-change. We could not then distinguish between sound-change and analogic change or borrowings of the type of E *bait* from ON *beita*, *beit*, replacing OE *bāt* 'esca'. We should have to give up, to take the classical instance, the sound-change discovered by Verner, for nothing is more common than the voicing of intervocalic spirants, and changes of this type occur progressively in various Germanic dialects. Had Verner countenanced the possibility of a change which passed sporadically from form to form, he could never have found the correlation of pre-Gic spirant-voicing with the place of the PIE accent. This example gets an added, if extraneous, interest from the fact that Verner, to all appearances, had not explicitly formulated the assumption of regular sound-change. Many of our problems, of course, would cease to exist. It would be incredibly naive of Hermann, for instance, to point out (15) the unsolved problem of PIE [oj] in Latin (*foedus* but *fūcus*), a problem which arises only under a refined application of the now existing comparative method, and then to solve this problem, as he claims to do, by a new method which admits of irregular sound-change. As a matter of fact, Hermann is far too practised in the present technique to commit such a blunder; the solution (*ū* originally imported from neighboring dialects) he proposes (56) falls under the present assumptions of linguistic borrowing and analogic change.

This confusion about our working methods originates in other than linguistic circles. The cheaper sort of philosophers and literary men are always devising half-baked theories which pretend to solve all problems, including ours, by means of grandiose but undefined catch-words (*idealistisch*, *geistesgeschichtlich*, *ganzheitlich*, *Spannung*, *Polarität*, and so on). Some of these people, having looked into linguistic books and found them difficult and void of popular-psychologic terms, direct their noise especially at the linguist, demanding that he conform henceforth to their theories. They affect a rakish up-to-dateness of phrase which is to show their possession of the important 'new' idea and casts a suspicion of idiocy upon anyone who has not yet adopted it. Now, the linguist enjoys less academic prestige and has less of a popular audience; he is methodically isolated by his divorcement from the common-sense notions (Wundt called them Vulgärpsychologie) which prevail not only in most other branches of human study, but in the linguist's own non-professional outlook; in his science he is perplexed by a host of unsolved problems; and, above all, he is imperfectly grounded in the presuppositions of the scientific method which he has learned to use. It is no wonder that he allows himself to be swept off his feet. To be sure, he cannot change his actual technique, but at least he supplements his work with inconsistent semi-popular theorizings, with polemics against the linguistic assumptions that do not fit into the new context, and with theoretical amendments which he does not state definitely enough to test their effect.[4]

In the present treatise Hermann seriously quotes amateur linguists (1, 17, 25, 41), though he rejects some of their notions, and once (85) betrays his real estimate of one of these authorities. Nevertheless, on the whole, they have convinced him.

At the outset (1), Hermann states the basis of his theory. We must seek out the Conditions (Bedingungen) and Driving Forces (treibende Kräfte) —it will not do to confuse these two—of linguistic change. The Conditions are three: the properties of vocal speech, the sensible qualities of the surrounding world, and the psycho-physical disposition of man. The Driving Forces involve all the Spiritual Powers of man, though, as is to be expected, these Impulsions (Triebe) cross one another and often conflict. The six principal Tendencies, according to Prof. W. Havers and in alphabetical order, are:

*Abbildetendenzen*, especially the tendency toward concrete forms of expression and the Instinct of Imitation;

*Ästhetische Tendenzen*, especially the expression of Mood and Feeling and the Striving for Beauty;

*Entspannungstendenzen*, the discharge of Emotion and Strong Feelings;

*Streben nach Kraftersparnis*, especially Inertia (Bequemlichkeit);

*Ordnungstendenzen*, especially Class-Formation, Striving for Clearness, Distinctness, Intelligibility, and Symmetry;

*sozialer Triebkreis*, especially Courtesy, Modesty, and Caution.

To these Conditions and Driving Forces, Havers would add two more great categories of explanation, namely Chance (Zufall) and Circumstances (Umstände), but these fail to meet with Hermann's approval.

Into these categories, which would delight an educationalist, we are to resolve the more superficial phenomena of linguistic change. Even thus, however, we might go wrong, if we failed to distinguish the many grada-

---

[4] He is the more excusable when we see ladies'-club books and Sunday-newspaper announcements claiming to abrogate the assumptions of even so solidly established a science as physics, because the authors (who, at that, may be excellent physicists) have discovered that position and velocity cannot be simultaneously determined—a parallel to which Dr. Ernest B. Zeisler calls my attention.

tions between the Conscious and the Unconscious (3). I have reproduced this passage at length, because here alone does Hermann give anything like an explicit statement of the assumptions which he wishes to substitute for those at present in use.

The first part of the treatise (4–62) is directed against the assumption of regular phonetic change. The statement of this assumption has always given pain to the tender-minded. Leskien said, 'Phonetic laws have no exceptions'. Today we realize that a linguistic change is not a 'law', but a historical event, and that the term 'exception', accordingly, is irrelevant. We formulate this type of change, rather, by saying that *phonemes change*. This is an assumption. It is made to fit the many cases where a phoneme or a combination of phonemes changes in a whole series of forms (G *stēn*, *stein*, *stuol*, *stahel*, . . . >[št-]). The wording of the assumption implies that the change is purely a change in the habit of producing phonemes and accordingly affects a phoneme or combination of phonemes at every utterance, no matter in what words or other significant forms the phoneme or combination may occur. Our assumption fits the fact that people articulate (or, rather, learn only under unusual circumstances, and then with difficulty, to articulate) sounds and combinations of sounds which are foreign to their language, and it fits the fact that the number of phonemes in a language is limited; in present-day standard English, for instance, we have no special words in which eighteenth-century [e:, o:, i:, u:] are preserved in undiphthongized form, and whoever undertakes to learn German or French, has a hard time learning to produce undiphthongal types. All this, of course, is what Leskien meant by his 'laws without exceptions'.

In his choice and presentation of examples and (except for one violation) in the use of the actual technique, Hermann shows himself as a skilful neogrammarian, but in matters of theory his details are as bad as his generalizations. He knew a Corean (12) 'der beim Deutschsprechen *l* und *r* dauernd durcheinander warf, ohne mit dem Ohre den Unterschied der von ihm selbst gesprochenen zwei Laute auffassen zu können'. Apparently it does not occur to Hermann that the Corean may have been substituting for both German *l* and *r* a single phoneme of intermediate acoustic type, which Hermann's German ear, in turn, intepreted now as *l* and now as *r*. Yet Hermann, of course, knows the principle which he words, perhaps somewhat ingenuously (21): 'Die Laute einer fremden Sprache machen gar nicht immer denselben Eindruck auf den Hörenden'.

Hermann does not recognize the phonemic principle as a formulation of working methods that are as familiar to him as to anyone else, but refers to it from time to time (iii, 49, 71, 196) with some anxiety; although he has read Trubetzkoy's excellent article on vowel systems (Travaux du Cercle Linguistique de Prague 1.39 [1929]). However, 'die ganze Lehre ist noch zu jung', and is confronted with a few stock difficulties of historical phonology (PIE [gʷ] in Greek, h- and f- in Latin, PIE [o:] in Lithuanian; p. 49). A false slant on the term *phoneme* appears also on page 54: 'Die Schrift kann den Schwankungen der gesprochenen Rede, d. h. den Wirkungen des Phonems, nicht gerecht werden. Wer je den Versuch gemacht hat, mundartliche Sprache phonetisch in der Schrift festzuhalten, weisz, wie grosz gerade auch von dieser Seite aus die Schwierigkeiten sind'. The phonemic principle tells us rather, that the only relevant notation is either a transcription in terms of phonemes or a mechanical record of acoustic features by means of precision instruments.[5]

As an illustration of how a language deals with troublesome homonymy, Hermann cites (18) the Chinese tones, as if they were something superadded to the ordinary, respectable phonemes; the extensive use of compound words in modern Chinese, which could have served here, is mentioned elsewhere (190), but also in a false light. The survival of Zakonian over the spread of the *Koiné* is adduced in connection with the phonetic conservatism of remote dialects (18). The Spanish of the Tagalogs (20; Schuchardt merely mentions it in Hermann's reference, Slawo-Deutsches 35; the proper reference is Vienna SB 105.111 [1884]) and the Italian (not, in this reference, the German) of Dalmatian Serbs, are brought in as if they illustrated substrata and not merely the difficulties of speaking a foreign language—a distinction which Schuchardt was careful to keep in the foreground. Yiddish, too, is to be examined for a substratum; its deviation from the other German dialects is not, one infers, to be explained by separation since the late Middle Ages.

The discussion of the results of dialect geography (27–42) contains the usual Idealistic line of reasoning: because the results of borrowing (a process recognized by nineteenth-century linguists, though they could not know its extent) are distinguishable by their phonetic deviations, therefore the assumption of regular phonetic change is invalid (so, especially, the example from Frisian, page 33). Since this fallacy has been repeatedly pointed out (28), Hermann props it by a more complicated one (32): If it were true that exceptionless sound-change occurred in a central community, then the results of sound-change would in this community present no exceptions; since actually, however, every dialect contains borrowed forms, the sound-change in all dialects, including the central community,

---

[5] The principle of the phoneme is implicit, of course, in all linguistic study, and, for that matter, in all alphabetic writing. The term *phoneme* in much the present value appears as early as de Saussure's Mémoire (1878). Explicit formulations will be found in Baudouin de Courtenay, Versuch einer Theorie der phonetischen Alternationen (1895), 9; Sweet, The Practical Study of Languages (1899), 18; Boas, BAE Bulletin 40, vol. 1 (1911), 16; [Daniel Jones] Principles of the International Phonetic Association (1912); de Saussure, Cours de linguistique générale² (1922), 55; 63 (first edition, 1915, from much older lecture notes); Sapir, Language (1921), 18, 47, 57, and in this journal 1.37 (1925); see also 2.157 (1926) and Modern Philology 25.216 (1927); not all these authors use the term *phoneme*, and the term *phoneme* has been used also in other senses.

must be subject to exceptions. A logician could point out the non-sequiturs, but this sort of dialectic is beside the point. The neo-grammarians do not suppose that the speakers ring a gong at the beginning and end of every sound-change and call time, in the interim, on all analogic change and borrowing, nor do they suppose that a community which has made a sound-change thereby becomes immune to analogic change and borrowing.

Alongside the general Alemannic *mir* 'we' for older *wir* (analogic generalization of a sandhi doublet), a small district has also *mō* 'where' for older *wō* (*wā*): this fact invalidates the assumption of regular sound-change (32). It is characteristic, however, that Hermann, in reality an excellent linguist, cannot refrain from stating two technically unexceptionable explanations of this *mō* and formulating the problem of a choice between them.

Hermann fails to understand (35) the exposition of method in LAN-GUAGE 4.99 (1928) [our B33—CFH] and in Sapir's contribution to Rice, Methods in Social Science (1931), 297. This exposition tells him only that sound-changes occur, forsooth, also in Indian languages, and that *some* sound-changes have no exceptions. Either by the rarest accident or by the use of black magic, then, Sapir and I must have hit upon sound-changes which belonged to this exceptionless type. Of course, Sapir's inferences and mine were only those which scientific men, including Hermann, make at every step; the point, which Hermann misses completely, is that the order in which the data came under observation revealed the adequacy of the method.[6]

The admission that *some* sound-changes 'have no exceptions', while it sounds like a harmless by-the-way concession, would really demand a recasting of Hermann's whole treatise. If Leskien's assumption does fit certain facts and leads to their classification and prediction, it has won its place; it then merely behooves Hermann to label his discrepant facts by some other name than *sound-change*, and, if they are not covered by any of the current assumptions, it behooves him to formulate his explanation in some additional assumption. This additional assumption, of course, must be consistent with the other assumptions which Hermann accepts (including, as we now learn, that of regular sound-change), and must be stated in linguistic terms.

Hermann makes another fatal concession when he says (40) that living phonetic alternations (such, to give an example, as [d:t] in G *Hunde* : *Hund* [hunt]) are free from exceptions, for these alternations are, of course, the

---

[6] It may not be amiss to state in this connection that Sapir and I are perhaps diametrically opposed as to proximate non-linguistic matters, such as psychology and the synthesis of linguistics with other sciences. Brugmann's experience (36) shared the chronological accident; however, it concerned not sound-change but analogic change.

results of conditioned sound-changes. One of Hermann's instances, however, the coincidence of PGic [þ] and [d] in Germanic dialects, is not an alternation, but the result of an ordinary sound-change.

Hermann quotes (27) Gilliéron as rejecting regular phonetic change, but no reference is given; I can recall only the reverse (cf. LANGUAGE 4.288 [1928]) [our B34, fn 6—CFH], nor can I recall Gilliéron's saying that a non-existent but threatening homonymy may prevent a sound-change ('dasz ein Lautwandel nicht eintritt, um eine Homonymie zu verhindern oder sie zu scheiden', p. 59, again without reference), and, indeed, this flatly contradicts the statement of Gilliéron's view on page 38, which I take to be the correct one. Hermann, however, says (59) that Italian *nove* 'nine' escaped the change *o > uo* because the result of this change would have been homonymous with the feminine plural, L *novae* > It *nuove*. The speakers (no doubt 'unconsciously' or 'subconsciously') foresaw what sound-change might do to their language, and therefore, by a concerted but unconscious act of will, forestalled the calamity. Gilliéron's method would suppose, rather, that the homonymy actually occurred, that the speakers knew also a non-homonymous regional (say, Tuscan) form, and favored it at the cost of the troublesome native doublet—all of which, in the case of a numeral, seems likely enough (cf. Wackernagel, Göttingen Nachr., Gesch. Mitt. 1904. 101). This indeed, is Hermann's only real deviation, so far as I can make out, from the actual working method of linguistics.

Under Hermann's New Method (52), the equation G *haben* : L *habēre* is acceptable, not on Kluge's quondam basis of PIE *[qhabhe:] but as a result of irregular sound-change; on the other hand, a similar explanation of the vowel of Attic Gk ['pous] 'scheint mir . . . ganz ausgeschlossen . . . Leischtsinnige Behauptungen, wie die, hier habe ausnahmsweise idg. ō im Attischen *ou* ergeben, müszten zum Chaos in der Sprachwissenschaft führen'. On this basis, how are adherents of the New Method to know whether the correspondence of, say, Gk [the'os]: L *deus*, is acceptable or, on the contrary, 'ausgeschlossen'? I submit that this method is not 'new', but was given more than a fair trial from the Renaissance until well into the nineteenth century.

The larger part of the treatise (72–192) deals with analogic change. Hermann shows (76 ff.) that we could motivate analogic changes more exactly if we discriminated among the model sets; thus, for the creation of L *senātī*, Paul's formula, *animus* : *animī* = *senātus* : *x*, is less illuminating than the formula *populus* : *populī* = *senātus* : *x*. The new formation is favored by model sets which are close formally, semantically, or in actual context (*senātus populusque*). This is a valuable refinement of our method, but it does not, as Hermann, by forcing the point too far, would make it seem, invalidate this method, and it does not necessitate denunciation of earlier work (73 ff.). Although Hermann at times (76, 86) accepts the proportional pattern, the main body of his text rejects it as irrelevant; Hermann prefers to reduce the ordinary cases of the proportional type to the status of the rarer contaminative type (L *gravis* > *grevis*, after *levis*), which under the current method is precisely the less understandable of the two. The reason is not clear, since Hermann's discussion consists of normal examples of both types, interspersed with deliberations about the degree of consciousness and the nature of the mental processes of the speakers who produce the new form. A long passage gives laborious recognition to the fact that the speakers do not formulate grammatical rules (101 ff.). The least obscure passage is probably the following (95): '... wenn ich z. B. von dem noch ungebräuchlichen Verbum *auteln* die von mire noch nie vernommene Erste Sing. des Präteritums *ich autelte* brauche. Hier wird ja auch nicht etwa die Proportion Präsens des schwachen Verbs -*e* : Präteritum -*te* = *autele* : *x*, *x* = *autelte* angewandt. Die Bildung der mir bis dahin unbekannten Form *autelte* geht vielmehr direkt vor sich· das Präteritum der schwachen Verba auf -*te* dient als Muster. Das geschieht im Unterbewusztsein. Eine Proportion würde schon einen Grad des Bewusztseins beanspruchen.' Here the phrase 'geht ... direkt vor sich' is meaningless, and the phrase 'dient als Muster' is a reminiscence of the current doctrine; the whole account merely says in a vague and unhelpful way exactly that which the linguist's proportion formula says in a compact and usable way. Apparently Hermann prefers the pre-scientific form of statement because it can be made to harmonize with popular-psychologic notions—a consideration totally irrelevant to linguistics.

'Die alte Methode mit Lautgesetz und Proportionsformel war zu grob und mechanisch. Sie musz einer feineren Methode weichen' (193).

Regrettable as it is that a swing of fashion can lead a scholar of Hermann's metal to waste his time on such theories as these, one feels yet somehow assured that in practice he will continue to use and to refine[7] the methods of our science. Science is materialistic and mechanical. Her truths are born as working assumptions and, if one scans them closely, never outgrow this estate. Some of her followers nevertheless see in her the only hope of mankind.

[7] See, for instance, Hermann's beautiful account of the rise of the Lithuanian standard language, Göttingen Nachr. 1929. 65.

# B40. The Structure of Learned Words

1933. *A Commemorative Volume Issued by The Institute for Research in English Teaching on the Occasion of The Tenth Annual Conference of English Teachers held under its Auspices*, 17–23; Tokyo.

The English vocabulary consists of three great types of words; the boundaries, to be sure, are not absolute. *Foreign* words are characterized by phonetic or phonologic peculiarities; they are isolated or else occur in very small morphologic sets; some of the nouns have a foreign plural. Examples are *mirage, intelligentsia, jiujitsu, alumnus (alumni), alumna (alumnae)*. The rest of the vocabulary divides itself into a *normal* ("native") and a *learned* (semi-foreign) type. For instance:

> Normal: *sing (sang, sung), song, singer, songster*
> Learned: *conceive, deceive, perceive, receive.*

To a large extent, these two types of words are made up of different constituents: normal roots combine with normal affixes, learned roots with learned affixes. The learned type uses more prefixes (*con-, de-, per-, re-,* etc.) than the normal; many learned words accent another than the radical syllable (*cóncept* beside *conceptual, invocátion* beside *invoke*). These and many other differences enable us to recognize learned affixes even in the cases where they are added to a normal root (*re-shape, right-eous*).

The historic origin of the learned vocabulary is familiar enough.[1] In the centuries after the Norman Conquest the language received many French loan-words. Among these were many *mots savants*, Latin forms which the French had taken from books and incorporated into their speech with certain phonetic and structural modifications, much as ordinary loan-words are incorporated. Thus, by ordinary (spoken) tradition, Latin *fragile* became Old French *fraile*; but the Latin word was known to the French from books, whence they took it, in the reading-pronunciation of their time, as *fragile.* Both forms were borrowed by English: *frail, fragile.* Along with the borrowing of French *mots savants*, the English acquired the habit of making them up: English writers and speakers use Latin

---

[1] See, of course, O. Jespersen, *Growth and Structure of the English Language*[4], London and New York (1929), pp. 84–153.

words (which they find in books). These words are re-shaped in accordance with the French *mots savants* and in accordance with the English phonetic development since the Norman borrowings. In fact, owing to the great number of these learned words, we are able to make new combinations of French and Latin-French elements (*mutinous, dutiable, eventual, fragmentary*).[2]

The outlines of this historical development have been fairly well traced, but a detailed study will be possible only when we have a systematic description. We need first an exact account of the present-day habits; then we must gather the evidence for past times, including not only the earlier occurrences of words (as listed, say, in the *New English Dictionary*), but also the evidence as to their phonetic shape, including, especially, the place of accent; finally, we shall need a description of the French speech that was brought to England.

The first step, then, is to describe the present-day forms. Although this description has not been made, we can gather some idea of what it will contain.

The present mass of English learned words does not entirely coincide with the words that the historian recognizes as borrowings; thus, the words *chair* and *cheer*, which, historically, are loans from French, are today normal words, showing none of the learned peculiarities. The grouping of English learned words into morphologic sets will perhaps often disagree with that of French or Latin. For instance, a descriptive analysis of present-day English will perhaps show (I do not know whether it will) that *atom* (*atomic, atomize,* older *atomy*) contains a root *at-* with a suffix *-om*, although the Latin (originally Greek) structure implied a root *-tom* 'cut' with a prefix *a-* 'not'. If this should prove true, then *atom* would not belong to the root-group of *microtome, appendectomy, tonsilectomy.* The grouping of learned words will be difficult, because the meanings are largely abstract and vague. In a set like *conceive, deceive, perceive, receive* this is offset by the phonetic steadiness of the form *-ceive,* but, as the phonetic shape of the learned morphemes, especially of the root, is subject to great fluctuation, this criterion also will be hard to apply.

The learned words, formed almost at will, often are carried along with little oral tradition; hence there may be great variety in their phonetic shape, especially as to accent; thus we have *hospítable* beside *hóspitable, revócable* beside *révocable, addréss* beside *áddress* (noun; the verb is always *addréss, ration* with [ej] or with [ɛ] in the first syllable.[3] A speaker may base his form on an imperfect hearing or on an imperfect observation of the printed symbols, so that he says, for instance, *portentious* instead of

---

[2] Jespersen, op. cit. p. 123.

[3] [Bloomfield here describes his transcription 'of Central-Western (Chicago) pronunciation'; see our B29.]

*portentous* (compare *pretentious, contentious*); thus, *morphodite* has become conventional, in sub-standard speech, for *hermaphrodite*. This merges with analogic creation on half-understood models, as in *normalcy* for *normality* (compare, perhaps, *bankrupt* : *bankruptcy, captain* : *captaincy, chaplain* : *chaplaincy*); a businessman wants to say *pneumogate* for 'travel by air' (compare *pneumatic* and *navigate*, where the compounding form of the first word would be *pneumato-* and the meaning 'travel' attaches not to the suffix-group *-igate*, but to the root *nav-* 'ship'). Further, we have to reckon with the fact that a complicated morphologic system leads to many smaller analogic modifications; some of these are furthered by spelling-pronunciation. This, *experiment* with [ij] in the second syllable (sub-standard) may be due to *experience* as well as to a false equation between spelling and spoken form. For *finality* we have forms with [i] and with [aj] in the first syllable; compare for the latter, *final* and the frequent use of the letter i for the sound [aj]. On the side of meaning the situation is much the same: striking departures from tradition are known as *malapropisms*, but there are also ordinary analogic developments, as in the case of *transpire* 'to leak out' (of news), and then merely 'to happen'.[4]

To illustrate the variability of learned roots, we may survey the group of *-ceive*:

(1) *conceive, deceive, perceive, receive*
   *conceivable (inconceivable), receivable*
(2) *accept, except*
   *cóncept, pércept, précept*
   *acceptable (acceptability)*
   *perceptible (perceptibility), imperceptible (imperceptibility)*
   *contraceptive, deceptive (deceptivity), inceptive, perceptive (perceptivity), receptive (receptivity)*
   *acceptance*
   *acceptátion*
   *conceptual (conceptualize), perceptual*
   *preceptor (preceptórial)*
   *conception, contraception (contraceptional), deception, exception (exceptional), inception, perception, reception*
(3) *incipient (incipience, incipiency), percipient, recipient*
(4) *conceit, deceit, receipt*
(5) *seize (seizure).*

The alternation of vowels in learned words consists largely in a distinction of two grades, diphthongal[5] (D) and monophthongal (M), as in the following examples:

---

[4] Jespersen, op. cit. p. 121.
[5] For the history, see K. Luick, *Historische Grammatik der englischen Sprache*, Leipzig 1913, pp. 439–469.

D [ij]   : M [e]:   *sequence*   :   *consecutive*
D [ej]   : M [ɛ]:   *profane*    :   *profanity*
D [aj]   : M [i]:   *finite*     :   *infinity*
D [juw]  : M [o]:   *produce*    :   *productive*
D [ow]   : M [ɑ]:   *cone*       :   *conic*
D [aw]   : M [o]:   *abound*     :   *abundant*

Both grades occur with various weakenings in unstressed position. Thus we have *finality* with D [fajn-] and with M [fin-]; *saline* with suffix D [-ajn] and M [-in]. There are various degrees of weakening, as *finality* with [fen-] or [fn̩-].

Irregular alternations of vowels are fairly frequent. Beside D [sijv] in *receive*, M [sept] in *receptive*, we have seen also M [sip] in *recipient*. The suffix D [-ijk] in *antique*, *oblique* has M [ikw] in *antiquity*, *obliquity*. A vowel may lose syllabic value; thus syllabic [er, r̩] appears in *refer*, *reference*, *differ*, *differential*, but non-syllabic [r] in *different*, *difference* [difrent, difrens]. Most important in this respect is the treatment of [ij] before vowels; in *curious* it may drop its [i] or keep it, so that the word has either two or three syllables; similarly, the [i] of [ij] is kept or dropped in *religiosity*; in *opinion* the [i] is dropped; in *religious* the entire [ij] is dropped.

These features are determined by the constituents of the form. Thus, the suffix -*ious* demands D [ej, ow] in the preceding syllable, as in *capacious*, *ferocious*, but in the alternation of [aj-i] it demands M [i], as in *religious*, *delicious* (*delight*), *vicious* (*vice*). The suffix -*ity* demands M in the preceding (stressed) syllable; *capacity*, *ferocity*, *brevity* (*brief*); of irregularities we may mention *scarce* : *scarcity* with D before -*ity*, and *clear* : *clarity* with alternation of D [ij] and M [ɛ].

The most regular consonant alternation is the coalescence of dentals with the [ij, j] of such suffixes as -*ion*, -*ial*, -*ious* (*opinion*, *perennial*, *curious*); here [t, s] with [ij, j] gives [š]: *delight* : *delicious*, *vice* : *vicious*. With the [j] of -*ion* [d, z] give [ž]: *erode* : *erosion*, *fuse* : *fusion*. Before these and certain other suffixes [k] is replaced by [s] and [g] by [j]: *public* : *publicity*, *theologue* : *theology*, and antevocalic [ij, j] coalesces with these sounds to [š, ǰ]: *optic* : *optician*, *theologue* : *theologian*. The coalescence of [t, d, s, z] with the [j] of suffixes like -*ue*, -*ure*, -*ule*, -*une*, gives [č, ǰ, š, ž]: *percept* : *perceptual*, *grade* : *gradual*, *sense* : *sensual*, *please* : *pleasure*, but there are also unaltered forms, with [tj] and so on, and the two are variously distributed: mostly (but not always) the unaltered variants are over-formal and semi-educated. The suffix -*ity* demands retention of [ij, j]: *religious* [-ǰos] but *religiosity* [-ǰi'jasitij], *artificial* [-šl] but *artificiality* [-š'jɛlitij], *precious* [-šos] but *preciosity* [-ši'jasitij]; *fatuous* has [č] rather than [tj], but *fatuity* has [tj] rather than [č]. At the beginning of a root, as in *produce*, *reduce*, *duke*; the coalescence is not made (in Chicago pronunciation, at least), hence *educate*, which has [j], cannot be grouped with the root [djuwk], but must be analyzed with a root [ed-]. This analysis happens to agree with the structure of the word in Latin, but it is the analysis, not the Latin structure, which makes the spelling-pronunciation with [dj] un-pleasing to our ears.

There are many irregular alternations of consonants, such as [gn] with [n] in *benignity : benign, dignity : condign, deign*. Voiced consonants alter-nate with unvoiced in certain forms: *anxious : anxiety*; beside *equate* we have *equation* with [š] or with [ž]. Especially, initial [s] is replaced by [z] after prefixes in certain forms: *session : possession, assume : presume, consent : resent*. Many roots have one or more alternant forms in which [t] is added, and this addition is made with various irregularities; thus, beside [sijv] *receive*, [sip] *recipient*, we have seen [sept] *receptive* and [sijt] *receipt*. Some roots appear in extremely deviant alternants whose classifi-cation offers difficulty, such as [sijz] *seize* beside [sijv]: historically these are due to the divergence of genuine French words from French *mots savants*, as *frail : fragile*. In the same way, we owe some irregularities to the circumstance that native English words have been drawn, through phonetic resemblance, into a learned group; thus, *flow* (native) is grouped with *fluent* (Latin).

The place of stress is determined by suffixes. One variety of -*y* (including the combination -*it-y*) demands stress on the third-last syllable: *rémedy, vorácity*; contrast *cóntroversy* with another variety of the -*y* suffix. Forms with suffix "zero"—that is, absence of a suffix—in certain cases accent the prefix: *convíct* (verb) : *cónvict* (noun)[6]. In some forms the prefix has a D vowel: *prótest* [ow], *rébate* [ij]; in others it has an M vowel: *próduct* [ɑ], *récord* [e].

Some affixes are accompanied by other peculiarities. When -*ity* is added to adjectives in -*ac-ious* and -*oc-ious*, the -*ious* is dropped: *capacious : ca-pacity, ferocious : ferocity*; in other cases, such as -*u-ous*, there are forms with loss of -*ous*, such as *vacuous : vacuity*, and others which keep -*ous*, such as *sinuous : sinuosity*; in the group -*it-ous* both suffixes are dropped: *fortuitous : fortuity*.

A systematic description of English morphology is desirable for its own sake, as a statement of facts. Without it, moreover, our historical account will fall short of what is attainable in the way of completeness and preci-sion. Aside from these theoretical benefits, however, a systematic descrip-tion of this kind, in the hands of the teacher (and perhaps even of the advanced students) would greatly help the foreign learner of English.

[6] K. H. Collitz in *Englische Studien* 43 (1911), 252.

# 41. Reviews of Bloomfield's *Language*

*Language*. By Leonard Bloomfield, Professor of Germanic Philology in the University of Chicago. New York: Henry Holt and Company, 1933. Pp ix + 564. $3.00.

British Edition. London: G. Allen and Unwin Ltd., 1935. Pp ix + 566. 15s. [Differs from the American edition in presenting British Public School pronunciation instead of Chicago English; in the use of the IPA alphabet without modifications; and in the presence of two pages of additions and corrections (551–552).]

'The Indo-European Language Family', in Donald W. Lee, *English Language Reader* (New York: Dodd, Mead and Co., 1963) is a reprint of a passage from Chapter 1, beginning with p. 7 line 11 and ending with the last full sentence on p. 14.

*Language History; from 'Language' (1933 edition)*. By Leonard Bloomfield; edited by Harry Hoijer. New York: Holt, Rinehart and Winston, Inc., 1965 [This reprints, unchanged, chapters 17–27; the notes of the original are amplified by Hoijer, to fill in otherwise dangling cross-references to the earlier chapters, and to take cognizance of works published since 1933.]

[Dedicated to A(lice) S(ayers) B(loomfield). Probably written at the University of Chicago, 1930–1932. The Preface is dated January 1933; but the book was off the presses in time for use in spring quarter courses at universities which operated on the quarter plan rather than with semesters. Chapters:

1. The Study of Language.
2. The Use of Language.
3. Speech-Communities.
4. The Languages of the World.
5. The Phoneme.
6. Types of Phonemes.
7. Modifications.
8. Phonetic Structure.
9. Meaning.
10. Grammatical Forms.
11. Sentence-Types.
12. Syntax.
13. Morphology.
14. Morphologic Types.
15. Substitution.
16. Form-Classes and Lexicon.
17. Written Records.
18. The Comparative Method.
19. Dialect Geography.
20. Phonetic Change.
21. Types of Phonetic Change.
22. Fluctuation in the Frequency of Forms.
23. Analogic Change.
24. Semantic Change.
25. Cultural Borrowing.

26. Intimate Borrowing.                    28. Applications and Outlook.
27. Dialect Borrowing.

The first 'criticism' I ever heard of this book was given orally by George M. Bolling in March 1933. I was a freshman at Ohio State and was permitted to register for 'Greek 701: Introduction to the Historical Study of Language'. At the first class meeting, Bolling said, with his usual slight stammer, 'for the first time since I began giving this course there is a textbook that completely satisfies me'—and told us to get Bloomfield's new book. The conduct of the class reflected Bolling's complete satisfaction. E. A. Esper tells me that in earlier years Bolling had lectured, in this course, from meticulously organized notes. This time there were no lectures. We read the successive chapters of the book first before class and then, together, in class, with interruptions, questions, and clarifications. We got through chapter 24 by the end of the course, and everyone got at least a B. (By repute, that was also the lowest grade Bolling would give anyone who was sufficiently out of tune with the temper of the times to register for Greek.)

The general critical reaction to the book was not so uniformly favorable as Bolling's comment. It is interesting to note, in the reviews that follow, that certain remarkably well-done parts of the book receive no detailed comment at all, favorable or unfavorable. For one just entering linguistics, no exposition could have been clearer or more helpful. For the experts, this simplicity was apparently deceptive and hard to interpret.

We do not reprint here a half-page notice by Carl F. Voegelin, followed by an equally brief comment from Daniel Jones, in *Le Maître Phonétique* III 43.53 (July–September 1933). The fourth brief note in B29 was Bloomfield's justification of his use of the term 'phoneme' in a way that puzzled and disturbed Jones.]

(1) Franklin Edgerton (Yale University), Journal of the American Oriental Society 53.295–297 (1933).

Tho called a "revised version of the author's *Introduction to the Study of Language*" (1914) this is really a wholly new work. It is a masterly one. It would be hard to exaggerate the quality of the performance. For the most part it is clear, simple, easy to read, and absorbingly interesting, as well as sound and authoritative. It presents the best opinion of linguistic scholars on all important aspects of their science, in a form which, with rare exceptions, can be easily followed by any intelligent layman. It is intended for laymen; yet it will help the most advanced linguistic scholar to clarify his ideas, at least; and surely few will be found so erudite that they cannot learn much from it. All teachers of languages ought to study it; unfortunately few of them have any real knowledge of linguistic science, and this is just the book they need.

There is only one important exception to its simplicity. Where Bloomfield develops his own (largely original) logical system of linguistic concepts, with corresponding terminology, summarized in tabular form on

p. 264, even his great skill fails to avoid what will seem to most laymen abstruseness and technicality. Such terms as *taxeme*, *tagmeme*, and *episememe* (p. 166), are indeed little used in the rest of the book, and most of it can be easily understood without reference to what the author means by them—which will interest linguists but hardly the general reader. It is a bit unfortunate that a few sections of this character had to be inserted at an early point in the text. I sincerely hope that they will not prove an insurmountable barrier to the many who could, and ought to, read the later parts, even if they find these few sections indigestible.

If this be called a criticism (and I do not suggest that I could have avoided the difficulty), it applies to form alone. Even in form few improvements would seem to me possible in the book. In substance it is even harder, for this reviewer at least, to find grounds for complaint. My only important disagreement concerns a few of the symbols chosen to represent phonemes in standard English (as spoken in Chicago, the dialect which the author adopts as most convenient for him).

For instance, the vowel sound in *up* is represented by [o]. I think this is unfortunate for two reasons. First, it is confusing to a layman because this sound is rarely represented by *o* in our conventional spelling. Even Bloomfield seems to me to have been led into inconsistencies by this violation of English spelling habits. He uses the same [o] for the vowel sound in *horse* (p. 125) and for that in the first syllable of *protest* (verb; p. 112). It seems to me that in so doing he represents three different phonemes by the one sign [o], and that of these three the sound in *up* is the one which English speakers would least naturally associate with [o]; yet it is just this one which Bloomfield invariably represents thereby. The use of [o] in the other two words named is, I think, almost unparalleled in the book, and I suspect these two cases are unintentional lapses, due to the influence of the spelling habits referred to.

My other objection is more serious, because it relates to scientific analysis, not conventional phonetic writing (which, of course, is arbitrary anyhow, so that the choice of one symbol rather than another is scientifically unimportant). The "compound phoneme" which we usually write *o*, as in *go*, is always represented by [ow]. "Compound phonemes" are defined (p. 90) as "combinations of simple phonemes. . . ." We must, therefore, assume that [ow] is a combination of [o] and [w]. But it seems to me that the vowel sound in *go* is certainly not a combination of the vowel sound in *up* with an element [w]; its first part is a quite different sound, at least in the dialect of Chicago and in all the United States. (It happens that standard British pronunciation does use, in such words as *oh!*, a diphthong which to my ear comes close to a combination of the vowel of *up* with a *w*; but Bloomfield was not referring to this.)— So also the first part of the "compound phoneme" [ej], as in *bay* [bej], is not identical with the simple phoneme represented by [e], as in *egg* [eg].

But these are trifles, which doubtless do not deserve so much space. In general, and in almost every detail, one is stimulated only to admiring appreciation of the author's rare combination of vast learning with the ability to present intricate facts in an orderly and easily comprehensible form.

Perhaps the high-water mark is the treatment of phonetic change and associated matters, a question on which distinguished linguists differ seriously, and which is hotly discussed among them today. Here Bloomfield's views are, as always, clear and definite, and may perhaps not be acceptable to some linguists. He adheres essentially to the "young grammarians." To me, at least, it seems that it will be hard for opponents to answer him; his is the best statement of the whole matter that I ever read.

The book is adequately indexed and contains an extensive and well selected bibliography, with special bibliographical notes to each chapter and to almost every one of the numbered sections into which the chapters are very conveniently divided.

(2) Samuel Kroesch (University of Minnesota), *Journal of English and Germanic Philology* 32.594–597 (1933).

When Bloomfield's *Introduction to the Study of Language* appeared in 1914 works of importance on general linguistics in English were, if we except Max Mueller's *Science of Language*, confined to Whitney's well-known study and to the translation of Paul's *Prinzipien*. In spite of the fact that in its psychological interpretations it inclined rather one-sidedly to the psychology of Wundt, it has nevertheless served a useful purpose, especially in courses on general linguistics in our schools. In these nineteen years linguistic study, stimulated in part by the controversies arising over Wundt's work and by the theories and publications of such scholars as de Saussure and his Geneva group, of Jespersen, Noreen, Meillet, Sapir, Pedersen among others, had made advances of such importance as to make a new edition of this work not only desirable but almost imperative.

The new edition has benefited by the author's thorough study of developments in the field of linguistics during these years, in which he has been not only a prominent teacher and investigator in the Indo-European field but also a student of languages outside this field. In the new edition he is not interested primarily in advocating certain theories concerning language but in presenting as objectively as possible a picture of the present status of the study of linguistics. It is natural in such a study that the IE languages and especially English should come in for the greater share of attention, but possibly to an even greater extent than in works of this type are languages outside of the IE field introduced for purposes of comparison. In addition to the languages considered in the first edition the author's special investigations into Tagalog, Menomini, and other American languages are utilized to throw additional light on linguistic problems. The new edition is, therefore, an entirely new work of at least twice the compass of its predecessor. The discussion of linguistics from the psychological standpoint is confined, in theory at least, to an objective presentation of the mentalistic and mechanistic viewpoints, although one suspects the author of mechanistic leanings. As a matter of fact, this distinction has less value than one might think, since one is not necessarily an out-and-out mentalist or mechanist but might adopt certain attitudes of both. While making use of the findings of psychology in so far as it has been of positive value in helping to solve linguistic problems, the author wisely emphasises the facts of language throughout rather than psychological interpretations.

To give the reader even a superficial idea of the contents of the work in the space allotted to me here is quite impossible. The twenty-eight chapters are subdivided into two hundred and fifty-nine sections, each of which treats a unit phase of the subject-matter of the chapter. The chapters themselves are arranged in a natural order so that subjects most closely related follow each other. The first four chapters beginning with a history of linguistic study and ending with a survey of the languages of the world may be regarded as an introduction to the main body of the work. The next four discuss the phonetic structure of language. Since it is the function of speech forms to convey meanings, a chapter on the psychological and semantic import of meaning follows. The grammatical, the largest group, embracing seven chapters deals with the morphological, syntactic, and lexical features of language. Three unrelated chapters, one on the history of writing, one on the comparative method of language study, and one on the often neglected study of dialect geography are followed by a group of five chapters treating the important subject of linguistic change (phonetic, analogic, semantic). The next three chapters on types of borrowing (cultural, intimate, dialect) might also be considered as treating forms of linguistic change. The last chapter, entitled "applications and outlook," discusses a number of more or less unrelated subjects affecting teachers and students of language (language teaching, phonetic spelling, artificial and universal languages). A section of notes, a bibliography, a short table of phonetic symbols, and an adequate index complete the work.

The impression left by an examination of the work is one of heightened respect for the breadth of knowledge, the industry, and the scholarly acumen of the author. The material is presented with an independence and objectivity which only years of familiarity with the subject can give. The book is intended, according to the author, "for the general reader and for the student who is entering upon linguistic work." The general reader will no doubt find interesting reading in a number of the chapters; nevertheless the author overestimates somewhat the general reader's capacity for assimilating linguistic abstractions. Certain chapters will require not only a beginning knowledge of linguistics but a familiarity of more or less long standing with the subject. In other words, it is primarily a book for the serious student of linguistics. To this end the full notes and bibliography make the study of sources and the formulation of an independent judgment, especially on controversial points at issue, not only possible but desirable.

In a work of such general excellence objections might seem out of place, and yet I cannot refrain from expressing my disagreement with the author on two points of the discussion in the chapters on phonetics. The one point is his failure to recognize high tense and high-mid tense vowel phonemes in Central-Western American. His simple vowels in these positions are all lax, or loose to use his expression; thus, [i] in *sin*, [u] in *put*, [e] in *egg*, [o] in *up*. The corresponding long vowel sounds are, therefore, all diphthongs, in unaccented as well as accented syllables, which are transcribed with the first element of the lax sounds with the above values. Examples: *see* [sij], *go* [gow], *vacate* [vejkejt], *few* [fjuw], *busy* [bizij]. This is a much closer approach to southern British English than I have ever heard in any part of the Midwest. The second point concerns his interpretation of the term phoneme and the use of the symbols for the phoneme. With his definition of the latter as "the distinctive feature of sound which the speaker has been trained to produce and recognize in the current of actual speech sound" I have no quarrel.[1] He recognizes further that since we have no way of recording all the non-distinctive features of a sound, a system of one sign for each phoneme of a language is all that is necessary to record it. The difficulty comes in his interpretation of the phonetic principle that where no ambiguity can result it may be advisable to depart even from this principle in order to save the use of extra symbols. This leads him, for example, to eliminate the slurred vowel symbol [ə] and to use [e] instead, thus employing one symbol for two of the most frequent phonemes in the English language, e.g., *address* (vb.) [edres]. To be sure, his contention would be that the unaccented position of the [e] would make it clear when the mid-mixed sound is written. This same feature he introduces into the German, whereas in French he is content to use the usual symbol [ə]. In German likewise he eliminates the symbol [ç] for the voiceless

---

[1] In a paper on the theory of phonemes reported in the Proceedings of the International Congress of Phonetic Sciences of July, 1932, Daniel Jones describes the phoneme as "a family of sounds in a given language, which are related in character and are such that no one of them ever occurs in the same surroundings as any other in words." He distinguishes further the diaphone and variphone as variations of phoneme types.

palatal continuant, using [x] for both palatal and velar sounds, thus *ich* [ix], *ach* [ax], "since the two varieties depend on the preceding phoneme." If he were writing *ich* in certain of the Alemanic dialects or in OHG or MHG he would of course expect the reader to know that the [x] here is velar. No teacher of German would want to add to the difficulties and confusion of these two sounds by adopting such a simplification. Such eliminations are for the expert in the phonology of the language, not for the general reader or the beginner in linguistics. For that reason some of these eliminations are particularly unfortunate in the author's own book where he uses phonetic transcriptions for many different dialects, both ancient and modern. Few of his readers will have either the necessary phonetic training or the command of the particular dialect to have an adequate idea of the value of these supposedly unambiguous symbols.

The chapter on semantic change is, on the whole, satisfactory. It would, however, have gained in breadth and definiteness of semantic classification by a study of Wellander's Studien zum Bedeutungswandel im Deutschen. I, II, III *Uppsala Universitets Årsskrift*, Upsala 1917, 1923, 1928. Though Paul and Wundt naturally come in for a share of the discussion no mention at all is made of this, in my opinion, the best discussion on semantics in German. For example, no reference is made to the subject of semantic ellipsis with which the whole of the second part of Wellander's work is concerned. On the other hand, Sperber's hypothesis of "*Affekt*" as a stimulus to semantic change is accorded recognition. The subject of semantic analogy is touched upon in the last few paragraphs of the chapter though the term analogy is not used in the discussion. Since the chapter on analogic change deals almost exclusively with phonetic and grammatical analogy, semantic analogy must still content itself with scattered, unlabeled illustrations in connection with other discussions. The infant, *semantic borrowing*, also stalks through the chapters on semantic change and borrowing, a nameless orphan. Some day, let us hope, the subject of semantic analogy will have attained sufficient dignity and importance to be accorded a section or mayhap even a chapter in some future edition.

In giving examples of illustrative English words the author might well have supplied cognates or analogous cases in the High German, such as for example: *bereit* in the discussion of NE *ready* (426); Bräutigam: bridegroom (423); Quehle, Zwehle: towel (460) etc. On one occasion (427) for some reason such cognates are given. A fuller use of these throughout would have been advisable. The proofreading was very carefully done. Only the following errors were noted: *irrevelantly* for *irrelevantly* (104), *thher* for *other* (329). The transcription of NHG *neunzig* as [nojntsik] (287) is certainly not *Bühnenaussprache*. I am not referring to the diphthong but to the last phoneme. In the notes to chapter 2 the reference 2.10 is an error, there being no section 10 in the chapter.[2] The bibliography and notes are excellent. There are no omissions of importance that have not already been mentioned in this discussion, unless one should regard Vendryes's *Language* as such. Graff, *Language and Languages* probably appeared after the work was in press.

These few objections and corrections seem petty indeed in consideration of the outstanding merit of the work. The author is to be congratulated on an achievement of the highest merit in the field of linguistics.

(3) Antoine Meillet (Paris), *Bulletin de la Société de Linguistique de Paris* 34:3.1–2 (1933).

M. L. Bloomfield a publié en 1914 un précis de linguistique générale fondé sur les théories de Wundt. Depuis il s'est aperçu que les linguistes n'ont pas suivi Wundt; au lieu de faire de son ancien ouvrage une édition corrigée, il a écrit un livre nouveau fondé sur des théories purement linguistiques. Destiné avant tout au public de langue anglaise, le livre a les caractères qui conviennent proprement à ce public: on y trouve beaucoup de données de fait, peu de théories abstraites, peu de formules générales. Il est clair et au courant des dernières publications; il rendra de bons services aux lecteurs qui voudront s'initier aux idées qui ont cours actuellement chez les linguistes. Professeur de germanique et s'adressant à des lecteurs de langue anglaise, M. L. Bloomfield prend une grande part de ses exemples dans l'anglais en particulier et, d'une manière générale, dans l'ensemble des langues germaniques. Ces exemples sont souvent suggestifs, ainsi quand il marque que les spirantes dentales ont été éliminées par la plupart des langues germaniques et que la conservation de ces spirantes en anglais est un fait de caractère exceptionnel.

Le peu de goût qu'a M. L. Bloomfield pour les théories est sensible dans le chapitre sur les changements phonétiques. Il ne cherche ni à les ramener, avec M. Grammont, à leurs conditions générales, ni à en chercher les conditions historiques; il n'analyse pas ce que l'on appelle les faits de substrat, et se contente de déclarer que les conditions du changement phonétique sont inconnues. Il a du reste une manière trop limitée d'envisager les changements. Il met hors du changement normal cas où, comme dans là dissimilation, l'assimilation à distance, la métathèse, il y a eu changement brusque d'un état phonétique donné; seuls, les changements lents et progressifs entrent pour lui dans la normale. Mais on ne peut ne pas tenir pour normal un changement tel que celui $k^w$ en $p$ qui a le

---

[2] [The three typographical errors noted in this paragraph remain uncorrected still in the April 1966 reprinting of the book, as do those noted near the end of Kent's review (5 below).]

même caractère de brusquerie que les faits cités plus haut. Il va jusqu'à mettre hors du changement normal le passage de *r* dental à *r* uvulaire qui a eu lieu notamment dans les parlers français urbains: ce changement fournit justement un bel exemple de loi phonétique rigoureuse et absolue.

Dans sa conclusion, M. L. Bloomfield est manifestement gêné par le manque d'utilité pratique de la linguistique: le mérite de la linguistique est d'être une science de caractère théorique propre à instruire, d'une manière désintéressée, sur l'esprit humain. Peu importe si la pédagogie n'en sait pas tirer profit. La tâche du linguiste est de rechercher la vérité sans se soucier du parti qu'on en tirera peut-être un jour ni même de savoir si jamais on s'en servira pratiquement.

(4) Edgar H. Sturtevant (Yale University), *The Classical Weekly* 27.159–160 (26 March 1934).

In his Preface (vii) Professor Bloomfield calls the book under review, Language, "a revised version of the author's *Introduction to the Study of Language*, which appeared in 1914 (New York, Henry Holt and Company). . . ." In reality, however, it is a new book. It is not merely larger by about 95 per cent; a very considerable part of the contents of the earlier work has been omitted or so far altered as to be scarcely recognizable.

The fundamental purpose remains the same (Preface, vii): "Like its predecessor, this book is intended for the general reader and for the student who is entering upon linguistic work. . . ." Any such book must at every turn combat the absurd pseudo-philosophical prejudices about language that many educated persons now hold, and it would be hard to imagine a more devastating attack upon this stronghold of ignorance. On the positive side Professor Bloomfield is generally conservative. When he treats disputed points, he never takes a dogmatic tone. Any person who masters this book will get as sound an outlook upon language as can be had. In that sense it may be called the best available introduction to linguistic science.

But an introduction must not make demands upon beginners that are beyond their powers. Professor Bloomfield's book is certainly a difficult book. Many readers will need fuller expositions and more illustrative material in order to grasp the unfamiliar point of view, but the chief difficulty lies in the technical terminology. Few books on language have presented so many new terms and new definitions of old terms. In as far as these are needed, it may be argued that their introduction really facilitates the mastery of the science; arithmetic is certainly made easier by the use of the necessary technical terms. At present, however, a large proportion of Professor Bloomfield's new terms occurs nowhere else; the reader must learn them purely for the sake of understanding this book. Besides, they are not always fully illustrated at their first occurrence, and they are rarely compared and contrasted with the grammatical terminology with which the reader is already familiar. One gets the impression that the author has such facility in originating new language that he underestimates the difficulty that results for the rest of us from such origination. Perhaps the book is not beyond the comprehension of a beginner of average intelligence, but it makes greater demands upon his attention than are usual in introductory treatises.

No such reservation is necessary in estimating the book as a contribution to linguistic science. The new terminology cannot fail to clarify our thinking; doubtless much of it will win general acceptance. The discrimination between descriptive grammar (Chapters 4–17: 3–296) and the historical and comparative study of language is by no means new, but it has rarely if ever been carried through so consistently. The former subject is here worked out largely on the basis of American English as spoken in Chicago, and there emerge from the discussion some main outlines of a descriptive grammar of English utterly unlike any yet published. One may hope that the task thus begun will presently be completed in the form of a new English Grammar. Such a book would finally banish the queer reflection of Latin grammar that has hitherto prevented an understanding of the structure of our native tongue.

Professor Bloomfield's statement of the case for the generally accepted axioms of linguistic science is the best we have.[1] In particular it is hard to see how any scholar can again assume 'sporadic' phonetic change. At the same time I hope to show elsewhere that we cannot be content with ascribing the regularity of this process to its gradual nature, as Professor Bloomfield does. He himself, I think, supplies the material for showing the falsity of his position. That again is a mark of a good book.

(5) Roland G. Kent (University of Pennsylvania), *Language* 10.40–48 (1934), with an added note (pp. 48–51) by George M. Bolling (Ohio State University), editor of the journal.

I cannot commend too highly Leonard Bloomfield's Language, published in 1933, a revised and enlarged form of his earlier Introduction to the Study of Language, published in 1914. Every serious student of linguistic science should read it, study it, digest it; he will profit by it, even as I have profited by it.

[1] [Sometime between 1936 and 1943 Sturtevant said, to a group that included me, 'What you young people should do is to write commentaries on Bloomfield's *Language*, like the commentaries on Panini'.—CFH]

I make this explicit statement of commendation because I propose to discuss certain features of it in a way that might seem disparaging, if I did not make such a preliminary statement of approval; and I do not wish to be regarded as condemning the work because I happen, on mature consideration, to disagree with the author on certain matters of presentation. He and I have discussed these points by letter, and I trust that I can present his side of them fairly.

These matters center around what may, for lack of a better term, be called 'phonetic transcription'; for lack of a better term, I say, for in it I include certain sub-topics which are not properly indicated by the phrase, yet are closely associated therewith.

Linguistic science labors under many difficulties, not the least of them being the necessity of presenting the material by symbols of a visual character: writing is a visual method, and what is written or printed must convey to the eye an impression that is interpretable to the ear as sounds and series of sounds, i.e., speech. When an author is dealing with one language only, and that a language well known to the reader, this difficulty may be minimized; but when he is discussing features of speech for which he must present examples from a number of languages, he runs into a very great difficulty.

Of course, for material drawn from a language already possessed of a literature, the author may use the conventional standard orthography of that language (Bloomfield 89); but to a reader who does not know the language, such a presentation will fail to convey the evidence on the point in hand, since he will not know how to interpret into sounds the symbols presented to his eyes. For example, the conventional orthography of English, French, Russian is far from presenting to the reader a simple and easily understood picture of the sounds involved; the orthography of Spanish, Italian, German is much more satisfactory, though not perfect. In such an instance, then, when the reader does not know the language, and his understanding of the discussion depends upon his appreciation of the sounds involved, the author must employ another system of notation, commonly called a 'phonetic writing', which may, as nearly as possible, be translated into sound by the reader without reference to whether he understands the language itself. This is obviously true also when the language is not yet possessed of a standard system of writing and must actually be reduced to written form.

Clearly there are limitations upon a phonetic writing: the varieties of sound are almost unlimited (Bloomfield 76), and it is quite impossible to devise a practical scheme of characters which shall distinguish every shade of sound employed in the speech of human beings. All these facts are not merely admitted by Bloomfield, but are emphasized by him; and as a practical solution of the problem he has taken refuge in a system of transcription which in his opinion minimizes them: it may be termed a 'phonemic transcription', though he does not use the term.

A 'phoneme' is a speech-feature, in most instances a sound, that is functionally distinctive in the language to which it belongs (Bloomfield 79–81). Thus the voiceless [θ] and the voiced [đ] are in English separate phonemes, because they serve, for example, to distinguish the noun *mouth* from the verb *mouthe* (Bloomfield 79); but the aspirated *p* in *pin* and the non-aspirated *p* in *spin* are in English one and the same phoneme, because the difference nowhere serves to distinguish different words (80). On the other hand, since speakers of one language do not by ear normally perceive and appreciate sounds of another language not occurring in their own speech, an English-speaking person does not (without instruction) observe that German *Buch* and *buk* end in different phonemes, a German thinks that *thin* and *tin* begin with the same phoneme, a Frenchman thinks that *think* and *sink* begin with the same phoneme, etc. (cf. Bloomfield 83).

Accordingly, says Bloomfield (84), if the transcriber is meticulously careful, he will encumber his phonetic notation with details (like the aspiration of the *p* of English *pin*) that have no functional existence; it is preferable to transcribe only by phonemes, disregarding the functionless variations. Yet he immediately meets the fact, which he admits and emphasizes (101), that what is a non-functional variation in one language is a functional distinction in another[1]: thus (though the example is not his at this point) the aspirated *p* and the non-aspirated *p* are separate phonemes in Ancient Greek, in Sanskrit, in many modern languages of India. The inevitable result is, that a distinction that is disregarded in the phonemic notation of English must be indicated in the phonemic notation of those languages, if examples should be drawn from them. There is also the converse case: in Japanese the sibilant [s] which stands before other vowels becomes approximately [š] before *i*.[2] The difference between [s] and [š] is functional in English: shall we disregard it in citing Japanese, because it is not functional—even though we have the machinery for marking the distinction?

Naturally the rigidity of any such scheme should be subject to relaxation; the author might indicate such non-phonemic differences as are con-

---

[1] Bloomfield instances the spirant [γ] in some types of German pronunciation, where it is a variant of the phoneme [g], stating that in Dutch and in Modern Greek [γ] and [g] occur as separate phonemes. But he himself now writes to me that these examples will not serve, for while the sounds are distinct in the languages named, [g] is in Dutch only a sandhi-product of [k] before [b] or [d], and in Modern Greek is the product of [k] after a nasal. For Modern Greek it might be added that [g] occurs initially in native words if a preceding nasal has disappeared and also in borrowings, such as [gaz] 'gas', written γκάζ. But he is right in separating [γ] and [g] in these languages, whereas they cannot be separated in German.

[2] For this statement, I refer to Hossfeld's Japanese Grammar, by H. J. Weintz (printed by Peter Reilly, Philadelphia, 1914).

veniently to be expressed in the notation which he is obliged to use for other languages. Such, I would hope, would be Bloomfield's procedure; for otherwise he would be under obligations to present a set of phonemes, with a statement of their automatic alterations, for each and every language which he plans to cite for illustration. And yet some of his usages indicate that he does not utilize the machinery at his command, when it comes to indicating non-phonemic distinctions. Thus (145) he transcribes German *Pferd* as [pfe:rt], although the vowel is made open by the following [r] (and is quite distinct in quality from that in *Bett* and from that in *Beet*), for the reason that this is an automatic variation, and does not produce a distinct phoneme.[3] On the other hand, he quotes French *vous aimez* as [vuz eme] (372), although the two vowels of the verb are recognized by the French as distinct, commonly indicated by *è* and *é* respectively. If, as he writes me, the French themselves habitually say [eme], or, as it were, *émé*, would not the closer sound of the prior vowel be an automatic variation which confused one phoneme with another, rather than an absence of a phonemic difference?[4] At the best, there is no warrant for writing [eme] rather than [ɛme], if the Russian word for 'city' is represented by ['gorot] rather than by ['gorət]—on which see my remarks below.

Another point that I would make, refers to Bloomfield's choice and use of phonetic or phonemic symbols. Among them (the list is on pp. 547–8) are the following:

[e]  as in Eng. *men*, and in French *gai*.
[ɛ]  as in Eng. *man*, and in French *dette*.
[i]  as in Eng. *tin*, and in French *fini*.
[o]  as in Eng. *sun*, *son*, and in French *beau*.
[ɔ]  as in Eng. *saw*, and in French *homme*.

Herein is much that is difficult for a speaker of English: the [ɛ] to designate the sound of the vowel in *man*, which English-speakers definitely associate with the first letter of the alphabet,[5] and the [o] for the sound which they associate with the letter *u*—though in both instances the most that we can

---

[3] Bloomfield writes me: 'German has only one vowel of the *e*-type, hence no [ɛ] appears in German transcriptions.' But to my ear, the vowels of *Bett* and *Beet* are quite distinct in quality as well as in quantity. On this, Bloomfield writes that he regards the sign of length in [be:t] = *Beet* as an adequate indication of the difference, especially since the *e*-vowel is not uniform in quality among native speakers of German.

[4] Cf. also footnote 9. My experience with speakers of French is that *é* in non-final syllables is likely to become *è* (i.e., [ɛ]), rather than the reverse. Thus I recall a Parisian professor who pronounces *répéter* as though *rè-pè-té* (or [rɛpɛte]), and my French colleagues tell me that his peculiarities of speech are typical of Parisian French of to-day.

[5] Of course it would be impossible to use [a], [e], [i], [o], [u], with their English values, in any system; English is too aberrant in its system of vowels and diphthongs, to be used as a basis for a notation, except with very great limitations.

expect is some less disturbing equation.[6] Worse is the fact that in these five instances the symbol designates sounds which are very different in the two languages, differences which, in fact, our teachers work hard to impress upon their pupils.

Bloomfield does indeed recognize this and provide against criticism when he says (88), 'If a language has two phonemes of the general type of our *e*-sound as in *pen*, we use the letter [e] for one of them, and the supplementary symbol [ɛ] for the other, as in *pan* [pɛn].' But is he quite justified in his procedure? For while English has two *e*-phonemes, and French likewise has two, it happens that the *e* of *dette* is very close to, though not identical with, the *e* of *men*; the other two sounds are very divergent, that of English being much opener and that of French being much closer. A series of three symbols is needed, to give any objective idea of the sounds: one for Eng. *man*, one for Eng. *men* and French *dette*, a third for French *été* (which I substitute for Bloomfield's *gai*[7]). For unless this be done, how shall we interpret citations from other languages, such as (219) Menomini [nenɛ:hkan] 'my hands'? Unless we know whether the *e*-phonemes are approximately those of English or those of French, we are left floundering.[8] It is no answer to say that it is immaterial which they are; it is disturbing to the reader, and puts an unfair obstacle in his way, if a better scheme is available.

Again, in pages 109–26, Bloomfield speaks of the reductions of vowels in unaccented syllables, and uses for certain examples a phonetic notation which indicates these reductions; see especially pages 111 and 113. And yet elsewhere in the same section he gives the phonemic values in square brackets, as in ['sekretejrij] for *secretary* (112), a pronunciation which, if unreduced, both he and I consider pedantic. Also, on page 111, the Russian word for 'city' is represented by ['gorot], although inevitably it is pronounced ['gorət], since there are changes in vowel quality effected in Russian by the lack of accent. On this point Bloomfield writes me: 'My pronunciation agrees with yours; I am merely trying to apply the principle of my preceding remark: an unstressed or low-stressed [ejr] (after the

[6] Cf. also the remarks of Franklin Edgerton in JAOS 53.295–7, on this and related matters, in a review of this same volume.

[7] The examples illustrating the sounds under discussion are not all well-chosen. French *gai* is given by the Petit Larousse of 1925 as *ghè*, i.e., with the vowel of *dette* (an older dictionary in my possession gives it as *ghé*); we might better substitute *été* in the table. Also, the use of English examples ending in a nasal makes the comparison difficult, since the nasal somewhat alters the preceding vowel-sound (but not enough to make of it a different phoneme!); one might better list *met, mat, bit, but* respectively, for the first four.

[8] For that matter, is not a third *e*-symbol required for French? The vowel that is nasalized in French *vin* is quite distinct from that in *dette*; but Bloomfield (228) transcribes [vɛⁿ], considering that the sign of nasalization is an adequate indication of automatic change of the sound. However, his phonemic writing seems to me to require [viⁿ] for 'structural' reasons (see latter part of review), cf. masc. *fin*, fem. *fine*.

stressed syllable) does not exist, but shades off to [er] or [r̩] invariably. Hence the stress-sign suffices to indicate the difference between the third syllables of *secretarial* [sekre'tejrijl] and of *secretary* ['sekretejrij].' The previous remark to which he alludes, is: 'Weakening of unstressed syllables in Russian is sufficiently indicated when the place of accent is given, i.e., ['gorot] but plural [goro'da] tells as much as ['gorət, gəra'da]: in fact, to the persons who know the rule which you cite, it tells more, since each of these transcriptions indicates both the accented and the unstressed forms of each vowel-phoneme, whereas ['gorət], for instance, fails to tell whether the second syllable has [o] or [a] or [i].'[9] His writing, it would seem, has here become virtually etymological; for it cannot be assumed that the majority even of the readers of the volume under discussion will know the automatic weakenings of the vowels in unstressed syllables of sundry languages.

He writes further, in a later letter: 'If a weakening is a regular and universal accompaniment of unstressed position, then we have the question which you raise: Shall we transcribe structurally, or shall we set down a systematic additional indication of weakening? I am trying the former, hitherto untried. In English, we have, of course, the further problem, quite distinct, as to what weakenings are actually "automatic". E.g., *final*: (1) *finality*; (2) *definite*; (3) *definitive*; in (1) we have automatic weakening, but the [aj] is often restored, especially by semi-educated speakers or by lecturers; in (2) the weakening is morphologic (alternation [aj – i]), and [aj] cannot be restored; proof of this last is form (3), with accented [i].'

In this manner, Bloomfield seems to me to have abandoned, in such unstressed syllables, even his own principle to which I have given the name of 'phonemic writing', and to have adopted an etymological system (he calls it 'structural'), which has many of the defects of the traditional standard orthography—neither system gives a fair idea of the sounds as they are in speech, but each represents a status that has passed away. This remark applied to citations from languages with a stress accent of variable position; for French, however, we find that his notations in square brackets are not strictly phonemic, but virtually phonetic, since they imply decisions on optional variations.

---

[9] Why should the 'structural' transcription be limited to vowels? Both in German and in Russian final voiced stops become voiceless; thus writings with [d], e.g. in German [pfe:rd] 'horse' and Russian ['gorod] 'city', are required in view of other case-forms, where [d] remains before the vowel of the flexional syllable. Bloomfield, however, writes that he 'transcribed [t] because in these languages [d] and [t] are distinct phonemes. Perhaps this principle is out of place, and I should really have used [d], but I believe the point is different from that of [ə] vs. [o] in the second syllable of the Russian word, or of [e] vs. [ɛ] in the German word.'

Just one more point. In deference to the high cost of typesetting non-Latin alphabets, Bloomfield has presented Greek words in transcription (cf. 89, end). The transcriptions are faithful to the Greek orthography, and yet he puts them in square brackets, the label of phonetic or phonemic notation: thus [sun'ejde:sis] for συνείδησις (456), although the first vowel is known to have been [y]; and ['genows] for γένους (362), although this word did not have a diphthong in the second syllable, but only a lengthened close [o], a sound represented in the Attic alphabet by O (like the short sound of the same quality), and only later written ου. This sound became [u:], and the transcription should therefore be ['genu:s].

It appears, then, that Bloomfield has placed in square brackets at least four kinds of transcriptions: phonemic, his preferred plan; phonetic, at times, to indicate the weakened vowels of unstressed syllables when this was the subject of discussion, and to some extent for French; etymologic (his 'structural'), showing the original values of the unstressed vowels subject to weakening; and mere transcriptional, as in the case of Greek.

This inconsistency does not seriously impair the great value of the book, but should suggest to us the importance of adopting some system of notation which does not ask the almost impossible of the scholarly reader, and the surely impossible of the less technical reader, to whom the volume brings a stimulating approach to the knowledge of language and of its behavior and processes. Bloomfield's system might be acceptable if he were treating a single language, and gave full explanations of the phenomena underlying or overlying his notations. But when many languages are called on for examples, what shall the author do, and what shall the reader have a right to expect?[10]

My suggestion is that the start for a phonetic notation should be made from the most generally used system; that modifications and additions should be such as not to confuse the reader who speaks the basic language of the book; that non-essential differences in sounds (like the aspiration of the *p* in Eng. *pin*, as contrasted with the non-aspiration of the *p* in *spin*) should be disregarded, unless examples from other languages are included where these differences are phonemic; that for purposes of notation the sounds of other languages be equated, as far as possible, with sounds

[10] I mean, of course, in a book of the type under discussion, where examples must be drawn from many languages. Where only one language is under discussion, either the phonetic transcription or the phonemic is practicable; there should in all cases be an accurate description of the values of the symbols, and for the phonemes there should be also a detailed account of their automatic variations and of the conditions in which the variations take place. The giving of such descriptions for a number of languages, which would be necessary for a book like Bloomfield's, would add unduly to its bulk. On the other hand, for a volume on a single language, the phonemic notation has many advantages, to which I am neither blind nor deaf; and for some purposes it is a great advance over the phonetic notation.

of the basic language of the book, but not equated unless there is a pretty close resemblance; that a brief account be given of such sounds of other languages as cannot be reasonably denoted in terms of the basic language; and finally, that mere transliterations, as of Greek, should never be put in square brackets.

On the other hand, I gladly admit that in this matter Bloomfield has courageously struck out into a new path; he may be right, and I wrong. But in his attempt to attain a simplification, he seems to me to have adopted an unnecessarily confusing scheme. It gives me pleasure to put on record that Bloomfield himself writes that our 'discussion will further the solving of the transcription problem, and is very welcome to me. Our difference of opinion is a good thing, because a premature agreement would slow up progress. The more we discuss the matter, the better we shall learn how to deal with it. I feel that we are close to a real advance in this old problem.'

In conclusion, I must pay tribute to Bloomfield's wide and accurate learning, and I acknowledge the great benefit that I have derived from the study of his book, verily a magnum opus, the careful assimilation of which I shall require of all students with a real interest in linguistics. Be it noted that the present critique is intended (and Bloomfield so understands it) to be not destructive, but constructive; and it is in the same spirit that for the benefit of the users of the book I append a brief list of corrections to his text:

59.11: For Faroese, read Faroe.

61.25–6: For in Switzerland, read in and near Switzerland.

62.3 (and elsewhere): For Albanese, read Albanian.

94.10 (and elsewhere): For vocal chords, read vocal cords (Bl. writes that he prefers chords as 'less misleading to beginners').

112.25: Read rather: *address*, verb [ɛ'dres].

112.30: Read rather: *atomic* [ɛ'tamik].

113.22: Read rather: *restituzione* [rɛstitutsi'jone].

116.39: For nine, read six (a slip to which Bl. himself calls my attention).

120.31: Read [bord] as phonemic value of *bird*, rather than [brd], which (to me, at least) represents a completely accentless state as in a compound *redbird*, but not in the second of the two separate words *red bird* (on this point, cf. 180, near bottom); but there may be a dialectal difference between Bloomfield and myself. A pronunciation [br:d], with a lengthened vowel, would not seem so strange to me in a stressed position, though I should never pronounce it that way myself.

122.37: Read *anatomy* [ɛ'nɛtamij] and not [e'nɛtṃij]; Bloomfield accepts the correction of the first sound on the basis that the stressed value of the vowel appears in *anagram*, etc. On the basis of the value of the stressed vowel in *anatomical*, I have changed the writing of the third vowel also.

238.15: *Thievess*, as fem. to *thief*, though properly formed, is not on record as ever having been used.

258.19: Delete comma after *this*.

284.18: For scratched, read pressed with a stilus.

350.20: Read rather [f, þ, h] for Pre-Italic and Pre-Latin.

363.29: Greek ἔλειψα (Bloomfield's [ˈelejpsa]) is not a real form; it did not occur in classical Greek, and if it is found at all, it is a new creation in Late Greek, and not an inheritance from Primitive Indo-European.

390.39: Read *quīnque*; 391.21–3: *\*nūtrī-trīx*, *nūtrīx*, *\*stīpi-pendium*, *stīpendium*, with the mark of length over the *i*'s.

396.28–9: Read rather: *s'en va* 'goes away'; for the liaison in *s'en aller* spoils the point of the citation.

446.30: Read rather [wi:n].

460.6–7: Read *compāniō* and *pānis*, with the mark of length over the *a*'s.


[Bolling's note:]

The editor is planning to review Bloomfield's book himself, but in the meantime is very glad to print Kent's discussion of the transcription problem. The book deserves indeed many reviews, for it is provocative of much thought; other discussions of questions raised by it will be welcome at any time.

The validity of Kent's objections seems to me to depend upon the attitude taken towards a paragraph (85), which deserves to be quoted.

'Only two kinds of linguistic records are scientifically relevant. One is a mechanical record of the gross acoustic features. . . . The other is a record in terms of phonemes, ignoring all features that are not distinctive in the language. Until our knowledge of acoustics has progressed far beyond its present state, only the latter kind of record can be used for any study that takes into consideration the meaning of what is spoken.'

Given the history of our studies, it is clear that this must be, at least for men of the older generations, a hard saying. Bloomfield's presentation of the case seems to me, however, entirely convincing, and Kent attempts no refutation of the general principle. If it is accepted there is obviously at present no place in our work for two methods of transcription, one 'phonemic' and one 'phonetic'.

Most of Kent's criticism seems to come from regarding the restriction to phonemes and nothing else merely as a refuge from the practical difficulties of transcription instead of seeing in it a principle of scientific value. It is perfectly easy to distinguish in writing or printing [s] from [š], [t] from [th], [p] from [b]; but, as a matter of principle (the reasons are given by

Bloomfield), we must not make these distinctions in dealing with Japanese, English, and Menomini, where they are meaningless; while we must make them in English, Sanskrit, English, and wherever else they carry differences of meaning.

The charge of inconsistency in the application of the phonemic principle is, in my opinion, not substantiated by reference to pages 111 and 113. Reductions in unstressed syllables may lead either to a change of phonemes, as in *isn't* [ˈizn̩t]; or to the non-distinctive modification of a sound, as in *business* [ˈbiznes]. The former must, of course, be recorded; the latter is sufficiently indicated by the stress-mark. To write [ˈbiznəs] would be like the meaningless underlining of a schoolgirl. Bloomfield refuses to do this; and the examples on pages 111 and 113 are all, either of the *isn't* type with the phonemes recorded, or of the *business* type with the non-distinctive modification indicated by the stress-mark alone.

The choice of symbols for the phonemes of any given language is always debatable, and in itself relatively unimportant. Bloomfield's transcription of English I find very satisfactory. The habits fostered by English orthography are so bad, that one must break with them sooner or later; and I cannot sympathise with the objections to such writings as *man* [mɛn], or *sun* [son]. On the other hand it is a matter of great importance to recognise that the selection of symbols is for each language an independent problem. The fact that [p] has been used for a certain phoneme in English must be no bar to its use in transcribing French or Menomini, even tho the sounds for which it will be used are noticeably different in all three languages. This will be generally conceded, and yet it is an exact parallel to the use of [ɛ] both in English [mɛn] and French [dɛt] to which exception is taken.

Our striving for an illusion of accuracy (cf. LANGUAGE 3.126) has led us to attach an exaggerated importance to the precise sounds of a language. Kent is of the opinion that Bloomfield should either have employed, as far as material circumstances permit, separate symbols for each shade of sound, so that any language cited in the book could be read by anyone with a pronunciation like (at least passably like) a native; or, if he wished to record phonemes alone, should have given for each language a phonetic description of its phonemes and a list of their automatic variations. I am in complete disagreement. For the first alternative should be substituted, on the principle enunciated in the paragraph already quoted, a request for phonographic records. Information of the sort desired in the second alternative is to be sought in the descriptive grammars of the languages involved. Bloomfield's book does not aim at imparting a native-like pronunciation of any language, and it is intelligible whether one possesses such ability or not. Kent denies this. Of Menomini [nenɛ:hkan] he says: 'Unless we know whether the *e*-phonemes are approximately those of English or those of French we are left floundering.'

Let us test this. We are told (219) that [nenɛ:h] makes it plural [nenɛ:hkan], [wi:ki:h] makes [wi:ki:hsan], etc. Bloomfield points out that the facts can be described in two ways. (1) Taking the singular as the basic form, the plural is made by adding a consonant (there are five possibilities) and the suffix [-an]; there will then be need of five lists to show which word adds which consonant. (2) Taking as basic the included forms [nenɛ:hk-], [wi:ki:hs-], etc., the plural is formed by the addition of [-an], the singular with zero suffix and observance of the rules for permitted finals. The latter method, which requires no list, is simpler and more natural. This I fancy I can understand, altho my pronunciation of Menomini is as bad as bad can be. The preceding paragraph in Bloomfield's book deals in somewhat similar fashion with German constructions such as [ˈgra:s] : [ˈgra:zen] but [ˈšpa:s] : [ˈšpa:sen]. Can it be maintained that one's ability to follow the argument depends upon the correctness of his pronunciation of German vowels? To take another example, no one who reads this would flounder in a morphologic or syntactic discussion because it used as English examples: *Enroughity is coming.—The Enroughities are coming.* Yet few of my readers can, I am sure, pronounce these examples correctly; and those who can probably secured the necessary information in a rather accidental way. In eastern Virginia there is said to be a family whose name is pronounced [ˈdabi] and written *Enroughity*. Whether the family is mythical or not, I do not know; but from boyhood I have been acquainted with two stories about them. One attempts to explain aitiologically the curious difference between the written and the oral form of the name; the other ascribes a military disaster to the inability of an officer from South Carolina to find the [ˈdabi ˈrowd] on his map. That is sufficient attestation for the forms. A reader who pronounced [*enˈrofiti], or anything else, could follow the supposed discussion as well as if he had said [ˈdabi].

In one important point I am in agreement with Kent against Bloomfield: the latter's transcription of Greek seems bad. Bloomfield (89–90) lays down excellent principles: for languages that use alphabets other than the Latin citation in the traditional form is to be deplored; we must have recourse either to transliteration or transcription, and for most linguistic purposes transcription is preferable. His square brackets seem to promise a transcription of Greek; but on examination their contents prove to be a transliteration, or something between the two.

As a transliteration it must be criticised for not showing a one-to-one correspondence between the alphabets, iota being represented both by *i* and *j*, upsilon by *u* and *w*. This comes, no doubt, from a crossing with the idea of transcription. As transcription his practise seems open to still greater criticism. His position, as I understand it, is that, if the Greek writing is phonemic, a transliteration of it will be phonemic also. Granted. But a transcription reached in this way may still be bad as distorting the pattern of the language. When Bloomfield symbolises a phoneme as [ej] the whole practise of his book suggests that the digraph stands for a compound phoneme; when we find other phonemes represented by [aj], [oj], we naturally infer that [ej] belongs in a series with them. But, on the ordinary view of Greek pronunciation (and Bloomfield has, I believe, no desire to dispute it), the phoneme [ej] has an entirely different position in the pattern, being paired with [e] as [i:] is with [i], or [a:] with [a]. Under these conditions [e:] would seem the only satisfactory transcription. The case of [ow] is somewhat similar, for it is not in a series with [aw], [ew]. The matter is more complicated, because the [o:] that once contrasted with [o] as did [e:] with [e], etc., had by classic times passed into a sound that may be represented best as [u:]. This in turn forces the use of other symbols (say [ü] and [ü:]) for the vowels written with upsilon. Bloomfield's best course would have been, in my opinion, to cite Greek forms in transliteration accompanied by transcription: *eimí* [e:'mi], *génous* ['genu:s].

It may be argued that symbols can represent whatever they are defined as representing. The principle is excellent, but there are limits to its application. These were recognized years ago, LANGUAGE 3.124 (1927), by Bloomfield and myself; and in his book Bloomfield has kept within these limits except in the present instance. At least I can recall no example of, say, [p] for a voiced velar spirant, [x] for a vowel, or a digraph for a non-compound phoneme. The present inconsistency is not harmless: if one attempts to describe the phonetic structure of Greek, as Bloomfield has described (130 ff.) that of English, the transcription will, as pointed out in the last paragraph, prove confusing.

There is no occasion to speak of the impersonal intent of these remarks, Kent has said all that is needed on that topic.


(6) George M. Bolling (Ohio State University), *Language* 11.251–252 (1935).


The appearance of this British Edition gives occasion to express briefly my opinion of Bloomfield's work.

It is built on Paul, the only secure foundation; and seems to me the only notable advance beyond the position reached in that scholar's work. The advance is made along two lines, the first of which is the stressing of the importance of the descriptive study of language. The argument that our historical studies are dependent upon our description, is incontrovertible; and will be especially appreciated by anyone who has worked at the language of the Homeric poems. Besides there is the outlook to the long future, to the time when trustworthy descriptions of the languages of the world will supply material for more fruitful inductions about language itself than can be made at the present time. The second drive has for its objective the elimination of 'psychological explanations' from our work. Again I am in hearty agreement with the author: even if the mechanistic view of human behavior be wrong, it is our province as linguists merely to report the facts that we can observe; the building of further theories upon these facts is the task of others, and will be hampered rather than helped by our interference. Such theories add nothing to our understanding of our own problems; Delbrück showed that, when he pointed out that one psychology (Herbart's) was as good as another (Wundt's) for our purposes.

There is no occasion to praise at length the manner in which the book is written:[1] its outstanding characteristics are orderliness of construction, and lucidity of exposition; the latter attained by a style that is almost studied in its simplicity and directness. The high points for me are: the two introductory chapters on 'The Use of Language' (21–41), 'Speech Communities' (42–56); the technique for describing the facts of a language purely in terms of linguistics (73–280); the discussion of phonetic change (346–68); and the presentation of semantic change (425–43) as a type of analogic change.

Linguistics seems to me to have been standing for some time at a crossroads. Is it to return to the place where Rask and Bopp and Grimm found it? The path is easy; and the mob, who 'because they speak, fancy they can speak about speech', call in that direction. Or, is it to continue the steep climb toward the heights to which the Neogrammarians pointed? I hope the latter. If so, it will take for its guide on the next stage the present book as, to adapt what it says of Paul, the standard work on the methods of linguistics.

(7) A. Debrunner (Bern), *Indogermanische Forschungen* 54. 148–149 (1936) ('Kleine Anzeigen').

Das Buch ist eine stark erweiterte Neuausgabe von Bloomfields Introduction to the Study of Language von 1914, die ich nicht kenne. Die britische Ausgabe ist ein mechanischer Abdruck der amerikanischen mit geringen Änderungen.

An "Einleitungen in die Sprachwissenschaft" ist ja in allen möglichen Sprachen kein Mangel; die meisten behandeln aber nur einige wenige Abschnitte aus dem ungeheuren Gesamtgebiet, das zwischen der Experimentalphonetik und den tiefsten Fragen der Sprachphilosophie liegt. Bei

---

[1] The changes in the new edition consist: . . .

The map on page 313 represents the Slavs as reaching the Aegean. This was certainly not done before the Great War, and the accompanying text would indicate that the map pictured much earlier conditions.

Bl. wird man weniger Abschnitte vermissen als bei den meisten andern. Das ist der erste Vorzug. Der zweite ist die starke Heranziehung nicht-indogermanischer Sprachen, die bei einem Germanisten besonders über-raschend ist; namentlich die Indianersprachen liefern dem Verfasser viel Vergleichsmaterial. Am besten haben mir die Kapitel "The comparative method" (S. 297 ff.; pädagogisch ausgezeichnete Beweisführung) und "Dialect geography" (S. 321 ff.; gute Beispiele aus allerlei Sprachgebieten mit klaren Sprachkarten) gefallen. Die erste Hälfte ist, zum mindesten für einen, der das Englische nicht völlig beherrscht, oft schwer verständ-lich; das liegt wohl daran, daß hier die Grammatik sehr stark logizistisch behandelt wird, und auch an einer übertriebenen Vorliebe für schemati-sierende Terminologie (z. B. S. 264 neben *phoneme* und *morpheme* auch *taxeme, glosseme, noeme, sememe, tagmeme, episememe*). Auch die Kapi-telüberschriften sind oft ungewöhnlich: "Types of phonemes" (S. 93 ff.) ist "Bildung der Laute", "Substitution" (S. 247 ff.) umfaßt Pronomina, Negationen, Zahlen, wobei der Verfasser zwischen psychologisch-gene-tischer und grammatisch-logizistischer Auffassung schwankt: "On the whole, then, substitution-types consist of elementary features of the situa-tion in which speech is uttered" (S. 249), aber "substitutes are, so to speak, linguistic forms of the second degree" (S. 250); "Dialect borrowing" (S. 476 ff.) behandelt die Entstehung von Hochsprachen, den Einfluß der Schrift auf die Aussprache, die Abkürzungssprache die Geschichte der Aussprache des c von den Römern bis heute, die "mots savants". Im Kapitel "Phonetic Change" (S. 346 ff.) steht mir die Auffassung "a pro-gressive favoring of variants in some one direction" (S. 365) zu sehr im Vordergrund; die ebenda nur vorübergehend erwähnten Momente "lin-guistic borrowing (imitation)" und "analogic change (systematization)" sind meines Erachtens wichtiger[1]; auch glaube ich, daß der sprunghafte Lautwandel, den Bl. (S. 390) für den Übergang vom Zungen-*r* zum Zäpf-chen-*r* nicht leugnen kann, viel häufiger ist, weil das Wesentliche am Lautwandel nicht das Artikulatorische, sondern das Soziologische ist. Das Schlußkapitel "Applications and outlook" (S. 496 ff.) bespricht Ge-genwartsfragen (Sprachunterricht, Weltsprachen); pädagogisch interes-sierten Lesern empfehle ich dringend, das bewegliche Klagelied über die Wirkungen des amerikanischen achtjährigen Elementarunterrichts (S. 504 f.) zu lesen, das ich nach meinen früheren Erfahrungen mit dem sechsjährigen ostschweizerischen nur zu gut verstehe.

Im ganzen wird man dem Buch am besten gerecht werden, wenn man es echt amerikanisch im besten Sinn nennt: 1. das Material ist sehr reich-haltig (das zwanzigseitige, kleingedruckte Literaturverzeichnis ist offen-bar nicht nur eine Sammlung aus andern Werken zusammengetragener

---

[1] Mein im Sept. 1932 erschienener Aufsatz 'Das Gefühl für grammatische Gesetze' (IF 50.177 ff.) konnte dem Verf. bei der Fertigstellung der Ausgabe noch nicht bekannt sein.

Titel), 2. die Vergleichung ist sauber und systematisch, 3. die Beurteilung und Darstellung ist sachlich-nüchtern (was heute als Gegengewicht gegen andre Bewegungen wieder nützlich ist). Die äußere Gestaltung: Einband, Sauberkeit des Schriftbilds, Korrektheit des Satzes, läßt nichts zu wünschen übrig.

# B42. Review of Havers

1934. *Language* 10.32–39.

*Handbuch der erklärenden Syntax: Ein Versuch zur Erforschung der Bedingungen und Triebkräfte in Syntax und Stilistik.* By Wilhelm Havers. (Indogermanische Bibliothek 1.1.20). Heidelberg: Winter, 1931. Pp 292.

This book presents, accurately and with great charm, a wealth of interesting phenomena in syntax and style. It contains excellent bibliographic notes and careful indices. The matter is arranged under the following heads (cf. LANGUAGE 8.227 [1932]) [our B39—CFH]: I. Conditions (1) inherent in the external form of language, (2) inherent in the psychophysical nature of man, (3) of the external world; II. Impulsive Forces, namely (1) the tendency toward concreteness, (2) the tendency toward emotional discharge, (3) the tendency toward economy of effort, (4) tendencies of order, (5) the tendency toward beauty of expression, (6) the sphere of social impulses. These headings are not intended to be mutually exclusive. The arrangement, in the eyes of the present reviewer, amounts largely to this: Havers describes in terms of popular psychology the connotation that is attached to a syntactically or stylistically peculiar speech-form, and then classifies this speech-form under one of the above-listed types. Everyone will agree that connotation is an important factor in the meaning of speech-forms; furthermore, since connotative values have so far eluded scientific classification, no one will object to an author's classifying them in terms of popular psychology, even though these terms do not furnish clear-cut and exclusive classes.

One must enter objection, however, to the claim that the description of these connotative values *explains the origin* of the speech-forms. Most readers, though not all, will grant this claim in matters of style,—that is, for features of speech-form which represent only the 'choice' of the speaker from a number of possibilities. Thus, Havers (179) calls upon the 'tendency toward beauty of expression' to explain speech-utterances of the pleonastic type of Greek *podániptra podôn* ('foot-washing water for feet', cf. *a shepherdess of sheep*). If the reader is a mentalist, he can probably accept this as an explanation; if he is a mechanist, he will object that Havers has not answered the question 'Why did the speaker use this and not a different speech-form?' but has merely reminded us of a second question: 'Why does this form of speech bear its peculiar connotation (of simplicity and grace) for members of the speaker's community?' The mechanist will say that neither of these questions has hitherto been answered, and that a mentalistic pseudo-solution can only discourage the search for real answers.

The author, however, does not confine this treatment to matters of style, but applies it also to forms that are obligatory in their language. Thus, he attributes (198) the lack of case-endings in the noun in German dialects (*der Mann, den Mann, dem Mann*) to 'avoidance of over-characterization', because the article suffices to show the case category. Here even few mentalists will follow him, for the linguistic study of the last century has shown that explanations of this sort are trivial. One asks immediately about the many German dialects where not only the noun but also its modifiers have lost the distinctions of case-form, quite as in Dutch *de man* and English *the man*, and one asks about the languages that show case-form in both noun and modifier. In this way one may easily lapse into pre-scientific notions about language (thus, 19: Kurze, einsilbige Wörtchen nützen sich im Gebrauch schneller ab). What saves the author from patent errors is only his familiarity with the results of the mechanistic language study of the last hundred years. For instance, he explains (2) the (now sub-standard) English usage in *His tears runs down his beard* by a 'tendency toward uniformizing and simplifying verb inflection', but he does not apply this explanation to the Attic type of singular verb with neuter plural noun subject (*gráphei tà paidía* 'the children are writing'); yet, to apply it to cases like this, in competition with the nineteenth-century method, would be the only fair test of his theory. This example is of paradigmatic importance, and I shall return to it.

In the study of man, pre-scientific modes of explanation hold sway; only small bits of territory have been gained by science, and the most promising of these is linguistics. Much of the publication of the last decades threatens us with the loss of this ground.[1]

From the point of view of linguistics, we can define *explanation* as a series of statements on various levels of generality.

In natural science one studies the correlations of events. One finds that an event of one type is often accompanied by an event of another type. When such a correlation has been established, the scientist can predict what will happen under certain circumstances; he predicts, for instance, that when we heat water from 0° to 4° centigrade, its volume will contract, but that if we then continue to raise the temperature, it will expand. At

---

[1] It is regrettable if the attempt to hold this ground should give offense to any students of language. The duty of the scientific worker is to seek the truth as best he can, without regard to consequences. The recognition of this duty should depersonalize all differences of opinion.

this stage, the scientist's prediction is based purely and simply upon the numerical correlation between the events: when the scientist speaks of 'cause' and 'effect', he means only this correlation and nothing more. Further, science studies more than one correlation for any type of event,— not only, for instance, the correlation between temperature and volume, but also that between pressure and volume. Any actual change, say of volume, is viewed in science not as the 'effect' of some one 'cause', but as a movement correlated with a practically infinite number of other movements.[2]

This, however, was not the medieval view and is not even now the popular view of correlated events. In the medieval and popular view, a favored earlier event, the 'cause', pulls a kind of invisible string which, in some metaphysical sense, *forces* the occurrence of a later event, the 'effect'. This view lends a philosophic cogency to correlations of events. It is a vestige of an older time when people took an animistic view of such correlations,—when one said, for instance, that 'water seeks its own level', or that 'Nature abhors a vacuum'. These statements describe the sequence of events, but they pretend to a deeper kind of truth than does the scientist's description. They describe the correlations as acts of a stubbornly consistent actor (*water* or *Nature*), and thus assure us of a kind of metaphysical necessity behind the observed correlations.

This animistic notion of 'causality' goes hand in hand with another pre-scientific notion, teleology. Human beings often tell us of some future act, and then proceed to perform it. In the popular view the preliminary speech guarantees a kind of spiritual pre-existence of the act: accordingly, the act, when performed, is the effect of its own spiritual pre-existence,— of the actor's 'desire' or 'tendency' to perform it. The teleologic notion is then applied also to inanimate agents: 'water *seeks* its own level', 'Nature *abhors* a vacuum'.

Havers did not do well to choose for the motto of his book this sentence of Ernst Otto:

> In der Entwicklungsgeschichte der Sprache können nicht 'kausale' Beziehungen aufgedeckt werden, sondern es ist vielmehr eine teleologische Betrachtungsweise geboten.

[2] The displacement of any particle is expressed by equations of the type

$$dx = \frac{\partial x}{\partial k} dk + \frac{\partial x}{\partial l} dl + \frac{\partial x}{\partial m} dm + \frac{\partial x}{\partial n} dn + \cdots,$$

with a practically endless number of terms on the right-hand side; those of the right-hand terms which are nearest to $dx$ in size are sometimes, loosely but conveniently, spoken of as 'causes' of $dx$.

All this is not to say that every student of physical science takes this view; many are quite naïve as to everything but the details of their technique. Pearson's Grammar of Science (2d ed., London, 1900; 3d ed., vol. 1, 1911) contains perhaps the clearest discussion of this matter. It is a classical treatise, which loses much, however, by ignoring linguistic values; thus, Pearson leaves otherwise simple things in a fog by saying 'conceptual' where the linguist would say 'verbal'.

Teleology does not stand in contrast with 'causality', but represents merely a more primitive form of the same age-old popular notion. A teleologic 'explanation' can be given without difficulty for any and every happening. If we create a vacuum over one end of a U-shaped tube containing water (the principle of the pump), the water will rise at this end: Nature abhors a vacuum. But the water rises only to a height of 33 feet above the level of the water outside: well, Nature's horror of a vacuum goes only so far and, after that, is offset by the weight of the water. Teleology cuts off investigation by providing a ready-made answer to any question we may ask.

The simple correlations of language consist of the linking of *meanings* (stimuli) with *linguistic forms* (speech-responses). In everyday life we assume the existence of these correlations: when anyone says anything, we proceed, in one way or another, to reckon with the meaning of his speech. If he says *There are some nice apples in the kitchen*, we may go to get one, or we may decide that the speaker is trying to fool us, but in any case we act upon his speech in specific ways. Our response differs from that which we would make to a different speech (e.g., *Look out, you'll knock over that jar*), and it contrasts with our lack of specific response to a speech in a language that we do not understand.

As a matter of scientific study, however, we are unable to demonstrate this correlation between the stimulus acting on a speaker (the meaning) and the speech-form which he utters. If a word like *apple* were spoken only by persons who at that moment were seeing or tasting an apple, we might establish such a correlation, but actually, of course, people often use the word *apple* when there is no apple in sight; from this power of displaced speech, indeed, we derive some of the greatest advantages of language. For science, accordingly, the correlation of meanings with speech-forms is merely an assumption, based upon our successful practice in everyday life, but incapable of proof: for this we shall have to wait until physiology has reached a state of perfection that is at present inconceivable.

The second level of scientific explanation consists of general statements that embrace larger and larger sets of correlations. The case of water 'seeking its own level' is included in modern science with many other petty generalizations in the statement that within a liquid the pressure exercised upon and by every part is the same in all directions. This statement enables us to predict with greater ease a greater variety of future events, in a way that gives us practical advantages in building locks, dams, tanks, and so on. The case of water rising under a vacuum is subsumed, by a similar generalization, along with the failure of the water to rise above a certain height, under the topic of atmospheric pressure. In short, explanation, at this level, consists of statements describing and therefore predicting wider and wider types of events. Its triumphs can be seen in the development of mechanics from Galileo to Newton, or in the growth of the modern theory of electricity, magnetism, and light.

As to language, this type of generalization appears in the statements of descriptive grammar. Granted the assumption that every speech-form has a stable meaning, we now observe uniformities among the speech-forms of a language; thus, we register the common element -*s* 'more than one' in forms like *hats, caps, books,* or the common features of congruence, word-order, and so on, which express the meaning 'actor performs action' in phrases like *horses run; the boy whistled; the dog came running.* We look forward to a larger synthesis, a General Grammar, which will register similarities between languages; lack of data forbids this, even as it frustrated the attempts of eighteenth-century scholars.

The teleologist submits the generalizations of descriptive grammar to his type of explanation. He postulates either a folk-psyche or a common mental attunement of the individuals in a speech-community, and then explains the grammatical features as effects of desires or tendencies. For the most part, he goes to this trouble only if the forms differ from those of his own language. If they differ but little, he gives explanations like the above-cited account of the lack of case-endings in the noun of German dialects, attributing these features to generally human tendencies or to the peculiarities of peasants' and common folks' minds. If the grammatical features differ too much from the familiar, the teleologist develops a fantastic psychology of exotic or savage peoples. Havers (111) repeats a time-honored example:

> Gewisse Objekte, besonders Körperteile, kann sich der Primitive kaum ausserhalb eines bestimmten Besitzverhältnisses vorstellen, es bedeutet also z. B. in der Sprache der Algonkins *noss* 'mein Vater', *koss* 'dein Vater' aber ein -*oss* besteht nicht. 'Das primitive Denken ist konkret', sagt Thurnwald . . . 'Wie wenig es begrifflich arbeitet, zeigt, dasz in den meisten primitiven Sprachen die menschlichen Körperteile nie als solche, als Arm, Bein, Nase vorgestellt werden, sondern nur in der konkreten Verbindung mit einer Persönlichkeit . . .'

Actually, the speaker of an Algonquian language behaves towards heads and towards fathers exactly as we do; the grammatical forms of his language are no more compulsive than are 'cultured' linguistic forms. He talks about heads and fathers in all the ways that we do, including the most abstract, e.g. Menomini [no:hnɛʔ] 'my father', [ko:hnɛʔ] 'thy father', [o:hnan] 'his father', [uwo:hnɛmaw] 'a father', [ne:s, ke:s, we:s] 'my, thy, his head', [me:s] 'a head', [we:nan] '(animals') heads (as at the butcher's shop)', and so on. As well might the Chinese speaker claim that speakers of English or German cannot think of 'trees' in the abstract, but only of 'one' or 'more than one' tree. There are no Primitive Languages, and there is no greater fallacy than that of the Idealist, who postulates an invisible, spiritual Inner Man and so gains the opportunity (since no one can observe this imaginary being) of pointing out the superiority of his Inner Man over the Inner Man of less deserving persons and communities.[3] The possessed-only noun belongs in grammar and will some day play its part in general grammar; its Psychological Interpretation belongs in a museum of superstitions. For this example, however, Havers is not to blame, for it is part of the traditional stock-in-trade of mentalism, and, indeed, he somewhat discounts it by citing a similar feature from Hungarian.

The generalizations of descriptive grammar are hampered by an appreciable amount of variation: languages change in the course of time. This brings us to a third level of explanation. Where the facts are accessible, we can define a feature of a language in terms of some earlier habit plus a change of habit. Thus, we can describe the use of the -s plural in English by stating the much narrower use of the -as plural in Old English and tracing the transferences of this suffix to new nouns, its phonetic modifications, and so on.

In the study of human affairs, where changes of this sort go on rapidly, the historical level of explanation has long been recognized. In geology and biology its recognition has come after a long struggle. Astronomers have had to set up a history, at any rate for the Solar System.[4] It may be that the 'laws' of physical science will someday turn out to be conditions which change in vast reaches of time; if so, they may become capable of historical explanation.

A consistent teleologist would have no use for historical explanation. If a speech-form is due to the 'desires' or 'impulses' of the speakers, then it is not due to the prevalence of a habit and even less to the tradition and modification of a habit in the course of time. It is only by an inconsistency that the teleologist attributes linguistic changes, in their turn, to universal manifestations of these same 'desires' or 'impulses'—and these, of course, the teleologist can summon to meet any need.

The ancients observed that in the Attic dialect of Greek, neuter plural noun subjects concorded with finite verbs in the singular number: *gráphei tà paidía* 'the children write' has a singular verb form, like *gráphei ho anē'r* 'the man writes', and contrasts with *gráphousin hoi ándres* 'the men write', with plural verb form. It seems that early students advanced a teleologic

---

[3] How does the 'savage' differ from us? Of course he entertains more superstitions and false beliefs as to historical fact, but this is not fundamental. In the ordinary run of speech and conduct, he is as reasonable and as clever as the 'civilized' man. The difference appears only in matters of theoretical generalization: here the civilized man often exercises the scientific method (which seems to the savage shockingly empty and cynical), whereas the savage *resorts to teleologic explanation*.

[4] See the admirable exposition in the late Hugh Elliot's Modern Science and Materialism, London, 1919.

explanation for this: 'Neuters have an affinity for the singular number'.[5] Apollonius Dyscolus preferred a different explanation: since the verb does not concord with accusative objects, the homonymy of nominative and accusative forms in the neuter gender made possible also the discordance of nominative subject and verb. Delbrück tried to correlate the distribution of singular and plural verbs for neuter plural noun subjects in Homer with the more or less unified meaning of the nouns.[6] Contrast with all this the historical explanation of Johannes Schmidt: the neuter noun plurals of Indo-European were formerly collective singulars; their endings are largely like those of the feminine singular; the Attic construction is the survival of an old habit of concord.[7]

The teleologist accepts the results of historical explanation where they bear overwhelming conviction, but he clings at the same time to notions which would have placed these results beyond our reach. Thus, Havers (16), mentioning the probable connotative value of the Attic construction, does not claim that this connotative value explains the origin of the construction, it is safe to conclude that Havers, like everyone else, accepts Schmidt's historical explanation. But where historical study does not provide a widely accepted explanation, the teleologist feels free to appeal to a 'tendency'. Thus, as we have seen, Havers (2) explains English forms like *His tears runs down his beard* and *Traitors hateth thee*, with plural subject and singular verb, as due to a 'tendency to uniformize and simplify verb inflection'. In that case, why is not the Attic construction due to the same tendency? May not the reason be that Johannes Schmidt's historical explanation of the latter figures in every Indo-Europeanist's training, but not the obvious explanation of the English forms,—namely that in Old English the present indicative plural ended in -*að*, a form which was gradually, but never completely, crowded out by the reflexes of OE -*en*, -*on*, endings of the subjunctive and past indicative plural?[8] And if a teleologist had not been furnished with the historical explanation of South German first person singular forms equivalent to a Standard German *ich spielen*, would he have any difficulty in discovering a 'tendency' which led

---

[5] *Tà oudétera harmódiá estin toîs henikoîs.* Apollonius Dyscolus begins his discussion by stating and refuting this view; edd. R. Schneider and G. Uhlig, 2.316 (Leipzig, 1910 = Grammatici Graeci 2.2); cf. R. Franz, De verbo apud Graecos coniuncto cum neutri generis subiecto plurali 3, diss., Bonn, 1875.

[6] Syntaktische Forschungen 4.25, Halle, 1879.

[7] Die Pluralbildungen der indogermanischen Neutra, 4 (Weimar, 1889).

[8] This is plainly the case with the -*eth* forms; the -*s* forms offer difficulty, but the ultimate explanation is the same; see Mätzner, Englische Grammatik[3], 1.361 (Berlin, 1880); H. C. Wyld, History of Modern Colloquial English 337 (London, 1920). Havers refers to Stoelke's dissertation (Heidelberg, 1913 = Anglistische Forschungen 49). Stoelke, however, did not sufficiently sift his material; thus, he includes examples of the normal OE construction of singular verb with numerals, as well as subjunctive plurals in -*e* (cf. JEGP 29.100 [1930]).

the speakers to use the infinitive or the plural instead of the congruence-form of the first person singular?

Linguistics, the most advanced of the human sciences, has developed also a still higher level of explanation, in that linguistic changes can largely be classed into a few types of process: phonetic change, analogic-semantic change, and borrowing. This generalization, effective as it has proved, offends popular common sense and therefore invites constant attack by vitalists and idealists.

We may seek, finally, yet another level of explanation, in which we could account for the occurrence of a certain linguistic change at a certain place and time, e.g., why did pre-Germanic change [p, t, k] to [f, þ, h], or why did English analogically extend the -s plural of nouns? The answer would be a correlation of linguistic changes with some other recognizable factor, enabling us to predict the occurrence of a linguistic change whenever this other factor was known.

# B43. The Stressed Vowels of American English

1935. *Language* 11.97–115.

[The following summary, appearing in brackets at the beginning of the article, reads as though it was supplied by the editor, Bolling, rather than by the author: 'Description of the stressed vowel phonemes of Central Western Standard-English as spoken in Chicago. The article possesses a more general interest as an example of the technique of analyzing phonemically the structure of a dialect.'

I have allowed myself more comments (in signed footnotes) here than for most of the articles included in this volume, but in all cases from Bloomfield's point of view (as far as that is possible), not from my own. In this same spirit, I believe that if Bloomfield's attention had been drawn to the matter, he would not have listed words like *rhythm* and *prism* as type 1 one-syllable words (he does, in the discussion of [i]), but as type 3 disyllables.]

**1.** The Central-Western (CW) type of American Standard English may be roughly defined as the type which preserves old [r] in final position and before consonants. Except for this archaism, its consonant structure is like that of Southern British Standard (B).[1] The syllabic phonemes, however, differ strikingly from those of B, both in acoustic shape and in distribution. CW is spoken by millions of people, and, in spite of general uniformity, presents many varieties of detail. I shall try here to describe the syllabic phonemes of the stressed syllables of educated speakers in Chicago,—that is, of persons whose speech does not plainly mark them as coming from a different region. Studies of American English have dealt mostly with types that are closer to B.[2] It is to be hoped that this sketch will be corrected and extended by other observers and with the use of mechanical methods. Unfortunately it is even at this day and age necessary to add that a priori speculation (about 'Standard English everywhere' or the like) can lead only to the most absurd results and to the confusion of issues.

CW, as spoken in Chicago, has two sub-types: some speakers, like B,

---

[1] H. Sweet, Primer of phonetics[3], Oxford, 1906; D. Jones, An English pronouncing dictionary, London, 1917 (second edition, 1926, not accessible to me); Outline of English phonetics[3], Leipzig, 1932.

[2] See the map by H. Kurath, LANG. 5.159 (1929). Statements about CW in Maître phonétique 3.5.40 (1927) and in L. Bloomfield, Language, New York, 1933.

distinguish seventeen syllabic phonemes in stressed syllables; the great majority, however, do not distinguish the vowel of *hot, sod, bomb* from that of *father, far, balm*, and accordingly have only sixteen such phonemes. Hence we require in principle seventeen symbols for our discussion; but, where no ambiguity results, we may lessen this number by the use of compound symbols. I use the following symbols: [i] *bit*, [e] *bet*, [ɛ] *bat*, [a] *balm*, [u] *put*, [o] *son, sun*, [ɔ] *saw*, [ɑ] *sod*, [ɽ] *fir, fur*, [ij] *see*, [ej] *say*, [aj] *sigh*, [ɔj] *boy*, [uw] *do*, [ow] *go*, [aw] *now*, [juw] *you, yew, ewe*. Most speakers, then, do not distinguish between [ɑ] and [a].[3]

**2.** The existence of these phonemes is established by 136 such pairs as *pit : pet, look : luck,. cam : calm, bomb : balm, see : say*. The biophysical description, in terms of speaker's movements, or of sound-waves, or of ear-drum vibrations, must be left to the laboratory. The biosocial description consists in a statement of the combinations in which these phonemes occur: which phonemes (including *zero*, the beginning of speech) may precede each of them, and which phonemes (including *zero*, the end of speech) may follow each of them. In this respect, the speech-forms of CW, as of B, fall into several types.

*Type 1.* As the basis of our description we take morphologically simple one-syllable words. Thus, we say that [i] occurs after [str] before [kt] in *strict*, and after zero before [f] in *if*, and we observe that [u], for example, does not occur in either of these positions. Such a list is needed, but since most of its features would not be peculiar to CW, I shall mention only the more noteworthy restrictions, in addition, of course, to the features in which CW deviates from B.

To the morpheme words of Type 1 there may be added suffixal and enclitic consonants:

*Type 1a.* Such combinations are made with suffixes and enclitics of the form [s, z, t, d], added without phonetic modification, under the usual

---

[3] Any transcription shocks and offends all but the few readers who have been inured to the free use of graphic symbols ('algebra'). When old-established renderings, such as [det] *debt* or [kam] *calm*, are denounced as dangerous innovations, the critics' choice of examples may perhaps give us a clue to the real difficulty: can it be that the disconcerting factor is really the absence of the letters *b* and *l*? Unaccustomed use of the symbol [o] is especially annoying, perhaps because this letter, whose shape resembles the shape of the lips in the utterance of its name, plays a dominant rôle in our first learning of the alphabet and retains this rôle in the graphic fetishism of later life.

The *shapes* of the graphic symbols scarcely deserve discussion. The reader who prefers the symbol [æ] where I use [ɛ] does not need any factual basis to justify his preference. Even the reader who claims that the symbol [o] for the vowel of *son, mother, come, love* is repugnant to the habits of English-speaking people, and therefore prefers to use a *v* upside down, may be guilty of several fallacies, but he is not tampering with the facts. If he replaces our [o] by this symbol everywhere except in digraph [ow], he will have the lay-out that is traditional in the transcription of B. But the *distribution* of the symbols is another matter. The theorist whose ratiocinations lead him to demand one and the same symbol for the vowels of *calm, psalm* and of *cam, Sam*, or to replace the symbol [č], as in *catch it*, by the symbols [t] plus [š] or the equivalent, will end with a sorry mess on his hands.

restrictions.[4] These combinations need not be listed; thus, when we have listed, under Type 1, the combination *look*, this implies the existence of *looks*, *looked*.

*Type 2.* In other cases, suffixes of the form [s, z, t, d] are added with phonetic modification, as in *says*, *has*, *kept*, or against the usual restrictions, as in *burnt*, or both, as in *lost*, *dreamt*. Thus there may arise combinations foreign to Type 1, such as [ɹnt, mt]. Or there may be added, with or without phonetic modification, other suffixal or enclitic consonants; these too may produce sequences foreign to Type 1. Thus, [al, fθ, ksθ, ownt] are final combinations foreign to Type 1, but they occur in Type 2: *pa'll* (*help us*), *fifth*, *sixth*, *don't*. A zero suffix may be added with phonetic modification; thus, *mouthe*, in Type 2, has a final [awð] that does occur in Type 1. In what follows I shall try to list the most striking sequences produced in Type 2.

*Type 2a.* To forms of Type 2 there may be added the normal forms of [s, z, t, d], as in *tenths*. These forms do not require listing.[5]

To any stressed syllable, be it a root syllable or a form of Types 1, 1a, 2, 2a, there may be added affixes and atonic words consisting of one or more unstressed syllables. After unstressed prefixes and proclitics, however, the onset of stress is in CW, as in B, plainly marked,[6] and the combinations which are interrupted by an onset of stress, as in *I'll look* [ajl ˈluk], *ahoy*, *convince*, and so on, seem to be only such as could be produced by a final of one of the preceding types plus an initial of Type 1; in this sketch, at any rate, they will be left out of account. Further, it seems that when unstressed suffixes and enclitics, added with or without modification, produce medial clusters of non-syllabics, the resulting sequences, again, are only such as could be produced by a final of the preceding types plus an initial of Type 1: *stronger* : *strong girl*, *timber* : *Tim burned*, *booklet* : *took letters*, *meanness* : *mean nest*. At any rate, we shall here disregard all medial clusters. This leaves for our consideration only the sequences of stressed syllabic plus single non-syllabic plus unstressed syllabic, such as *singer*, *father*, *pussy*.

*Type 1b.* To words of Types 1, 1a, 2, 2a there may be added, without modification, syllable-forming suffixes or enclitics: *sing-er*, *law-yer*, *saw it*, *saws it*, *has it*. These forms need not be listed.

*Type 3.* Stressed syllables not occurring as independent words (i.e., roots) occur with syllable-forming suffixes. These forms may contain sequences foreign to the other types. Thus, [að, er] do not occur in the

---

[4] See my Language 132 ff.

[5] The plural of *sixth* is in CW usually [siks] *sixths*; here the suffix [s] is added with modification, and the form belongs to Type 2 twice over.

[6] It produces such distinctions as *a name* : *an aim*; *that stuff* : *that's tough*; see D. Jones in Maître phonétique 3.9.60 (1931).

other types, but appear in Type 3: *father, berry*. On the other hand, Type 3 suffers under special restrictions. Thus, [us] occurs in Type 1, *puss*, and accordingly in Type 1b, *pussy*, but [us] plus syllabic is foreign to Type 3. Type 3 never has simple [ŋ], which Type 1 has in *sing*, 1b *sing-er*. We place into Type 3 also cases where a syllable-forming suffix is added with phonetic modification to a word of Type 1, such as *soft-en* ['sɔfn̩]. It seems, however, that nearly all such cases result in consonant clusters, as in *long-er* ['lɔŋɡr̩].

**3.** Some of the restrictions which appear in a survey of the phoneme sequences open the possibility of using compound symbols for some of our stressed syllabic phonemes.

(1) Six of our stressed syllabics, [i, e, ɛ, u, o, ɑ], as in *pit, pet, pat, put, nut, pot*, do not occur before syllabics or before [j, w] or at the end of a word. Therefore digraphs consisting of one of the letters [i, e, ɛ, u, o, ɑ] plus [j] or [w] or any symbol of a syllabic phoneme, such as [i] or [u], can create no ambiguity. Transcribers of English, accordingly, use digraphs for some of the stressed syllabics other than these six, e.g., [ei] or [ej] for the syllabic of *say*. For the second character of such digraphs [j, w] seem preferable, since this leaves the syllabic symbols, such as [i, u] free to indicate a new syllable at every occurrence.

(2) Two of our stressed syllabics, [a, ɔ] do not occur before [j, w] in Type 1, but do occur in final position, as in *pa, saw*, and may therefore precede syllabics and [j, w] in forms of Type 1b: *pa* and *ma* ['pan̩ 'ma], *saw it* ['sɔit], *they'll haha you* [ha'haju] *out of the place; pa will* ['pawl̩] *help us; lawyer* ['lɔjr̩]; *Shaw will* ['šɔwl̩] *be there*. The combinations [aj, aw, ɔj] which arise in this way, resemble the syllabic phonemes of *high, how, boy*. The forms *pa will hit him*, with *will* in the weak form [wl̩], and *Powell hit him* are probably homonymous on the lips of most Chicagoans. If we believe that these equations are true, then we must use the digraphs [aj, aw, ɔj] for the syllabic phonemes of *high, how, boy*; this is the course which I follow. If we believe that these equations are inexact, then we cannot use these digraphs, but may resort to symbols of class (1) and transcribe [hɑj, hɑw, bɔj].[7]

Having chosen digraphs for the syllabics of *high, how, boy*, we avail ourselves of (1) to form digraphs also for the syllabics of *see, say, do, go* [sij, sej, duw, gow]. The latter part of the syllabic phoneme in *you, yew, ewe* is equal to the [uw] of *do*, and the first part of it to the [j] of *yes*. For this reason we transcribe it by the trigraph [juw]. The eight phonemes which we transcribe by compound symbols are conventionally called *diphthongs*; among them, [juw] is called also by the special name

---

[7] For the majority of CW speakers, who have not the distinction of [a] and [ɑ], we transcribe *pa, hot* [pa, hat]; the question as to the digraphs remains as above, except that if the second alternative is chosen, the symbol [ɑ] in *high, how* occurs only in these digraphs.

*triphthong*. In contrast, the remaining syllabic phonemes are called *simple vowels*.[8]

**4.** The CW simple vowels are produced with loose muscles. In the diphthongs the latter part of the phoneme is more tense; before [r], moreover, [ij, ej, uw, ow] seem to be somewhat tense throughout, so that the sounds in *share, more* are as near as CW can get to the French vowels in *cher, mort*.

All the CW vowels are unrounded, except the four diphthongs which we transcribe with [w], that is [uw, juw, ow, aw], as in *do, few, go, how*. In these the latter part is slightly rounded.

Four of the stressed syllabics are shorter than the rest: [i, e, u, o], as in *pit, pet, put, nut*. Within each of the two classes thus created, stressed syllabics and combinations of stressed syllabic with [m, n, ŋ, l] are somewhat shortened (and have usually a simplified intonation) before unvoiced consonants. Thus, in the short class, *bit, bet, book, but* have shorter vowels than *bid, bed, bull, bud*, and [im] is shorter in *limp* than in *limb* or in *limber*. In the long class, *hat, bought, beat* have shorter syllabics than *bad, sawed, bead*, and the [ɛn] in *cant* is shorter than in *canned, can*.

These relations, however, do not hold for the diphthongs [ɔj], as in *boy*, or before [r] plus consonant: in these cases only the longer quantity seems to occur in what we may call the solemn or basic form of words. In formal enunciation (when asked, for instance, to read or pronounce a single word) a speaker will usually produce the long quantity in *dark, sharp, start, starch*, and the like. Nevertheless, in current speech some of these words seem to have variants (S) with shorter vowels and simpler intonation. Thus, *starch* seems always to have the longer quantity, but *march, March* occur also with the shorter. The occurrence of these S forms is an elusive sub-phonemic feature; it is with the greatest diffidence that I shall list the forms as I seem to hear and speak them.[9] Strangely enough, S forms seem

---

[8] The customary alternative statement is this: The phonemes [i, e, a, ɔ] occur before [j], as in *hee, hay, buy, boy*, and the phonemes [u, o, a] occur before [w], as in *do, go, now*, but in these combinations both the syllabic and the following [j, w] deviate acoustically from their usual shape, especially before [r], as in *fear, fair, fire, poor, pour, sour*. This statement is equivalent to the one in the text above, and preferable in the way of brevity and clearness, but it annoys some students.

The acoustic analysis of [juw] is so obvious that one hesitates to call it a phoneme. However, it appears only within morphologic units, and it alone enables anything like [j] to occur after initial consonants and clusters, as in *few, skew*. The only exception to the latter statement seems to be the variant ['pjɛnow] beside [pi'jɛnow] *piano*; the derivative ['pjɛnist] beside [pi'jɛnist] *pianist* seems to offer difficulty, for a less urbane ['pijṇist] is perhaps the prevalent form.

[9] In view of my complex linguistic background, both personal and professional, I have tried to describe not my own speech, but that of the people about me. So far as phonemic differences are concerned, this seems to offer little difficulty. As to sub-phonemic features, however, the situation is more complex, and seems to be somewhat as follows: (1) One does not ordinarily react to sub-phonemic differences. (2) When a sub-phonemic difference is

to occur also before [r] plus voiced consonant,—for instance, in *garden*, but not in *harden*,—and in a very few words, such as *here*, *there*, even before final [r]. In the case of the diphthongs [ij, ej, ow] the S forms result in a sound resembling the ordinary forms of the phonemes [i, e, o, ɔ]; e.g., *here*, *there*, *horse*, *wart* are practically [hir, ðer, hors, wɔrt] beside the solemn variants [hijr, ðejr, howrs, wowrt]. Since precisely these phonemes do not otherwise occur before final [r] or [r] plus consonant, we are free to use these symbols to indicate the S forms. This, indeed, is advisable if I am right in believing that the occurrence of S forms really differs for different words. Thus, *worn* [wowrn] seems to be incapable of S, whereas *warn* is either [wowrn] or [wɔrn]; if we use the latter transcription, we tell the whole story.

5. The following outline gives the more important features of occurrence of the stressed syllabics of CW, especially where CW contrasts with B. We give for each phoneme (a) occurrence before single non-syllabics in Types 1 and 3, with special attention to zero and [r], and no mention of the usual lack of [ž] in Type 1 or of the complete lack of [ŋ] in Type 3; (b) occurrence before final clusters in Type 1, together with unusual combinations in Type 2; (c) a few observations as to occurrence initially and after [w].

[i], as in *bit*; high front short; perhaps somewhat looser than the corresponding B vowel, Sweet's and Jones' [i].

(a) It does not occur in final position or before syllabics or [j, w]. It does not occur before final [r]; cf. however, the S form of [ij]. Hence it does not occur before [r] plus syllabic in Type 1b, but it does occur in Type 3: *mirror*, *virile*, *spirit*, *lyric*; here *syrup* has an inelegant by-form ['srop]. [ð] Type 1, only *with*, and even this has a widely used by-form [wiθ]; 3 in a few words: *wither*. [θ] 1 *smith*, hence 1b *smithy*, but 3 lacking. The form *been* has only [i], never [ij]; *get*, *again* with [i] are sub-standard. Occurrence: *tip, ripple, bit, bitter, stick, liquor, rib, ribbon, lid, riddle, pig, wriggle, rich, pitcher, ridge, pigeon, cliff, piffle, kiss, thistle, fish, mission, live, river, fizz, busy, vision, rim, simmer, pin, minute, ring, bill, pillow.*

(b) It is unpronounceable before [r] plus consonant; other clusters occur in great variety: *crypt, strict, fix, lift, wisp, fist, risk, rhythm, prism, limp, nymph, lint, wind, plinth, mince, pink, lynx, quilt, milk, gild, filch,*

striking (as, in a speaker from a distant part of the area) or has been marked out by some special circumstance (such as phonetic training of the observer), it receives a regional or social connotation, and after that: (a) A sub-phonemic variation which the observer himself uses will generally escape his notice; if he tries to observe it, he will suspect himself (rightly or wrongly) of attributing it to speakers who do not use it, and will end in uncertainty. This is my experience with the S forms. (b) A sub-phonemic variation foreign to the observer's own habit is noticeable and seems either provincial (e.g., for me, the backing of [ɛ], as in *hat*, southern) or over-refined (e.g., for me, excessive diphthongization of [ow]) or else clumsy (e.g., for me, the use of an S vowel in the word *fork*).

*bilge, sylph, filth* (historically Type 2), *film, kiln*; cf. Dickens' *Quilp*. From 2 we add *sixth, width, fifth*.

[e] as in *bet*; higher mid front, short, like the corresponding B vowel, Sweet's and Jones' [e].

(a) It does not occur in final position or before syllabics or [j, w], or before final [r]; but cf. the S form of [ej]. Hence it does not occur before [r] plus syllabic in Type 1b, but it occurs freely in this position in Type 3: *berry, merit, error*; here *bury* has a by-form with [ɛ]. [f] 1 is rare: the name of the letter F and the short-name *Jeff*; 3 *heifer, effort, Jefferson*. [θ] rare: 1 *Beth, Seth*; 2 *breath, death*; 3 *method, ethics*. [v] 1 lacking; 3 occurs freely: *never*; *nephew* has [f] or [v]. [ð] 1 lacking; 3 freely: *leather*. [z] rare: 1 *fez*; 2 *says*; 3 *embezzle*. [ŋ] lacking. The word *again* has [e], not [ej]; there is also a sub-standard form with [i]; *catch* has a sub-standard form with [e]. Other consonants: *step, epic, let, letter, wreck, second, ebb, pebble, bed, meddle, beg, legate, etch, lecher, edge, ledger, mess, lesson, mesh, session, measure, gem, lemon, pen, henna, sell, cellar*.

(b) It is unpronounceable before [r] plus consonant; other clusters occur in great variety: *sept, sect, sex, text, deft, rest, Kemp, tent, tense, help, melt, elk, weld, belch, shelf, wealth, else, Welsh* (the last three are historically of Type 2), *delve, elm*. Type 2 adds *depth, breadth, dreamt, tenth*, and, with [ŋ], *length, strength*.

[u], as in *put*; high back, short; unrounded and looser than the corresponding B vowel, Sweet's and Jones' [u]. It is of very restricted occurrence.

(a) It does not occur finally, before syllabics, before [j, w], or before [r]; see, however, the S form of [uw]. It is lacking also before [b, j, ð, n, ŋ]; before [p, f, m] it occurs only as a by-form of [uw]. [t] *put, foot*, and variants, beside [uw], of *root, soot*. [k] *book, cook*, etc. [d] *good, hood*, etc.; 2 *could*, etc., 3 *pudding*. [g] 1 lacking; 3 *sugar*. [č] 1 only *Butch* as a nickname; 3 *butcher*. [s] *puss*. [š] *push, bush, Cushman*; 3 *cushion*. [z] 3 *bosom*. [l] *bull, full*, etc.; 3 *bullet*.

(b) Only *wolf*.

(c) It differs from all the other stressed syllabics in not occurring initially.

[o] as in *son, sun*; higher mid back, short; like the corresponding B vowel, Sweet's and Jones' [ʌ], but lacks the more open and fronted variants that are common in B.

(a) It does not occur finally, before syllabics or [j, w, r]; cf., however, the S form of [ow]. [θ] only in the archaic 2 *doth* and in *Cuthbert*. [ð] 1 lacking; 2 *other, mother, brother*. Other consonants: *cup, supper, nut, flutter, luck, bucket, rub, rubber, bud, rudder, rug, juggle, fuss, hustle, rush, Russia, love, oven, buzz, cousin, come, summer, done, funnel, tongue, dull, gully*.

(b) It is lacking before [r] plus consonant; but cf. the S forms of [ow].

Other clusters are varied: *corrupt, duct, cusp, rust, husk, jump, hunt, month, dunce, trunk, gulp, cult, hulk, gulch, bulge, gulf, pulse, culm.*

[ɛ] as in *hat*; lower mid front; lower and decidedly longer than the corresponding B vowel, Sweet's and Jones' [æ].

(a) It does not occur finally or before syllabics or [j, w]; however, in 3 the name *Gawain* is pronounceable. Before [r] 1 is lacking, but 3 occurs freely: *carry, carrot, marrow, charity*; many learned words, such as *various, apparent*, have [ɛ] or [ej]. [ð] 1 lacking; 2 *baths*; 3 *gather*, etc. [z] 1 *jazz, razz* (slang 'mock, taunt'), *raspberry*; 2 *has*; 3 *hazard, dazzle.* [ž] 3 *azure*. [l] 1 rare: *pal* (historically a loan from Romany), *gal* (mock-dialectal for *girl*, short-names *Al, Hal, Sal*; 3 freely: *alley, salad, palace.*[10] The words *thresh, wrestle* have homely by-forms with [ɛ]. Occurrence: *map, apple, hat, rattle, lack, tackle, grab, dabble, sad, saddle, rag, haggard, laugh, taffy, bath, catholic, pass, castle, mash, passion, have, havoc, cam, hammer, can, cannon, bang.*

(b) It is unpronounceable before [r] plus consonant; [l] plus consonant seems to occur only in the archaic 2 *shalt*. There is a moderate array of clusters: *apt, lapse, act, axe, raft, clasp, cast, ask, chasm, lamp, pant, Banff, chance, rank, Manx.*

(c) After [w] it occurs only before velars: *wag, waggle, swag, swagger, whack, thwack, wax, Wacker, whang, swang, swank.*

A nasalized foreign form occurs among educated speakers: *fin-de-siècle, Lebrun* ['fɛⁿde'sjejkl̩, le'brɛⁿ].

Before certain non-syllabics CW [ɛ] corresponds not to B [æ] but to B [ɑ:]. I list the forms with these non-syllabics, placing a star before words in which B has [ɑ:], and a star in parentheses before words in which B has both [æ] and [ɑ:].

[f] *draff, riffraff, *epitaph, *photograph, *calf, *chaff, *half, *laugh, *staff*; 3 *daffy,*[11] *taffy* (B has [ɔ], the normal correspondent of CW [ɑ], and writes *toffee*).

[ft] *haft, *aft (*after), *daft, *draught, *graft, *raft, *shaft, (*) Taft*; cf. *laughter, *rafter, *Grafton; *waft* is read also with [ɔ] and [ɑ].

[v] *have, *salve*; 2 *calve, *halve (*calves, *halves)*; 3 *avid, gravity*, etc.

[θ] *(homeo)path, (after)math, math* (students' slang for *mathematics*), *Gath, McGrath, *bath, *lath, *path*; in *wrath* B has [ɔ:], the normal correspondent of CW [ɔ]; 3 rare: *Catherine,* (*) *catholic.*

[ð] 2 *baths*; *laths* has also a form with [θs]; 3 *gather, Mather,* (*) *lather, *rather*; this last word occurs also with [a]; *father* has always [a].

[s] *bass, basswood, crass, gas, lass, mass, High* (*) *Mass, sass* (homely:

---

[10] The late C. W. Alvord insisted upon [ɛ], not [ɔ], in his name.

[11] The B form of this word is unknown to me; B has [ɑ] in *daft*, and NED gives [ɑ] for the dialectal *daff* 'simpleton'.

*Don't sass back* 'don't retort impudently'),[12] (*) *ass*, *\*brass*, *\*class*, *\*glass*, *\*pass*, (*) *morass*; 3 *cassock*, *facile*, etc., *\*castle*.

[sp] (*) *asp*, *\*clasp*, *\*gasp*, (*) *hasp*, *\*rasp*; cf. *aspect*, *aspen*, *Caspian*, *aspic*, *aspirate*, (*) *Jasper*.

[st] *bast*, *\*cast*, *\*caste*, *\*fast*, *\*aghast*, *\*last*, *\*mast*, (*) *contrast*, *\*vast*; 2 *\*past*; cf. *bastard*, *bastion*, *dastardly*, *plastic*, *\*aster*, *\*asterisk*, *\*castor*, *\*master*, *\*nasty*, *\*pastor*, *\*plaster*, *mastiff*, *masticate*.

[sk] *casque*, (*) *basque*, *\*bask*, *\*cask*, *\*task*, *\*mask*, *\*ask*; cf. *\*basket*, *\*casket*, *\*rascal*, *gasket*, *Gaskell*, *Ascot*, *Asquith*.

[nt] *brant*, *cant*, *pant*, *rant*, *scant*, *Levant*, (*) *ant*, *\*aunt*, *\*grant*, *\*slant*; 2 *\*can't*, *\*shan't*; cf. *antics*, *antlers*, *banter*, *bantam*, *canter*, *mantle*, *shanty*, *pantry*.

[nd] *and*, *hand*, *land*, etc., *expand*, *\*command* (*\*demand*, *\*reprimand*, *\*remand*); cf. *candy*, *candle*, *gander*, etc.

[nč] *\*blanch*, *\*branch*, (*) *ranch*, *\*stanch*.

[ns] *romance* [ra'mɛns, 'row₁mɛns], with both forms apparently in all meanings of the word, *\*dance*, *\*chance*, *\*France*, etc.; cf. *fancy*.[13]

[nš] *\*Blanche*.

Isolated forms: *\*moustache* [ma'stɛš, 'mos₁tɛš], *\*example*; the word *\*almond* occasionally has an elegant [a]; *\*drama* has both [ɛ] and [a].

The use of [ɑ:] in these forms is the deviant feature of B that is best known to speakers of CW. So far as mere sound is concerned, it is easy to imitate, since CW [a] as in *calm* (and for most speakers also in *sod*) is acoustically the same thing as B's [ɑ:]. Hence the 'compromise vowel' which is reported for some types of Standard English, does not occur in CW.[14] Schoolteachers who are otherwise innocent of any attempt at B pronunciation, will try to make their pupils use [a] in a few words like *laugh*. Social climbers betray themselves by hyperurbanisms, such as [a] in *bass* or *lass*, or even in *and*, *man*, *shadow*. These, however, are isolated phenomena; both among the masses and among better educated speakers [ɛ] is entirely stable in the starred words, excepting *rather*, *drama*, and perhaps *almond*.

[a], as in *far*; low, quite like the corresponding vowel of B, Sweet's [aa], Jones' [ɑ:]. Most CW speakers merge [a] and [ɑ] into one phoneme; see under [ɑ] below. For the occurrence of [a] as a variant of [ɛ], see above, under [ɛ].

[12] The word *sauce* 'gravy' has [ɔ], corresponding to B's [ɔ:]; *saucy* has [ɔ] but also a homely by-form with [ɛ].

[13] A mock-B form of *fancy* with [a] and, in grotesque exaggeration, with [ɔ], is used in CW as a witticism. B, of course, has [æ].

[14] A 'compromise vowel' in the forms that are here starred would remove words like *pass*, *glass*, *grass* from the [ɛ] group of *gas*, *bass*, *lass*. Hence the 'compromise vowel' in such types of Standard English is not part of the [ɛ] phoneme. If one may judge by the forms listed in Jones' Outline 74, the 'compromise vowel' is part of the [ɑ:] phoneme, with distribution dependent upon the following consonant.

(a) It occurs in final position, but only in peculiar words: *pa, ma* (*pápa, máma*) are childish; *fa, la, fra, spa, shah, papá, mamá* are foreign-sounding; *ah, ha, aha, hahá* (slang, *the merry háha*), *rah-rah, baa, blah* ('nonsense, turgid speech') are interjectional. Types 1a, 2, 1b bring [a] into position before syllabics and unusual non-syllabics: *pa's, pa'll* (*help us*), *pa'd* (*help us*), *rah-rah-ing*. The combinations [aj, aw] that arise in this way, as in *it doesn't baa yet, it doesn't baa well*, are probably equal to the phonemes [aj, aw], as in *buy it, Powell*; cf. §4, above. [a] occurs freely before final [r], where the other simple vowels (except perhaps for certain S forms) are lacking: *star, jar*; 1b *starry, jarring*. On the other hand, [a] does not occur before [r] in Type 3, where [i, e, ɛ, ɔ, a] occur freely. Before non-syllabics other than [r] the phoneme is severely restricted: [v] in foreign *lava, bravo, caviar*; [đ] only in 3 *father*; [m] *balm, calm, palm, alms, qualms*; [ž] in the foreign suffix [až]: *mirage, garage*. It is used rather freely, however, in rendering foreign words: *da capo, adagio, da Gama, Bach, Prague, Jeanne* [žan]; the name *Chicago* has a by-form with [a] beside more usual [ɔ]; for *tomato*, see [ej].[15]

(b) The only clusters are [r] plus consonant, but these occur freely. The types or words in which I seem to hear S forms are marked S; this indication holds up to the next cluster. [rp] S *sharp, carpet*; [rt] *art* (*artful, arty* 'pretentiously artistic') *heart* (*hearty, hearten*), etc.; S only in certain derivatives: *artist, artisan, artifice, artificial, party, partner, partisan*; forms of Type 3 seem to be always capable of S variants: *barter, Carter, garter, marten, Martin, martyr, Spartan*; contrast, in 1b, *carter, starter*, where S seems impossible; [rk] S *dark, market*; [rb] S *garb, garbage, marble*; [rd] *hard* (*harder, -est, -ly, -y, -en*), *guard, lard* (*lard-er* would be 'one who lards'), *Hardy*, etc.; but 3 seems to allow of S: *garden, larder, pardon, tardy, ardent*; [rg] only 3, S *argue, cargo, largo, embargo, Margaret, target*; [rč] *starch*; S *arch, march, March, larch, parch*; [rǰ] *large*; S *barge*; 3, S *margin, sergeant, argyrol, Argentine*; [rf] S *scarf*; [rθ] S *hearth, Arthur*; [rs] S *parse, parson*; [rš] S *marsh, marshal*; [rv] S (?) *carve*; 2 *scarves*; 3 *marvel, harvest*; [rz] *Mars, Tarzan*; [rm] S (?) *arm, charm, farm*; 3, S *army, armor*; [rn] *darn*; 3 seems to permit S: *varnish, tarnish*; [rl] S (?) *Carl, gnarled, Charles, parlor*.

(c) [a] occurs after [w] only in the bookish word *qualms*.

There is a nasalized [a] in foreign words, among educated and semi-educated speakers, as in *carte blanche* ['kart 'blaⁿš]. There is a widespread elegant middle-class form ['aⁿvelowp] *envelope*, beside the normal ['envelowp, 'envelop]; the verb is always [en'velop].[16]

---

[15] In *yacht*, where B has [ɔ], the CW speakers who distinguish [a] and [a] seem to use [a].

[16] The rapid cultural advance, during the last fifty years, of the CW area involves universal schooling by semi-educated teachers, and wide reading; hence there occur elegant reading forms which are foreign to the best educated persons. Thus, the normal CW form of *valet* is

[ɔ] as in *saw*; lower mid back; unrounded, hence differing somewhat from the corresponding vowel of B, Sweet's and Jones' [ɔ:]. Many words with [ɔ] have by-forms with [ɑ]; after [w] these seem to be for the most part of indifferent connotation, but after other consonants they are more elegant than the variants with [ɔ]. Most of the variants with [ɑ] occur in words in which B has [ɔ], the vowel which corresponds systematically to CW [ɑ]. Thus, the normal CW form is [fɔg] *fog*, and the more elevated form is [fɑg], which corresponds systematically to B [fɔg]. Acoustically, however, CW [ɔ] is closer to B [ɔ] than is CW [ɑ]. Direct imitation of B would therefore favor CW [ɔ], whereas in the ordinary run of CW connotations the variants with [ɑ] are higher-toned. This incongruity probably plays a part in the variations of the word *god*. The words which in B have [ɔ] are starred below; those which in B have [ɔ:] or [ɒ] have a star in parentheses. The occurrence of CW [ɔ] after [w] differs from that in other positions and is disregarded in (a) and (b).

(a) It occurs in final position, as in *saw*. This brings it, in forms of Type 1b, into position before syllabics and [j, w], as in *saw it, saw you, lawyer, Shaw will*; here *drawer* 'tiroir', *drawers* 'undergarment' are disyllabic, like *drawer* 'one who draws' and *saw 'er*. The combination [ɔj] that arises in this way seems to be equal to the diphthong in *boy*, so that *lawyer* rimes exactly with *annoyer*; cf. §4, above. The vowel [ɔ], except after [w], is unpronounceable before final [r], but occurs before [r] in Type 3, probably always beside more elevated variants with [ɑ]· *oral*,[17] *aural, aurist*, (*) *laurel, Laura*, (*) *Lawrence*. In some words the variant with [ɑ] is quite common: *coral, *moral, *oracle, *orator, *coroner*. In others [ɑ] is the normal form, and [ɔ] has an inferior connotation: *foreign, *forest, *horrid, *horrible, *orange, *Florence. *Morris*. [p] is lacking, though I seem to have heard a slang *yawp* 'talk loudly and petulantly'.[18] [t] 1 scarce: *taut, nought* (popular and childish for 'zero'), *naught* (archaic, as in *dreadnaught*); 2 *bought, caught, ought*, etc.; 3 *autumn, naughty, cauterize*. [k] *talk*, etc.; 3 seems to be lacking. [b] *daub*. [d] *broad, fraud*; 3 *caudal*; in *god* the form with [ɔ] is coarse (in exclamations), but also elevated (in prayer); the variant with [ɑ] is the normal form. Before [g], where B has only [ɔ], CW has by-forms with [ɑ], but the forms with [ɔ] prevail entirely in the homely words *dog, *hog*; less exclusively in *cog, *fog, *frog, *log*; in less common words [ɑ] has a better chance, e.g. *bog, *flog, *jog*; 3 *soggy*; *Chicago* has [ɔ], but [a] is also common. [č, ǰ] are lacking. Before

['vɛlej], and the educated speaker uses either this or the B form ['vɛlet], but there is also an elegant middle-class form [ve'let], due perhaps to a confused theoretical knowledge of the B form. To this type belong such eccentric forms as ['fɛčizm] *fascism*, ['lɛveljej] *lavallière*, ['šejz 'lɔⁿž] *chaise longue*.

[17] The B variant of *oral* with [ow], given in NED, occurs also in American English.

[18] [It probably slipped Bloomfield's memory that *yawp* occurs in the poetry of Walt Whitman: 'sound my barbaric yawp over the roofs of the world'.—CFH]

[f] the variants with [ɑ] are uncommon and decidedly elegant: *cough*, *\*off*; *\*often*, *\*soften*, (\*)*coffee*, *\*offer*, *\*office*, *\*officer*, *\*coffin*; [ɑ] is commoner than [ɔ] in bookish words like *\*doff*, *\*coffer*, *\*proffer*. [θ] (\*)*cloth*, (\*)*moth*, *author* have prevalently [ɔ]; *\*broth*, *\*froth* have both vowels; in learned words, like *\*Gothic*, [ɑ] prevails, but variants with [ɔ] occur. Before [s] by-forms with [ɑ] occur in all words of Type 1; least often perhaps in *\*boss*, (\*)*cross*, *\*loss*, *\*moss*, *\*toss*, *sauce*; more frequently in *\*dross*, *\*floss*, *\*gloss*, *\*joss*, *\*Ross*; 3 *faucet* has [ɔ]; in learned words [ɑ] prevails: *\*process* (the B form with [ow] occurs in CW only as a pedantic elegancy), *\*fossil*, *\*apostle*, *\*glossary*, *\*docile*.[19] [š] is lacking, except after [w]. [v] only *mauve*, beside [ow], which is B's vowel. [ð] only 2 (\*)*cloths*. [z] *cause*, *hawser*, etc. [m] is lacking. [n] *dawn*, etc.; only 2 (\*)*gone* has a very refined variant with [ɑ]; stressed *\*on* has usually [ɑ], but there is a less polite variant with [ɔ]. Before [ŋ], where B has only [ɔ], the [ɑ] variants are rare and elegant in *\*long*, *\*song*, *\*strong*, *\*wrong*, occasional in *\*belong*, and perhaps as common as [ɔ] in *\*gong*, *\*prong*, *\*thong*, *\*throng*. [l] *ball*, etc.; *\*cauliflower* occurs also with [ɑ]; *\*doll* has prevalently [ɑ]; the form with [ɔ] is coarse or childish.

(b) Clusters are few: *haunt*, *Faunce*, (\*)*fault*, (\*)*falter*, (\*)*false*; [ft] *\*soft*; *\*loft* (\*)*aloft*) seems to have an [ɑ] variant. [st] *\*cost*, *\*frost*, 2 *\*lost* with over-elegant [ɑ] variants; *\*foster* has perhaps more often [ɔ] than [ɑ]; *caustic*. [nč] *launch*, *paunch*, *haunch*, *staunch* have by-forms with [ɑ], against B, which has, however, by-forms with [ɑ:]. Before [r] plus consonant [ɔ] is unpronounceable, except after [w].

(c) After [w the vowel [ɔ] is very common, but most of the forms have variants with [ɑ]. Final: *squaw*. Before final [r] and [r] plus consonant, only the S variants of some words with [ow] seem to be acoustically equal to [ɔr]; see below, under [ow]; in Type 3, however, we have *\*warren*, *\*warrant*, *\*quarry*, *\*quarrel*, all with [ɔ] or [ɑ]. [p] only in homely words, but in these, strangely enough, [ɑ] prevails over [ɔ]: *\*swap*, *wop* 'Italian', *\*whopper*. [t] *\*swat*, *\*squat* favor [ɑ]; the stressed form of *\*what* is [wɔt, hwɔt] or, a bit elegantly, [hwat], beside unstressed [wot, hwot]; 3 *water*, *quarter*, *\*quatrain*; only this last, a bookish word, could be read with [ɑ]. [k] only *walk*, *squawk* (without [ɑ] variants), in contrast with the free occurrence of [ɛ] in this position. Before [b] the [ɑ] form prevails in *\*swab*, *\*squab*, *\*squabble*, *Schwab*, and especially in *\*wobble*, (\*)*wobbly*). Before [d] variants with [ɑ] are common: *\*wad*, *\*squad*, etc. [g] is lacking, in contrast with [ɛ], above. [č] *\*watch*, with [ɑ] variant. [j] is lacking. [f] *\*quaff*, *\*waft* are reading forms, produced with [ɑ, ɔ, ɛ]. [θ] *\*swath*, similarly. [sp] *\*wasp*, with [ɑ] variant. [š] *\*wash*, *\*quash*, *\*squash*, *\*Washington*, all with [ɑ] variants. [z] only in the stressed form of *\*was*, which has

---

[19] The B variant of *docile* with [ow] would sound striking in CW.

persistently [ɔ], and [ɑ] only in elegant diction; the unstressed form is [woz]. [n] *swan, with [ɑ] variant; the book word *wan has [ɑ, ɔ, ε]. [nt] *want, *quantity, with [ɑ] variants; speakers who distinguish use [ɑ], not [a], in these variants. [nd] *wand, *squander, *wander, with [ɑ] variants. [l] wall, squall, Waller, Walter, Walton seem to have always [ɔ]; Waldorf, (*) Waldo, *swallow, *quality, *squalid have [ɔ] or [ɑ]; the book word *squalor is read also with [ej]. [lts] *waltz has at least prevalently [ɔ]. [lš] (*) Walsh has prevalently [ɔ].

In foreign forms educated speakers have a nasalized form of this vowel, as in salon [seˈlɔⁿ, ˈsεǀlɔⁿ, ˈsεǀlɑn].

[ɑ] as in sod; low, slightly more retracted than [a]; aside from the total lack of rounding, it is longer and lower than the corresponding B vowel, Sweet's and Jones' [ɔ]. Most speakers have only one phoneme for [ɑ] and [a]; acoustically it seems to equal rather the [a] of the speakers who make the distinction. Even these latter have difficulty in imitating B's [ɔ]; actors who 'drop their R's' and use [a] in pass, etc., often lapse into the open unrounded CW [ɑ] or [a] in words like hot, got, not. The merging of [ɑ] and [a] produces only one pair of homonyms, bomb : balm, aside from theoretical constructions, such as my pod shut up : my pa'd shut up. It can be tested also in rime forms, such as bother : father, sorry : starry. I do not know whether the distinction of [ɑ] and [a] is a survival or a renovation based on the written form.

The words in which [ɑ] competes with [ɔ] have been mentioned under that vowel; these include all occurrences before [g, f, s, ŋ].

(a) It does not occur finally, before syllabics, or before [j, w]. It is unpronounceable before final [r], but [ɑr] occurs in Type 3, both as a variant of [ɔ] and in sorry, borrow, tomorrow. [š] is rare: gosh, josh; also in the bookish bosh, tosh. [v] 3 only: novel, Ovid. [ð] 3 only: bother and the bookish pother. [z] 1 Boz; 3 common: nozzle, closet, rosin. [m] 1 bomb; 3 common: vomit, comet, hominy, omelette. Other consonants: stop, opera, spot, bottle, stock, stocking, rob, robin, odd, model, botch, crotchet, dodge, codger, don, bonnet, moll, hollow.

(b) Clusters are few: adopt, copse, concoct, box, mosque, romp, fond, sconce, bronze, honk; [l] plus consonant only in [lv]: solve (dissolve, revolve, etc.).

(c) After [w] hornswoggle; in all others it competes with [ɔ], but prevails in homely words, wop, wobble, swat; cf. under [ɔ], above.

[ɽ] as in fur, fir; differs greatly from the corresponding B vowel, Sweet's [əə], Jones' [əː]. The tip of the tongue is raised toward the highest point of the palate. This syllabic [ɽ] is formed like the non-syllabic [r]; its syllabic character is due, in most instances, merely to the less sonorous surroundings: bird, stir, urge, err [ɽ]. Before syllabics, a syllabic [ɽ] differs from a non-syllabic [r] by a moment of greater stress; this distinguishes, for instance, *stirring* ['stɽiŋ] from *string* [striŋ]; in such forms B has [ər].[20]

(a) It occurs freely in final position: *err, stir* (*stirs, stirred, stirring, stirrer* ['stɽɽ]). Unlike the other simple vowels, it occurs freely before syllabics in forms of Type 3: *hurry, furrow, squirrel* ['skwɽl]. It occurs rarely before [j, w]: *furrier* ['fɽjɽ, 'fɽijɽ], *Erwin*. It does not occur before [r] within a word; compare phrases, such as *Sir Richard*. B has [ɑ:], the normal correspondent of CW [ar], in *clerk, derby, Berkeley*. In this last, CW occasionally uses [ar]; this variant, as well as the form *varsity* ('pertaining to the university', of athletic organizations) is in imitation of B. The form *were* is always [wɽ].

[p] 1 only slang *purp* 'dog'; 3 *serpent, purple*. [š] 3 only: *exertion*. [ð] 3 *further*. [z] *furze*. [ž] 3 *excursion, version* (B has [š] in some of these forms.) [ŋ] is unpronounceable. Others: *dirt, curtain, work, turkey, curb, Herbert, bird, murder, burg, burgle, birch, mérchant, urge, virgin, surf, surface, earth* (3 lacking?), *curse, person, serve, scurvy, worm, hermit, turn, journey, girl, surly*.

(b) Clusters are very few: *excerpt, thirst*; 2 *burnt*.

[ij] as in *see*; high front diphthongal, like the corresponding B phoneme, Sweet's [ij], Jones' [i:].

(a) It occurs finally, as in *see*. In 1b the occasional agent nouns and comparatives with *-er*, such as *freer, seer* ['sijɽ] 'one who sees' are probably always disyllabic, contrasting with one-syllable forms like *seer* 'prophet', *sear, sere* [sijr]. In Type 3 [ij] occurs before syllabics in forms like *Leon, peony*. Combinations with following [j, w] are possible in 1b: *see you, Lee will* (*help us*).

It occurs freely before [r], as in *cheer, era*. In this position the latter part of the articulation is somewhat lowered, and the whole phoneme takes on the character of a slightly tense uniform vowel. A few words of this shape seem to have S forms which are acoustically equivalent to [ir], a final combination that does not otherwise occur. The S forms appear in the words *here, hear, ear, year, dear, dearest*, the last two only as terms of address. Thus, *Come here!* seems to be indifferently, with a mere sub-phonemic variation, [kom 'hijr] or [kom 'hir, kom 'ir]; *Yes, dear* is ['jes 'dijr] or ['jes 'dir]; but *Butter is dear* ['dijr] has not the S form; *ten years* [jijrz, jirz].[21] The great mass of [ijr] words, such as *fear, cheer, mere, beer*, are not capable of S.

[b] rare; *grebe, glebe* are book words; 3 *feeble*. [ž] 3 *lesion*, etc. [ŋ] is unpronounceable. Others: *cheap, steeple, meat, beetle, speak, deacon, weed, wheedle, league, eager, peach, feature, siege, region, leaf, reefer,*

---

[20] Similarly, unstressed syllabic [ɽ] is marked as syllabic by its surroundings, as in *better* ['betɽ], or by a slight stress, as in *error, pattern, pickerel* ['erɽ, 'pɛtɽn, 'pikɽl].

[21] Can forms like these be the factual basis for the superstition, common among B speakers, that CW uses [ɽ] for sequences of vowel plus [r], as in *America*?

*wreath, ether, cease* (3 lacking?), *leash, secretion, leave, evil, seethe, either,*[22] *please, measles, seem, demon, mean, Venus, feel, Keeley.*

(b) Clusters are very few: [st] *east*, etc.; [ld] *yield*, etc.; [nd] only in *fiend*; [rs] only *fierce, pierce.*

[ej] as in *say*; mid front diphthongal, like the corresponding B phoneme, Sweet's and Jones' [ei], but even sub-standard CW lacks the B Cockney variant approaching [aj].

(a) It occurs in final position, as in *pray*, and, consequently, before syllabics and [j, w] in 1b, as in *praying, may you, May will.* . . . However, the suffix *-er* receives peculiar treatment: the agent suffix and the comparative suffix are added without modification, as in *prayer* 'one who prays', *grayer* 'more gray' ['prejr̩, 'grejr̩], but other suffixes of this form show elevated variants with non-syllabic [r]: *prayer* 'oratio', *layer* 'stratum' ['prejr, prejr, 'lejr̩, lejr]; this last variant is homonymous with *lair*.

It occurs freely before [r]: *pear, pair, pare, vary, Mary.* In this position the diphthong is modified into a slightly tense and rather open long vowel. Many words of the learned type vary between [ejr] and [ɛr]; cf. above, under [ɛ]. S variants, in which [ejr] seems to be acoustically equivalent to an otherwise unpronounceable final [er], occur in the words *there, where*, as in *Who's there?* [huwz 'ðejr? huwz 'ðer?], differing from *their*, which seems to have no S variant, even in unstressed position. In *tomato* the B form with [a] is in CW an occasional elegancy. [b] 1 only *babe*[23]; 3 *able*, etc. [č] in the name of the letter H; 3 *nature.* [f] *chafe*; 3 *cockchafer*, a book word. [θ] *faith, wraith*; 3 seems to be lacking. [š] 3 *nation*, etc. [ð] *lathe*; 2 *bathe*; 3 only *Mather*, beside the usual form with [ɛ]. [ž] *beige*; 3 *invasion*, etc.; *equation* has [ž] rather than [š], against B. [ŋ] is unpronounceable. Others: *drape, caper, bait, cater, shake, bacon, aid, cradle, vague, sago, sage, agent, case, mason, cave, favor, raise, razor, frame, amiable, vain, banal, fail, tailor.*

(b) Clusters are few: [st] *taste*, etc. [nt] *paint*, etc.; the homely 2 *ain't* 'am not' has always [ej]. [nj] *strange*, etc. Others only in isolated words: *traipse, scarce.* The forms *laird, cairn, bairn* keep their Scottish connotation. In 2 we have *eighth.*

[uw] as in *do*; high back diphthongal, like the corresponding B phoneme, Sweet's [uw], Jones' [u:]. I treat here also [juw] as in *ewe.*

(a) These phonemes occur in final position: *woo* (*woos, wooed, wooing, knew you, who will* . . .), *few.* They occur before vowels in Type 3: *Louis* ['luwij, 'luwis], *suet, cruel.* In both 1b and 3, forms with the suffix *-er*, such as *wooer, doer, booer* ['buwr̩], *ewer, skewer*, differ from one-syllable forms, such as *boor* [buwr].

---

[22] In *either, neither* CW has [ij]; the forms with [aj] are studied elegancies.
[23] [Add Lewis Carroll's *wabe* and *outgrabe*, in *Jabberwocky.*—CFH]

Before [r], as in *boor*, *sewer* 'égout', *pure*, *jury*, *fury*, the [uw] is lowered into a slightly tense long vowel; CW has no variants corresponding to B's usual [ɔə, ɔ:] in *poor*, *sure*, *your*. The word *your* (*yours*) has an S form containing the otherwise unpronounceable sequence [ur]. This seems to be not merely an unstressed form, as in *yourself*, *your friend* [jur 'frend, jr̩ 'frend], but also a stressed variant, as in *It's yours* [its 'juwrz, its 'jur̩z].

Before other consonants 3 is rare or lacking. [p] *stoop, cooper, cupid*; here *hoop* has an inelegant by-form with [u]. [t] *boot, cute* 'cunning', *beauty*; *soot* has a common variant with [u]; in *root* [u] is homely. [k] is rare: *spook, puke, fluke, duke, euchre*. [b] is rare: *Rube, Reuben, goober*, 'earth nut' (usually called *peanut* ['pijnot], without secondary stress). [d] *food, feud, boodle*. [g] is rare: *fugue, nougat, Hugo*. [č] only in slang words: *mooch* 'to spy', *hooch* 'illicit liquor', *pooch* 'dog'. [j] is rare: *huge, stooge* 'henchman, foil for a comedian' (cf. Dickens' *Scrooge*). [f] only in *hoof, roof*, which have commonly [u], but elegantly [uw]; slang *goof* 'fool'. [θ] *booth, ruthless*; 2 *truth*. [s] *loose, lucid*. [š] rare, foreign: *douche, ruche*. [v] rare: *move, groove, Hoover*; in 2 the archaic plurals *rooves, hooves*. [ð] only *smooth, soothe*. [z] *choose*, etc. [ž] 1 only the foreign *rouge*; 3 common: *hoosier, fusion*. [m] *doom, fume, rumor, humor*; here *room, broom, groom* have commonly [u], beside more formal variants with [uw]. [n] *moon, lunar*. [ŋ] is unpronounceable. [l] *cool, coolie*.

(b) Clusters are very few: *boost, roost, wound*.

(c) The triphthong [juw] is restricted as to initials. It occurs after zero, [p, sp, k, sk, b, f, v, m, h], as in *ewe, pew, spew, cure, skew, beauty, few, view, muse, hew*. After [g]: the book word *gules* is easily pronounced. After [n] most speakers have [uw] rather than [juw], but the latter prevails among the more privileged and educated; a speaker may treat different words differently. After [t, d, st] the diphthong prevails decidedly over the more elegant triphthong, but there are speakers who use the latter, at least in most words, or most of the time. After [s] and [l], as in *suet, lute*, the triphthong is decidedly rare and elegant; it seems to be fairly common, however, in medial position: *assume, consume, allure*, and after [z] in *resume, presume*.

[ow] as in *go*; mid back diphthongal, like the corresponding B phoneme, Sweet's and Jones' [ou].

(a) It occurs freely in final position: *sew* (*sews, sewed, sewing, sewer, know you, Joe will*), less often in Type 3 before syllabics: *poet, Joel*. With *-er* it makes two-syllable forms in Type 1b: *slower, sower, sewer* ['sowr̩], 'one who sews', distinct from *sore* [sowr].

It occurs before [r], lowered into a fairly tense long vowel: *sore, floor, story*. The word *war* has an S variant, practically [wɔr], contrasting with *wore* [wowr], which has no S variant. The words *or, nor* have S variants, practically [or, nor], in contrast with *for*, which is shortened only in atonic use.

[š] only in learned words of Type 3: *ocean, motion*. [ð] only in 2 *loathe*. [ž] foreign in *doge, loge*; 3 learned words: *erosion*. [j] is lacking; [ŋ] is unpronounceable. The form 2 *shone* has only [ow]. Other consonants: *hope, open, boat, total, oak, broker, robe, sober, road, odor, vogue, ogle, coach* (3 lacking) *loaf, chauffeur* ['šowfr̩] beside [šo'fejr], *both* (3 lacking), *gross, grocer, stove, over, nose, ozone, home, Homer, bone, onus, coal, holy*.

(b) Clusters other than with [r] are few: *roast, bolt, bold, hoax*; [nt] only in 2 *don't, won't*. Before the clusters of [r] plus consonant, some words have S variants; these approach the character of [or] after consonants other than [w], and of [ɔr] after [w]. [rp] S *torpid, warp*. [rt] *court, sort, short*; S *sport, snort, fort, forty, fourteen, port, important, extort, exhort*, with S variants practically [ort], and *wart, quart, thwart*, with S variants practically [ɔrt]; cf. *quartz*, with S (?). [rk] *fork* in ordinary CW never S; *stork* S?; S in *cork, pork, orchid, orchestra*. [rb] S *orb, orbit, absorb, morbid, Corbett*; *warble*. [rd] *board, cord, chord, border, accord, according*; S in *ford, order, Gordon, accordion, cordial, sordid*; *ward, reward, warden*. [rg] S *morgue, organ*. [rč] S *porch, torch, scorch, fortune, torture, orchard*. [rǰ] *George*; S perhaps in *gorge, forge, orgy*. [rf] S *morphine, orphan*; *wharf* [wowrf, wɔrf]. [rθ] S *forth, fourth, north*. [rs] *coarse, hoarse*; S *force, horse, Morse, Norse, torso, forceps*; *course* seems to have S only in the phrase *of course*. [rš] S *portion*, etc. [rv] 2 *wharves* [wowrvz]. [rð] cf. S *northern*. [rm] S *storm, form, normal, torment*; *warm, warmth, swarm*. [rn] *mourn* (*mourning*); 2 *born, torn, shorn, worn, forlorn*; S *corn, horn, thorn, morning, hornet, corner*; *warn, Warner*. Test pairs for S would be *hoarse : horse, mourning : morning, wore : war, worn : warn*, but they cannot be deliberately applied, since S forms seem to be rare in the enunciation of single words. Spelling pronunciation may be involved, at least in some of the contrasts.

[aj] as in *I, eye*; diphthongal, low to mid front, like the corresponding B diphthong, Sweet's and Jones' [ai].

(a) It occurs freely in final position: *cry* (*buy it, spy you, Guy will*) and in Type 3 before syllabics: *lion, pious*. Forms of Type 1b with suffix *-er*, such as *liar, higher* ['hajr̩], differ from one-syllable forms, such as *lyre, hire* [hajr]. It occurs freely before [r]: *hire, Myron*. [b] 1 only *jibe*[24]; 3 is commoner: *fibre, libel, bible*. [g] 1 only *Tige*; 3 *tiger*. [j] rare: *Elijah*. [θ] only *Smythe*; 3 *python*. [š] only *Elisha*. [ð] *scythe, lithe, writhe*; 3 in

---

[24] [Here Bloomfield missed a perfectly common type 1 word that he himself had many occasions to use: *tribe*. In doing so he illustrated a point that he expressed many times (though in this particular article he left it unstated, as obvious): that even the best memories or the fullest records can fail.—CFH]

the elegant by-forms of *either, neither*. [č] is lacking[25], [ŋ] unpronounce-able. Others: *wipe, viper, bite, mitre, spike, icon, side, bridle, life, trifle, ice, isolate, hive, ivy, wise, Liza, time, Lima, sign, minor, file, silent*.

(b) Clusters are very few: [nd] *bind*, etc., [ld] *wild*, etc.; isolated forms *pint, Christ*; 2 *ninth*; *height* has a common inelegant by-form with [tθ].

[aw] as in *now*; diphthongal, low to mid back, like the corresponding B diphthong, Sweet's and Jones' [au].

(a) It occurs finally, as in *allow* (*allowance, allow you, how will*). Forms of Type 1b with *-er*, such as *bower* 'one who bows', *allower, endower*, seem to keep the suffix syllabic: ['bawr̩]. Type 3 forms with [aw] before a syllabic are few: *coward, Powell*; here *towel, trowel* have predominant one-syllable by-forms, but the school word *vowel* seems to be always disyllabic.

Final [r] is common: *our, hour, dour, flour, flower, sour, scour, shower, tower*, but all these words seem to vary freely between one-syllable forms [flawr] and homelier two-syllable forms ['flawr̩]; likewise *flowery* ['flawr̩ij, 'flawrij] but 3 *dowry* has only two syllables ['dawrij].

[p] only in the spelling pronunciation of *Cowper*, beside [uw].[26] [j] only *gouge*. [ð] only 2 *mouthe*. [k, b, g, f, š, v, m] seem to be lacking; [ŋ] is un-pronounceable. Other consonants, with 3 largely lacking: *out, crowd, powder, mouth, mouse, rouse, trousers, down, Downer, foul*.

(b) Clusters are few: *oust, count, sound, bounce*; [nǰ] only in *lounge*.

(c) After [w] only the past tense form 2 *wound*.

[ɔj] as in *boy*; diphthongal, lower mid back to mid front, like the corre-sponding B diphthong, Sweet's and Jones' [ɔi]. Its occurrence is very much restricted. It seems to permit of S forms before [l, n], as in *boil, coin*, and in the words *point, ointment, oyster* (contrast *joint, boisterous*).

(a) Final: *enjoy* (*enjoying, annoy you, Roy will*); 3 *royal*. It is lacking before [r]. Simple consonants: [t] *quoit, Hoyt, loiter*. [d] *Lloyd, hoyden*. [f] *coif*. [s] *choice, moisten*. [z] *noise, poison*. [n] *coin, poignant*. [l] *oil, doily*.

(b) Clusters: [st] *moist, oyster*; [nt] *point*.

(c) After [w] only *quoit*.

[25] [Type 2 *righteous* would be a case, unless Bloomfield pronounced the word in an unusual way.—CFH]

[26] [The dates of publication suggest that Bloomfield must have been working on this article and on B44 at the same time. For B44 fn 3 he invented a word (type 1 ?) *cowp*, showing that the combination of stressed vowel and final mentioned here is not 'unpronounceable', only unused. Had he ever happened to meet anyone with the surname *Shoup* (as I did in 1955), he would have had also this example.—CFH]

# B44. Linguistic Aspects of Science
## (*article*)

1935. *Philosophy of Science* 2.499–517.

I

Scientific method interests the linguist not only as it interests every scientific worker, but also in a special way, because the scientist, as part of his method, utters certain very peculiar speech-forms. The linguist naturally divides scientific activity into two phases. the scientist performs "handling" actions (observation, collecting of specimens, experiment) and utters speech (report, classification, hypothesis, prediction).[1] The speech-forms which the scientist utters are peculiar both in their form and in their effect upon hearers.

The forms of the scientist's speech are so peculiar in vocabulary and syntax that most members of his speech-community do not understand them. If one wants to read an English treatise on mechanics, it is not sufficient that one be a native speaker of English: one needs also a severe supplementary training.

The effect upon hearers of the scientist's speech is even more remarkable. In a brief utterance the scientist manages to say things which in ordinary language would require a vast amount of talk. He "manages to say things" —that is, his hearers respond uniformly and in a predictable way. Indeed, their response is even more uniform and predictable than is the hearers' response to ordinary speeches. This appears strikingly in self-stimulation: by the use of scientific speech-forms (notably, mathematical calculation) we may successfully plan procedures which we could not plan in ordinary language. Moreover, the scientist manages to say very complex things: if his statements were put into ordinary language, the phrases would become so involved (especially in the way of box-within-box syntactic constructions) that the hearers would not "understand"—that is, they could make no conventionally adequate (uniform and predictable) response. Also, it is a remarkable fact, and of great linguistic interest, that many of

---

[1] This division is the natural one for a linguist; it is necessary also for psychology; see A. P. Weiss, *A theoretical basis of human behavior*, second edition, Columbus, 1929, p. 307.

the scientist's utterances cannot be made in actual speech, but only in writing: their structure is so complex that a visual record, for simultaneous survey and back-reference, is indispensable.[2]

It is evident that the speech-forms of the scientist constitute a highly specialized linguistic phenomenon. To describe and evaluate this phenomenon is first and foremost a problem of linguistics. The linguist may fail to go very far toward the solution of this problem, especially if he lacks competence in branches of science other than his own. It is with the greatest diffidence that the present writer dares touch upon it. But it is the linguist and only the linguist who can take the first steps toward its solution; to attack this problem without competence in linguistics is to court disaster. The endless confusion of what is written about the foundations of science or of mathematics is due very largely to the authors' lack of linguistic information. To mention an elementary point: the relation of writing to language appears in a peculiar and highly specialized shape, as we have seen, in the utterances of the scientist. It would be easy to show by examples that a student who blunders as to the relation of ordinary writing to language cannot be expected to make clear formulation of this complex special case.[3]

[2] It is necessary that we understand that writing is not "language," but a device for recording language utterances. The utterances that are made in any one language consist structurally of a finite number of recurrent units, and this on two levels. In the first place, the utterances in a language consist of various combinations of smallest units (*words*) that can be spoken alone. Of these there are in any one speech-community some tens of thousands. Hence a language can be replaced by some tens of thousands of unit signals (say, visual marks), each of which replaces the utterance of one word. This is the principle of Chinese writing. In the second place, the words in any one language consist of various combinations of a few dozen typical sounds (*phonemes*). Hence a language can be replaced by a few dozen unit signals (say, visual marks), each of which replace the utterance of a phoneme. This is the principle of alphabetic writing. All writing is a relatively recent invention, whose use until yesterday, was confined to a few favored persons. A system of writing opens the possibility of graphic notations that cannot be successfully paralleled in actual speech. This is true because visual symbols possess characteristics that are foreign to the sound-waves of speech: chiefly, they provide an enduring instead of an immediately vanishing stimulus, and offer possibilities of arrangement (tabulation) that cannot be matched in the succession of acoustic stimuli. Graphic notations that cannot be matched in actual speech have arisen in the case of classical Chinese (which is unintelligible in modern pronunciation, but is read and written by Chinese scholars; cf. B. Karlgren, *Sound and symbol in Chinese*, London, 1923) and in the case which here interests us, of mathematical and allied notations.

[3] A less elementary point of the same sort appears in the "heterological" contradiction: An adjective which describes itself is *autological* (e.g., *short* is autological, since the adjective *short* is actually a short word). An adjective which is not autological is *heterological* (e.g., *long* is not a long word). Is the adjective *heterological* heterological? If it is heterological, it describes itself and is therefore autological. If it is autological, it does not describe itself and therefore is heterological.—The fallacy is due to misuse of linguistic terms: the phrase "an adjective which describes itself" makes no sense in any usable terminology of linguistics; the example of *short* illustrates a situation which could be described only in a different discourse. E.g.: We may set up, without very rigid boundaries, as to meaning, various classes of adjectives. An adjective which describes a phonetic feature of words is *morphonymic* (e.g., *short, long, monosyllabic*). A morphonymic adjective which describes a phonetic feature of

Among the confusions of this sort there is one which runs deepest,— so deep, in fact, that some non-linguistic students have discovered it for themselves and in more recent discussions have managed to avoid it: the naïve transition from speech to inner goings-on. In everyday life, upon the instant that a speech strikes our ears, we respond only to its meaning; that is, we very properly respond to the speech upon the basis of the normal habits of language, and we do not stop to examine the sounds of the speech or to analyze its grammatical structure. When someone says "I'm thirsty," we all say "He is thirsty," and proceed to treat him as one in need of drink. The linguist alone, when acting in his professional capacity, responds to the structure (phonetic, grammatical, lexical) of the utterance. In the matter which here concerns us, this difference is important, because the speech-forms of scientific discourse are not a part of everyday speech and do not serve as everyman's signals for simple actions such as drawing a cup of water. When the scientist utters one of his queer speeches, the non-linguist cannot summarize the situation by any such unambiguous résumé as the phrase "He is thirsty." Lacking this, he has developed, in the course of history, a substitute formula. If the scientist says "Two $n$-spaces in an $(n+1)$-space have at least an $(n-1)$-space in common," the non-linguist says of the scientist "He has a *concept* of a space of $n$ dimensions, a *concept* of a space of $n$ plus one dimensions, a *concept* of a space of $n$ minus one dimensions," and so on. This formula is an uncritical reproduction of the everyday formula of the type "He is thirsty." When anyone says "I'm thirsty," we at once behave on the premise that certain things, invisible to us, are happening inside him. Physiology confirms this supposition. Accordingly, when the scientist makes his utterance, we naïvely proceed to make a parallel supposition, to the effect that, inside him, invisible to us, and distinct from his mere speech, there is occurring a Something (a "concept") which is "represented" or "communicated" (in one-to-one correspondence) by his speech, just as a speaker's condition of thirst (an unmistakable physiological process) is "represented" or "communicated" by the speech of the thirsty man. Physiology has never confirmed this supposition, and, indeed, one does not expect her to, but resorts to the claim that the Concepts are invisible, intangible, and, in short, non-material entities.

Although I am one of those who believe this claim and the entire baggage of mentalism to be empty and useless, I need not here attempt to re-argue the matter, for the Concept hypothesis, even if one accepts it, is totally

itself is *autological*. A morphonymic adjective which is not autological is *heterological*. The adjectives *autological* and *heterological* designate meanings of adjectives and not phonetic features; hence they are not morphonymic.—Contrast the following sensible discourse: A *hakab* is a word that ends in a bilabial stop (p, b). A word that is not a hakab is a *cowp*. The words *hakab* and *cowp* are hakabs.

irrelevant to the workings of scientific speech. It is one of the very first rules of scientific discourse that the hearers respond only to the (spoken or written) statements of the scientist, and that they do not respond to anything that may be going on inside him; in particular, they do not respond to any supplementary statement about goings-on inside the scientist. Science, we say, is "objective." And when his turn comes to speak, the scientist knows that he may not expect any allowance to be made for his "subjective" adventures,—for anything that may be going on inside him,—and that his audience will respond only to the exact stimulus-value of his words, determined according to well-fixed conventions. A scientific utterance differs from an ordinary utterance in this, that the conventional response does not allow of variations based upon goings-on inside the person of the speaker or of the hearer. To seek the foundations of scientific terminology in the world of Concepts is to create confusion and paradox. In sum, the goings-on within the scientist,— regard them as physiological or as "mental,"—are explicitly ruled out from the conventional response to scientific speech: the scientist's "concepts," "notions," "ideas," stomach-aches, and what not play no part in the communication, and what is spoken is accepted only at face value.

## II

A typical linguistic situation is that of a person who has been off exploring and returns with a speech: "There is a steep cliff at the far side of that rise in the land," "Cranberries grow in that marsh," "There are some good apples in the pantry," and so on. We call such speeches reports, and we may also call them predictions, for they imply that if you make such and such movements you will incur such and such a stimulus. We respond to them as we do to other speeches, in various ways, and often with error and confusion. It is for the good of the community, in a simple biological sense, that this error and confusion be kept to a minimum. The limiting case would be a report so phrased that, as to any biologically or socially relevant features of the response, every member of the community would respond in exactly the same way. In any community, some reports come nearer than others to this limiting case. Some such may be preserved in the way of tradition. In a highly organized community there are specialists in such reporting and in receiving such reports, and the traditional body of these reports is held fast in written form, constituting the "body" of science, and there is developed, as time goes on, a special vocabulary and phraseology suited to the optimum sureness of report,— the terminology of science.

In the phase of observation and experiment we are aware of our limitations and illustrate them by saying that we have no absolute guarantee that the sun will rise tomorrow; in the same way, there is no scientific report to which all qualified persons (and who are they?) will respond in exactly the same way. On the other hand, we probably cannot draw any sharp line between ordinary and scientific reports. Hence, lacking an absolute definition of science, we can say with sureness "This is science" and "This is not science" only part of the time, and we can describe the characteristics of science but cannot sharply define them. One of the most important of these characteristics is to be found in the linguistic phase of science: science uses language-forms to which all qualified persons respond in as nearly as possible the same way. Qualified persons are those who, under the division of labor, have been trained to respond to the language-forms used in science, for these language-forms differ from those of every-day life and most persons cannot respond to them at all. The linguist is interested in studying the origin of these language-forms, their relation to everyday language-forms, their structure, the way the scientist uses them, and so on.

The language-forms which serve us best in this matter are the number-words of everyday speech (*one, two, three,* . . .) and expressions defined in terms of these.

It is at this point that the non-linguist will make a detour. Suppose that we found the word *elephant* to play an important part in all scientific discourse. The non-linguist would pay scant attention to the word itself, but would insist upon a thorough study of elephants, in the way of zoology, before he went on, and if this could not be carried to a conclusion, would insist upon the paradox of our uncertainty about the ultimate nature of elephants, which conflicted with the usefulness of the word *elephant* in scientific discourse,—an evil paradox, indeed, since, uncertain about the very nature of scientific discourse, we cannot hope to rationalize our knowledge of elephants.

Now, we are not concerned with elephants, and must take them for granted and leave the zoologist to study them. We cannot study every-thing at once, and must accept with humility the vicious circle of science, as of life, finding our test of success in our ability to predict and to create. We need ask only how the word *elephant* came to play its part in scientific discourse, what service it does, how it works along with the other terms of scientific speech, and so on.

In every speech-community there are certain speech-forms toward which our response is relatively constant and uniform. The physicist, physiologist, psychologist, and anthropologist who study the situations in which these speech-forms are uttered and the responses which a hearer makes to these speech-forms, may not find them simple at all, but that is none of our present concern. We are concerned merely with the fact that our responses (including further speech) to certain speech-forms are relatively constant and uniform, and that these speech-forms constitute the basis of scientific speech. Here again, there is no absolute boundary: the more constant and uniform our use of a speech-form, the better suited is this speech-form to scientific reporting. Other things being equal, the more narrowly we restrict a scientific report to speech-forms of maximum response-uniformity, the better will be the success of that report.

## III

Limiting our consideration, for the present, to the English language, let us examine a few of the speech-forms which call forth the most uniform response and have passed, accordingly, into the special dialect of the scientist.

One is the word *not*. It is seldom uttered alone, but appears usually in phrases, such as *Don't!—Mustn't!—There aren't any berries over there.*[4] To state the meaning of this word is a problem for the physiologist, psychologist, and anthropologist. We should be wrong, however, if we quit work until these students came to a satisfactory definition of the English word *not*. They would very properly retort by laying down their tools and saying "We cannot go ahead until you have given us the foundations of science. We cannot give you a definition of the word *not* until you have established a terminology in which definitions are to be given." It is evident that we must content ourselves with a provisional definition which will be improved or replaced as the psychologist, anthropologist, and so on make progress; they, in turn, will make revision of their results whenever this is demanded by our general principles of scientific discourse. Nowadays we should define the word *not* as the linguistic *inhibitor* in our speech-community.[5] This is plain in the most elementary of the phrases containing it, the inhibition *Don't!* In the scientist's speeches, whose typical form is prediction, the word *not* inhibits the hearer who might otherwise move in a certain direction or utter certain speech-forms. The two statements,

> *There are berries behind that hill;*
> *There aren't any berries behind that hill,*

are such that a hearer cannot make any one type of conventional response to both at the same time; thus, he cannot at the same time go behind the hill with his berry-basket and stay at home. The utterance, in a phrase, of

---

[4] The parallel phrase without *not* of the last example is *There are berries over there*. The plus of the word *any* in the example illustrates the special twists, often quite bizarre, which we find in different languages; in setting up rules for scientific speech, we exclude these features or try to make them innocuous. A striking example is the troublesome adjectival *no* of English (*No cat has nine tails*, etc.).

[5] *Inhibition* is here a physiological term (Pavlov): all English-speaking persons have been trained so that hearing the word *not* inhibits them in certain definable ways.

the word *not* produces a phrase such that simultaneous parallel response to both this phrase and the parallel phrase without *not* cannot be made. Such a word can exist because the human body occupies only one continuous region in the space-time world. We observe especially that the human body is condemned to incessant travel, always in one sense, along the axis of time. The chief point for us, however, is this, that although many men now living can improve upon the above description of the word *not*, none can give a rigid and satisfying definition for our present use, simply because any definition, if rigid, presupposes a scientific vocabulary which in turn presupposes the word *not*. No matter how we describe the scientific vocabulary, we must begin with a set of undefined terms.

Mathematicians have long recognized this;[6] a linguist will add merely a comment on the nature of the undefined terms. The undefined terms could be treated by a process of demonstration. This is the process by which a child learns to speak. The inventor or transmitter of the scientific terminology would repeatedly perform handling actions (such as touching or moving certain objects) and at the same time utter the undefined technical term. He would repeat this until his listeners were able to utter the appropriate technical term whenever the demonstrator performed the handling action, and to perform the appropriate handling action whenever they heard the technical term.[7] If this were done, the scientific terms would actually constitute a "language." Ordinary languages are acquired by infants who have no earlier speech; this language would be acquired by persons who already spoke some ordinary language. It would differ from ordinary languages also in the smaller range and greater regularity of its vocabulary and syntax. It would deserve the name "language," however, because its speech-forms would be defined for each speaker in terms of handling actions, and not in terms of another language. For obvious reasons, such as the abstract character of the meanings, we create and transmit scientific speech-forms not by demonstration, but by explanation in terms of an ordinary language, such as English. Therefore the speech of the scientist constitutes not a "language," but a technical dialect within an ordinary language. The logistician who calls his system of symbols a "language" is using a dangerous metaphor. When he tells us that the system is complete in itself, that the symbols are to be defined only by their interplay within the "language," this may mean one of two things. It may mean that the hearer (reader) is to respond to the symbols in such ways and only in such ways as have been agreed upon. This is a self-evident demand. It may mean, however, that the author believes that,

[6] This recognition appears in an admirable way, both explicitly and in the structure of the discourse, in O. Veblen and J. W. Young, *Projective geometry*, Boston, 1918.

[7] On demonstration, see Weiss, *op. cit.*, 21.

by this fiat, he can wipe out his own English explanation. If so, he is mistaken. The hearer (reader) must in one way or another be trained to respond to the symbols. A treatise written entirely in logistic symbols would be unintelligible to readers who had not been told the meaning of the symbols.

When we have introduced the word *not*, we have created two classes of statements. Once a statement has appeared in any given discourse, then there cannot appear in this same discourse a statement differing only by the presence (plus or minus) of the word *not*. There must be some additional difference, either in the words of the two statements or in their syntactic structure or position (e.g., one of them may be part of a larger statement). Thus we have, in any discourse, statements which have been made (within this discourse they are *true* statements) and statements which have been excluded (for this discourse they are *false* statements). A new statement must be tested before it can be added to a given body of discourse. It dare not belong (directly or by implication) to the excluded group. If it has not been excluded, it may turn out, under the permanent conventions of our terminology and the temporary conventions of this particular discourse, to be a mere re-wording of a statement or statements (or parts of such) which are already in the discourse; then it is already *true* and *implied*. Or it may be indifferent, neither excluded nor implied; in this case we may add it to our discourse and make it true, or exclude it and make it false (either of these is done by an *assumption*), or we may leave it alone; in actual practice, what we do depends upon the stimuli provided by our object of study (observation, experiment, verbal record of earlier studies, etc.). Even discourses that concern probability are subject, in the first place, to this dichotomy: it comes before all questions of content.

## IV

Systems by which English-speaking persons may be taught to understand and to utter scientific speech could be constructed in various ways. I have chosen the word *not* as an example of an indefined term taken over from everyday speech, because one would probably make this choice. In the same way, other undefined terms have to be created,—such, for example, as a word in the sphere of the English words *and*, *or*, *if*; a word for equality ("*A* may in all discourse be replaced by *B*"); a word for class; for appurtenance to a class; and so on. There is one set of terms, however, defined and undefined, which deserves mention. In every community children are taught to recite certain words in a fixed order; these words have no meaning, outside of the fact that there exists this conventional way of reciting them.[8] These are the cardinal numerals. The tenuity of their meaning makes them ideal for scientific discourse. Nevertheless, this meaning involves certain features of man and his world, such as the linear character of our movement in time. We cannot escape some undefined terms of the character of *before* (or *predecessor* or the like). The cardinal numerals have a variety of uses in ordinary speech. The simplest is that of putting sets of objects into one-to-one correspondence without actually confronting them. Since in this operation human beings show great uniformity of response, it plays an important part in science; probably every science that is to speak in numerical terms will have to presuppose the existence of distinct objects and our trick of assigning objects to classes, often in arbitrary ways,—a long chapter of psychology and anthropology.

In some languages the cardinal numerals are said to be very few, e.g. three or four. In English and many other languages they are systematized, by features of morphology and syntax, in such a manner that, given any numeral word or phrase, a hearer can utter a numeral word or phrase in a stated before-and-after relation to the given numeral; for instance, we can (uniformly and predictably) name the immediate successor of any cardinal numeral. There is nothing mysterious about this, since all that is required is a verbal habit: the phrase *immediate successor of . . .* would suffice. This enables us to utter discourses of the familiar type:

> *If a positive integer is blue, its immediate successor is blue;*
> *The first positive integer is blue;*
> *Every positive integer is blue.*

Our certainty that the combination of the first two statements will evoke the same reponses, so far as scientific speech is concerned, as will the third statement, is due not to "innate judgments a priori" or the like, but simply to the fact that we have made certain conventions (acquired certain habits) as to the use of words. A positive integer is by definition a word or phrase which has a definite place in the recitation of number-expressions (*one, two, three, . . .*). We learn to begin this recitation by saying *one*; then we learn to recite up to *twelve*; we learn the place also of *hundred, thousand, million*. Other words have components which indicate their place in the recitation, in part with irregularities of form: *thirteen, twenty, thirty, billion, trillion*. The rest are phrasal combinations which explicitly state their place in the recitation: *twenty-one, two hundred sixty-four*, etc. Whatever positive integer we may name, a speaker of English can "count" up to it. However, he need not waste his time in this way, since in any actual use we are concerned only with some of the successor-relations of the

[8] This is not strictly true; the numeral *thirteen*, for instance, has another phase of meaning in our superstitious response; however, these non-serial phases of meaning are easily eliminated for scientific use.

integer that has been named. When we say that the English language provides an "infinity" of positive integers, we do not mean that anybody can go on counting forever; we mean only that our language has speech-forms for saying "the immediate successor of" any integer. When we say that a class is "infinite," we do not mean that any person or set of persons has made an endless series of responses; we mean only that we have agreed upon a conventional response (a *function*) to some type of stimulus (*argument*) and have by demonstration or verbal instruction fixed our agreement so well that we respond uniformly to any new stimulus of this type. The values of an argument need not be enumerable.[9] Where it is found useful for scientific speech, we can distinguish by using *every* with enumerable arguments and *any* with non-enumerable ("every positive integer less than 13" but "any positive integer greater than 13"), leaving *all* as an indifferent word for both cases.

## V

As we proceed with the use of numbers, we find operations which make new words convenient. For instance, if we use numbers in talking about the giving and returning of objects, we shall find it convenient to have two parallel sets of numbers (positive and negative) and a *zero* for "quits." The most serious step of this kind is the creation of *fractions*; in the enlarged system (*rational numbers*) counting is no longer possible, but it is still true that we shall unmistakably agree upon the before-and-after relation of any two numbers. We then go on to say (Dedekind's Postulate) that we will use any phrase which is so defined that this agreement can be maintained.

We have found it useful, also, to employ speech-forms (*higher numbers*) which consist of two or more real numbers in a fixed order. The terms defined in connection with real numbers will affect these higher numbers in various ways; the details will depend upon which conventions of real-number discourse we want to maintain for higher numbers. Thus, our agreements about two-placed higher numbers (*complex numbers*) are aptly summarized by the use of the phrase "square root of minus one," written $\sqrt{-1}$ or $i$. Three-placed higher numbers (ordinary *vectors*) are in the same way subjected to certain conventions which are aptly summarized in certain theorems about the *scalar product* and the *vector product* of two vectors. Since our space is three-dimensional (this is for the psy-

[9] [Bloomfield is not here using the word *enumerable* in the technical sense given to it in mathematics (*enumerable* = *denumerable* = *countable*: of a set the elements of which can be put into one-to-one correspondence with the set of all positive integers). He means the word in an everyday sense, for which mathematicians use the term *finite*. The views Bloomfield expressed in this article may be controversial, but the controversy should not be hung up on a mere choice of terms.—CFH]

chologist and anthropologist to explain), three-placed vectors are useful for geometrical discourse. It is surprising to see the tenacity with which writers on this subject confuse the terminology (vectors) with the geometrical application, as though we had not learned that the spatial relations of objects are not a matter of verbal agreement (mathematics), but demand observation. Given a vector $X = \{X_1, X_2, X_3\}$, we define the number $[(X_1)^2 + (X_2)^2 + (X_3)^2]^{\frac{1}{2}}$ as mg(X), and we define the vector $\{X_1/mg(X), X_2/mg(X), X_3/mg(X)\}$ as di(X) or simply x. We do this because in Euclidean space, when a straight-line interval is described, in Cartesian coordinates, by X, the length of this interval is described by mg(X), and its direction by di(X). The description is purely verbal (numerical), but the things described are certain very general characteristics of the objects in our world; since we have learned that this description is only approximate, it should be impossible to confuse the description with the objects. To make this confusion,—to insist that a "vector" is not merely an ordered set of three numbers, but possesses also some other characteristics,—is to forego the advantage of mathematical terminology. This terminology includes, for instance, terms like *differential* and *gradient*, whose definition makes it easy to show the truth of the statement: "The gradient of a scalar function of a vector has the direction of the greatest rate of change of the scalar function." Instead of the simple and rigorous arithmetical proof, we find in our physics books a horrid little diagram, with the differentials drawn in as short lines. This diagram is more abstract than the numerical statement. By looking at the diagram and at the same time reading a not entirely numerical proof (whose rigor is hard to control), we arrive finally at the above statement.[10]

Since I am not a mathematician, I shall not attempt to carry this farther, beyond expressing the suspicion that the same confusion exists in the matter of tensors, which are perhaps to be defined as ordered sets of ordered sets of numbers (matrices); the behavior of tensors under a change of coordinates characterizes merely one of the operations that may be performed upon them, an operation useful in the application to geometry and physics, but by no means necessary (and indeed damaging) to their definition.

Mathematics is not on a level with the other sciences; it is in principle a part of every science; it is the technique of making statements in the speech-forms which elicit the most uniform response. The logical calculus and the phoneme notation of linguistics are mathematical; as numerical discourse seems to secure the greatest uniformity of response, it may be advisable to reduce such non-numerical types, in theory at least, to numerical form.

---

[10] On vectors, see E. Study, *Einleitung in die Theorie der Invarianten*, Brunswick, 1923.

## VI

A report or prediction is limited in extent. The reporter does not continue indefinitely to make speech-responses to the object. In describing a tree we do not count its leaves. In scientific work, the selection of useful features for report is one of the criteria of skill. Perhaps every scientific worker has had the chastening experience of hearing someone else base a useful classification or prediction upon features which he had seen and passed by as unessential. Since the scientist's report omits many verbal responses that can be made, it does not fully describe the "actual object." The non-linguist, unaccustomed to a persistent study of mere speech, jumps to the fiction of a "conceptual" object which does correspond exactly to the scientist's report. For instance, in geometry we may discuss relations which concern only one dimension; we may discuss *lines*, *curves*, and so on, mentioning only the length relations of objects and refraining from discussion of their width and thickness. If a record of observations is tabulated by dots on a chart and these dots come close to a simply definable curve, it may be useful to name this curve, as an approximate description of the placing of the dots. Such statements are verbal, not "conceptual."

In particular, the scientist's use of the number system is distressing to the non-linguist. When we ask the distance to the nearest town and receive the answer "Five miles," we know that this is not the minutely measured straight-line Euclidean distance from the tip of our left boot to the nearest point of the city limits. No one marvels at this or draws philosophic conclusions. Various degrees of approximation are used, down to the point where our handling responses, with the best instruments, cease to yield uniform results. In the speech of the scientist two conventions are useful:

(1) Earlier approximations do not limit the scope (verbal freedom) of later approximations. Having spoken of "five miles" and "six miles" (or millimeters) does not preclude our speaking, upon another occasion, of "five and one half miles." The scientist reserves the right of making free use of intermediate number expressions whenever he is stimulated to do so either by a more minute handling of objects or by a new scheme of reporting. The number system has no contiguously closed divisions: it is *dense*.

(2) The fear of future discourse does not limit the scope (verbal freedom) of numerical discourse. In any single instance where the scientist's report says "five miles" (or "$\sqrt{2}$ millimeters," etc.), it may be that some other report, about a different object, or after new observations, or perhaps merely under a different scheme of reporting, will say "four and nine tenths miles" or "five and one tenth miles" (or "1.4142 millimeters," and

so on). The scientist reserves the right of not worrying about this eventuality, and of using any number expression that is intelligible under the conventions of arithmetic (such as real numbers under the Dedekind Postulate). The number system has no contiguously open divisions: it is *continuous*.[11]

Physicists seem to be especially given to non-linguistic treatment of linguistic forms, such as attributing a mystical character to the form of a verbal report. Some, for instance, are afraid to define *force* in terms of mass and acceleration: there is a something there that does not appear in the mere equations. Finding that the act of observation alters the state of certain objects, the physicist may (legitimately or even necessarily) decide upon a form of report which takes this circumstance into consideration, but he is merely making a mistake in linguistics if he then tries to elevate this scheme of reporting into a metaphysical principle. If we said that the inside of every opaque solid is green until the solid is cut or broken or subjected to other than the usual conditions of illumination, we should have a statement (useless, to be sure) of the same metaphysical validity as this physicist's (useful and acceptable) form of reporting.

## VII

The speech-forms of scientific discourse include grammatical features. Two of these are especially important: the sentence-form of *statements* and the structural feature of *subordination*.[12] In scientific speech these features are limited, just as are the words which scientific speech takes over from ordinary language.

In any one utterance, a *sentence* is a word or phrase which, within the arrangement habits (*grammar*) of the language, is not a part, in this utterance, of any larger phrase. A *statement*, in English, is a sentence of a particular type, defined by grammatical features: it consists of a substantive expression (*actor*) and a finite verb expression (*action*), spoken in one

[11] In its everyday meaning, the term *continuous* is not particularly descriptive of convention (2); it was chosen, of course, on account of the simple geometrical bearing of this convention.

Translated into everyday language, Dedekind's postulate amounts roughly to this: We shall use in numerical discourse any word or phrase which we can define in such a way that its before-and-after relation to any rational number whatever is unmistakably determined. —It is true that at the bottom of our discourse there lie undefined words which may arise to trouble us. However, our terminology of numbers is sound enough to prevent this in all but the most unusual situations, and even in these unusual situations a realistic diagnosis will show also the cure.

[12] In linguistics the term *statement* applies only to sentences of a certain type (*John runs*). When the phrase *John runs* appears as part of a sentence (*If John runs, he will fall*), then this phrase is not a statement. In logic, however, the term *statement* is used also of expressions which are part of larger expressions; the term is so used in III, above.

of certain types of order, with the falling type of final pitch.[13] The meaning common to all English statements in contrast with all English sentences that are not statements, is for the psychologist and sociologist to define. Provisionally we may say: A (full-sentence) statement is the grammatical form which insures response of the hearer. That is, whether the hearer has or has not been stimulated by a given event or by a linguistic report of this event, the statement conventionally makes him respond to this event: the hearer's actions (including speech) are thereafter such as are appropriate to a person who has been stimulated by this event. If they are not, then the speaker is not making the normal response to the statement: he has "failed to understand" it, "disbelieves" it, and so on. The convention of scientific discourse is to use only statements. A description of scientific terminology will define a very few types of statements that are to be permitted. This can be done, for English, by naming the finite verbs which are permissible: *exists*, *equals*, *implies*, *is a member of* . . . , and so on, and by naming the permissible accompaniments. Ultimately, of course, the definitions of *statement* and of the permissible forms will contain undefined terms, taken over with as good an explanation as may be, from everyday language.

In a sentence, the smallest meaningful elements of a language are not merely strung along in succession; various relations between these elements act as conventional stimuli. The meaning of a succession of elements depends upon which elements appear with which (e.g., *Drink milk* is a command, but *fresh milk* is not), upon the order of the elements (*John hit Bill* : *Bill hit John*), upon modifications of their phonetic shape (of this there is little in English; compare perhaps *re-solve* 'solve again' with *resolve*), and upon certain phonetic features which are reserved for this use (in English, certain conventional features of stress and pitch; compare *convict'* : *con'vict* or *It's four o'clock*, statement, with falling pitch, versus *It's four o'clock?* question, with rising pitch). The meaning of a sentence depends upon *constructions* which are definable in terms of these structural features.[14] One type is *syntactic subordination*. The grammatical function of a phrase may be the same (or within certain restrictions the same) as that of a word or phrase which appears within it. In *Drink fresh milk* the function of *fresh milk* is the same as that of *milk* in *Drink milk*. The word *milk* is the "head" of the phrase *fresh milk*, and the word *fresh* is "subordinated" to the word *milk*. Even an actor-action phrase may be subordinated (e.g., *John runs* in *If John runs, he will fall*).[15] A certain rigid minimum of this habit is taken over into scientific speech and there luxuriates to such an extent as to render this speech unintelligible in normal spoken shape and intelligible only in the written record. In short, the

[13] For sentence-types, see L. Bloomfield, *Language*, New York, 1933, p. 170.
[14] *Ibid.*, 158.
[15] *Ibid.*, 194.

parentheses of logic and mathematics are not to be taken for granted, but carry over a feature of ordinary language which requires, at bottom, certain undefined terms that can be illuminated only by a serious psychological and anthropological discussion.

## VIII

The speech-forms of the English-speaking scientist are not a "language," but merely a special vocabulary and phraseology within the English language. It appears, however, that a scientific discourse which most nearly insures uniform response in its own language (e.g., English) is also most easily translated into another language (e.g., French or German). This is due, in part, to the historical circumstance that scientific terms are coined in one language and then translated, by explicit definition, into others. This, however, is not true of the most elementary forms. When we adopt and limit or define speech-forms such as *not, one, two, three, implies, exists*, for maximum uniformity of response, we come finally to anthropologic common factors: a practically equivalent adoption or redefinition of everyday words will be possible in any other language. The explanation of the undefined terms will be different for different languages, but the meanings finally reached will be the same.

In our numerals and other mathematical terms we have reached a maximum of uniformity between languages: under certain conventions the same graphs can be used for different languages. It is true that 91, for instance, which in Chinese has the arithmetically perfect speech-form "nine ten one," exhibits in English the slightly irregular shape *nine-ty-one*, and in German is "one and ninety," in French "four twenty eleven," and in Danish "one and half five-times." Under a simple convention, however, the same graphic mark, 91, is used in writing all these languages. This feature of writing is a superficial symptom of the linguistic circumstance that a number, such as *ninety-one*, is perfectly translatable, as to scientific meaning, from one language into another. The substructure of adoption and definition of everyday words and grammatical features differs for different languages, but the actual terminology and syntax of scientific discourse tends to be conventionalized,—and in the case of mathematics has already been conventionalized,—to such an extent that the difference between languages is an infinitesimal of higher order than the difference between individual speakers of the same language.

# B45. Language or Ideas?

1936. *Language* 12.89–95.

[Bloomfield was President of the Linguistic Society of America in 1935, and this paper—or an oral version of it, without the critical apparatus—was in effect his Presidential Address to the Society in New York in December of that year. A bracketed summary at the beginning of the printed version in *Language*, possibly written by the Editor (Bolling), reads as follows: 'The logicians of the Vienna Circle have independently reached the conclusion of *physicalism*: any scientifically meaningful statement reports a movement in space and time. This confirms the conclusion of A. P. Weiss and other American workers: the universe of science is a physical universe. This conclusion implies that statements about "ideas" are to be translated into statements about speech-forms.']

Some years ago I had the honor of addressing the Linguistic Society of America and one of the sister societies upon a prescribed subject 'Linguistics as a science'.[1] The views which I was bound to express were shared by so few people that it seemed natural to state them in the form of prediction rather than of dogma. Linguistics as actually practised employs only such terms as are translatable into the language of physical and biological science; in this linguistics differs from nearly all other discussion of human affairs. Within the next generations mankind will learn that only such terms are usable in any science. The terminology in which at present we try to speak of human affairs—the terminology of 'consciousness', 'mind', 'perception', 'ideas', and so on—in sum, the terminology of mentalism and animism—will be discarded, much as we have discarded Ptolemaic astronomy, and will be replaced in minor part by physiological terms and in major part by terms of linguistics.

This prediction was based not only upon what seem to me to be the striking features of linguistic methodology, but in far greater measure upon the doctrine of non-animistic students of human behavior, especially upon the conclusions of our late colleague, Albert Paul Weiss.

A prophecy of this sort, no matter how deep the conviction from which it springs, is so pitifully subject to individual prejudices and errors that

[1] Studies in philology 27.553 (1930) [our B36.—CFH]. The summary which follows above is stated so as to bring out the accord with the Viennese conclusions (see below).

even more than most statements it needs to be confirmed or refuted. Within the last years a group of philosophers and logicians, known as the Vienna Circle, has arrived at the same conclusion concerning language.[2] Subjecting various branches of science to logical scrutiny, Rudolf Carnap and Otto Neurath have found that all scientifically meaningful statements are translatable into physical terms—that is, into statements about movements which can be observed and described in coordinates of space and time. Statements that are not made in these terms are either scientifically meaningless or else make sense only if they are translated into statements about language. The former, entirely meaningless type may be illustrated by the sentence: *The world is known to me only through my perceptions.* This statement is scientifically meaningless, for it directs us to no observation at any place or time; it predicts nothing.[3] The second type may be exemplified by the sentence: *Redness is a concept.* This makes sense only if it is translated into a statement about language, namely: *In the English language the word redness is a noun.*[4]

The path by which Carnap and Neurath reach this conclusion is thorny. It is the path of 'pure' formal logic, with abstraction from all empirical content. Carnap employs mentalistic terms and has to struggle with them; both Carnap and Neurath use linguistic terms without reference to their

[2] R. Carnap, 'Ueberwindung der Metaphysik,' Erkenntnis 2.219 (1931); also in a French translation, which I have not seen, La science et la métaphysique, Paris 1934 (=Actualités scientifiques, vol. 172); 'Die physikalische Sprache,' Erkenntnis 2.432 (1931); also in an English translation, which I have not seen, The unity of science, London 1934 (=Psyche miniatures, General series, No. 63); 'Psychologie in physikalischer Sprache,' Erkenntnis 3.107 (1932); 'Les concepts psychologiques,' Revue de synthèse 10.45 (1935); Logische Syntax der Sprache, Vienna 1934 (=Schriften zur wissenschaftlichen Weltauffassung, 8); Philosophy and logical syntax, London 1935 (=Psyche miniatures, General series, No. 70).

O. Neurath, 'Physikalismus,' Scientia 50.297 (1931); 'Physicalism,' The monist 41.618 (1931); 'Soziologie und Physikalismus,' Erkenntnis 2.393 (1931); Einheitswissenschaft und Psychologie, Vienna 1933 (=Einheitswissenschaft, Heft 1); Le développement du cercle de Vienne, Paris 1935 (=Actualités scientifiques, vol. 290).

[3] This example is modeled on Carnap's examples in Philosophy and Logical Syntax, 16 ff.; for a thoroughgoing analysis see Weiss's article on solipsism, Psychological Review 38.474 (1931).

[4] Compare Carnap, 62, who uses *thing-word* for *noun.* The term *noun* (or *thing-word*), of course,—though Carnap does not mention this—must then be defined, for English grammar, and the term *word* for language in general, as technical terms of linguistics; this definition, moreover, must be made in terms of the postulates, undefined basic terms, and earlier definitions of linguistics—not by definitions of meaning and not in metaphysical terms. Thus, a *word* is the smallest meaningful unit that can be spoken alone. In English, a *noun* is a word which enters centrally into endocentric phrases with preceding adjective modifiers, serves as an actor with a finite verb, as the goal of a verb or preposition, and as a predicate complement, appears always in one of two sub-classes, singular and plural, and joins with the suffix [-ez, -z, -s] to form an adjective. Carnap, so far as I have found, nowhere mentions the fact that the discourse of logic presupposes descriptive linguistics and uses the technical terms of this empirical science. The complex linguistic background of logical and mathematical statement is generally ignored by philosophers and logicians; an informal outline of it will be found in Philosophy of Science 2.499 (1935); more formally in my Language, New York 1933, chapters 2 to 16.

empiric background. These defects keep our authors from attaining to the mathematical elegance and cogency, the surgical precision, or the vast human scope of Weiss's 'Theoretical Basis'. Yet their thornier path follows the same direction. A summary of their argument, given in non-mentalistic terms, could serve directly as a formal résumé of the steps by which Max F. Meyer or A. P. Weiss reach the same goal.[5]

Carnap and Neurath agree, then, with the American students in saying that mentalistic phraseology, in so far as it is not nonsensical, is only a troublesome duplication of linguistic phraseology. The most important feature of this agreement is the circumstance that Carnap and Neurath have done their work in complete independence of their American predecessors. They mention American work a very few times, and then in such manner as to guarantee their lack of familiarity with it. It is safe to say that we have here a highly significant confirmation; the Vienna authors, working independently and with a different method, have reached the same conclusion, stating it in terms which need not even be 'translated' to show the equivalence.[6]

---

[5] Max F. Meyer, The Psychology of the Other One, second edition, Columbia, Missouri, 1922.

Albert Paul Weiss, A Theoretical Basis of Human Behavior, second edition, Columbus, 1929.

[6] In Der logische Aufbau der Welt (Berlin 1928) 81, Carnap mentions Watson and, of all people, Dewey, as behaviorists; in Erkenntnis 3.124 (1932) he mentions a German translation (1930) of Watson's Behaviorism. Neurath, Einheitswissenschaft 20, analyzes a paragraph of this German translation and finds that Watson's use of the terms *good* and *bad* violates the rule of physicalism; from this, Neurath seems to draw the conclusion that Watson and all other American students fail to satisfy the demand of physicalism. As a matter of fact, Watson has in the original text (New York, 1924, page 41) the words 'good' and 'bad' in quotation marks plainly as citations from everyday speech. Moreover, without prejudice to Watson's merits as an investigator and as a popularizer, his Behaviorism has the familiar faults of popularization and cannot be seriously used as Neurath uses it. In order to compare the Vienna students' physicalism with serious American work, one must study the latter as well as the former.

Yet Neurath's point is not without interest. In correcting the passage from Watson, he can find only an ethnological translation for the words *good* and *bad*; meanwhile Weiss, Theoretical Basis 102 ff., 446 ff. has given a strictly physical translation of these words in terms of the *variability of a system*.

Neurath proposes (Einheitswissenschaft 17) to designate his group as *Behavioristiker* and their discipline as *Behavioristik*, in contrast with the American *behaviorists* (*Behavioristen*) and *behaviorism* (*Behaviorismus*). The distinction is illusory, since it is based upon lapses from exactitude, real or apparent, such as are to be found also in the writings of the Vienna circle. We shall do well not to insist upon such deviations, but rather to concentrate upon the necessary and sufficient rule: Every scientific statement is made in physical terms. The most perfect formulation of this, so far as I know, and the best exemplification, are to be found in Weiss's Theoretical Basis. As to the name *behaviorism* (which Weiss disliked), it is in many ways objectionable and has been adopted by writers who fail, not only in the way of lapses, but in actual operation, to fulfil the essential demand (Carnap, Erkenntnis 3.125, 'unechter Behaviorismus'). *Physicalism* is a much better word. We should stress our agreement as to the essential point and join in defending it from misinterpretation. Note, for instance, the striking accord between Neurath's 'zweites Menschlein' (Einheitswissenschaft

The realization that science can speak only in physical terms will not down. One cannot read modern writings without meeting it again and again, expressed by students who, to all appearance, have reached it independently. The early papers of Pavlov show dramatically how a group of physiologists is forced to accept this discipline.[7] In England, Lancelot Hogben demonstrates keenly and brilliantly how biology forces it upon us.[8] For physical science it is a working rule, but even when physicists look beyond this, some of them arrive at our conclusion. Thus, P. W. Bridgman, in spite of a perfunctory and otiose profession of mentalism, and in spite of much animistic verbiage which could be easily translated away— Bridgman always says 'concept' when he means simply 'word' or 'technical term'—formulates and applies an 'operational' rule for all definitions in physics, to the effect that terms which do not speak of operations are meaningless.[9] Doubtless also there is more than one isolated instance, such as the medical dissertation of H. Ahlenstiel, Der Begriff psychisch und die Auffassungen vom Wesen der Wissenschaft.[10] All these students, however, like their predecessors, the 'materialists' of the eighteenth and nineteenth centuries, are left with the problem: How do ideas arise from mere matter?[11] The students of the Vienna group, alone, it would seem, agree with their American colleagues in viewing this as a pseudo-problem, because such terms as 'idea' are merely misnomers for linguistic events.

*     *     *

The testing of this hypothesis of *physicalism* will be a task of the next generations, and linguists will have to perform an important part of the work. Non-linguists (unless they happen to be physicalists) constantly forget that a speaker is making noise, and credit him, instead, with the possession of impalpable 'ideas'. It remains for linguists to show, in detail, that the speaker has no 'ideas', and that the noise is sufficient— for the speaker's words act with a trigger-effect upon the nervous systems of his speech-fellows. Linguists, then, will have to read the description of the universe, as men have written it, and wherever they come upon the

16) and Weiss's early essay, 'The mind and the man within', Psychological Review 26. 327 (1919).

[7] I. P. Pavlov, Conditioned Reflexes, translated by G. V. Anrep, Oxford 1927.

[8] L. Hogben, The Nature of Living Matter, London 1930.

[9] P. W. Bridgman, The Logic of Modern Physics, New York 1932; profession of mentalism (x); operational principle (5); application (28, an excellent example, whose very wording agrees with Carnap); 56 (an important point); 94; 130; 139; 153; 166; 203.

[10] Printed summary on a leaflet, Kiel 1921; the original dissertation is typewritten only, and I have not seen it.

[11] Here we must include the doctrine predominant among Russian scholars. For example, R. Shor's article on Linguistics in the Encyclopedia (Bol'shaja sovetskaja enciklopedija, 65.392, Moscow 1931) represents not 'materialism' in any strict sense, but rather the normal nineteenth-century dualism.

mention of an 'idea' (or any synonym, such as 'concept', 'notion', or the like), they will have to replace this mention by terms relating to language. If the description so revised is better than the old—simpler and fruitful of sounder and easier prediction—, then the hypothesis will have been confirmed and mankind will accept it as we accept the Copernican astronomy.

We may illustrate this by a simple instance of a typical sort. Here is a passage from a most admirable treatise on the foundations of scientific method:[12]

> The geometrical ideas of line and plane involve absolute sameness in all their elements and absolute continuity. Every element of a straight line can in conception be made to fit every other element, and this however it be turned about its terminal points. . . . Further, every element of a straight line or plane, however often divided up, is in conception, when magnified up, still an element of straight line or plane.
>
> The geometrical ideas correspond to absolute sameness and continuity, but do we experience anything like these in our perceptions? . . .
>
> The fact remains, that however great care we take in the preparation of a plane surface, either a microscope or other means can be found of sufficient power to show that it is not a plane surface. It is precisely the same with a straight line; however accurate it appears at first to be, exact methods of investigation invariably show it to be widely removed from the conceptual straight line of geometry. . . . *Our experience gives us no reason to suppose that with any amount of care we could obtain a perceptual straight line or plane, the elements of which would on indefinite magnification satisfy the condition of ultimate sameness involved in the geometrical definitions.* We are thus forced to conclude that the geometrical definitions are the results of processes which may be started, but the limits of which can never be reached in perception; they are pure conceptions having no correspondence with any possible perceptual experience.

The terms 'perceptual' and 'conceptual' derive from the following consideration: 'My universe consists necessarily and exclusively of my experiences'. This, the solipsistic axiom, tells us nothing about anything *within* the universe; whatever its value for other activities, it has no bearing on science. Hence for 'perceptual' we shall say *actual*, and for 'conceptual' we shall say *verbal*.

Pearson speaks here of three things: (1) actual ('perceptual') objects, (2) speech-forms, namely geometrical definitions, and (3) 'ideas' or 'concepts', such as 'the concept of a straight line'. It is our hypothesis that (3) is merely a traditional but useless and confusing way of talking about (2); that we find in our universe (that is: require in our discourse) only (1) actual objects and (2) speech-forms which serve as conventional responses to certain features that are common to a class of objects.

Suppose that we know nothing of geometry. We have a great many

---

[12] Karl Pearson, The Grammar of Science[3] 1.197 (London 1911).

little spots all over the floor, including two red ones, some distance apart, which we will call *A* and *B*; and we have a great many rods or strips of metal, of various shapes. We take these rods of metal and lay first one then another so as to cover both of the red spots *A* and *B*. We soon find that the metal rods are of two kinds. Some of them, when we lay them so as to cover *A* and *B*, cover always the same other spots, no matter how we lay them or which rod we use. We call these rods 'straight'. Of the remaining rods this is not true; one and the same rod can be laid in various ways so as to cover spots *A* and *B*; it will cover now some of the black spots and now others. Any two rods of this second class can be laid so as to cover different spots, always including *A* and *B*.

The geometrician gives us a succinct statement of this. Given a set of things called 'points', we define classes of these. The classes called 'straight lines' are classes such that on any two points there is one and only one straight line.

Now, it is probable that if we make the spots very small and place them very close together and examine the placing of the rods with a microscope, no rod will ever satisfy the geometric definition of 'straight'. Also, this definition does not mention the width, thickness, weight, temperature, color, and so on, of the rods, although every rod presents features of this sort. In these respects the term 'straight' resembles all other speech-forms; it is in such forms that we discourse and co-operate.

Now let us re-word the statement in non-mentalistic terms:

> The geometrical definitions of line and plane say that lines and planes are absolutely alike in all their elements and absolutely continuous. They say that every element of a straight line can be made to fit every other element, and this however it be turned about its terminal points. . . . Further, every element of a straight line or plane, however often divided up, is still, according to the geometrical definition, an element of straight line or plane.
>
> The geometrical definitions imply absolute sameness and continuity, but we find no objects with these characteristics. . . .
>
> The fact remains, that however great care we take in the preparation of a plane surface, either a microscope or other means can be found of sufficient power to show that it is not a plane surface. It is precisely the same with a straight line; however accurate a straight edge appears at first to be, exact methods of investigation invariably show it to be far from satisfying the geometric definition. . . . Our measurements give us no reason to suppose that with any amount of care we shall ever obtain a straight-edged or plane-surfaced object which will under careful observation satisfy the geometric definitions. We are thus forced to conclude that the geometrical definitions are simple verbal descriptions which roughly describe classes of objects but do not exactly describe any given object. In this the geometrical terms are like all other speech-forms.

It is our hypothesis that the terms 'concept', 'idea', and so on add nothing to this. We suppose that the person who says 'I was having an idea of a straight line' is telling us: 'I uttered out loud or produced by inner speech movements the words *straight line*, and at the same time I made some obscure visceral reactions with which I habitually accompany the sight or feel of a straight edge or the utterance or hearing of the word *straight*.' Of all this, only the verbal action is constant from person to person. If we are right, then the term 'idea' is simply a traditional obscure synonym for 'speech-form', and it will appear that what we now call 'mental' events are in part private and unimportant events of physiology and in part social events (responses which in their turn act as stimuli upon other persons or upon the responder himself), namely acts of speech. If this is true, then linguistics in the future will deal with much wider problems than today.

# B46. Review of Bentley

1936. *Language* 12.137–141.

*Linguistic Analysis of Mathematics.* By Arthur F. Bentley. Bloomington, Indiana: The Principia Press, 1932.

*Behavior, Knowledge, Fact.* By Arthur F. Bentley. Bloomington, Indiana: The Principia Press, 1935.

These books deal with several topics which your reviewer believes can be usefully studied in the light of linguistics. One of the books has the word 'linguistic' in its title, and the words 'language' and 'linguistic' occur very frequently on the pages of both. Moreover, they contain many sentences which, torn out of context, would hold the same promise, such as LA 38: 'Every exact analysis, in, of, or by means of language, rests in preliminary provisional dissection and organization of linguistic materials.' 59: '. . . we proceed to examine linguistic phenomena in full play.' 63: 'We proceed, thus, under a full linguistic-semantic inspection.' BKF 9: 'A science of language exists, of course, just as much as does a science of psychology', and so on.

This appearance, however, is deceptive. The word 'language', with its derivative 'linguistic', in these books does not mean that which linguists and many other people call 'language'. What it does mean, your reviewer, after careful reading, is unable to say. LA 32 we read: 'Language may be studied in terms of printed page, writing hand, reading eye, hearing ear or speaking voice.' In this statement any linguist will recognize a widespread popular error. The next sentence, however, says, 'In such specialized studies we have here no technical interest.' Then, 33: 'Language is a functional of Experience, of Knowledge and of Fact: and Experience, Knowledge and Fact are functionals of it, and of another', and 35: 'Language subdivides most generally into (a) Inchoate Implication. (b) Words-common. (c) Terms. (d) Symbols.' These subdivisions are then explained. Then again, BKF 131: 'Language, so viewed, is no such limited abstraction as is the "language" of the grammarian or philologist . . .' 145: 'We proceed now to the linguistic aspect', but again the linguistic reader's hopes are shattered, for the next sentence reads: 'Aristotle studied language and gave us laws of reasoning.'

Now and then, to be sure (as in LA 32, quoted above), Bentley does speak of 'language' as linguists use the term, and when he does so, it is not in a way to inspire confidence. Thus, LA 18: 'the "Essai de sémantique" of Michel Bréal, who concentrated attention upon evolutions of linguistic meaning as contrasted with the prevalent philologies specializing upon linguistic form', where, aside from the false emphasis, the plural of 'prevalent philologies' is puzzling. The most astounding passage of this sort is BKF 9: 'Neither the "abstraction" set up for language by the professional philologist, nor a close specialization for "behavior" in some narrowly "mechanistic" or "mental" form, will show language and science themselves in wide spatial and durational spreads.' This simply does not make sense; one can infer only that the whole body of nineteenth-century linguistic work, which deals almost exclusively with the 'spatial and durational spreads' of language, does not exist for Bentley.

A large section (BKF 229–82), finally, develops the foundations of linguistics without benefit of the generations of work that have been devoted to this subject—and the result is just about what one might expect of such an attempt.

A writer, of course, has the privilege of defining and using words in any way he sees fit. If we are right in assuming that Bentley wishes to redefine (in the vaguest of terms, to be sure), the words 'language' and 'linguistic', then some of his statements about 'language', 'philology', and the like are lapses from his new definition into the current meaning of the terms, and they are unfortunate lapses, because he is evidently innocent of linguistics.

Confusion is all the more likely since some students believe that the topics with which Bentley is dealing receive a great deal of light from the study of language. The only psychologist, so far as I know, who has appreciated the working of language in human behavior, is A. P. Weiss. Occasionally Bentley writes as though he followed Weiss; thus, BKF 149: 'Language, taken in this way, absorbs very largely—in the end, we may even find, entirely—the meanings or references which are commonly ascribed to "thought" and assumed to inhabit the region at the far side of the "physical-to-psychical" jump.' However, it always turns out that Bentley does not mean 'language' in the linguist's sense of the word. In fact, Bentley's summary of Weiss's system (BKF 58) shows that Bentley fails to understand precisely this aspect of Weiss's work. Bentley does not grasp the linguistic basis of Weiss's 'biosocial' classification ('social factor', 'response', etc.), or the central position of these terms in Weiss's system. Instead, Bentley views these terms as a discordant element arising in spite of Weiss's strictly physical hypothesis and threatening to break it down; thus, 81: 'We find Weiss, in his movement-space, overwhelmed by something called "social".'

Perhaps the case of Bentley gives us the explanation for the fact that many keen students fail to understand Weiss's meticulously clear exposition. When Weiss speaks of 'language' he means exactly what he says, the language which is studied by linguists, the noise you make with your face. The linguistically untrained reader is so thoroughly accustomed to regarding (or rather, disregarding) language as some sort of mere subsidiary noise for the 'expression of ideas', that he fails to accept Weiss's words in their plain meaning. It is as though a citizen, going to court for some minor business, were greeted by the judge with the words, 'Good morning, I sentence you to death'. Under all the presuppositions of our place and time, the citizen would fail to accept these words until he felt the noose round his neck. One cannot imagine a clearer statement than Weiss's; the difficulty is only that many readers cannot take his words at their face value because these words utterly contradict the readers' presuppositions, and this is especially the case of readers who are not accustomed to discourse about language.

We may go a step farther. Weiss believed, and this reviewer believes, that the topics which Bentley is discussing cannot be elucidated without linguistics. In simple cases even the reviewer can see how the lack of linguistics hampers Bentley's discussion of cognate matters. Thus, BKF 59: 'We need spend no time on Weiss' electron-proton theory, which has merely the status of a counterblast to the "mentalists"; it is just one dogma against another. As an unused hypothesis it is psychologically sterile. . . .' Yet Weiss plainly says (Theoretical Basis[2] 16 footnote 1929) that this is not his hypothesis, but the hypothesis of physics at the time of writing; that physics is sure to change its basic hypotheses; that the only important point for us is that we discuss human behavior in physical terms. The same conclusion has since then been reached, independently and along the route of logical analysis, by H. Neurath and R. Carnap (see, for instance, the latter's Unity of Science, London, 1934). Their rule of 'physicalism' says that scientific discourse makes sense only when it speaks in physical terms. Be this as it may, when Weiss tells us from where he is taking the undefined terms of his system, he is neither enouncing a dogma nor giving us an unused hypothesis. Bentley's lapse here seems to result from a failure to grasp the linguistic conditions of scientific discourse.

Again, LF 16: 'A fully clarified postulation is, however, not attained until all alternative postulates are explored. Illustrative of this is the Euclidean parallel axiom.' Bentley's demand here is impossible, since one could go on inventing ('alternative') postulates for ever. That this demand rests upon a misunderstanding of the linguistic situation appears in the explanatory footnote: 'Until alternative axioms were brought to light and studied a century ago, there was a defect in Euclidean geometry yet waiting to be revealed. This defect was realistic, under the distinctions of the text.' Actually, the question, open until a century ago, about Euclid's parallel axiom, was a question of independence: was Euclid right in making this statement an axiom, or could the statement be proved as a theorem on the basis of Euclid's other axioms? When it was shown that consistent geometries could be developed without this statement, it appeared that Euclid was right, that, emphatically, this was not a defect in the Euclidean geometry. It is Bentley who here makes a 'realistic' lapse, and this lapse is due to Bentley's non-linguistic approach.

Similarly, Bentley's sketch of a definition of the mathematical term 'group' (LA 81) omits the features that are most important for the discussion in hand, and his claim that mathematicians speak of a group alternatively as a mathematical operation upon the objects or as itself a mathematical thing 'in which latter case the original objects appear as operations within it' contains several misapprehensions of a kind that will scarcely be made by a linguistically trained student, even if his mathematics be as poor as the reviewer's.

The chapter on the denumerability of decimals (LF 181) is a good illustration of non-linguistic attempts at discussing the foundations of mathematics. Since mathematics is a form of speech, information about its necessary modicum of undefined terms can be obtained only by linguistic considerations. Beyond this, the mathematician may occasionally, by way of luxury, ask for a report upon the linguistic character of a defined term, such as 'infinity'. The linguist's contribution will be rather trivial, but may give comfort. Thus, it requires no great linguistic insight to show that the mathematician's 'denumerable infinity' and 'non-denumerable infinity' name two different types of convention as to the use of words. The thing can be proved within mathematics, without discussion of the linguistic background. However, instead of supplying the linguistic scholium, Bentley confuses what the mathematicians have not confused.

A linguist will naturally object to a treatise which claims to deal with 'language' but is at no point in touch with the methods and results of linguistic science, and he will naturally question whether a system of psychology that is so constructed can add anything to what we know.

# B47. *Fragments of*
# The Language of Science

1937 (unpublished).

[The linguistic nature of mathematics concerned Bloomfield deeply in the 1930's. That his basic approach to the subject had evolved much earlier is attested by the following footnote, which appears on page 14 of the first edition (1925) of A. P. Weiss's *A Theoretical Basis of Human Behavior*:

> The conception of mathematics as an ideal language should be credited to Professor Leonard Bloomfield of Ohio State University. The writer, and this seems to have been the experience of others, has never been able to "place" mathematics satisfactorily among the sciences on account of the absence of any subject-matter. However, when mathematics is regarded from the linguistic point of view represented by Dr. Bloomfield, its function (as a recording and defining mechanism which is practically unlimited by the quantitative or qualitative restrictions of ordinary language) in science immediately becomes apparent.

There are hints in the 1933 book (see its index, s.v. 'mathematics'). Then came the pieces we reprint as B44, B45, and B46. At the 1936 Annual Meeting of the Linguistic Society, in Chicago, he gave a paper (never published) on 'Infinite Classes'. The 1939 monograph *Linguistic Aspects of Science*, an expansion of the 1936 article of that title, touches on the topic, but only in passing.

Late in 1937, however, Bloomfield submitted to the Committee on Research of the Linguistic Society a manuscript of some three hundred pages entitled *The Language of Science*. His approach is clear. He accepted the discourse of mathematicians as a corpus, and treated that corpus by much the same sort of analysis to which he subjected Tagalog or Menomini texts, or any other body of data— of course, with differences stemming from the fact that mathematical discourse is a specialization from everyday discourse in whatever ordinary language may be involved, and from the fact that much mathematical discourse is only possible in written form, not in speech.

Edgar H. Sturtevant, for the Committee, sought mathematical consultants; Oystein Öre of the Department of Mathematics at Yale directed him to Haskell B. Curry of Pennsylvania State College (now The Pennsylvanian State University). It is through the kindness of Professor Curry that I have been able to see the correspondence.

The judgment was friendly, cautious because linguistics was not the reviewer's field of competence, but critical in that the reviewer had found certain clear mathematical errors as well as some ineptnesses. For example, Bloomfield had used the expression 'algebraic number' in a sense different from that in which it is customarily used by mathematicians. If I may judge from Professor Curry's comments, from the fragments of the work that remain, and from a brief remark Bloomfield made to me several years later, Bloomfield seems also to have attempted to demonstrate that mathematicians are talking nonsense when they speak of the nondenumerability of the real numbers. (One school of philosophers of mathematics—the so-called 'intuitionists'—seem vaguely to share this view, but for entirely different reasons.)

Professor Curry's meticulous comments were forwarded by Sturtevant to Bloomfield, who then wrote to Professor Curry as follows (12 November 1937): 'Your report . . . reached me yesterday, and I am very much indebted to you for your careful reading and comment. Criticism and correction from someone interested in the subject and familiar with mathematics is something I very much wanted and seemed unable to get. Assuming that the main contentions of the MS are correct, then, in order to be of use, it would still have to be intelligible and interesting to linguists and, even though contradicting the beliefs of mathematicians, it would have to be free from mathematical errors. Whether I can give it these two qualities seems extremely doubtful. . . .' Apparently he decided that he could not, and in due time destroyed the manuscript.

I cannot refrain from expressing my regrets at this loss. Had he lived to rework the topic, benefiting from Professor Curry's suggestions (even if not accepting them all), some of his successors, who have concerned themselves with the interrelations of language and mathematics, might have been helped to avoid various stupid errors.

Bloomfield saved paper. When an article had been printed, rejected, or abandoned, he turned the sheets over and used the blank sides for handwritten drafts of whatever he was working on. Thus it is that some of the Algonquian materials transmitted to me after his death were on sheets the other sides of which had bits of various published or unpublished works. And in this way seven pages of the manuscript of *The Language of Science* were saved: one in duplicate, and one with the top margin cut off so that we do not know the page number.]

[Page 2 is the Preface:]

Scientific discussion is carried on in a peculiar form of speech. This appears plainly in the use of formulae, and most plainly in mathematical calculation. The language of science claims our interest because it is an abnormal and yet a very important type of speech. To see that it is abnormal we need only recall that a scientific treatise is unintelligible to most persons: it is not enough that one be a speaker of the language (say, English) in which the treatise is written, but one needs also a special supplementary training. To show that scientific speech is important would be to recite the impressive list of our advances in material culture during the last few centuries: most of our discoveries and inventions—in sanitation and medicine, in the supply of food, clothing, shelter, and implements, in transportation, and in construction of every sort—would have been impossible in a society which had not the art of scientific calculation.

It seems, strangely enough, that no student of human speech has ever made a study of this queer and useful outgrowth of language. Having made the attempt, the present writer has reached the conclusion that such a study, apart from its linguistic interest, leads to the solution of certain problems which have baffled non-linguistic attack—the problems which concern the foundations of mathematics. If this conclusion is justified, the following pages should be of wider than linguistic interest.

[Page 3 is the Table of Contents, not complete because there were 31 chapters in all:]

[Page 103 is a carbon copy, in which there are blanks where Bloomfield had inserted penned write-ins in the ribbon copy; but these were not added to the carbon and I cannot guess at them. Therefore I indicate the location of the blanks by an empty pair of brackets·]

The postulates which we have so far adopted promise only that *two*, defined as the Immediate Successor of *one*, is distinct from *one*. They leave open the possibility that *one* may be the Immediate Successor of *two* or of some later term; for instance, the chain of [] might be

$$1, 2, 3, 4, 0, 1, 2, \ldots$$

Systems of arithmetic where this is the case are *modular* systems. The number system of English and of ordinary arithmetic, by contrast, is an infinite system. For it, we must rule out the recurrence of *one* in the chain of the operator *Immediate Successor of*. This demands a recursive definition of the serial operator *Sequent of*, as above given. Then the postulate is:

(05) $x$ [] $y$
    implies
    not $x$ [] $y$.

It is important to observe that this serial operator is not the same as the operator *Successor of* which is used in algebra, for the field of this latter includes speech-forms, such as fractions, which are not in the field of the operator *Immediate Successor of*; hence *Successor of* cannot, like *Sequent of*, be defined in terms of the operator *Immediate Successor of*.

It would be redundant to specify also that *one* is the only thing-noun of whic

Our postulates (O and P) suffice to say that the class Positive Integer is an infinite chain, with first member *one*, of the operator *Immediate Successor of*. It differs from the field of this operator only in that we have left open the possibility of defining speech-forms for the field which will precede *one*, and therefore will not be members of the class Positive Integer. Under the current view, however, the

[Page 163 begins with notations that it is impossible to interpret without the definitions on earlier (missing) pages. At the bottom there is this passage:]

Except for certain special cases of multiplication, we cannot [yet, in terms of the definitions so far given] subject the irrational numbers to ordinary algebraic operations. We still have to adopt postulates defining these in such manner that the rational and irrational numbers will enter consistently into the operations. We can save repetition, however, if we define these operations not merely for algebraic numbers, but for all real numbers that may be defined at any

[Page 179:]

calculate members of an infinite class with limit $\sqrt{2}$ is only a way of confirming the legitimacy of this definition. In fact, we have not even produced a succinct formula to define our infinite class, but have resorted to trial and error to find successive members of it; given a likely-sounding rational number, such as 1.41421, we have to make a calculation to see whether it is a member of the class. An irrational number named by an algebraic formula, such as $\sqrt{2}$ or $72^{\frac{1}{2}} + 3^{\frac{1}{2}}$, is, on the face of it, something very different from a formula defining an infinite class of speech-forms. It is quite another matter that some numbers are defined by means of formulas which name an infinite class of speech-forms.

Any number, indeed, can be defined as a limit. Thus, $\sqrt{2}$ can be named as

$$\lim_{x=2} \sqrt{x},$$

In this instance, however, and generally in the case of irrational numbers of the algebraic type, this formula furnishes no immediate key for the naming of an infinite class of speech-forms with the number as a limit. There are two cases where the limit formula is applicable. On the one hand, every rational number can be named as the limit of a succinctly definable infinite class; on the other hand, there are succinct limit formulas which name irrational numbers. So long as the formula has a place in the field of numerical successorship and is utterable, it will satisfy the definition of a real number.

Let us take first the case of rational numbers. The most familiar method of defining numbers as limits is to name them as sums of fractions and at the same time to use in the denominators of these fractions only some one integer and the integral powers of this integer. If the number to be named has in its denominator some factor which is not a factor of the standard denominator, the

[I think that the page whose number is missing belongs next, but this is not certain:]

For any terminating decimal denotes a rational number, and any circulating [=repeating; this was a perfectly standard term, no longer much used] decimal has a rational number as its limit. Therefore, if we attempt to name a series of the decimal type whose limit will be an irrational number, we must calculate the digits one by one: the decimal will be endless but non-circulating. No matter now many digits we may calculate, the naming will be incomplete. The members of the summation series can be obtained one by one, but we have no finite formula for the direct naming or recognition of these members. To prescribe the naming, in this form, of an irrational number, is to insist that our hearers *complete the recitation* of an infinite class of speech-forms. This fallacy is still current among mathematicians; we shall return to it in Chapter 22.

We have yet to consider the third method of defining irrational numbers: a formula defines an infinite class of rational numbers and orders this class so as to make it approach a limit; this limit then satisfies the definition of a real number, and may be irrational. The following is an important example. The product of the first $n$ positive integers,

$$1 \cdot 2 \cdot 3 \cdot \ldots \cdot n,$$

is called *factorial n*, and is written $n!$ or $\lfloor n$. Thus, $3! = 6$, and $4! = 24$. Now let the class $K$ consist of all numbers of the form $1/n!$ and let this class be well-ordered according to the natural order of $n$; then the sequence is:

$$1, 1/2, 1/6, 1/24, 1/120, \ldots,$$

and it evidently has the limit zero. The summation sequence is:

$$1, 1+1/2, 1+1/2+1/6, \ldots,$$

and the limit of this summation sequence is named by the serial sum

$$\lim_{n=\infty} 1 + 1/2! + 1/3! + \cdots + 1/n! + \cdots.$$

[Page 213:]

We now change to a level of discourse where the $R$'s are thing-nouns. They are members of a class $\Phi$, which is defined as follows. (1) Say *decimal point*; (2) recite any sequence of digits or none; (3) name a second sequence of digits, not all zeros, as a circulating sequence; if you want to avoid duplicates, this sequence must not be the same as the end of the sequence (2). Then any speech-form of the shape (1)–(2)–(3) or of the shape (1)–(3) is a member of the class $\Phi$.

It may be worth noticing, by way of parenthesis, that we cannot reverse this formula so as to put the class of all decimals that have no integral part into one-one correspondence with the class of all integers. If we named integers in the reverse of the usual order, first the units, then the tens, and so on, only terminating decimals would correspond to integers; non-terminating decimals would correspond to infinite recitations of digits, which are not numbers.

Given the class $\Phi$, together with a formula for well-ordering it, such as that in the above array, we can define, *as functions of* $\Phi$, infinite classes of speech-forms of the type $N$. For instance, we add 1 to the $k$th digit of the $k$th $R$, except that when the sum is 10 we replace it by 1. We thus obtain the infinite class of speech-forms $N^1$, the non-circulating decimals whose first ten digits are .5471111117. This formula for naming $N^1$, is stated in terms of $\Phi$ and its well-ordering: a digit of $N^1$ can be named only if one first names $k$ digits of the $k$th $R$. Hence to calculate and recite digits of $N^1$ to the end of one's patience is not to name a number: it is only the formula $N^1$, interpreted as above, which names a number.

# B48. Initial [k-] in German

1938. *Language* 14.178–186.

[Delivered at the first Summer Meeting of the Linguistic Society, Ann Arbor. We omit the bracketed summary printed at the beginning of the article.]

It is generally said that the HG dialects have shifted WGic initial [p-, t-, k-] to affricates [pf-, ts-, kx-]: *pound, ten, cold* appear as [pfunt, tsɛːn, kxalt].[1] The shifted form of [t-] runs north roughly to the Benrath Line (*machen* : *maken*). The shifted form of [p-] covers in the west a smaller area: Spires, Mannheim, Fulda have [p-], as appears on Map 3 of Wrede, Deutscher, Sprachatlas, Marburg 1926 ff. In the East Central dialects, [pf-] has largely undergone a further shift to [f-]. The shift of [k-] to [kx-] seems to cover a much smaller territory: Switzerland (except Basle) and some adjoining districts. In most of this area there has been a further shift of [kx-] to [x-]. It is only this latter representation that can be plotted on maps, such as Map 3 of the Atlas. Where [k-] has not been shifted to [kx-] or [x-], it appears as an aspirated fortis stop. As the distinction between affricate and aspirated fortis is merely one of degree, we cannot draw a line between dialects which have shifted WGic [k-] and those which have not. This, the accepted view, will be found, for instance, in Behaghel, Geschichte der deutschen Sprache[5] (=Paul, Grundriss 3) 421 ff., Berlin 1928.

Braune Althochdeutsche Grammatik[3] 75, Halle 1911, stated the matter differently: the shift was [k-] > [kh-] and extended, at any rate in OHG

---

[1] G: German; Gic: Germanic; H: high; M: middle; O: old; W: west.

Author's name and date replace the full citation of a title in the following cases: the study is listed in Mentz, Bibliographie der deutschen Mundartenforschung, Leipzig 1892 (=Sammlung kurzer Grammatiken deutscher Mundarten 2) or in Martin, Bibliographie zur deutschen Mundartforschung und -dichtung in den Jahren 1921–1926, Bonn 1929 (=Teuthonista, Beiheft 2); the study appeared in ZfdMa, Teuthonista, or ZfdMundartforschung before 1938; the study was reviewed in one of these journals or listed in Jahresbericht fgPh in the year of publication or in the next following year. As the studies are mostly short, and the treatment of [k-] easily found, I have not cluttered the text with page references.

Forms in brackets are normalized from the transcriptions of the various authors, or else are normalized OHG; starred forms in brackets are typical G, with unshifted consonants and weakening of unstressed vowels, or else typical pre-G.

times, over Bavarian and Alemannic, but not into Franconian. This comes nearer the truth, but still falls short of it.

For practical phonetics, from the standpoint of North German, Standard German, or general European pronunciation, the current statement is fair enough, but its value is only 'practical': it is irrelevant to the phoneme system of the HG dialects—and this system is the only relevant frame of reference for a definition of shifted and unshifted consonants.

The term 'affricate' is trivial, since in HG, as perhaps in all Gic speech, a succession of stop plus spirant is spoken always in the affricate manner, with the organs as far as possible in position for the spirant at the moment when the stop is opened. We should say, therefore, that in the HG dialects which shift WGic [p-, t-, k-], these sounds are represented by combinations of a stop and a spirant formed in the same general region of the mouth. Thus, in some dialects, the genitive [ts] *des* is homonymous with the short form of the preposition [ts] *zu*, and a syntactic combination like [t supə] *die Suppe* has the same initial as [tsi:t] *Zeit*; similarly, such a dialect may have [p fyəss] *die Füsze* with the same initial as [pfunt] *Pfund*; see, for instance, Winteler 44 ff. (1876).

A distinction between an affricate [kx-] and an aspirated stop [kh-] can be made in few of the dialects, perhaps only in some of those which have the further shift to [x-]. Some such dialects distinguish [kxy:t] *gekaut*, [k xuə] *die Kuh* from [kholt] *geholt*, [khai] *kein*; compare Winteler 136. The [x-] dialects, however, offer no difficulty: they have shifted WGic [k-] and they are plainly distinguishable from the rest. The distinction between an affricate (as a shifted [k-]) and an aspirated stop (as an unshifted [k-]) is needed under the current formulation precisely for the dialects that do not have the further shift to [x-]. Within these dialects there is no such distinction, and it has been repeatedly observed that, passing from one dialect to another, we can draw no line between dialects that have an 'affricate' and dialects that have an 'unshifted' but 'aspirated' stop; see, for instance, Bohnenberger, ZfdA 45.368 (1913). Whether a dialect has an 'affricate' or an 'aspirated stop' for WGic [k-] is a question irrelevant to the phoneme system of these dialects. It has no meaning, unless, indeed, we decide to set up a precise but arbitrary distinction, in terms of sound waves or articulatory movements, and make mechanical records for each dialect. If the laboratory is equipped to do this, one may still question whether the results would be of any interest.

When we say that WGic [p-, t-, k-] appear in HG dialects which shift them, as combinations of stop plus related spirant (apart, always, from the further shifts to [f-] and [x-]), then the special character of these combinations is determined for each dialect. Most HG dialects conform to Heusler's Law (Heusler 24 [1888]): in clusters of unvoiced sounds (that is, stops and spirants) there is no distinction of lenis and fortis, but uniformly an intermediate sound. Some HG dialects, to be sure, are not covered by Heusler's Law and are capable of such distinctions as [kne:xd] *Knecht*, plural [knexxt] *Knechte*; cf. Nagl 396 (1886). As for clusters in word initial, however, barring, as always, the [x-] dialects, and apart from phenomena of sandhi, only one type seems to occur in any one dialect. Exceptions, real or apparent, will concern us below.

In the phoneme system of our dialects, then, WGic [k-] is represented, apart from further shifting to [x-], quite like [p-] and [t-], by the combination of stop plus related spirant: [kx-, kh-, gh-], quite like [ts-] or [ds-] and [pf-] or [bf-]. The shifted form covers a large area, larger, in the west, than the shifted form of [p-].

A historical accident gives us the evidence for this statement. Over the southerly portion of the HG area, the prefixes [bə-] and [gə-] have lost their vowel before various initial consonants. Hence a form like [pfoktə] *bevogten* (Winteler 54) could be adduced to show that a form like [pfunt] *Pfund* contains phonemically stop plus spirant. Similarly, in a large block of HG dialects a form like [kxaltən, khaltən, ghaltən] *gehalten* has the same initial as a form like [kxalt, khalt, ghalt] *kalt*. Generally [kxain, khain, ghain] *kein* < *[bəh-ain] has the same initial. Hence, apart from the dialects which have [x-], we obtain proof, for a large body of dialects, that WGic [k-] before vowel has gone through the HG consonant shift and is represented by a combination of stop plus spirant.

The shift of [k-] in most dialects has taken place only before vowels. Before [l, r, n] WGic initial [k-] has remained as a stop and has, accordingly, coincided with WGic [g-]: [klain, glain] *klein* like [kla:s, gla:s] *Glas*, [kru:t, gru:t] *Kraut* like [kra:s, gra:s] *Gras*, [knext, gnext] *Knecht* like [kna:d, gna:d] *Gnade* < *[gəna:bə] with old loss of prefix vowel. In the same way, unshifted WGic [t-] before [r] has coincided with WGic [d-]: *treten* like *Traum*. Only the [x-] dialects and a southern portion of the [kx-] dialects distinguish between WGic [k-] in the form [x-] or [kx-] and WGic [g-] in the form [k-] or [g-] before [l, r, n]. There is also an intermediate type of dialect in which WGic [kl-, kn-] coincide with WGic[gl-, gn-], but [kr-] (as also the reflex of [gə-r-]) appears as [kxr-], while [gr-] is kept; see Jutz, Teuthonista 6.46 (1929).

Some of the authors who describe our dialects state explicitly that the reflex of [k-] before vowels coincides with that of [gə-h-]; others show by their transcription that the two have coincided; the actual shape of the transcription [kx-, kh-, gh-, k-] does not matter. Now and then, to be sure, an author writes [k-] or [kh-] for WGic [k-] but [gh-] for [gə-]; this does not always mean that a phonetic distinction is intended. Texts in traditional orthography occasionally yield evidence by writing *k-* in words that have or once upon a time had the structure [gə-h-]. For the loss of vowel in [gə-h-] we cannot use Map 28 of the Atlas, which plots the forms of *ge(brochen)*, since the treatment of the prefix differs before different consonants.

Our citations, then, show that the coincidence of [k-] as in [ghalt] *kalt*, with [gəh-] as in [ghaltən] *gehalten*, extends over the entire area that has lost the vowel of the prefix [gə-] before [h-]. Beyond this, to the north, our criterion fails. Better knowledge of the phonemics of the dialects would doubtless reveal other criteria, and these would show that the shift of WGic [k-] extends farther toward the north. Apparently the full form of [gə-] has been gaining ground at the expense of the shortened form; hence relic words with [gəh-]=[k-] occasionally furnish a clue.

Finally, a word about the origin of our forms. Before the HG consonant shift, the language had the WGic unvoiced stops [p, t, k], the voiced (later unvoiced lenis) stops [b, d, g], and the unvoiced spirants [f, þ, s, h]—or was [þ] already voiced? The shift of initial [p-, t-, k-] consisted in their replacement by a phoneme of the second series plus a phoneme of the third series; apart from conditions peculiar to the cluster and from later changes, this produced phonemically [bf-, ds-, gh-]. The old spellings of *ch-* for WGic [k-], appropriate to both [x-] and [kx-, kh-], cannot guide us to regional pronunciations.[2]

Our listing of references is greatly facilitated by the publication of Map 56 of the Atlas, which gives Wrede's beautiful classification of the G dialects—this in spite of many drawbacks, above all, the omission of Dutch-Flemish, Swiss, Austrian, Yiddish, and the other colonial dialects. In the pamphlet which accompanies the map, we correct two misprints: on page 248, the third line from the bottom (*ββ. Osthochalemannisch: mähet*) should be at the foot of the page, below the lines that are numbered 1, 1 and 2, 2; on page 251, after line 8 (aa. Bolchen-Birkenfeld: *fescht*), there has dropped out a line containing something like ' bb. Trier-Koblenz: *fest*'. After these corrections are made, we shall replace the very cumbersome sigla by consecutive numbering of the smallest divisions. Thus, the *ich-Apfel* dialects run from 1 to 29; the *ich-Appel* dialects from 30 to 61; and the *ik* dialects from 62 to 99.[3]

---

[2] Of the long fortis spirants which replaced postvocalic [p, t, k], only one was a new phoneme: [Z] from [t], as in [eZZan] 'eat'; the other two, [ff] from [p] and [hh] from [k], coincided, so far as one can see, with sounds already in the language: [offan] 'open' like [heffen] 'heave' <*[haffjan], and [mahho:n] 'make' like [hlahhen] 'laugh'<*[hlahhjan]. New phonemes arose through (later) shortening of these long spirants, [sla:fan] 'sleep' contrasting with [gira:vo] 'reeve' and [bru:xan] 'brook' with [li-han] 'leihen'. In the later development, the spirant of [ts] seems to have resembled the new [Z] rather than the old [s].

[3] Needless to say, we follow the scheme mechanically. However, I have included references to Vienna among Types 1 to 6, even though it is an island of *euch* in the area of *enk*. Wrede's scheme raises a few difficulties of this kind Thus, among the *ich, Apfel, Kind* dialects (Types 10 to 23), it provides for the combination of *Is, Hus* (Baden type) with *mähet* (Swabian type) for a southern region, Type 14; but this combination occurs also farther toward the north. For the *ik* dialects the scheme is self-contradictory. If one knows the geographic provenience of a dialect to begin with, this does no harm; for an *ik* dialect spoken, say, in Iowa, Wrede's

We are concerned, in Wrede's classification, only with the HG or *ich* dialects, Types 1 to 61.

Types 1 to 29 *Apfel* (Upper German) all shift [k-] before vowels, and this appears plainly by our criterion, since here the prefix [gə-] loses its vowel before [h-].

Types 1 to 6 *enk* (Bavarian). Schmeller 1821 did not register our phenomenon; he came close to it in the interesting footnote on page 105. It appears in the studies of Beranek, Die Mundarten von Südmähren, Reichenberg 1936 (= Beiträge zur Kunde sudetendeutscher Mundarten 7): Eichhorn 1928; Gartner 1900; Haasbauer 1924; Hajnal, Az isztiméri német nyelvjárás hangtana, Budapest 1906 (= Magyarországi német nyelvjárások 4): Micko 1930; Nagl 1886; Pfalz 1913; Weigl 1924.

The southernmost of these dialects have the shift also before [l, r, n]: Egger 1909; Gröger 1924; Rudolf 1934; Schatz 1897. Intermediate dialects have the shift before [r], but not before [l, n]: Himmelstosz 1893; Lessiak 1903; Schieszl 1909, 1914; Schöpf 1866 (explicit statement, 297).

In literary sources, the equivalence of [k-] and [gəh-] appears in the conventional spelling of the word *Kälter, Kalter* 'container', representing *Gehälter, Gehalter*: Castelli 1847; Jakob 1929; Mareta 1861; Schmeller-Fromann 1872 (oldest occurrence, 1558). Another such spelling is *keien* 'throw, vex,' representing *geheien*: Hintner 1878; Jakob 1929; Lexer 1862; Mayr 1930; Zaupser 1789. Zaupser has also *kolpet* 'uneven', presumably *geholpicht*. Similarly, dialect texts in conventional spelling; thus, Firmenich, Germaniens Völkerstimmen, vol. 2, Berlin 1846, has 682 *ket'n*, 698 *keit* (Bavaria); 707 *kert* 'gehört', 783 *Koamnusz* 'Geheimnis', 784 *kot* 'gehabt,' 786 *katzt* 'geheizt' (Carinthia); 790 *käu'n* (Lower Austria): vol. 3 (1854) 607 *keiat* 'gehört' (Eger Region).

Types 7 to 29 *euch* (Alemannic-Franconian). For a large body of these dialects, Jutz 1931, 220, states the equivalence of [k-] and [gəh-].

Types 7 to 9 *fescht, Chind* (Upper Alemannic) have [x-] and need not concern us here. An interesting singularity appears in the dialect spoken

scheme would not work. Doubtless, the discussion of the scheme promised for a forthcoming number of Deutsche Dialektgeographie will clear up such matters. Whoever has tried to classify dialects will appreciate Wrede's skill. The divisions make solid blocks and are based on common forms and on differences recognizable even in the poorest transcription.

Even so, we shall sometimes go wrong in placing a dialect. Strange as it may seem, extensive essays about a dialect sometimes fail to give us such forms as *us* or *you* or the imperative *be*. Powerful and deep-seated inhibitions block the study of language, especially of one's own language. One seeks means of evasion, and these may in time grow conventional. In the nineteenth century, the recording of G dialects was usually replaced by a meagre listing of correspondences with MHG. Today the convention leans rather to geographic discussion of borrowing; here too the information often runs very thin, with sometimes scarcely a speech form to a page. The genuine record of a dialect, such as we have in Roedder's Volkssprache und Wortschatz, New York 1936, is almost or altogether unique. Yet without the protocol, there is little value in scientific pretensions.

References which deal with more than one dialect may appear under several types.

on the Tann Mountain (Type 9, Rudolf 1934). This dialect has [x-] not only in [xind] *Kind*, but also for [gəh-], as in [xolfa] *geholfen* or [xeŋ] *Gehänge*. Presumably the [x-] pronunciation was here borrowed by speakers of [kx-] in whose dialect [k-] and [gə-h] had already coincided.

Types 10, 11 *fescht, Kind, Is, Hüs* (Alsatian types). Here Martin-Lienhart 1899 print [khalt] for both *kalt* and *Gehalt*. Menges, Volksmundart und Volksschule im Elsasz 20, Gebweiler 1893, says: 'Nur wenn b und g vor h stehen, werden sie zu p und k. Behalten und gehören heiszen mundartlich palte und kere'. Special studies: Enterle, Die Mundarten der Landschaft Freiburg im Breisgau, Bühl 1936 (=Bausteine zur Volkskunde und Religionswissenschaft 14): Heimburger 1888; Henry 1900; Kilian 1935; Lienhart 1891; Mankel 1886; Schwend 1900; Sütterlin 1892.

Types 12 to 14 *fescht, Kind, Is, Hus* (Black Forest type). Ehret 1911 in the phonetic part of his study says (34) that his [k-] represents MHG [k-] before vowels as well as the prefix [gə-] before (he means plus) [h-]; in the historical part (39, 49) he says, however, that [gə-] before (read plus) [h-] appears as a strongly aspirated [kh-], more strongly aspirated than the reflex of [k-]. Heilig 1900, for Bahlingen (97) has [kummə] *kommen* and both [ka:] and [gha:] *gehabt*; for Kenzingen (168, 361) he gives [kumə] and [ka:] as well as [kaldə] *gehalten*, and so for all past particles of verbs in [h-] except [kho:lt] *geholt*. On page 93 he has [kepf] *Köpfe* and [ghalda] *gehalten*. Also Lau 1903 has [kennə] *kennen* but [khaltə] *gehalten*; he has, however, [kin] *kein*. Against this, the usual state of affairs is attested by Dreher, Laut- und Flexionslehre der Mundart von Liggersdorf und Umgebung, dissertation Tübingen 1919; Heilig 1897, 1914; Heusler 1888; Jäger 1903; Ketterer 1930; Kilian 1935; Schlager 1931; Staedele 1927; Wasmer 1915 (he writes [k-] and [gh-] but on page 336 says they are alike); Weik, Lautlehre der Mundart von Rheinbischofsheim, dissertation of Freiburg i. B., Halle 1913. Likewise, for the intermediate southern type, Marte 1910; for the full southern type, Jutz 1925.

Types 15 to 19 *fescht, Kind, Eis mähet* (Swabian). For this group as a whole, Bohnenberger 1928 and Kauffmann 1890 attest [k-]=[gəh-]. Fischer, in his Geographie 66 (1895), has [kx-, kh-] for [k-] and, page 63, [gh-] for [gə-]; in his Wörterbuch 1904 ff., however, he expressly discusses (3.111) the coincidence of [k-] and [gə-] and refers to spellings of *k-* for [gə-], such as *kaim* for *geheim*, and to inverse spellings, such as *Gehebs* for *Kebse* (date, 1350). The special studies confirm this: Bopp, Der Vokalismus des Schwäbischen in der Mundart von Münsingen, dissertation Straszburg 1890; Haag, Die Mundarten des oberen Nackar- und Donaulandes, school program, Reutlingen 1898; Heissl 1935; Keinath 1930; Knupfer 1912; Meisinger, Die Rappenauer Mundart, I. Lautlehre, dissertation Heidelberg 1901; Theodor Müller 1911; Rudolf 1934; Schlager 1931; Veit 1901 (p. 9: [ghed] *gehabt*, [kald] *kalt*, 'trotz des völlig identischen Anlauts der beiden Wörter'; censured by Meisinger ZfdMa 2.283 [1901]); Vogt 1931; Wagner 1889, 1891; Weishaupt 1935; Zinser 1933. In traditional orthography, *k*- for [gǝh-] appears in Firmenich, vol. 2, 427 *keiht*, 435 *keia*, 442 *keiha*, 469 *kaihr* 'gehöre', 487 *koit*.

For colonial dialects of this type (Type 19) in Transcaucasia, Schirmunski 1928 transcribes both [k-] and [gǝh-] as [kh-] but says that the latter has stronger aspiration.

Types 20 to 23 *fescht, Kind, Eis, mähe* (Alemannic-Franconian border type). Braun 1906 has [komǝ] *kommen*, [kuǝ] *Kuh*, and [khe:rd] *gehört* for some of his localities, but [ke:rd] *gehört* for others. All the other evidence is for [k-] = [gǝh-]: Blumenstock 1911; Boger 1935; Breunig, Die laute der Mundart von Buchen, school program, Tauberbischofsheim 1891; Dietzel 1908; Knupfer 1912; Lauinger, Lautlehre der Mundart des Dorfes Spessart, Heidelberg dissertation, Leipzig 1929; Mangold 1930; Meisinger 1901; Nohe 1901; Reichert 1914; Roedder, Volkssprache und Wortschatz des badischen Frankenlandes, New York 1936; Sander 1916; F. G. G. Schmidt 1898; Sexauer 1927; Waibel 1932; Wanner 1907, 1908.

For the colonial dialect near Leningrad (Type 22), Ströhm 1926.

Types 24 to 29 *fest* (Upper Franconia, Thuringia). Our criterion applies to only part of the area, since the more northerly districts keep the vowel in [gǝ-].

Type 24 (Nuremberg): Gebhardt 1907 has, for instance, [gha:ut] *gehauen* and [khu:ǝrn] *Korn*, but in his phonetic survey says not a word about this. Hans Sachs wrote *Gehalter* with *k*- (Schmeller-Frommann, s. v.) and Hanz Folz' printers render the word with *k*- in verse 103 of the poem reprinted by Keller, Fastnachtspiele, vol. 3 (=Bibliothek des Stuttgarter Literarischen Vereins 30 [1853]), p. 1215; the facsimile of a different printing in Hampe, Drucke und Holzschnitte, vol. 2, Straszburg 1899, has the same spelling; and so has a third printing, preserved at Wolfenbüttel (photostat in University of Chicago Library).

Type 25 (Ansbach, Bamberg, Hof): Batz 1912 (Bamberg); Schübel, Versuch einer Charakteristik und Phonetik der Bamberger Mundart von Stadtsteinach, Munich dissertation, Halle 1911.

Type 26 (Vogtland). Our criterion holds only for the southern part: Gerbet 1908; this is confirmed for Schöneck by Hedrich 1891.

Type 27 (Rothenburg, Würzburg, Meiningen, Salzungen) yields evidence for the south: Foerster 1913 (Neustadt); Heilig 1898 (Taubergrund); Lenz 1887 (Handschuhsheim).

Types 28 and 29 give no evidence, since here [gǝ-] keeps its vowel.

Types 30 to 61, *Appel* dialects (Central German).

Types 30 to 47 *Pund* (Western). The shift of [k-] extends to dialects that have not shifted [p-].

Type 31 *was, fescht, Eis, gebroch* (Western Palatinate) keeps the vowel of [gə-]; however, Christmann 1927 has [kärmsə] 'sich härmen', which is evidently a relic with [gəh-] = [k-]. The colonial dialect in Hungary described by Lindenschmidt, A verbászi német nyelvjárás alaktana, Budapest 1905 (= Magyarországi német nyelvjárások 2) belongs to this type but has preserved the shortened form of the prefix and has [k-] = [gəh-].

Type 32 *gebroche* (Eastern Palatinate) consistently has [k-] = [gəh-] wherever the prefix has lost its vowel: Bertram, Die Mundart der mittleren Vorderpfalz, Erlangen 1937 (= Fränkische Forschungen 7) for the district just west of Spires; Bräutigam 1934 (Mannheim); Freiling 1929 (Odenwald, about Zell); Heeger 1896 (Lingenfeld, Landau, Rheinzabern); Treiber 1931 (Plankstatt); Wenz 1911 (Beerfelden in the southern Odenwald).

The same holds true of colonial dialects in this type: in Hungary, Kräuter, A niczkyfalvai német nyelvjárás hangtana, Budapest 1907 (= Magyarországi német nyelvjárások 5); Heinrich F. Schmidt 1911; in the Banat, Weifert 1935; in the Neva Region in Russia, Ströhm 1926.

Types 33 to 38 *fest* (Hessian) generally retain the vowel of [gə-]; only for the district Fürth, Lindenfels, Reisen (the upper Weschnitz valley) Weber 1908 attests [k-] = [gəh-] for a dialect of Type 35. In Hungary, Schäfer, A kalaznoi német nyelvjárás hangtana, Budapest 1908 (= Magyarországi német nyelvjárások 6), belonging in Type 35 or 36, has [k-] = [gəh-].

Types 48 to 61 *Fund* (Eastern). Our evidence extends only to Type 50 (Southern Upper Saxon), since only here does [gə-] lose its vowel: Gerbet 1900 (Klingenthal); Goepfert 1878 (Freiberg and environs); Hausenblas 1898 (Brüx); 1914 (Brüx, Postelberg). Farther north in Type 50, [gə-] has kept its vowel. For Zwickau, Gerbet 1900 gives the relic form [khak] *Gehäcke*, with initial like that of [khumə] *kommen*. Philipp 1897 says that the lower-class speech of Zwickau drops the vowel of [gə-], but he gives no example of this before [h-].

For colonial dialects, we have [k-] = [gə-] in Weifert 1934 (Weisskirchen, Bela Crkva, in the Banat); this dialect uses [eŋk] for 'you' dative and accusative plural, but belongs in Wrede's Type 50. Similarly, Gréb 1922 (Deutsch-Pilsen). The Zips dialect described by Gröger 1911 belongs in Type 50; it preserves the vowel of [gə-] but has (58) [ka:jə'ra:j] 'vexation', from [gəh-], with the same initial as [kimt] *kommt*.

# B49. Obituary of Prokosch

1938. *Language* 14.310–313.

Eduard Prokosch was born in Eger, Bohemia, on the 15th of May, 1876. His father was the principal of a grammar school. Prokosch graduated from the classical gymnasium of his native city in 1894, and then studied law in Prague and Vienna, passing the state bar examination in 1897. He came to the United States in 1898 and served for a time as secretary of the Austrian vice-consulate in Milwaukee. In 1900 he completed a course of training at the German-American Teachers' Seminary.

Prokosch was married in 1901 to Mathilde Dapprich of Baltimore; his wife survives him, as do their three children, Gertrude, who is the wife of Professor Hans Kurath of Brown University, Frederic, well known as a poet and novelist, and Walther, an architect.

From 1901 to 1904 Prokosch served as an instructor in German at the University of Chicago; at the same time he pursued his studies, receiving the degree of M.A. in 1901. During the summer semester of 1904 he studied at Heidelberg, and during the following two semesters at Leipsic, where in 1905 he took his doctor's degree under Sievers. His thesis was entitled: Beiträge zur Lehre vom Demonstrativpronomen in den altgermanischen Dialekten.[1]

From 1905 to 1913 Prokosch taught at the University of Wisconsin. In the latter year he was called to the University of Texas as professor of Germanic philology; he lost this position during the war, chiefly because of a correct factual statement in his text book Introduction to German (published in 1911) concerning the representation, under the Empire, of the German people in the Reichstag.

An enlightened administration called Prokosch to Bryn Mawr College; he taught there from 1919 to 1928. During the academic year 1927–28, in addition to his professorship at Bryn Mawr, Prokosch held a research fellowship at Yale and served as head of the department of German at New York University; this latter position he held also during the next year. In 1929 he was called to Yale University as professor (after 1930, Stirling professor) of Germanic languages.

---

[1] Published Halle a. S., 1906.

Prokosch was a Signer of the Call that lead to the foundation of the Linguistic Society of America, president of the Society in 1930, and its delegate to the American Council of Learned Societies at the time of his death. For several summers he taught in the Linguistic Institute of the Society.

He took an equally active part in the Modern Language Association of America, serving as treasurer 1924–8, on the Executive Council, on the Committee on Research Activities, and as president in 1937.

In recent years he has helped many displaced German scholars start life anew in this country.

His life ended in an automobile accident on August 11, 1938.

Eduard Prokosch found it possible to work sixteen hours a day; he forgot nothing that he had attentively heard or read; he did not know the meaning of worry, pain, or fear and he dealt kindly and understandingly with people and with dogs. His knowledge was vast, not only in his professional domain and in German literature (which he treated as a hobby), but also in apparently remote matters of science and of practical life. He walked, skated, and swam without fatigue, made himself equally at home in forest or city, and dealt plainly and agreeably with all manners of persons and situations. His sense of humor was excellent and even boisterous, but one was likely to find humor in his serious speech, for, seeing more clearly than most men, he ignored so many pretences, postures, and superstitions that his serious statements had often the devastating effect of sheer humor. Affairs of society and politics, including even the Great War, left him intellectually unmoved, however senseless he might find them. He once called himself an anarchist, a puzzling description, since he belonged to no sect; doubtless he meant to indicate his failure to participate in obnoxious or merely pompous conventions. One evening, watering the lawn, he laid down the hose to step toward me, who had come for a visit; his three-year-old daughter picked up the hose and drenched him. 'Now Papa will have to go upstairs', he said, 'and change his clothes.' This method of educating children as well as pupils succeeded admirably, though lesser men might not be well advised to try it.

Of Prokosch as a teacher one can speak only in personal terms. In the summer of 1906 I came, fresh out of college, to Madison, to be looked over for an assistantship. Desiring to earn an academic living, I had developed no understanding or inclination for any branch of science. The kindly Professor Hohlfeld delegated Prokosch, one of his young instructors, to entertain me for the day. On a small table in Prokosch's dining room there stood a dozen technical books (I seem to remember that Leskien's Old Bulgarian grammar was among them) and in the interval before lunch Prokosch explained to me their use and content. By the time we sat down to the meal, a matter perhaps of fifteen minutes, I had decided that I should always work in linguistics. At the end of the two years of pupilhood that followed, I knew no greater intellectual pleasure than to listen to Prokosch. Apart from the specific direction to linguistics, this incident must be multiplied into hundreds, if one would estimate the effect of Prokosch as a guide to younger people.

Beside his graduate classes, Prokosch taught his quota of sections of elementary German. The vague optimism of treatises on Methods of Teaching Foreign Languages turned into dust when Prokosch explained the nature of this work. Every form, lexical or grammatical, which he uttered before the class, was registered in a card index, with provision for its recurrence. He used, of course, the 'direct method', though these words may mean little or nothing. Copious deliberations and surveys have brought this matter no farther today than Prokosch had carried it in 1906. His Introduction to German is probably still the best beginner's German book, but it is scholarly, requiring study on the part of the pupil and a command of German on the part of the teacher.[2] Later, less sinewy versions and supplements adapted the content to more popular use.[3] The beginner's book in Russian covers less ground, but dealing with a more difficult language, serves better to illustrate the methodical approach.[4]

Of Prokosch's scientific publications, Sounds and History of the German Language and An Outline History of the German Language pursue a pedagogic aim, but contain many original views.[5] The Faust essay was the outgrowth of a hobby.[6] Prokosch's more strictly technical studies—apart from the comparative grammar of the Germanic languages, which is still in press—sufficed to give him an international reputation and to put him easily at the head of Germanic students in our country.[7] One

[2] New York (Holt) 1911.

[3] German for beginners, 1913; Deutsches Lese- und Übungsbuch, 1913; Deutscher Lehrgang. Erstes Jahr, 1916; First German lessons in phonetic spelling, 1916; Konversations- und Lesebuch (with C. M. Purin), 1916; all published by Holt in New York. Compare also The teaching of German in secondary schools, Austin, Texas, 1915 (Bulletin of the University of Texas, Number 4); I have not seen The college teaching of German, 1920.

[4] Elementary Russian grammar, Chicago (University of Chicago Press) 1920.

[5] The former was published in 1916 by Holt, the latter in 1934 by the Oxford Press.

[6] In Studies in German literature in honor of A. R. Hohlfeld 184–216. Madison, Wisconsin, 1925. (University of Wisconsin studies in language and literature, Number 22.)

[7] The following is surely an incomplete list: AJP 32.434 (1911); 33.195 (1912); 38.432 (1917); GR 1.47 (1926); JEGP 11.1 (1912); 16.1 (1917); 20.468 (1921); 21.119 (1922); MP 11.71 (1913); 26.459 (1929); IF 33.377 (1914); PMLA 42.331 (1927); Studies in English philology in honor of F. Klaeber 196 (1929); Studies in honor of H. Collitz 70 (1930); a series of articles in the 1930 volume of Monatshefte für deutsche Sprache und Pädagogik, Milwaukee. Reviews: JEGP 21.353 (1922); 22.298 (1923); 24.135 (1925); 32.225 (1933); MP 15.59 (1917); 21.331 (1923); LANGUAGE 9.89 (1933). [The work awaiting publication at the time of Prokosch's death appeared in 1939: A Comparative Germanic Grammar (William Dwight Whitney Linguistic Series, Special Publications of the Linguistic Society of America), Philadelphia. Hans Kurath saw this work through the press, with assistance from Bernard Bloch and Margaret Chase George.—CFH]

finds here clarity, originality, and an immediate grasp of the concrete. Nevertheless, those who knew Prokosch found that these writings expressed only a minor phase of the man. He strode gallantly and brightly through a world that was not ready to make full use of his powers.

# B50. Menomini Morphophonemics

1939. *Études phonologiques dédiées à la mémoire de N. S. Trubetzkoy* (*Travaux du Cercle Linguistique de Prague* 8) 105–115.

[Bloomfield was like other scholars of his generation—and of ours—in his participation in volumes prepared to honor a fellow scholar or his memory. Apparently, when the invitation came to contribute something to this particular memorial volume, he drew on his ongoing and constantly-revised grammar of Menomini, rewriting the section on morphophonemics to stand as an independent article rather than as a connected part of a book. He had not been too happy about the technical term 'morphophonemics' and had rarely used it before 1939 (it does not appear in the 1933 textbook); yet the article here reprinted has been hailed as one of the two germinal papers in American morphophonemic theory, the other being M. Swadesh and C. F. Voegelin's 'A Problem in Phonological Alternation,' which was published in the same year (*Language* 15.1–10).

Except for one point, the information about Menomini in this article is all included, with improved organization, in Bloomfield's *The Menomini Language* (†1962), most of it in chapter 4. The one exception is serious. In his constantly manifested desire to write as simply and clearly as the facts allowed, he revised one series of statements in such a way that they are wrong. The formulation of alternation of vowel length in §4.52 of the book is in error; the earlier statement, in §§32–33 of this paper, is difficult to follow but correct. As Editor of Bloomfield's Algonquian materials for posthumous publication I did not catch this; it was pointed out to me in the fall of 1967 by K. V. Teeter. To make the matter clear, I have inserted directly after §§32–33 below a paraphrase in modern 'how to do it' terms. The insertion is marked as from my pen—the style of presentation is not at all like Bloomfield's.

The passage from this article to which reference has most often been made in recent years is §4, where Bloomfield describes the extent to which the morphophonemic adjustments of the present-day language and the history of the language can be viewed as parallel.]

**1.** The Menomini language is spoken by some 1700 people in Wisconsin; most, but not all, speak English as a first or second language; some, especially among the pagans, have also a speaking knowledge of Ojibwa or Potawatomi. Menomini texts will be found in Publications of the American Ethnological Society, volume 12 (New York 1928). Menomini belongs to the widespread Algonquian family of languages; see Michelson in the 28th Annual Report of the American Bureau of Ethnology (Washington 1912).

**2.** Analysis of Menomini speech-forms by formal-semantic resemblances yields a fairly clean division of forms into phrases, compound words, and simple words. The words in a phrase and the members in a compound word differ but little in different combinations; such variations as occur, constitute the *external* or *syntactic* sandhi of the language and will not be discussed in this paper. Simple words and the members of compounds, in turn, resolve themselves, under analysis, into morphologic elements which vary greatly in different combinations; the present paper describes these variations, the *internal sandhi* or *morphophonemics* of the language.

**3.** It is necessary to distinguish these morphophonemic alternations from certain others, which we may call *morpholexical* variations. In Menomini, as in other Algonquian languages, different words often contain morphological elements of otherwise identical meaning but differing somewhat in form. Thus, the word tahkīkamiw *it is cold water* contains a suffix -kamy- *water*, *liquid*, but this form of the suffix occurs only in a few words; the freely usable form of the suffix is -ākamy-, which may, of course, be described as consisting of -kamy- and a presuffixal element -ā-: menwākamiw *it is a good liquid*, apīsākamiw *it is black liquid*, maskāwākamiw *it is strong liquid*, and so on. These morpholexical variations are quite distinct from internal sandhi; we shall deal with them only to the extent that they appear in the necessary preliminary survey of morphology, §§6 to 9.

**4.** The process of description leads us to set up each morphological element in a theoretical *basic* form, and then to state the deviations from this basic form which appear when the element is combined with other elements. If one starts with the basic forms and applies our statements (§§10 and following) in the order in which we give them, one will arrive finally at the forms of words as they are actually spoken. Our basic forms are not ancient forms, say of the Proto-Algonquian parent language, and our statements of internal sandhi are not historical but descriptive, and appear in a purely *descriptive order*. However, our basic forms do bear some resemblance to those which would be set up for a description of Proto-Algonquian, some of our statements of alternation (namely, those in §§10 to 18) resemble those which would appear in a description of Proto-Algonquian, and the rest (§§19 and following), as to content and order, approximate the historical development from Proto-Algonquian to present-day Menomini.

In our theoretical forms we shall separate morphologic constituents by hyphens. The symbol ~ means "is replaced in alternation by". The colon (:) means "appearing in the actual Menomini word"; the word cited after a colon will generally involve alternations which have not yet been stated at the time of citation, but a reader who has gone through all of our statements will be able, returning to the citation, to account for all of these features.

5. The morphophonemes in our basic forms are:

Syllabics (short and long vowels)

|         | front |   |   | back |   |   |
|---------|-------|---|---|------|---|---|
| higher  | e ē   |   |   | o u ō |  |   |
| lower   | ə ɛ ɛ̄ |   |   | a ā  |   |   |

Non-Syllabics

| semivowels  | y w |   |   |   |   |   |   |   |   |   |
|-------------|-----|---|---|---|---|---|---|---|---|---|
| consonants  | p   | t | k | č | s | h | ʔ | m | n | N |

In actual speech, ə is replaced by e, §36, and N by n, §13. On the other hand, the alternations result in two additional phonemes i and ī §§20, 35 and a semi-phoneme ū, §35. The morphophoneme u seems to occur in only one suffix, -uw- forming transitive verbs, as pītuwɛw *he brings it to him*; in the actual language, u arises also by the alternation of §35. Hence the actual Menomini phonemes are

Syllabics (short and long vowels)

|       | front |   | back    |
|-------|-------|---|---------|
| high  | i ī   |   | u (ū)   |
| mid   | e ē   |   | o ō     |
| low   | ɛ ɛ̄   |   | a ā     |

Non-Syllabics

| semivowels  | y | w |   |   |   |   |   |   |   |
|-------------|---|---|---|---|---|---|---|---|---|
| consonants  | p | t | k | č | s | h | ʔ | m | n |

The *clusters* in our basic forms are

| č | before | p, k |
|---|--------|------|
| s | before | p, t, k |
| ʔ | before | p, t, k, č, s, n |
| h | before | p, t, k, č, s, n |
| n | before | p, t, k, č, s |

In the actual language, the basic clusters of n plus consonant are replaced by those with h plus consonant, §23. In the basic forms, any consonant or cluster may be followed by one or two semivowels; in the actual language such combinations are greatly restricted by §16 and §20.[1]

---

[1] A few phonetic indications, while not strictly relevant, may be of interest. The high vowels, i, ī, u, ū, are much as in French *mis*, *mise*, *doux*, *blouse*; the long mid vowels ē, ō

**6.** The morphologic features of Algonquian appear in three layers: inflection, secondary derivation, and primary formation. All three consist chiefly in the use of suffixes. Processes other than suffixation demand some preliminary comment (§§7 to 9).

**7.** In inflection, suffixes are added to stems of nouns, verbs, and a few particles. Four prefixes are used in inflection: kɛ- *thou*, Nɛ- *I*, wɛ *he*, and, occurring only in some dependent nouns (§9), mɛ- *indefinite personal possessor*: kenɛh *they hand or arm*, kenɛhkenawan *our (inclusive) hands*, kenɛhkowawan *your hands*, nenɛh *my hand*, nenɛhkenawan *our (exclusive) hands*, onɛh *his hand* (§17), onɛhkowawan *their hands*, menɛh *someone's hand, a hand*. Before a vowel, the prefixes (in their basic form, hence by morpholexical variation, §3), add t: ōs *canoe*, ketōs *they canoe*, otōnowaw *their canoe*, and so on.

There are certain irregularities of prefixation, of which we shall mention only one: before dependent noun stems (§9) in ē- and ō-, the prefixes drop their vowel: kēyaw *thy body*, nēyaw *my body*, wēyaw *his body*, kōhnɛʔ *thy father*, nōhnɛʔ *my father*, w-ōhn- : ōhnan *his father* (§17), cf. owōhnemaw *the father, a father*.

**8.** Certain inflectional forms of verbs have *initial change*: the first vowel of the stem is altered as follows:

a, ɛ ~ ē: aʔtɛw *it is in place*, ēʔtɛk *that which is in place*; kɛmew- : kemēwah *if it rains*, kēmew- : kēmewah *when it rained*; wɛn-ɛt- : onēt *it is pretty*, wēn-ɛt-k- : wēnɛh *that which is pretty*.

o ~ ō: koskōset *if he wakes up*, kōskoset *when he woke up*.

y- prefixes a: yāčehtok *if he renews it*, ayāčehtok *when he renewed it*.

Stems beginning with consonant plus y or w prefix ay to the y or w: pyāt *if he comes*, payyāt *when he came*; kwāhnɛt *if he jumps*, kaywāhnɛt *when he jumped*.

Otherwise, long vowel prefixes ay: wāpamak *if I look at him*, wayāpamak

---

much as in German *weh, wo*; the short mid vowels e, o somewhat as in English *pit, put*, but ow is somewhat as in English *sowing*; ɛ, ē are even lower than the vowels of American English *bed, bad*; short a ranges from German *hat* to English *hut*; ā from French *pâte* to English *saw*. The semivowels y, w are as in English, but after a non-syllabic, yā, wā are falling diphthongs: payyāt *when he came*, kwāhnɛw *he jumps* are phonetically [payi:at, ku:ahnɛw]. Of the consonants, only m, n are voiced; ʔ is a well-marked glottal stop, often with vocalic echo; p, t, k, č, s are lenes with slow opening. Non-syllabics are often strongly palatalized or labiovelarized by the preceding vowel, initial non-syllabics by the following vowel: mīp *early in the morning* (both consonants palatalized); mwāk *loon* (both consonants labiovelarized); nekiʔs *my son* (palatal k); okīʔsan *his son* (labiovelar k). In word, compound, or close-knit phrase, a long vowel in the next-to-last syllable and a long vowel followed in the next syllable by a short vowel, have a strong stress accent: pakāmɛw *he struck him* (stress on -kā-); pemātɛsew *he lives* (stress on -mā-). This seems to be the only actualized difference between ow and ōw: nēmowak *they dance* (stress on nē-) manētōwak *game animals* (stress on -tō-). Successions of syllables that do not contain such an accent, are varied by less stable ups and downs of stress: pɛʔtɛnamoken *it is said that they touched it by error* will be stressed on the first and third, or on the second and fourth syllables, or in other ways.

*when I looked at him*; āčemit *if he narrates*, ayāčemit *when he narrated*; pōneʔtat *if he ceases*, payōneʔtat *when he ceased*.

There are some irregularities, which we shall not here describe.

**9.** Features of inflection are in some cases retained in secondary derivation. Apart from this, secondary derivation consists in the addition of suffixes to the stems of nouns or verbs, as enēniw *man*, enēniwew *he is a man, manly*.

In primary formation suffixes are added to a root: root mat- *bad*, suffix -aʔnɛmw- *dog*: matāʔnɛm *nasty cur*.

Throughout the morphology, zero suffixes must sometimes be set up. It is a striking feature of Algonquian that in certain cases we must set up the root of a word as zero. In a few verb forms the stem is replaced by zero; thus, the stem ɛn- *say so to* is replaced by zero before the inflectional suffix -ək-: enēw *he says so to him*, ekwāh *the other one says so to him*, netɛkwah *he says so to me*. A large class of noun stems and certain particles contain no root and occur only with the prefixes of §7: these are *dependent* nouns and particles, such as -nɛhk-, -ēyaw-, -ōhn- in §7, or, say (with two suffixes), -ēt-aʔnɛmw- in kētaʔnɛm *thy fellow-cur*, wētaʔnɛmon *his fellow-cur*. No root begins with a cluster; since every word begins with a root or one of the four prefixes, no Menomini word begins with a cluster. The vowel e is probably nowhere to be set up in the first syllable of a basic form.

Roots, like suffixes, show morpholexical variation. Reduplication is the commonest form of this. Normally, it consists in prefixing the first non-syllabic followed by ā: pakam- : pakāmēw *he strikes him*, pā-pakam- : pāpakamēw *he beats him*. There are also irregular types of reduplication, as pōhkonam *he breaks it across by hand*, pōʔpōhkonam *he repeatedly breaks it*.

**10.** When an element ending in non-syllabic precedes an element beginning with a consonant, a *connective* -e- is inserted. Thus, root pōN- *cease* with suffix -m- *by speech* gives pōN-e-m- : pōnemɛw *he stops talking to him*. Contrast, on the one hand, pōN-ɛNem- : pōnēnemɛw *he stops thinking of him*, and, on the other hand, kēhkā-m- : kēhkamɛw *he berates him*.

**11.** If an element ending in vowel plus w precedes an element with initial w, the -e- is used: kaw-e-wēp- : kawēwēpɛnɛw *he flings him prostrate*; contrast kaw-ɛN- : kawēnēw *he lays him prostrate*, and sēk-wēp- : sīkwēpɛnam *he flings it scattering*.

Irregularly, -e- is used between consonant and w in a few combinations, as ɛsp-e-wēp- : espēwēpahɛw *he tosses him aloft by tool or on horns*.

**12.** Irregularly, certain combinations do not take connective -e-. Root ɛn- *thither, thus* with suffix -pahtā- *run*, gives ɛn-pahtā- : ehpāhtaw *he runs thither*; cf. ɛn-ɛNem- : enēnemɛw *he thinks so of him*, and wāk-e-pahtā- :

wākepāhtaw *he runs a crooked course.* Verb stem kɛmewan-, with initial change (§8) kēmewan-, with inflectional suffix -k- gives kēmewan-k- : kēmewāhken *whenever it rains,* kēmewah *when it rained;* cf. kemēwan *it is raining* and ēʔtɛken *whenever it is in place,* ēʔtɛk *when it was in place.*

In such forms, if the first consonant is other than n, it is replaced by h: sēnak-at-k- : sēnakāhken *whenever it is difficult,* sēnakah *when it was difficult;* cf. sanākat *it is difficult;* atōt-pw-: atūhpwan *table,* cf. atōtapiw *he sits on something,* sakīpwak *if I bite him.*

**13.** Before e, ē, y, final t∼č and n∼s. Thus, pyēt-e-m-∼pyēčem- : pīčemɛw *he calls him hither;* cf. pyēt-ohnē- : pītohnɛw *he walks hither.* ɛn-yā-∼ɛsyā- : esyāt *if he goes thither;* cf. ɛn-ohnē- : enōhnɛt *if he walks thither or thus.* -ēn-e-∼-ēse- : wēs *his head;* cf. wēnowawan *their heads.* ōn-e-∼ōse- : ōs *canoe;* cf. ōnan *canoes.* pɛʔt-e-∼pɛʔče- : pēʔč *by error;* cf. pɛʔtɛnam *he touches or handles it by error.*

In a few cases, the mutation is made before the suffix -əh- which derives local particles from nouns: wēseh beside wēneh *on his head.*

Certain n's are not subject to this alternation; we designate these in our basic forms by N; in actual speech, then, this theoretical N is replaced by n.

**14.** Irregularly, in certain forms, t is replaced by s before ɛ and ā. So always before -ɛhk- *by foot or body movement* and -āp- *look:* pyēt- ɛhk-∼ pyēsɛhk- : pīsɛhkaw *it moves hither;* wɛht-āp- : ohsāpomɛw *he looks at him from there,* cf. wɛht-ɛN- : ohtēnam *he takes it from there.* Other suffixes, less often: wɛht-ɛčyē- : ohsēčīnam *he takes it bodily from there.*

**15.** Successive vowels are in every instance modified.

After long, short other than o drops: asyē-ɛN- : asyēN- : asīnam *he pushes it back, rejects it,* cf. kāhtɛnam *he shoves it.* nakā-ɛN- : nakānam *he stops it by hand,* cf. nakāʔtaw *he stops, comes to a standstill.*

ā-o∼ō: kyāʔtā-ohnē : kyāʔtōhnɛw *he walks in a circle,* cf. kyāʔtā-hsemw- : kyāʔtāhsemow *he dances in a circle* and pōN-e-hsemw- : pōne-hsemow *he stops dancing.*

ē-o∼yā: asyē-ohnē- : asyāhnɛw *he walks backwards.*

ā-ā∼ā: nakā-āpyē- : nakāpīnaʔsow *he brings his horses to a stop,* cf. mat-āpyē- : matāpīnaʔsow *he drives badly.*

Between other long vowels, y is inserted. akwā-ēʔn- : akwāyēʔnɛn *it is blown to shore,* cf. akwā-čemē- : akwāčemɛw *he paddles to shore;* asyē-ēʔn- ∼asyēyēʔn- : asīyēʔnemɛw *he blows him back;* wɛNē-āhkw- : onīyāhkwa-hɛw *he gets him up from bed,* cf. wēNē- : onēw *he gets up.*

**16.** After consonant, the first of two semivowels is dropped: ahkɛhkw-yān- : ahkēhkyan *hearth,* cf. ahkēhkoh *in the kettle* (§20); aʔsɛNy-wēk-∼ aʔsɛnwēk- : aʔsɛnīkat *it is hard-woven cloth,* cf. aʔsɛnyak *stones,* wāpesk-wēk- : wāpeskīkan *white linen,* wāpeskɛsew *he is white;* mɛhkw-wēk-∼ mɛhkwēk- : mɛhkīkan *red flannel,* cf. mɛhkwākom *red blanket,* netākom *my blanket.* In some basic forms, we write twy instead of ty merely to bar

§13; thus, we set up pēnt-ēkon-āhtwy- to give pēhčekonāh *sacred bundle*, plural pēhčekonāhtyan.

**17.** Initial w-ō-~ō-: with kēyaw, nēyaw, wēyaw compare kōhnɛʔ, nōhnɛʔ, w-ōhn- : ōhnan in §7.

Initial w-ɛ-~o-: with the preceding compare the normal forms of the prefixes: kɛ-, etc., as ketān *thy daughter*, netān *my daughter*, wɛ-tāN- : otānan *his daughter*, otānew *he has a daughter*, but, with initial change, wētānet *the parent of a daughter*.

Initial w does not occur before o; initial y does not occur before short vowels, either in basic forms or in the actual language.

Initial wyē-~ī- is set up for a few forms like wyēw-ēw : īwēw *futuit illam*.

**18.** When an element in vowel plus w precedes an element with initial ɛ or ə, the combination is normally retained, as kaw-ɛN- : nekāwɛnan *I lay it flat*. Irregularly, however, in certain forms, a replacement is made. This happens always when the w ends a verb stem and the ɛ or ə begins an inflectional ending, but there are also other cases. The following rules hold for ə as well as for ɛ.

awɛ, āwɛ, owɛ~ō: kɛt-ɛnaw-ɛnɛ~kɛtɛnōnɛ- : ketēnōn *I resemble thee*, cf. kɛt-ɛnaw-e-m : ketēnawem *thou resemblest me*; -amow-ɛnɛ-~amōnɛ- : kesākaʔsamōn *I give thee tobacco*, cf. kesākaʔsamowem *thou givest me tobacco*; Nɛt-ɛhtanaw-ɛm-~nɛtɛhtanōm- : netēhtanom *my domestic animal*.

Before k, t, s, however, verb stems in -aw- and -amow- have ā instead of ō: ɛnaw-əkw- : enāk *the other one resembles him*; -amow-əkw- : nesākaʔsamāk *he gives me tobacco*; ɛnaw-ɛtw- : enātowak *they resemble each other*; -amow-ɛsw- : nātamasow *he helps himself*, cf. nātamowēw *he helps him*.

uwɛ, wāwɛ~wā: pyɛ́t-uw-əkw-~pyɛtwākw- : pītwāk *the other brings it to him*, cf. pītuwɛw *he brings it to the other*; mamwāw-əkw- : mamwāk *the other takes it from him*, cf. mamwāwēw *he takes it from the other*.

ewɛ, ēwɛ, ɛ̄wɛ, yāwɛ~yā: wēt-yēw-əkw-~wečyākw- : wičyāk *the other one accompanies him*, cf. wīčiwēw *he accompanies the other*; -nɛNyew-ɛhkwēw-~-nɛnyāhkwēw- : maskīhkīwenɛnyāhkiw *medicine woman*, cf. maskīhkīwenɛniw *medicine man* and pītɛhkiwēw *he brings a woman*; omēʔnomenēw-ɛhkwēw- ; ǫmēʔnomenyāhkiw *Menomini woman*; cf. omḗʔnomenēw *Menomini*; nēw-əkw- : nyāk *the other sees him*, cf. nēwɛw *he sees the other*; kyāw-ɛhkom- : kyāhkomɛw *he is jealous of him*, cf. kyāwēw *he is jealous*.

In a few forms, however, ēwɛ, ɛ̄wɛ is replaced by īyo : wyēw-əkw-~īw-əkw- : īyok *fututa est ab illo*; wyēw-ɛtw-~īw-ɛtw- : iyotowak *alter alteram futuunt*.

**19.** Irregularly, in a few forms, vowel plus w contracts with other vowels, chiefly aw-ā ~ wā : kēsaw-ākamy- ~ kēswākamy- : kīswākamiw *it is warm liquid*, cf. kēsawan *it is warm*.

**20.** After consonant, y, w plus vowel other than a, ā are replaced by vowels.

yē ~ ē: kōNy-ēwe- : kōnēwew *it is snowy*, cf. kōNy- : kōn *snow*, plural kōNy-ak : kūnyak *lumps or masses of snow*, and awētok-ēwe- : awētoke-wew *he, it is of spirit nature*, from awētok *spirit*, plural awētokak.

wē ~ ō: Nētyānw-ēwe- : nīčyānōwew *he is childish*, cf. Nētyānw- : nīčyān *child*, plural Nētyānw-ak : nīčyānok (§21) *children*.

ye, we ~ i: Nε-mεnw-e-hsenē- ~ nεmεnihsenē- : nemēnihsenēm *I am well placed*, cf. mεnw-āp-ant- : menwāpahtam *he sees it well*. yē, wē ~ ī mεnw-ēNent- : menīnehtam *he likes it*, cf. εn-ēNent- : enēnehtam *he thinks so of it*; pyē-w : pīw *he comes*, cf. pyā-t : pyāt *if he comes*, and for the morpholexical variation of ā and ē, nepēw *he sleeps*, nepāt *if he sleeps*. To stems which we set up with wyē- (§17), the prefixes are added with t and the replacement is made: kεt-wyēw-āw : ketīwāw *futuis eam*. Similarly, kεt-wyēw-εnε- : ketīyon (§18) *te futuo*. However, wē after consonant is kept in -wēp- *throw* (§7) and in a few words such as mahwēw *wolf*, moswēn *shawl*.

yε, yə ~ e: aʔnapy-εhkē- : aʔnapehkεw *he makes nets*, cf. aʔnap *net*, aʔnapyak *nets*, and wēkewamεhkεw *he builds houses*, wēkewam *house*, plural wēkewaman; aʔsεNy-ah : aʔsεneh *on the stone*, cf. aʔsεn *stone*, aʔsεnyak *stones*, and wēkewameh *in the house*; aʔsεNy-εns-ak ~ aʔsεnen-sak : aʔsεnēhsak *little stones*, cf. wēkewām-εns-an- : wēkewamēhsan (§§ 22, 34) *little houses*.

wε, wa ~ o: ahkεhkw-εhkē- : ahkēhkohkεw *he makes kettles*, cf. ahkεhkw- : ahkēh *kettle*, ahkεhkw-ak : ahkēhkok (§21) *kettles*; ahkεhkw-əh : ahkēhkoh *in the kettle*; ahkεhkw-εns-ak ~ ahkēhkon-sak : ahkēh-kōhsak *little pails*; sak-e-pw-εnt- ~ sakepont- : sakēpoh *if he is bitten*, cf. sak-e-pw-ak : sakīpwak *if I bite him*, and suffix -εnt- in pakam-εnt- : pakāmeh *if he is struck*; sak-e-pw-əkw- ~ sakepokw- : sakēpok *the other bit him*, cf. pakam-əkw- : pakāmek *the other struck him*. To initial wε- the prefixes are added with t and replacement is made: Nεt-wεtāNe- ~ nεto-tāne- : netōtānem *I have a daughter*, cf. wεtāNe- : otānew *he has a daughter*, from wε-tāN- : otānan *his daughter*.

For yō, yo I can cite no cases.

wō ~ ō: there seems to be no example in my notes; as I am not a native speaker, I cannot guarantee words which I form, but I should not hesitate to say ēhkw-ōnt- : ēhkōhtah *as far as he carried it on his back*, cf. ēhkwahah *as far as he went into the water*, and panōhtam *he dropped it from his back*.

wo ~ o: ēhkw-ohnē- : ēhkohnεt *as far as he walked*, cf. ēn-ohnē- : ēnohnεt *the way he walked*.

**21.** ya, wa, yā, wā are retained: aʔsεnyak *stones*, mεʔtεkwak *trees*, pyāt *if he comes*, mwāk *loon*. In actual sound, yā, wā after non-syllabic are falling diphthongs [i:a, u:a].

Irregularly, in certain forms, wa after consonant is replaced by o. This occurs when the a begins an inflectional ending in the paradigms of most nouns and verbs: ahkɛhkw-ak : ahkēhkok *kettles*; contrast, with wa kept, mɛʔtɛkwak *trees*; mɛhk-amw-ak : mɛhkāmok they find it, cf. mɛhk-amw- : mɛhkām *he finds it*, and pītāwak *they bring it*, beside pītāw *he brings it*. In word-formation less often: wāp-osw-akom- : wāposokom beside wāpos-wakom *rabbit skin*, but always apēhs-osw-akom- : apēhsosokom *deerskin*, cf. wāpos *rabbit*, apɛhsos *deer*, with plurals wāposok, apēhsosok.

**22.** Before n plus consonant, ɛ is replaced by e: pakam-ɛnt ∼ pakament- : pakāmeh *if he is struck*; ɛn-ɛnt- ∼ ɛnent- : enēh (§31) *if he is called so*; kɛ-set-ɛns-an ∼ kɛsetens-an : kesētēhsan (§34) *thy toes*; mēt-ɛnkwāmw- ∼ mētenkwāmw- : mītehkwamow *dormiens se concacat*.

**23.** Clusters of n plus consonant are replaced by h plus consonant; examples in §22.

**24.** Final vowels are dropped: āsetē- : āset *in return*, cf. āsetē-hsem- : āsetēhsemɛw *he lays them to overlap*, āsetē-ɛhkaw- : āsetēhkawɛw *he crosses paths with him*; contrast the treatment of final t before -ɛhk- in §14; ōse- : ōs *canoe*, etc., §13.

**25.** Final non-syllabics are dropped until only one is left: mɛʔtɛkw- : mɛʔtɛk *tree*, cf. mēʔtɛkwak *trees*; ahkɛhkw- : ahkēh *kettle*; aʔnapy- : aʔnap *net*, cf. aʔnapyak *nets*.

Excepted are the clusters ʔč and ʔs: pɛʔt-e- ∼ pɛʔče- : pēʔč *by error*; namēʔs- : namēʔs *fish*.

**26.** Irregularly, in certain forms, one of two like consonants together with the intervening vowel, is dropped (haplology): sēhk-ākamy- : sēhkamiw *it is open accessible water*, cf. sēhkehnɛn *it lies beached*; kɛhk-e-kātē- ∼ kɛhkātē : nekēhkatɛp *my garter*, cf., without haplology, kɛhk-e-kātē- : kɛhkēkātēp *garter*.

**27.** Metathesis and distant dissimilation occur in a very few forms: wēskew-ɛse- ∼ wēskyāse- : wyāskɛsew *he is good*, cf. wēskew-at-w- : wēskewat *it is good*, and mat-ɛse- : matēsew *he is bad, ugly*; mɛ-motwy-ens- : menūtīh *someone's bag, a bag*, cf. kemūtīh *thy bag*, nemūtīh *my bag*, omūtīh *his bag*.

**28.** Alternation of short and long vowels is complex but very regular. In this alternation, the long vowel corresponding to ə is ē: for basic u I have no example. Certain words are excepted from this alternation; we shall call them *atonics*.[2]

---

[2] Historically, they are either words which were atonic at a bygone time when the language had a stress accent which produced the present alternations of quantity, or loan words from languages which have not the Menomini alternation. Stress is not distinctive in the present-day language. [For this reason, Bloomfield subsequently revised his terminology, calling atonic words 'static', tonic words 'mobile'.—CFH]

**29.** In monosyllables, short vowels are replaced by long: pɛʔt-e ∼ pɛʔč- : pɛ̄ʔč *by error*; mw-əkw- ∼ mok- : mōk *the other eats him*. Contrast atonics: sew *as it were*.

**30.** A syllable whose vowel is followed by a cluster is *closed*; any other syllable is *open*. After a closed syllable, a long vowel in an open syllable is replaced by a short vowel: kōhn-ɛw : kōhnɛw *he swallows him*, cf. mēnɛw *he gives it to him*; mɛtɛhn-ɛw : metɛ̄hnɛw *he tracks him*; nɛʔn-ɛw : nɛʔnɛw *he kills him*; kēhkā-m- : kēhkamɛw *he berates him*, cf. kēhkā-nt- : kēhkāhtam *he berates it*. Exceptions, e.g. anohkīw *he works*, maskīhkīwenɛniw *medicine man*.

**31.** If the first two vowels of a word are short, the second is replaced by a long. Excepted are *glottal* words, whose first syllable contains a short vowel followed by ʔ. Nɛ-pɛmāt-ɛse- : nepēmātɛsem *I live*, cf. pemātɛsew *he lives*; pɛm-ohnē- : pemōhnɛw *he walks along*, cf. pītohnɛw *he walks hither*, Nɛ-pɛm-ohnē- : nepēmohnɛm *I walk along*, pēm-ohnē- : pēmohnɛt *when he walked by*; kan-əkw- : kanēk *the other escaped him*, cf. pakam-əkw- : pakāmek *the other struck him*; ɛn-ɛnt- ∼ ɛnent- : enēh *if he is called so*, cf. pakam-ɛnt- : pakāmeh *if he is struck*; Nɛt-ahkow-əkw- ∼ nɛtahkōkw- : netāhkok *he comes next after me*, cf. ahkow-akw- : ahkōk *the other comes next after him*, so also in the compound word nenaw-ahkōk *he will come next after me*, for internal sandhi does not carry across the suture of compound words. Further, for instance, mɛhk-amw- : mɛhkām *he finds it*, Nɛ-mɛhk-ān- : nemēhkan *I find it*, but, in compound, nekēsmɛhkān *I have found it*; contrast pōn-amw- : pōnam *he puts it in the pot*, nepōnān *I put it in the pot*.

Glottal words are excepted: nɛʔnɛw *he kills him*; when a prefix is added, the resulting form is not a glottal word: Nɛ-nɛʔn- : nenēʔnaw *I killed him*; pɛʔtɛnam *he takes it by error*. Atonic, for example, nekot *one* (but nekōtēs *at one time*); mesek *and, also*; anohkīw *he works* (but netānohkim *I work*).

**32.** If the even (second, fourth, etc.) syllable after the next preceding long vowel or after the beginning of a glottal word, is open and has a long vowel, this long vowel is replaced by short: nōhtaw-ēw : nōhtawɛw *he hears him*, cf. pakam-ēw : pakāmēw *he strikes him*, pāpakam-ēw : pāpakamēw *he beats him*; pā-pɛm-e-ke-h-ēw : pāpɛmekehɛw *he brings him up*; ačet-e-kāpowe-h-ēw : ačēčekapowehēw *he stands him upside down*, cf. ɛn-e-kāpowe- : esēkāpowew *he stands so*; Nɛ-kɛhken-ān- : nekēhkenan *I know it*, cf. nenaw-kɛhkēnān *I shall know it*; aʔsek-ɛN-ēw : aʔsekɛnɛw *he picks them up*, cf. pɛʔt-ɛN-ēw : pɛʔtɛnɛw *he touches him by error*.

**33.** If the even syllable (as in §32) is closed and contains a short vowel, this short vowel is replaced by a long: kēhken-ank-wāʔ : kēhkenāhkwaʔ *that which they know*, cf. kēhken-ank- : kēhkenah *that which he knows*, kɛhken-ank-wāʔ : kɛhkīnahkwaʔ *if they know it*, kɛhken-ank- : kɛhkēnah *if he knows it*; kēmew-an-ken- : kēme-wāhken *whenever it rains*, cf.

kɛmew-an-k- : kēmewah *when it rained*, kɛmew-an-k- : kemēwah *if it rains*;
māmat-ɛhkā- : māmasēhkaw *it goes poorly*, cf. pōnɛhkaw *it stops going*;
koʔt-ank-wāʔ : kuʔtāhkwaʔ *if they fear it*, cf. koʔtah *if he fears it*, and,
with initial change (not a glottal word, since the first vowel is long),
kōʔt-ank-wāʔ : kūʔtahkwaʔ *that which they fear*; aʔsek-ɛN-ank-waʔ :
aʔse-kɛnāhkwaʔ *if they pick it up*, cf. aʔsekɛnah *if he picks it up*, pɛtʔɛ-
nahkwaʔ *if they take it by accident*.

[The following paraphrase of §§30–33, covering all non-atonic words
except monosyllables, may be easier to follow:

1. If the first two vowels of a nonglottal word are both short, lengthen
the second.

2. Anywhere after the first long vowel of a nonglottal word, and anywhere in a glottal word, if a long vowel is preceded by a consonant cluster
and not followed by a consonant cluster, shorten it.

3a. In a nonglottal word mark the first short vowel after the first long
vowel 'odd'. In a glottal word mark the first vowel 'odd'.

3b. In any such word (glottal or nonglottal), after the vowel marked
'odd', mark successive subsequent vowels alternatively with 'even' and
'odd', except that if in this process a long vowel is marked 'odd', mark
the next vowel 'odd' also and start the alternation of marking over again
from that point.

3c. If a vowel marked 'even' is followed by a single consonant, shorten
it. If a short vowel marked 'even' is followed by two consonants, lengthen
it.—CFH]

**34.** Certain forms retain a long vowel against the above habits. So the
suffix -wēk- *cloth*, as wāpeskīkan *white linen*; the word onāwanīk *brown
squirrel*. The diminutive suffix -ɛns- (together with its variations, such as
-ons- §20) always lengthens its vowel: kesētēhsan *thy toes*, anɛmw-ɛns-~
anɛmons- : anēmōhsak *little dogs*. Some alternations of quantity are
morpholexical rather than morphophonemic. Thus, when the abstract
noun suffix -N is added to verb stems in -kē-, the result is -kaN : kēskɛse-
kɛw *he cuts things through*, kēskɛsekan *scythe*.

**35.** If postconsonantal y, w, or any one of the high vowels, i, ī, u, ū,
follows anywhere in the word, the vowels ē and ō are raised to ī and ū,
and the vowel o in the first syllable of a glottal word is raised to u : mayīce-
kwaʔ *that which they eat*, cf. mayēcek *that which he eats*; ātɛʔnūhkuwɛw
*he tells him a sacred story*, cf. ātɛʔnōhkɛw *he tells a sacred story*; sɛhk-e-
hsen-k-wāʔ ~ sɛhk-ē-hsehkwāʔ : sɛhkīhsehkwaʔ *if they lie down*, cf. sɛh-
kēhseh *if he lies down*; kuʔnatwāʔ *if they fear him*, cf. koʔnačen *if he fears
him*. This alternation sometimes fails to take place in long words: kēwaskɛ-
pīw beside kīwaskɛpīw *he is drunk*. On the other hand, it is often extended
to compound words and short phrases: kīs-pīw beside kēs-pīw *he has
come*. Since ū occurs only in this alternation, it is not a full phoneme.

**36.** The morphophoneme ə is replaced by e: pakam-əkw- : pakāmek *the other one struck him*; wēkewam-əh : wēkewameh *in the house*.

**37.** The vowel ɛ is replaced by e in the first syllable of words except before a cluster of h or ʔ plus consonant: pɛmohnē- : pemōhnɛw *he walks along*; Nɛset- : nesēt *my foot*. Contrast Nɛhsehs- : nɛhsēh *my younger brother or sister*; Nɛʔnɛhs- : nɛʔnɛh *my elder brother*; pɛʔtɛnam *he touches it by error*; kɛhkēnam *he knows it*.

**38.** The forms now arrived at are *phonemic* forms of the actual Menomini language. Menomini phonetics, however, allows a great deal of latitude to some of its phonemes, and of some overlapping between phonemes. Thus, phonemic ɛ is rather widely replaced by e, except where h, ʔ plus consonant follows; we have used the morphophoneme ə for the cases where this replacement is universal and therefore phonemic. Some speakers partially and some quite constantly replace i by e.

# B51. From *Linguistic Aspects of Science* (monograph)

1939. *Linguistic Aspects of Science* (*International Encyclopedia of Unified Science*, edited by Otto Neurath, 1:4). Chicago: The University of Chicago Press (ninth impression 1965).

[Reviewed in *Journal of Philosophy* 36.613 (1939) by E. N. (=Ernest Nagel?), in *Philosophical Review* 49.678–680 (1940) by Frederick B. Fitch (only two-paragraph mention; the review is of three of the fascicles of Vol. 1 of the *International Encyclopedia of Unified Science*), and in *Language* 16.347–351 (1940) by James W. Wilson.

The last of these reviews was arranged for by Bernard Bloch, as he assumed the editorship of *Language* in 1940; he thought it might be interesting and worthwhile to arrange for a scientist from some field other than linguistics to react to Bloomfield's work. The result was deplorable. Wilson, doubtless an excellent craftsman in his own field (biology), was totally unable to follow Bloomfield's argument (the two reviewers in the philosophical journals scarcely did better), and expressed what he believed was Bloomfield's conclusion by the phrase 'the world of science is an ideal world'! In a letter to Bloomfield, Bloch apologized and admitted that his experiment had been a failure, offering a chance for a rebuttal. In place of a rebuttal, Bloomfield supplied merely the brief sarcastic note 'Ideals and Idealists', *Language* 17.59 (1941), referring the reviewer (and others) for clarification to the very monograph that had been 'reviewed'.

Our brief excerpt is from p. 34. We reproduce this paragraph because it is one of Bloomfield's clearest statements of the importance of everyday reality as the point of departure for all theory and all science.]

The welfare of a community depends, so far as the actions of people are concerned, most directly upon simple handling activities whose occasion and performance are plainly observable—activities such as the gathering of food, hunting, fishing, construction of dwellings, boats, and containers, manufacture of clothing and tools, etc. These are manipulations of non-human objects, satisfactory in their biophysical aspect. Even where human bodies figure as objects, as in surgery or conflict, these actions suffice in themselves, with a minimum of biosocial significance. The situation in which an act of this sort will succeed does not always present itself in full to the performer; another person may mediate by speech:

'There are berries beyond the cliff'; 'The fish are biting today'; 'My moccasins need patching'; etc. Reports like these concern matters where behavior is uniform: in general, people will agree on the outcome of a test. This is the sphere of ordinary life out of which science grows forth. Natural science grows forth directly; the scientific study of man is hampered by the difficulty of subjecting biosocially conditioned behavior to such simple and testable reports.

# B52. Review of Gray

1939. *Modern Language Forum* 24.198–199.

[Like most of us, Bloomfield would often, in private, express strong opinions in violent terms; unlike some of us, he found ways of depersonalizing such views before putting them into the permanent record of print. When he and I had both just seen this book, I asked him what he thought of it; he replied 'It's dreadful!' The review, by being gentler and more explicit, is also much more useful.]

*Foundations of Language.* By Louis H. Gray. New York: The Macmillan Company, 1939. Pp xv + 530. $7.00.

Of recent years quite a few books have appeared which deal in the most general way with the subject of human speech—books intended for the general reader, for workers in related fields, and for beginners in linguistic study.

What these books say about the shape and the history of various languages, and especially of the English language, is bound to be much the same: one naturally speaks here of well established facts. Yet each new book of this sort is to be welcomed, because it will show a new form of exposition, and even more because it will treat also of a subject about which there is no agreement at all: the place of language in life and in the universe.

Here lies the great difficulty which besets the author of a general book about language: just here, where he must speak most simply and precisely, he has to deal with unsolved problems that concern not only his own science but also such twilit realms as anthropology, psychology, and philosophy.

On this, the uncertain and troublesome phase of his subject, Professor Gray holds an extreme view. He says (p. 13) that language is a means of expressing emotional and mental concepts—this, indeed, is part of his definition of language. The present reviewer believes that such terms as "emotional and mental concepts" are merely ill-defined names for phenomena which, in the main, are outgrowths of language. The reviewer, if he were forced to talk about "concepts," would describe them as rudimentary acts of speech. Perhaps only because of this wide divergence, it seems to the reviewer that Gray has stated his belief with too little mention of opposite and intermediate opinions.

When Gray speaks of matters within the usual bounds of linguistics he offers generously of his encyclopedic knowledge. His book is a mine of information; apart from the very full etymologies, this is true especially of the last chapters, which list the languages of the world and tell briefly the history of linguistic science.

The present reviewer differs from Gray also upon a pedagogic question. Except for those excellent last chapters, the wealth of detailed examples, given with little or no explanation of all the detail, seems likely to overwhelm and confuse most readers. A scholar of Gray's mettle no doubt finds it irksome to confine himself to well-worn standard examples and to tell the thrice-told tales which explain them; yet this, your reviewer believes, is required of an introductory book.

The linguistic reader will be startled, now and then, by what he meets, until he realizes that the text implies a new and original view of some technical matter. For instance, Gray's Proto-Teutonic (as it appears, for instance, on pages 67, 69, 81) differs much from the Proto-Germanic of our handbooks. A new and original view of such matters, however justified, should not be presented, by subtle implication, to readers who want elementary facts.

In sum, professional students of language will find in this book much interest and stimulation, but the general reader will do well to limit himself to the last three chapters.

# B53. *From* Letters to Bernard Bloch

1937–1940.

[Bloch asks: Can one say that taxemes are features of morphology, tagmemes features of syntax? On 17 May 1937 Bloomfield replies:]

No; that is not the distinction I meant. Taxeme is any feature of arrangement that can be defined but not further broken up; tagmeme is a combination of such features (in the limiting case, one) which has a meaning, but cannot be analysed into smaller meaningful features. Examples from morphology would be hard to give in English. Sanskrit daiva- *divine* as deriv of deva- *god* shows 2 taxemes, acct shift & vowel subst; they combine into a tagmeme, with meaning, say, *pertaining to*. This is parallel to the way 2 phonemes (meaningless) combine into a morpheme (meaningful). See table on p. 264 [of *Language* (1933)].

[Bloch is working towards his paper 'Phonemic Overlapping' (*American Speech* 16.278–284, 1941) and the paper done with G. L. Trager 'The Syllabic Phonemes of English' (*Language* 17.223–245, 1941). He has presumably seen Bloomfield's 'Menomini Morphophonemics' (our B50). He asks for a clarification of the Menomini situation. On 28 December 1940 Bloomfield replies:]

The M affair is morphophonemically quite clear, since there is living alternation of short and long vowels. We are concerned with the front vowels. I shall use ⟨ ⟩ for morphophonemes. Then we have ⟨i, e, ε⟩ alternating with ⟨i·, e·, ε·⟩. The question is what are the phonemes. The long are clear: three phonemes. E.g. contrasts like [ni·s] *two* : [ne·s] *my head*. As to the shorts: ⟨i⟩ is or was by some older people quite consistently represented by a phoneme [i], resembling French [i] in *fini*, e.g. contrast [a·cemit] *if he tells his story* : [a·cemet] *if he tells the story about me*. But these older people, I think, sometimes use [e] for ⟨i⟩, and younger speakers do so with varying degrees of frequency; I know one younger man who seems never to use [i] but always [e]. Yet all alternations are with everyone, so far as I can see, suited to morphophoneme ⟨i⟩, e.g. [ne·mow] *he dances* : [ni·mit] *if he dances*, younger speaker [ni·met], with effect of ⟨i⟩ on preceding vowel. ⟨e⟩ seems to be universally [e], resembling Am Eng (Chicago?) [i] in *pit*. ⟨ε⟩ is the most difficult. Before [h, ʔ]

apparently in most instances represented by [ɛ], a very open front vowel (Finnish *ä*, which I have heard only a few times, sounded like it to me). E.g. [nɛhse·h] *my younger brother or sister* : [nɛʔnɛh] *my elder brother*. We have in word-initial only [e], e.g. [ehpa·htaw] *he runs thither*, morphophoneme ⟨ɛ⟩, cf. [ɛ·hpahtok] *whither he ran*. Otherwise also in the 1st syllable of a word, ⟨ɛ⟩ seems before [h, ʔ] in some words to appear as [e] oftener than as [ɛ], e.g. [nɛhta·wak, nehta·wak] *my ear*. I think this never happens if the 2d syllable contains [e·]. Before sounds other than [h, ʔ], ⟨ɛ⟩ in the first syllable is always, I think, an [e]: [newiahkwan] *my hat*, [pemo·hnɛw] *he walks along*: this is ⟨ɛ⟩, e.g. [pɛ·mohnɛt] *when he walked along*. In syllables other than the first, ⟨ɛ⟩ appears as [ɛ] rather consistently before [h, ʔ, y, w], e.g. [nɛ·hnɛw] *he breathes*, [awɛ·hsɛh] *bear*; however, [e] appears occasionally in some forms, e.g. [nɛ·hnew] *he breathes* (but never, I think, in the suffix that you see in the word for *bear*, e.g. [menɛ·hsɛh] *small island* versus [menɛ·hseh] *on the island*). Perhaps these [e]'s are phonemically separate forms, doublets, formed by analogic change on account of the next feature. Before consonants other than [h, ʔ, y, w], ⟨ɛ⟩ appears consistently as [e] in syllables immediately after a long-vowel syllable: [nɛ·hnet] *if he breathes*, [pemo·hnet] *if he walks*, [nenɛ·hnem] *I breathe*. Here, I think, [ɛ] is rare or perhaps excluded. The trouble is that phonetically all sorts of shades between mid and very low seem to occur, and I don't know where to draw the line between phoneme [e] and phoneme [ɛ]. In all other positions (in non-first syllable before consonant other than [h, ʔ, w, y] and not after long-vowel syllable), both phonetic types seem to occur for ⟨ɛ⟩; in some words [ɛ] seems commoner, in others [e], and I simply set up phoneme [ɛ], which in these positions is anywhere from 1/10 to 9/10 of the time replaced by phoneme [e], depending on word and on speaker: [aʔsɛn] *stone*, [nepɛ·mohnɛm] *I walk along*, [pɛ·mohnɛt] *when he walked along*, [kɛ·sepɛnam] *he fiddles with it, fingers it, handles it in a useless way*.

   If one ignores morphophonemic structure, the problem becomes one of establishing negative statements: an "[e]" which, in a given form, never has variants with [i] or with [ɛ] by its side is really phoneme [e]; an "[e]" which has variants with [i] by its side is phoneme [i]; an "[e]" which has variants with [ɛ] by its side is phoneme [ɛ]. And conversely: every "[i]" has variants with [e] by its side and represents phoneme [i]; "[ɛ]" may occur without variants of "[e]" or with less frequent or more frequent variants of [e], and all these represent phoneme [ɛ].

   Swadesh, recording more accurately as to ear than I, and not knowing the language, confirmed the above in main outline.

# B54. *From* Letters to Charles F. Hockett

1938–1941.

[My itinerary and activities are relevant for interpreting the excerpts that follow. Summer 1937: with Potawatomi in northern Wisconsin. 1937–1938: Yale. Summer 1938: about three weeks in southern Ontario with various Ojibwa groups, then back to the Potawatomi, but with a couple of days at Ann Arbor where Bloomfield was teaching in the Linguistic Institute (and working on Ojibwa with Mr. Andrew Medler of Walpole Island, Ontario); this was our first meeting. Fall 1938: Shawnee, Oklahoma, working with Kickapoo. Winter–Spring 1939: Yale, working up the Potawatomi material as my Doctoral Dissertation, under the direction of Murray Emeneau. Summer 1939: at the Linguistic Institute at Ann Arbor, seeing Bloomfield occasionally. Fall 1939: Mexico. Winter–Spring 1940: studying under Bloomfield at the University of Chicago; five weeks during the Spring back with the Potawatomi (on funds that were supplied, anonymously, by Bloomfield). Summer 1940 until February 1942: in Ann Arbor.

Of our correspondence during this period, only Bloomfield's letters to me have survived. At first the subject was Potawatomi, then Ojibwa, and Algonquian in general; but concerns of methodology and of theory soon appeared. The period was one of great unrest about phonetics, phonemics, and morphophonemics. Partly under the influence of George L. Trager, I had begun to evolve an understanding of all this that differed from Bloomfield's; in particular, I was unwilling to accept 'words' as initial givens in all languages, feeling that phonemic analysis should be based on whole utterances, and I supposed that when things sounded the same they had to be the same phonemically, however different the 'same' words or morphemes might sound in other arrangements. But I was not yet able to express this viewpoint with any clarity, getting the important notions all mixed up with extraneous matters. This shows in my 1942 paper ('A System of Descriptive Phonology', *Language* 18.3–21—Bloch softened my original title by adding the first three words), and must have made matters even more obscure in my hastily written letters. My concern with Ojibwa was more as materials for theoretical discussion than as data. Bloomfield was primarily concerned with accurate reporting of facts. As a result, much of the latter part of this correspondence was at cross-purposes. Bloomfield was unable to dig out the few crucial points I had buried in awkward verbiage, and so never (during these years or later) pondered them to formulate a considered opinion. He did not like my 1942 paper, though he took pains not to let me know this (I learned of it indirectly); of course, I have not liked it myself for many years now, but for rather different reasons. (In general, Bloomfield, Edgerton, and some of the other elder statesmen of the Linguistic

Society were gently urging Bloch, in the early years of his editorship, to try to cut down on the number of articles on phonemics and to focus more attention on other aspects of language.) But if Bloomfield could not see my points, I was totally unable at the time to see his. I think I can see them now, and I consider them important and valid, in no way in conflict with what I was trying so desperately to say.

I have retained, in the excerpts that follow, Bloomfield's words of kindness and encouragement as well as his unrelenting criticism, because the former as well as the latter were characteristic of his way of dealing with colleagues, particularly younger ones, and their work.]

U of C Sept 28 '38

It has been a great joy to read your MS. As time permits (I am loaded up with all sorts of obligations) I shall study it and also the texts. Even one reading has taught me a lot—especially about the reduced vowel business, which had quite stumped me in eastern Chippewa. The comments and suggestions below are naturally concerned with points where I think you could improve the MS; you will see that they are few and deal with minor or surface things.

Living with Fox-speaking family should be very good. [I never managed to arrange this.—CFH] Please let me know whether you hear only two sibilant phonemes [s, š] or more, e.g. [s, hs, š, hš] or the like.

Plan for Kickapoo, apart from external matters . . ., is due to a consideration which I don't like to urge: our Fox is all ritual of linguistically dull nature. I have put much of it on slips and it is very discouraging. Excepting only Jones' texts and the autob of a Fox woman; and the former are badly transcribed and almost entirely in "quotative" (conjunct) form. Hence Fox everyday speech is an urgent need for Alg.
. . .

P1. First three §§ are scaffolding, and should not be presented to the reader. Throughout, you leave too many such parts. If you want to tell the reader how you worked your way through to the final statements, do it in a preface or in a separate essay.

P3. You evidently agree with me that we can treat technical terms as Humpty Dumpty treated words. The trouble is that many readers get a fixation on some such feature and ignore what you are telling them. This is sure to happen when you make *cluster* include single non-syllabic. Some other word (e.g. *block* or —— [here Bloomfield's hand was illegible, and when I asked what word he had written the reply was again illegible— CFH]) will save you many enmities—the word is not too strong.
. . .

P4. Not "rules-of-thumb," for what is here involved is not merely our convenience, but the speakers' habit of correlating morphologic complexes. To be sure, we take the liberty of inventing a basic (morphophonemic) formula and then telling how it is to be modified to produce the actual (phonemic) utterance, but this is merely a descriptive device: the actual forms do stand in the correlations which we describe. You should say: from our morphophonemic (*basic* is a shorter word) formulae the phonemic forms are derived as follows: 1) if a weak and a strong vowel come into contact, the weak vowel disappears (or: the strong vowel only remains), . . . It's not you or the reader who does these things.

. . .

P7. The troublesome table, hard to type, print, or read, turns out to be superfluous: a simple formula will cover nearly all cases; the exceptional ones will then be much more forcibly set off. . . .

. . .

P10. . . . Are these forms so rare? And even if they are, does that affect the matter? Are they anomalies? I should take it merely as an ordinary instance of homonymy.

P13. Since you are not giving history, the remark at the top of the page troubles me: why touch on history just here? Moreover, you are too sure. . . .

P14. . . . "that is, the fact that . . . *analyze* were related." Scaffolding, merely a preliminary consideration to the preceding (relevant and sufficient) statement. Moreover, example is not good, since English has its own morphology of learned words, in which *analyze : analysis* are connected. I'll send you a reprint about this. But it doesn't matter for Pott-[awatomi].

. . .

P23. Don't say "I'll be God-damned" (1) It offends sanctimonious readers, including deans, trustees, and some professors, and these last will undergo fixation and fail to understand your text; (2) it is stylistically out of harmony with your matter and makes the impression of an undigested rendering of yours or informant's.

P24. *Substantive* and *adverb* are bad terms here, since they are tied up for all readers as names of form-classes and not of positions. I am well inured to redefinitions, but found the next pages hard reading, what with effort to remember which things were positions and which form-classes. *Clause-word* is less troublesome, but also bothers a little. Get four terms like *predicator* which will clearly refer to syntactic positions.

P33. "The determination . . ." Whenever one lands in this statement (I don't know how often it's happened to me) it is time to revise: we have postulated something that isn't in the language.

P42. "Gender and dependency intersect" This is true; but the mere fact that you say it will confuse a reader who does not know. Keep the two topics apart.

P43. "Must" is a bad word which has come to us from (non-linguist) writers of language text-books. We are not laying down rules for the speakers. . . .

The use or non-use of possessive -m- and the treatment of noun-stems before inflectional suffixes call for more definite statements. I grant that we have not learned to draw a line between grammar and lexicon. But we can't send our readers to go through the whole lexicon and pick out the nouns which add some vowel before a plural suffix, and similar classes. (I think even gender should be completely given in the grammar, contrary to our custom.) Well, this means more or more exact morphophonemic machinery. The *stem* must contain some indication of what the forms are; hence it must be based on plural (or obv[iative]) rather than singular. The irregular nouns that are left (don't say they are "*historically* regular"— if that means anything, it goes without saying, but what does it mean?) should be listed.

P47. . . .Don't say *cases* for number and obviation; this will just get a lot of people mad. Why not simply *inflections* or *flections* or the like?
. . .

P51. Quotes in parenthesis near foot of page are confusing. If your terminology here turns out to be insufficient, nail it up better, but don't appeal in this way to the reader's sympathetic understanding, for he generally has none.
. . .

P62. Simplify table or break it up into formulae? I speak with hesitation, since I don't know how we can make these paradigms clear to a reader. But there is some system in them which should stand forth in our description.

————

1030 East 49th St
Chicago
Oct. 3 '38

. . .

As to technical terms, *cluster*, *case*, etc., I am not the one who will find fault, since I believe in your right to set up your own terms; my comment here was Jesuitical, with an eye only on other readers. This applies even to the things which I call "form-classes" and "positions"—although here your terminology gave me some labor, I still assert your right to it. By *position* I mean any place in a syntactic frame (e.g., your *predicator*); by *form-class*, the set of all forms which can *fill* a given position. Thus, your *adverb* is in my terminology a position, which can be filled, e.g., by a noun in local case. . . .

————

U of C
Nov 8 '38

Thank you very much for carbon of Ojibwa paper. There is not only the pleasure of reading and learning, but what is much better, the knowledge that you young people are going to carry on—and with increasing effectiveness at that. . . .

. . .

It seems to me you give too little phonemic value to the reduced vowels [in Ojibwa]. Thus škotē (1) can be spoken with a vowel before the cluster, (2) begins with a cluster, hence is not a type that ever appears as unalterable word-form, but rather a type that appears as [a] variant, (3) is preceded by ʔ in close phrase after vowel (I have mēkwē-ʔškotēnk *in the fire*), (4) will have a vowel after pers[onal] prefix (thus, would it not be nəntaš-k°tēm *my fire*? nəntašk°tēsə man *my matches*?), (5) will make initial change on basis of an initial vowel (thus, would it not be ēšk°tēwik *when it had fire on it, that which has fire on it*?)

You tell about the reduced forms, but not about the basic forms. These are plain enough where there is alternation, and it is our job then to find them. What puzzles me, is the cases where there is no alternation. Thus, kək·ina. I take the first vowel to be a, but this is not dependable, since I know Cree kahkiyaw and have read Jones' Oj kahkina. So I dare not say that for Mr. Medler it is an a, and don't even know that for him it is any vowel at all except just our reduced ə-zero. Only I think ə-zero is not a phoneme, but only an alternant of a and i. What's the answer?

To what extent does the morphophonemic vowel, a, i, o, wa, wi, determine the character of the reduced vowel—i.e., how many reduced vowels are there? My guess is, two, viz. ə representing a, i and o representing o, wa, wi. Sometimes Mr. Medler [from Walpole Island, Ontario; served as Ojibwa informant for Bloomfield's class at the Linguistic Institute in the summer of 1938] seemed to distinguish between dependent noun with o- *third person possessor* and i- (that is, ə-) *indefinite possessor* (<*me-?). . . .

———

1030 E. 49th St.,
Chicago, Nov. 14 '38.

. . . Your statement of Ojibwa a, i : ə is one way (or rather 2 ways) of saying the thing, but the 3d (a : ə and i : ə) may be useful in some cases (and I think Oj is such a case)—as PIE ā, ē, ō : ə. . . .

———

The University of Chicago
Department of Linguistics
Jan. 23 '39.

. . . Don't go too far in accepting suggestions about Pot. Gr. or other matters. Most of our original ideas are wrong, but the few that are right constitute progress. . . .

———

U of C
Aug 18, 1939.

. . . If you have been talking with Emeneau, I can say that I agree with him about phoneme matters, but have probably not formulated things as definitely as he. I don't understand what you (and Trager) are trying to get at; this may mean, of course, that you are on the verge of finding something that is new to me.

Example. Standard German has non-final bdgzv and ptksf, but in final position only the latter set. In morphology former in word-final ~ [is replaced in alternation by] latter: rund-e : runt, cf. bunt-e : bunt. (Against Twaddell, if I understand him aright, we identify medial and final ptksf.) Now, these are the facts which the language gives us—the things the speakers do. I don't understand such questions as "*Is* a final p the same phoneme as a medial p or as a medial b or a third phoneme?" The only question I can see is a choice that is entirely in our hands: we can describe the facts in various ways. This is something I should take in my stride, changing perhaps, as work progressed, from one scheme to another.

As to Oj[ibwa]. (1) nasals n, m before stops (b d g ǰ) have only one shape: one could $\left\{ \begin{array}{l} \text{systematize} \\ \text{transcribe} \end{array} \right\}$ (a) mb, nd, ng, nǰ or (b) mb, nd, ng, nǰ or (c) use only one symbol (say n) in this position.

In word-final, nasal + g is usually replaced by a nasal sound phonetically distinct from n or m. Hence we may $\left\{ \begin{array}{l} \text{systematize} \\ \text{transcribe} \end{array} \right\}$ wa·baṇ 'tomorrow' or wa·bang. The former would be consistent with (a) above, but it seems to me wasteful to use ŋ—a question of style $\left\{ \begin{array}{l} \text{versus(!)} \\ \text{and} \end{array} \right\}$ pedagogy.

Before sibilants only one nasal occurs: in sound it resembles n, but more usually appears as strong nasalization of a preceding vowel. Hence we can systematize as ⁿ (anusvara) or as n. I prefer the latter, because it saves one unit or one symbol or what you will.

Before ʔ and y no nasals occur, but the strong nasalization (of long vowel) does. Hence we may transcribe ⁿ or n. I prefer the latter (for same reason as above): ebino·ji·nʔewi, ebino·ji·nyag.

In word-final, nasalization + y is always replaced by mere nasalization. Hence we may write ⁿ or ny (cf. -ng above). I prefer the latter: ebino·ji·ny. This may well be open to objection on stylistic or pedagogic grounds: in principle, as a form of description, either statement fits the facts.

(I suspect that nasalization plus ʔ would vanish if we knew more about the language: merely a replacement for nasalization plus y before front vowels (?) and reduced vowels (?).)

(2) If your rule [governing the syllables within an Ojibwa word in which short vowels are reduced] held in all cases, we could deal with reduced vowels as a phonetic matter. In the reduced positions o and postconsonantal wa and postconsonantal wi (but I think not a and i before w—am in doubt as to this) coincide; and a and i (when not after postconsonantal w) coincide. This is one of the places where an "is" or "is really" or the like means nothing to me. If your rule held good in all forms, I should systematize reduced vowels with short unreduced. If I used separate symbols, it would be only for stylistic or pedagogic reasons.

In fact, it seems that occasionally, in adding prefixes, one keeps the vowels of the prefixless form: òmìtigwa·bi·n beside mìtigwa·b [the grave accent here represents 'vowel reduction']. If this is true, then such cases could be marked by special symbols, e.g. write merely mitigwa·b, oskinawe·wiya·n, etc., but omìtigwa·bi·n or the like. Or, we could decide to indicate reduction even though in nearly all instances it is covered by your rule. If we indicate reduction, I can see four schemes: (a) two special symbols for reduced vowels, e.g. ⁱ ° or e, u; (b) two vowel symbols with a sign of reduction, as ì ò (your present scheme); (c) three special symbols for reduced vowels, and indication of postconsonantal w, e.g. ° ⁱ ᵃ (wⁱ wᵃ) or u e ʌ (we, wʌ); (d) three vowel symbols with a sign of reduction ò, ì, à (wì, wà).

In preparing my data, I have wavered between (a) e, u and (c) u, e, ʌ (we, wʌ). [The first of these two is the notation Bloomfield finally settled on: see his *Eastern Ojibwa* †1958.] A single sign of reduction is better, if we can find a way of printing it. But type c-d is better than type a-b, because it tells the reader what unreduced vowel is involved.

[inserted to illustrate this:]     (ᵃkik, nⁱndakik)

If I knew it in every instance I should not hesitate. This is not a question about the language: it is a question as to the clearest and most convenient way of telling about the language.

(3) Using one device, such as ʔ, to mark all the long fortes, seems very good to me. Stylistically and pedagogically ʔ may not be a good choice. My inclination is to use h rather than ʔ and to use h also for the glottal

stop (gᵃwahang): this, too, is open to objection from the pedagogic angle.

Initial glottal stop I should not recognize in the phoneme system: any and every initial vowel is sometimes formed with this sound and sometimes without. Hence we can put ʔ (or h) before every "initial" vowel or leave it off all the time—no matter at all. For purely stylistic reasons I leave it off.

(Mr. Medler twice gave the word for some sort of screech owl with intervocalic h not ʔ: I don't know what to make of that—shall simply mention the fact that here ʔ (or h) sounds like a glottal spirant.)

All this strikes me as of tertiary importance. What I want to get is the forms of the language. The system, unless we go completely haywire (miss distinctions of sound, etc.), will take care of itself.

---

1030 East 49th St
Chicago, Illinois
(August 22, '40)

. . . Shall be here till Sept 4; we expect to reach New Haven Sept 8.

---

Yale University
New Haven, Connectic
Jan 28 '41

. . . Glad to hear from you, but have not been writing much, because my wife has been very sick, with a severe depression, since September 5, in hospital since Oct 24. . . .

# B55. The Picture Country

1940. *Teaching Children to Read.* By Leonard Bloomfield. Copyright 1940 by Leonard Bloomfield (in dittographed form from typescript).

[Bloomfield's concern with the use of linguistic knowledge in the teaching of reading apparently began when he prepared some materials to use with one of his own children. This direction of practical application of linguistics is not mentioned in the 1914 *Introduction*, but is touched on in §2.2 of the 1933 *Language*. A fuller development of the materials was undertaken with the encouragement of Clarence L. Barnhart, who tells the sad tale of the long battle against the educational powers that be—a battle that has still not been won—in 'The Story of the Bloomfield System', in Bloomfield and Barnhart *Let's Read: A Linguistic Approach* (Detroit: Wayne State University Press, †1961), pp 9–17. Bloomfield's original explanatory introduction to *Teaching Children to Read* is printed in full in the same volume, pp 19–42; an abridged reworking by Bloomfield himself was published in 1942 and constitutes our item B56.

The story we reprint here is the last one in the materials—the one for Book VI, Lesson 15. In editing the materials for their long-delayed publication, Barnhart was forced to eliminate, shorten, or completely replace some of the things Bloomfield had designed as reading exercises. This is, in one way, regrettable: Bloomfield had included a story of a boy captured and raised by Indians, a version of the Windigo myth, and various other bits which in his treatment were surely calculated to have a beneficial impact on the young of our society. One of the characters in one of the late stories is a Mr. Pentstemon—a touch that it is unfortunate to lose. I am not, of course, criticizing Barnhart's editorial decisions; he is wiser and better informed in these matters than I. Barnhart retains the story we give here, with only minor revisions. However, we give the original version from 1940, except for one brief sentence that Bloomfield himself had lined out in the copy of the materials to which I have had access. After considerable agonizing, I have decided that I cannot even delete the terminal paragraph, though I think that to do so would be an improvement.

The reader should remember that in writing this story Bloomfield was working within two sets of constraints, one overt, one covert. The overt constraints are that he can use only words that are spelled regularly or semiregularly, by his own careful classification, plus just such irregularly spelled words as have been explicitly introduced and drilled before the child reaches this story. The hidden constraints are that, although Bloomfield wants to encourage the development of the child's imagination, he will not permit any topic or turn of phrase that would lead the child towards empty, pompous discourse or into mentalistic or metaphysical nonsense.]

Florence was a girl who lived in a big city. Florence and her father and mother lived in an apartment in a big building. They had two rooms: in one room they slept, and in the other room they cooked and ate their meals. There were no trees in the street where they lived; it was a very busy street and very noisy, with many trucks and vans and cars going by all day and all night. When Florence went downstairs, she was not allowed to go into the street, because she might get run over. Florence and the children she played with had to play indoors or in the hallways or on the sidewalk, and even the sidewalk was crowded most of the time with people who were going this way and that. So there was not much to do for the children, and when Florence stayed upstairs at home, she was lonesome, for she had no brothers or sisters. Sometimes she tagged after her mother and bothered her, but her mother did not get cross.

"Poor little creature!" her mother would say; "She has not much to do. It's natural that she gets bored. I wish she could live in the country, the way I did when I was a child."

Then she would turn to Florence and tell her about the way children lived in the open country, where there was lots of space to play in and many things to do.

Then one day something strange happened. It was a hot day in the summer before Florence started to go to school. She was just six years old. The door-bell rang and Florence opened the door that led from the outside hall into the kitchen. There stood a queer-looking old man. He had a long gray beard, and he carried several big boxes and bundles slung over his back, and hanging round his neck he had an open tray with all kinds of things on it: pins and ribbons and shoelaces and combs and little mirrors. He was going around from house to house and selling these things. When Florence's mother went to the door, the old man asked her if she did not want to buy some of his things. He began lifting things up from the tray and showing them, and telling about the other things he had in his boxes and bundles.

"I'm very sorry," said Florence's mother, "but I haven't any extra money that I could spend on things like these. I am sure your things are very nice, and I thank you for letting me see some of them, but I really can't afford to buy any."

The old man smiled and thanked her and started down the hall toward the stairway that went up to the next floor of the building. He walked very slowly.

'Oh, Mother," said Florence, "That man is very tired. Look at the way he walks. Maybe he would like to come in and rest."

Florence's mother patted her on the head and said, "That's right, child. It's a very hot day and he has a heavy load. Run and ask him to come in and rest and have a cup of tea."

Florence ran down the hall and caught up to the old man and said, "Please, sir, won't you come in and rest? My mother wants you to have a cup of tea."

The old man laughed and said, "Thank you, dear," and went back with Florence. He put down all his boxes and bundles and his tray, and Florence's mother had him sit in the big chair by the window, and then she made a cup of tea for him. While the old man rested and drank the tea, he talked with Florence's mother. They talked about the city and the country and about how hard it was for children, living in the city, where there was so little room to play. Florence did not understand everything they said. She listened because she liked the old man. From time to time he looked at Florence and smiled. His beard and moustache covered his mouth, but in his little blue eyes you could see when he was smiling.

When the old man got up to go, he opened one of his boxes and said, "This little young lady, your daughter Florence, has been very kind to me. I wish I could give her a present. I can't do that, but I have a picture here that will please her. I will lend it to her for one year. Hang it up on the wall and it will give her a great deal of pleasure. A year from now I will come back and get it."

Then the old man got out a big picture in a wooden frame. The picture showed a great stretch of land, with a lake or perhaps the ocean showing at one side. On the lake or the ocean there was a big steamship and there were several little sailboats with men and women and boys and girls in them. At the edge of the water there were people fishing and there was a landing place with some people just getting into a little launch to go for a ride. Then, on the land, you could see many things, too. There was a track with a railroad train steaming along, and you could see people sitting in the train, at the windows. The train was just coming to a station, and there were people waiting at the station, men and women and boys and girls. Then, beyond the tracks there was a big farm with men plowing, and a woman tending to a herd of cows, and children playing under the trees in an orchard. Another thing you could see in the picture was a road with motor cars and horses and wagons on it. In another place there were some soldiers marching along, with guns on their shoulders and flags flying. The top of the picture showed the blue sky with white clouds in it and a flock of birds flying and a balloon going up in the air.

Florence and her mother thanked the old man for letting them have the picture.

Then, when Florence opened the door for him to go out, he leaned down and said in a low voice to Florence, "Child, when you are lonesome or have nothing to do, you can walk into the picture and let all kinds of things happen. You needn't be afraid, because nothing really happens. It's just for amusement. Whenever you are alone in the room, you can walk right out into the picture. Good-by, my child!"

When Florence's father came home that evening, Florence and her mother told him about the old man. Florence's father hung the picture up on the wall opposite the window, above the sofa.

"It's not a very beautiful picture," he said; "There are too many things in it. But the colors are bright and it will amuse Florence to look at all the different things and people."

The next day Florence's father was away, as usual, at work. Then, in the forenoon, Florence's mother had to go out marketing, and Florence was left alone in the apartment. She stood looking at the picture, and then after a while she remembered what the old man had said to her. The picture was up on the wall, higher than Florence's head.

"It doesn't seem natural that I could walk into it," she thought; "I wonder how I can step through the frame."

She stepped toward the picture and then she got the answer to her question. The picture seemed to get bigger and bigger and to reach right down to the floor, as if the sofa were not there at all, and Florence found herself stepping on the soft grass at the edge of the orchard.

There she was, under the trees, with the children that were playing in the orchard! The first one to notice her was a girl about her own age.

"Hello!" said the girl to Florence; "What's your name?"

"Florence Riley," said Florence; "What's your name?"

At that moment Florence had a feeling that she wanted this girl's name to be Mary Eliot. Mary Eliot was the name of one of the girls she played with, in her real playing, round the house.

"My name's Mary Eliot," said the girl.

That was the way it went on. Florence played with the children, and they all had a very good time. But whenever Florence had a feeling that she wanted something to be a certain way, then that was the way things would go. One boy climbed way up to the top of a tree, and Florence thought, "He might fall down now, but I don't want him to get hurt. Anyway, he wouldn't get hurt, because the whole thing isn't real."

And there! The boy lost his hold and came crashing through the branches and tumbling down on the grass right in front of Florence. He got up and laughed and said, "It didn't hurt me at all; I just had a good tumble."

After a while Florence said to Mary, "Let's go ride on the train. The train will take us to the seashore."

The railway station seemed to be miles away, down in the valley. But Florence and Mary walked just a little while; they went around some big bushes, and there right before them was the station. They went inside the station, to the ticket window, and Florence asked the man for two tickets to go all the way to the seashore.

The man said, "Two dollars, please," and there, in Florence's hand, were two one-dollar bills!

So she paid for the tickets, and she and Mary went out on the platform, and soon the train came steaming in.

"All aboard!" cried the brakeman, and Florence and Mary climbed into a coach and found two seats by a window. Then the train started, and the girls looked out of the window and had a great time watching the country and the people at the stations. A man came through the train selling pop corn, and all Florence had to do was to reach into the pocket of her dress, and there was a dime to buy pop corn.

At last the train came to a station at the seashore, and Florence and Mary got out. They ran down to the landing place. Two men, dressed in sailor suits, were just getting ready to take a party of children out sailing.

"I am sure they will invite us to go along," thought Florence.

Then one of the sailors turned round and said, "Come on, little girls; there's just room for two more in the boat."

Florence and Mary got in the boat. Then the sailors hoisted the sail and pushed off from the shore, and the boat sped through the water. The spray flew in the children's faces. How fast they went! They sailed far out on the sea, and then they turned round and sailed back. When they got back to the landing place, Florence thought it must be nearly lunch time.

"I must go home now," she said to Mary.

Then she ran along the beach and thought, "Now I am coming to the end of the picture; I'll just step out of it and into our room."

She took a step or two, and there she was, back in the room, standing with her back to the picture; only the picture was up over her head, on the wall. Her mother was in the room, getting ready for lunch.

"Well, Florence," said Mother; "where have you been all this time? Downstairs, playing with Mary?"

Florence did not quite know how to answer her mother's question.

"Why, Mother," she said, "it seems to me as if I had been in that picture the old man lent us —as if I had been playing there, with those children."

Her mother smiled and said, "That's natural enough!" and asked no more questions.

After that, Florence never was lonely. Whenever she was alone at home, she walked into the picture and let all kinds of things happen. Mostly she played and looked at things and explored the country. Sometimes strange or scary things happened. Florence could wish them to stop or she could let them go on. Once the soldiers came marching along the road, and the children got in their way, and the soldiers caught them and took them off to prison. Florence let it happen because she wanted to see what the prison was like, and she knew that the things that happened were not real, anyway. And besides, if she did not like the way things were in the picture, she could always step right back into the room, and the picture would be just hanging up there on the wall.

No matter how long Florence stayed away in the picture, her mother never seemed to be worried or anxious. Her mother seemed to understand about the picture and to think that Florence's trips were quite natural.

That autumn, Florence began going to school. She did not have so much time, now, to walk into the picture. Still, on Saturdays and Sundays and holidays she often went there and had all kinds of exciting times.

Toward the end of the school year, in spring, Florence began to bring home books from school, because by this time she could read quite well. Then one day her father bought her a story book. Florence liked the stories in the book. The next Saturday and Sunday she was alone quite a bit, and she spent the time reading in her book and did not once walk off into the picture. After the end of the school year, when she was at home much more, she spent more time reading than she did in the picture.

Then one day the door-bell rang, and there was the old man with his boxes and bundles and his tray.

"Oh, how do you do, sir! Do come in and have a cup of tea," said Florence; "I want to tell you what wonderful times I've had walking into the picture and playing there."

The old man smiled at Florence with his blue eyes and said, "I am glad, child, that you liked the picture. But I know you haven't been going into it so much lately. All the picture was good for was to amuse you until you learned to read. Now you can read about much more wonderful things than just the few things that are in this picture. In the future, you will want only books for the time when you are alone. You will not want the picture any more. So now I am going to take it and lend it to some other child that has not yet learned how to read books."

Florence's mother helped the old man take the picture down from the wall. The old man opened one of the boxes that he carried and put the picture into it. Then Florence's mother made some tea, and while they drank tea, Florence listened to what the old man and her mother were saying. She did not understand all of what they said, but she knew that they were talking about books and reading and about children's games and children playing out of doors.

When the old man got up to go, Florence went with him to the door. He looked down at her with his little blue eyes and said, "Perhaps, some day, if you need something, I shall come to see you again. But it won't be for quite a long time, because now you know how to read and need never feel bored and unhappy when you are alone."

Then he said good-by and went away.

Florence missed the picture at first, but after all, her books were more amusing than the picture had been. Besides, she was older now and could play more with her friends; she did not have to stay alone so much as before.

# B56. Linguistics and Reading

1942. *The Elementary English Review* 19.125–130, 183–186.

[1939–1940 was Bloomfield's last year at Chicago, 1940–1941 his first at Yale. This article may have been reworked for publication at Yale, but had originally been written in Chicago; see our prefatory remarks to B55. The same applies to B65. B57–B64, and B67, were surely written at Yale.]

Any large gain in the speed and effectiveness of reading instruction in our schools would bring great advantage to the community. Saving years of every child's school time, it would open the way for other improvements in education. To the writer of this essay it seems very likely that such a gain could be effected with small trouble beyond what is involved in the discarding of a few long-established prejudices.

As to motivation and as to most aspects of classroom procedure, our reading methods have been admirably developed; the time should be ripe for the application, in the classroom, of the facts about reading which today are recognized by all professed students of language. A procedure which takes account of these facts, when tried out with individual children, has proved very successful. Trial in the classroom can be made only with the co-operation of schoolmen. It has been begun on a small scale; the present writer would be glad indeed if this essay should lead teachers and school authorities to co-operate in such attempts.

In this essay I shall outline the main facts about reading which are known to linguists. These facts will here be set forth somewhat dogmatically, since space forbids an account of how they were discovered; such an account would have to tell a large part of the history of linguistic science during the last hundred years.[1]

The art of writing is not a part of language, but rather a comparatively modern invention for recording and broadcasting what is spoken; it is comparable, in a way, with the phonograph or with such a recent invention as the radio. Every human society that has come within our ken possesses a fully developed language, but, until recently, only a few communities have practised writing. Until one or two centuries ago, moreover, in com-

---

[1] This history is very interestingly presented in H. Pedersen's *Linguistic science in the nineteenth century*, translated by J. Spargo, Cambridge, Massachusetts, 1931.

munities like our own, which practised writing, this art was carried on only by a very small minority of the population.

Writing is merely an attempt, more or less systematic, at making permanent visual records of language utterances. It is evident, of course, that by learning to read and write, the individual greatly extends his linguistic horizon and that such developments as the growth of his vocabulary are from then on largely tied up with his reading. Nevertheless, it is a great mistake to confuse the acquisition of literacy with the acquisition of speech: the two processes are entirely different.

Writing seems in every instance to have grown out of *picturing*. Picturing (or *picture writing*) consists in drawing pictures to represent a message. The elements in the pictures, such as figures of different animals, are conventionalized, so that one need not depend too much on draughtsmanship.[2]

The important feature of picture writing is that it is not based upon language at all. A reader who knows the conventions by which the pictures are drawn, can read the message even if he does not understand the language which the writer speaks. If the reader knows that the picture of an animal with a big tail means a beaver, he can get this part of the message, even though he does not know how the word for a beaver would sound in the writer's language. In fact, he can read the picture correctly, even if he does not know what language the writer speaks. Without going too far into the psychology of the thing, we may say that the reader does not get the speech-sounds (the words or sentences) which the writer might use in conversation, but he gets the practical content (the "idea") which in conversation he would have got from hearing those speech-sounds.

The second main type of writing is *word-writing*. In word writing each word is represented by a conventional sign, and these signs are arranged in the same order as the words in speech, Chinese writing is the most perfect system of this kind. There is a conventional character for every word in the language. Each character represents some one Chinese word. As the vocabulary of a literate person runs to about twenty thousand words, this means that in order to read even moderately well, one must know thousands of characters. Learning to read Chinese is a difficult task, and if the Chinese reader does not keep in practice, he is likely to lose his fluency.

It is probable that word writing grew out of picture writing; at any rate, in the systems known to us, some of the characters resemble conventionalized pictures. However, the difference between these two kinds of writing is far more important for our purpose than any historical connection. The

---

[2] The best examples are to be found in G. Mallery's study, published in the 4th and 10th *Annual Reports* of the Bureau of American Ethnology, Smithsonian Institution, Washington, 1886 and 1893.

characters of word writing are attached to words, and not to "ideas." In picture writing you could not distinguish such near-synonyms as, say, *horse*, *nag*, *steed*, but in word writing each one of these words would be represented by a different character. In picture writing very many words cannot be represented at all—words like *and*, *or*, *but*, *if*, *because*, *is*, *was*, and abstract words like *kindness*, *knowledge*, *please*, *care*—but in word writing each word has a conventional symbol of its own.

We ourselves use word writing in a very limited way in our numerals, and in signs like &, +, −, =, and the like. The symbol 5, for instance, by an arbitrary convention, represents the word *five*, and there is no question of spelling or sound involved here: the symbol is arbitrarily assigned to the word. The characteristic feature of word writing, from the point of view of people who are used to alphabetic writing, is that the characters, like 5 or 7, do not indicate the separate sounds which make up the word, but that each character, as a whole, indicates a word, as a whole. Viewing it practically, from the standpoint of the teacher and pupil, we may say that there is no spelling: the written sign for each of the words (four, seven, etc.) has to be learned by itself. You either know that the character 7 represents the word *seven*, or you don't know it; there is no way of figuring it out on the basis of sounds or letters, and there is no way of figuring out the value of an unfamiliar character.

Word writing has one great advantage: since a character says nothing about the sound of the word, the same characters can be used for writing different languages. For instance, our numeral digits (which, as we have seen, form a small system of word writing) are used by many nations, although the corresponding words have entirely different sounds.

The third main type of writing is *alphabetic writing*. In alphabetic writing each character represents a *unit speech-sound*. The literate Chinese, with his system of word writing, has to memorize thousands of characters— one for every word in his language,—whereas, with an alphabetic system, the literate person needs to know only a few dozen characters,—one for each unit speech-sound of his language. In order to understand the nature of alphabetic writing we need to know only what is meant by the term *unit speech-sound*, or, as the linguist calls it, by the term *phoneme*.

The existence of unit speech-sounds or phonemes is one of the discoveries of the language study of the last hundred years. A short speech, —say, a sentence,—in any language consists of an unbroken succession of all sorts of sounds. Systematic study has shown, however, that in every language the meaning of words is attached to certain characteristic features of sound. These features are very stable and their number ranges anywhere from fifteen to around fifty, differing for different languages. These features are the unit speech-sounds or phonemes. Each word consists of a fixed combination of phonemes. Therefore, if we have a written character for each phoneme of a language, the sum total of characters will range anywhere from fifteen to fifty, and with these characters we shall be able to write down any word of that language.

The existence of phonemes and the identity of each individual phoneme are by no means obvious: it took several generations of study before linguists became fully aware of this important feature of human speech. It is remarkable that long before scientific students of language had made this discovery, there had arisen a system of alphabetic writing,—a system in which each character represented a phoneme. It seems that alphabetic writing developed out of word writing, and that this remarkable development has taken place only once in the history of mankind,—somewhere between 2000 and 1000 B.C. at the eastern end of the Mediterranean, with Egyptians, the Semitic-speaking peoples (such as the Phoenicians), and the Greeks, successively playing the principal role. All forms of alphabetic writing, then, are offshoots of a single original system. The details of this origin, and of the later history, so far as we can get at them, are of great interest, but would carry us too far afield. It is important for us to know that alphabetic writing was not invented at one stroke, as a finished system, but that it grew gradually and, one could almost say, by a series of accidents, out of a system of word writing. Neither then nor at any time since was there any body of experts who understood the system of phonemes and regulated the habits of writing. Among modern nations, some have almost perfect alphabetic systems, such as the Spanish, Bohemian, and Finnish systems of writing, but others have relatively imperfect systems, such as the Italian, Dutch, or German, and still others have extremely imperfect and arbitrary systems, such as the modern Greek, the French, and the English.

We can illustrate the nature of alphabetic writing by means of English examples, for, in spite of its many imperfections, our system of writing is in origin and in its main features alphabetic. This is proved by the simple fact that we can write all English words by means of only twenty-six characters, whereas a system of word writing would demand many thousands. As an illustration we may take the written representation of the word *pin*. It consists of three characters, and each of these three represents a single phoneme. If anyone told us to use these three characters to represent the word *needle*, we should find the suggestion absurd, because these characters do not *fit the sound* of the word *needle*. That is, each of three characters, *p i n*, is used conventionally to represent a unit *sound* of our language. This appears plainly if we compare the written symbols for other words, such as *pig*, *pit*, or *bin*, *din*, or *pan*, *pun*, or if we reverse the order of the letters and read *nip*.

The alphabetic nature of our writing appears most plainly of all, however, when we put together a combination of letters that does not make a word and yet find ourselves clearly guided to the utterance of English speech-sounds; thus, nobody will have trouble in reading such nonsense-syllables, as *nin, mip, lib*.

If our system of writing were perfectly alphabetic, then anyone who knew the value of each letter could read or write any word. In reading, he would simply pronounce the phonemes indicated by the letters, and in writing he would put down the appropriate letter for each phoneme. The fact that we actually can do both of these things in the case of nonsense words such as *nin* or *mip*, shows that our system of writing is alphabetic.

In order to read alphabetic writing one must have an ingrained habit of producing the sounds of one's language when one sees the written marks which conventionally represent the phonemes. A well-trained reader, of course, for the most part reads silently, but we shall do better for the present to ignore this, especially as we know that the child learns first to read aloud.

The accomplished reader of English, then, has an over-practiced and ingrained habit of uttering one sound of the English language when he sees the letter *p*, another sound when he sees the letter *i*, another when he sees the letter *n*, and so on. In this way, he utters the conventionally accepted word when he sees a combination of letters like *pin, nip, pit, tip*, and, what is more, all readers will agree as to the sounds they utter when they see unconventional combinations, such as *pid, nin, pim*. It is this habit which we must set up in the child who is to acquire the art of reading. If we pursue any other course, we are merely delaying him until he acquires this habit in spite of our bad guidance.

English writing is alphabetic, but not perfectly so. For many words we have a conventional rule of writing which does not agree with the sound of the word. Take, for instance, the two words which are pronounced *nit*. One is actually spelled *nit*, but the other is spelled *knit*, with an extra letter *k* at the beginning, a letter which ordinarily represents one of the phonemes of our language.

Now someone may ask whether the spelling of *knit* with *k* does not serve to distinguish this word from *nit* "the egg of a louse." Of course it does, and this is exactly where our writing lapses from the alphabetic principle back into the older scheme of word writing. Alphabetic writing, which indicates all the significant speech-sounds of each word, is just as clear as actual speech, which means that it is clear enough. Word writing, on the other hand, provides a separate character for every word, regardless of its sound, and at the cost of tremendous labor to everyone who learns to read and write. Our spelling the verb *knit* with an extra *k* (and the noun *nit* without this extra *k*) is a step in the direction of word writing. This convention goes a little way toward giving us a special picture for the verb *knit*, as opposed to its homonym, and it does this at the cost of a certain amount of labor, since the reader must learn to ignore initial $k$ before $n$, and the writer must learn where to place it and where not to place it. It is none the less important to see that in its basic character our system of writing is alphabetic—witness merely the fact that we get along with twenty-six characters instead of twenty-six thousand.

The letters of the alphabet are signs which direct us to produce sounds of our language. A confused and vague appreciation of this fact has given rise to the so-called "phonic" methods of teaching children to read. These methods suffer from several serious faults.

The inventors of these methods confuse writing with speech. They plan the work as though the child were being taught to pronounce—that is, as if the child were being taught to speak. They give advice about phonetics, about clear utterance, and other matters of this sort. This confuses the issue. Alphabetic writing merely directs the reader to produce certain speech-sounds. A person who cannot produce these sounds, cannot get the message of a piece of alphabetic writing. If a child has not learned to utter the speech-sounds of our language, the only sensible course is to postpone reading until he has learned to speak. As a matter of fact, nearly all six-year-old children have long ago learned to speak their native language; they have no need whatever of the drill which is given by phonic methods.

The second error of the phonic methods is that of isolating the speech-sounds. The authors of these methods tell us to show the child a letter, say $t$, and to make him react by uttering the ($t$) sound. This sound is to be uttered either all by itself or else with an obscure vowel sound after it. Now, English-speaking people, children or adults, are not accustomed to make that kind of a noise. The sound ($t$) does not occur alone in English utterance; neither does the sound ($t$) followed by an obscure vowel sound. If we insist on making the child perform unaccustomed feats with his vocal organs, we are bound to confuse his response to the printed signs. In any language, most phonemes do not occur by themselves, in isolated utterance, and even most of the successions of phonemes which one could theoretically devise, are never so uttered. We must not complicate our task by unusual demands on the child's power of pronouncing. To be sure, we intend to apply phonetics to our reading instruction, but this does not mean that we are going to try to teach phonetics to young children. In the absurdity of trying this we see the greatest fault of the so-called phonic methods.

In spite of the special methods, such as the "phonic" method, which have been advocated at various times, the actual instruction in our schools consists almost entirely of something much simpler, which we may call the *word-method*. The word-method teaches the child to utter a word when he sees the printed symbols for this word; it does not pretend to any phonetic breaking-up of the word. The child learns the printed symbols, to be sure, by "spelling" the word,—that is by naming, in proper succession, the letters which make up the written representation of the word, as *see-aye-tee*: *cat*, and so on. No attempt is made, however, to take advantage of the alphabetic principle. If one examines the primers and first readers which exemplify the various methods that have been advocated, one is struck by the fact that the differences are very slight: the great bulk of the work is word-learning. The authors are so saturated with this, the conventional method, that they carry their innovations only a very short way; they evidently lack the linguistic knowledge that would enable them to grade the matter according to relations between sound and spelling. It is safe to say that nearly all of us were taught to read by the word-method.

The word-method proceeds as though our writing were word-writing. Every word has to be learned as an arbitrary unit; this task is simplified only by the fact that all these word-characters are made up out of twenty-six constituent units, the letters. In order to read a new word, the child must learn the new word character; he can best do this by memorizing the letters which make up this new word-character, but these letters are arbitrarily presented and have nothing to do with the sound of the word.

The most serious drawback of all the English reading instruction known to me, regardless of the special method that is in each case advocated, is the drawback of the word-method. The written forms for words are presented to the child in an order which conceals the alphabetic principle. For instance, if near the beginning of instruction, we present the words *get* and *gem*, we cannot expect the child to develop any fixed and fluent response to the sight of the letter *g*. If we talk to him about the "hard" and "soft" sounds of the letter *g*, we shall only confuse him the more. The irregularities of our spelling—that is, its deviations from the alphabetic principle—demand careful handling if they are not to confuse the child and to delay his acquisition of the alphabetic habit.

Our teaching ought to distinguish, then, between *regular* spellings, which involve only the alphabetic principle, and *irregular* spellings, which depart from this principle, and it ought to classify the irregular spellings according to the various types of deviation from the alphabetic principle. We must train the child to respond vocally to the sight of letters, and this can be done by presenting regular spellings; we must train him, also, to make exceptional vocal responses to irregular spellings, and this can be done by presenting systematically the various types of irregular spelling. For instance, we must train the child to respond by the *k*-sound to the sight of the letter *k* in words like *kiss, kid, kin, kit*, but we must also train him not to try pronouncing a *k*-sound when he sees the written *k* in the words like *knit, knife, knee, knight*.

The knowledge required to make this classification is not very profound.

Although this knowledge is easily gained, persons who lack it are likely to make troublesome mistakes. The author of a text-book and the classroom teacher does not need a profound knowledge of phonetics; he needs only to realize that information on this subject is available and that he need not grope about in the dark.

Although the various methods that have been advanced are, in practice, only slight adaptations of the universal method of word-reading, it will be worth our while to glance at one of them which has some vogue, namely the *sentence method* or *ideational reading*. This method attempts to train the child to get the "idea" or content directly from the printed page.

When a literate adult reads, he passes his eyes rapidly over the printed text, and, scarcely noticing the individual words or letters, grasps the content of what he has read. This appears plainly in the fact that we do not often notice the misprints on the page we are reading. The literate adult now observes the laborious reading of the child, who stumbles along and spells out the words and in the end fails to grasp the content of what he has read. The adult concludes that the child is going at the thing in a wrong way and should be taught to seize the "ideas" instead of watching the individual letters.

The trouble with the child, however, is simply that he lacks the long practice which enables the adult to read rapidly; the child puzzles out the words so slowly that he has forgotten the beginning of the sentence before he reaches the end; consequently he cannot grasp the content. The adult's reading is so highly practiced and so free from difficulty that he does not realize any transition between his glance at the page and his acceptance of the content. Therefore he makes the mistake of thinking that no such transition takes place,—that he gets the "ideas" directly from the printed signs.

This mistake is all the more natural because the adult reads silently; since he does not utter any speech-sounds, he concludes that speech-sounds play no part in the process of reading and that the printed marks lead directly to "ideas." Nothing could be farther from the truth.

The child does his first reading out loud. Then, under the instruction or example of his elders, he economizes by reading in a whisper. Soon he reduces this to scarcely audible movements of speech; later these become entirely inaudible. Many adults who are not very literate, move their lips while reading. The fully literate person has succeeded in reducing these speech-movements to the point where they are not even visible. That is, he has developed a system of internal substitute movements which serve him, for private purposes, such as thinking and silent reading, in place of audible speech-sounds. When the literate adult reads very carefully,—as, when he is reading poetry or difficult scientific matter or a text in a foreign language,—he actually goes through this process of internal speech; his conventional way of reporting this is that he internally pronounces or "hears himself say" the words of the text. The highly skilled reader has trained himself beyond this: he can actually shunt out some of the internal speech-movements and respond to a text without seizing every word. If you ask him to read aloud, he will often replace words or phrases of the printed text by equivalent ones; he has seized only the high spots of the printed text. Now this highly skilled adult has forgotten the earlier stages of his own development and wants the child to jump directly from an illiterate state to that of an over-trained reader.

It is true, of course, that many children in the upper grades—and even, for that matter, many post-graduate students in the university—fail to seize the content of what they read. It was this unfortunate situation which led to the invention of ideational methods in reading instruction. This however, meant confusing two entirely different things. So much can be said, however; the child who fails to grasp the content of what he reads is usually a poor reader in the mechanical sense. He fails to grasp the content because he is too busy with the letters. The cure for this is not to be sought in ideational methods, but in better training at the stage where the letters are being associated with sounds.

The extreme type of ideational method is the so-called "non-oral" method, where children are required not to pronounce words but to respond directly to the content. They are shown a printed sentence such as *Skip round the room*, and the correct answer is not to say anything, but to perform the indicated act. Nothing could be less in accord with the nature of our system of writing or with the reading process such as, in the end, it must be acquired.

The stories in a child's first reader are of little use, because the child is too busy with the mechanics of reading to get anything of the content. He gets the content when the teacher reads the story out loud and, later on, when he has mastered all the words in the story, he can get it for himself, but during the actual process of learning to read the words he does not concern himself with the content. This does not mean that we must forego the use of sentences and connected stories, but it does mean that these are not essential to the first steps. We need not fear to use disconnected words and even senseless syllables, and, above all, we must not, for the sake of a story, upset the child's scarcely formed habits by presenting him with irregularities of spelling for which he is not prepared. Purely formal exercises that would be irksome to an adult, are not irksome to a child, provided he sees himself gaining in power. In the early stages of reading, a nonsense syllable like *nin* will give pleasure to the child who finds himself able to read it, whereas at the same stage a word of irregular spelling, such as *gem*, even if introduced in a story, will discourage the child and delay the sureness of his reactions.

There is always something artificial about reducing a problem to simple mechanical terms, but the whole history of science shows that simple mechanical terms are the only terms in which our limited human capacity can solve a problem. The lesser variables have to wait until the main outline has been ascertained, and this is true even when these lesser variables are the very things that make our problem worth solving. The authors of books on reading methods devote much space to telling why reading is worth while. The authors of these books would have done far better to stress the fact that the practical and cultural values of reading can play no part in the elementary stages. The only practical value of responding correctly to the letters of the alphabet lies in the messages which reach us through the written or printed page, but we cannot expect the child to listen to these messages when he has only begun to respond correctly to the sight of the letters. If we insist upon his listening, we merely delay the fundamental response.

If you want to play the piano with feeling and expression, you must master the keyboard and learn to use your fingers on it. The chief source of difficulty in getting the content of reading is imperfect mastery of the mechanics of reading.

Space forbids our giving more than a meager outline of a system of reading instruction based upon the facts which have been set forth on the preceding pages.

The first step, which may be divorced from all subsequent ones, is the recognition of the letters. We say that the child *recognizes* a letter when he can, upon request, make some specific response to it. One could, for instance, train him to whistle when he saw an A, to clap his hands when he saw a B, to stamp his foot when he saw a C, and so on. The conventional responses to the sight of the letters are their names, *aye*, *bee*, *see*, *dee*, and so on, down to *zee* (which in England is called *zed*). There is not the slightest reason for using any other responses.

It is an open question whether all the letters, small and capital (in printed form, of course) should be taught before reading begins.

At the pre-primer stage the habit of left-to-right scanning should be developed by means of appropriate exercises, which may well afford, at the same time, an introduction to the letters and the numeral digits.

Our first reading material must show each letter in only one phonetic value; thus, if we have words with g in the value that it has in *get*, *got*, *gun*, our first material must not contain words like *gem*, where the same letter has a different value; similarly, if we have words like *cat*, *can*, *cot*, our first material must not contain words like *cent*. Our first material should contain no words with silent letters (such as *knit* or *gnat*) and none with double letters, either in the value of single sounds (as in *add*, *bell*) or in special values (as in *see*, *too*), and none with combinations of letters having a special value (as *th* in *thin* or *ea* in *bean*). The letter *x* cannot be used, because it represents two phonemes (*ks* or *gz*), and the letter *q* cannot be used, because it occurs only in connection with an unusual value of the letter *u* (for *w*).

Our first reading material will consist of two-letter and three-letter words in which the letters have the sound-values assigned at the outset. Since the vowel letters are the ones which, later on, will present the greatest difficulty, we shall do best to divide this material into five groups, according to the vowel letter.

The work of this first stage is all-important and should be continued until the pupils are very thoroughly trained. Nonsense syllables, such as *bam*, *bap*, *mim*, *mip*, should be included. Words unfamiliar to the child, such as perhaps *van*, *vat*, should not be avoided; they should be treated as nonsense syllables or, if there is time, accompanied by a very brief explanation of their meaning.

Short sentences of the type *Nat had a bat* can be used at this stage.

The second stage takes up regular spellings in which double consonants and other digraphs appear in consistent uses, e.g. *ll* as in *well*, *th* as in *thin*, *sh* as in *shin*, *ch* as in *chin*, *ee* as in *see*, *ea* as in *sea*, *oa* as in *road*, *oo* as in *spoon*. If a very few words of irregular spelling are introduced at this stage (e.g., *is*, *was*, *the*), it is possible to devise connected reading of reasonably varied content.

The third stage takes up words whose spellings may be called *semi-irregular*, for example the type of *line*, *shine*, *mile*, *while* or the type of *bone*, *stone*, *hole*, *pole*. At this stage, also, two-syllable words whose spelling is consistent with the other materials, can be taken in: *winter*, *summer*, *butter*, *sister* (but not, for instance, *father*, *mother*, *brother*). A small set of the commonest irregular words (pronouns, forms of the verbs *be*, *have*, *do*, and *go*) is included because it enables us to give extended readings of connected text.

The last stage takes up irregularly spelled words, such as *father*, *mother*, *night*, *all*, *rough*, *cough*, *though*. It is only here that the question of reading vocabulary need be considered. In the first three stages an individual word (apart from the small stock of irregular ones that have been taken in) offers no problem: all that is needed is the habit of connecting letters with sounds. At those stages, unfamiliar words like *van*, *moot*, *mote*, afford good practice precisely because they are unfamiliar, and the same can be said of nonsense syllables. At the fourth and last stage, however, each word, being entirely irregular in shape, is a separate item to be memorized. At this last stage, accordingly, we use only familiar words which are needed for reading.

No matter how well we plan in other respects, our teaching will yield inferior results so long as the material which we present is clumsily chosen.

Only if we choose our material in accordance with the nature of English writing, will the classroom procedure which we have so carefully developed, produce proper results. The children will learn to read in a much shorter time, and they will read more accurately, more smoothly, and with better understanding of the content.

# B57. Philosophical Aspects of Language

1942. *Studies in the History of Culture: The Disciplines of the Humanities* (presented to Waldo Gifford Leland), Menasha, Wisconsin, pp 173–177.

[The paper 'Linguistic Aspects of Philosophy', delivered by Bloomfield at the Fourth Summer Meeting of the Linguistic Society in Chapel Hill, N.C., in 1941, may have been a version of this.]

The persons in a speech community coördinate their actions by means of language. Language bridges the gap between the individual nervous systems: a stimulus acting upon any one person may call out a response action by any other person in the community. Language unites individuals into a *social organism*.

In a way, language is to the social organism what the nervous system is to the individual. A stimulus acting upon any part of an animal may call forth a movement in any other part: the nervous system serves as a connection. Pinch a dog's tail and his mouth will snap at you. In the social organism a stimulus acting upon one person may produce a response in any other person: the connection is produced by language.

As a simple instance, suppose that Jack and Jill are walking down a lane: Jill is hungry and thirsty and she sees some apples in a tree, but she cannot climb fences or trees. So far as her own non-linguistic bodily equipment is concerned, she would have to stay hungry. However, she utters some conventional speech sounds, and at once Jack climbs over the fence and up the tree and brings her an apple. Jack has responded to the stimulus of Jill's hunger. As a speaking person, Jill commands the varied powers of many individuals—ultimately, of all the persons in her speech community and even beyond.

This instance is so simple that it may be paralleled among speechless animals. Language, however, produces very exact coöperation. Speechless animal communities are either very loosely knit, or else, as among ants or bees, they are restricted to a few rigid schemes of operation. In a human community, every child is trained in a twofold system of habits. He is taught to respond to situations not only with non-linguistic bodily movements, but also with conventional speech sounds. At the same time, he is taught to respond to these conventional speech sounds when he hears them from other persons: the other person's speech acts as a stimulus of a special sort ("stimulus-on-other-person," in our example, "Jill's-hunger").

The person who receives the stimulus and the person who acts upon it need not be near each other. If some farmers want a bridge across a river, their speech need not reach the ears of the bridge builders: many relays of speech, through a town meeting, a legislature, various officials, an engineer's office, and a contractor's staff, will finally lead to the point where workmen actually perform the movements of building a bridge.

In such ways language gives man a great biological advantage. This appears in exact coöperation in small-scale activities, such as hunting, fishing, or warding off wild animals. It leads later to the division of labor in large societies like our own. In a community of the latter kind, even the least favored individual has at his service a great variety of human performance, far beyond the strength and skill of his own body.

We do not know what connection, beyond mere coincidence, there may have been between language and the use of fire and tools; whatever the connection, it cannot detract from the import of this basic function of language.

When we say that a speech community is a *social organism*, we are not using a figure of speech. A person's membership in a speech community is not merely something superadded to his existence as a biological unit. Human behavior is entirely permeated by social factors. With the possible exception of some physiological processes, the activities of a human individual cannot be classified or predicted on the sole basis of biological equipment, but depend very largely upon the society in which he lives and upon his place in this society.

Each community is formed by the activity of language; speech utterances give us the most direct insight into its working and play a part in everything that is done. In order to observe a human group, we must understand its speech. If we want to probe deeper into the ways of the community and their historical origin, we must possess, to begin with, a systematic description of its language. In order to know anything about mankind, we must study in this way a varied set of communities. What little we know about man has come from study of this kind. Without such knowledge, we are slaves, in this matter, to rationalization, prejudice, and superstition.

The existence of an individual depends upon his membership in a speech community, to such an extent that every phase of his behavior contains linguistic elements. His *I* and *you*, his *good* and *bad*, his *will* and *must*, and so on, are largely conditioned by language and can be most plainly observed in the utterance of speech. In this sphere we may single out, on account of its cosmic importance, the power of *calculation*.

An untrained individual's response to any complex set of objects is extremely uncertain and often disadvantageous. This can be seen in the behavior of young children or of persons confronted with complexities (for example, in the way of mechanical devices) which are beyond their training. In language, however, the individual has a set of responses which have been practised by many persons and are less whimsical than untrained individual reactions. The human adult, accordingly, responds to a complex situation by a series of speech utterances (audible or internal, or, in modern times, written) which we call a *calculation*. At the end of the calculation he proceeds to make a final response, verbal or manual, whose form is dictated by the intermediate speeches. In many instances, to be sure, the conventional speeches are faulty and lead to a poor response: every community is beset with tribal superstitions, tabus, and dyspraxies. On the other hand, we find remarkably clever actions customary among savage tribes; these culminate in modern scientific procedures. In the case of these latter, the verbal calculation takes largely the form of *mathematics*.

Here again, of course, we see the division of labor: physicists, chemists, engineers, and other scientists and technical workers act for us in complex situations, and they, in turn, call upon mathematicians for the verbal reckoning. In the favorable case, then, we have the highly civilized society which meets the situations of life rationally and advantageously, for the most part by securing the operation of specialized individuals.

The social organism is the highest type of organization within our cosmos. It is wellnigh immortal, and can deal with almost any situation and secure almost any advantage. Even upon this level of biological success, the ethical consequences are self-evident. The social organism will function successfully to the extent that a stimulus upon any member will produce a response in the suitable member; for instance, if the hunger or pain of any person is speedily and smoothly dealt with by the appropriate members of the community. The social organism will function successfully to the extent that it contains enough persons who are trained to respond to its situations; for instance, if for a large population of food growers there are also enough teachers to secure rational behavior and enough physicians and sanitarians to secure the health of the community.

However, in order to draw ethical consequences, we must know what "good" is to be sought. In the light of the linguistic and coöperative character of society, this goal seems to be *variability*, both of the individual and of the social organism. The social organism, to function smoothly, must contain persons of the most various and specialized training and must set them into action appropriately and speedily. Within such an organism, the individual must perform extremely varied responses, delicately attuned to every situation—responses which, of course, in nearly every instance involve the coöperation of other individuals. It is probably the approximation to this state which we mean when in everyday speech we use the term *well-being* or *happiness*, and it is, more certainly, the inability to respond to a situation which we mean by the reverse of these terms.

Beyond all this, there is a cosmic significance to the linguistic actions of society. Modern means of recording speech utterance enable us to store up valuable responses. Here we have notably the devices of writing and printing. A great library, today, contains, recorded and available, the best responses that have been made to almost everything in the accessible world. Even now, at the dawn of civilization and with our primitive equipment, we approach the limit where everything in the accessible universe is paralleled by a recorded human response in the form of a speech utterance, and where all these records are available, at need, to any person. To the extent that irrationality and superstition are discarded, and to the extent that the social organism fosters variability in its members—and these are largely linguistic developments—to that extent will the social organism approach a state which, in contrast with the powers of less developed people, and in the eyes of such people, could be characterized as omniscience and omnipotence.

The development here is not constantly forward. Irrational and self-destructive activities are often preserved by means of language. A frequent error of societies is to make inadequate response to things, and to hope that verbal calculating will make up for imperfect observation: this is the nature of so-called *a priori* reasoning, scholasticism, and other forms of pseudo-philosophizing. Given, however, an adequate observation of things language acts to eliminate irrational patterns of behavior. For this reason, to the extent that a community carries on disadvantageous conventions, the persons or groups at the focus of disease try to prevent not only rational observation but also the free use of language. As the social organism develops, it tends more and more to abandon self-destructive actions and to conventionalize those which embody a successful response. This process depends largely upon speech—argument, debate, exposition, scientific treatises, and so on. As examples we may cite, on the one hand, the abolition of private warfare or of slavery, and, on the other hand, the rise and the conventional application of present-day physics, engineering, medicine, and sanitation.

The outline here given is based upon the treatise of Albert Paul Weiss, *A theoretical basis of human behavior* (second edition, Columbus, Ohio, 1929) and upon the same author's essay, *Linguistics and psychology*, in the journal *Language*, volume I, 1925.

# B58. Meaning

1943. *Monatshefte für Deutschen Unterricht* 35.101–106.

The meaning of speech forms presents various problems in the theoretical study of language and in practical applications, such as language learning.

The question "What is *meaning*?" approaches these problems at an awkward angle. A familiar term of popular or scholastic discourse, such as the term *meaning*, means different things in different contexts; it can be defined in various ways and with varying emphasis. If we start from the familiar term and try to define it, we are led into pseudo-problems and fruitless debates. An instance of this may be seen in the arid discussions of the term *sentence* which are summarized in Ries's book *Was ist ein Satz?* (second edition, Prague, 1931).

Experience shows that it is not profitable to begin the study of a subject by trying to define the popular or technical terms that are connected with it. It is much better simply to examine the objects of one's curiosity and then, when one comes across some feature which seems to deserve a name, to assign to this feature a familiar term which seems roughly to fit the case. Or else, we may prefer to invent some new word to name the feature we have seen.

Suppose that some intelligent observer came to us from another planet, where vocal language was unknown. This observer would see that men differed from animals, among other things, by constant and minutely adjusted cooperation and division of labor, and by a cumulative system of adaptations, which enabled them to avoid the errors and to adopt the successful actions of earlier persons. He would see also that during our various activities we made chattering noises with our mouths. In time, he would learn to distinguish the different noises and to see that certain noises were connected with certain types of things and events; for instance, he would observe that a person who had been out of doors might say *It's raining* and that then another person, who had not been out of doors and had not seen the rain, would adjust his actions to the condition of rainfall. Or he would observe that when one person said *Shut the door*, another would usually go and shut the door. After a time, the observer would even see the point of such utterances as *It was raining yesterday afternoon* and

*It looks like rain* and *I'm going to shut the door*. Finally, he would learn to recognize recurrent parts of utterances, and to see that words like *shut*, *door*, *apple* occurred in speeches that were connected with acts of shutting something and objects of certain definite types.

Now when our observer went back to his planet and made his report about us, he would need, in whatever system of communication was there in use, a general term to cover the objects and events which are typically connected with any one terrestrial speech form. The actual student of language, to return to him, faces the same necessity, and, if he does not want to coin a new term, he will naturally choose the traditional term *meaning*. He will say that every speech form is connected with certain typical features in the situation of the speaker and with certain typical actions of the hearer. He will make some such definition as this: The features of situation and action which are common to all utterances of a speech form are the *meaning* of that speech form.

This definition (or rather, this way of looking at the matter) sets off a great many problems. What is the "meaning" of words like *but*, *if*, *because*? How about a speaker who starts talking about *apples* when he has not seen any apples for a long time? What are the situations which prompt people to talk about *centaurs* or *unicorns*? One can easily avoid these and many similar problems if one adopts the popular (*mentalistic*) view and says that speech forms reflect unobservable, non-physical events in the *minds* of speakers and hearers: for every speech form that is uttered, one need only then claim the occurrence of a corresponding *mental* event. If, on the contrary, these general problems of meaning are to be studied, they will concern physiology, psychology, and sociology rather than linguistics alone.

In language, forms cannot be separated from their meanings. It would be uninteresting and perhaps not very profitable to study the mere sound of a language without any consideration of meaning. Even in laboratory phonetics one specifies what word or what part of a word is being analyzed. In studying a language, we can single out the relevant features of sound only if we know something about the meaning. This appears plainly when one confronts an unfamiliar language. An observer who first hears the Chippewa of Wisconsin or Michigan will note down such forms as [gi:žik, gi.šik, ki:žik, ki:šik], and he will not know whether he has recorded one, two, three, or four different words. Only when he learns that all four indifferently mean 'sky' and when he finds similar variations for other unit meanings, will he realize that these variations are not significant. On the other hand, the difference between the final consonants of such forms as [ki:šik] and [ki:šikk] will perhaps at first escape the observer or seem to him to be trifling or irrelevant, until he realizes that this difference goes hand in hand with a gross difference of meaning, since only the forms with a shorter and weaker final consonant mean 'sky', while the others mean 'cedar'. It is only the differences of meaning which decide that most of the inevitable variations of sound are irrelevant and only certain ones play a part in communication. In short, the significant features of sound (the *phonemes*) of a language are, of course, those which involve a difference of meaning.

There is scarcely any limit to the varieties of meaning, but the significant features of sound in any one language are never more than a few dozen. It is the very nature of language that the infinite, flowing, and unexplored variety of things and happenings is represented (imperfectly, of course) by combinations of a few dozen recognizable elements of sound. It results from this that language is abstract: if a thing has certain characteristics we call it an *apple* and let it go at that. Every apple has a color, but we need not bother to include the color in our signal. If the color interests us, we can speak of a *red apple*, but to describe the particular apple in full detail might take many hours. On the other hand, the forms of language are arbitrary: if we insert the sound [m] and say *ample*, we have an entirely different signal, just as in Ojibwa [ki:šik] 'sky' and [ki:šikk] 'cedar' have nothing to do with each other. The forms of a language are simple in structure, consisting of sequences of a few dozen phonemes, but the meanings are complex, because they include everything in the life of the speakers.

It follows from this that in all study of language we must start from forms and not from meanings. For instance, our school grammars give such definitions as these: "A noun is the name of a person, place, or thing"; "An adjective is a word which describes or limits a substantive"; "A verb is a word which can assert something (usually an action) concerning a person, place, or thing." The interpretation or application of statements like these would lead to disputes even in a college of metaphysicians; they can only baffle and confuse the pupils and this, indeed, may account for many people's dislike and fear of statements about language. If we said, for instance, that a noun is any word which can be preceded by the word *the* to form a unit phrase, we should have a usable criterion which would offer only slight difficulty in the case of names (*the Tom I know*).

In short, it is easy to describe, classify, and arrange the forms of a language, but even if we commanded the entire range of present-day knowledge, we should still be unable to describe, classify, or arrange the meanings which are expressed by these forms. Take for instance the directory of a city with many thousands of inhabitants: there is no dispute about its arrangement and we can all use it with ease because the names are listed alphabetically, according to their form, but this would not be the case if we tried to arrange the directory by meaning—that is, according to features of the inhabitants, such as stature, age, wealth, or intelligence.

To earlier students, language appeared to have a third aspect, intermediate between form and meaning; this aspect was usually called *function*. Thus, a word like *apple* not only meant a certain kind of fruit, but also functioned as a noun, serving as the subject of verbs, as the object of prepositions and transitive verbs, and so on. Careful study, however, showed that features like these are a part of the form; they are the formal features which come into being when two or more forms are combined in a larger form. Thus the word *apple* enters into phrases with preceding adjectives and, except for certain very special expressions, is always so preceded (*an apple, the apple*); the phrases so formed enter into larger phrases with following finite verb expressions (*the apple tastes sour*); the word *apple* is matched by a plural form *apples*; and so on. A form's privilege of occurring in any one position is *a function* of that form, and all its various functions together make up its *function*. In sum, the function of a speech form consists merely of formal features which appear when it serves as part of a more inclusive form.

It is very difficult to state the meaning of a word or form, because the things and happenings in the world are many and varied and also because different languages classify them in different ways. If we have a complete botanical description and classification of all the plants of a region, we can define every plant name used by the speakers of this region; after each name we shall list the species (one or more) which it designates, and when any one species is called by more than one name we can use notes and cross-references. But when we come to expressions for states of a person, such as *sad, happy, jolly, merry* or for types of friendship and affection between persons, there is no system of hard and fast descriptions and classifications by which we could register the meanings so that everyone would interpret our report in a uniform way, as was the case with our plant names. In such matters we should have to wait for manuals of physiology and sociology that would read as unambiguously as do our present manuals of botany.

This lack of a fixed scale or standard troubles us especially when we try to state the meaning of the very commonest types of expression in a language. H. W. Nagl, describing his native Austrian dialect (*Da Roanad*, Vienna, 1886), takes nine pages of fine print to tell the meaning of the adverb *halt*. Thus, a teacher of French, Spanish, or German may spend hours explaining the meaning of the subjunctive mode. Since we have no clear terms for stating such things, the time will usually be wasted, except for the examples which are presented in the course of the attempted explanation. Recognizing this, the late M. J. Andrade, an excellent teacher, used to present the Spanish subjunctive by simply having his pupils memorize a dozen or so of typical sentences. Until some new branch of science furnishes a scale of measurement for discourse about topics like these, the work of stating such meanings will have to be done by examples rather than by explicit definition. This is one of the features which lend great value to minute and leisurely studies of a dialect, with plentiful citation, such as our teacher Roedder's *Volkssprache und Wortschatz* (New York, 1936). There are few such studies, even for familiar languages.

It is difficult to state the meaning of the speech forms of a language which one knows; it is even more difficult to find out the meaning of speech forms in an unfamiliar language. The demand for full and exact statements of meaning in descriptions of exotic languages is certainly justified, but it can be fulfilled only in the rare cases where the investigator has, after years of association, acquired something like the mastery of a native. In the ordinary case, one can furnish only a very rough indication, with here and there a distinction or a clarifying restriction which one has been lucky enough to observe. Similarly in ancient languages, one may be lucky enough, through careful study of texts, to discover one or another clearcut feature of meaning. It may be questioned whether any present-day scholar is ever satisfied with his understanding of any one page, say, of Middle High German. It is an unfortunate fashion which leads to the writings of essays and dissertations on "semantic fields" of the most difficult and abstract sort in older languages; if one were to take concrete fields, such as names of plants or of household utensils or terms for cutting and carving, the difficulty would be less, but would appear more plainly.

In language teaching the difficulty of describing meanings makes a great deal of trouble. By tradition we assign a meaning, in the shape of a brief English definition, to each foreign word; then, whenever the foreign language does not agree with our grammatical rules and our definitions, we say that it has an "idiom". This plan works (to be sure, very poorly) because the languages usually taught resemble English quite closely both in cultural background and in the general grammatical structure which they inherit in common. Even here, however, the plan breaks down as soon as we pay close attention to almost any one form. Prokosch used to point out that the German noun *Tisch*, apart from the matter of gender, differed from English *table* in never being applied to such things as a table of statistics. In fact, everything in a language is "idiom" and, strictly speaking, this term would have to be applied to every form of the foreign language.

A clever and linguistically sensitive teacher who used the dictionaries and disposed of many apt examples, could compose a brief essay to describe the meaning of each foreign form—even of such elusive words as the German adverb particles (*ja, doch, zwar, noch, schon, erst, eben, denn,* and so on)—and a very gifted pupil might conceivably remember and apply all this doctrine. One could imagine a very interesting text book which presented such discussions for a thousand or so of the commonest words of a foreign language. It seems likely, however, that even when teachers go pretty far in this direction, the pupils profit by the examples that accompany the explanation, rather than by the explanation itself. Moreover, now that war conditions are forcing some of us to give instruction at a very rapid pace and in more distant languages, it seems to be getting clearer and clearer that the activity which far exceeds all others as to economy of time and as to sureness of results is hearing and trying to speak. If this is confirmed, then obviously any explanation, including explanation of meanings, that is presented in English, is given at a great cost, and should perhaps be confined to brief printed form in the text book and never allowed to take up the precious classroom moments when the pupil might be hearing the foreign language.

Even so, the management of meanings is bound to give trouble. We acquire our native language by hearing and speaking in a myriad of real situations. The things and happenings of which one speaks are not present in the classroom. Some beginners' books (including my German one) try to meet this difficulty by introducing a great deal of talk about classroom situations, but this is too narrow and uninteresting a range. One thing is certain: the traditional fables, stories, and anecdotes, silly in content (but often literary or stilted in expression) serve very poorly, especially because they introduce vocabulary in the wrong order. I once used a German beginner's book which, on one of the first pages, contained the absurd sentence *Die Katze verzehrte die Maus*—when the pupils had not met the words *essen* and *fressen*. This presentation distorts and in the end confuses the learner's reception of meaning. One may suspect that the use of simple or silly content in inconsiderate form arose through a mistaken adoption of materials from early reading books for native children.

Perhaps the greatest problem of foreign language teaching (alongside, to be sure, of the phonetic problem) will turn out to be one which we have never placed in this rank: the problem of talking, with controlled vocabulary, in the classroom, about all the topics that the student is to master, and of doing this in such a way that the meaning appears not in the shape of English expressions, but in the actual situation of the learner.

# B59. Review of Swadesh

1943. *Language* 19.168–170.

*La Nueva Filología.* By Mauricio Swadesh. With appendix: La uniformización de los alfabetos del mundo, by Norman A. McQuown. (Collección 'Siglo XX'; Biblioteca del Maestro, Vol. 4.) Mexico City: El Nacional (Organo Oficial del Gobierno de Mexico), 1941. Pp 288.

This is an excellent introduction to linguistics. It covers the usual topics; the chapter headings are: 1. Origen y rasgos generales de la nueva filología; 2. Supersticiones populares sobre la lengua; 3. Los sonidos del habla humana; 4. La síntesis fonémica de la fonética; 5. La escritura; 6. El análisis estructural; 7. La cadenación gramatical; 8. Inflexión y clasificación; 9. La historia del lenguaje; 10. La linguística y la enseñanza. There is an appendix by N. A. McQuown, outlining practical phonetic alphabets for Castilian Spanish, American English, German, Chinese, French, Italian, Russian, Arabic, Malay, Quechua, Zulu, Nahuatl, Totonac, Tarascan, Mazatec, and Navaho, and citing some of the resolutions of the first Congreso indigenista interamericano sobre la educación indígena.

Not only in Chapter 2, but in many parts of the book, Swadesh carefully tries to remove the false notions about language which are traditional among his readers.

The word 'new' in the title disturbs the present reviewer. When a linguist has occasion to present to teachers, educationalists, or other laymen some long-established and commonplace result of our science, he is likely to be dealt with as if he were propounding haphazard and eccentric notions of his own. On the other hand, some linguistic students, especially abroad, are prone to din out the 'newness' of every new statement or new emphasis, false or true, proclaiming revolutions in our science and setting out to found new 'schools' at the drop of a hat. Accordingly, your reviewer believes that this form of the title does an injustice to Swadesh's excellent book.

The examples, taken from a great variety of languages, are well chosen and neatly presented.[1]

---

[1] On page 172, the first Russian example is wrong. On page 236, there is the statement that in some types of English the words *matter* and *madder* coincide in sound; I know of no report of such an observation; rather, the tongue-flip variant of /t/ seems everywhere to contrast with /d/.

Your reviewer finds serious fault only with some of the later parts of the book. Chapter 7 begins with a vague passage setting up two technical terms *utilization* and *creation* ('más o menos una idea original mía'— hence scarcely appropriate in a beginner's manual). These two terms are not clearly defined and there are no examples except the statement that these terms themselves are an instance of 'creation'. From that point on, the chapter lapses into traditional philosophic jargon: 'términos', 'relaciones', 'entidades', and so on; *aquí* equals 'en este lugar'; *trabaja* equals 'es hacedor de trabajo', where the word *es* 'expresa la pura predicación' (165), and we learn (179) about 'la gran variedad de conceptos que se pueden representar en la forma de términos. Una clasificación completa sería un examen minucioso de las posibilidades de conceptualización de la mente humana.' We even get, on page 213, the conventional bit of philosophy about there really being a past and future but no such time as the present. This is a statement (perhaps a postulate) in the realm of elementary physics. It seems to mean that the utterance *It's raining* cannot possibly be made during a rainfall. Why does it appear in discourses about language? Is there any aspect or part of the universe that can be explored by sheer common sense, cleverness, or what is known as dialectic? In order to state the meanings of speech forms we should need scientific classifications and definitions of everything in the world; in practice, we make shift largely with rough statements in the everyday terms or semi-scholastic verbiage of our community. From this situation there arose, long before the time of serious linguistic study, the notion that, beforehand and independently of any particular act of observation, one could formulate, by virtue of some sort of philosophic acumen, a realistic outline of the universe which would serve as a frame of reference for statements of the meaning of linguistic forms. We need not here dwell upon the prescientific and indeed barbarous character of this notion, for, strangely enough, our author himself performs this task on pages 221 and 222 of his book. To be sure, he returns to speculation on pages 246 and 249, anent the origin of language.

These 'philosophic' passages stand out darkly against the rational and humane illumination which pervades the treatise. They could serve as an instance of vestigial traits in culture: shreds of medieval speculation still hanging to the propellers of science and sometimes fouling them. The lesson of this contrast is brought home to the reader because the rest of the book speaks clearly with the voice of enlightenment. Philosophic and political meditations have no place in a scientific manual.

# B60. Obituary of Boas

1943. *Language* 19.198.

Franz Boas, a signer of the Call which led to the founding of the Linguistic Society of America, and the Society's President in 1928, died on December 21, 1942, at the age of 84.

He was German by birth. His early training was in physics and geography. At the age of 25 he spent a year with the Eskimos on Baffin Land; at this time, his interest turned to anthropology and linguistics. He came to the United States in 1886. From 1896 on he taught at Columbia University.

He worked in various branches of anthropology. Most interesting to linguists, perhaps, were his studies of what is popularly called 'race'. We can no longer plead ignorance as an excuse for the brutal and harmful superstitions on this theme, such as prevail in most communities and not least in our own.

Perhaps his greatest contribution to science, and, at any rate, the one we can best appreciate, was the development of descriptive language study. The native languages of our country had been studied by some very gifted men, but none had succeeded in putting this study upon a scientific basis. The scientific equipment of linguists, on the other hand, contained few keen tools except the comparative method, and this could not yet be here applied. Boas amassed a tremendous body of observation, including much carefully recorded text, and forged, almost single-handed, the tools of phonetic and structural description. This achievement is briefly and modestly summarized in the Introduction to the Handbook of American Indian Languages (Smithsonian Institution, Bureau of American Ethnology, Bulletin 40; Washington, 1911). The progress which has since been made in the recording and description of human speech has merely grown forth from the roots, stem, and mighty branches of Boas' life work. Boas himself tended this growth: he taught William Jones, Truman Michelson, Edward Sapir, and others now living, and with unfailing kindness he helped many who were not formally his pupils.

All this arose from his immediate greatness as a man. Above all, Boas was good; his kindness and generosity knew no bounds. He cast a saintly blessing over his family, his friends, and his students. He fought with supreme valor against any evil that came within his ken. He gave all his strength unflaggingly to the search for truth. Those who knew him, seeking for the best example of a man of science as a member of society and as a citizen, will think of Franz Boas.[1]

[1] [Bloomfield was asked to write a preface for *Linguistic Structures of Native America* (the volume from which our B65 is taken). His preface is dated 1944, and reads as follows: 'This volume, dedicated to the memory of Franz Boas, was planned by Edward Sapir. The contributors have been deprived of the help and encouragement that Sapir would have given; the reader has been deprived of the contribution that Sapir would have written with insight, grace, and power. The dedication is as Sapir intended it, though now we must speak of memory. In our work we have thought of Franz Boas, the pioneer and master in the study of American languages and the teacher, in one or another sense, of us all.'

Note also the pointed mention of Boas in the first paragraph of *About Foreign Language Teaching* (B63).—CFH]

# B61. Review of Bodmer

1944. *American Speech* 19.211–213.

*The Loom of Language.* By Frederick Bodmer. New York: W. W. Norton and Company, [1944]. Pp x + 692, illustrated.

What would one say of a chemical textbook sponsored by an authority on the history of music and written by a man who had made extensive use of paints, drugs, and cosmetics, but had never troubled himself to acquire so much as the rudiments of chemistry? What publisher, indeed, would think of issuing such a book, what critic of seriously considering its merits? To a student of language it is shocking and humiliating to see how little of the results of linguistic science has reached even the upper levels of our culture. The methodical and cumulative study of language, dating from about the year 1800, is approximately as old as that of chemistry. Its results have been plentiful and often unexpected. Here perhaps more than at any other point of attack, science has gained systematic and other than trivial knowledge about specifically human behavior—a notable result, since the study of language seemed at first to hold out no such promise.

The book here under review intends to inform the general reader about language. Its author is evidently an educated man with some knowledge of several European languages. His book is recommended and prefaced by an eminent man of science (in another field, of course), it is being energetically distributed by a reputable publisher, and it has been praised by critics who know nothing about its subject. If one were willing to ignore the tiresome, sciolistically facetious, and repetitious style of this book, its total lack of clarity and structure, and the errors and misunderstandings in which it abounds, there would remain the fact that in the state of its information it lies some decades behind Whitney's excellent popular books, *Language and the Study of Language* (1867) and *The Life and Growth of Language* (1874).

Franz Bopp, the pioneer of comparative grammar, receives some mention, and there is frequent reference to the Indo-European family of languages—to be sure, under the once customary name of 'Aryan,' which in present-day terminology applies only to the Indo-Iranian branch of the Indo-European family. Nevertheless, the reader learns almost nothing of the results of comparative and historical linguistics, and what little he gets is largely wrong. Absent also are the results of the later directions of linguistic research: dialect geography and descriptive analysis.

This last omission is especially striking, since one of the chief aims of the book is to help the reader to 'learn' foreign languages. This application of linguistic science is the subject of Henry Sweet's classical treatise on *The Practical Study of Languages* (1900). In place of what is there set forth and of what has since been learned, the present book offers a jumble of haphazard fantasies, untried and untriable, such as might occur to anyone who started from scratch to improvise upon this theme. So far as the present reviewer can see, this book would not help, but only befuddle a person who wanted to study a foreign language.

Another principal aim of the book concerns the social significance of language. The author understands this only as it is understood in the popular view of our time. He dwells upon Basic English and upon artificial languages, in the usual hope that some kind of linguistic invention will overcome the social barriers of language. He does not speak of the fundamental and pervasive role of language in human behavior as it has occupied linguists during the present century, although he names Sapir's *Language* (1921) in one of the apparently otiose lists of books which come at the ends of some chapters.

Confusion of writing with language appears in many passages. The terms 'self-expression' and 'correspondence' play a big part in the advice for 'learning' foreign languages; apparently one is to find a foreigner who is willing (and able) to correct one's mistakes in letters (of all things) which one is to write in his language. The difference between complex and simple sentences is illustrated (on pages 165 and following) by two versions of a before-and-after testimonial about a young woman who was greatly benefited by reading *The Loom of Language*; among other things, she started writing to a 'boy friend' in Sweden.

On page 71 there is a table of the English vowels in 'phonetic script': *a* as in *hat*, and so on; the example for *ai* is the name *Einstein*.

Humboldt's distinction (1836) of 'isolating,' 'inflectional,' and 'agglutinative' languages, with 'incorporating' languages as a supplementary type, still appears (page 209) in this very form, except for a strange but characteristic miscomprehension:

> At one time comparative linguists distinguished an *incorporating* or *holophrastic* type to accommodate the Amerindian languages, which illustrate another peculiarity of sound pattern. It is extremely difficult to recognize where one word begins and another ends in the language of the Greenland Eskimo. The same is true of a great variety of indigenous, totally unrelated, vernaculars of the American continent. How far people distinguish one word from the next, especially in rapid speech, varies from one dialect to another within a small group. In a large family such as the Aryan, we find examples

of highly holophrastic languages such as French or highly staccato languages such as German.

There is much sprightly reference to 'grammarians,' 'grammar books,' and the like; indeed, the author seems dimly to realize that linguists have ceased to force the description of languages into the framework of traditional Latin grammar. Ignorant, however, of descriptive linguistics, he gives only a garbled version of this same traditional doctrine. His sketches of the principal Romance and Germanic languages amount to no more than a hurried and jumbled summary of what is more clearly stated in any school grammar. This confusion is increased by occasional attempts at dealing with more than one language at a time; for instance (page 270): '. . . *telefoneeren* (Dutch), *telefonieren* (German). German and Dutch verbs of this class have past participles without the *ge-* prefix, e.g. *ich habe telegrafiert*' (this, of course, is not true of Dutch). Elsewhere, also, Dutch fares pretty badly; page 283: '*ik leer, ik leerde; ik lach, ik lachte*. The past participle is formed by putting *ge-* in front of the root and adding *-d* or *-t . . . ik hab geleerd*' (read *heb*; the past participle of *lachen* is *gelachen*); page 282; '*kammer—kammers*' (meaning 'room—rooms'; read *kamer—kamers*). Instead of warning the reader against trying to study more than one language at a time, the author, irresponsibly and in the face of all experience, goes so far as to tell him (page 8) that he may 'benefit by trying to learn German along with Dutch.'

Although most of the book consists in tramping round and round again over a dozen or so of trivial topics, a student of language will find much comic relief: queer misconceptions, alternating attempts at jocularity and at improvisation of scientific judgments, and a generally bizarre and cockeyed picture of the world of language in which he spends his working days.

# B62. Secondary and Tertiary Responses to Language

1944. *Language* 20.45 55.

[For how this article came to be written, see fn 17 of Bloch's obituary notice (70(1)), and the next to the last paragraph of Hall's notice (70(4)). The 'chamber of horrors' portion of the article was reprinted in Harold B. Allen, ed., *Readings in Applied English Linguistics* (New York: Appleton-Century-Crofts, Inc., 1958) pp 195–202; second edition (1964) pp 274–281.]

Utterances about language may be called SECONDARY RESPONSES to language. For us, the most important are those which are made in the systematic study of language—the utterances, above all, which, recorded in books and essays, embody the past results of linguistic science. They will not concern us here; to the extent that we succeed in working scientifically, the verbal phase of our work takes on the general characteristics of scientific utterance.

On other than a scientific level, our culture maintains a loosely organized but fairly uniform system of pronouncements about language. Deviant speech forms in dialects other than the standard dialect are described as corruptions of the standard forms ('mistakes', 'bad grammar') or branded as entirely out of bounds, on a par with the solecisms of a foreign speaker ('not English'). The forms of the standard dialect are justified on grounds of 'logic'. Either on the strength of logical consistency or in pursuance of largely conventional authoritative rules, which constitute a minor tradition within the main one (for instance, the rules about *shall* and *will*), certain forms are theoretically prescribed for the standard dialect. When it is noticed that speakers of the standard dialect do not use these forms or use others beside them, these deviations are again branded as 'mistakes' or, less often, attributed to 'usage', which appears here only as a special and limited factor, mentioned doubtfully as interfering with more legitimate controls.

Traditional lore of this kind is occasionally put into literary form and developed in detail, as in the well-known treatise of Richard Grant White,

Words and their uses, past and present: a study of the English language (New York, 1870).[1]

The speaker is able to discourse also upon more remote topics. In spite of the degenerative character of dialects other than the standard one, some distant local dialects are said to maintain pure Elizabethan English.[2] As a dim reflex of statements concerning linguistic relationships, one hears that the Finnish and Hungarian (or the Bengali and Lithuanian, or the Basque and Malayalam) languages are mutually intelligible. Some ignorant people and some savage tribes are said to have a vocabulary of only a few hundred words. This may be attributed to illiteracy, for 'spoken language' fleetingly renders the forms which have their basic and permanent existence in the 'written language'. The latter 'fixes' and 'preserves' linguistic tradition. Operations upon the system of writing immediately affect a language. The following press releases embody various other phases of popular linguistics, but are especially illuminating on the matter of language and writing.

From the Tulsa Daily World of February 27, 1941:

### TULSAN WANTS SEQUOYAH'S ALPHABET TAUGHT IN PUBLIC SCHOOLS

Sequoyah's alphabet should become a part of the standard equipment in Oklahoma schools, a Tulsan declared Tuesday as he mailed letters to officials at the state capitol proposing that the Cherokee language be made a part of the regular curriculum in all state high schools.

"It's the only native tongue conceived and taught as a language in America," Dr. C. Sterling Cooley, 415 South Guthrie, wrote A. L. Crable, Oklahoma superintendent of public instruction. Copies were sent to Senator Henry Timmons and Representative W. H. Langley of the state legislature which is now in session at Oklahoma City. . . .

Possibility that Sequoyah's languages could fool the Germans again, however, was just a minor point in the doctor's contention the Cherokee tongue should be taught in school like English, French or Latin.

"Oklahoma schools have taught a lot of subjects a lot more useless," Doctor Cooley said. . . .

Doctor Cooley said the 86 characters of Sequoyah's famous alphabet were memorized by some cherokees in as little time as three days.

"One-semester course should be sufficient for Oklahoma students to learn the subject," he said.

---

[1] Contemporary with Whitney's Language and the study of language (1867) and Life and growth of language (1874). Our undergraduate instructors advised us to read Richard Grant White; Whitney was not mentioned.

[2] An Associated Press dispatch (New York Times, November 26, 1939) is headed 'Fishermen speak in Middle English'. Part of the wording is as follows: 'A touch of Elizabethan England still flourishes on the "outer banks," a serpentine strand off North Carolina's coast. . . . one hears on the "outer banks" words and phrases so similar to the language of Queen Elizabeth's day that philologists and historians see a distinct connection.'

For this and most of the following citations, as well as for much kind help and criticism, I am indebted to Bernard Bloch.

Doctor Cooley's letter to Superintendent Crable follows:

"Dear Sir:

"To perpetuate a beautiful language that would prove uniquely useful in time of war; to preserve the only native tongue conceived and taught as a language in America; to offer something better than the "trial of tears" as a memory of our treatment of them and to honor a great leader of an historic people I believe Oklahoma ought to make it possible for its citizens to choose the syllabus of Sequoyah as an elective study in the curriculum of any public school where languages in addition to English are taught.

"I propose this to you because you are logically the one who can best open the door of opportunity to any and all who wish to learn the tongue of the Cherokees, the language of Indians everywhere, and I shall be grateful to you if you will advise how others and myself may help to make it possible for our schools to perpetuate a language that is solely American in origin."

Doctor Cooley said he sent a copy of the letter to Representative Langley because, to his knowledge he is the nearest full-blood Cherokee Indian in the legislature and might be interested in furthering the proposal.

## From the Tulsa Daily World of April 2, 1941:

### CRABLE INDORSES SEQUOYAH'S LANGUAGE AS COLLEGE COURSE

Indorsement of a proposal for teaching Sequoyah's alphabet in public schools, coupled with a recommendation as to where the subject might be experimented with was received here Tuesday from A. L. Crable, state superintendent of public instruction.

In a letter to Dr. C. Sterling Cooley, originator of the proposal which has grown, more or less, into a movement, Crable said, "I am in thorough sympathy with your interest in the syllabary of Sequoyah," and suggest that the State Teachers college in Tahlequah would be the school in which the course should be instituted as an elective study.

"Probably all the colleges of the state would be interested in the effort to perpetuate the great work of Sequoyah, in the way you suggest," the state superintendent's letter to Doctor Cooley read. However, the education executive specifically recommended that the Tulsan take the matter to the president of Northeastern State college in Tahlequah, capital of the Cherokee Nation. This Doctor Cooley indicated he would do.

The movement to perpetuate Sequoyah's alphabet and tongue has reached into states other than Oklahoma. Doctor Cooley pointed out after receiving a letter Tuesday from a Mrs. F. P. Arthurs who wrote in behalf of the department of modern languages at Western State College of Colorado at Gunnison. Mrs. Arthur, who Doctor Cooley believes to be officially connected with the college, asked for references on the life of Sequoyah and inquired about the progress of the Sequoyah movement in Oklahoma.

"I shall write her," said the Tulsan, "that the movement has plenty of encouragement, but no official action—as yet."

Turning back pages of history to 1917, at which time the unveiling of Sequoyah's statue took place in the national capitol's hall of fame, Doctor Cooley found the kind of praise for the Cherokee Indian he has been looking for.

"Sequoyah invented the only sensible alphabet in the world," the Tulsan quoted the late Speaker Chomp Clark[3] of Missouri as saying at the unveiling ceremonies. "It has one letter for each and every sound the human throat can make," the speaker added in praising phonetics of the language. "If he (Sequoyah) had lived 2,000 years ago, one-fifth of the usual time of life could be saved." Here Clark said it took years of schooling to acquire even a fair command of the English language, while the Sequoyah alphabet could be learned in only a few days.

On the same occasion, the late Senator Owen of Oklahoma said: 'It is a strange thing that no alphabet in all the world reaches the dignity, the simplicity, and the value of the Cherogee[3] alphabet, the Cherokee could learn to spell in one day."

The alphabet, containing 85 characters, was invented in 1821 by the Cherokee, whose name it bears, after 12 years of study. Sequoyah could neither speak nor write the English language.

For release September 3, 1941:

Tulsa, Oklahoma:—Bookkeeping, Typing, Shorthand and kindred subjects for business people, will move over slightly, to make room for a subject never before taught the white man. An Indian language, the tongue of the Cherokees, from the syllabus of Sequoyah, is to be offered as a special course with real Indian full-bloods as teachers.

To preserve the only native tongue in America before it is too late, Leon E. Crawford, President of the American Business College here, announced today he had made arrangements to bring an octogenarian from out of the hills of eastern Oklahoma, the only Indian alive who can set Cherokee type, to Tulsa to start work on grammars and dictionaries, necessary for class room instruction. Crawford explained ordinary adults can learn the tongue in a couple of semesters of easy lessons, which he plans to give at night, to scores of business and professional men and woman, who have expressed a desire to study Cherokee, in an endeavor to perpetuate it.

Levi Gritts, last elected Chief of the Cherokees, and his wife, together with J. B. Shunatonna, Chief of the Otoe tribe, all Oklahoma Indians, will supervise the classroom attempt to have Indians teach the white man how to speak and write the only printable language indigenous to North America.

In more abstruse matters our tradition gives the speaker some freedom of improvisation, but even here the pattern is fairly uniform. Theories about the origin of language and suggestions for research on this problem run along certain well-fixed lines.[4] The speaker has the right to improvise

---

[3] So spelled in our reprint of the release.

[4] The following, from a reader's letter to the New York Times, dated August 6, 1937, is quite characteristic.

'Some years ago a scientist lived in a land of monkeys to learn their language. I suggest that the study of language begin there with the primitive sounds of animals, followed by a survey of what is known of the speech of savages. After this might come a review of the most ancient fragments of recorded tongues, tracing them down into the developed languages of Egypt, Mesopotamia, Persia, India, China and elsewhere. Some idea of a dispersal of tongues from a common Asiatic center might thus be had and the earliest roots of our commonest words be learned. A brief survey, in translation, of the recorded literature of these dispersal tongues would bring us down through the ancient classics in all lands to the Greek and Roman

etymologies; these, however, adhere to a rather simple scheme.[5] This phase of popular lore also is capable of development in literary hands.[6]

The speaker who discourses about language sometimes adds that he himself has not a perfect command of his native language—the reasons differ with biographic details—but is aware of his weakness and tries to overcome it; he alludes patronizingly to other speakers who do not know enough to make a similar effort. In fact, it soon appears that the speaker possesses a fairly extensive stock of authoritative knowledge which enables him to condemn many forms that are used by other speakers.

Several peculiarities of these secondary responses deserve further study. The speaker, when making the secondary response, shows alertness. His eyes are bright, and he seems to be enjoying himself. No matter how closely his statement adheres to tradition, he proffers it as something new, often as his own observation or as that of some acquaintance, and he is likely to describe it as interesting. If he knows that he is talking to a professional student of language, he first alleges ignorance and alludes modestly to the status of his own speech, but then advances the traditional lore in a fully authoritative tone. The whole process is, as we say, pleasurable.[7]

The linguist's cue in this situation is to observe; but if, giving in to a natural impulse (or else, by way of experiment), he tries to enlighten the speaker, he encounters a TERTIARY RESPONSE to language. The tertiary response occurs almost inevitably when the conventional secondary response is subjected to question. The tertiary response is hostile; the speaker

cultures, where we should learn not merely a few pages of Xenophon and Homer; of Caesar, Cicero, Virgil and Horace, but, in translations, the whole glorious range of Greek and Latin literary, poetic, scientific and philosophic accomplishment, and the bearing of it all on our modern thought.'

[5] A letter to the New York Times, dated Caracas, Venezuela, November 18, 1939, contains the following characteristic passage: 'But from what root did the word "Reich" grow up? Certainly not from the same as the word "realm." I rather believe that "Reich" has something to do with the German word "reichen" (i.e., reach). On this basis I think I have a more satisfactory explanation of the designation of "Deutsches Reich" and "Frankreich," as those countries or lands that "reach" (or embrace within their respective boundaries, present or former) the Germans, respectively the French (or Franks, originally). . . . a long time ago, probably after the division of Charlemagne's Holy Roman Empire, the western part (chiefly present-day France) came to be designated by the German word Frankreich (although probably spelled in the then prevailing German), i.e., the realm, or rather the land within which "reached" the Franks, from which word afterward a new word, France, resulted.'
Cf. the discussion of a similar instance by R. G. Kent, JAOS 55.115 9 (1935).

[6] Thus, a fairly elaborate theory is built up by Burton Rascoe, Titans of literature, from Homer to the present 48 ff. (New York, 1932).

[7] Undefined popular terms, such as *pleasure* or *anger*, are here used because there is not (or I have not) enough physiology and sociology to redefine them. See, for the rest, A. P. Weiss, A theoretical basis of human behavior, revised edition 419 ff. (Columbus, 1929). Similarly, I use terms like *mechanist* or *non-mentalist*: in a community where nearly everyone believed that the moon is made of green cheese, students who constructed nautical almanacs without reference to cheese, would have to be designated by some special term, such as *non-cheesists*.

grows contemptuous or angry. He will impatiently reaffirm the secondary response, or, more often, he will resort to one of a few well-fixed formulas of confutation.

Invariably in my experience, the linguist's counter-statements are treated as eccentric personal notions—even by speakers who otherwise are aware of the cumulative character of science.[8] The knowledge that the linguist has in person investigated the topic under discussion does not alter this response.[9] Statements about the relation of standard and non-standard forms are likely to be interpreted as 'defense' or 'advocacy' of the latter.[10] Especially, linguistic statements about the relation of writing to language conflict so violently with self-evident truth that they can be interpreted only as a perverse refusal to consider certain facts.[11] A cultured speaker, in confuting the linguist's statements, is likely to appeal, without making clear the connection, to the existence of great writers in his language.[12]

A literary instance of the irate tertiary response is the controversy be-

---

[8] After I had outlined the relation of writing to speech, with explicit reference to the history of our science, before a group of educationists who were interested in elementary reading instruction, I was finally refuted by the statement that 'you'll have to SHOW the modern educationist'.

[9] A physician, of good general background and education, who had been hunting in the north woods, told me that the Chippewa language contains only a few hundred words. Upon question, he said that he got this information from his guide, a Chippewa Indian. When I tried to state the diagnostic setting, the physician, our host, briefly and with signs of displeasure repeated his statement and then turned his back on me. A third person, observing this discourtesy, explained that I had some experience of the language in question. This information had no effect.

[10] 'You surely don't expect me (You wouldn't want your children) to go around saying things like *I seen it* or *I done it*.' A college administrator expressed his wonder at the very 'liberal' attitude of linguists in matters of 'grammar'.

[11] Having read a few sentences about the difference between language and writing, a philosopher concludes that the linguistic author refuses to talk about writing. This conclusion is not shaken by a following fairly wordy passage about the use of graphic signs. To say that writing is not the central and basic form of language is simply to ignore writing altogether. See Journal of Philosophy 36.613 (1939).

Naive invention of phonetic alphabets is not uncommon. The inventor usually believes that he has made an important discovery. Usually, also, he views this discovery as capable of immediately affecting language—removing language barriers or the like. Thus, Senator Robert L. Owen of Oklahoma invented a 'global alphabet' (78th Congress, 1st Session; Senate Document No. 49, Government Printing Office, 1943). The New York Times (July 29, 1943) quotes Senator Owen as follows: 'Through it I can teach any reasonably intelligent man Chinese in two months,' he asserted. 'It is a means by which we can teach the English language to all the world at high speed and negligible cost. It will pay its own way.'

[12] A Russian savant was shocked, in the classical manner described by Jespersen, Grundfragen der Phonetik 56 (Leipzig, 1904), at the sight of the transcriptions used in an elementary Russian course for American students, transcriptions which deviate from the conventional orthography, such as /trúpka/ for graphic *trubka*, /sát/ for graphic *sad*, /búdjit/ for graphic *budet*. In his complaint to an administrative officer he alluded at some length to 'the written and spoken language . . . of Turgeniev, Tolstoy and Chekhov', and to the circumstance that one of his schoolmates later became well-known as a poet.

tween George Washington Moon and Dean Alford. Neither contestant had any knowledge of the subject, but one had questioned the other's secondary response.[13]

The ordinary speaker makes a response of the tertiary type only when some secondary response of his is questioned or contradicted; but, on a higher and semi-learned plane, a tertiary response may be aroused in a speaker who merely hears or reads linguistic statements and possesses enough sophistication to see that they conflict with his habitual secondary responses. Thus, Oscar Cargill, Intellectual America 521 (New York, 1941), writes:

> One cannot ignore the weight of Freeman's essay, "Race and Language" (1885), upon the efforts of these pure scholars. His praise of philology and his use of it as a test of nationality tickled the egos of these new scientists who fancied that their researches would be of the utmost consequence to society. Further and further back into German forests, up Scandinavian fjords, and over Icelandic barriers they pushed their quests for the origin of words. Now, while it is true that the commonest words in English speech have Anglo-Saxon originals and these in turn have Gothic counterparts, not one of these scholars has demonstrated that the ideational content of these limited Northern vocabularies was a heavy burden for the intellect of a moron. Words like *the, is, have, sleep, drink* and *eat* represent the profundity of primitive Anglo-Saxon thought. Pundits, of whom the revered Walter W. Skeat, Litt.D., LL.D, D.C.L., Ph.D., F.B.A., of the University of Cambridge, is typical, have laboriously traced *Ha* (interj. E.) back to Old Friesic *haha* (to denote laughter!) and to German *he*; but it is said that Caligula quite unethically uttered a similar sound when he ordered Pomposo, the philologist, thrown to the lions. In all the northern vocabularies there are no equivalents for such words as *democracy, politics, morals, aesthetics*, and—horror of horrors—*scholarship!* The wolfish pursuit of moronic vocabularies and the ghoulish unearthing of the kennings and pennings of the Northern barbarians diverted young students from the true historical fount of wisdom—the Greek and Roman classics, which fell into the greatest disuse in Western history. There was treachery, alas, among the teachers of classics themselves; for under the leadership of Basil Gildersleeve (educated at Berlin, Bonn, and Göttingen, though a graduate of Princeton), who was appointed Professor of Greek at Hopkins in 1876 and editor of *The American Journal of Philology* in 1880, American classical scholars turned away from the teaching of concepts to the venal study of syntax and word origins. Before long there were no classical scholars in the old sense in America but only philologists, papyri readers, and robbers of tombs. On every front save that of history the triumph of *Kultur* over culture was complete.

[13] Henry Alford, The Queen's English (London, 1864 [1863]); George Washington Moon, A defence of the Queen's English (London, 1863); The Dean's English (London, 1864). These books went into several editions, taking the shape of a polemic; see the entries in A. G. Kennedy, A bibliography of writings on the English language (New York, 1927). Alford and Moon develop the art of finding 'errors' in English to a point where probably no utterance could escape censure. On Alford, see W. D. Whitney, Oriental and linguistic studies 2.166 (New York, 1874).

The following remarks are briefer, but perhaps diagnostically even more significant:[14]

> The study of language today is not the learning to speak and write or even read: it is a technical subject, excessively dry, largely wrong, and thoroughly repellent. Yet an appreciation of language and its uses may be about as enlightening as any discipline we have. Enlightenment, however, is not a matter of accidence, morphology, and other technical aspects so dear to the German-trained and inspired. We give pretty much the same course in "English" from the grades through a couple of years of college—and yet we insist that we enlighten our students. Truly, we are fatuous as well as conceited!

It is only in recent years that I have learned to observe these secondary and tertiary responses in anything like a systematic manner, and I confess that I cannot explain them—that is, correlate them with anything else. The explanation will doubtless be a matter of psychology and sociology. The general background, however, has become apparent to me through certain observations of a more special sort.

It happens that, within the domain of linguistics, I am one of a number of workers who believe that animistic and teleological terminology (*mind*, *consciousness*, *concept*, and so on) does no good and much harm in linguistics, or, for that matter, in any branch of science. In this position one encounters, on a higher and more specialized plane, to be sure, responses of the same general type as the popular ones that were outlined above. I am not alluding here to reasoned discussion of scientific method or of special postulates and methods in linguistics. Of this, in fact, one gets very little. Animistic terminology is so deeply rooted in our culture that its application seems self-evident; perhaps it is incapable of formulation in postulates and definitions which could be confronted, in the way of a philosophical or methodological comparison, with the postulates and definitions of non-animistic science.[15] At any rate, the student who undertakes to eliminate mentalistic terminology from his work meets with types of response which resemble the popular responses to linguistic science in general.

Whoever resolves to forgo in linguistics the use of mentalistic terms, will find himself accused of ignoring segments of human behavior. According to our cultural tradition, certain activities are so obviously and indisputably 'mental' that anyone who says that he will not use mentalistic terms or explanations is understood to mean simply that he will not recognize the existence of these activities.[16] In an essay on word-meaning (un-

[14] S. A. Nock of the Kansas State College of Agriculture and Mechanic Arts, in the Bulletin of the American Association of University Professors 29.202 (1943).

[15] A. P. Weiss ix.

[16] Counter-statements are of no avail, e.g. Weiss vii:
'When Watson maintains that he will not discuss consciousness, this is generally interpreted by psychologists to be an arbitrary elimination of the essential part of human behavior.

published) a leading linguist argues that mechanists cannot successfully speak of meaning because they undertake to ignore certain phases of human response. This undertaking he assumes as a fact admitted by both parties to the dispute. Thus, he argues, the mechanist cannot consider the ethnologic features of meaning, such as connotative colorings or social levels. The mechanist's definition of a plant-name, for instance, cannot (he thinks) extend beyond the definition which appears in a handbook of botany: it cannot deal with ethnically conditioned features of meaning. One reads all this with wonderment and surprise until one realizes what is involved. The realm of the physical is covered by physical and biological science. Everything else is assumed to be obviously and indisputably 'mental'. Hence a linguist who refuses to speak of mental things comes to be viewed as refusing to speak of anything which lies outside the borders of physics and biology.[17]

This interpretation of mechanistic work may go so far as to assert that mechanists undertake to ignore a large domain of directly observable events, such as facial mimicry or even audibly uttered speech. This distortion, entirely at odds with any program announced by mechanists, is hard to understand until one realizes that it is made in all innocence. A large domain of observable events, including even uttered speech, appears to the common sense of our time so directly and unquestionably to represent 'mental' processes that he who refuses to speak of the latter is likely to be understood as refusing also to consider those observable events.[18]

To these it seems as if the behaviorists ignore consciousness because it is too difficult, or because it is a phase in the study of human behavior with which they do not wish to be bothered. Of course, no such inference is warranted. Behaviorism claims to render a *more* complete and a *more* scientific account of the totality of human achievement *without* the conception of consciousness, than traditional psychology is able to render *with* it. The factors which traditional psychology vaguely classifies as conscious or mental elements merely *vanish* without a remainder into the biological and social components of the behavioristic analysis.'

[17] The actual claim of the mechanist, regardless of its merits, that was to be met, is of course an entirely different one. Mechanists and mentalists will in principle give the same definitions for the meaning of a word; only, the latter, in principle if not in actual usage, prefix to each definition some such phrase as *the image of, the concept of, the idea of*; L. Bloomfield, Language 143 f. (New York, 1933); see also p. 38. My statement of the difference may be all wrong, but one cannot do away with it by inventing some entirely different and plainly absurd statement, attributing it to the mechanist, and then refuting it.

[18] An extreme instance, worthy of quotation:
'This paper proposes to discuss the phonemics of bilinguals from the standpoint of their conceptions as well as their speech, an aspect which will be considered unscientific by . . . confirmed behaviorists. . . . However, we offer as evidence only objectively observable behavior, what people say and what people do. Like all scientific evidence, introspective report requires critical handling. We do not offer as established fact every golden remark of the native informant, but check it against the phonetics of his utterance, his handling of an experimental alphabet, his facial and verbal reactions to our attempts to speak words of his language, his pronunciation of other languages we know, and any other item that may suggest something. This is Sapir's method, the critical use of every bit of evidence. It refuses

To say that the mechanist denies himself access to certain features of human behavior sounds to him like question-begging, but actually such statements arise merely from a failure to realize that the mechanist quite simply denies the existence of anything like a special 'mental factor' in human conduct. The 'mental' nature of certain aspects of human behavior seems obvious to the common sense of most men, including many good linguistic scholars. Hence they find it hard to interpret a proposal to exclude 'mental' factors otherwise than as a refusal to observe those features of behavior which they attribute to the action of the 'mind'. It is otherwise with some disputants—and, again, I allude here not to reasoned discussion, but to more immediate socially conditioned responses. Here we meet with accusations of ignorance and iniquity. The mechanist is described as merely repeating the errors of early 'materialistic' philosophers.[19] The painted wooden revolver of solipsism is leveled at the offender: the mechanist can work, after all, only with his mind, which is inferior to the minds of the great philosophers of the past.[20] His approach to solemn questions is crude, rough, and ignorant. He is cynical and insensitive, and cannot 'explain' the finer aspects of human culture and achievement. The following passage is worth quoting in full as an illustration perfect in every detail.[21]

> My paper, based as it is on aesthetic and psychological considerations, will probably prove unpalatable to the anti-mentalistic school of linguistics. According to B. Bloch, *Language*, XVII, 351, "most American linguists probably agree with Bloomfield that a mentalistic approach to linguistic problems can only obscure the issue and 'short-circuit' inquiry." Just how the anti-mentalists would reduce the aesthetic factor in linguistics to a matter of "unofficial" private taste (—to the level, that is, of superstition, or some such inevitable residue of primitive human nature) is clearly brought out by the following lines of the same writer:
>
>> We can describe and codify the facts of language, and we can explain them within the framework of our science, by historical statements; to judge their usefulness or their beauty is to go outside that framework. This does not mean, of course, that a linguist is debarred by his profession from having opinions or tastes. In his unofficial [!] capacity as a

to be restricted to using only half the observable facts, and is not frightened at such stigmas as "mentalist."'—M. Swadesh in Language, culture, and personality: essays in memory of Edward Sapir 59 (Menasha, 1941). One wonders which half of the observable facts is not included in what people say and what people do, and is accessible to the mentalist but not to the mechanist.

[19] That is, the mechanist is repeating the mistakes of philosophers who took no account of the effects of language. It is customary to condemn any aberrant doctrine by identifying it with any other, on the strength of any common feature whatever (compare, for instance, the political-sociological series *slum clearance*, *socialized medicine*, *New Deal*, *communism*, *free love*). Here again, counter-statement does not help, e.g. Weiss 303 f.

[20] L. Bloomfield, Linguistic aspects of science 13 f. (International Encyclopedia of Unified Science 1.4; Chicago, 1939).

[21] Leo Spitzer, Why does language change? MLQ 4.430 fn. 23 (1943).

human being and a user of language he can no more help [!] making judgments than anyone else.

The anti-mentalistic attitude has its origin in the fear of introducing "unknowns" into linguistics; it is no far cry from this attitude to that of denying the very existence of some basic factor of human speech because this factor is not easily traceable in detail; but, out of fear before the "unknown" that may be connected with a certain factor, to introduce the notion of its inexistence is to sin against the known, against knowledge itself. First one says: "let us not speak of the human mind because this would 'obscure our notions'"; later one behaves as though this human mind did not exist at all; this would be an anti-scientific, sophistical attitude; this is the attitude of this school of linguists who would prefer any mechanical and matter-of-fact explanation to a spiritual one. And to admit of a schism between the scholar-as-a-human being, and the "official scholar," as Bloch proposes, is to betray a lack of ambition toward the goal of a unification of human nature; it is a surrender to modern mental disintegration.

Ironically enough, the antimentalists seem to consider their pronunciamentos in favor of a fragmentary outlook on life to be the very paragon of scholarliness. Thus we learn by an authoritative statement of L. Bloomfield (*Language*, XIX, 170) that "philosophic passages have nothing to do in linguistic treatises";[22] they are "vestigial traits in culture," "shreds of medieval speculation"—whereas what is desirable is "rational and humane illumination." He does not seem to realize that such a statement itself constitutes a "philosophy" (albeit a very shallow decoction of eighteenth-century theories of the *philosophes*) and that a linguistic treatise based on this anti-philosophic philosophy is necessarily bound to be a mentalistic philosophy (of the Leonard Bloomfield brand of mentalism, of course). I surmise that the antimentalists can only afford to call themselves "unbiased by philosophy" because they suppose that what they ignore (or are ignorant of) can be eliminated at will and does not exist—in them, in spite of them.

In another passage (*Language*, XIX, 199) B. Bloch writes: "What 'mechanists' usually criticize in the work of 'mentalists' . . . is the circularity of their argument: the explanation of a linguistic fact by an assumed psychological process for which the only evidence is the fact to be explained." Such a statement betrays lack of familiarity with a current philosophical thought such as that expressed in Goethe's profound aphorism: "Das Höchste wäre zu begreifen dass alles Faktische schon Theorie ist." I suppose the antimentalists take it as a 'fact' that there are such things as 'Proto-Romance,' 'Germanic languages,' without realizing that these 'factual' expressions imply a theory, a speculation: indeed, there is here underlying the Goethian idea of the *Urpflanze* (an "unknown"!), a principle not present in any particular branch but unfolding in them all. Thus the antimentalists do not hesitate to accept the results of speculation (when these have become commonplace, mechanized 'speech-habits'); they accept the canned fruit but reject the live tree of speculation itself; they *want* to live on the *dead* residues of the past, not in the living present. And this school would be a school of the future?

Furthermore the above-mentioned passage contains a reference to the "circularity of reasoning" characteristic of the mentalists. It is as if Schleiermacher and Dilthey had never taught that the "philologischer Zirkelschluss" is the basic operation in the humanities: thus it was that Diez started with the

---

[22] Misquotation; the expression is not in my dialect.

observation (contrary to the assertion of Raynouard that Provençal was the mother language) that no one Romance language is reducible to another, and then proceeded to construct his ' Urpflanze,' the "unknown quantity" Proto-Romance = Vulgar Latin, finally concluding with the reverse procedure by which he verified his assumption that 'Vulgar Latin' as conceived by him, could explain all the Romance languages. Nothing is more orthodox than such "circular reasoning." Similarly, when I have observed what I call a ' stylistic fact' (which is already a ' speculation,' see above) in the language of a writer, I tentatively suggest a possible psychological root, in the writer, of this particular usage—later to test whether the assumed psychological root is able to explain other stylistic observations which may be made concerning his individual language. (It is hardly correct to say that 'the mentalists' base their psychological analysis on *one* fact alone.) There is the same circularity here as in the reasoning of Diez: both speculations are in fact based on the ' idea' of the organicity of development (the ' organism' of Vulgar Latin, 'the organism of the psyche of an individual writer'—both of which unfold). Of the two speculations, the bolder would seem to be the one of Diez! Thus, far from being a logical error, as Mr. Bloch believes, the circularity of argument is the main operation in sciences of the human mind.

The anti-mentalistic bias which pervades the publications of the Linguistic Society of America can be shown on nearly every page;[23] I shall offer only one specimen. In dissertation no. 17, "The Neuter Plural in Vergil" (1934), J. F. Gummere seeks to prove by statistics that the use in Latin dactylic verse of the (nom. and acc.) plural of neuters is due to their greater metrical convenience; by analogy an "illogical" use of the plural in the place of the singular was brought about, and "the so-called 'poetic' plurals are merely [!] these illogical plurals." He cites lines 645 seq. of the *Aeneid*:

    interiora domus inrumpit *limina*, et altos
    conscendit furibunda *rogos* ensemque recludit
    Dardanium, non hos quaesitum munus in *usus*.

It apparently satisfies the unpoetic mind of this writer ("Du gleichst dem Geist, den du begreifst!") to see an *ultima ratio* in "metrical convenience"; this seems to him to be *a causa sui*, whereas the "poetic" qualities of vagueness, majesty, etc., are probably Hecuba to him. Any normal human being could analyze this mythologem of "metrical convenience"—which introduces an "unknown" (of mentalistic origin at that) much more detrimental

---

[23] Whether the publications of the Society are pervaded by such a bias may be determined by any reader. If articles of any one trend should appear to predominate, the reason would doubtless be the same as that stated by the Editor in Bulletin 15.18 (1942): 'LANGUAGE is not the organ of any one school of linguistic theory, but of the Linguistic Society as a whole. It may publish controversial views, and occasionally it may seem to give more space to one side of a controversy than to another, if supporters of that side happen to send in more material; but the Committee on Publications, in their official capacity, have no interest in promoting any special cause beyond the one for whose advancement our Society was organized.' It accords with this statement that five articles by Spitzer have appeared in the journal during the past four years (LANG. 16.213–4; 17.50–3, 253–5; 19.156–61, 258–61).

The passage cited by Spitzer as an instance of anti-mentalism is taken from a ten-year-old Language Dissertation. Without prejudice to the merits of that work, it is to be noted that the following statement appears on its inside back cover: 'The Society does not pass upon the scholarly merit nor upon the validity of the theses propounded in the dissertations.' If examples of an anti-mentalistic bias occur on nearly every page of the Society's publications, an example should not have been so far to seek.

to the understanding of the linguistic phenomenon in question (which is the basis of the Vulgar Latin and Romance morphological type *gaudia > joie*) than the legitimate, if difficult, question of its psychological and aesthetic radix.

A healthy opposition to undisciplined mentalism is to be welcomed, but here the opposition has developed into a wholesale negation of much of the finest thought in linguistic philosophy since Herder. What a cruel self-mutilation of the human mind!

Non-animistic and non-teleological procedures and statements are simple necessary things, carried on without much comment until they are systematized; only then do they arouse hostility. From its beginnings, in the person of Galileo, modern science has been assailed as cynical, impious, and superficial. Our grandfathers witnessed this struggle in the matter of geology and biology. It is an interesting trait of culture that scientific workers in domains from which animism and teleology have been banished, feel free to demand the use of these notions in less developed branches of science, such as our own.

We have acquired understanding and the power of prediction and control and have reaped vast benefit in the domains where we have developed non-animistic and non-teleologic science. We remain ignorant and helpless in the domains where we have failed to develop that kind of science, namely, in human affairs, such as the correlation of incentive with the distribution of economic goods, or the disposal of conflicting national interests.

The only exception here is our relatively good knowledge of the structure and history of languages, a body of knowledge which, against the predisposition and expectation of the discoverers, turned out to imply no animistic or teleological factors. Although this situation gives us no certainty, it offers a strong probability in favor of extending the methods that have been successful to replace those which have yielded no success. Mankind has always found such steps difficult and has resisted them with more than mere inertia. Obscurantism, the articulate vanguard of that resistance, has never employed rational argument, but only invective and, from the time of Galileo to our own, every degree of irrational sanction.

# B63. About Foreign Language Teaching

1945. *The Yale Review* 34.625–641.

[The linguists at Yale, like those everywhere, became deeply involved in practical language-teaching during World War II; in addition to other activities along this line, they had to provide for instruction in various unusual languages for service personnel, in locally housed segments of the Army Specialized Training Program. Some of the administrative authorities of the University, and doubtless some of its alumni, were somewhat disturbed about the educational and scholarly propriety of these involvements. The preparation and publication of the present article by the acknowledged intellectual leader of the group was intended to explain matters and to allay fears.]

Every language serves as the bearer of a culture. If you speak a language you take part, to some degree, in the way of living represented by that language. Each system of culture has its own way of looking at things and people and of dealing with them. To the extent that you have learned to speak and understand a foreign tongue, to that extent you have learned to respond with a different selection and emphasis to the world around you, and for your relations with people you have gained a new system of sensibilities, considerations, conventions, and restraints. All this has come to you in part unnoticed and in part through incidents which you remember, some of them painful and some pleasurable. If the culture is remote from your own, many of its habits differ very widely from those of your community. No exception is to be made here for the peoples whom we are inclined to describe as savage or primitive; for science and mechanical invention, in which we excel them, represent only one phase of culture, and the sensitivity of these peoples, though different, is no less than our own. A deep experience among such peoples may account in part for the rich and noble personality of men like John Eliot, Roger Williams, James Schoolcraft, or, in our time, Franz Boas. It would be superfluous to speak of the great civilizations of the Orient, such as the Islamic, the Hindu, and the Chinese. Even where a culture is very close to ours, as in western Europe or even in the Balkans or in Russia, the gain is no less, since the angle of approach, the shadings of response, still differ from what is native to us. But they differ more finely; the likenesses may deceive us into attempting a crude and superficial approach.

The language of a community which possesses a written literature offers something in addition, since, if you speak it and have lived in it even a little, you can read with understanding. To persons who have never spoken the language, the written literature presents a pitfall. With the aid of a grammar and a dictionary, one can puzzle out a text, "translating" each word or phrase by an English equivalent, and obtaining a discourse which lacks the color and distorts the lines of the original. Bare facts can be reached in this kind of reading; the worker in any branch of science gets the gist of foreign books and periodicals. Poetry, drama, and fiction, philosophy and history, cannot be grasped in this way. "Reading" them by piecing together English words from grammar and glossary yields but small return for much labor.

How difficult it is to understand, beyond the measure of a mere crude translation, the literature of a language in which one has not lived, appears plainly in the case of our written heritage from ancient Greece and Rome. Here are cultures very close to our own, and indeed, to a large extent, earlier stages of our own; yet, after centuries of scholarship, few of us but lifelong students of classical philology can appreciate what we read. Even the professed philologian, with his library of apparatus, is never quite satisfied with what he grasps. If he could but go and live for a while in ancient Athens or Rome, upon his return he would rank above all masters of his craft.

We are accustomed to take a superficial view of human societies and of the languages in which they have their being. The words of different languages are not just externally different labels for the same things; they apply to different ranges of objects and events. The differences are subtle and extend to flavor and connotation. Unlike the native child, whose linguistic experience registers on a blank slate, the learner of a foreign language errs constantly through the prepossessions of his own language. Few ever become perfect; to the extent that one does, it is by living experience. The quintessence of meaning and its most delicate variations are drawn upon in literature, the artistic use of words.

I have mentioned first the cultural and biographic value of foreign languages, because it is something which we are likely to underestimate. The practical value of a foreign language, as a tool or means, is more evident. So far as it is concerned, practice regulates itself: in a community which needs foreign languages, many people will acquire them. To some nationalities we attribute a talent in this direction, when, in fact, they have only a need. This is the case of the small countries of western Europe. Also, in Russia, under the old régime, the children of many wealthy families were brought up with a succession of foreign governesses; Russians have not the special talent for foreign languages which is commonly attributed to them. The same thing appears in communities of simpler civilization. I knew an old woman of the Menomini tribe of Wisconsin who, in addition to her native language, spoke fluently in Chippewa and Potawatomi and had a smattering of Winnebago and of English; she could not read or write. Though the occasion in such cases is practical, here, too, a living experience has produced a facility which cannot be got from textbooks or even from phonograph records.

Hitherto, in the United States, we have had neither the practical need for speaking foreign languages nor the biographical and sentimental experience of them. Exceptions have been numerous, but not enough to change the large picture: persons who lived closely with the aborigines of our continent; settlers of other than English speech who came in cohesive groups or stood high enough culturally to maintain, sometimes for generations, a bilingual status; in recent times, members of that wealthy stratum of society which is known as the international set. Mostly, however, the situation has been such as to create no impulse for acquiring what foreign languages one heard on the lips of hostile Indians, of later immigrants, or of neighbors such as the Mexicans or the French of Canada.

In our system of education, modern foreign languages appear as a hothouse growth, and as one that is neither wisely planted nor well tended. Two, three, or four years of French, German, or Spanish in high school and perhaps a few more in college produce no sensible result. The alumnus neither speaks nor understands his foreign language; he has learned to decode short stories and novels by thumbing a glossary, but a wise instinct leads him to drop this occupation as soon as he has completed his course of study. It would be of little interest here to describe the reasons for this failure. What we know about language has been learned since the beginning of the nineteenth century, but our schools still adhere to the traditions of an earlier time. It is safe to say that not one in a hundred of our teachers of foreign languages has read such books as Henry Sweet's "Practical Study of Languages," Otto Jespersen's "How To Teach a Foreign Language," Harold E. Palmer's "Principles of Language Study," or, for that matter, any respectable handbook of linguistics. The fault lies not with the teachers but in their training and direction, which is entirely in the hands of educationists and professors of literature.

Improved methods of communication and travel and the exigencies of war have confronted us with the need for foreign languages. In such things there is a lag until pressure results in a shock. In the year 1941 officials of our government saw that we should need men who could speak various foreign languages; we could no longer depend on outsiders. After Pearl Harbor this need became immediate and urgent. The army needed men who could converse in a number of languages most of which had not been taught in our schools and colleges, and it needed these men as quickly as possible. The army stated its needs to the American Council of Learned Societies, a cooperative organization comprising professional associations of workers in humanistic subjects. The Council presented the problem to members of one of its constituent societies, the Linguistic Society of America. Most of the members of this society are teachers of foreign languages, but they belong to a small minority among these teachers—the minority which studies linguistics. The result was that the army's directives for foreign language instruction embodied certain results of linguistic science that had not generally figured in the teaching of our schools and colleges, and discountenanced certain practices that had there prevailed but are supposed by workers in linguistics to be irrelevant or injurious.

This is not to say that students of linguistics had at their disposal any "method," quicker, easier, or more effective than traditional practice, for teaching languages. If anything of the kind exists in the empyrean realm of Platonic ideas, it has certainly not been discovered. General pedagogic devices and precautions go only a little ways; beyond that, teaching is a craft and an art and at its best varies with teacher, student, and subject. But there is one tangible factor that is often neglected in our schools, and almost always so in their linguistic operations: it is advisable that the teacher know as much as possible about the subject of instruction. All that the student of linguistics could offer, beyond whatever competence he shared with other teachers, was a knowledge of the past results of linguistic science.

The scientific study of human speech had its beginnings early in the nineteenth century. The topic which first presented itself was the comparison of the languages which belong to the great Indo-European family: Latin, Greek, Indo-Iranian (including, especially, Sanskrit), Celtic, Slavic, Germanic (including English), and some others. In the course of fifty years' work, chiefly on this problem, linguistic students obtained an outline knowledge of the big things about human speech: how languages change; how languages are related to each other and how they influence one another; how systems of writing arise and how writing differs from language. They traced the history of the various languages of our family, and they identified, in the main, the many other families of languages that are spoken by mankind. The results of this period of linguistic science were admirably summed up and presented to the general reader by William Dwight Whitney, Professor of Sanskrit and Comparative Philology at Yale, in "Language and the Study of Language" (1867) and "The Life and Growth of Language" (1874).

A second period of linguistic science may be said to run to the end of the nineteenth century. The main results of this period concerned the physiology of language—how speech sounds are produced—and the more exact formulation of linguistic changes.

With the present century there came a broadening of the linguistic horizon, due chiefly to the study, by American workers, of the Indian languages of our continent. Here one found a multitude of independent linguistic families, differing greatly in sound and structure. Some notion of this broader view can be got from the fascinating book "Language" (1921) by Edward Sapir. This growth of knowledge was important for the work with which we are here concerned: it was largely through the observation of American Indian tongues that linguistic students learned to describe the structure of languages in realistic and intelligible terms—and not in the traditional pseudo-philosophical jargon of our school grammars.

This, roughly, was the equipment of the linguistic workers who faced the problem of teaching some thousands of our fellow citizens in government service to speak foreign languages. This equipment sufficed to establish certain broad recommendations which seem self-evident in the light of past results of linguistic science. Students are to be trained in the colloquial spoken form of the language that is to be learned. They are to spend most of their classroom hours in small groups (ten men at most) listening to a native speaker, imitating him, and, as soon as possible, conversing with him. An instructor is to supervise this work and to give a few lectures each week on the structure of the language. These few prescriptions by no means amount to anything that can be called a method, and the directive for the Army Specialized Training Program in language scarcely went beyond them. It may be of interest to explain briefly the reasons for them, and to say something about their practical effect.

One learns to understand and speak a language by hearing and imitating native speakers. In rare instances, a foreign speaker who has acquired the language will speak it as well as a native and, accordingly, could serve equally well as a model, but such persons are hard to find and hard to identify. Nearly always, a foreign speaker falls short in accuracy and sureness. Accordingly, in the army language courses each student was given copious opportunity to hear and to imitate a native speaker of the language that he was to acquire. These native speakers were at first designated by the term "informants," which is current among linguists and anthropologists. Some of the native speakers, to whom this word was unfamiliar, found it offensive; some term such as "tutor," "guide," or "speaker" seems preferable. We shall here refer to the informant as the "native speaker."

In a language that is spoken by any large number of people there are great differences of dialect. Usually there is some one preferred dialect which is used when speakers from different parts of the country have occasion to speak to each other—a *standard dialect*, which is understood in all parts of the area. It is necessary, therefore, that the native speaker use the standard dialect without too much local coloring. Fortunately, under modern conditions many people are able to speak the standard dialect of their language, and this is true of nearly any foreigner who is travelled enough to find himself in the United States. In the case of immigrants' languages, such as Italian or Russian, only those speakers can be used for our purpose who have brought with them a command of the standard dialect.

There is no such thing as a person speaking "incorrectly" in his native dialect; the worst thing that can be said of the native speaker is that he speaks a dialect which we do not want to learn. We face trouble in the speaker whose command of the standard dialect is imperfect; from him we may get forms of speech which sound rude or laughable to persons from other parts of the area. A more frequent difficulty is presented by the speaker who has acquired the standard dialect in school and along with it a mass of false tradition, such as exists in most literate communities, as to how the language "ought to" be spoken, especially grammatical rules (like ours about *shall* and *will*) that have no basis in actual speech. Such a speaker will use stilted or bizarre expressions when he recalls the "rules" and, worse yet, he may try to reproduce his own schoolroom experience by talking *about* his language instead of *in* it, repeating or improvising a more or less fanciful body of doctrine.

When we have found a speaker who can talk naturally in the standard dialect of his language, we must still train him to do this before the students. Experience has shown that one must make it a rule that the native speaker use no English whatever. Beyond this, it is well to prescribe that the native speaker is never to say anything *about* his language; he is to correct his students' mistakes by simply repeating the correct form for them to imitate. It is important to keep in view that our students must learn to understand the language as it is really spoken, and not the archaic or falsified forms that exist only in schoolrooms.

The time the student in our army courses is to spend with the native speaker was set at a minimum of ten hours a week. Some linguists believe that it is better to have more time, and best, indeed, to hear the foreign language through all one's waking hours, to the total exclusion of English. Not all agree to this, and, in any case, practical conditions set a limit. In some courses, the number of hours has been well above the minimum; in a few, such as the very intensive Yale Chinese course for officers, the students hear the foreign language nearly all through the day. Actually, we do not know how effectiveness varies with time spent in hearing the language. As to calendar time, the army was able to allow only nine months, in some cases twelve, in others only six, and in some pressing instances even less. This was not a matter of choice, but it appears that even these last groups, under a full-time working schedule, were able to get fairly good results; some of their alumni are now serving effectively in the foreign country.

The meetings with the native speaker are known as "drill sessions." Not more than ten students attend such a session; six or eight do better than ten. Each student has a mimeographed copy of the expressions that are to be practised. The native speaker pronounces these for the students to imitate and continues with this until the students reproduce the forms intelligibly. Then the drill changes to questions and answers based on these expressions, and, at later stages, to more or less free conversation within the scope of the mimeographed material. Here, of course, much depends on the personality, tact, and skill of the native speaker, and upon the guidance which he receives from the instructor who is in charge of the work.

These drill sessions are the most important part of the work, for in them the student gets his experience of the language. Taken alone, however, and without careful guidance, they would give an uncertain result, somewhat like that of a very brief visit to a foreign country. What is said and done in the drill session must be planned and supplemented by a competent instructor.

The task of the instructor is to direct the native speakers, to supervise the drill sessions, to plan the topics and choose the forms which are to appear in practice and conversation, and, wherever it seems helpful, to explain the forms of the language.

The basic requirement and, as experience has shown, that which, more than anything else, determines the success of the work, is the instructor's ability to do these things—his technical competence in certain phases of linguistics. If the instructor is himself a native speaker of the language to be learned, he can do all this more easily and much better, provided he has also the necessary technical competence. A native instructor without technical competence is hindered rather than helped by his command of the language. The forms of his native speech seem to him self-evident, and the students' inability to use them seems stupid and perverse. A native instructor who is at the same time competent in linguistics could be found in extremely few instances; for most of the languages no such person was available.

Next best is a competent instructor who has a good artificial command of the language that is to be learned. In some respects he does better even than a linguistically trained native instructor, since he can recall the ups and downs of his own learning. For some of the languages not even this demand could be met: among the few persons who had learned to speak these languages, none possessed the necessary technical competence.

Accordingly, in quite a few instances linguistic workers had to serve as instructors for a language that was strange to them. Fortunately, they had from six months to a year in which to work with a native speaker before the dread day on which "the soldiers came." This is not as bad as it may appear, for a skilled worker can analyze the sounds and forms of a strange language in a relatively short time; some, in addition, have the knack of learning to talk pretty quickly. At any rate, it turned out that some of the most successful courses were among those which began in this rather terrifying way: Thai (Siamese), Burmese, Malay, Turkish, Japanese. With surprising regularity the outcome of the courses correlates not with the instructor's background in the language, but with his competence and skill in the technical aspects of the work.

From the very outset the student faces the problem of foreign sounds. The native speakers must be trained to speak naturally and at normal conversational speed. Anyone who is placed in the abnormal situation of speaking his language to uncomprehending foreigners is likely to slow up his speech and to distort it. An English-speaker, for instance, is likely to replace the slurred vowels of unstressed syllables by the full and distinct vowels which we use under stress; speakers of other languages will make the same or similar distortions. To the naïve speaker this distortion seems to make things easier, but actually it has the opposite effect, since, to mention only the most obvious result, it leaves the learner unable to comprehend normal speech.

At ordinary conversational speed, a foreign language sounds rapid, blurred, and vague. Some essential distinctions of sound escape the learner because they are absent in his language. A German, for instance, cannot at first hear the difference between English words like *bag* and *back*; in the same way, we are likely to miss such essential features as the tonal distinctions in Swedish or in Chinese or the distinction of plain and nasalized vowels in French. For the most part, both in hearing and in reproducing a foreign language, we are likely to replace the foreign sounds by the nearest sounds of our own language.

The first task of the instructor, accordingly, is to awaken the students to the foreign sounds, to train them to imitate exactly, and to point out elusive distinctions. When this is done, some students are able to mimic, but others cannot: one has to show them what to do with their tongue, lips, and other organs of speech, and to exercise them in the new positions and movements. For all this, of course, the instructor must be competent in phonetics—that is, he must know how speech sounds are produced.

The second task of the instructor is to choose the phrases which are to be learned. These should be natural, beginning with the commonest and most useful expressions, such as greetings, formulas of courtesy, and requests for food, drink, or information. Strangely enough, this is not always evident to persons untrained in linguistics; thus, some of our conventional elementary textbooks for foreign languages begin with bizarre and unusual discourses, such as the telling of a child's fable in stilted literary language.

Beyond this, one must regulate the occurrence of the forms: new ones must not come too many at a time, and old ones must be persistently repeated. The locutions are practised until the students can use them fluently, and, in addition, each student is supplied with a written record of the forms that are presented; this enables him to survey them and, to some extent to study them outside the meetings. This record is made in a simple phonetic alphabet—that is, in an alphabet which shows only the essential features of sound, but omits none of these, including stress, intonation, and the like. Nearly all the conventional systems of writing that prevail for different languages involve confusing features, in the way of inconsistencies, omission of essential features, and other defects. Conventional orthography is presented to the student only after he is so sure of the forms as to be proof against these misleading quirks and able to supply the deficient features. Chinese and Japanese writing, which employs thousands of characters with no indication of the sound, can be treated only as a separate branch of study—far more difficult than the acquisition of the language.

Different languages say things in different ways. Where we say "I'm hungry," the French say "I have hunger" and the Japanese say "Stomach is empty." Our schoolroom tradition applies the term "idiom" to the more surprising phrases of a foreign language. It would be more correct to say that everything in any language is "idiom," even in the instances where, superficially at least, the foreign turn of speech accords with our own. The inexperienced learner expects a foreign language to contain words with the same coverage of meaning as English words; the foreign language puzzles him by using several different words for one "idea" (that is, for one English word) or one word for several "ideas" (that is, for several English words). The beginner is puzzled also by such things as inflectional differences (German *an die Wand, an der Wand*, both apparently meaning "on the wall"). He wants to have these things explained; if this want is not met he is likely to lose confidence and to develop blockages. The ultimate explanation for the forms of any language is historical: the speakers use the forms which they have heard from other speakers. This has to be made clear to the student, who otherwise will waste his time in "logical" or "psychological" rationalizing. He must learn that his task is simply to practise the foreign locutions until he can understand them and utter them without hesitation or difficulty.

Nevertheless, we cannot depend entirely upon this procedure, even when the materials for study are very well selected and very thoroughly learned. Although this is the way infants acquire their native language, it cannot with any economy be applied to the later acquisition of a foreign language. The child takes several years to master his native language, and during this time he hears and speaks as much in a month as our students would in a year. The child hears and speaks in real situations, with powerful motives, rewards, and penalties. Most important of all, the child gets his impressions on a blank slate, while our students have at every point to overcome lifelong habits of muscular action, of naming, classification, and combinatory patterns peculiar to their native language. Complete success in this is very rare: hardly anyone, as we know, ever learns to speak a foreign language exactly as it is spoken by natives. Every language, moreover, serves as the bearer of a complex culture. The child acquires this culture along with his speech, regarding it unquestioningly, as part of the nature of things. In the case of European languages, which stand culturally very close to ours, it is the details and nuances which escape us. Cultures more remote from our own appear to a wholly unskilled observer as no culture at all; at a later stage of learning they bewilder one with their odd complications; yet one can converse intelligibly only if one knows what situations arise and what speeches they demand. And this, by the way, is the only sound approach to the study of a foreign literature.

All these problems have to be met by the instructor. He assembles the locutions that have been learned, shows their common features and their points of difference, and indicates, so far as possible, the range of validity of each new expression and the extent to which a pattern may be transferred to new locations. What this amounts to is the grammar—inflection, word-formation, and syntax—and the lexicon of the language. The statements of traditional grammar (in the languages that have such a thing) are mostly inept, when they are not untrue or meaningless. If the instructor is at the same time a native speaker of the language to be taught, he can get at the facts by introspection, but to do so and to state the results demands a high degree of linguistic skill. The worst possible instructor is an educated native speaker without linguistic competence but with traditional scholastic preconceptions about his language.

From three to five hours a week were allotted to the instructor, who meets the class as a whole, regardless of its size. In the early stages of the work, while phonetics and the basic structure have to be explained, this is not too much. After these early stages, it has been found better to devote some of these hours to additional practice; beyond answering students' questions, there is little to say that equals practice in value. Throughout, it is important to stress practice rather than theory; it is an easy downhill path which leads from the severe but rewarding labor of practice to the easy but unfruitful field of grammatical theorizing. It should be noted that in the lecture hours the instructor presents forms of the language by eliciting them from a native speaker and not by producing them from his own knowledge. Even some instructors who are native speakers of the language that is being taught prefer to elicit the forms from an assistant, so important is it for the students to understand the difference between the instructor and the drill master. It is a fatal mistake of linguistically naïve persons to confuse the native's command of his language with the smattering of a foreign speaker: the failure to distinguish these two has done only less harm in our schools and colleges than the failure to recognize the need of linguistic competence in a teacher of language.

Beyond all this, success depends in large measure upon an imponderable: the atmosphere created by the instructor and by the native speakers. The native speaker, to return to him, bears the brunt of this. He needs no technical knowledge, but very much depends on his willingness and patience, his tact and his personality, much also upon the guidance and supervision which he receives from the instructor.

This outline of what was recommended and supplemented by experience will suffice perhaps to show that nothing has been evolved which would fairly deserve the designation of a "method." All that can be said is: Do whatever is indicated by mankind's accumulated knowledge about human speech; fill in the details with whatever pedagogic knowledge or skill you may command. The army work in languages has been attacked by some teachers and educators on the supposition that it embodies some new "method" in rivalry with the "methods" of "old-fashioned language teachers." Only results can tell. The present writer, being an "old-fashioned language teacher" and, at the same time, somewhat concerned in the planning of the army courses, could hardly expect much weight to be given to his claims of success. Foreign visitors and Americans who have lived in foreign parts have again and again expressed their amazement at our students' facility. Some of our men, after nine months or a year of instruction, are now overseas, making their way in languages which were formerly thought to defy approach even after years of residence. For the rest, we may refer to more impartial statements, such as the account in the "Survey of Language Classes in the Army Specialized Training Program" prepared for the Commission on Trends in Education of the Modern Language Association of America.

To what extent can our schools and colleges profit from the experience that was gained in the army courses in foreign languages? To what extent does the arrangement of these courses deserve to be transferred to foreign language teaching in normal times?

The army courses were planned to supply an immediate and pressing need. They did not develop a cut-and-dried method, they varied greatly as to details of procedure and as to effectiveness, they were conducted under circumstances very different from those of ordinary schooling, and they did not look forward to the study of literature. Experience with the army courses has doubtless proved valuable to the teachers who were engaged in them, but few of these teachers would be likely to advocate a direct transfer of the army arrangements to our schools and colleges. What one wants to transfer is simply the broad principles which were embodied, beforehand, in the army's directives for language teaching. These principles amount only to what linguistic science tells us about language learning. They apply to all study of foreign languages, regardless of special conditions or ultimate aims.

The most important requirement here is that of linguistic competence in the teacher. Language teaching in our schools and colleges is ineffective because it ignores the knowledge about human speech which has been gained during the last hundred and fifty years. No one would consult a chemist whose state of information was that of the eighteenth century. Thus there is one prediction, but a very important one, which we can make with assurance: the language work of our schools and colleges will be greatly improved when the persons who plan it and the teachers who conduct it have a reasonable command of linguistic science.

This, in fact, applies not only to the study of foreign languages but also to the other linguistic activities of our schools. Thus, their ever-shifting methods of teaching children to read are devised by schoolmen who do not know the relation of writing to language. The result is that years of every child's time are wasted; we actually have "remedial reading" classes in our high schools. We could make a great economic gain and a great gain in genuine literacy—that is, in the ability to read with understanding —if our grade-school teachers had some elementary training in linguistics. The unsatisfactory results which our educational system obtains in foreign language teaching are on a par with the results which it obtains in other linguistic disciplines: reading; teaching children who speak non-standard forms of English to speak the standard language; English composition; understanding of literature.

If foreign language study in our schools is to be put on a sound basis, we shall face the need for native or nearly native presentation of the foreign language, since without such a presentation the subject can hardly be of value. Some of the larger universities now employ native informants for their regular civilian courses. A teacher with a reasonable amount of training in linguistics will usually be able to acquire a nearly native command of his foreign language by visits to the country where it is spoken. As a substitute for such visits, there are full-time special courses; the best known, perhaps, are the summer sessions offered in French, German, and Spanish by Middlebury College in Vermont. A few years hence we may find that many students from foreign countries are eager to come to the United States on some plan of exchange; it should be feasible to employ these students for part-time work as speakers in our foreign language courses in high schools and colleges. Ultimately, if the need persists, there will be many Americans who speak foreign languages well enough to serve as teachers.

The time to be devoted to foreign language study presents a mechanical but troublesome problem of administration. A similar problem has been solved in the case of laboratory work in physical and biological science. We shall do well to arrange things in much the same way, giving, say, ten class hours a week to foreign language, but treating most of these hours as laboratory work which requires no outside preparation. It will be more difficult, of course, to restrict the numbers of students in these laboratory hours. In the language classes it may also prove more difficult than it is in the science laboratory to hold the adolescent's attention. Only experience can provide the answer to this question.

The outlay of time and money for frequent meetings and small classes should be at least partially offset by the reduction of calendar time. Each student should be given one year of intensive work in a foreign language, a year devoted mainly to speaking and only in part, towards the end, to reading. A second year, on an ordinary schedule of three to five hours a week, should be given to reading in the geography, history, and literature of the foreign country. Any work beyond this, such as further conversational practice, wider study of history or literature, or study of a second language, should be entirely optional and a matter of specialization.

Our experience with the army courses probably cannot guide us as to the stage of schooling at which it is best to begin the study of a foreign language, or as to the classroom procedure and scheduling which would yield the best results in ordinary schools. Most linguists will agree that college is not the place for elementary instruction in foreign languages. In those European countries which in the past have produced a relatively high number of good foreign language speakers, training has begun quite early. Many well-to-do families employed foreign governesses for their children, and in school a foreign language was taken up in the fifth or sixth year. It seems that young children find conversational drill less irksome and take more pleasure in phonetic and verbal achievement. If this is correct, it bears out the opinion that our present eight-year grammar school curriculum is too long and that the subjects which are now taken up in high school could better be begun some years earlier. Our army experience, however, has little bearing on these questions. As to such matters, and especially as to details, prediction is likely to go wrong; trial and experience can tell us what to do. The only certain prediction—the prediction which led to the success of the army courses—appears in the demand that the planners and textbook writers and teachers who carry on the language work of our schools be trained in the relevant branches of linguistic science.

# B64. *From* On Describing Inflection

1945. *Festschrift für M. Blakemore Evans* (*Monatshefte für deutschen Unterricht* 37:4–5) 8–13.

[Our excerpt consists of the first paragraph and about two-thirds of the second. The balance of the paper is a treatment of current French verb inflection, intended to show how a 'less rigorous' statement of such morphological facts may be 'more useful even for scientific purposes' than a 'rigorous' statement that becomes overly cumbersome. Bloomfield's example of the latter is George L. Trager's 'The Verb Morphology of Spoken French', *Language* 20.131–141 (1944). But the bulk of the paper, here omitted, is not the best example of Bloomfield's way of combining precision and clarity in the statement of grammatical patterns. Much better are the appropriate chapters of the posthumously published grammars of Ojibwa and of Menomini.]

Traditional grammars base their description on orthography, they sometimes employ clumsy procedures, and often they resort to repetition instead of assembling forms which present a common feature. This last habit is pedagogically useful, when one does not carry it to the length of causing difficulty by sheer bulk, so as to swamp the noteworthy features.

Systematic description, on the other hand, tries to assemble all forms that have any common feature and to unite them under a single statement. Now, the basic uniformity in language is the mere recurrence of forms and constructions. The partial resemblances between forms which we describe in morphology are often so whimsically irregular that a rigorous statement has practical disadvantages. It may take more discourse to describe a few eccentric forms than it would merely to cite them. The author of a rigorous description finds difficulty in making it watertight; even Panini left some holes. The reader finds difficulty in interpreting, applying, and combining the separate statements; this, too, would be true of Panini's grammar even if one could mend the superficial faults (such as unwritten ditto marks). A less rigorous statement may be more useful even for scientific purposes.

# B65. Algonquian

1946. Harry Hoijer and others, *Linguistic Structures of Native America*
(*Viking Fund Publications in Anthropology* 6; New York) 85–129.

[For Bloomfield's brief dedication of this volume, see our remarks at the end
of B60. Bloomfield's contribution to the volume, here reprinted, was essentially
completed by 1940, for I read it in typescript during that year. Subsequent re-
working, before the long-delayed publication, was confined largely to additions
to the bibliography.

The errata reported by me in *International Journal of American Linguistics* 19.78
(1953) have been corrected for the new printing.

The paper supersedes B19 and B22 (our brief excerpts from which are given
for other reasons, not because of their treatment of Algonquian).]

§1. The grouping of the Algonquian languages is uncertain, since most
of them are scantily or poorly recorded. Following, in the main, Michelson,
we may list them as follows:[1]

    I. Central-Eastern:
        A. Central Type: Cree-Montagnais-Naskapi, Menomini, Fox-
           Sauk-Kickapoo, Shawnee, Peoria-Miami, Potawatomi, Ojib-
           wa-Ottawa-Algonquin-Salteaux, Delaware, Powhatan.
        B. New England Type: Natick-Narragansett, Mohegan-Pequot,
           Penobscot-Abnaki, Passamaquoddy-Malecite, Micmac.
    II. Blackfoot.
    III. Cheyenne.
    IV. Arapaho-Atsina-Nawathinehena.

Two languages of California, Wiyot and Yurok, have been suspected
of kinship with Algonquian.[2]

---

[1] Truman Michelson, *Preliminary Report on the Linguistic Classification of Algonquian
Tribes* (28th Annual Report of the Bureau of American Ethnology, Washington, 1912,
pp. 221–290).

[2] A. L. Kroeber, *The Languages of the Coast of California North of San Francisco* (University of California Publications in American Archaeology and Ethnology, vol. 9, Berkeley,
1910–1911, pp. 384–412, and 414–426); Truman Michelson, *Two Alleged Algonquian Languages of California* (American Anthropologist, n.s., vol. 16, Lancaster, Pa., 1914, pp. 361–
367) and *Rejoinder* [to Sapir] (American Anthropologist, n.s., vol. 17, Lancaster, Pa., 1915,
pp. 194–198); Gladys Reichard, *Wiyot Grammar and Texts* (University of California Publications in American Archaeology and Ethnology, vol. 22, Berkeley, 1925, pp. 1–215); Edward

§2. Our reconstructions are based, to begin with, on the four best-known languages: Fox, Cree, Menomini, and Ojibwa. Michelson's brilliant study of the divergent western languages (Blackfoot, Cheyenne, and the Arapaho group), showed that these reconstructions will, in the main, fit all the languages and can accordingly be viewed as Proto-Algonquian.[3] Since then, however, Siebert has shown that F, C, M, O have all merged two consonant clusters, θk and xk, which are distinct in Delaware and the New England languages;[4] for this feature, at any rate, an eastern language is necessary in the reconstruction of PA.[5]

## 3-15. SOUNDS

§3. PA had four vowels, each in short and long quantities: high front i, ii; low front e, ee; high back o, oo; low back a, aa.

We use the term *nonsyllabic* of any phoneme other than a vowel and of any sequence of phonemes not containing a vowel.

The PA vowel system is preserved in F; only initial PA e- > F i-, form 13, and F has a few assimilative (?) changes of short vowels, as in form 100.

PA i and e are merged to i in C and O.

PA i, ii are broken up in M into a high vowel, M i, ii and a mid vowel, M e, ee. Similarly, PA o, oo yield M u, uu and M o, oo. PA e appears in M partly as e (coinciding with e from PA i) and partly as a very open vowel, M ɛ. PA cc > M cc. Moreover, M has made complex but regular changes of vowel quantity.

Examples of PA vowels: *1* \*aθemwa "dog": Kickapoo anemwa, C atim, M anɛɛm, O anim. *2* \*pemaatesiwa "he lives": F pemaatesiwa, C pimaatisiw, M pemaatesew, O pimaatisi. *3* \*seekesiwa "he is afraid": F seekesiwa, C seekisiw, M sɛɛkesew, O seekisi. *4* \*wentenamwa "he

Sapir, *The Algonkin Affinity of Yurok and Wiyot Kinship Terms* (Journal de la Société des Américanistes, n.s., vol. 15, Paris, 1923, pp. 37–74); C. C. Uhlenbeck, *Infigeering op het gebied der Algonkin-Talen* (Mededeelingen der Koninklijke Akademie van Wetenschappen, Afdeeling Letterkunde, Ser. A., vol. 69, Amsterdam, 1930, pp. 111–116).

[3] Truman Michelson, *Phonetic Shifts in Algonquian Languages* (International Journal of American Linguistics, vol. 8, New York, 1935, pp. 131–171).

[4] Frank T. Siebert, Jr., *Certain Proto-Algonquian Consonant Clusters* (Language, vol. 17, Baltimore, 1941, pp. 298–303).

[5] Forms are cited in uniform inflection; especially, verbs are cited in the third person singular independent indicative (transitive verbs with obviative object), except for Ojibwa transitive verbs, where we give the conjunct form, because there the independent indicative has been replaced by another inflection (§42). Often, therefore, the cited inflectional form has been made by me from stems recorded in some other form of the paradigm.

Starred forms or forms with hyphens at the beginning or end are Proto-Algonquian. (Etymologies are preceded by numbers in *italics* for reference.) Abbreviations: > = "became"; < = "coming from"; ~ = "is replaced in alternation by"; an. = "animate"; C = "Cree"; exc. = "exclusive"; F = "Fox"; inan. = "inanimate"; inc. = "inclusive"; intr. = "intransitive"; M = "Menomini"; O = "Ojibwa"; obv. = "obviative"; PA = "Proto-Algonquian"; pl. = "plural"; sg. = "singular"; tr. = "transitive"; V = "vowel."

takes it from there ": F otenamwa, C ohtinam, M ohtɛɛnam, O ontinank.[6]
5 *poosiwa "he embarks": F poosiwa, C poosiw, M poosew, O poosi.
6 *kiiškahamwa "he chops it through": F kiiškahamwa, C kiiskaham, M keeskaham, O kiiškaqank.

§4. Before syllabic vowels, PA i, o are nonsyllabic; we write y, w:[7]
7 *wiiyawi "his body": F wiiyawi, C wiyaw, M weeyaw, O wiiyaw.

§5. PA ya between consonants > F yee, O ii: 8 *aqsenyali "stones": F asenyeeni, C asiniya, M aqsɛnyak (an. form), O assiniin.

PA yaa > F aa after č, š and C, O aa after all nonsyllabics. PA yaa, waa > M ia, ua (falling diphthongs) after nonsyllabics when not shortened: 9 *neniičyaanehsa "my child"; F neniičaanesa, M neniičianɛh, O niniičaaniss. 10 *kyaataawa "he hides it": C kaataaw, M kiataaw, O kaatoot; reshaped in F kyaatamwa.

PA yee > F ee after č, š; C ee after all nonsyllabics; M ii after all nonsyllabics; O ee after š, 86, ii after other nonsyllabics: 11 *pyeetaawa "he brings it": F pyeetoowa (inflectional ending reshaped), M piitaaw, O piitoot.

PA wee > M ii after nonsyllabic: 12 *pyeetweeweekesiwa "he comes with noise": F pyeetweeweekesiwa, M piitiiwɛɛkesew, O piitweeweekisi.

PA yi > i after nonsyllabic in all the languages for which we have data, but in M this i is distinct from e < PA i: 13 *elenyiwa "man": F ineniwa, C iyiniw, M enɛɛniw, O inini.

PA wi > F, O i after t, l (the exact conditions are obscured by new formations); C o, M i (o before w) after all nonsyllabics: 14 *piintwikeewa "he enters a dwelling": F piitikeewa, C piihtokeew, M piihtikɛw, O piintikee.[8]

PA yii > ii in all the languages for which we have data, but in M this ii is distinct from ee < PA ii: 15 *kešyiipisowa "he speeds": M kesiipesow O kišiipiso.

PA wii > M ii after nonsyllabic: 16 *kwiiθomeewa "he longs for him": F kwiinomeewa, M kiinomɛw, O kwiinomaat.

In word initial, PA we > o in most of the languages, 4.

§6. The PA simple consonants were p, t, k, č, s, š, θ, l, m, n. The last three were voiced. The rest were voiceless, probably lenis; in some dialects of O they are largely voiced. Medial k is often voiced in F and C. In O, PA h appears as a glottal stop, for which we write q.

PA θ (unvoiced interdental or lateral?) and l coincide in most languages. Shawnee, Delaware, the Peoria group, and the New England languages have l. Blackfoot, Cheyenne, and Nawathinehena have t, coinciding with

---

[6] The O form is in conjunct mode: "if he takes it from there"; cf. footnote 5.

[7] We use y, w because it is likely that in some of the languages the syllabic and nonsyllabic values are no longer mechanically determined. Also, we set up such theoretical elements as nyeeww- "four."

[8] In setting up postconsonantal wi, yi for PA, we depart from earlier conclusions, which were prompted, at bottom, by the mistaken assumption that in PA l alternated with š.

PA t; M, F, O, and Potawatomi have n, coinciding with PA n, but differing from the latter in morphologic treatment, §20. The remaining languages distinguish as follows:

|  | PA θ | PA l |
|---|---|---|
| Atsina | t | n |
| Arapaho (except Atsina and Nawathinehena) θ | | l |
| Cree-Montagnais | t | y |

Northern C dialects represent PA l variously by n, l, r, or by an interdental voiced spirant.

C has PA t, θ > č originally in diminutives, secondarily also in some other forms.[9]

C and M merge PA s and š in s, an intermediate sound. PA s > Shawnee θ. The consonants appear in 1 to 16.

§7. Clusters of two consonants occur medially. They consist of ordinary consonants preceded by obscure elements which we render by arbitrary symbols.

Where northern O dialects represent the prior element of a cluster as h, there most O dialects have a fortis or ambisyllabic unvoiced consonant, e.g., PA hs > northern O hs, general O ss.

§8. Clusters with second member p:

| PA | F | C | M | O |
|---|---|---|---|---|
| mp | p | hp | hp | mp |
| hp | ? | hp | hp | pp |
| xp | hp | sp | hp | pp |
| čp | ? | sp | čp | pp |
| šp | hp | sp | sp | šp |

17 *wempenamwa "he lifts it up": C ohpinam, O ompinank: compare F opaaškeewi "it flies up" and M ohpεεqnen "it is blown upward." 18 *koohpačiheewa "he ruins him": C koohpačiheew, M koohpačehεεw, O kooppačiqaat. 19 *axpeelemowa "he places reliance": F ahpeenemowa, C aspeeyimow, M ahpεεnemow, O apeenimo. 20 *noočpinatamwa "he pursues it": C noospinatam, O nooppinatank; compare M noočpenεεhtaw. 21 *ešpemenki "up above": F ahpemeki, C ispimihk, O išpimink; reshaped M espεεmiah (< -iiwenki).

§9. Clusters with second member t:

| PA | F | C | M | O |
|---|---|---|---|---|
| nt | t | ht | ht | nt |
| ht | ht | ht | ht | tt |

---

[9] Recognition of this fact dispenses with the cluster θš formerly set up for PA.

| qt | ht | st | qt | tt |
|----|----|----|----|----|
| št | ? | st | ? | št |

For nt, see 4.  *22* *ešihtaawa "he makes it so": F išihtoowa (ending re-shaped), C, isiihtaaw, M eseehtaw, O išittoot.  *23* *peqtenamwa "he takes it by error": C pistinam, M pɛqtɛnam, O pittinank; compare F pehtena-weewa "he shoots him by error."  *24* *weštikwaani "his head": C ostik-waan, O oštikwaan.

§10.  Clusters with second member k:

| PA | F | C | M | O | |
|----|---|---|---|---|---|
| nk | k | hk | hk | nk | |
| hk | hk | hk | hk | kk | |
| xk | hk | sk | hk | kk | Delaware hVk, New England hk |
| θk | hk | sk | hk | kk | Delaware xk, New England sk |
| çk | šk | hk | hk | sk | Northern Cree htk[10] |
| čk | hk | sk | čk | šk | |
| šk | šk | sk | sk | šk | |

*25* *tankeškaweewa "he kicks him": F takeškaweewa, C tahkiska-weew, M tahkɛɛskawɛw, O tankiškawaat.  *26* *noohkomehsa "my grand-mother": F noohkomesa, C noohkom (without diminutive suffix), M noohkomɛh, O nookkomiss.  *27* *axkyi "earth, land": F ahki, C askiy, M ahkeew (ending reshaped), O akki, Penobscot kki (nətahki "my land").  *28* *nemeθkawaawa "I find him": F nemehkawaawa, C nimiskawaaw, M nemɛɛhkawaw, O nimikkawaa, Penobscot nəməskawɑ.  *29* *meçko-siwa "he is red": F meškosiwa, C mihkosiw (Swampy Cree mihtkosiw), O miskosi; compare M mɛhkoon.  *30* *nooçkwaatamwa "he licks it": F nooškwaatamwa, C noohkwaatam, M nuuhkwatam, O nooskwaatank.  *31* *nalakačkwi "my palate": C nayakašk; the first syllable is reshaped in M nenaakačkon (plural only), O ninakašk; compare M kakiipana-kačkow "he is dumb."  *32* *kečkyeewa "he is old": F kehkyeewa, M kečkiiw. šk in 25.

There were perhaps other clusters with k. M has qk, as in poohkeqkow "he is one-eyed." There are quite a few discrepant sets, but some of them are doubtless due to reshaping of words in one or another language: F eemehkwaahi "spoon," C eemihkwaan, O eemikkwaan, but M ɛɛmesk-wan; F nehtooškwani "my elbow," M nɛhtuuhkwan, O nintooskwan, but C nitooskwan; M kayaah "gull" (plural kayaahkok), but O kayaašk.[11]

---

[10] The fuss and trouble behind my note in Language (Vol. 4, pp. 99–100, 1928) would have been avoided if I had listened to O, which plainly distinguishes sk (<PA çk) from šk (<PA š k); instead, I depended on printed records which failed to show the distinction.

[11] James A. Geary, *Proto-Algonquian *çk: Further Examples* (Language, vol. 17, p. 307, 1941) shows what may lie behind some of the apparent discrepancies.

§11. Clusters with second member č:

| PA | F | C | M | O |
|----|---|---|---|---|
| nč | č | hč | hč | nč |
| hč | hč | hč | hč | čč |
| qč | hč | sč | qč | čč |

*33* *wenčiiwa "he comes from there": F očiiwa, C ohčiiw, M ohčeew, O ončii. *34* *ešihčikeewa "he makes things so": F išihčikeewa, C isiihči-keew, M cseehčekɛw, O išiččikee. *35* *keqči "big, much": F kehči, C kisči, M kɛɛqč, O kičči.

§12. Clusters with second member s:

| PA | F | C | M | O |
|----|---|---|---|---|
| ns | s | s | hs | ns |
| hs | s | s | hs | ss |
| qs | s | s | qs | ss |

*36* *wensaapameewa "he sees him from there": F osaapameewa, C osaapameew, M ohsaapamɛw, O onsaapamaat. *37* *nemihsa "my elder sister": F nemiseeha (diminutive), C nimis, M nemeeh (pl. nemeehsak), O nimisseenq (diminutive). *38* *nekwiqsa "my son": F nekwisa, C nikosis (diminutive), M nekiiqs, O ninkwiss.

§13. Clusters with second member š.

| PA | F | C | M | O |
|----|---|---|---|---|
| nš | š | s | hs | nš |
| hš | š | s | hs | šš |
| qš | š | s | qs | šš |

*39* *neškiinšekwi "my eye": F neškiišekwi, C niskiisik, M neskeehsek, O niškiinšik. *40* *wemehšoomehsali "his grandfather": F omešoome-sani, C omosooma (without diminutive suffix), M omɛɛhsomɛɛhsan, O omiššoomissan. *41* *kawenkwaqšiwa "he is sleepy": F kawekwašiwa, C kawihkwasiw, M kakuuhkwaqsew (reduplicated and contracted, §19), O kawinkwašši.

§14. Clusters with second member θ.

| PA | Ꞁ | C | M | Ω |
|----|---|---|---|---|
| nθ | ? | ht | hn | n |
| hθ | s | ht | hn | ss |
| qθ | s | st | qn | ss |

*42* *wanahanθeewa "he loses the trail of him": C wanahahteew, M wawaanahaahnɛw (reduplicated); compare O pimaqanaat "he tracks him" (with root pem-). *43* *ešihθenwi "it falls or lies thus": F išisenwi,

C isihtin, M eseehnen, O išissin. *44* \*koqθeewa "he fears him": F kosee-wa, C kosteew, M koqnεw, O kossaat.

§15. Clusters with second member l.

| PA | F | C | M | O |
|----|---|----|----|----|
| nl | n | hy | hn | n |
| hl | s | hy | hn | ss |
| ql | s | hy | qn | ss |

In C hy, the h or the y mostly drops; the conditions have been obscured by leveling.

*45* \*wiinleewa "he names him": F wiineewa, C wiiheew, M weehnεw, O wiinaat. *46* \*leehleewa "he breathes": F neeseewa "he is saved," C yeehyeew "he breathes," M nεεhnεw, O neessee. *47* \*aqleewa "he places him": F aseewa, C aheew, M aqnεw, O assaat.

## 16–24. INTERNAL COMBINATION

§16. In the combination of word-forming elements, when an element ending in a nonsyllabic is followed by an element beginning with a con-sonant or cluster, a *connective* -i- appears between them. Thus, the root poon- "cease" combines directly with a suffix like -eele "think": *48* \*pooneelemeewa "he stops thinking of him": F pooneenemeewa, C pooneeyimeew, M poonεεnemεw, O pooneenimaat. Similarly, a root like kiihkaa- "berate" combines directly with a suffix such as -m "act by speech on an animate object": *49* \*kiihkaameewa "he berates him": C kiihkaameew, M keehkamεw, O kiikkaamaat. But when poon- com-bines with -m, the connective -i- appears between them: *50* \*poonimeewa "he stops talking to him": F poonimeewa, C poonimeew, M poonemεw, O poonimaat.

§17. Irregularly, in certain combinations, the connective -i- is not used before p, t, k. In these combinations, t-p, θ-p ~ xp; t-k ~ θk; nasal is assimi-lated as to position. Our examples show first the root eθ- "thither, thus" before a suffix with initial vowel, then the suffix -pahtoo "run" preceded by connective -i-, and then the irregular combination of eθ- with -pahtoo: *51* \*eθahkamikesiwa "he carries on so": F inahkamikesiwa, C itahkami-kisiw, M enaahkamekεsew, O inakkamikisi; *52* \*pemipahtaawa "he runs by": C pimipahtaaw, M pemeepahtaw, O pimipattoo (inflection re-shaped); compare F pemipahowa; *53* \*expahtaawa "he runs thither": C ispahtaaw, M ehpaahtaw, O ippattoo; compare F ihpahowa. The root atoot- "on something," as in M atootapew "he sits on something," com-bines thus with -po "eat": *54* \*atooxpowa "he eats from upon some-thing": F atoohpowa, C atoospow, M atoohpow, O atooppo. The root, wiit- "along, with," §103, combines with a unique suffix -pee "sleep":

*55* \*wiixpeewa "he sleeps with someone": F wiihpeewa, M weehpɛw; \*wiixpeemeewa "he sleeps with him": F wiihpeemeewa, M weehpemɛw; but C has here hp (loanword?): wiihpeemeew. Our next examples show first a verb stem in t, then the ending -ki after a verb stem in vowel, and then the combination, always made without connective -i-, of a verb stem in t with the ending -ki: *56* \*kiišekatwi "it is day": F kiišekatwi, M keesekat, O kiišikat; *57* \*aqteeki "when it is there": F ahteeki, C asteek, M aqtɛk, O atteek; *58* \*kiišekaθki "when it is day": F kiiše-kahki, M keesekah, O kiišikakk.

Similarly after n: *59* \*kemiwanwi "it rains": C, O kimiwan, M kemee-wan; *60* \*kemiwanki "when it rains": C kimiwahk, M kemeewah, O kimiwank.

§18. Between consonants, ye∼i and we∼o. Thus, the local suffix of nouns is -enki-: *61* \*wiikenki "at his house": F owiikeki, C wiikihk, M weekeh. With the noun stem aqseny-, 8: *62* \*aqseninki "on the stone": F aseniki, M aqsɛneh. On a noun in consonant plus w it appears as follows: *63* \*meqtekwi "stick": F mehtekwi, C mistik (pl. -wa), M mɛqtek (pl. -wan), O mittik (pl. -oon); *64* \*meqtekonki "on a stick or tree": F mehtekoki, C mistikohk, M mɛqtekoh, O mittikonk.

After consonants, wiiw∼oow, as illustrated in §67.

In all positions, apparently, woo∼oo. Thus, the prefixes ne- of the first person and we- of the third appear as n-, w- before ii: *65* \*niiyawi "my body": F niiyawi, C niyaw, M neeyaw, O niiyaw; \*wiiyawi "his body," 7; but as n- and zero in \*noohkomehsa "my grandmother," 26, and *66* \*oohkomehsali "his grandmother": F oohkomesani, C ooh-koma, M oohkomɛɛhsan, O ookkomissan.

After consonant plus w, y is dropped; thus, with suffix -yaa: *67* \*tahk-yaaki "when it is cool": F tahkyaaki, C tahkaak, O takkaak; reshaped M tahkiik (representing -yee, transferred from a different inflectional form); *68* \*meçkwaaki "when it is red": F meškwaaki, C mihkwaak, O miskwaak; reshaped in M mɛhkiik.

§19. Irregularly, in certain forms, awe∼aa before t, k, s, and ∼oo before other consonants. This *contraction* always takes place when the e begins an inflectional ending. We illustrate first the endings -ekwa "he—me" and -eθene "I—thee," then a verb stem ending in aw, and then its combination with these endings: *69* \*newaapamekwa "he looks at me": F newaapamekwa, C, O niwaapamik, M newaapamek; *70* \*kewaapa-meθene "I look at thee": C kewaapamitin; the other languages have haplologic forms: F kewaapamene, M kewaapamen, O kiwaapamin; *71* \*newiintamawaawa "I tell it to him": F newiitamawaawa, C niwiih-tamawaaw, M neweehtamowaaw, O niwiintamawaa; *72* \*newiintamaak-wa "he tells it to me": F newiitamaakwa, C niwiihtamaak, M neweeh-tamak, O niwiintamaak; *73* \*kewiintamooθene "I tell it to thee": F kewiitamoone, M keweehtamon, O kiwiintamoon (all haplologic); C kiwiihtamaatin has analogic aa for oo.

In general, however, the sequence awe is undisturbed: *74* \*kaweneewa "he prostrates him by hand": F kaweneewa, C kawineew, M kawεεnεεw, O kawinaat.

M has various other contractions of Vwe; some may date from PA.

§20. Before i, ii, y, PA t~č and θ~š: *75* \*pemaačiheewa "he makes him live, restores him to life": C pimaačiheew, M pemaačehεw, O pimaačiqaat; compare pemaat-, 2. *76* \*pyeečimeewa "he calls him hither": C peečimeew, M piičemεw; compare pyeet-, 12. *77* \*piinčihšinwa "he falls into an enclosed place": C piihčisin, M peehcehsen; compare piint-, 14. Similarly, compare went-, 4, and wenč-ii-, 33; -htoo-, -htaa-, 22, with -hč-i-kee, 34. *78* \*miikaaθeewa "he fights him": F miikaaneewa, M meekaanεεw, O miikaanaat; *79* \*miikaaši "fight thou him": F miikaaši, M meekaasin (extended by particle \*na or otherwise reshaped), O miikaaš. With eθ-, 51, compare eš-i-, 22, 43.

This alternation distinguishes n < PA θ, in F, M, O, and Potawatomi, from n < PA n. Thus, the imperative "thou—him" form of a stem like kawen-, 74, keeps n before i: *80* \*kaweni "lay thou him prostrate": F kaweni, C, O kawin, M kawεεnen. These languages, however, have extended the alternation analogically to forms with n < PA l: *81* \*miileewa "he gives it to him": F miineewa, C miyeew (Woodland C miineew), M meenεεw, O miinaat; compare Shawnee nimiila "I give it to him"; *82* \*miili "give thou it to him": C miyi (Woodland C miini), Shawnee miili; but reshaped in F miiši, M meesen, O miiš.

§21. Irregularly, in certain forms, PA t~s before aa and e; so always before the suffixes -ehk "by foot" and -aap "look." Thus, compare went-, 4, with wens-aap-, 36.

The same alternation appears in the sequence iitii~iisii: *83* \*miitenkwaamwa "he defecates in his sleep": C miitihkwaamiw (ending reshaped), M miitehkwamow (ending reshaped), O miitinkwaam; *84* \*miisiiwa "he defecates": F miisiiwa, C miisiiw, M meeseew, O miisii.

§22. A short vowel drops before or after a long vowel. Thus, the prefix ne-, 9, 28, 37, appears as n- where it is added to ii-, 65, and to oo-, 26; similarly, we-, 24, 40, appears as w- before ii-, 7, 61, and as zero before oo-, 66. The suffix -en "by hand," 74, loses its vowel after such roots as nakaa- "stop," ašyee- "back": *85* \*nakaaneewa "he stops him by hand": C nakaaneew, M nakaanεεw, O nakaanaat; *86* \*ašyeenamwa "he pushes it back, rejects it": C aseenam, M asiinam, O ašeenank.

§23. Between long vowels the sound y is inserted, at least if one is a front vowel. Thus, F has pemaamowa "he flees by," but ašeeyaamowa "he flees back"; and M has pemεεqnen "it is blown by," but asiiyεεqnen "it is blown back."

§24. In word final position, PA apparently shortened long vowels: F nepaate "if he sleeps," stem nepaa-, but, with zero ending, nenepa "I sleep."

## 25. THE WORD

§25. In PA the word began with a vowel or with a simple nonsyllabic or with consonant plus y, w. Between the vowels of a word there was a semivowel, or a consonant, or a cluster, or one of these followed by y or w. The word ended in a short vowel. The vowel of the first syllable was never i.

Members of compound words were treated phonetically like words.

Before an initial vowel of the next word or compound-member, the final vowel dropped or else h was inserted: F pešekesiw-owiiwina, pešekesiwih-owiiwina "deer-horn."

Many of the languages (not F, Shawnee, Peoria) lost the final vowel as well as a preceding postconsonantal w, l. M and O lost also a preceding postconsontal y, but C has iy: *87* *aqsenya "stone": F asenya, C asiniy, M aqsen, O assin. C lost also a preceding h or l, 8.[12] M further lost all but the first sound of a preceding cluster, 9, except qč, qs, 35.

However, in two-syllable words with short vowels (C also in others) these languages keep the final intact, M adding h: *88* *ehkwa "louse": F, C ihkwa, M ehkuah, O ikkwa. *89* *nepyi "water": F nepi, C nipiy, O nimpi, ᵣeshapcd M nepeew.

Most types of O insert a nasal after initial m, n, plus short vowel before a simple stop, 38, 89, but not, apparently, in nak-, 85.

Particlcs which precede nouns and verbs in composition keep their final vowel (mostly it is the particle final suffix -i) not only in F and Shawnee, but also in C and O; in M they are treated like other words. *90* *weepi "begin": F weepi-pyeetoseewa "he starts to walk hither," M wɛɛp-piitohncw, O weepi-kimiwan "it starts to rain." *91* *meeqči "to exhaustion": C meesči-nipaheew "he kills them all," M nemɛɛqč-aqsekɛnan "I pick it all up." *92* *weški "new": C oski-wiikihtowak "they are newly married," M oskeeh-weekehtowak.

## 26–29. INFLECTION

§26. The inflectional types are *noun, verb* (in four subtypes), and (uninflected) *particle*, including *pronouns*.

Nouns are in two *gender* classes, *inanimate* and *animate*; the latter includes all persons, animals, spirits, and large trees, and some other objects, such as tobacco, maize, apple, raspberry (but not strawberry), calf of leg

---

[12] Actually, all final vowels of C have an h-like off-glide.

(but not thigh), stomach, spittle, feather, bird's tail, horn, kettle, pipe for smoking, snowshoe.

*Number* is *singular* and *plural*.

*Person* is *first*, *second*, and *third*, with distinction of exclusive and inclusive first person plural: M netaanenaw "our daughter" (parent speaking to another person), ketaanen "our daughter" (one parent speaking to the other). If an animate third person occurs in a phrase, any other animate third person and any inanimate verb in this phrase has a distinguishing form, the *obviative*. Thus, C, talking about a chief (okimaaw): okimaaw iskweewa kitoteew "the chief talks to a woman," okimaaw iskweewa kitotik "a woman talks to the chief," where iskweewa is the obviative of iskweew "woman"; okimaaw nikitotaaw "I speak to the chief," okimaaw okosisa nikitotimaawa "I speak to the chief's son," tipiskaaw "it was dark," eeh-takohteet tipiskaayiw "when he arrived it was dark." A few inflectional forms distinguish a nearer and a farther obviative: C okimaaw oteema "the chief's horse (obv.)," okimaaw okosisa oteemiyiwah "the chief's son's (obv.) horse (farther obv.)." C, M, and most O dialects have lost the distinction of number in the obviative; in C this is due to phonetic development. In general, the finer distinctions of obviation (such as transitive verb forms for "I—obv.," "thou—obv.," "obv.—me," and so on) have been lost in most of the languages; C and O best preserve them.

§27. The noun is inflected for number, with different endings for the two genders; the animate noun also for obviation and for address. All inflected forms, except unpossessed nouns, contain personal-anaphoric reference (by gender, person, and number) to some object: possessed nouns to a *possessor*, verbs (except in the *passive*) to an *actor*, transitive verbs also to a *goal-object*. These can be named specifically by words in cross-reference: M okeemaaw otaanan "(the chief his-daughter), the chief's daughter"; nenah nenɛɛwaaw enoh okeemaaw "I I-see-him that chief (as for me, I see the chief)."

Verbs are *intransitive* and *transitive*. The former are divided into those which refer to an animate actor, *animate intransitive* verbs, M paapɛhcen "he falls," and those which refer to an inanimate actor, *inanimate intransitive* verbs, M paapɛhnɛn "it falls." Transitive verbs are divided into those which refer to an animate goal, *transitive animate* verbs, M nemuawak "I eat them" (as, anoohkanak "raspberries," animate) and those which refer to an inanimate goal, *transitive inanimate* verbs, M nemeečenan "I eat them" (as, atɛɛhemenan "strawberries," inanimate).

However, some intransitive verbs are used habitually with *implied goals*; thus M menuah "he drinks (it)" is intr. in form, but in general makes sense only with a pseudo-object: nepeew menuah "he drinks some water," and M netooweematem "I have a friend" is freely used also with a pseudo-object: čaan netooweematem "I have John as a friend." About half the tr. an. verbs are matched not by tr. inan. verbs, but by *pseudo-transitive* verbs, namely intr. verbs formed mostly with the suffixes -too, -htoo and taking implied objects: F wiikiyaapyeeni ašihtoowa "he builds houses," where the verb is intr. in form. Some of the languages, however, as M and O, have reshaped these verbs into a special tr. inan. type. Some tr. an. verbs (*double-goal* verbs) imply a second goal in addition to the one for which they are inflected: M soopomah enɛɛsenamaaq "hand me the sugar," where the verb is inflected for "thou—me," but its structure implies a second goal, here soopomah "sugar."

Conversely, some tr. inan. verbs refer to no identifiable object, but have a merely *formal* goal: M noqnonam "he swims"; also M nemaamiiqtɛh-kooskanan "I go bare-legged," with the formal goal in plural inflection. These forms, too, have been reshaped in O.

§28. There are four inflectional prefixes. Three of them, ke- "thou," ne- "I," we- "he, it," appear on both noun and verb. The fourth, me-, appears only on certain nouns, §32. Where more than one person is involved as possessor, actor, or goal, the preference is in the order given; thus "we inc." has ke-, but "we exc." has ne-; tr. forms for "I—thee" and "thou—me" both have ke-: M kenian "I see thee," kenɛɛwem "thou seest me."

The prefixes add t before a vowel: *93* *netaqlaawa "I place him": F netasaawa, C nitahyaa, M netaaqnaw, O nintassaa; compare *aqleewa "he places him," 47; contrast *nemeθkawaawa "I find him," 28. However, before the vowels of certain stems no t was added, 7, 26, 31 (where C probably preserves the old form), 61, 65, 66.

§29. Among endings common to noun and verb are those of the third person: an. sg. -a, pl. -aki, obv. sg. -ali, pl. -ahi; inan. sg. -i, pl. -ali: F ineniwa "man," ineniwaki "men"; ineniwani "(other) man," ineniwahi "(other) men"; miišaami "sacred bundle," miišaamani "sacred bundles."

## 30–32. INFLECTION OF THE NOUN

§30. In addition to the forms just cited, the an. noun has forms for address: F ineniwc "man!" ineniwetike "men!"

The noun makes *possessed themes*, which are then inflected like unpossessed nouns, except that an an. noun with third person an. possessor is necessarily obviative. Possessed themes take a suffix -em. Thus *ehkwa "louse," 88, gives rise to forms like the following: *94* *netehkoma "my louse": F netehkoma, C nitihkom, M netɛɛhkom, O nintikkom; *95* *ketehkomaki "thy lice": F ketehkomaki, C kitihkomak, M ketɛɛh-komak, O kitikkomak; *96* *wetehkomali "his louse": F otehkomani,

C otihkoma, M otɛɛhkoman, O otikkoman; 97 *wetehkomahi "his lice": F otehkomahi, C otihkoma, O (Lake Superior) otihkomaq; M and most O dialects use the singular form for both numbers.

The forms for plural possessor add -enaan for the first person, -waaw- for the second and third: F ketehkomenaanaki "our (inc.) lice," ketehkomwaawaki "your lice," otehkomwaawahi "their lice." An obv. possessor is indicated by -eliw: C otihkomiyiwa "the other's (sg. or pl.) louse or lice."

§31. There are many irregularities in the formation of possessed themes. Some do not take -em; so especially the abstract nouns derived from verbs with the suffix -n and various extensions of it: 98 *pemaatesiweni "life": F pemaatesiweni, C, O pimaatisiwin, M pemaatesewen; 99 *wepemaatesiweni "his life": F opemaatesiweni, C, O opimaatisiwin, M opɛɛmaatesewen. Also, certain objects of intimate possession do not take -em: 100 *axkehkwa "kettle": F ahkohkwa, C askihk, M ahkɛɛh (pl. -kok), O akkikk; 101 *netaxkehkwa "my kettle": F netahkohkwa, C nitaskihk, M netaahkɛh, O nintakkikk.

§32. Certain stems, dependent nouns, occur only in possessed form, nearly all without -em.

One type, denoting parts of the body and a few intimate possessions, uses the prefix me- for an indefinite personal possessor; so 24, 31, 39, 61; 102 *keteehi "thy heart": F keteehi, C kitee, M ketɛɛh, O kiteeq; compare M metɛɛh "a (human) heart," metɛɛhyan "(human) hearts." The form with third person singular possessor is used as an indefinite possessor form for parts of animals' bodies: M otɛɛh "his heart, its heart; an animal's heart (as, at the butcher's)," otɛɛhyan "animals' hearts," contrasting with otɛɛhowawan "their hearts." Some languages, such as O, have lost the form with me-.

The other class of dependent nouns, terms of relationship, have no form with me-, but use verbal derivatives, §82. Thus, beside *nekwiqsa "my son," 38, there are such derived forms as M okiiqsemaw "a son, the son," wɛɛkiqset "one who has a son." Examples in 26, 37, 40, 66. Some of these have irregular forms for address: 103 *noohko "O my grandmother": F anoohko, C noohko, M nohkoq, O nookko; compare 26.

Some dependent nouns have irregularities of prefixation. Some of the stems begin with a cluster, impossible in word initial, 24, 39. Some that begin with ii do not add t to the prefixes, 7, 61, 65; 104 *niiθemwa "my sister-in-law (man speaking), my brother-in-law (woman speaking)": F niinemwa, C niitim, M nenem, O niinim. Three terms of relationship have initial oo with the same peculiarity: *noohkomehsa 26, 66; 105 *oohθali "his father": F oosani, C oohtaawiya (reshaped), M oohnan, O oossan; 106 *noohšihsema "my grandchild": F noošisema, C noosisim, M noohsehsɛh (diminutive -ehs replacing -em), O noošiss (-em lacking). In PA, t was absent also in some that began with other vowels; C has many traces of this, as in 31.

Dependent nouns are formable from the pseudo-root -iit- and by composition with the dependent prenoun -iiči, §100.

## 33. INFLECTION OF THE VERB

§33. Intransitive verb stems end in a vowel, transitive verb stems in a nonsyllabic.

The forms of the verb fall into five *orders*. Each order consists of one or more *modes*, each with a full set of forms. The *independent* order takes prefixes; its principal mode, however, the *indicative*, has zero instead of we- for the third person. The other orders take no prefixes. The *imperative* has forms for second person actor only, and only one mode. The *prohibitive* has two modes with the same restriction, but also a third mode, the *potential*, with a full set of forms. The *conjunct* and *interrogative* orders are used only in subordinate clauses and as participles. The languages differ widely in their stock of modal forms; all seem to have lost a few, and some languages have created new ones.

## 34–42. INDEPENDENT ORDER

§34. The chief mode of the independent order is the *indicative*, used in ordinary statements.

The an. intr. verb here has the ending -w in the third person, with -li before it in the obviative; then come the usual third person endings. Thus, *pemaatesiwa "he lives," 2; *107* *pemaatesiwaki "they live": F pemaatesiwaki, C pimaatisiwak, M pemaatesewak, O pimaatisiwak; *108* *pemaatesiliwali "the other lives": F pemaatesiniwani, C pimaatisiyiwa; simplified in M pemaatesewan, O pimaatisiwan; *109* *pemaatesiliwahi "the others live": F pemaatesiniwahi, C pimaatisiyiwa. The first and second persons singular have no ending; M adds an m, C an n: *110* *kepemaatesi "thou livest": F kepemaatesi, C kipimaatisin, M kepɛɛmaatesem, O kipimaatis.

The languages disagree as to the plural forms of first and second persons. For the first pl F has -pena (some eastern languages agree with this); C has exc. -naan, inc. -naw or -naanaw; M exc. -menaw, inc. -q; O -min. The second person is pluralized by F -pwa (so also in some eastern languages), C -naawaaw, M -muaw, O -m.

Before the -w of the third person endings the final vowel of the stem is subject to alternations; these have been largely leveled out in the different languages, least so perhaps in M. Thus, the numerous (pseudo-tr.) stems in oo: *111* *nepyeeto "I bring it": F nepiito, M nepiitoon, O nimpiitoon (here M and O have added a tr. inan. ending), but *pyeetaawa "he brings it," 11. Some stems in aa have ee before w: *112* *nenepa "I sleep": F nenepa, C ninipaan, M nenεεpaam, O ninipaa; *113* *nepeewa "he sleeps": F nepeewa, M nepεεw, O (Algonquin) nipee; leveled out in C nipaaw, O nimpaa. Stems in e drop it before w: *114* *nenepe "I die": F nenepe, C ninipin, M nenεεpem, O ninip; *115* *nepwa "he dies": F nepwa, M nepuah, O nimpo (reshaped with o for wa); leveled out in C nipiw. *116* *nemene "I drink (it, implied goal)": F nemene, M nemεε-nem; *117* *menwa "he drinks (it)": F menwa, M menuah. *118* *nenaate "I fetch it" (pseudo-tr.): F nenaate, C ninaatin, M nenaaten, O ninaatin; the last three with tr. inan. ending added; *119* *naatwa "he fetches it": F naatwa, M naatwah (second syllable restored on the model of stems with short vowel in the first syllable), O naati (leveled out), C naatam (reshaped into tr. inan. inflection).

The stem si- "say so" is entirely irregular: *120* *nesi "I say so": F nesi, M neseem; *121* *ewa "he says so": F iwa, M ewaah.

§35. The inan. intr. verb is like the third person of the an. intr., with inan. endings: sg. -wi, F pyeemikatwi "it comes": pl. -wali, F pyeemika-tooni "the things come"; obv. sg. -liwi, F pyeemikateniwi; obv. pl. -liwali, F pyeemikateniwani.

The preceding F example shows a stem in e dropping this vowel before w. The alternation of aa ~ ee appears, for instance, in a stem like meçkwaa-, 68: *122* *meçkweewi "it is red": M mεhkiiw; leveled out in F mešk-waawi, C mihkwaaw, O miskwaa.

§36. The independent indicative forms of the tr. an. verb fall into four sets. The first two sets involve not more than one of the first two persons; the other two sets involve both first and second person as actor and goal.

§37. In the first set of forms the prefix, determined by §28, accords with the actor: first or second person acts on third; third acts on obviative. The ending -aa ~ -ee is added to the stem, and the *theme* so formed is inflected much like an an. intr. verb: *123* *newaapamaawa "I look at him": F newaapamaawa, C niwaapamaaw, M newaapamaw, O niwaapamaa; *124* *kewaapamaawaki "thou lookest at them": F kewaapamaawaki, C kiwaapamaawak, M kewaapamawak, O kiwaapamaak; *125* *waapa-meewa "he looks at the other one": F waapameewa, C waapameew, M waapamεw; O has lost this form, replacing it by one of a different mode, §42.

The forms with first and second person plural actors diverge: F kewaa-pamaapena "we (inc.) look at him or them," C kiwaapamaanawak "we (inc.) look at them," M kewaapamonawak, O kiwaapaminaanik. Here belong also the passive forms of the third person: *126* *waapamaawa "he is looked at": C waapamaaw, M waapamaw, O waapamaa. Forms with obv. goal take -em before the -aa: C niwaapamimaawa "I see the other one."

§38. In the second set of forms the prefix, determined by §28, accords with the goal: third person acts upon first or second, obv. upon third. Here belong also the forms for inan. actor and the passives of first and second person. The theme is formed by the ending -eke, with inflection like an. intr. verb, with loss of e before -w. Thus, *newaapamekwa "he looks at me," 69; *127* *waapamekwa "the other looks at him": F waapamekwa, C waapamik, M waapamek; O uses a form originally of different mode, §42.

The stem eθ- "say so to" is reduced to zero before -eke: *128* *eθeewa "he says so to him": F ineewa, C iteew, M enɛɛw, O inaat; *129* *ketekwa "he says so to thee": F ketekwa, C, O kitik, M ketɛɛkwah; *130* *ekwa "the other says so to him": F ekwa, M ekuah; C (regularized) itik.

§39. In the third set of forms the actor is the second person (agreeing with the prefix) and the goal the first person. The theme is formed with suffix -i: *131* *kewaapami "thou lookest at me": F kewaapami, C kiwaapamin, M kewaapamem, O kiwaapam; *132* *keteši "thou sayest so to me": F keteši, C kitisin, M ketɛɛsem, O kitiš. As before, the plural forms diverge: F kewaapamipwa "ye look at me," C kewaapaminaawaaw, M kewaapamemuaw, O kiwaapamim.

§40. In the fourth set of forms the actor is the first person and the goal (agreeing with the prefix) is the second person. The theme is made with a suffix -eθene, which, especially when final, is largely reduced by haplology in the n-languages: *kewaapameθene, 70. The plural forms are discrepant: F kewaapamenepwa "I look at you," C kiwaapamitinaawaaw, M kewaapamenenɛmuaw (without haplology), O kiwaapamininim, kiwaapaminim. The stem eθ- is here, as in §38, reduced to zero: *133* *keteθene "I say so to thee": F ketene (haplologic), C kititin, M ketɛɛnen, O kitinin.

§41. The tr. inan. verb has an ending -am for the third person; this is followed by -w and the usual third person endings: *134* *waapantamwa "he looks at it": F waapatamwa, C, M waapahtam. O here uses a form of a different mode, §42, but has -am in verbs with formal goal: ineentam "he thinks so." The first and second persons singular have an ending -aa: *135* *newaapanta "I look at it": F newaapata, M newaapahtan, O niwaapantaan; leveled out, C niwaapahteen. The first and second persons plural have -ee, followed by plural endings: C kiwaapahteenaawaaw "ye look at it," M kewaapahtɛmuaw.

§42. The languages differ greatly as to modes of the independent order other than the indicative.

A mode which took all three prefixes and had apparently an l in its endings appears in C as a preterit, in M as a negative, and in O tr. verbs replaces the old third person forms of the indicative: C opimaatisi "he once lived," kipee-waapamiti "I came to see thee (but thou wast not there)"; M kan opɛɛmaatesenan "he is not living," kan owaapamanan "he does not look at him"; kan owaapahtanan "he does not look at it"; O owaapamaan "he sees him, owaapantaan "he sees it."

C, M, O have an emphatic preterit with -pa: *136* *pemaatesipanyeeki "they once lived": C, O pimaatisipaniik, M pemaatesyapanik (reshaped; -sya- represents -siwe-).

F, C, O have a dubitative mode with -tok: *137* *pemaatesitoke "he probably lives": F pemaatesitoke, C pimaatisitokee (extended ending, perhaps < -tokeeli), O pimaatesitok; *138* *pemaatesitokeeniki "they probably live": C, O pimaatisitokeenik.

M has an interrogative mode: kewaapahtɛmet "dost thou look at it?" and an emphatic present: pemaatesyasah "so he is alive!" pemaatesyasapanik "so they are alive!"

O has a negative mode with -ssii (perhaps in origin a diminutive suffix): kaa wiin pimaatisissii "he is not alive."

## 43. IMPERATIVE ORDER

§43. In the imperative order, an. intr. verbs have the ending -lo for the singular: *139* *poosilo "embark thou": F. poosino, C poosi, M poosenon (extended, perhaps with particle *na), O poosin. The plural ending is -ko: *140* *poosiko "embark ye": F poosiko, C, O poosik, M (extended) poosekon.

The tr. an. verb has the following endings: "thou—me" -ilo; "ye—me" -iko; "thou—us, ye—us" -inaanke; "thou—him, thou—them" -i, 79, 80, 82; "ye—him, ye—them" -ehko: *141* *waapamehko "look ye at him, them": F waapamehko, C waapamihk, M (extended) waapamɛɛhkon, O waapamikk.

The tr. inan. verb has sg. -anlo: *142* *waapantanlo "look thou at it": F waapatano, C waapahta, M waapahtah, O waapantan. The plural ending is -amoko.

## 44. PROHIBITIVE ORDER

§44. The forms of the prohibitive order have hk in most of the endings. F has a *prohibitive* mode, used in negative commands and in statements of undesired occurrence; corresponding forms, for second person actor only, appear in C and O for future commands: *143* *maačyiihkani: F kaata maačiihkani "do thou not move"; maačiihkani "thou mightst move"; C maačiihkan "do thou later go on a hunt"; O maačiikkan "do thou later go away." F has forms for all persons: pyaahkiči "he might (undesiredly) have come"; the endings, after the -hk, resemble those of the conjunct order.

F has also a *potential* mode for statements of hypothetical occurrence: maačiihkapa "thou wouldst go," okimaawisa "he would be chief."

O has second person forms with longer endings in negative commands: keekwa maačiikkeen "do thou not go away."

## 45–49. CONJUNCT ORDER

§45. The verb forms of the conjunct order have personal endings quite different from those of the independent order. These endings are followed by various mode signs.

The *indicative* mode used in ordinary subordinate clauses, ends in -i (though F, which best preserves these endings, has -e in some of the inflections): F pemaatesiči "that he lives; when he lives."

The *changed* mode has the same ending, together with *initial change*, a modification of the first vowel of the verb stem: a, e~ee; o~oo; to a long vowel ay is prefixed (but F leaves long vowels unchanged; O and, in traces C, has ii~aa). The changed conjunct is used in *when*-clauses of a single past occurrence, and as a *relative* conjunct, §102:   *144* *neqθaawa "he was killed": M nεqnaw, O nissaa;   *145* *neeqθenči "when he was killed": F neeseči, M nεεqneh, O neessint (final consonant restored, t for č). Stems beginning with the roots tahθ- "so many" and taθ- "there," and the an. intr. stem taa- "exist, dwell," 248, prefix een- for initial change: *146* *tahšiwaki "they (an.) are so many": F tašiwaki, C tasiwak, M tahseewak, O taššiwak;   *147* *eentahšiwaači "as many as they are": F eetašiwaači, C eehtasiwaat (final consonant restored), M εεhtahsetuaq (ending reshaped), O eentaššiwaat (in some dialects eentaššiwaač).

The changed conjunct of stems containing a particle eeh (this is the changed form; the simple form does not occur) is common in C: eeh-takohteet "when he arrived." It occurs occasionally in O; in F this form serves also for nonsubordinate statements in hearsay narrative: eeh-pyaači "when he came; he came (it is said)."

The *subjunctive* mode ends in -e; it is used in subordinate clauses of events which have not yet occurred: F kiiši-nepaate "when he has gone to sleep" (then do you . . .); M piat "if, when he comes."

The *iterative* mode ends in -ini and has initial change; it is used in clauses of repeated occurrence: F peemaatesičini "whenever one lives," M pεε-maatesečen. In F these forms, without initial change, are used in negative non-subordinate sentences: aakwi pemaatesičini "he does not live."

The *participle* of the conjunct order has the ending -a for the animate singular and -i for the inanimate singular, with initial change. The participle denotes an actor, a goal, or an implied goal: F peemaatesita "one who lives," neesaata "he who killed the other," miinaki "that which I gave to him" (ending -ak "I—him"). The plural forms are not made with the usual conjunct endings, but are derived from the singulars with endings like those of §29: an. pl. -iki: F peemaatesičiki "they who live," inan. pl. -ili: F miinakini "those which I gave him." The obviatives are based on the usual conjunct endings, the singular adding -ili, the plural -ihi: F peemaatesiničini "the other who lives," peemaatesiničihi "those others who live."

C and O have a preterit conjunct with -pa; O has also a negative conjunct with -ssi.

§46. In the an. intr. verb, the personal endings (which precede the mode signs of §45) are: "I" -aan; "thou" -an; "we exc." -aank; "we inc." -ankw; "ye" -eekw; "he" -t; passive -nk. The third person is pluralized by -waa before or after the -t, and made obviative (without distinction of number) by -li before the -t. After a vowel, the first five prefix y: *148* *pemaatesiyaane "if I live": F pemaatesiyaane, C, O pimaatisiyaan, M pemaateseyan; *149* *pemaatesite "if he lives": F pemaatesite, C, O pimaatisit, M pemaateset.

Many stems in ne drop e; for instance, those ending in -hšine "fall, lie": *150* *šenkihšinaane "if I lie down": F šekišinaane, M sɛhkeehsenan, O šinkiššinaan. These and most other stems in e have -k for "he": *151* *šeenkihšinka "one who lies down": F šeekišika, M sɛɛhkehseh, O šeenkiššink; *152* *nepeke "if he dies": F nepeke, M nepɛɛk.

§47. The inan. intr. conjunct has, for both sg. and pl., -k, obv. -lik: 57, 58, 60, 67, 68.

§48. The personal endings of the tr. an. verb fall into four sets. In each set the third person is pluralized by -waa and made obviative by -em.

The first set, with no theme sign, has the following endings: "I—him" -ak; "thou—him" -at; "we exc.—him" -akent; "we inc.—him" -ankw; "ye—him" -eekw; "he—obv." -aat; "he, passive" -ent ("I—obv." -emak, "they—obv." -aawaat or -aatwaa, and so on): *153* *waapamate "if thou lookest at him": F waapamate, C, M, O waapamat.

The second set has the theme sign -eke, as in §38, followed by -w wherever a third person is involved. Here belongs the form for "obv.—him," -ekot: *154* *waapamekote "if the other looks at him": F waapamekote, C, O waapamikot, M waapamekot. Here belong also the forms for inanimate actor; these have the endings of §46, but the languages differ as to the vowel after the -ek: F nesekwiči "if it kills him," M nɛqnekot. C, M, O have similar formations for the passives of the first and second persons, but F has special forms for these in the third and fourth sets.

The third set of forms has the theme sign -i, as in §39: "he—me" -it; "he—us exc." -iyament; "thou—me" -iyan; "thou—us, ye—us" -iyaank; "ye—me" -iyeekw: *155* *waapamiyamente "if he looks at us exc.":

F waapamiyamete, C waapamiyamiht, M waapameyameh, O waapamiya-mint.

The fourth set of forms has the theme sign -eθ, as in §40: "he—thee" -eθk; "he—us inc." -eθankw; "he—you" -eθeekw; "I—thee" -eθaan; "we—thee, we—you" -eθaank; "I—you" -eθakokw: *156* *waapa-meθankwe "if he looks at us inc.": F waapamenakwe, C waapamitahk, M waapamenah, O waapaminank.

§49. The tr. inan. verb has -am, followed by the endings of §46: "I—it" -amaan; "thou—it" -aman; "we exc.—it" -amaank; "we inc.—it" -amankw; "ye—it" -ameekw; "he—it" -ank; "they—it" -amowaat; "obv.—it" -amilit; "it, passive" -amenk; except for participles, sg. and pl. objects are not distinguished. *157* *waapantameekwe "if ye look at it": F waapatameekwe, C waapahtameek, M waapahtameek, O waapan-tameek; *158* *waapantanke "if he looks at it": F waapatake, C waa-pahtahk, M waapahtah, O waapantank; *159* *waapantamenke "if it is looked at": F waapatameke, C waapahtamihk, M waapahtameh, O waapantamink.

## 50. INTERROGATIVE ORDER

§50. The forms of the interrogative order, used in subordinate clauses of question or probability, have an ending -eeli, added to personal endings which resemble those of the conjunct, the chief differences being extensive use of a theme sign -aaw for the third person, and of -kw instead of -t (or -k) as a third person ending. In C and O there is only one mode, with initial change; F has also a mode without initial change and a participle. C and O have a preterit with -pa; O has also a negative with -ssi. *160* *peemaatesikweeli "whether he live": F peemaatesikweeni, C peemaati-sikwee, O peemaatisikween; *161* *wayaapamaawateeli "whether thou lookest at him": F waapamaawateeni, C wayaapamaawatee, O wayaa-pamaawateen.

## 51. WORD FORMATION

§51. In *composition*, one or more *prior members* are prefixed to a noun stem, a verb stem, or a particle; the members are treated phonetically like words in a phrase, suffering little or no modification. In *derivation*, suffixes are added to stems (*secondary* derivation) or to roots (*primary* derivation), and these components are subject to internal sandhi. Both compound stems and derived stems are subject to inflection; prefixes and initial change appear at the beginning (in compounds, on the first member) and inflectional endings at the end.

The distinction between compounds and derived words is not removed by the fact that some suffixes are homonymous with independent stems. Thus, beside the an. intr. stem api- (C apiw "he sits") there is a suffix -api "sit," forming an. intr. verbs; yet there is a sharp formal distinction between, say, C isih-apiw "and thus he sits" (nitisih-apin "and so I sit," eesih-apit "when he accordingly sat") and C itapiw "he sits so" (nititapin "I sit so," eetapit "the way he sits"). The former is a compound, with the particle isi (< PA *eši) "thus" as prior member; this particle is formed from the root eθ- "thither, thus" with the particle-forming suffix -i. The latter is a primary derivative in which the root eθ- is followed by the suffix -api, which is deverbal from the stem api-, §56.


## 52–54. COMPOSITION

§52. Certain particles, *preverbs*, freely precede verb stems: M kees-pes-nɛɛwɛɛw "he has seen him on the way," nekees-pes-nɛɛwaaw "I saw him on the way," kayees-pes-nɛɛwak "when I had seen him on the way": kees "completion," pes (used only as a preverb) "hither"; F weepi-pyeeči-teteposeewa "he begins to approach walking in a circle." Particles and even longer words are often *included* between the members of such compounds: M nekees-pes-tɛh-wenah-nɛɛwaaw "but I did see him on the way," with tɛh wenah "however" included; F nepyeeči-ketaanesa-naa-naawa "I have come to fetch thy daughter," with ketaanesa "thy daughter" included.

Some particles occur only as prior members: wiih "future" in F, C, O; kiih "past" in C and O; eeh in F, C, O, §45. On the other hand, particles formed with suffix -i added to roots are freely formed (§91) and freely used as preverbs.

§53. Noun stems with an ending -i and an. intr. verb stems with an ending -wi (properly, agent nouns formed with -w) are used as prior members with nouns: F manetoowi-wiikiyaapi "a manitou lodge" (manetoowa "manitou"); niimihetiwi-nakamooni "dancing song" (niimihetiwaki "they dance together").

Particles (*prenouns*) appear before nouns in less variety than before verbs: *162* *waapi "white": F waapi-nenoswa "white buffalo," C waapi-maakwa "white loon," M waap-mianiiw "white owl," O waapi-kaak "white porcupine"; *163* *mači "bad": F mači-metemooha "bad old woman," C mači-maskisin "worthless shoe," M mačeeq-mahkɛɛsen, O mači-očiččaak "evil spirit." The prenoun -iiči "fellow" yields dependent compound nouns, §100.

§54. Certain particles, denoting position or number, form *exocentric* particle compounds with a following noun stem; the suffix -e is added: F ahkwič-asenye "on top of a stone," nesw-eesepane "three raccoons' worth."

## 55–58. DERIVATION

§55. In general, the same suffixes are used for both primary and secondary derivation, though some are predominantly secondary.

*Final* suffixes appear at the end of the stem; without a sharp boundary, we can distinguish between *abstract* finals, which merely determine the form-class (noun, four types of verbs, or particle) and *concrete* finals, which add some more palpable meaning. Thus, -esi an. intr., 2, 3, is abstract, but -piso an. intr. "move without obstruction, glide," 15, is concrete. Unanalyzable stems, such as aθemw- "dog" in 1, are sometimes conveniently described as having a final of the form *zero*.

In primary derivation, the final suffix is often preceded by a *medial* suffix, such as -weeweek- "noise," 12. Medial suffixes have concrete meaning. Dependent noun stems contain a medial suffix but no root; thus -teeh- "heart," 102.

§56. Some concrete finals and some medials are *deverbal*, resembling a word-stem either in the way of homonymy or with some formal deviation, most usually loss of an initial nonsyllabic: *164* \*apiwa "he is in place, he sits": F apiwa, C apiw, M apeew, O api, stem api-; *165* \*eθapiwa "he sits so": F inapiwa, C itapiw, M enaapew, O inapi; final suffix -api. Beside the tr. an. stem \*waapam-, 125, there is the tr. an. final suffix -aapam, 36.

§57. Suffixes appear in divergent forms, so that we set off *accretive elements*: *premedials, postmedials, prefinals*. Some prefinal elements appear in more than one final and in part carry a meaning; we call them *significant prefinals*. Thus, the an. intr. finals -enkwaqši, 41, and -enkwaame, 83, both mean "sleep" and have a common prefinal -enkw-. More often, a significant prefinal appears in a set of four verb finals; thus, -hθ "fall, lie" appears in an. intr. -hšine, 77, 150; inan. intr. -hθen, 43; tr. an. -hšim and pseudo-tr. inan. -hθetoo: *166* \*ešihšimeewa "he lays him so": C isisimeew, M eseehsemɛw, O išiššimaat; *167* \*ešihθetaawa "he lays it so": F išise-toowa, C isihtitaaw, M eseehnetaw, O išissitoot.

§58. Noun stems often lose final w when a secondary derivative suffix is added, as in 198. An. intr. verb stems, on the other hand, often add w to their final vowel before a suffix of secondary derivation, as in 197.

Dependent nouns take the prefix we-when secondary derivation is made from them, 184; those which take the prefixes without t (before ii and oo, §32) here prefix wew-; see, for instance, §68.

## 59–65. NOUN FINALS

§59. Many primary nouns show no analysis; we may say that they consist of a noun root and a final suffix of the form *zero*, 27, 63, 87–89; *168* *miinali "berries, blueberries" (sg. rarely used): C miinisa (diminutive), M meenan, O miinan; *169* *šiiqšiipa "duck": F šiišiipa, C siisiip, M seeqsep, O šiiššiip; *170* *aakima "snowshoe": M aakem, O aakim. Many such nouns end in w: 1, 88, 100; *171* *wekimaawa "chief": F okimaawa, C okimaaw, M okeemaaw, O okimaa; *172* *eškoteewi "fire": F aškoteewi, C iskoteew, M eskootɛɛw, O iškotee: *173* *eθkweewa "woman": F ihkweewa, C iskweew, O ikkwee, Delaware xkweew; *174* *atehkwa "caribou": C atihk, M atɛɛh (pl. -kok), O atikk.

A very few nouns appear in sets, with a common noun root and different finals: *175* *nameewa "sturgeon": C nameew, M namɛɛw, O namee; *176* *nameeqsa "fish": F nameesa, M namɛɛqs; this is perhaps to be described as an irregularly formed diminutive of the preceding; *177* *nameekohsa "trout": C nameekos, M namɛɛkoh (pl. -sak), O nameekoss, diminutive of a stem nameekw-, compare §65; *178* *nameepila "carp, sucker": C nameepiy, M namɛɛpen, O nameepin.

§60. Scarcely any primary nouns are formed from general roots (that is, from roots which appear in primary verbs and particles) with an abstract final suffix. A noun of this exceptional kind is *elenyiwa "man," 13, with root elen- "ordinary, plain": *179* *eleni (prenoun) "ordinary, plain": C iyini, M enɛɛn (as enɛɛn-apuan "ordinary roast: corn bread"); *180* *eleneqšipa "ordinary duck, mallard": C iyinisip, O ininiššip.

In contrast with this, many nouns consist of a general root with a concrete suffix. The concrete suffix may be a noun final deverbal from a noun stem; thus -eqšip "duck," 180, deverbal from *šiiqšiipa, 169. Similarly, -aqθemw "dog," deverbal from *aθemwa, 1: *181* *waapaqθemwa "white dog": C waapastim, M waapeskaaqnem (longer form of the root), O waapassim. Or the concrete suffix may be a medial suffix followed by an abstract noun final, as -aapeθk- "stone, metal," with noun final -w: *182* *piiwaapeθkwi "iron": F piiwaapehkwi, C piiwaapisk, O piiwaapikk; compare M enɛɛnaapɛh (pl. -kon) "axe," Penobscot wɑpahpeskʷ "white rock." Or, finally, the concrete suffix may be a medial with noun final zero, as -aaxkw- "wood, tree, solid": *183* *šenkwaaxkwa "pine tree": F šekwaahkwa, O šinkwaakk; compare M askaah (pl. -kok) "white pine."

Among the noun stems that are formed with a medial are the dependent nouns, §32; the medial suffixes which appear in dependent nouns of relationship, however, do not occur elsewhere. A few noun stems consist of a medial suffix with the third person prefix we- or, less often, me-, §103.

§61. Noun final -w is freely added to intr. verb stems, forming agent nouns, as M čeepaahkow "he cooks"; as noun, "cook," nečeepaahkom "my cook, my wife," As a primary suffix it appears after some medials, as in 182.

Final -aa-w is added to tr. an. verb stems, forming nouns of undergoer: *184* *wekwiqsemeewa "he has him as a son": F okwisemeewa, M okiiqsemɛw, O okwissimaat; *185* \*wekwiqsemaawa "one who is a son": F okwisemaawa, M okiiqsemaw.

§62. Noun final -n forms actions, products, and instruments from an. intr. stems: *186* \*meteewiwa "he takes part in the Mystic Rite": C miteewiw, M metɛɛwew, O miteewi; *187* \*meteewini "the Mystic Rite": M metɛɛwen, O miteewin; here C miteewiwin has a longer suffix; see below. Before this -n, the an. intr. final -kee has replacement of ee by a: *188* \*paaškesikeewa "he shoots with a gun": F paaškesikeewa, C paaskisikeew, O paaškisikee; compare, with medial -ečyee-, M paaskečisekɛw; *189* \*paaškesikani "gun": F paaškesikani, C paaskisikan, O paaškisikan; compare M paaskečisekan.[13] Otherwise, ee∼aa, as in M ahpɛɛsaawaan "bark mixed with tobacco," from ahpɛɛsaawɛɛw "he mixes something into his tobacco"; O kittikaan "field, farm" from kittikee "he farms" (<keqt-wik-ee-).

An extension of this -n is -wen, as in \*peemaatesiweni "life," 98, from the an. intr. stem pemaatesi-, 2.

Another extended form is -kan, as in F išiteehaakani "thought," from išiteeheewa "he thinks so."

An extended form -aakan is added to some tr. an. stems, forming undergoers: *190* \*wiičyeeweewa "he accompanies him": F wiičeeweewa, C wiičeeweew, M wiičiiwɛɛw, O wiičiiwaat; *191* \*wiičyeewaakana "companion": C wiičeewaakan, O wiičiiwaakan.

Some unanalyzable nouns end in -n: *192* \*maxkesini "moccasin": F mahkeseehi (diminutive), C maskisin, M mahkɛɛsen, O makkisin, Penobscot maksən.

§63. Diminutive formations differ in the different languages; s-clusters and, less often, h, appear in the suffixes, e.g., from \*aθemwa, 1, we find F anemooha, C ačimosis, M anɛɛmoohsɛh, O animoonss and pejorative animošš. Finals of this type are -ehs, 9, 26, 40; -hs, 37, 106; -qs, 38, 176.

§64. Few concrete noun finals are unanalyzable; the commonest is perhaps -aahtekw "stick, wood, tree": *193* \*elenaahtekwa "ordinary wood or tree": M enɛɛnaahtek "hardwood," O ininaattik "maple." This is common as a secondary suffix, as M kohkaanaahtek "fish pole" from kohkaan "fish hook."

More commonly, concrete noun finals contain medials, as in 182, 183. Common in secondary derivation is -wikamikw "house," with medial -wik- "dwell": *194* \*ataaweewa "he trades, sells": F ataaweewa, C ataaweew, M ataawɛɛw, O ataawee; *195* \*ataaweewikamikwi "trading post, store": C, O ataaweewikamik, M ataawɛɛwikamek (with i generalized from cases where -wik- comes after a consonant, §5).

Common in secondary formations is -aapoow "liquid," with medial

---

[13] Here, as in other examples, the meaning is modern, but the habit of formation is old.

-aapw-; thus, from *eškoteewi "fire," 172: *196* *eškoteewaapoowi "fire water, whisky": C iskoteewaapoy, M eskooteεwaapoh (ending reshaped), O iškoteewaapoo.

§65. Most concrete noun finals are deverbal, as -eqšip, 180, from šiiqšiip- "duck," 169; -aqθemw, 181, from aθemw- "dog," 1. These occur also in secondary derivation, as M awεεtokaaqnem "bloodhound," from awεεtok "spirit." From elenyiw- "man," 13, there is the final -lenyiw, common in secondary use; thus, from ataawee- "trade," 194: *197* *ataaweewilenyiwa "trader": M ataawεεwenεniw, O ataaweewinini; compare F ataaweeneniwa, without addition of -w, §58. From eθkweew- "woman," 173, there is deverbal -eθkweew; thus, added to wekimaaw-, 171: *198* *wekimaaθkweewa "chief's woman": C okimaaskweew, O okimaakkwee; compare M okiimuuhkiw, without dropping of the final w of the underlying stem, §58, and with contraction. From miin- "berry," 168, there is -min: *199* *waapimina (an.), *waapimini (inan.): F waapimini "maize," C waapimin "white bead," M waapemen (an.) "maize," O (Cuoq) waapimin "apple." From nameekw- "fish," in 177, there is formed -ameekw: *200* *myaalameekwa "catfish": F myaanameekwa, C maayameek, O maanameek; *201* *aθameekwa "dead fish": C atameek, M anaamεεk. Secondary, from atehkw- "caribou," 174, with unusual loss of postconsonantal w: *202* *atehkameekwa C atihkameek, O atikkameek. Another deverbal noun final is -aapeew "male, man": *203* *meqθaapeewa "giant": C mistaapeew, M mεqnapεεw, O missaapee. This is deverbal from *204* *naapeewa "male, man": F naapeewa, C naapeew, M naapεεw, O naapee.


## 66–73. INTRANSITIVE VERB FINALS, SECONDARY

§66. Intransitive verb finals go largely in pairs, for an. and inan. actors. Where there is no special inan. formation, an inan. intr. stem is derived from the an. intr. with -makate: *205* *pyeewa "he comes": F pyeewa, M piiw; *206* *pyeemakatwi "it comes": F pyeemikatwi, M piimakat. Similarly, M pemaatesemakat "it lives," from 2.

§67. In both genders -i added to noun stems in vowel plus w makes verbs of being. Thus, an. intr. meteewi-, 186, is derived from the noun *207* *meteewa "shaman": C miteew, M metεεw, O mitee. From wekimaaw-, 171: *208* *wekimaawiwa "he is a chief": F okimaawiwa, C okimaawiw, M okeemaawew, O okimaawi. To noun stems not ending in vowel plus w, suffix -eewi is added for verbs of being, as M meniikaaneewew "it is a town," from meniikaan "town." Similarly, from aθemw- 1, M anεεmoowew "he is a dog," §18.

§68. An. intr. -i is added to possessed noun themes with third person

singular possessor, making verbs of possession. Thus from wetehkom-
"his louse," 94–97: *209* \*wetehkomiwa "he has lice": C otihkomiw,
M otɛɛhkomew, O otikkomi. Dependent nouns which have this theme in
wii- prefix we- to it: M oweeyawew "he has a body," from weeyaw, 7;
those which have oo- prefix wew-: M owoohkomɛɛhsew "he has a grandmother," from oohkomɛɛhsan, 66; see §58.

§69. An. intr. verbs of gathering and producing are derived from nouns
with final -ehkee: *210* \*wiikopihkeewa "he gathers basswood bark": F
wiikopihkeewa, M weekopeehkɛw; the underlying noun is *211* \*wiikop-
yi "basswood bark": F wiikopi, M weekop, O wiikop.

§70. An. intr. verbs of action on indefinite inanimate objects are derived
from tr. inan. stems by means of -kee. Thus, paaškesikee-, 188, is derived
from *212* \*paaškesamwa "he shoots it": C paaskisam, O paaškisank;
compare M paaskečisam. Pseudo-tr. inan. stems in -too, -htoo drop oo;
thus ešihčikee-, 34, is derived from ešihtoo-, 22.

However, the tr. inan. stems whose tr. an. pendant has -aw, §85, take
-aakee: *213* \*noontaakeewa "he hears something": F nootaakeewa, O
noontaakee, from *214* \*noontamwa "he hears it": M noohtam, O noon-
tank; the tr. an. pendant of this is *215* \*noontaweewa "he hears him":
F nootaweewa, M noohtawɛw, O noontawaat.

§71. An. intr. verbs of action on indefinite animate objects are derived
from tr. an. verbs by means of -iwee: *216* \*niimyiheewa "he makes him
dance": F niimiheewa, C niimiheew, M niimihɛw, O niimiqaat; *217*
\*niimyihiweewa "he makes people dance": F niimihiweewa, M niimi-
hewɛɛw. From some stems, however, these an. intr. derivatives are
made in other ways; thus to miikaaθ-, 78, suffix -kyee is added without
connective: *218* \*miikaaθkyeewa "he fights people": M meekaahkow
(inflection reshaped, compare the conjunct miikaahkit "if he fights"), O
miikaakkii.

§72. An. intr. verbs of *reciprocal action* are derived with -etwi from tr.
an. verbs; thus, from 216: *219* \*niimyihetwiwaki "they make each other
dance, they dance together": F niimihetiwaki, C niimihitowak, M niimi-
hɛtowak, O niimiqitiwak. In some cases, however, this derivative is made
with -wi from the tr. inan. verb; so in the case of 78: *220* \*miikaatamwa
"he fights it": M meekaatam, O miikaatank; *221* \*miikaatwiwaki "they
fight each other": F miikaatiwaki, M meekaatowak, O miikaatiwak.
Similarly, beside tr. an. waapam-, 125; tr. inan. waapant-, 134: *222*
\*waapantwiwaki "they look at each other": F waapatiwaki, M waapahto-
wak, O waapantiwak.

§73. Reflexive an. intr. verbs are derived with -eso from tr. an. stems.
Thus, from pemaačih-, 75: *223* \*pemaačihesowa "he restores himself to
life, he saves his (own) life": C pimaačihisow, M pemaačehɛsow. However, there are quite a few special formations, such as -wiso added to the

tr. inan. stem; from 134: *224* \*waapantwisowa "he looks at himself":
F waapatisowa, O waapantiso.

Some of these special formations occur in both genders and show primary rather than secondary structure. These have a less explicitly reflexive meaning; we call them *middle reflexives*. Thus, beside tr. an. -esw, tr. inan. -es "by heat," there are middle reflexives in an. intr. -eso, inan. intr. -etee: *225* \*kiišesweewa "he cooks him done": C kiisisweew, M kiisesiw, O kiišiswaat; *226* \*kiišesamwa "he cooks it done": F kiišesamwa, C kiisisam, M keesesam, O kiišisank; *227* \*kiišesowa "he is cooked done": F kiišesowa, C kiisisowa, M keesesow, O kiišiso; *228* \*kiišeteewi "it is cooked done": F kiišeteewi, C kiisiteew, M keesetεw, O kiišitee. Similarly, beside divergent forms (§84) of these tr. finals: *229* \*wensweewa "he brings him to boiling": M ohsiiw, O onswaat; *230* \*wensamwa "he brings it to boiling": M ohsaam, O onsank; *231* \*wensowa "he comes to a boil": M ohsoow, O onso; *232* \*wenteewi "it comes to a boil": M ohtεεw, O ontee.

Beside tr. an. -θ, tr. inan. -t or pseudo-tr. -too, there is very often a middle reflexive pair with an. intr. -so, inan. intr. -tee: *233* \*kyaaθeewa "he hides him": C kaateew, M kianεεw, O kaanaat; pseudo-tr. inan. kyaatoo-, 10; *234* \*kyaasowa "he hides himself, he is hidden": F kyaasowa, C kaasow, M kiasow, O kaaso; *235* \*kyaateewi "it is hidden": C kaateew, M kiatεεw.

In some instances, tr. an. -m, tr. inan, -nt are matched by middle reflexive an. intr. -nso, inan. intr. -ntee: *236* \*eθakimeewa "he counts, values him so": C itakimeew, M enaakemεw, O inakimaat; *237* \*eθakintamwa "he counts, values it so": C itakihtam, M enaakehtam, O inakintank; *238* \*eθakinsowa "he is counted, valued so": C itakisow, M enaakehsow, O inakiso (reshaped from -inso); *239* \*eθakinteewi "it is counted, valued so": F inakihteewi, M enaakehtεw, O inakintee.

Beside tr. an aql-, 47, pseudo-tr. inan. aqtoo-: *240* \*aqtaawa "he places it, has it": F ahtoowa, C astaaw, M aqtaw, O attoot, the middle reflexive inan. intr. is aqtee-, 57, but the middle reflexive an. intr. is suppletive api-, 164.

A freely formed type of middle reflexive, *verbs of undergoing*, adds an. intr. -kaaso, inan. intr. -kaatee to tr. inan. stems. In structure, these verbs are middle reflexives of stems in tr. an. -θ, tr. inan. -t, -too, §81, based on an. intr. stems in -kee, §70. Thus, from pseudo-tr. inan. ešihtoo-, 22, and beside the an. intr. derivative ešihčikee-, 34, the verbs of undergoing are: *241* \*ešihčikaasowa "he is (generally) made so": M eseehčekasow, O išiččikaaso; *242* \*ešihčikaateewi "it is (generally) made so": C isiihčikaateew, M eseehčekatεεw, O išiččikaatee.

Some an. middle reflexives merely add -o to the tr. an. stem. The commonest verb of this sort is *243* \*aačimeewa "he tells of him": F aačimeewa, C aačimeew, M aačemɛw, O aačimaat; *244* *aačimowa "he tells of himself, he narrates (his own experience)": F aačimowa, C aačimow, M aačemow, O aačimo. Similarly -po, 54, beside -pw, 311, 312; -eelemo, 19, beside -eelem, 48.

## 74–78. INTRANSITIVE VERB FINALS, PRIMARY

§74. The final vowels of an. intr. stems can always be described as suffixal. Often enough, however, the part of the stem which precedes the final vowel seems to occur in no other primary word. Thus, -i appears in esi- (si-, e-) "say so," 120, 121, and in poosi- "embark," 5. Similarly: *245* *niimyiwa "he dances": F niimiwa, C niimiw, M neemow (inflection reshaped), O niimi. The pseudo-tr. inan. in -i that serves as pendant to tr. an. amw- "eat," 317, is of this character: *246* *miičiwa "he eats it": F miičiwa, C miičiw, M miičwah (inflection reshaped), O miiči.

In other instances, -i is added to a recurring root: *247* *waapiwa "he looks on": F waapiwa, C waapiw, M waapew, O waapi.

The final vowel is -e in a few, such as nepe- "die," 114, 115; mene- "drink (it)," 116, 117; naatc- "fetch (it)," 118, 119.

Final -aa (replaced by -ee before -w in inflection) appears in pyaa- "come," 205. Similarly, taa-: *248* *teewa "he exists": M tɛɛw, O tee; compare M netaam "I exist," O eentaat "where he dwells" (with irregular initial change, §45); M has a corresponding inan. intr. takuah "it exists," takiik "if it exists"; compare O eentakween "I wonder whether it is the case."

An. intr. -ee appears in leehlee- "breathe," 46. Similarly: *249* *ahkeewa (prior element of cluster uncertain) "he extracts marrow": M ahkɛɛw, O akkee. In analyzable stems, -ee is very common after medials, as in *piint-wikeewa "he enters a dwelling," 14, with medial -wik-.

An. intr. -ii appears after recognizable roots, for instance in 33, 84.

§75. More recognizable abstract finals, mostly occurring in pairs, an. and inan., are fairly numerous.

A very common pair in primary derivation is an. intr. -esi, inan. intr. -ate: *250* *sanakesiwa "he is difficult, he is hard to get": F sanakesiwa, M sanaakesew, O sanakisi; *251* *sanakatwi "it is difficult": F sanakatwi, M sanaakɑt, O sanakat.

Another such pair is an. intr. -esi, inan. intr. -yaa. Thus, beside inan. meçkwaa-, 68, 122, there is an. meçkosi-, 29; *252* *kenosiwa "he is long": F kenosiwa, C kinosiw, M kenoosew, O kinosi; *253* *kenweewi "it is long": M keniiw; reshaped in C kinwaaw, O kinwaa.

A less common pair is -esi, -ete, as in M matɛɛsew, matɛɛt "he, it is bad, ugly."

Another an. final appears in -aθe, inan. -ane: *254* *kosekwaθwa "he is heavy": M kosɛɛkwan, O kosikwan; inflection reshaped in C kosikwatiw; 255 *kosekwanwi "it is heavy": C, O kosikwan, M kosɛɛkwan. In C, this inan. -ane everywhere replaces -ate.

Somewhat different is -eθe, inan. -ane, as in M weehken, weehkan "he, it tastes good"; M has this -eθe in mɛhkoon "he is red," 29.

A few pairs have -ekeθe, inan. -yaa: 256 *meqθekeθwa "he is big": M mɛqnekɛn, C (reshaped) misikitiw; 257 *meqšyeewi "it is big": M mɛqsiw; inflection reshaped in F mešaawi, C misaaw.

Suffixes of this kind appear after medials; thus, -esi appears after -wee-week- "noise" in 12, and after -ahkamik- "place, space" in 51.

Suffixes like these are not always paired; thus, an. intr. -esi occurs without an inan. pendant in pemaatesi-, 2, seekesi-, 3, and inan. intr. -ane without an an. pendant in kemiwane-, 59. This last has a unique root; a root found also in other words appears in the following, without an. pendant: 258 *waapanwi "it dawns": F waapanwi, M, C, O waapan.

§76. More concrete finals are largely analyzable into prefinal and final parts; often also the same prefinal appears in transitive suffixes. Thus, prefinal -k appears in intr. verbs for growth and shape, an. intr. -ki, inan. intr. -kene: 259 *ešikiwa "he grows so, is so, fares so": F išikiwa, M eseekew; 260 *ešikenwi "it grows so, is so": F išikenwi, M eseeken. Prefinal -at "cold" appears with the same finals in an. -ači, inan. -atene: 261 *kawačiwa "he freezes to prostration": C kawačiw, M kawaačew, O kawači; 262 *kepatenwi "it freezes over": F kepatenwi, M kepaaten, O kipatin.

Very common is -hšine, -hθene with prefinal -hθ "fall, lie," 77, 150. The pendant of inan. ešihθene-, 43, is 263 *ešihšinwa "he falls so, he lies so": C isisin, M eseehsen, O išiššin.

Prefinal -nt "in water" is followed by an. -ne, inan. -ee: 264 *akwinčinwa "he is in water": C akohčin, M akiihčen, O akwinčin; 265 *akwinteewi "it is in water": F akwiteewi, C akohteew, M akiihtɛw, O akwintee.

Prefinal -ešk "movement of foot or body" appears in -eškaa, for both genders: 266 *papaameškaawa "he goes about": C papaamiskaaw, M papaameskaw, O papaamiškaa. There is also a form -ehk of this prefinal, with apparently dissimilative distribution, though the languages differ: 267 *peesehkaawa "he moves slowly": M pɛɛsɛhkaw, O peesikkaa, but C peesiskaaw, probably reshaped; the root is peet-. Compare §85.

§77. Other finals have fairly definite meanings but are not analyzable. Thus, an. intr. -eente "stay away": 268 *eθeentwa "he stays away so long": F ineetwa, M enɛɛhtwah, O (inflection reshaped) eneenti. Very common is an. intr. -ohθee "walk": 269 *pemohθeewa "he walks along": F pemoseewa, C pimohteew, M pemoohnɛw, O pimossee.

§78. Deverbal finals are numerous. Thus, from an. intr. waapi-, 247, there is an. intr. -aapi "look": 270 *eθaapiwa "he looks thither or thus":

F. inaapiwa, C itaapiw, O inaapi; *271* \*natawaapiwa "he looks to see":
F natawaapiwa, C nitawaapiw, M mataawaapew, O nantawaapi; root
nataw- "try, seek." From this last stem M in turn derives an an. intr.
-atawaapi: menuatawapew "he has good eyesight," root melw- "good."
Similarly, from inan. intr. waapane-, 258, there is a deverbal -aapane
"dawn": *272* \*pyeetaapanwi "dawn approaches": F pyeetaapanwi, C
peetaapan, O piitaapan.


## 79–87. TRANSITIVE FINALS

§79. Transitive verb finals or *instrumentals* go in pairs, tr. an. and tr.
inan.; hence some analysis always presents itself. Instead of a tr. inan.
there is often a pseudo-tr. in -too or-htoo, with inflection reshaped in M
and O in the direction of tr. inan. endings.

§80. The most abstract pair is tr. an. -h, tr. inan. -htoo. In secondary
use it is added to an. intr. stems. Thus. niimyih- "cause to dance," 216, is
derived from niimyi "dance," 245; the pseudo-tr. inan. is *273* \*niimyih-
taawa "he makes it dance": F niimihtoowa, M niimihtaw, O niimittoot.

This pair freely makes primary verbs: *274* \*ešiheewa "he makes him
so": C isiiheew, M eseehεεw, O išiqaat; pseudo-tr. inan. ešihtoo-, 22.
*275* \*pooniheewa "he ceases from him, leaves him alone": C pooniheew,
M poonehεw, O pooniqaat; *276* \*poonihtaawa "he ceases from it": F
poonihtoowa, C poonihtaaw, M poonehtaw, O poonittoot. Other examples are 18, 52 (pseudo-tr. with formal object, so also 53), 75.

§81. Quite abstract also is tr. an. -θ, tr. inan. -t (often pseudo-tr. inan.
-too). In secondary use it is added to an. intr. stems in -ee; this vowel is
replaced in some words by aa, in others by a. Thus, from piintwikee-, 14:
*277* \*piintwikaθeewa "he brings him inside": F piitikaneewa, M piihti-
kanεεw, O piintikanaat; here C has the reshaped piihtokaheew, with -h,
§80; *278* \*piintwikataawa "he brings it inside": F piitikatoowa, C
piihtokataaw, M piihtikataaw, O piintikatoot. This pair is added to pyaa-
"come," 205, with the unique irregularity of aa∼ee: *279* \*pyeeθeewa
"he brings him": F pyeeneewa, M piinεεw, O piinaat; tr. inan. pyeetoo-,
11, 111.

There are many primary formations, such as miikaaθ-, 78, miikaat-,
220, "fight." Similarly, kyaaθ , 233, kyaatoo-, 10, "hide." *280* \*nooçk-
waaθeewa "he licks him": C noohkwaateew, M nuuhkwanεw, O noosk-
waanaat; tr. inan. nooçkwaat-, 30.

An odd pseudo-tr. inan. is naate-, 118, 119, which goes with tr. an naaθ-:
*281* \*naaθeewa "he fetches him": F naaneewa, C naateew, M naanεεw,
O naanaat. Another odd pair is tr. an. eθ- (with irregularity of inflection,
§§38, 40) and tr. inan. et-: *282* \*etamwa "he says so to it, calls it so, says
it so": F itamwa, C itam, M etaam, O itank. Somewhat different are tr.

an. koqθ- "fear," 44, and neqθ- "kill," 144. The tr. inan. mates are not alike: *283* *koqtamwa "he fears it": F kohtamwa, C kostam, M koqtam, O kottank; *284* *neqtaawa "he kills it": F nehtoowa (with the usual leveling of the vowel), M nεqtaw, O nittoot.

Longer forms, analyzable into prefinal plus final, have definite meanings, as -ahanθ "track, trail," 42; the tr. inan is -ahantoo: M wawaanahaahtaw "he loses track of it," O pimaqatoot "he follows the track of it."

§82. Tr. an. -m, with various tr. inan. pendants, has the specialized meaning "by speech, by thought." Commonest is tr. inan. -nt; thus, to kiihkaam-, 49, there corresponds *285* *kiihkaantamwa "he berates it": C kiihkaahtam, M keehkaahtam, O kiikkaantank; *286* *akimeewa "he counts him, them": C akimeew, M akeemεεw, O akimaat; *287* *akintamwa "he counts it, them": C akihtam, M akeehtam, O akintank. From this there is a deverbal pair -akim, -akint, 236, 237.

Other instances, of tr. an. -m are 16, 50, 76.

Peculiar is -m, -ot in aačim-, 243, and *288* *aatotamwa "he tells of it": C, M aatotam, O aatotank.

The longer form -am, -ant means "by mouth, eat, bite": *289* *eθameewa "he bites or eats him so": M enaamεεw, O inamaat; *290* *eθantamwa "he bites or eats it so": F inatamwa, M enaahtam, O inantank.

With a longer prefinal, -eelem, -eelent means "by thought," as in 48; *291* *pooneelentamwa "he ceases thinking of it": F pooneenetamwa, C pooneeyihtam, M poonεεnehtam, O pooneentank.

In many formations, however, tr. an. -m, with its various inan. pendants, has not this specialized meaning; thus, waapam-, 125, waapant-, 134, mean "look at." From this pair there is derived a pair of deverbal suffixes -aapam, -aapant: *292* *eθaapameewa "he looks at him so": F inaapameewa, C itaapameew, M enaapamεw, O inaapamaat; *293* *eθaapantamwa "he looks at it so": F inaapatamwa, C itaapahtam, M enaapahtam, O inaapantank.

Another common pair with unspecialized meaning is *294* *pakameewa "he strikes him": F pakameewa, M pakaamεεw; *295* *pakantamwa "he strikes it": F pakatamwa, M pakaahtam.

A common extended form is -oom, -oont "carry on one's back": *296* *pyeetoomeewa "he carries him hither on his back": F pyeetoomeewa, M piitoomεεw, O piitoomaat; *297* *pyeetoontamwa "he carries it hither on his back": F pyeetootamwa, M piitoohtam, O piitoontank.

The common pair -hšim, -hθetoo has the prefinal part -hθ which occurs also in other formations, §57, examples 166, 167. Similarly, with prefinal -nt, 264, 265, the tr. suffixes are -nčim, -nčitoo: *298* *akwinčimeewa "he puts him in water": M akiihčemεw, O akwinčimaat; *299* *akwinčitaawa "he puts it in water": M akiihčetaw, O akwinčitoot.

Tr. an. -em is added to possessed noun themes: from wekwiqs- "his son," 38, there is tr. an. wekwiqsem- "have or treat as a son," 184.

Tr. an. -m is added to an. intr. stems that contain the root wiit- "along with," §103, making verbs of accompaniment; thus, from wiixpee- "sleep with others," there is wiixpeem- "sleep with," 55. The underlying stem need not occur in inflected forms. Thus, an an. intr. stem wiitapi- "sit with others" is not quotable, but the derived tr. an. is usual: *300* \*wiitapimeewa "he sits with him" (especially, "with her," as a symbol of marriage): C wiitapimeew, M weetapemɛɛw, O wiitapimaat. Often the underlying stem is a compound with the preverb \*wiiči "along": O anokkii "he works," wiiči-anokkiimaat "he works along with him"; C meetaweew "he contends, he plays," wiiči-meetaweemeew "he contends or plays with him."

§83. A very common pair is tr. an. and inan. -en "by hand." Thus, our examples, 4, 17, 23, 74, 85, 86, are matched as follows: *301* \*wenteneewa "he takes him from there by hand": F oteneewa, C ohtineew, M ohtɛɛnɛɛw, O ontinaat; *302* \*wempeneewa "he lifts him up": C ohpineew, O ompinaat; *303* \*peqteneewa "he takes him by mistake": C pistineew, M pɛqtɛnɛɛw; *304* \*kawenamwa "he knocks it down by hand": C kawinam, M kawɛɛnam, O kawinank; *305* \*nakaanamwa "he stops it by hand": C, M nakaanam; *306* \*ašyeeneewa "he pushes him back, rejects him": C aseeneew, M asiinɛɛw, O ašeenaat.

§84. In some pairs the tr. an. differs from the tr. inan. by a plus of w.

Very common is -ahw, -ah "by tool, instrument, or medium." Thus, beside 6, there is *307* \*kiiškahweewa "he chops him through": C kiiskahweew, M keeskahɛw, O kiiškawaat.[14]

Also common is -esw, -es "by heat," 225, 226. With 212 compare the tr. an. *308* \*paaškesweewa "he shoots him with a gun": F paaškesweewa, C paaskisweew, O paaškiswaat; M, with medial -ečyee- "whole body, belly," paaskecisiiw. In some stems the suffixes are -sw, -s, preceded by various consonants; thus wensw-, wens-, 229, 230.

Another common pair of this type is -ešw, -eš "by cutting edge": *309* \*kiiškešweewa "he slices him through": F kiiškešweewa, C kiiskisweew, M kiiskesiw. O kiiškišwaat; *310* \*kiiškešamwa "he slices it through"; F kiiškešamwa, C kiiskisam, M keeskesam, O kiiškišank.

Somewhat different and far less common is the pair -pw, -pot "by mouth": *311* \*sakipweewa "he bites him": M sakiipiiw, Shawnee neθakipwa "I bite him"; *312* \*sakipotamwa "he bites it": M sakeepotam, Shawnee neθakipota "I bite it." These last two pairs also have variants with clusters instead of simple š and p.

There are a few short verbs of this general type: *313* \*mešweewa "he

---

[14] Wherever the w of the suffix tr. an. -ahw is not merged with a following e to yield PA o (§18), there O drops the preceding q (< h) and M drops the w.

hits him with a missile ": F mešweewa, C misweew, M mesiiw, O mišwaat;
*314* *mešotamwa "he hits it with a missile ": M mesootam, O mišotank;
for C Lacombe gives misam. *315* *pemweewa "he shoots him ": F pemweewa, C pimweew, M pemiiw, O pimwaat; *316* *pemotamwa "he
shoots it ": F pemotamwa, C pimotam, M pemootam, O pimotank. Tr.
an. only is the common verb *317* *amweewa "he eats him ": F amweewa,
O amwaat; C moweew, M miiw lack the initial vowel, but it is present in
the deverbal suffix -amw: C kitamweew "he eats all of him," M ketaamiiw;
M mɛɛqtamiw "he eats them till all are gone." The place of a tr. inan. is
taken by the pseudo-transitive an. intr. miiči-, 246.

§85. In various pairs the tr. an. has a plus of -aw. Some of these admit
of no plain analysis. Thus, beside tr. an. meθkaw-, 28, there is tr. inan.
meθk-: *318* *meθkamwa "he finds it ": F mehkamwa, C miskam, M
mɛhkaam, O mikkank. Another unique pair is noontaw-, noont-, 214, 215.

Other pairs have more clear-cut suffixes. Thus, -qtaw, -qt is added to
an. intr. stems, for action relative to an object, as in the following set:
*319* *aθoxkyeewa "he works ": F anohkyeewa, C atoskeew, M anohkiiw
(with irregular vowel quantities, perhaps borrowed from O) O anokkii,
Penobscot alohke; *320* *aθoxkyeeqtaweewa "he works for or at him ":
C atoskeestaweew, M anohkiiqtawɛw, O anokkiittawaat; *321* *aθox-
kyeeqtamwa "he works at it ": M anohkiiqtam, O anokkiittank.

Very common in primary derivation is -eškaw, -ešk "by foot or body-
movement," with a probably dissimilative variant -ehkaw, -ehk; -ešk, -ehk
reappear in the intransitive finals -eškaa, -ehkaa, 266, 267. Thus, beside
tankeškaw-, 25, the tr. inan. is *322* *tankeškamwa "he kicks it ": F takeš-
kamwa, C tahkiskam, M tahkɛɛskam, O tankiškank; *323* *neqtaaseh-
kaweewa "he comes to him relieving his loneliness ": C nistaasihkaweew,
M nɛqtasɛhkawɛɛw, O nittaasikkawaat.

Another common pair is -ehtaw, -eht "hear ": *324* *natohtaweewa
"he tries to hear him, listens for him ": C nitohtaweew, M natoohtawɛw,
O nantottawaat; *325* *natohtamwa "he listens for it ": C natohtam,
M natoohtam, O nantottank.

The pair -naw, -n has to do with perception, especially "by sight ":
*326* *ešinaweewa "he sees him so ": C isinaweew, O išinawaat; *327*
*ešinamwa "he sees it so ": C isinam, O išinank.

The pair -elaw, -el means "shoot (with arrow or gun) ": *328* *wentela-
weewa "he shoots him from there ": F otenaweewa, M ohtɛɛnawɛw, O
ontinawaat; compare C niisoyaweew "he shoots two of them " (root
niišw- "two "): *329* *wentelamwa "he shoots it from there ": M ohtɛɛnam, O ontinank.

§86. Tr. an. -amaw is added to tr. inan. stems, forming double-goal
verbs, §27. Thus, from waapant- "look at," 134: *330* *waapantama-
weewa "he looks at something for or on him ": F waapatamaweewa, C

waapahtamaweew, O waapantamawaat. Similarly, wiintamaw-, 71, is made from wiint-, 334.

One common verb has no underlying tr. inan. and diverges in having no second object: *331* \*naatamaweewa "he helps him": C naatamaweew, M naatamowεεw, O naatamawaat.

The few recorded tr. inan. forms corresponding to tr. an. -amaw (e.g., M naatamatam "he helps it") diverge too greatly to permit of a reconstruction.

When the tr. inan. member of a pair is pseudo-transitive, the double-object derivative is made with -aw (M has the phonetically queer -uw), before which the final vowel of the pseudo-tr. is dropped. Thus, from ešihtoo-, 22: *332* \*ešihtaweewa "he makes it so for him": F išihtaweewa, M esiihtuwεw, O išittawaat. Similarly, from naate-, 118, 119: *333* \*naataweewa "he fetches it for him": F naataweewa, M naatuwεw.

§87. We come now to a number of common but isolated verbs. Tr. an. miil- "give something to," 81, has no tr. inan. by its side and functions as a double-object verb. A few tr. an. verbs end in clusters with l, as aql- "place," 47; its pendant is the pseudo-tr. aqtoo-, 240. Beside wiinl- "name," 45, there is *334* \*wiintamwa "he names it, tells it": C wiihtam, M weehtam, O wiintank. No tr. inan. is recorded for *335* \*noonleewa "she suckles him": C nooheew, M noohnεw, O noonaat.

Other divergent verbs end in w, as wiičyeew-, 190: *336* \*neeweewa "he sees him": F neeweewa, M nεεwεεw. F has here the tr. inan. neetamwa "he sees it"; M has a pseudo-tr. nεεmwah (representing a stem neeme-).


## 88, 89. PRONOUNS

§88. A set of *personal* pronouns is based on a suffix -iil- with prefixes. Singulars have an ending -a; plurals have endings like those of §30, in part differing in the different languages: *337* \*niila "I": F niina, C niya, M nenah, O niin; *338* \*wiila "he, it": C wiya, M wenah, O wiin; *339* \*niilaana "we excl.": F niinaana, C niyaan; *340* \*kiilwaawa "ye": F kiinwaawa, C kiyawaaw, M kenuaq, O kiinawaa.

§89. The languages agree in having other sets of pronouns: *demonstrative*, *indefinite*, and *interrogative*, each in several varieties, but there is little agreement among them. The following are some of the few agreements. *341* \*awiyaka "someone, anyone" (sg. or pl.): C awiyak, M weyak; but O awiya. C and M have a special obviative form for this: *342* \*awiyali "some (other) one, any (other) one": C awiyah, M weyan. *343* \*keekoohi "something, anything" (sg. or pl.): F keekoohi, M kεεkooh, O keekoo; but C keekwa, kiikwa diverges. *344* \*aween- "who is it?": F weeneeha; M awεεq, awεεniq, O aweeneešš; but C awiina. *345* \*weekw- "what is it?": F weekoncehi, M wεεkiq, O weekoneešš. The interrogative pronouns are predicative, hence an accompanying verb is in conjunct or interrogative order: M piiw "he comes"; awɛɛq payiat? "who (is it that) comes?"

In general, pronouns are capable of predicative use: F iin ee-nepeyaani "this (is) when I die." In M, pronouns have special predicative inflections: eneh "that," but eneq as nepɛɛyan "this (is) when I die." O has a special predicative particle mii: mii šikwa wii-ni-maačaayaan "now (is when) soon I must go."

## 90–93. PARTICLE FINALS

§90. Many particles, differing from language to language, cannot be referred to recurrent roots. There are a very few correspondences: *346* *keehi "additive limiting" (placed after the first word of the modified expression): F keehi, M kɛɛh; for instance M eneq kɛɛh nenah "that is enough for me" (eneq "it is that," nenah "I").

Especially as to particles of negation there is great discrepancy: F aakwi, awita (with potential), kaata (with prohibitive); C nama (nama wiya), eekaa (in clause and prohibition); M kan, kat (in clause), poon (in prohibition); O kaa (kaa wiin), keekwa (in prohibition); Shawnee mata; Potawatomi čoo.

§91. Many particles were made from roots with suffix -i. Thus, from eθ- "thus, thither": *347* *eši "thus, thither": F iši (preverb), C isi (also preverb and prenoun), M es (preverb), eseeh (prenoun), O iši (preverb and prenoun). Other examples 35, 90, 91, 92, 162, 163, 179.

The lower numeral particles are of this form: *348* *nekotwi "one": F nekoti, M nekot. C and O have this root in other words, but for the independent particle O has peešik (which appears also in some of the New England languages) and C the unique peeyak. *349* *niišwi "two": F niišwi, C niiso, M niis, O niiš. *350* *neqθwi "three": F neswi, C nisto, M nɛqniw, O nisswi. *351* *nyeewwi "four": F nyeewi, C neewo, M niiw, O niiwin. *352* *nyaalanwi "five": F nyaananwi, M nianan, O naanan; C niyaanan is probably a borrowed form.

The higher numbers are made with longer suffixes, partly from the same roots, but there is much divergence among the languages: *353* *nekot-waašika "six": F nekotwaašika, C nikotwaasik; but M nekuutuasetah and O ninkotwaasso diverge. *354* *neqšwaašika "eight": F nešwaašika, M suasek (reshaped initial); but O niššwaasswi. *355* *metaatahθe "ten": C mitaataht, M metaatah; but F metaaswi, O mintaasswi.

§92. Particles of place are derived from noun stems by suffix -enki, 61, 62, 64; -enki is less common as a primary final, 21.

§93. The suffix -e is added to combinations of root and medial, forming particles of exocentric meaning, parallel with the compound noun forms of §54. *356* \*nekotwikamike "in one houseful": F nekotikamike, M nekuutikamek, O ninkotokamik. *357* \*piintwike "in the house, inside": F piitike, M piihtik, O piintik. Some formations of this kind had -i, if we may judge by F: *358* \*niišwaapyeeki "in two strings": F niišwaapyeeki, C niiswaapeek, M niisuapiik. *359* \*aθaamepyeeki "under the water": F naamepyeeki, C ataamipeek, M anaamepik; O anaamipiink has the ending reshaped, as though with -enki, §92.

## 94–100. MEDIAL SUFFIXES

§94. Medial suffixes appear in nouns, either with a noun final (182, -aapeθk- "stone, metal" with noun final -w) or alone (183, -aaxkw- "wood solid"). No line can be drawn between medials in this use and concrete noun finals; we call a suffix medial when it appears also in other uses. When no root is present, the noun is dependent (-yaw- "body," 7; -štik-waan- "head," 24; -alakačkw- "palate," 31; -škiinšekw- "eye, face," 39; -teeh- "heart," 102). In intransitive verbs, medials appear before final suffixes, mostly an. intr. -ee (-wik- "dwelling," 14) and -esi, -at (ahkamik- "space," 51) or else suffixes of more concrete meaning. In transitive verbs, medials appear before the finals (as in the M forms of 188, 189, 212, 308, with -ečyee- "whole body, belly"). In particles they appear in the types of §93 (-wik-, -wikamik- "dwelling," -aapyeek- "elongated thing, string, row," -epyeek- "water, liquid").

Some medials do not form dependent nouns; others, especially those in dependent nouns of relationship, appear only here (26, 37, 38, 40, 104, 105, 106). In a dependent noun a medial often has a divergent form, especially a premedial extension.

§95. An extremely common medial is -aaxkw- "wood, solid"; its shape is entirely stable and it makes no dependent noun. In nouns it appears with zero final, as in 183. Occasionally it (that is, strictly speaking, the combination of medial -aaxkw- plus noun final *zero*) serves as a secondary suffix. Thus, from aakim-, 170: *360* \*aakimaaxkwa "white ash tree": C aakimaask,[15] O aakimaakk, Penobscot ɑkəmahkw. Similarly, from the theme with prefix we- of a dependent noun, M oseetaah (pl. -kon) "axe handle" (possessed netoosetah "my ax handle") from oseet "his foot," 377 With an. intr. -ee it appears in such forms as M keeskahaahkow "he fells trees," O kiiškaqaakkwee. With other intr. finals: *361* \*pemaax-kwihšinwa "he lies lengthwise as or on a solid": M pemaahkihsen. O pimaakkwiššin; *362* \*pemaaxkwihθenwi "it lies lengthwise as or on a solid": F pemaahkwisenwi, M pemaahkihnɛn, O pimaakkwissin. *363* \*kenwaaxkosiwa "he is a tall tree": C kinwaaskosiw, M kenuah-

---

[15] Cited Language (vol. 17, p. 307, 1941); not known to me.

kosew, O kinwaakkosi; *364* \*kenwaaxkwatwi "it is a long stick":
M kenuahkwat, O kinwaakkwat. With transitive finals: *365* \*eθaax-
koneewa "he places him thus by hand as or on a solid; he thus arranges
for him": M enaahkonεw, O inaakkonaat. *366* \*sakaaxkwahamwa
"he fastens it by tool to or as a solid": F sakaahkwahamwa, C sakaask-
waham, M sakaahkwaham, O sakaakkwaqank. With particle final -e, it
appears in forms like F otaahkwe "from the wood, on that side of the
wood," čiikaahkwe "close to the solid."

Similar to this is -aapeθk- "stone, metal." It, however, takes final -w in
nouns, 182. With intr. final: *367* \*kiiškaapeθkyaa- "be a cut-off rock":
C kiiskaapiskaaw, O kiiškaapikkaa. With tr. finals: *368* \*kešyaapeθkes-
weewa "he heats him as stone or metal": C kisaapiskisweew, M kesia-
pεhkεsiiw, O kišaapikkiswaat; *369* \*kešyaapeθkesamwa "he heats it as
stone or metal": C kisaapiskisam, M kesiapεhkεsam, O kišaapikkisank.
In particles: *370* \*niišwaapeθke "two pieces of metal; two coins, two
dollars": C niiswaapisk, M niisuapεh, O niišwaapikk.

§96. As an example of a medial with variable form we may cite -kamy-
"liquid," which appears also with premedial -aa; in M, for instance, only
this extended form is used in new formations. *371* \*keqčikamyi "sea":
M kεqčekam, Shawnee kčikami; compare C kihčikamihk "in the sea"
and F kehčikamiiwi "sea." *372* \*tahkikamyiwi "it is cold water": C
tahkikamiw, M tahkiikamiw, O takkikami. With premedial -aa: *373*
\*meçkwaakamyiwi "it is red liquid": C mihkwaakamiw, M mεhkua-
kamiw, O miskwaakamiw.

§97. Among postmedial accretions, -ee and -ak are frequent, the latter
especially before an. intr. -esi and inan. intr. -at. Both are present, for
instance, in -epyeek- "water, liquid," 359; the simple form -epy- appears
in forms like M omaanep (pl. -yan) "spring of water," mooskenεpiiw "he,
it is full of liquid" (with intr. final -ee); -epyee- appears in forms like M
siinepinam "he wrings it out" (with tr. inan. final -en "by hand"). Post-
medial -ak is present in -aapyeek- "string," 358; compare -aapy- in forms
like M meqtekuap "bowstring" and --aapyee- in forms like M sakaa-
piinεεw "he holds him by a string, by reins" (with tr. an. -en "by hand").
Similarly, -weeweek- "noise," 12, has -ee and -ak added to -weew-, as in
M piitiiwεεw "it sounds hither" (< pyeet-weew-ee-); this, in turn, is an
extension of -wee-, as in M eniitam "he makes it sound so" (< eθ-wee-t-).
Similarly, -ekon- "day" appears in particles: *374* \*nyeewokoni "four
days": F nyeewokoni, M niiwokon, O niiyokon; and -ekonak- in verbs:
*375* \*nyeewokonakatwi "it is four days": F nyeewokonakatwi, M
niiwokonakat. O niiyokonakat.

§98. Deverbal medials are largely the same as deverbal noun finals.
Thus, the noun final -eθkweew "woman," 198, appears as a medial before
an. intr. -ee: *376* \*pyeeteθkweeweewa "he brings a woman or women":

F pyeetehkweeweewa, M piitɛhkiwɛɛw, O piitikkweewee; compare C nootiskweeweew "he seeks a woman." Similarly, -aqθemw "dog," 181, in C sinikonastimweew "he pets his dog(s)"; -eqšip "duck," 180, in C nootisipeew "he hunts ducks."

§99. Some medials occur unchanged as dependent noun stems, thus, -sit- "foot": *377* \*nesitali "my feet": F nesitani, C nisita, M neseetan, O nisitan. This medial appears as a noun final, for instance, in M nekɛɛq- česct "my big toe" (normally in possessed form, but not a dependent noun, since it has the root keqt- "big"); before an. intr. -ee, M keeskese- tɛɛw "he is cut off at the foot"; with postmedial -ee before tr. an. -ahw in M keeskesetɛɛhɛɛw "he chops off his foot," O kiiškisiteepinaat "he tears off his foot"; with premedial -tala in F teewitanasiteekaapaawa "he stands with aching feet."

Other medials have a discrepant form in dependent noun stems. Thus, -iipit- occurs as a dependent noun: *378* \*niipitali "my teeth": F niipitani, C niipita, M neepetan, O niipitan, but everywhere else the suffix is -aapit-: *379* \*saakaapiteewa "he teethes": M saakaapetɛw, O saakaapitee. Ex- tended -aapitak- appears in M nɛqnwapetakat "it is three-pronged."

Some medials which begin with p, t, k have xp, ht, θk or xk in dependent nouns: *380* \*nexkaatali "my legs": F nehkaatani, C niskaata, M nɛh- kaatan, O nikkaatan; compare Penobscot nkɑt "my leg." In all other uses the form is -kaat-: C kiiskikaat "person or animal with a leg cut off"; *381* \*kiiškikaateewa "he is cut off at the leg": C kiiskikaateew, M keeske- katɛɛw. Extended -kaatee-, for instance in M čeeqčepekaatɛɛqtaw "he jerks his legs."

§100. The *pseudo-root* -iit- "along, with, fellow" behaves like a root in every way except that, like medials, it never begins a word. It forms de- pendent nouns, such as M keetaqnɛm "thy fellow cur," weetaqnɛmon "his fellow cur"; and it forms the dependent prenoun particle -iiči: *382* \*niiči-elenyiwa "my fellow man": C niiči-iyiniw, M neeč-enɛɛniw, O niiči-inini.

A pseudo-root -iil- appears in the personal pronouns, §88.

## 101-107. ROOTS

§101. Roots are the most numerous type of morphologic element. Noun roots appear in a single primary noun, mostly with no plain suffix (miin-, 168), though many such stems end in w (aθemw-, 1). Rarely there is more than one noun (namee-, 175, 177, 178). General roots appear in primary verbs and particles and in nouns with concrete suffixes (elen-, 180, 193). Some general roots, especially some short ones, occur in only one primary form or one pair or set of verbs: a-, 317; a- or aq-, 47, 57, 240; e-, 128, 282; keeh-, 346; ko- or koq-, 44, 283; mii-, 81; ne- or ncq-,

144, 284; nee-, 336; pe-, 315; py-, 205; t-, 248. A root me- is demanded by 28, 318, but also, with divergent meaning, by 313. Other roots range through all degrees of freedom, with much difference among the languages. The following are examples of freely used roots: akw- "adhere, be on," 264, 265, 298, 299; ašyee- "reverse direction, back," 86, 306; atoot- "on something," 54; aθaam- "underneath," 201, 359; elen- "ordinary," 13, 179, 180, 193; ešp- "high," 21; kaw- "prostrate," 41, 74, 261, 304; kenw- "long," 252, 253, 363, 364; kep- "cover up," 262; keqt- "big," 35, 371; kešy- "hot," 368, 369; kešyii- "speedy," 15; kiiš- "finish, done," 225–228; kiišk- "cut through, sever," 6, 307, 309, 310, 367, 381; koohpat- "useless," 18; maat- "move," 142; mat- "bad," 163; meçkw- "red," 29, 68, 373; meeqt- "exhaust," 91; melw- "good," 397; meqθ- "big," 203, 256, 257; miit- "defecate," 83, 84; myaal- "spotted," 200; nakaa- "stop," 85, 305; nekotw- "one," 348, 353, 356; niišw- "two," 349, 358, 370; paašk- "burst," 188, 189, 212, 308; peet- "slow," 267; pem- "along in space or time," 52, 269, 361, 362; peqt- "by accident," 23, 303; poon- "cease," 48, 50, 275, 276, 291; saak- "protrude, emerge," 379; sak- "seize hold," 311, 312, 366; sanak- "difficult," 250, 251; seek- "fright," 3; tahk- "cool," 67, 372; waap- "look; white; dawn," 125, 134, 162, 181, 199, 247, 258; wan- "disappear," 42; weep- "begin," 90; wemp- "upward," 17, 302; wešk- "new, young," 92.

No root is present in dependent stems and in certain verb inflections, 129, 130, 133.

§102. *Relative* roots refer to an *antecedent* in the phrase. For instance, a word containing the relative root eθ- "thither, thus," 22 (34, 241, 242, 332), 43, 51, 53, 165–167, 236–239, 259, 260, 263, 268, 270, 274, 289, 290, 292, 293, 326, 327, 347, 365, 392, such as M eseekew "he is thus, fares thus" or eseemen "such fruit," makes sense only in phrases like kamaač eseekew "he is contrary," kakiihkih eseemen "all kinds of fruit." The antecedent is sometimes a particle in composition: M mεεhnow-eseekew "he is of good disposition." However, the changed conjunct of a verb containing a relative root serves without an antecedent as a *relative conjunct*: M εεseket "the way he is, the way he fares," εεs-pemₐateset "the way he lives." These forms appear especially as complements of nonverbal predicative forms (§89): F iin eeši-kanoonaači "that was the way he spoke to him"; M eneq εεseket "that is the way he is," taaq εεs-pemaateseyan "how is it that thou farest?" The relative roots are ahkw- (cluster uncertain) "so far," ahpiiht- (clusters uncertain) "to such intensity," eθ- "thither, thus," taθ- "there," tahθ- "so many," 146, 147, went- "from there, therefore," 4, 33, 36, 301, 328, 329: *383* \*eehkopyeekaθki "as far as the water extends": F eehkopyeekahki, M εεhkopikah, O eekkopii- kakk. *384* \*eehpiihtesiyaani "as powerful or as old as I am": F eehpiih- tesiyaani, M εεhpeehteseyan, O eeppiittisiyaan. *385* \*eentaθesiyani "where thou art active, where thou dwellest": F eetanesiyani, M εεhta-nεseyan, O eentanisiyan.

§103. Some roots in the several languages are derived from stems and themes, largely from nouns with the third person prefix we-; some such forms are inherited.

The most important instance is the root wiit- "along, with others," 55, 190, 300, derived from the pseudo-root -iit-, §100; it appears also in the common preverb, *386* \*wiiči "along, with": C, O wiiči, §82, M weeč, as in weeč-asaaqsow "he is enrolled along with the others."

Similarly, beside the dependent noun stem -iik- "dwelling," 61, there is a root wiik- "dwell": *387* \*wiikiwa "he dwells": C wiikiw, M weekew (neweekem "I dwell"). This verb is distinct from the verb of possession, §68: *388* \*wewiikiwa "he owns a dwelling": C owiikiw, M oweekew (netooweekem "I own a dwelling"). M has also wiikiahtam "he dwells on the bank of it (a body of water)". Nouns containing this root seem once to have been dependent: *389* \*wiikiwaami "house": M weekewam, O wiikiwaam, but O (Algonquin) miikiwaam. Similarly F wiikiyaapi "house," but C miikiwaahp. There is some confusion between secondary derivatives of the dependent noun -iik- and derivatives of the root wiik-; thus F has owiikiwa "he dwells" and M makes rare possessed themes of the shape netooweekewam "the house I own" (in contrast with neek "my dwelling").

Similarly, a few noun stems consist of a medial suffix with third person prefix, as though a theme of a dependent noun had been isolated: *390* \*wexpenya "tuber, potato": F ahpenya, M ohpεεn, O oppin, Penobscot ppən "ground nut." Compare with this the medial suffix -xpeny-: M moonehpεniiw "he digs potatoes."

Occasionally a theme with prefix me- is elevated into a root. Thus, M meewahkapetaw "he ties it up in a pack" (<miiwaθkaa- ?) and F nemii-wašiweni "my pack" appear beside the dependent stem -iiwaθ-: *391* \*niiwaši "my pack": C niiwas (pl. niiwata), M neewas "my pack" (pl. neewanan), meewas "someone's pack, a pack"; O wiiwaš "his pack"; the F noun is not quotable, but the verb of possession (§68) is recorded as owiiwašiwa "he has a pack."

§104. Some roots appear with *postradical* extensions. In a few cases these are meaningful, thus, pemaat- "live," 2, 75, beside pem-, §101. Similarly, beside eθ-, §102, there is eθaat-: *392* \*eθaatesiwa "he is of that character": C itaatisiw, M enaatesew, O inaatisi.

Most postradicals, however, have no clear meaning. Thus, beside w̄aap-"white," 162, 181, 199, there is waapešk-: *393* \*waapeškesiwa "he is white": F waapeškesiwa, C waapiskisiw, O waapiškisi; compare M waa-peskεn; *394* \*waapeškyeewi "it is white": F waapeškyaawi, C waapis-kaaw, M waapeskiw, O waapiškaa.

A plus of postconsonantal w is especially common. Thus, some forms have kep-, 262, but others kepw-: *395* *kepahamwa "he closes the opening of it with something:" C kipaham, M kepaaham, O kipaqank; compare F kepahikani "stopper"; *396* *keponamwa "he covers the opening of it with his hand": C kiponam, M kepoonam. There are various such pairs; most roots in consonant plus w, on the other hand, never lack the w, as, for instance, the very common root melw- "good": *397* *melweelemeewa "he likes him": F menweenemeewa, C miyweeyimeew, M meniinemɛw, O minweenimaat.

Quite a few roots appear sometimes with postconsonantal w and sometimes with aw. Thus, beside kwiiθw-, 16, certain stems have kwiiθaw-: *398* *kwiiθaweelemeewa "he yearns for him": C kwiitaweeyimeew, O kwiinaweenimaat. A common pair of this kind is natw- "seek," 324, 325, nataw-, 271.

§105. Often the extended root has the shape of a stem, especially of a tr. inan. stem, as M keeskahaahkow "he fells trees," §95, formed from a root M keeskah-, homonymous with (and historically no doubt abstracted from) the stem of tr. inan. keeskaham, 6. In a number of instances the simple root occurs only in one or two stems and it is only the extended root, with the shape of a tr. inan. stem, that is freely used. Thus, naa- "fetch" occurs only in tr. an. naaθ-, 281, and pseudo-tr. inan. naate-, 119, but the extended naat- is freely used: *399* *naatoontamwa "he fetches it carrying it on his back": F naatootamwa, M naatoohtam. Similarly, py- "come" occurs only in an. intr. pyaa-, 205; this has the secondary derivatives tr. an. pyeeθ-, 279, pseudo-tr. inan. pyeetoo-, 11, but, resembling this last stem, the extended root pyeet- is freely used, 12, 76, 272, 296, 297, 376. An odd but important root of this sort is pii- "enclose, inside." The simple root occurs only in a pair of middle reflexive verbs: *400* *piinsowa "he is enclosed": M peehsow, O piinso; *401* *piinteewi "it is enclosed": M peehtɛw, O piintee. The corresponding tr. verbs would be tr. an. piinl-, tr. inan. piint-; these forms occur nowhere, apparently, as verb stems, but everywhere as extended roots. The form piinl- appears in one pair of tr. verbs: *402* *piinlahweewa "he encloses him in something": F piinahweewa, M peehnahɛw, O piinawaat; *403* *piinlahamwa "he encloses it in something": F piinahamwa, M peehnaham, O piinaqank. Except for these forms, all stems are made from the extended root piint-, 14, 77, 357.

§106. *Reduplicated* roots occur especially in verb forms, with meanings such as repetition, plurality, or intensity. The regular type of reduplication prefixes the initial nonsyllabic plus aa: F waawaapameewa "he keeps looking at him" (beside 125), M naaniis "two each" (beside 349); before a vowel, aay- is prefixed: M aayaačemow "he keeps narrating" (beside 244). There are various irregular types of reduplication: F kehkahweewa "he decides about him," kekyeehkahweewa "he repeatedly decides about him"; M keeskeeskaham "he repeatedly chops it through" (beside 6); M poohkonam "he breaks it across by hand," pooqpoohkonam "he repeatedly breaks it across." More remote is papaam-, 266, beside pem-, §101. The noun šiiqšiip-, 169, seems to show reduplication in a noun root.

§107. In some cases the reduplicated root tends to suppletive use for plurals. Beside kenw- "long," 252, 253, 363, 364, the irregularly reduplicated kakaanw- is used where more than one long thing is involved, as M kakaanuahkosewak "they are tall trees" (beside 363 for the singular), kakaanuahkwaton "they are long sticks" (sg. 364); *404* *kakaanwaanexkweewa "he has long hair": M kakaanuanɛhkow, O kakaanwaanikkwee; compare F kakaanohkweewa, Natick quanonuhquoant "having long hair" (Trumbull). Similarly M enɛɛken "he is so big," ayiinekɛnok "they are so big" (would be ayyeeθ- beside eθ-); mɛqnekɛn "he is big," 256, mamaahkekɛnok "they are big"; mɛqsiw "it is big," 257, mamaahkiwan "they (inan.) are big"; nahɛɛnesew "he is small," nahɛɛnet "it is small," papiasewak "they are small," papeewaton "they (inan.) are small"; likewise the prenouns: mɛɛqč-enɛɛniw "big man," mamaah-enɛɛniwak "big men."

## BIBLIOGRAPHY OF ALGONQUIAN ACCORDING TO LANGUAGE GROUPS

### General Sources

MURDOCK, G. P., *Ethnographic Bibliography of North America* (Yale Anthropological Studies, vol. 1, New Haven, 1941).

PILLING, J. C., *Bibliography of the Algonquian Languages* (Bureau of American Ethnology, Bulletin 13, Washington, 1891).

VOEGELIN, C. F., *Bibliography of American Indian Linguistics 1938–41* (Language, vol. 18, pp. 133–139, Baltimore, 1942).

Items from these sources are in general not repeated below.

### Comparative Studies

BLOOMFIELD, LEONARD, *A Note on Sound-Change* (Language, vol. 4, pp. 99–100, Baltimore, 1928).

　*Proto-Algonquian -iit- 'Fellow'* (Language, vol. 17, pp. 292–297, Baltimore, 1941).

　*On the Sound System of Central Algonquian* (Language, vol. 1, pp. 130–156, Baltimore, 1925).

　*The Word-Stems of Central Algonquian* (In *Festschrift Meinhof*, pp. 393–402, Hamburg, 1927).

GEARY, JAMES A., *Proto-Algonquian *çk: Further Examples* (Language, vol. 17, pp. 304–310, Baltimore, 1941).

MICHELSON, TRUMAN, *Algonquian Linguistic Miscellany* (Journal of the Washington Academy of Sciences, vol. 4, pp. 402–409, Washington, 1914).

*Algonquiana Parerga* (International Journal of American Linguistics, vol. 8, pp. 39–44, New York, 1933).

*An Archetype Vindicated* (Language, vol. 11, p. 148, Baltimore, 1935).

*The Fundamental Principles of Algonquian Languages* (Journal of the Washington Academy of Sciences, vol. 16, pp. 369–371, Washington, 1926).

*Miscellanea Algonquiana* (International Journal of American Linguistics, vol. 7, p. 93, New York, 1932).

*Notes on Algonquian Languages* (International Journal of American Linguistics, vol. 1, pp. 50–57, New York, 1917).

*The Proto-Algonquian Archetype of "Five"* (Language, vol. 9, pp. 270–272, Baltimore, 1933).

*Remarks on Terms of Relationship* (Journal of the Washington Academy of Sciences, vol. 7, pp. 181–184, Washington, 1917).

*Some Algonquian Kinship Terms* (American Anthropologist, n.s., vol. 34, pp. 357–359, Menasha, Wis., 1932).

*Terms of Relationship and Social Organization* (Proceedings of the National Academy of Sciences, vol. 2, pp. 297–300, Washington, 1916).

*Two Phonetic Shifts Occurring in Many Algonquian Languages* (International Journal of American Linguistics, vol. 1, pp. 300–304, New York, 1920).

*Two Proto-Algonquian Phonetic Shifts* (Journal of the Washington Academy of Sciences, vol. 9, pp. 333–334, Washington, 1919).

*Varia Algonquiana* (International Journal of American Linguistics, vol. 5, pp. 116–117, New York, 1929).

SIEBERT, FRANK T. JR., *Certain Proto-Algonquian Consonant Clusters* (Language, vol. 17, pp. 298–303, Baltimore, 1941).

UHLENBECK, C. C., *Ontwerp van Eene Vergelijkende Vormleer van Eenige Algonkin-Talen* (Verhandelingen der Koninklijke Akademie van Wetenschappen, Afdeeling Letterkunde, n.s., vol. 11, no. 3, pp. 1–67, Amsterdam, 1910).

*Het Passieve Karakter van het Verbum Transitivum of van het Verbum Actionis in Talen van Noord-Amerika* (Verslagen en Mededeelingen der Koninklijke Akademie van Wetenschappen, Afdeeling Letterkunde, ser. 5, vol. 2, pp. 187–216, Amsterdam, 1917).

## Cree

BLOOMFIELD, LEONARD, *The Plains Cree Language* (Proceedings of the Twenty-second International Congress of Americanists, vol. 2, pp. 427–431, Rome, 1928).

*Plains Cree Texts* (Publications of the American Ethnological Society, vol. 16, pp. 1–309, New York, 1934).

*Sacred Stories of the Sweet Grass Cree* (National Museum of Canada, Bulletin 60, Ottawa, 1930).

COOPER, J. M., *Some Notes on the Waswanipi* (Proceedings of the Twenty-second International Congress of Americanists, vol. 2, pp. 459–461, Rome, 1928).

MICHELSON, TRUMAN, *Indian Language Studies on James and Hudson's Bays, Canada* (Explorations and Field Work of the Smithsonian Institution in 1935, pp. 75–80, Washington, 1936).

*The Linguistic Classification of Rupert's House and East Main Cree* (American Anthropologist, n.s., vol. 26, p. 295, Menasha, Wis., 1924).

*The Linguistic Classification of Tete de Boule* (American Anthropologist, n.s., vol. 35, p. 396, Menasha, Wis., 1933).

*A Report on a Linguistic Expedition to James and Hudson's Bays* (Language, vol. 12, pp. 135–136, Baltimore, 1936).
*Some Linguistic Features of Speck's "Naskapi"* (American Anthropologist, n.s., vol. 39, pp. 370–372, Menasha, Wis., 1937).
*Studies among the Montagnais-Naskapi Indians of the Northern Shore of the St. Lawrence River* (Explorations and Field Work of the Smithsonian Institution in 1937, pp. 119–122, Washington, 1938).
SPECK, F. G., *Naskapi* (Norman, Oklahoma, 1935).

## Menomini

BLOOMFIELD, LEONARD, *The Menomini Language* (Proceedings of the Twenty-first International Congress of Americanists, vol. 2, pp. 336–343, Hague, 1924).
*Menomini Texts* (Publications of the American Ethnological Society, vol. 12, pp. 1–607, New York, 1928).
MICHELSON, TRUMAN, Review of *Menomini Texts* by Leonard Bloomfield (Language, vol. 5, pp. 189–190, Baltimore, 1929).
SWADESH, MORRIS, Unpublished data.

## Fox Group

BLOOMFIELD, LEONARD, *Notes on the Fox Language* (International Journal of American Linguistics, vol. 3, pp. 219–232, 1925, and vol. 4, pp. 181–219, New York, 1927).
Review of *The Owl Sacred Pack of the Fox Indians* by Truman Michelson (American Journal of Philology, vol. 43, pp. 276–281, Baltimore, 1922).
JONES, WILLIAM, *Algonquian (Fox)*, (Bureau of American Ethnology, Bulletin 40, pt. 1, pp. 735–873, Washington, 1911).
*Fox Texts* (Publication of the American Ethnological Society, vol. 1, pp. 1–9, New York, 1907); compare H. M. Rideout, *William Jones* (New York, 1912).
*Kickapoo Ethnological Notes* (American Anthropologist, n.s., vol. 15, pp. 332–335, Lancaster, Pa., 1913).
*Some Principles of Algonquian Word-Formation* (American Anthropologist, n.s., vol. 6, pp. 369–411, Lancaster, Pa., 1904).
MICHELSON, TRUMAN, *The Autobiography of a Fox Indian Woman* (40th Annual Report of the Bureau of American Ethnology, pp. 291–349, Washington, 1925).
*Contributions to Algonquian Grammar* (American Anthropologist, n.s., vol. 15, pp. 470–476, Lancaster, Pa., 1913).
*Contributions to the Fox Ethnology* (Bureau of American Ethnology, Bulletin 85, Washington, 1927, and Bulletin 95, Washington, 1930).
*Fox Kemiyāwi "It Rains"* (Language, vol. 13, pp. 73–75, Baltimore, 1937).
*Fox Linguistic Notes* (In *Festschrift Meinhof*, pp. 403–408, Hamburg, 1927).
*Fox Miscellany* (Bureau of American Ethnology, Bulletin 114, Washington, 1937).
*On the Future of the Independent Mode in Fox* (American Anthropologist, n.s., vol. 13, pp. 171–172, Lancaster, Pa., 1911).
*Linguistic Miscellany* (In *Studies in Honor of H. Collitz*, pp. 37–40, Baltimore, 1930).

*Mesawi'ka, and Fox Sociology* (American Anthropologist, n.s., vol. 35, p. 397, Menasha, Wis., 1933).

*Notes on the Buffalo-Head Dance of the Thunder Gens of the Fox Indians* (Bureau of American Ethnology, Bulletin 87, Washington, 1928).

*Notes on the Fox Negative Particle of the Conjunctive Mode* (American Anthropologist, vol. 15, p. 364, Lancaster, Pa., 1913).

*Notes on the Fox Wapanowiweni* (Bureau of American Ethnology, Bulletin 105, Washington, 1932).

*Notes on the Social Organization of the Fox Indians* (American Anthropologist, n.s., vol. 15, pp. 691–693, Lancaster, Pa., 1913).

*Observations on the Thunder Dance of the Bear Gens of the Fox Indians* (Bureau of American Ethnology, Bulletin 89, Washington, 1929).

*The Owl Sacred Pack of the Fox Indians* (Bureau of American Ethnology, Bulletin 72, Washington, 1921).

*Rejoinder* (to the Bloomfield review of *Owl Sacred Pack*) (American Journal of Philology, vol. 44, pp. 285–286, Baltimore, 1923).

Review of *Observations on the Ethnology of the Sauk Indians* by Alanson Skinner (American Anthropologist, n.s., vol. 26, pp. 93–100, Menasha, Wis., 1924).

*The So-Called Stems of the Algonquian Verbal Complexes* (Proceedings of the Nineteenth International Congress of Americanists, pp. 541–544, Washington, 1917).

*Some General Notes on the Fox Indians* (Journal of the Washington Academy of Sciences, vol. 9, pp. 483–494; 521–528; 593–596, Washington, 1919).

*Vocalic Harmony in Fox* (American Journal of Philology, vol. 41, pp. 181–183, Baltimore, 1920).

*Who Were the Padouca?* (American Anthropologist, n.s., vol. 23, p. 101, Menasha, Wis., 1921).

## Shawnee

VOEGELIN, C. F., *Productive Paradigms in Shawnee* (In *Essays in Anthropology in Honor of Alfred Louis Kroeber*, pp. 391–403, Berkeley, 1936).

*Shawnee Phonemes* (Language, vol. 11, pp. 23–37, Baltimore, 1935).

## Peoria Group

VOEGELIN, C. F., *Shawnee Stems and the Jacob P. Dunn Miami Dictionary* (Indiana Historical Society, Prehistory Research Series, vol. 1, pp. 63–108; 135–167; 289–341; 345–406; 409–478, Indianapolis, 1937–1940).

## Potawatomi

HOCKETT, C., *Potawatomi Syntax* (Language, vol. 15, pp. 235–248, Baltimore, 1939).

Unpublished data.

MICHELSON, TRUMAN, *The Linguistic Classification of Potawatomi* (Proceedings of the National Academy of Sciences, vol. 1, pp. 450–452, Washington, 1915).

## Ojibwa Group

CUOQ, J. A., *Grammaire de la Langue Algonquine* (Proceedings and Transactions of the Royal Society of Canada, 1st ser., vol. 9, pp. 85 ff., 1891, and vol. 10, pp. 41 ff., Ottawa, 1892).

HALLOWELL, IRVING, *Was Cross-Cousin Marriage Practised by the North-Central Algonquian?* (Proceedings of the Twenty-third International Congress of Americanists, pp. 519–544, New York, 1930).

JONES, WILLIAM, *Ojibwa Texts* (Publications of the American Ethnological Society, vol. 7, pt. 1, pp. 1–501, 1917; pt. 2, pp. 1–771, New York, 1919).

JOSSELIN DE JONG, J. P. B. de, *A Few Otchipwe Songs* (Internationales Archiv für Ethnographie, vol. 20, pp. 189–190, Leiden, 1912).
*Original Odzibwe Texts* (Baessler Archiv, Beiheft 5, pp. 1–54, Leipzig and Berlin, 1913).

MICHELSON, TRUMAN, Review of *The Ojibwa Indians of Parry Island, Their Social and Religious Life* by Diamond Jenness (American Anthropologist, n.s., vol. 38, pp. 657–659, Menasha, Wis., 1936).

VOEGELIN, C. F., Unpublished data.

## Delaware

SPECK, F. G., *Oklahoma Delaware Ceremonies, Dances and Feasts* (Memoirs of the American Philosophical Society, vol. 7, pp. 1–161, Philadelphia, 1937).
*A Study of the Delaware Big House Ceremony* (Publications of the Pennsylvania Historical Commission, vol. 2, pp. 5–192, Harrisburg, 1931).

VOEGELIN, C. F., *Proto-Algonquian Consonant Clusters in Delaware* (Language, vol. 17, pp. 143–147, Baltimore, 1941).

## Powhatan

GERARD, W. R., *The Tapehanek Dialect of Virginia* (American Anthropologist, n.s., vol. 6, pp. 313–330, Lancaster, Pa., 1904).

MICHELSON, TRUMAN, *The Linguistic Classification of Powhatan* (American Anthropologist, n.s., vol. 35, p. 549, Menasha, Wis., 1933).

## Natick Group

GERARD, W. R., *The Root Kompau: Its Forms and Meaning* (American Anthropologist, n.s., vol. 14, pp. 574–576, Lancaster, Pa.).

MICHELSON, TRUMAN, *On the Etymology of the Natick Word Kompau, 'He Stands Erect'* (American Anthropologist, n.s., vol. 13, p. 339, Lancaster, Pa., 1911).
*Mr. Gerard and the Root "Kompau"* (American Anthropologist, n.s., vol. 14, p. 577, Lancaster, Pa., 1912).

TRUMBELL, J. H., *Natick Dictionary* (Bureau of American Ethnology, Bulletin 25, Washington, 1903).

## Penobscot Group

MICHELSON, TRUMAN, *The Linguistic Classification of the Shinnecock Indians* (American Anthropologist, n.s., vol. 26, p. 427, Menasha, Wis., 1924).

*The Passamaquoddy Indians of Maine* (Explorations and Field Work of the Smithsonian Institution in 1934, pp. 85–88, Washington, 1935).

*Review of Penobscot Transformer Tales* by F. G. Speck (American Journal of Philology, vol. 41, pp. 305–306, Baltimore, 1920).

PRINCE, J. D., *The Differentiation between the Penobscot and the Canadian Abenaki Dialects* (American Anthropologist, n.s., vol. 4, pp. 17–32, New York, 1902).

*The Modern Dialect of the Canadian Abenakis* (In *Miscellanea Linguistica in onore di Graziadio Ascoli*, pp. 343–362, Turin, 1901).

*A Passamaquoddy Tobacco Famine* (International Journal of American Linguistics, vol. 1, pp. 58–63, New York, 1917).

*The Penobscot Language of Maine* (American Anthropologist, n.s., vol. 12, pp. 183–208, Lancaster, Pa., 1910).

*A Tale in the Hudson River Indian Language* (American Anthropologist, n.s., vol. 7, pp. 74–84, Lancaster, Pa., 1905).

PRINCE, J. D. AND F. G. SPECK, *Dying American Speech-Echoes from Connecticut* (Proceedings of the American Philosophical Society, vol. 42, pp. 346–352, Philadelphia, 1903).

*Glossary of the Mohegan-Pequot Language* (American Anthropologist, n.s., vol. 6, pp. 18–45, Lancaster, Pa., 1904).

*The Modern Pequots and Their Language* (American Anthropologist, n.s., vol. 5, pp. 193–212, Lancaster, Pa., 1903).

SPECK, F. G., *A Modern Mohegan-Pequot Text* (American Anthropologist, n.s., vol. 6, pp. 469–476, Lancaster, Pa., 1904).

*Native Tribes and Dialects of Connecticut: A Mohegan-Pequot Diary* (43rd Annual Report of the Bureau of American Ethnology, pp. 199–287, Washington, 1928).

*Penobscot Transformer Tales* (International Journal of American Linguistics, vol. 1, pp. 187–244, New York, 1920).

*Wawenock Myth Texts from Maine* (43rd Annual Report of the Bureau of American Ethnology, pp. 165–197, Washington, 1928).

## Micmac

SPECK, F. G., *Beothuk and Micmac* (Indian Notes and Monographs, ser. 2, no. 22, New York, 1922).

## Blackfoot

JOSSELIN DE JONG, J. P. B. de, *Social Organization of the Southern Piegans* (Internationales Archiv für Ethnographie, vol. 20, pp. 191–197, Leiden, 1912).

KROEBER, A. L., Review of *The Adverbial and Prepositional Prefixes in Blackfoot* by G. J. Geers (International Journal of American Linguistics, vol. 1, pp. 184–185, New York, 1918).

MICHELSON, TRUMAN, *Notes on the Piegan System of Consanguinity* (In *Holmes Anniversary Volume*, pp. 320–333, Washington, 1916).

*Notes on Some Word-Comparisons between Blackfoot and Other Algonquian Languages* (International Journal of American Linguistics, vol. 3, pp. 233–235, New York, 1925).

Review of *Original Blackfoot Texts* by C. C. Uhlenbeck (American Anthropologist, n.s., vol. 13, pp. 326–330, Lancaster, Pa., 1911).

UHLENBECK, C. C., *De Afwezigheid der Datief-Conceptie in het Blackfoot* (In *Symbolae Rozwadowski* pp. 72–82, Cracow, 1927).

*Blackfoot Notes* (International Journal of American Linguistics, vol. 2, p. 181, 1923; vol. 5, pp. 119–120, 1929; and vol. 9, p. 76, New York, 1936).

*A Concise Blackfoot Grammar* (Verhandlingen der Koninklijke Akademie van Wetenschappen, Afdeeling Letterkunds, n.s., vol. 41, pp. 1–240, Amsterdam, 1938).

*Het Emphatisch Gebruik van Relatief Pronominale Uitgangen in het Blackfoot* (In *Festschrift P. W. Schmidt*, pp. 148–156, Vienna, 1928).

*Infigeering op het Gebied der Algonkin-Talen* (Mededeelingen der Koninklijke Akademie van Wetenschappen, Afdeeling Letterkunde, ser. A, vol. 69, no. 3, pp. 11–116, Amsterdam, 1930).

*Some Word-Comparisons between Blackfoot and Other Algonquian Languages* (International Journal of American Linguistics, vol. 3, pp. 103–108, New York, 1924).

UHLENBECK, C. C. AND R. H. VAN GULICK, *A Blackfoot-English Dictionary* (Verhandlingen der Koninklijke Akademie van Wetenschappen, Afdeeling Letterkunde, n.s., vol. 33, no. 2, pp. 1–380, Amsterdam, 1934).

*An English-Blackfoot Dictionary* (Verhandlingen der Koninklijke Akademie van Wetenschappen, Afdeeling Letterkunde, n.s., vol. 29, no. 4, pp. 1–261, Amsterdam, 1930).

## Cheyenne

GRINNELL, G. B., *Notes on Some Cheyenne Songs* (American Anthropologist, n.s., vol. 5, pp. 312–322, Lancaster, Pa., 1903).

MICHELSON, TRUMAN, *American Linguistics* (Science, vol. 76, pp. 55–56, New York, 1932).

*Anthropological Studies in Oklahoma and Iowa* (Explorations and Field Work of the Smithsonian Institution in 1932, pp. 89–92, Washington, 1933).

*Anthropological Studies in Oklahoma, Iowa, and Montana* (Explorations and Field Work of the Smithsonian Institution in 1931, pp. 179–182, Washington, 1932).

*Phonetic Shifts in Cheyenne* (International Journal of American Linguistics, vol. 8, p. 78, New York, 1933).

*Studies of the Algonquian Tribes of Iowa and Oklahoma* (Explorations and Field Work of the Smithsonian Institution in 1929, pp. 207–212, Washington, 1930).

*Studies of the Cheyenne, Kickapoo, and Fox* (Explorations and Field Work of the Smithsonian Institution in 1930, pp. 207–210, Washington, 1931).

PETTER, R., *Sketch of the Cheyenne Grammar* (Memoirs of the American Anthropological Association, vol. 1, pp. 443–478, Lancaster, Pa., 1907).

SAPIR, E., *Algonkin p and s in Cheyenne* (American Anthropologist, n.s., vol. 15, pp. 538–439, Lancaster, Pa., 1913).

## Arapaho Group

KROEBER, A. L., *The Arapaho* (Bulletin of the American Museum of Natural History, vol. 18, pp. 1–229, New York, 1902).
*Arapaho Dialects* (University of California Publications in American Archeology and Ethnology, vol. 12, no. 3, pp. 71–138, Berkeley, 1916).
MICHELSON, TRUMAN, *Algonquian Tribes of Oklahoma and Iowa* (Explorations and Field Work of the Smithsonian Institution in 1928, pp. 183–188, Washington, 1929).
*Language Studies among the Fox and Northern Arapaho Indians* (Explorations and Field Work of the Smithsonian Institution in 1927, pp. 179–182, Washington, 1928).
*Some Arapaho Kinship Terms and Social Usages* (American Anthropologist, n.s., vol. 36, pp. 137–139, Menasha, Wis., 1934).
UHLENBECK, C. C., *Additional Blackfoot-Arapaho Comparisons* (International Journal of American Linguistics, vol. 4, pp. 227–228, New York, 1927).

# B66. From *The Menomini Language*

[The date of this passage is not known, though it was most likely written some-time in 1940–1946, when Bloomfield, as other duties allowed, turned to the continuing revision of his description of Menomini. The book was published in †1962 (New Haven and London: Yale University Press; William Dwight Whitney Linguistic Series). We place the excerpt here because B67, known to be the last article he wrote, should come at the end. Chapter 22, *Phrase Structure*, is the first of the two chapters on syntax; our passage appears on pp. 440–441.]

## 22.18–20. STYLISTIC VARIATION

22.18. The description of phrase structure is rendered partly indeterminate by stylistic variations of various sorts.

The constituents of a phrase often appear in other than the usual order, or separated by other words, or with pause intonation between them, or with two or all three of these. Forms of this kind imply special emphasis, especially on a constituent that is spoken first; sometimes they seem to involve connotative meanings, and sometimes they seem to be purely rhetorical, involving some rhythmic feature:

> *o·s eneh* 'that canoe, that thing', usually depreciative, beside colorless
> *eneh o·s* 'that canoe';
> *meta·tah nenɛ·qnawak mesɛ·wak* 'I have killed ten rabbits', emphasis
> on the number;
> *yɛ·n eneh ɛ·qtek we·kewam* 'that house which is on the farther side';
> the emphatic word *yɛ·n* 'on the farther side' comes first, with the
> pronoun between it and its verb.

22.19. In most instances, however, variations of this kind represent merely *waves* of speech response. The great freedom of word order and pause intonation, especially in constructions of concord, allows the speaker to develop his sentence with lesser impulses or waves before, during, and after the main part.

Thus, he may *anticipate* a form, adding something at the beginning: *maski·hki·wenɛni·hsɛh, enoq kaya·kɛhkeno·hamowa·cen* 'Little-Doctor, he is the one who teaches him'.

He may insert a form by way of parenthesis: *enoq, maski·hki·wenɛni·hsɛh, kaya·kεhkeno·hamowa·cen* 'he is the one, Little-Doctor [is], who teaches him'.

He may add a form by way of *afterthought*: *enoq kaya·kεhkeno·hamowa·cen, maski·hki·wenεni·hsεh* 'he is the one who teaches him, Little-Doctor [is]'.

These forms are all commoner than the unified and completely deliberate version, which would presumably be *maski·hki·wenεni·hsεh-ε·h kaya·kεhkeno·hamowa·cen* 'Little Doctor is the person who teaches him'.

22.20. No sharp line can be drawn between unified phrases and expressions in more or less separate waves: *si·piah*(,) *eneq as aki·htek* 'in the river(, there) it is afloat'; *eneq*(,) *si·piah*(,) *as aki·htek* 'there(,) in the river(,) it is afloat'; *eneq as aki·htek*(,) *si·piah* 'there it is afloat(,) in the river'.

# B67. Twenty-One Years of the Linguistic Society

1946. *Language* 22.1–3.

The Linguistic Society of America has come of age. An account of its origin is to be found in the first number of this journal, dated March 1925 (LANG. 1.1–5). There also something is said about the state of affairs which prompted the founding of the Society—a state of affairs now remembered only by those who have reached middle age.

Before there was a Linguistic Society, separate pairs or small groups of linguists used to meet and discuss their problems at the gatherings of professional associations—such as the American Philological Association, the Modern Language Association of America, the American Oriental Society, and the American Anthropological Association—whose fields of interest included some phase or branch of linguistics. Then, as now, these associations dealt generously with their linguistic members: at their meetings they gave time to papers on language, and they published these papers in their journals. Later, indeed, they welcomed, some of them officially, the founding of the Linguistic Society. Most of us continue to adhere to one or more of these societies. The boundaries between fields of science, like the boundaries between the States of our Nation, are but imaginary lines, serving a methodical and administrative convenience; our welfare demands that they be crossed in every direction and with the utmost freedom.

Thus linguists met, pleasantly and profitably, but only in several disconnected groups, each of which appeared as a small and subsidiary cell within a larger society. There was no place where all linguists could meet, no reunion devoted entirely to linguistic discussion, and no journal devoted to our subject.[1]

It would be hard to estimate the pleasure and satisfaction and, above all, the stimulation which the new Linguistic Society brought to students of

---

[1] Franz Boas began publishing the International Journal of American Linguistics as early as 1920; yet it may be not unreasonable to attribute the quality and volume of its later years in part to the stimulus of our Society. Beginning with Volume 6 (1930) this journal has borne the imprint of the Linguistic Society.

language. We now met fellow-workers whom we had never met before; we heard and debated new topics; we learned from each other, formed lasting friendships, and gained immeasurably in the vividness of our professional life.

Much of this, though not all, can be inferred from the files of our journal. The range of topics treated in the pages of LANGUAGE is vast; but as one might expect, the three leading fields are comparative Indo-European grammar, the Romance languages, and English. The tone and quality of these volumes strike one as bold, imaginative, workmanlike, straightforward. Each contributor, of those who survive, would doubtless point out errors and shortcomings in what he wrote; but the total effect is cumulative, arising from the zest and the inventiveness that pervade, in varying degrees, a great number of the contributions.[2] The two supplementary series of Language Monographs and Language Dissertations (the latter perhaps less directly) and the Special Publications bear witness to the same effect.

Only those who, before the year 1925, worked in almost complete isolation can appreciate the change that came about with the existence of the Linguistic Society.

The improvement in the professional happiness of linguistic workers is only the subjective aspect of an improvement in the continuity and social cohesion of our work. Linguistics has come more and more to resemble, in its social complexion, the type of the better established branches of science—say physics, chemistry, and biology.

Most plainly to be ascribed to the existence of our Society is our tendency toward cumulative progress. The younger workers in these two decades have started where the older workers left off. Some of our young doctors—even some students before their doctorate—have performed tasks which we of the older generation approached ineptly and fearsomely. Nowadays the older worker in linguistics often learns from the younger, and has the supreme professional satisfaction of knowing that the next generation is going forward from the frontiers of what is known today.

Less plainly due, perhaps, to the existence of our Society, and yet doubtless furthered by the experience of assembly and the give-and-take of discussion, is our increasing social maturity, the obsolescence of pre-scientific reactions, and the growing prevalence of impersonal and rational

---

[2] The editors have had little to do in the way of selection: the manuscripts that came to them have maintained a high level of merit, and only a small proportion have been rejected. Anyone who has been in close touch with the editors (as has the present writer) will testify to their impersonal and painstaking service, their refusal to give weight to private theories, and their exclusive attention to the quality and workmanship of whatever was submitted. As to the work of editing, it is hard to realize how much patient, meticulous toil has gone into every issue of LANGUAGE—a labor of love for which we all owe a debt of gratitude to these two men.

procedure. In this respect, the attitude of linguistic workers seems to be approaching that of workers in older branches of science. Linguists who, in these decades, have expressed unpopular views have often met with dissent and with counter-argument, but only rarely with invective. We are learning to correct errors of fact by further observation, and errors of theory by more careful calculation; we are coming to see more and more clearly how unimportant it is whether this man or that was originally right. This form of interaction can be observed especially among our younger linguists. It resembles the procedure within more mature branches of science and contrasts with what may be seen in less developed fields or among workers who are less familiar with the traditions of our Society. Here the demands of science concord with our folkways: we have no prima donnas.[3]

It may not be altogether wrong to say that the existence of the Linguistic Society has saved us from the blight of the odium theologicum and the postulation of 'schools'. When several American linguists find themselves sharing some interest or opinion, they do not make it into a King Charles's Head, proclaiming themselves a 'school' and denouncing all persons who disagree or who merely choose to talk about something else. Nor do they, with few exceptions, bring against others the charge of forming a 'school' and thus initiate a rule of collective responsibility.

The struggle with recalcitrant facts, unyielding in their complexity, trains everyone who works actively in science to be humble, and accustoms him to impersonal acknowledgment of error; but in no small measure this humility is reenforced and expanded into tolerance and cooperation by the companionship and social discipline of membership in a society of persons who work in the same field. A colleague (often a younger one) makes a statement that seems to be quite wrong, until, in the ensuing conversation, we realize that his statement is based on wider or more exact observation, or on a calculation that is neater or more appropriate, and we carry away an insight that working alone we never could have got.

Yet much remains to be done. Like similar benefits on a larger political scale, the advantages that we get from our Society can be kept only by persistent practice. If work ceases, inertia and entropy will have free play.

The external status of our science leaves much to be desired, though there has been some improvement. The projects for the study of native American languages and for the American dialect atlas have gone a long way toward realization, thanks to the organized work of the Linguistic Society. When our country faced a troublesome emergency in the use of foreign languages, the Army, through the American Council of Learned

[3] The editors of LANGUAGE, who have the unpleasant duty of sometimes rejecting manuscripts, report that we who suffer the rejections (the present writer is proud to be included) almost universally accept the editors' decision as impersonally as it is made.

Societies, turned to the Linguistic Society and obtained the best professional guidance that its members were able to give. And the administra-
tions of at least some universities have come to understand the place of
linguistics in the domain of science. Nevertheless, the community at large
does not yet recognize even that a body of linguistic knowledge exists.
The basic teaching of our schools, in reading and writing, in standard
language and composition (and in their incredible courses on 'general
language'), is dominated still by educationists who, knowing nothing
about language, waste years of every child's time, and leave our community semi-literate. In the teaching of foreign languages there has been
at least some unsettlement in consequence of the Army courses, but this
too often involves consideration of the mere externals of the work that
was done, with no understanding of the essential condition of professional
guidance. Even academic groups and learned periodicals in other fields of
science are sometimes unaware that there exists any cumulative body of
information about language, and go for linguistic counsel to persons who,
quite evidently, have made no use of it.

It is hard to popularize our knowledge, which contradicts at many
points the ancient doctrines of popular belief. Even the student or the
reader who is willing to learn is so hampered and confused by prejudg-
ments that he finds our simplest statements hard to understand. Perhaps
it would have been equally difficult, a few centuries ago, to popularize the
science of physics; but there the motive of technical application and
economic advantage forced the audience to overcome its blockage. The
cure for this ill would seem to lie in repeated and progressively better
attempts to popularize what we know—a matter of individual effort. But
beyond this, our Society, by its weight and its working, is bound to exercise
increasing pressure upon the community.

# 68. C. F. Hockett: Implications of Bloomfield's Algonquian Studies

1948. *Language* 24.117–131.

[The issue of *Language* in which this appeared (24:1, January–March 1948) was dedicated to Leonard Bloomfield. This article was reprinted in Dell Hymes, *Language in Culture and Society* (New York: Harper and Row, 1964), pp. 599–609. Here, as in that reprinting, the term 'phonemic change', which appeared in the original as an occasional (but misleading) synonym of 'sound change', has everywhere been replaced by the clearer term. For this reprinting I have made only one or two very minor improvements of wording. The views expressed are those of 1948.

The list of articles and books on Algonquian in footnote 2 inadvertently omitted Bloomfield's 'Menomini Morphophonemics', *Travaux du Cercle Linguistique de Prague* 8.105–115 (1939), our B50.

On §10 point (1) see now *International Journal of American Linguistics* 32.59 (1966), fn 3. However, there is no reason to alter principle (p) at the end of §10.]

It is generally known[1] that one of Leonard Bloomfield's life works is the descriptive and comparative study of Algonquian.[2] It is also generally

---

[1] Many of the non-Algonquian references given in the footnotes of this paper were found with the assistance of Robert A. Hall Jr. For my understanding of the 'almost mystical' version of the drift theory (see §8), I am indebted to Gordon H. Fairbanks (who is not a proponent of this version of the theory). All of my colleagues at Cornell have participated in instructive discussion of this paper, and to all of them I express my thanks.

[2] Bloomfield's publications on Algonquian are listed here, approximately in order of publication. They will be referred to hereafter as 'Ref. 1' and so on, except that the third and twelfth items will be termed, respectively, the Sound System and the Sketch. The latter includes a bibliography of Algonquian which is complete save for a few items which have appeared since 1941.

(1) Review of The Owl Sacred Pack of the Fox Indians, by Truman Michelson, AJP 43.276–81 (1922).

(2) The Menomini Language, Proceedings of the Twenty-first International Congress of Americanists 336–43 (The Hague, 1924).

(3) On the Sound System of Central Algonquian, Lang. 1.130–56 (1925).

(4) The Word-Stems of Central Algonquian, Festschrift Meinhof 393–402 (Hamburg, 1927).

(5) Notes on the Fox Language, IJAL 3.219–32 (1924), 4.181–219 (1927).

(6) A Note on Sound Change, Lang. 5.99–100 (1928).

(7) The Plains Cree Language, Proceedings of the Twenty-second International Congress of Americanists 427–31 (Rome, 1928).

conceded that his work in this field is of considerable importance.[3] But most of those who are quite willing to admit this do so on indirect evidence: since Bloomfield's other work proves him a sound scholar, his Algonquian studies must be sound too. Algonquian, after all, is an out-of-the-way language family, and few have concerned themselves with it. In view, particularly, of Bloomfield's endeavors in this field, this neglect is unfortunate. To the writer the following points seem beyond dispute: (1) careful study of Algonquian as Bloomfield has described it can be a fascinating, enlightening, and rewarding experience even for established comparatists and historical linguists; (2) for the newcomer to linguistics, a reading of Bloomfield's Algonquian works is one of the finest indoctrinations into the best of linguistic method.

In a sense, any body of data on any group of languages can serve in both these roles. But, if, for example, the would-be linguist attempts to learn the elementary principles of comparative method in terms of Indo-European, or even of Germanic or Romance, the external difficulties are great: the material is widely scattered and bulky, some of it is old and hard to interpret, some of it is excellent but some is extremely bad. On the other hand, even though the Algonquian languages are 'exotic' (whatever that may mean), they are phonetically simple, not too widely divergent from the familiar Indo-European languages in structure—remarkably similar, in some ways, to older Germanic—and Bloomfield's treatment is compact, uniform in approach, and uniformly excellent.[4]

Most of the lessons which can be learned from Bloomfield's Algonquian are apparent to anyone who reads, with suitable diligence, his Sketch.[5] There are, in addition, a few important points which are not apparent from that paper alone, nor even necessarily from that paper together with his other writings in this field, save to someone who has had some independent first-hand contact with the extant Algonquian languages and with earlier

(8) Menomini Texts, Publications of the American Ethnological Society, Vol. 12 (New York, 1928).

(9) Sacred Stories of the Sweet Grass Cree, Bulletin 60, National Museum of Canada (Ottawa, 1930).

(10) Plains Cree Texts, Publications of the American Ethnological Society, Vol. 16 (New York, 1934).

(11) Proto-Algonquian -iit- 'Fellow', LANG. 17.292–7 (1941).

(12) Algonquian, in Linguistic Structures of Native America 85–129 (Viking Fund Publications in Anthropology, Number 6; New York, 1946).

[3] 'A remarkable contribution', says Sturtevant of Bloomfield's Sketch, LANG. 23.314 (1947).

[4] Bloomfield has noted the resemblance to older Germanic several times in conversation but not, so far as I know, in print; in Ref. 5, 4.191, the comparison is rather with Indo-European as a whole. Needless to say, the attempts of Reider T. Sherwin, The Viking and the Red Man (4 vols. to date; New York, 1940–46), to establish a genetic connection between Algonquian and Germanic are entirely misguided.

[5] See fn. 2.

efforts, mainly by missionaries, to describe this or that language of the group. It is our purpose here to list those principles and procedures of historical and comparative linguistics which seem to emerge with especial clarity and force from Bloomfield's Algonquian studies. It is the writer's hope that this listing and discussion will serve to focus more attention on the work dealt with, and to be of some assistance to the person who does undertake the study recommended.[6]

We shall discuss the following points:

(1) Description and history
(2) The evaluation of written records
(3) The use of phonemic notation
(4) Preliminary internal reconstruction
(5) Assumptions about directions of linguistic change
(6) The assumption of regular sound change
(7) The Wörter-und-Sachen technique
(8) Drift
(9) The significance of starred forms
(10) Negative lessons

On each of these there has been, and is, disagreement among those who occupy professional posts in which they purport to deal with language. On each point (save the last), Bloomfield's Algonquian material unambiguously indicates one answer, to the exclusion of the various alternatives that have been proposed.

1. DESCRIPTION AND HISTORY. There are still extremists who say that descriptive linguistics is balderdash,[7] and a few, equally extreme, who scorn the comparative method in historical linguistics as irrelevant antiquarianism and, at best, guess work.[8] Some of the disagreement is genuine; but some stems simply from the insufficient complexity of our terminology for different types of linguistic operation. In order to see the genuine issue we must clear away the terminological obscurities.

A SYNCHRONIC analysis describes the speech habits of an individual or a relatively homogeneous group at a particular time.[9] It ignores what interpersonal differences may be known, and makes no mention of changes in habits that take place during the period from which the evidence dates. A CONTRASTIVE study compares the speech habits of different individuals

---

[6] The principles itemized in this paper are by no means intended to constitute a complete canon of historical or comparative linguistics. The choice is based on the nature of the Algonquian material, not on a general analysis of linguistic method.

[7] Classical Philology 38.210–11 (1943), 39.218–22 (1944); also the implications of the review in LANG. 16.216–31 (1940).

[8] Acta Linguistica 2.1–22 (1940–1); IJAL 10.192–3 (1944); and see Robert A. Hall Jr., Bàrtoli's 'Neolinguistica', LANG. 22.273–83 (1946).

[9] The terms 'synchronic' and 'diachronic' date at least from Ferdinand de Saussure, Cours de Linguistique Générale (Lausanne, 1916).

or groups and tallies the similarities and differences—regardless of the relative position of the speakers or groups in space or time.[10] A DIA-CHRONIC analysis states the changes in speech habits in a single community from one point in time to a later period. Occasionally one can observe marked personal differences even in a small community, or clear instances of change of habit during a very short span of time; when such observations are included in a monograph which is mainly synchronic, that does not necessitate any change in the definition of 'synchronic', but simply means that the content of the monograph is not purely synchronic. This comment should not be interpreted as an objection to the practice, which is often valuable.[11]

In the gathering of information, for synchronic, contrastive, or diachronic purposes, there are several different methods. The CONTACT method consists in first-hand observation of the speakers. The PHILO-LOGICAL method consists in the interpretation of written records. The COMPARATIVE method extrapolates backwards from the earliest evidence available (or the earliest used) from two or more dialects or languages which seem to be related. Between these methods there is no sharp line of demarcation. The field worker, though he uses the contact method, later studies his own notes and in so doing involves himself in a kind of philological method; another linguist may read the notes, or the completed report, of the first, and so places himself in a position somewhat analogous to that of the interpreter of written records which date from earlier generations. The close intertwining of the philological and comparative methods is obvious.[12]

The extraneous sources of argument about 'description' and 'history' stem from the ambiguity in the use of those two terms (or of others used in place of them). 'Description' sometimes refers to synchronic analysis, sometimes to contact method. 'History' sometimes means diachronic analysis, sometimes philological or comparative method or both. With the more narrowly defined terms, the logical interrelationships are easy to see:[13]

[10] 'Contrastive' is Whorf's proposal (I cannot find the reference), made because the more natural term 'comparative' is already pre-empted for a different technical use.

[11] Good illustrations of the value of mixed synchronic and diachronic discussion are Ref. 4, 401—which includes also some extremely penetrating remarks on the relation between the synchronic and diachronic points of view—and Bloomfield's paper Literate and Illiterate Speech, American Speech 2.432–9 (1927).

[12] This three-by-three categorization of types of linguistic activity is more general in its application than here indicated: it applies, as a matter of fact, to all the subject-matter of cultural anthropology, of which linguistics is logically a subdivision. This is clearly indicated in Sapir, Time Perspective in Aboriginal American Culture (Ottawa, 1916). There are doubtless some types of fruitful and valid investigation, of language or of culture as a whole, not subsumed in the classification.

[13] The methodolical points or 'principles' drawn from the discussion are lettered serially through the paper, from (a) to (p).

(a) Synchronic analysis may be based on any of the three methods, or on combinations of them. Synchronic analysis of a language no longer spoken, obviously, cannot involve the contact method; that of a language for which there are no direct records has to be based on the comparative method. In this sense, 'description' is not logically prior to 'history'.

(b) Either diachronic or contrastive analysis involves prior synchronic analysis. In this sense, 'description' is logically prior to 'history'.

(c) The comparative method has to involve comparison of something. The data to which the comparative method is applied consist of bodies of synchronic descriptions of related languages. The assumptions which underlie the comparative method are distilled from diachronic analyses of bodies of synchronic material, all of which are based, in turn, on a method other than the comparative method.[14]

These interrelations are complex. The virtue of Bloomfield's Algonquian studies on this score is that the interrelations not only are perfectly clear to Bloomfield, but are made equally clear to his reader. His sketch, for example, is at one and the same time all of the following: (1) a brief synchronic outline grammar of four Algonquian languages still extant;[15] (2) a brief synchronic outline grammar of their parent; (3) a contrastive analysis of the four modern languages and the parent language; (4) an outline of the diachronic analysis of the continuum from the parent to each of the modern languages; and (5) a demonstration of the application of the comparative method to the modern data for the reconstruction of the parent language. The Sketch does not take up these problems one by one, but rather gives a composite picture. A single careful reading produces an accurate and realistic general impression of Algonquian structure. A subsequent reading with special attention to any of the facets listed above can give more detailed information. In such successive readings, one is never at a loss to know the range of applica-

---

[14] That is, we derive our notions of linguistic change in the first instance from the history of those languages, such as English, French, and German, for which there is documentary evidence over a considerable span of time. We then make a comparative analysis of some group of languages whose common ancestor is known to us independently—for example, Romance—assuming the kinds of linguistic change discovered by the first operation, and comparing our reconstruction with the documentary evidence for the parent. Since our inverted predictions in such cases have a considerable degree of accuracy, we feel confident of at least statistically accurate results when the same comparative method is applied to a group of languages for whose parent there is no other evidence. It is true that linguistic science in the 19th century did not follow this course in its chronological development; but this does not invalidate the logical statement. Until the logical interrelationships had clearly emerged, the statements of historical linguistics were somewhat more tentative than afterwards.

[15] That is, Fox (F), Cree (C), Menomini (M), and Ojibwa (O). The abbreviations indicated will be used in the rest of this paper, together with 'PA' for Proto-Algonquian, the reconstructed parent (but see §10).

tion of each individual statement: it applies just to F, or just to the development of F from PA, or just to PA, or to all the languages, and so on.

Bloomfield's Sketch, then, is a model useful to anyone who faces the task of organizing information about a family of languages into an arrangement that makes synchronic, diachronic, and contrastive sense.

2. THE EVALUATION OF WRITTEN RECORDS. The documentary material on which Bloomfield bases his Algonquian analysis is of several types: (1) his own field records of M and C, made with full benefit of phonemic theory; (2) F records from William Jones, a native speaker of F who was trained under Boas and Michelson in phonetics, but not in phonemics;[16] (3) O records from the same person; (4) earlier records by missionaries and traders, without benefit of either phonetics or phonemics, and with English or French as native language, but with the advantage of long residence with the Indians and constant practical use of the languages. Since Bloomfield's first publications, others trained under him or within his sphere of influence have recorded F and O,[17] and Bloomfield himself has recorded O. We thus have a check on the accuracy of older reports, except for the negligible extent to which speech patterns may have changed between missionary times and the present.

Jones's F materials are overloaded with superfluous diacritics, indicating evanescent distinctions or subphonemic differences, but in general no phonemic contrast is omitted. O materials from the same observer have the same unnecessary indication of minutiae, but in addition obscure certain phonemic contrasts which are of considerable comparative importance—for example, the contrast between *sk* and *šk*. Certainly there is a relationship between these facts and Jones's background. F does not have the contrast *sk* : *šk*; it is not surprising that as a native speaker of F, Jones missed the contrast when listening to the rather similar O. His phonetic training, without phonemics, led to the overly minute recording of what he had happened to be trained to hear; his native control of F prevented omission of contrasts that were relevant there.[18]

[16] For references see the Sketch. Later contributions by Michelson use approximately the same notation. It is not clear whether this notation was a joint product of Jones and Michelson, or was worked out by one and passed on to the other.

[17] F: at least J. M. Cowan, Carl F. Voegelin, and the present writer; O: the latter two, J. A. Geary (other dialects), F. T. Siebert Jr, and—in the summers when O was the language studied in the field-methods course at the Linguistic Institute—a good many others.

[18] It would be tempting to generalize as follows. If a native speaker of a language is trained in phonetics in such a way that he will hear, in any language, at least all those contrasts which are distinctive for his own speech, and will have the symbols easily at hand to record them, he will, in recording his own language, sometimes include subphonemic contrasts, but will never omit contrasts that count. But this statement is far from obviously true. Suggestions of this kind were made by Sapir in Sound Patterns in Language, LANG. 1.37–51 (1925), and more elaborately in La réalité psychologique des phonèmes, Journal de

As might be expected, the missionary records are much less satisfactory. Some of them consistently fail to indicate such important features as vowel length; some of them write subphonemic distinctions heard at one time or another, because those distinctions were present phonemically in French or in English; sometimes certain contrasts are recorded irregularly. As a result of the last, when one desires to check on some feature of a particular word, one often finds that the missionary recording is unreliable on that point.[19]

We may distil from this the following methodological observations:

(d) The extent to which one can use written records made by an untrained person can only be determined by direct observation of the language by a trained person. For a language no longer spoken, this is of course impossible.

(e) When a direct check is impossible, records made by a native speaker are more trustworthy than those made by a foreigner; those made by a person with some training (as Jones' training in phonetics to the exclusion of phonemics) are more trustworthy than those from a person with no training at all; obviously, records from a person with long practical contact, other things being equal, are more trustworthy than those from the casual passer-by.

3. THE USE OF PHONEMIC NOTATION. If one compares Bloomfield's Sketch with a recent paper by Geary[20] one difference is striking. All forms cited in Bloomfield's paper are phonemicized, and the choice of symbols for each language is such as to render the switch from one language to another as easy as possible for the reader. Geary could not validly do this; for his object was to cull from all sources, including the missionary records, forms which are evidence for a particular PA consonant cluster; of necessity he cites each form from an older record in the graphic shape in which it was found. Anyone can read Bloomfield; only an Algonquianist can really read Geary.

Further scrutiny of these two papers, and of some of the older records, shows that the close relationship of the Algonquian languages is immediately apparent from the missionary records; but it would be almost impossible to attempt the reconstruction of PA on the basis of the missionary records alone. On the other hand, once something is known of the structure of PA, many of the missionary records can be used, though sometimes with uncertainty, to find additional cases of this or that correspondence.

Psychologie 30.247–65 (1933), but Twaddell's discussion, On Defining the Phoneme 8–16 (LSA Monograph 16 [1935]), raises serious doubts.

[19] Some such cases are discussed in J. A. Geary, Proto-Algonquian *çk: Further Examples, LANG. 17.304–10 (1941).

[20] See fn. 19.

This further supports points (d) and (e), and suggests the following:

(f) Written records are a means to an end, and there is no justification for holding them in high esteem, or even in reverence (as is sometimes the case) EXCEPT as indirect evidence for what one is trying to discover.[21]

(g) When his only evidence consists of written records, the analyst should attempt a phonemic interpretation of the material. He can achieve accuracy in his synchronic description, in his diachronic deductions, and in his use of the material for comparative purposes, only to the extent that the phonemic interpretation of the written records is feasible without ambiguity.[22] Furthermore, he should make his phonemic interpretation clearly recognizable to his readers, by including for every form cited, explicitly or by implication, a possible phonemicization.[23] Failure to do the former impairs his own results; failure to do the latter hampers his readers.

Some of the undue esteem in which written records are held has probably been supported by the following additional principle, which is not deducible from Bloomfield's Sketch, but does appear in some of his earlier writings and quite clearly in Geary's paper:

(h) When the interpretation of written records cannot be completely free from ambiguity, the graphic shape actually occurrent in the source should be included along with the attempted phonemicization—or, when more convenient, a transliteration of the original graphic shape. The reader is then in the best possible position to reexamine the evidence and draw his own conclusions.

**4.** PRELIMINARY INTERNAL RECONSTRUCTION. The statement made above that in Bloomfield's Sketch all forms are phonemicized now has to be modified. His notation for O, and possibly for M and F, deviates from the phonemic 'ideal' in being somewhat more than phonemic.

In Southern O occur three varieties of vowels: long /ii ee aa oo/, short /i a o/, and ultra-short /ə u/. Within the limits of a word, the distribution of short and ultra-short vowels is almost, but not quite, predictable in terms of environment. Since the predictability is not complete, the distinction is phonemic: one must write /i a o/ and /ə u/ as they are heard. Bloomfield does not do so: he writes only *ii ee aa oo* and *i a o*, e.g. *mittik* instead of *məttik* 'tree'. For most Southern O dialects, one cannot tell whether

---

[21] LANG. 22.256 (1946); French Review 17.168–70 (1944).

[22] Disagreements about METHODS of phonemicization are another matter. If 'phonemic solutions' are non-unique, as seems likely to me at the present moment, any alternative one will do. There is a gain in clarity and simplicity if each of a set of languages to be compared is phonemicized by the same principles, but if this is not done reconstruction is still perfectly feasible. Against phonemics of any kind: Archivio Glottologico Italiano 31.159 (1940)—one instance of many.

[23] Bloomfield, Language §5.10 (New York, 1933).

the vowel in the first syllable—an ultra-short one—is /i/ or /a/, and phonemically one would have to use a special symbol /ə/; the same symbol would have to be used in a completely phonemic transcription of what Bloomfield transcribes as *akkikk* 'kettle', rather than the initial *a* of that form. O itself, and the diachronic analysis of the continuum from PA to O, are treated by Bloomfield in terms of this normalized notation. Can this procedure be justified?

The answer is yes. Bloomfield's notation is based on the preliminary internal reconstruction[24] of an O dialect-type that must have preceded the current dialects by only a relatively short period of time. The reconstruction is internal, not based on comparison of dialects, since the earlier stage can be postulated with validity on the basis of the data for any one dialect. If one compares phonemic /məttik/ 'tree' with /nəmittəkoom/ 'my tree', and /əkkikk/ 'kettle' with /nəntakkəkkoom/ 'my kettle', one observes that /ə/ alternates (under statable conditions of word-rhythm) with both /i/ and /a/. There are a few cases in which no larger form can be found of the right rhythmic pattern to determine whether the alternation is with /i/ or with /a/, and in most of the dialects there are a few cases in which ultra-short vowels have disappeared altogether. Even in a synchronic description of O, however, the restoration of /i/ and /a/ rather than /ə/ in all such cases, with statements on the reduction of short vowels in words of each rhythmic pattern, is a necessary step for efficient treatment. One's working notation then becomes morphophonemic rather than purely phonemic; from the graphs /mɪttɪk/, /nimittikoom/, /akkikk/, /nintakkikkoom/, and the statements, one can infer the actual phonemic shape with very little difficulty.

In other words, what Bloomfield does in the case of O is to use a morphophonemically regularized notation instead of a straight phonemic transcription. There is evidence of such regularization in M and F too. F forms are given with intervocalic /w/ and /y/, which are morphophonemically correct and which must have been phonemically correct in a slightly earlier stage, rather than with the curious alternation and evanescence that those morphophonemes now exhibit.[25] M is cited with six short and six long vowels, though Bloomfield himself has said that in actual pronunciation the three-way distinction of /i/ : /e/ : /ɛ/ is partly obscured.[26]

---

[24] H. M. Hoenigswald, Internal Reconstruction, SIL 2.78–87 (1944); Sound Change and Linguistic Structure, LANG. 22.138–43 (1946).

[25] Obvious from Jones's texts; observed by the present writer in the Kickapoo and Sauk dialects of Fox.

[26] Ref. 8, xiv: 'The texts are here recorded as they struck my ear. Analysis shows that this record (and therefore, if I heard aright, the actual pronunciation) largely obscures the distinction between three short front-vowel phonemes, which here appear as *i* and *e*.' Since Bloomfield became a fluent speaker of Menomini (a fact which he does not admit, but which is fairly obvious from his discussions), his recording is probably accurate. Nowadays

We infer the following principle:

(i) Before comparative analysis is undertaken, each body of synchronic data should be examined carefully to see whether there are not internal clues, mainly morphophonemic, to the structure of the language at a slightly earlier stage. When there are, any possible internal reconstruction should be undertaken, since it will dispose of later innovations in each language, getting them out of the way for a clearer view of the deeper time-perspective of external comparison.

5. ASSUMPTIONS ABOUT DIRECTIONS OF LINGUISTIC CHANGE. Bloomfield's description of Proto-Algonquian reveals it as a language of approximately the same degree of complexity as any one of the modern languages. Each of the modern languages has retained some of the features of the parent, lost some, and developed some new ones. F has the vocalic system of PA; C and O have one vowel fewer than PA; M has two more. The number of individual consonants in PA (excluding first members of clusters, §9) is greater than in any of the modern languages; it seems highly probable, however, that $\theta$ and $\check{s}$, and similarly $t$ and $\check{c}$, which stand in close morphophonemic relation in PA, were at a slightly earlier stage allophones of single phonemes—perhaps, indeed, this was true even in PA times. The larger number of consonants in PA, then, was a temporary matter, the result of certain sound changes and analogic changes, and the number was later reduced in each line of development. The modal systems of verbs in the daughter languages correlate exactly only in a few cases. One suspects that some of the modes present in PA have split in some of the modern languages, and have been lost in others; certainly the total number of modes in PA did not exceed the rather large number in present-day F.[27]

(j) In undertaking a reconstruction, there is no justification for any of the following a-priori assumptions: (1) that the parent language was simpler than the descendants; (2) that it was more complex than the descendants; or (3) that it manifested about the same degree of complexity as the descendants.

The first of these a-priori assumptions is the old theory of the 'primitiveness' of 'early' language, and of contemporary languages spoken by 'simple' peoples.[28] The second is the inversion of the first brought about

---

we would cast his statement in the terminology of morphophonemics rather than phonemics, but the fact stated would not be altered.

[27] Sketch §33.

[28] Max Muller's myth of speakers with vocabularies of only a few hundred words is related. W. von Humboldt, Die Verschiedenheit des menschlichen Sprachbaues §19, gives three stages in the history of language: 'growth' before IE, a 'state of perfection' in IE, and 'decay' since then; for other early references see LANG. 12.101 (1936) and Italica 18.145–54 (1941). Later survivals of these older notions: the subject of review in LANG. 11.154–60

primarily by Jespersen's discussion.[29] More concrete suggestions, akin to one or the other, are also found.[30] All such theories derive from a hope which a hundred years ago was legitimate: that comparative linguistics might in time push our perspective on the history of language appreciably nearer the beginnings of human speech. Now that we realize how old is human speech, and what a scratch on the surface of that depth is our deepest reconstruction, the hope must be abandoned.

Bloomfield's PA reconstruction speaks not only against assumptions (1) and (2), but against any a-priori assumption of this kind whatsoever. In his paper of 1925 (Ref. 3), Bloomfield postulated two more vowels and one more consonant for PA than are included in the Sketch. Since then he has discovered the analogical bases, in certain of the individual languages, for the complications that had earlier led him to assume these additional phonemes. The first, more complex system was not set up because Bloomfield thought that an older language 'should be' more complex; nor did he later simplify the picture through any conviction that an older language 'should not be' more complex. In each case the assumed degree of complexity was simply an inference from the facts known about the modern languages.

**6.** THE ASSUMPTION OF REGULAR SOUND CHANGE. One story in the slow development of our understanding of PA is worth telling in detail, even though it is already perhaps the most generally known phase of Algonquian linguistics.

In his Sound System (Ref. 3), Bloomfield postulated the PA cluster *çk* (F O *šk*, C M *hk*) on very slim evidence. There was only one stem, meaning 'red', to be found which showed just this correspondence in the extant languages, and each of those languages had the cluster in question also as a reflex of one or more other PA clusters. Yet there seemed to be no analogical basis in any of the languages whereby a reconstruction could be made with a better attested PA cluster, and borrowing seemed unlikely in view of the meaning of the stem. There were a few other sets of apparently related words showing unique correspondences of clusters—'spoon' has F C *hk*, O *kk*, as though from PA *hk*, but M has *sk* instead of the *hk* which would arise from the latter. But these other cases are in morpho-

---

(1935); Emérita 3.257–76 (1935), esp. 272, 274–5; Alf Sommerfelt, La langue et la société (Oslo, 1938).

[29] Otto Jespersen, Progress in Language (London, 1894): cf. also his Efficiency in Linguistic Change (Copenhagen, 1941), and the review in LANG. 17.350–3 (1941). Bernhard Karlgren, in reconstructing ancient and archaic Chinese, posits extremely complex phonological structure for those stages of Chinese, and seems (though without explicit reference) to justify this greater complexity for the older stage in terms of Jespersen's theory; see his Philology and Ancient China, esp. 16–18 (Oslo, 1926).

[30] See more recent references in fn. 28.

logically isolated words, whereas the PA stem 'red' underlies many derivatives in every language.

A year or so later, it was discovered that Swampy Cree, a dialect from which records had not earlier been available, had in words containing this stem not *hk* but *htk*, a cluster not found in Swampy Cree as the reflex of any other PA cluster so far set up. Here was not merely an exceptional correspondence between usual clusters, but an extant dialect in which the postulated PA cluster is kept separate from all others. Bloomfield published a note giving this as evidence for the productivity of the assumption of regular sound change.[31] Sapir cited the case, together with a similar one from his own Athabascan work, in an article on the comparative method as one of the methods of social science.[32]

But the story did not end there. New investigators discovered that Jones had consistently misheard the O forms: the O words with this stem have *sk*, not *šk*, and this *sk* is not found as a reflex of any other PA cluster.[33] Swampy Cree no longer stood as the only extant dialect to keep PA *çk* separate; O was now known to do so too. Geary examined the missionary sources and discovered a number of other cases of the same correspondence, so that the stem for 'red' was no longer isolated—even though PA *çk* still seemed to be relatively rare. In his Sketch, Bloomfield includes a footnote: 'The fuss and trouble behind my note in Language [see above] ... would have been avoided if I had listened to O, which plainly distinguishes *sk* ( < PA *çk*) from *šk* ( < PA *šk*); instead, I depended on printed records which failed to show the distinction.'[34]

It should be clear that the wording of Bloomfield's note detracts in no way from the importance of the sequence of events outlined above as evidence for the productivity of the assumption we are discussing. After the publication of the Sound System, events might conceivably have taken a different turn. Instead of discovering additional cases of the same correspondence, Jones's error, and the special reflex in Swampy Cree, Algonquianists might have found an analogical basis or an opportunity for borrowing whereby PA *çk* could be eliminated. This turn of events would also have proved the fruitfulness of the assumption.

For what we mean in this case by 'productivity' or 'fruitfulness' is just what Bloomfield states in his book Language (§20.5): residual forms, not accounted for at a particular stage in the history of the reconstruction of a particular parent language either by well-attested sound change or by analogical formations or borrowing, or accounted for by postulated

---

[31] Ref. 6.

[32] Edward Sapir, The Concept of Phonetic Law as Tested in Primitive Languages by Leonard Bloomfield, Methods in Social Science 297–306 (ed. Stuart A. Rice; Chicago, 1931). Also Bloomfield, Language §20.8 (end).

[33] See fn. 17, and Geary, loc. cit.

[34] Sketch, fn. 10.

changes for which there is very little evidence—such residual forms STIMULATE FURTHER INVESTIGATION. As a basis for further investigation, the linguist sets up hypotheses to explain what might have been the past history of certain forms. Many such hypotheses remain unproved, because additional investigation reveals no additional evidence; others are disproved by new evidence that is uncovered. But some of them are proved right. Slowly but surely the stock of residual forms is reduced, though it may never be exhausted. The contrary fundamental assumption—that sound changes proceed at random—produces nothing at all, because there are never any problems: given any form that won't fit the sound changes so far observed, one simply assumes a sporadic change of a different sort.

(k) We must assume regularity of sound change.

7. THE WÖRTER-UND-SACHEN TECHNIQUE.[35] Bloomfield reconstructs PA *paaškesikani* 'gun' and *eškoteewaapoowi* 'whisky', both on the basis of perfectly normal correspondences between whole words in the extant languages. The items named by these terms, of course, are post-Columbian. The forms are compound; Bloomfield says in a footnote to the first that 'here, as in some other examples, the meaning is modern, but the habit of formation is old.'[36]

If only this is to be ascribed to pre-Columbian times, then each of the modern languages concerned has coined new terms for the new items of material culture, using identical (cognate) morphemes according to identical patterns of formation, in such a way that the phonemic correspondences between the whole words are perfect. But it might also be that the terms themselves date from PA times, and that since the introduction of whisky and guns by Europeans the semantic shifts have been parallel in the various languages. Or, as European influence spread, the forms may have been invented by the speakers of one language and then borrowed by loan-translation into the other languages.[37]

It does not matter, for our present purpose, which of these alternatives is true. The fact that from well-attested modern forms one can reconstruct PA forms with meanings that were obviously impossible for PA is a clear indication of danger in the Wörter-und-Sachen technique. We deduce the following composite principle:

(1) Attempts to infer the culture of the speakers of a reconstructed parent language wholly from the forms and meanings of the daughter languages are always dangerous. The danger is less, though probably still

---

[35] Bloomfield, Language §18.14, and his references.

[36] Sketch, fn. 13.

[37] The English expression *fire-water* may be a loan-translation from Algonquian; if the former is older, then one or more Algonquian languages may have loan-translated the English.

considerable, if the forms compared are morphologically simple than if they are compounds.

**8. DRIFT.** There are two versions of the theory of drift. One is almost mystical: in a particular linguistic continuum the same sound shifts may happen over and over again; there is something in the genius of the language which leads to these sound shifts rather than to others.[38] The other is realistic, and fairly simple: when a speech community has split, inherited speech habits are for a while fairly similar, and may lead to the independent analogical development of forms which look like inherited cognates. If at a later date the descendant languages are compared with a view to reconstruction of the parent, some such pseudo-cognates may be falsely ascribed to the parent language.[39] The Algonquian words for 'gun' and 'whisky', in all probability, are illustrations of this, though we cannot be absolutely sure.

(m) Any INDIVIDUAL reconstructed form is suspect because of the possible influence of drift (in the second sense). In comparative linguistics one may achieve only statistical accuracy.

**9. THE SIGNIFICANCE OF STARRED FORMS.** There have been two theories of reconstructed forms.[40] The so-called 'realistic' theory holds that in reconstructing the phonemic pattern of a parent language, one should try to arrive at a set of phonemes bearing a relation to each other of the kind that is known to exist in languages more directly observed. The 'formula' theory, on the other hand, holds that reconstructions are simply short notations representing sets of correspondences.

Bloomfield's Algonquian reconstructions show clearly the circumstances under which the first practice is possible, and those under which the second is necessary. The vowel system postulated for PA is certainly phonemically realistic, being identical with that of one modern language, F. The fundamental consonant system is also: $p$ $t$ $\check{c}$ (possibly an allophone of $t$) $k$ $s$ $\theta$ $\check{s}$ (possibly an allophone of $\theta$) $h$ $l$ $m$ $n$ $w$ $y$ (the last two possibly

---

[38] E. Prokosch, A Comparative Germanic Grammar, esp. 34 ff. (Philadelphia, 1939).

[39] The discussion in Sapir's Language, chapters 7–8 (New York, 1921), is sufficiently broad to justify (apparently) either interpretation; for the realistic theory, see 184–5 in particular.

[40] Cogently discussed by C. D. Buck, Some Questions of Practice in the Notation of Reconstructed IE Forms, LANG. 2.99–107 (1926). Buck says (102): the purpose of reconstructions 'is not to furnish a picture of the parent speech for its own sake, but as a background of the historical relations.' This is in part an answer to the charge of 'irrelevant antiquarianism' sometimes levelled at the comparative method; even so, we should say that 'a picture of the parent speech for its own sake', to the degree attainable, is also a legitimate aim.

When this problem was discussed at Yale in the late thirties, one person cited Sapir as a proponent of the realistic theory, in contrast to Bloomfield as a supporter of formulas. It will be clear from the present discussion that this interpretation of Bloomfield was wrong.

allophones respectively of *o* and *i*). Of these, *l m n* (*w y*) were in all probability voiced; the others may have been voiced or voiceless, or perhaps were sometimes one and sometimes the other, without phonemic distinction.[41] *θ* may have been a voiceless lateral rather than an interdental spirant, or, again, perhaps both, depending on dialect or on environment.[42] The phonetic details are naturally obscure; it is the phonemic pattern which we claim to be 'realistic'.[43] The only type of doubt which could be raised as to the status of these elements as the actual phonemes of PA would be purely logistic: if, for example, every daughter language had, independently, changed PA *m* to *n* and PA *n* to *m*, no one could be the wiser. One could even claim that such a change would be subphonemic; in any case such possibilities need not disturb us.

When it comes to medial clusters, the situation is different. Medial clusters consist of two members; the second is always clearly identifiable as one of the ordinary consonants; but the multiplicity of correspondences requires the postulation of a somewhat larger number of purely arbitrary elements as prior members.[44] Thirty-one different medial clusters are attested; no one of them has identical reflexes in all four of the modern languages.[45]

In this case all one can do is to choose for the prior members a set of symbols which will have, if possible, some mnemonic value; e.g. PA *mp nt nč nk ns nš nθ nl* for clusters which in O have a nasal as first element, especially since such clusters in O occur only as reflexes of this set in PA.

Similarly, instead of writing *çk* for the PA cluster which gives F *šk*, C M *hk*, O *sk*, one could write *sk*, which is not otherwise used. It may well be that the PA clusters customarily written *mp*, *nt*, etc. actually had a nasal as first element. It may also be that PA *çk* was phonemically *sk*, the first element being phonemically identical with the independently occurring PA *s*. But the use of these notations for mnemonic reasons IS NOT EVIDENCE for such a phonemic interpretation: one may attain a spurious appearance of realism, but the actual phonemic nature of the first members of the clusters is still as obscure as before.

That the number of medial clusters in PA was larger than the number in any descendant language is surprising only to one who is not familiar with aspects of Algonquian linguistics other than phonology. In most of

---

[41] Sketch, §6.

[42] Loc. cit.

[43] In several recent papers (LANG. 20.84–6 [1944], 23.34–42 [1947]), Herbert Penzl has demonstrated, in connection with problems of early English, the difference between phonemic realism and what might be meant by phonetic realism.

[44] Sketch, §7.

[45] Since the phonemic systems of the modern languages are different, 'identical' must be interpreted relatively: since F and O *š* and *k* are elements in differing sets of contrasts, F *šk* and O *šk* are not in any absolute sense 'identical'.

the modern languages there is a sandhi habit whereby an element ending in a consonant, when due to be followed in the same word by one beginning with a consonant, is separated therefrom by a non-morphemic *i*.[46] This habit existed in PA times, but was then apparently rather new. The new habit prevented the re-formation of many clusters that had formerly existed; but formations surviving from an earlier stage retained the more complex consonantism. The trend towards simplification of the cluster system was a characteristic of PA which continued in the various separate dialects after their split, but the details varied from one dialect to another. Some of the pre-PA compounds are reconstructible from the modern languages, giving an essential clue to the statements just made; most, however, remain obscure.[47]

Thus it is quite possible that Algonquian research may in time produce evidence that will make the interpretation of the prior members of PA consonant clusters less purely algebraic. Only a deeper time-perspective, achieved by more detailed comparisons with Algonquian languages not of the Central Algonquian type, can do this. In the meantime, to underscore the point, 'realism' in this phase of the reconstruction of PA can only be spurious.

(n) Reconstruction should be phonemically realistic whenever possible.

(o) When realistic reconstruction is not possible, arbitrary indices of correspondences must be used. The fact that they are arbitrary, and the reasons which necessitate this arbitrariness, should be clearly stated. This practice will prevent a spurious impression of realism on the reader, and will obviate futile speculation on his part as to what the arbitrarily symbolized elements may 'really' have been.

**10.** NEGATIVE LESSONS. This paper could not serve its purpose fully without mentioning a few points on which, in the present writer's opinion, Bloomfield's Sketch can be misleading.

(1) Bloomfield labels his reconstructed prototype 'Proto-Algonquian'. It is based mainly on the comparison of F, C, M, and O; eastern Algonquian and the three groups of Plains languages are not often brought into the picture. Indeed, it would be difficult to include more mention of them in the present state of our knowledge. In feeling that the PA reconstructed in his Sketch will take care of the Plains languages, Bloomfield gives Michelson's work in the comparative analysis of the latter languages more credit than it deserves.[48] The course of wisdom for the reader of Bloom-

---

[46] Sketch, §16.

[47] Sketch, §17.

[48] Sketch, §2, referring to T. Michelson, Phonetic Shifts in Algonquian Languages, IJAL 8.131–71 (1935). The implication here is not that Michelson's study is not 'brilliant', as Bloomfield terms it, but that the synchronic information on Plains Algonquian available to Michelson was unsatisfactory.

field's Sketch is to replace 'PA' everywhere by 'PCA', standing for 'Proto-CENTRAL-Algonquian', and to withhold judgment on the status of the eastern and Plains languages until a good deal more of descriptive and comparative work has been done.

(2) Bloomfield says, 'before syllabic vowels, PA *i, o* are nonsyllabic; we write *y, w*.'[49] The phonemic status of *y* and *w* is another point on which judgment is best reserved. Bloomfield's notation (with all four symbols *i o y w*) is good; his statement seems hasty.

(3) Bloomfield cites Penobscot forms from Siebert, following Siebert's orthography except that accent marks are omitted. This conceals the fact that a number of the eastern languages of the family have an accentual system, more or less complex but definitely phonemic; these accentual systems have to be taken care of in the reconstruction of anything that can be called Proto-Algonquian. Exact citation of Siebert's forms, including the accent marks (perhaps with a footnote), would have been more in line with the general principles on which Bloomfield's work is based.

Point (3) turns on the discussion of §2 and §3 in this paper. Point (2) is connected with the content of §9. From point (1) we derive our last principle:

(p) A parent language reconstructed from the comparison of a certain set of daughter languages can be regarded as the parent only of the languages so used. Information from languages not previously used may change the reconstruction, deepen the time-perspective with a new reconstruction of an earlier stage, or demonstrate that the reconstruction already made is capable of handling the new data also.[50]

CONCLUSION. The sixteen principles which have been listed in the course of our discussion are not new or startling; indeed, by this time each of them ought to be so generally agreed upon that any mention of them, save in the most elementary textbooks of linguistics, would be ridiculous. We have unhappily not yet reached such uniformity of opinion about fundamentals. Yet if, for any one of the sixteen, Bloomfield's Algonquian evidence stood alone—if there were no comparative Germanic, comparative Romance, comparative Indo-European, comparative Semitic, and so on—that isolated support for the principle would still be persuasively solid.

[49] Sketch, §4.

[50] Thus Potawatomi is probably historically analyzable on the basis of Bloomfield's P(C)A without modification thereof (C. F. Hockett, The Position of Potawatomi in Central Algonkian, Papers of the Michigan Academy of Sciences, Arts, and Letters 28.537–42 [1942]); but Delaware is probably not (C. F. Voegelin, Proto-Algonquian Consonant Clusters in Delaware, LANG. 17.143–7 [1941]).

# 69. William G. Moulton:
## Leonard Bloomfield as Germanist

[The author, Professor of Linguistics at Princeton University and President of the Linguistic Society of America in 1967, was kind enough to prepare this paper especially for the present volume.]

It is not usual to speak of Bloomfield as a Germanist. We think of him rather as one of the founders of linguistics as a discipline, as a scholar in the field of American Indian languages, and—above all—as the author of an immensely influential book, his 1933 *Language*. These were the things that made him the dean of American linguists during his lifetime, and these are the things for which we remember him today. Yet Bloomfield was also a Germanist: primarily so during the early years of his scholarly life, and at least partly so even during his later years. Because his role as Germanist does not appear clearly in the writings of these later years, I hope I may be pardoned for beginning these remarks with some personal reminiscences from this period. Throughout his life, Bloomfield taught many Germanists. Curiously, he directed the dissertations of very few students—in Germanics or any other field. I was one of those lucky few.

My acquaintance with Bloomfield began in the fall of 1940, when he came to Yale as Sterling Professor of Linguistics. I had entered the Yale Graduate School four years earlier in order to study "German"—by which I understood, rather vaguely, studies that would somehow combine literature and language in the Germanic field. In that fall of 1936 the adviser to new graduate students of German (there were only two of us) was Eduard Prokosch—the same great teacher who had so inspired the young Bloomfield at Wisconsin in 1906. Prokosch suggested that I enroll in his course in Gothic. I did so; and under his influence I soon decided, like Bloomfield thirty years earlier, "that I should always work in linguistics." As Bloomfield describes his first meeting with Prokosch (*Language* 14.312, 1938 [B49]), he reached this decision in "a matter perhaps of fifteen minutes"; it took me perhaps three class meetings.

The Yale of those years was an ideal place for a young man who had decided that he should "always work in linguistics." Among the teachers available to us, there was not only Prokosch but also Edward Sapir,

Franklin Edgerton, and Edgar H. Sturtevant—to mention only those under whom I personally studied. Two of these great men, however, were soon lost to us. Prokosch died in an automobile accident in August 1938; Sapir became seriously ill late in 1938 and died the following February.

During the next two academic years the few of us who were graduate students in one branch or another of linguistics wondered how these two great men could possibly be replaced. We were of course able to continue our studies because of the presence at Yale of men like Edgerton and Sturtevant, as well as of Hans Kurath who came down from Brown University two days each week. But I in particular felt uneasy. I was now writing a dissertation on a topic that Prokosch had approved, and I could not help worrying whether his eventual successor would also approve it.

In the spring of 1940 we finally received the news we had been waiting for: Leonard Bloomfield was coming to Yale in the fall. Insofar as any one person could replace both Sapir (for general linguistics) and Prokosch (for Germanic linguistics), Bloomfield was the man. The joy of other students was unalloyed; my own was mixed with apprehension as to how Bloomfield would receive my dissertation, now nearing completion—or so I thought.

My memory of Bloomfield that first fall is one of gratitude tinged with sadness. He was a lonely man; no sooner had he arrived in New Haven than Mrs. Bloomfield became ill and was hospitalized for many months. I hesitated to bother him with my own problems. Yet when I finally dared approach him, I found him warm, friendly, immensely patient, and perhaps even more shy than I. When I told him that Prokosch had started me on my dissertation, his eyes lit up and said, quite simply: "He was my teacher, too." And when I then described the problem on which I had been working—one improbably combining Swiss German dialects and Old High German vowel length—he immediately expressed interest, was eager to see what I had written, and clearly wanted me to talk with him as a fellow Germanist. Relieved, I brought him the "final draft" that I had completed toward the end of the summer.

Perhaps a week later I stopped by to see Bloomfield again and found that he had already read the draft that I had given him. His first words were encouraging: the problem was worth investigating, I had gone about it in a reasonable way, and my results were useful. "But," he went on, "you have made things very hard for your reader. He cannot follow your argument unless he first makes himself as much of an expert on these matters as you are." (He might have quoted, though he did not, one of his favorite aphorisms: "Man kann sich den Leser nie dumm genug vorstellen.") Then, leaning back in his chair and staring off into space as he so often did, he continued: "You know, I once wrote a book, and people say that parts of it are hard to read. Some younger man should revise it and make it simpler." And he looked back and smiled at me as if I might be that younger man. Not until after I had left his office did I realize that the "book" he had spoken of so casually was his great work *Language*.

Though I was crestfallen that my "final draft" must now be rewritten so as to make it clearer and simpler, I was at least relieved that Bloomfield had approved it in general and had welcomed me as a fellow Germanist. Some three months later I gave him a second "final draft"—written this time, as I thought, so that *anyone* could read it. In retrospect, I believe this version must have been even worse than the first: I must have gone to the opposite extreme and tried to redo the whole thing in popular magazine style. With infinite patience Bloomfield read it all, made innumerable comments, and even rewrote a large part of one chapter; and with infinite kindness he urged me to write yet a third "final draft" that would strike a balance between my first two attempts. Now seeing my own foolishness, I spent another three months doing so—and at last produced a readable version. When it was done, and duly defended and accepted, Bloomfield urged me to publish it even if this meant (on my instructor's salary) some personal financial sacrifice. "Never pay to have anything else you write published; but pay for the publication of your dissertation if you have to." The dissertation appeared the following fall as a supplement to the journal *Language*; and even the critical eye of Bernard Bloch, then in his second year as Editor, found not a word that needed to be changed. Possibly the dissertation is still readable, even today. If so, it is an example of the kind of indirect influence that Bloomfield had in his later years, through his students, on Germanistic studies in this country.

That Bloomfield should have begun his scholarly life as a Germanist was apparently a matter of chance—as such things are in the lives of so many of us. "In the summer of 1906 I came, fresh out of college [he received his A.B. from Harvard at age 19], to Madison, to be looked over for an assistantship. Desiring to earn an academic living, I had developed no understanding or inclination for any branch of science. The kindly Professor Hohlfeld delegated Prokosch, one of his young instructors, to entertain me for the day" (*Language* 14.311–2, 1938 [B49]). And then follows the remark that perhaps fifteen minutes of talk with Prokosch were enough to convince him that he should always work in linguistics.

Bloomfield's early writings show that he fell very strongly under the spell of Prokosch at Wisconsin (where he stayed during the academic years 1906–1907 and 1907–1908) and then of Francis A. Wood at Chicago (where he completed his dissertation in 1909, age 22). Both Prokosch and Wood were Germanists and comparative philologists in the German Neo-Grammarian tradition; and for the next thirty-one years (until he became Professor of Linguistics at Yale) Bloomfield was a member of German departments at all the universities at which he served. The Germanistic element in his training was further strengthened by a year of study in Germany (1913–1914, at Leipzig and Göttingen). Such study in Germany was obligatory for any member of a German department who hoped for academic advancement. As Bloomfield once told the story to me: "The chairman of my department called me in one day and said that I was one of two instructors being considered for promotion, but that only one of us could be chosen. Though the department preferred me, they could not favor me over the other man because he had studied in Germany whereas I had not. If I would arrange to spend a year in Germany, they could promote me." And so Bloomfield went to Germany, and was duly promoted.

Bloomfield's Germanistic writings extend chronologically from 1909–1910 (the publication of his dissertation, in two parts, in *Modern Philology* [B1]) to 1938 (an article on "Initial [k] in German" [B48]). They fall roughly into four categories: (1) his dissertation, and works deriving from it; (2) a number of painstaking philological articles which reveal curiously little of the Bloomfield we know from non-Germanic works; (3) barely two articles showing what most of us would think of as the "true" Bloomfield; and (4) for a while, at least, a stream of reviews. The chronology and the relationship to non-Germanic works are interesting. Most of the Germanic works were published during his years at Illinois (1910–1921) and during the first three of his years at Chicago (1927–1940). But Bloomfield the "general linguist" of course appears as early as 1914 in *An Introduction to the Study of Language*; and after 1930 he published only two articles on Germanic (one in 1937, one in 1938). Significantly, many of the later Germanic articles appeared in *Festschriften* of various sorts. The fact that Bloomfield was invited to make these contributions shows that he was recognized as a Germanist, both in this country and abroad; but the articles themselves give the impression of being works which had lain in his desk for some years, perhaps half completed, and which he now put into final, publishable form.

There is little that need be said here about the various philological articles which Bloomfield wrote—"The *e* Sounds in the Language of Hans Sachs" (1912), "Notes on the Preverb *ge-* in Alfredian English" (1929), "Otfridiana" (1929), "Salic *litus*" (1930), "OHG *eino*, OE *ana* 'solus'" (1930), "Old English Plural Subjunctives in *-e*" (1930), or even the late "Notes on Germanic Compounds" (1937). These are painstaking and valuable works—and sometimes rather dull. Their one "Bloomfieldian" aspect is the immense amount of sheer labor that they reveal. Bloomfield was never afraid of hard work.

Far more interesting—and far more "Bloomfieldian"—are his dissertation and the many works which later, in one way or another, grew out of it. As a young man trained in the Neo-Grammarian tradition, Bloomfield was apparently struck by the fact that a large part of the Germanic vocabulary cannot be accounted for by the Neo-Grammarian theory of regular sound change. There must also be in human language a creative element which permits new forms to be produced on the analogy of old ones; and this process must be subject to systematic investigation just as much as is sound change. This was hardly a new thought. What *was* new was Bloomfield's insistence in carrying out this investigation without appealing to vague ideas of sound symbolism and without assuming innumerable *ad hoc* solutions.

In his dissertation, with its awkward title "A Semasiologic Differentiation in Germanic Secondary Ablaut," the 22-year-old Bloomfield chose to investigate one aspect of this creative element in Germanic. The text of some of the initial paragraphs is worth quoting, and is found in the present volume in B1. The remainder of the dissertation consists largely of 249 numbered sets of forms illustrating "secondary ablaut" discussed in the introduction.

The general theme of this dissertation was to reappear during the following years in a whole series of articles and reviews. We find it in the 1911 article "Etymologisches," published in perhaps the most illustrious German philological journal, the famous "Paul und Braunes *Beiträge*." The first paragraph is worth quoting in full:

> Ein grosser teil des germanischen wortschatzes scheint sich keiner vergleichung mit auswärtigen formen zu fügen. Im versuche, solches material etymologisch zu beleuchten, macht die forschung besonders zwei fehler. Der eine besteht darin, dass man die betreffenden wortsippen schlechthin als 'schallmalend', 'lautnachahmend', oder 'onomatopoietisch' stempelt, und meint, damit die sache abgetan zu haben. Der andere, in letzter zeit häufige, ist, dass man durch ad hoc aufgestellte lautgesetze die dunkeln formen als sandhidoubletten und dergleichen mit deutbaren wörtern verbindet.

We must admire the courage of a budding Germanist, who has just published his dissertation, now writing an article in German—for the leading German journal of his field. And we cannot help being struck by the second sentence, which seems to reveal a colossal arrogance in the 24-year-old scholar: "Die forschung macht besonders zwei fehler." Indeed! This is an aspect of Bloomfield that was to appear often in his later writings. Yet for those of us who knew the gentle person that Bloomfield was, it is not really arrogance at all—merely a kind of childlike directness. It appeared often in his professional writings, but never in direct personal relations.

The young Bloomfield was so caught up in these ideas that he could not resist repeating them in no less than three reviews he published this same year (1911). Of Richard Loewe's *Deutsches Wörterbuch* he wrote: This book could give the layman (for whom it was intended) "no idea of the wonderful creative vigor of Germanic, of the fact that a vast part of its words are new formations or new creations—certainly no idea as to the nature and means of such creation." He chided Heinrich Schröder, *Ablautstudien*, for dealing only with "sound laws,—which will not and cannot, by themselves, account for the Germanic Word-treasure." And in a review of *Indo-European a : $a^x i$ : $a^x u$*, by his teacher Francis A. Wood [B3], he wrote that "the vocabulary of the IE. languages as we have it is the product of countless analogic and 'contaminative' developments, formations, and re-formations, the result of a myriad workings and changes of human language tendencies and habits. It exhibits numberless groups of rime-words, ablaut-parallels, and other traces of associational and emotional activity of the human mind." A year later (1912) he wrote, in "A Type of Scandinavian Word-formation": "In this way the Germanic languages formed whole groups of rime-words. If we had complete records we could observe these being formed one after the other: as it is we must be content, in most cases, to determine which words date from an earlier stratum of language and which are analogic formations." In the same year, reviewing the 3rd-4th edition of Wilhelm Braune, *Althochdeutsche Grammatik*, he chided the author for "explaining" such things as the -*kk*- of German *zucken* as "lautsymbolische verstärkungen bei intensivbildungen." For Bloomfield this was no explanation at all. He adds delightfully: "Of course no sounds could be so expressive of 'zucken' to a German-speaking person as those in the word *zucken*; to the English *twitch* says exactly what it means, and so on through the dictionary; but this is not linguistic history and will not account for origins. The models for the intensive verbs and the shortened names (note of course the *n*-inflection of the latter) with double consonants were, so far as we know, cases of *n*-assimilation; where the *n*-assimilation did not actually take place its results were imitated: the words were certainly not formed by some mystic symbolism to suit the idea."

The most mature presentation of these ideas occurs in the article "Einiges vom germanischen Wortschatz" [B20], published in the 1925 *Festschrift* for the great German scholar Eduard Sievers but perhaps written in part at an earlier period. Bloomfield begins by pointing out the two great achievements of 19th century historical linguistics: first, the knowledge that was gained about the history of the Indo-European languages; second, the methods that were evolved to attain this knowledge. Though much was learned in this way, a large part of the vocabulary of Germanic (and of other branches of Indo-European) still remains etymologically unexplained. "In dieser Sachlage ist man darauf gekommen, das oben genannte zweite Ergebnis der Sprachforschung aufzuopfern, um dann bei loserer Methode alles eklären zu können. So wird vor allem der aus vorwissenschaftlicher Zeit stammende Begriff der 'Lautsymbolik' ohne weitere Kritik wieder aufgefrischt . . ., oder es werden sonstige Theorien über Wortschöpfung erfunden, oder der germ. Wortschatz wird etwa aus weit entfernten und ganz unbekannten Sprachen abgeleitet." "Wie werden sich nun die Probleme lösen, welche der grösste Teil des germ. Wortschatzes aufwirft?" His answer is delightful: "Zum Teil gar nicht," followed by the typically Bloomfieldian aphorism: "Man muss eben nicht alles wissen wollen." But then his real answer is given: "Nur dies wissen wir seit der Junggrammatikerbewegung: die Vorgänge, die wir nicht kennen, verliefen ebenso wie diejenigen, welche wir kennen." This adamant refusal to abandon a sound methodology merely because its application becomes more difficult was an attitude which Bloomfield maintained all his life, and he could be quite abrupt about the matter. I remember that, in one of the "final drafts" of my dissertation, I had suggested suspending the workings of regular sound change in order to account for an inflectional ending which carried (as I thought) a particularly valuable grammatical meaning. (The idea was of course not original with me; I had copied it from a renowned German scholar.) Bloomfield would have none of it. Either we believe in regular sound change or we don't. If we do, we can continue the wonderful work of our Neo-Grammarian predecessors and try to enlarge upon it. If we don't, we are charlatans.

The many articles and reviews that grew, directly or indirectly, out of his dissertation show a characteristic that appears in nearly all of Bloomfield's writings, Germanic as well as non-Germanic: a willingness to work through great masses of data in order to arrive at general principles. From this point of view the many articles on the Germanic vocabulary are as important in revealing Bloomfield the general linguist as they are in revealing Bloomfield the Germanist. Yet Bloomfield also loved the data themselves, as any good philologist must; and I believe it was this love of data which accounts for the various articles that I have somewhat impatiently classified as merely "philological." These articles alone would have made the reputation of a lesser man. For all their philological value, however, I am still puzzled that they should show so little of Bloomfield the general linguist; and I do not know why so many of them should have appeared in 1929 and 1930, right after he had gone to Chicago.

The only Germanic articles which fully reveal Bloomfield the general linguist are "German ç and x" (1930 [B29]) and "Initial [k] in German" (1938 [B48]). The former, barely a page in length, seems at first glance to be quite inconsequential: it merely tells us that German [ç] and [x] can be analyzed as allophones of a single phoneme. But its terse wording reveals a principle which somehow never emerges clearly in the phonological chapters of his great book *Language*: that a phonemic analysis should be made with due regard to grammatical boundaries. Within morphemes (as we would now say), German [x] occurs only after /a aː o oː u uː au/, whereas [ç] occurs in all other positions, including initially. "German treats compound members and suffixes with initial consonant phonetically as separate words. . . . Hence the [ç] of the suffix [-çən] is treated as if it were in word-initial, as in [çeˈmiː] *Chemie*, and forms like [ˈfrau-çən] *Frauchen*, [ˈpfau-çən] *Pfauchen*, [ˈkuː-çən] Kuhchen merely illustrate initial [ç]." (I have here changed a few details of Bloomfield's analysis of German, though none that concern the principle involved.) Perhaps because, in *Language*, Bloomfield did not clearly discuss the relevance of grammatical boundaries to phonemic analysis, younger American linguists later devoted a number of articles to this topic. It is interesting that, in this tiny article, Bloomfield clearly anticipated the position which most of us now hold.

Though we might expect that Bloomfield would have applied the principles of phonemic analysis to many other problems of Germanic, there is only one other article in which he did so: the 1938 "Initial [k] in German" [B48]. This is a masterful treatment of the topic and shows an exhaustive acquaintance with the data involved. Classic descriptions of the High German Consonant Shift, as it appears in modern dialects, are distressingly inconsistent. They treat the shift of Germanic initial *t-* and *p-* in parallel fashion: the voiceless stop *t-* was shifted to the affricate *ts-* throughout all of the south (cf. English *ten*, German *zehn*; the *t-/ts-* line, with others parallel to it, is used to delimit the High German area); and the voiceless stop *p-* was shifted to the affricate *pf-* throughout much of the south (cf. English *pound*, German *Pfund*; the *p-/pf-* line is used to delimit, within High German, the West Middle German area). So far, so good. But then the shift of *k-* is usually treated in quite another way. This appears in most of the High German area as [kh-], in a narrow southern strip as [kx-], and in the extreme south (through an obviously secondary development) as [x-]. Because it is not possible to distinguish clearly between [kx-] and [kh-], and because this latter cannot be distinguished clearly from northern aspirated [kʰ-], it is customary to use the *x-/kx-, kh-, kʰ-* line as the northern boundary of "shifted" *k-*. But this is of course absurd, since [x-] is so obviously a secondary development.

Bloomfield's solution to this problem is ingenious, and disarmingly simple. It is based upon a phonemic, rather than a phonetic, definition of the High German consonant shift. (In the following quotations I shall write phonemic forms within slant lines, phonetic forms within square brackets, as is now the custom; Bloomfield used only square brackets.) "Before the High German consonant shift, the language had the West Germanic unvoiced stops /p t k/, the voiced (later unvoiced lenis) stops /b d g/, and the unvoiced spirants /f þ s h/—or was /þ/ already voiced? The shift of initial /p- t- k-/ consisted in their replacement by a phoneme of the second series plus a phoneme of the third series"—that is to say, the shift of a stop to the sequence "stop plus spirant." In the case of *p*- and *t*-, phonetic criteria are still adequate to suggest where this phonemic shift took place; and clear phonemic evidence can be obtained by an appeal to grammatical criteria. Thus "a syntactic combination like /t supə/ *die Suppe* has the same initial as /tsi:t/ *Zeit*; similarly, such a dialect may have /p fyəss/ *die Füsse* with the same initial as /pfunt/ *Pfund* . . . ." In the case of *k*-, on the other hand, phonetic criteria are adequate only where earlier *k*- now appears (via secondary development from *kx*-) as *x*-; elsewhere we must rely on grammatical criteria. A historical accident—the loss of unstressed /ə/—gives us the needed evidence. Where earlier /gəh-/ (as in *gehalten*) now appears as [kx-], [kh-], or [gh-] ([kxaltən, khaltən, ghaltən]), this phonetic sequence surely represents the phonemic sequence /kx-/, /kh-/, or /gh-/—that is to say, the phonemic sequence "stop plus spirant." Where in these same areas earlier /k-/ (as in *kalt*) now also appears as [kx-], [kh-], or [gh-] ([kxalt, khalt, ghalt]), this must also represent the phonemic sequence /kx-/, /kh-/, or /gh-/. "Hence, apart from the dialects which have /x-/, we obtain proof, for a large body of dialects, that West Germanic /k-/ before vowel has gone through the High German consonant shift and is represented by a combination of stop plus spirant." The bulk of the article consists of a listing of the dialects where, in this phonemic sense, the "shift" of *k*- can be said to have taken place. "Our citations, then, show that the coincidence of [earlier] /k-/ as in /ghalt/ *kalt*, with [earlier] /gəh-/ as in /ghaltən/ *gehalten*, extends over the entire area that has lost the vowel of the prefix /gə-/ before /h-/. Beyond this, to the north, our criterion fails. Better knowledge of the phonemics of the dialects would doubtless reveal other criteria, and these would show that the shift of West Germanic /k-/ extends farther toward the north."

Bloomfield's discussion of "Initial [k] in German" is surely not the last word on the subject. Among other things, it places us in a curious dilemma: though the phonetic shift of Germanic *k*- presumably took place at an early date, we cannot demonstrate its phonemic shift until after the much later loss of unstressed *e* in the prefix *ge*-. Despite any such weaknesses, however, the article represents an immense advance beyond the obviously unacceptable treatments of initial *k*- that appear in German discussions of the topic. Perhaps because the article appeared such a short time before the outbreak of World War II, it does not seem to have influenced subsequent German discussion of the matter. This may also be because German scholars were, until recently, not interested in phonemics.

No discussion of Bloomfield as Germanist would be complete without at least brief mention of Bloomfield as language teacher. In 1906, age 19, he went to Wisconsin as graduate student *and* as assistant in German (which presumably meant teaching "baby German"). In 1942, age 55, he wrote his *Outline Guide for the Practical Study of Foreign Languages*. During the following wartime years he not only served as mentor for all of us who were writing the many volumes of the *Spoken Language* series (my wife Jenni Karding Moulton and I, as authors of *Spoken German*, owed much to his example, as did all the other authors in this series); he also took time out to write *Colloquial Dutch* (1944), and *Spoken Dutch* (2 vols., 1945), and to rescue a foundering *Spoken Russian* by rewriting the first volume and authoring the second volume. (He listed himself as co-author of the second volume, together with his informant Luba Petrova; because he was unhappy about the first volume, which he had largely "inherited" from others, he listed himself only under the amusing pseudonym of I. M. Lesnin.) In between these dates he published in 1923 an elementary German text entitled *First German Book*. His own explanation of this book, as he once related it to me, was: "I told my colleagues that I didn't like any of the elementary texts we used. They said that if I felt like that I would have to write my own book. So I did." Though I never taught from this book, and hence cannot judge its practical merits, it is certainly far more "modern" than anything else that I know from the 1920's. It must have been useful, because it was reprinted in a second edition in 1928. The only books that I can judge from personal experience are his *Colloquial Dutch* and *Spoken Dutch*. I used both of these to teach myself Dutch, in preparation for a year in Holland, and they enabled me to arrive in Holland with a highly useful control of Dutch; I later used them once very successfully with a small class of students. The book *Spoken Dutch* contains a lovely example of Bloomfield's humor. Lesson 8 is entitled "Barber and Laundry," Lesson 9 is entitled "Eating." And the "Listening In" section of Lesson 9, which was intended (according to the instructions given to all of us) to combine new material with old, has a conversation that begins with the following immortal words:

Guest: Kellner! Kom eens hier als 't u blieft.   Waiter! Come here, please.
Waiter: Ik kom dadelijk bij u, mijnheer.          I shall be right with you, sir.
Guest: Er is een haar in mijn soep.               There's a hair in my soup.

I hope I may again be forgiven if I close this discussion of Bloomfield as Germanist, just as I began it, with some personal reminiscences. Though it may seem hard to believe for those who know him only as the author of *Language*, or of the "Postulates," or of "Menomini Morphophonemics," Bloomfield remained all his life a devoted Germanist and philologist. I can document this from two personal memories. Immediately after the stumbling completion of my dissertation, Bloomfield arranged to have me teach a graduate course in Old High German. (As I recall, I had one student.) In preparing for this course I became greatly interested in one of the scribes of the Old High German *Tatian*—a 9th century translation of a Latin gospel harmony—and spent many months writing an article on the topic. This was traditional philology with a vengeance. When I had completed my article, I showed it to Bloomfield and asked him whether it was worth publishing. He read it eagerly and agreed with me that it should be submitted to the *Publications of the Modern Language Association*. When the reader for this estimable journal criticized my work because I had not clearly shown who had translated which parts of the Old High German text, Bloomfield reassured me: "This is the mistake they all make: they don't distinguish between the translators and the scribes. You are only talking about the latter, and his criticisms have nothing to do with what you wrote." Though I should have known better, I was amazed that Bloomfield should be so well informed about such a minor point of Old High German philology. The article was duly published in 1944, and I was henceforth immortalized in a series of footnotes in subsequent editions of Braune's *Althochdeutsche Grammatik*.

During these same wartime years when we were all so busy with so many other things, the lonely Bloomfield (Mrs. Bloomfield was again hospitalized) one day asked me whether he and I could not meet once a week and read some *Otfrid*. This is a 9th century German life of Christ written in rhymed verse (end-rhyme here appears for the first time in German) by a monk at the monastery of Weissenburg about whom we know little but his name, "Otfrid." The work is philologically important because, among other reasons, Otfrid himself almost certainly looked over one of the manuscripts we have and added the corrections that he thought necessary. And so I came to Bloomfield's office; and for many weeks in the spring of 1942 (I think that was the date) we read Otfrid. I shall never forget the experience. I was fresh from a Ph.D in Germanic linguistics and was teaching a course in Old High German; and I still labored under the delusion that Bloomfield was primarily a specialist in general linguistics and Algonquian. But his knowledge of Germanic in general, and of Old High German and Otfrid in particular, was overwhelming. I discovered that he had an almost complete set of reprints of the many articles and dissertations that had been written on Otfrid. And I discovered that, compared to Bloomfield, I was a complete ignoramus. I can see him now, pulling the Gothic Bible from his bookshelf and showing me a form or a construction that was parallel to something we had just read in Otfrid. In retrospect, I can only marvel at my youthful resilience: if I had had any sense, I would have given up Germanic linguistics and philology then and there.

But of course I did not. For Bloomfield's vast knowledge had a double quality: it was both humbling and inspiring. And so I continued my work in Germanic linguistics and philology, as best I could. As I write these lines, just twenty years after I last saw Bloomfield (I left Yale in 1947), I am again filled with gratitude tinged with sadness. The triumph of his life was that, largely through his writings, he influenced a whole generation of American linguists. The tragedy of his life was a double one: that he was not able to live out his scholarly life to the full, and that he personally supervised the studies of so few students, particularly in the field of Germanics, where he had so much to offer.

# 70. Obituary Notices and Additional Data

[We reprint only those notices that give independent information, deleting certain repetitions in those by Sturtevant and Hall. We thus omit that supplied by Bloch for the 45th Anniversary Report on the Harvard Class of 1906 (Associated Harvard Alumni) and that by George L. Trager in *Le Maître Phonétique* III.92.24–26 (July–December 1949). Certain information not given in any of the obituaries is presented below in (2); some of this will be found in the article on Leonard Bloomfield in the *Encyclopedia of the Social Sciences*, 1967 edition.]

(1)  Bernard Bloch (Yale University), *Language* 25.87–94 (1949)

Leonard Bloomfield died on April 18, 1949, at the age of 62, after nearly three years of crippling illness. He was a signer of the Call that led to the founding of the Linguistic Society, and the Society's President in 1935.

Bloomfield was born in Chicago on April 1, 1887, the son of Sigmund and Carola Buber Bloomfield. His aunt was Fannie Bloomfield Zeisler, a concert pianist of international repute; his uncle was Maurice Bloomfield, for many years Professor of Sanskrit and Comparative Philology in the Johns Hopkins University—like his nephew, one of the great figures in American linguistics, and the second President of the Linguistic Society.[1]

When Bloomfield was nine years old, his family moved to the village of Elkhart Lake, Wisconsin, where his father was proprietor of a hotel. Here the boy lived until he was old enough to go to high school, except for two winters spent in Europe with his family (1898–9 and 1900–1). The village school did not agree with him: it came to be a standing joke in his family that he found it hard, and that once he failed of promotion to a higher grade—perhaps because he disapproved of the teaching methods in use there.[2] In spite of these difficulties, and largely as a result of his mother's tutoring, he passed the high-school entrance examination required in those days and returned to Chicago to attend the North Division (now the Waller) School.

In 1903 he entered Harvard College, to be graduated three years later. The course that he liked best and found most valuable there was the one

---

[1] See the obituary of Maurice Bloomfield by George M. Bolling in Lg. 4.214–7 (1928).
[2] Personal communication from Mr. Grover Bloomfield of Milwaukee.

in daily themes, conducted by the late Professor Charles Townsend Copeland. Because it forced him to put something down on paper day after day, week after week through the year, knowing that every careless word and every awkward sentence would be mercilessly exposed, this course, he used to say, taught him not only to write but also to think.

At the age of nineteen, with his A.B. from Harvard, Bloomfield went to the University of Wisconsin to begin his graduate work and serve at the same time as Assistant in German. Here he met Eduard Prokosch, his senior by nine years, and fell at once under the spell of the older man's personality. The meeting was an important event in Bloomfield's life; for it marked the birth of his career as a linguist. The incident is charmingly described in Bloomfield's obituary of Prokosch.[3]

> ... In the summer of 1906 I came, fresh out of college, to Madison, to be looked over for an assistantship. Desiring to earn an academic living, I had developed no understanding or inclination for any branch of science. The kindly Professor Hohlfeld delegated Prokosch, one of his young instructors, to entertain me for the day. On a small table in Prokosch's dining room there stood a dozen technical books (I seem to remember that Leskien's Old Bulgarian grammar was among them) and in the interval before lunch Prokosch explained to me their use and content. By the time we sat down to the meal, a matter perhaps of fifteen minutes, I had decided that I should always work in linguistics.

After two years of teaching and study at Wisconsin, Bloomfield went to the University of Chicago, where he continued both activities under the direction of Professor Francis A. Wood. It was Wood who chose the subject for his dissertation: 'a semasiologic differentiation in Germanic secondary ablaut'. He received his doctorate from the University of Chicago in 1909. On March 18 of the same year he had married Miss Alice Sayers of St. Louis.

In 1913 and 1914 he further extended his knowledge of linguistics through study at the Universities of Leipzig and Göttingen; among the scholars with whom he worked in Germany were August Leskien, Karl Brugmann, and Hermann Oldenberg. But in spite of the veneration in which he held these men, it was always Prokosch whom he called his teacher. 'At the end of the two years of pupilhood (in Madison),' he wrote,[4] 'I knew no greater intellectual pleasure than to listen to Prokosch.'

Bloomfield's teaching career is shown in the barest outline by the following dates: 1909–10, Instructor in German, University of Cincinnati; 1910–13, the same, University of Illinois; 1913–21, Assistant Professor of Comparative Philology and German, University of Illinois; 1921–27, Professor of German and Linguistics, Ohio State University; 1927–40, Professor of Germanic Philology, University of Chicago; 1940–49, Sterling Professor

---

[3] Lg. 14.311–2 (1938) [B49].
[4] Lg. 14.312.

of Linguistics, Yale University. In the summer of 1925 he served as Assistant Ethnologist in the Canadian Department of Mines; for three summers (1938, '39, and '40) he was on the staff of the Linguistic Institute in Ann Arbor.

At the time of his death he was a member of the following professional organizations: the Linguistic Society of America, the American Oriental Society, the American Philological Association, the American Ethnological Society, the Modern Language Association of America, the American Association for the Advancement of Science, the Society for the Advancement of Scandinavian Studies, the International Phonetic Association, the American Philosophical Society [elected to membership 1942 —CFH], and the Royal Danish Academy of Science. He was also one of the two American members of the Comité International Permanent de Linguistes.

Bloomfield's scholarly writings were at first concerned with rather small details of Indo-European (and especially Germanic) phonology and morphology. But soon his interest in the larger aspects of linguistic science came to be reflected in wider-ranging and more general studies. In 1914 he published his first inclusive survey of the field, *An introduction to the study of language*. His Tagalog texts appeared in 1917, a product of his increasingly varied research in languages outside the Indo-European orbit; and five years later, in a review of Michelson's work on Fox, he wrote the first of his many contributions to the descriptive and comparative study of the Algonquian languages.

Bloomfield's masterpiece is unquestionably his book *Language*, published in 1933: a work without an equal as an exposition and synthesis of linguistic science. He called it, in the Preface (vii), 'a revision of the author's *Introduction to the Study of Language*'; but it is in fact a new work in every detail of its plan and execution. Even the author's fundamental point of view is wholly different in the two books. In 1914 Bloomfield had viewed language from the position of Wilhelm Wundt, whose 'Völkerpsychologie' is accordingly reflected in the earlier book. By 1933, partly as a result of his association with the psychologist Albert Paul Weiss,[5] he had become a behaviorist. But what is more important, he had convinced himself, as he was later to convince so many others, that it does not matter what particular brand of psychology a linguist finds attractive, so long as he keeps it out of his linguistic writings. Because of this teaching, which now is a commonplace among American linguists, Bloomfield has been repeatedly charged with denying some of the most vital features of human behavior—as if an ethnologist who chose to describe social organization

---

[5] Weiss's chief work, *A theoretical basis of human behavior* (Columbus, Ohio, 1924; rev. ed. 1929), had a profound influence on Bloomfield. See also the shorter statement of Weiss's view in Lg. 1.52–7 (1925) and Bloomfield's obituary in Lg. 7.219–21 (1931) [B38].

without reference to physiology should be accused of denying the circulation of the blood.

His absorbing interest in linguistics as a science did not prevent him from devoting himself also—more diligently than the majority of linguists —to its practical applications, especially in the teaching of reading and the study of foreign languages. In opposition to many scholars with far less understanding of science, he felt that scientific inquiry was by no means wholly its own justification, which lay rather in the hope that it might lead us ultimately 'toward the understanding and control of human events'.[6] Among the more utilitarian products of this conviction are his German beginners' book (1923, 2nd ed. 1928) and his English primer, a complete course for teaching school-children to read and write, based on the true relation of writing to speech and carefully planned to illustrate all regular spellings before proceeding to the irregular. This primer was used experimentally in Chicago parochial schools in the early 1940's and proved its worth in the classroom; but it was never published—partly because 'the basic teaching of our schools, in reading and writing, in standard language and composition . . ., is dominated still by educationists who, knowing nothing about language, waste years of every child's life, and leave our community semi-literate.'[7]

It was during the last war that Bloomfield's concern for foreign language teaching bore fruit. The history of the Intensive Language Program is familiar to most members of the Linguistic Society: how it was organized in 1941 by the American Council of Learned Societies to train teachers and prepare textbooks of strategically important languages; how it supervised the methods of instruction in the Army Specialized Training Program throughout the country; and how it published, through the Linguistic Society, a series of practical manuals written by trained linguists and applying the latest results of our science to the problem of teaching foreign languages. What is not so widely known is the part that Bloomfield played in these activities. Although he was not a member of the committees that nominally directed the Intensive Language Program, and remained by preference in the background of its operations, there is no one to whom the Program is more deeply indebted. The influence of his teachings is obvious in every phase of its work: many of the younger men and women who took part in it learned their trade from him or from his book *Language*; and he himself contributed no fewer than four works to the series which the Program sponsored in 1942, when it was not yet clear what direction the Program would take, he wrote one of the Program's two booklets on descriptive methodology: his *Outline guide for the practical*

---

[6] *Language* 509. The whole last chapter of *Language* is an expression of this hope and a discussion of the special fields where it may be most directly realized.

[7] Lg. 22.3 (1946) [B66].

*study of foreign languages,* a brief but lucid statement of how the linguist works with an informant. Later he wrote three of the practical manuals: two for Dutch and one for Russian, devoting months of gruelling work to the task. In addition, he found time and strength to prepare a grammatical introduction for the War Department's Russian dictionary.

Bloomfield's relation to the Linguistic Society was peculiarly intimate. He was a member (with George M. Bolling and Edgar H. Sturtevant) of the organizing committee that first conceived the possibility of an association devoted wholly to linguistics; he himself wrote the Call for the Organization Meeting,[8] as well as the first article published in *Language* (1.1–5), setting forth the reasons for establishing a Linguistic Society. In the days of the Society's early struggle for recognition he was one of its most convinced and convincing supporters; when it had come to be internationally respected as a professional and scientific body, he continued to work for it with quiet devotion. It is not inappropriate that the last article from his pen is a summary of the Linguistic Society's development.[9]

Bloomfield's greatness as a scholar was not limited to any one branch or aspect of linguistics. He was intimately acquainted with much of the vast literature of our science; and what he once read remained active in his prodigious memory. This reading gave him a profound sense of indebtedness to earlier workers in the field: he would often emphasize the cumulative nature of science, which enables each new generation to begin where the old one left off. But the ties that linked him to his predecessors did not fetter his imagination, or prevent him from exploring new languages and new techniques. Few men have been at home in so many corners of linguistics. Trained as an Indo-Europeanist in the great tradition of the neo-grammarians, he had also a specialist's knowledge of at least four groups within the general field: Germanic, Indic, Slavic, and Greek. Moreover, with a breadth of understanding rare among scholars of similar background, he appreciated not only the value of comparative and historical grammar but that of descriptive grammar as well. His interest in the latter subject, and the depth of insight that he brought to it— both stemming perhaps from his intimate study of Pāṇini—are notably reflected in his book *Language,* where more than a third of his exposition is concerned with it.[10]

Nor did he confine himself within the bounds of Indo-European; he had a wide acquaintance with languages in other families also. His firsthand investigation of several Malayo-Polynesian languages was one of the pioneer works in a little-known field. And as everyone knows, his descriptive and comparative studies of the Algonquian languages are

[8] Printed in Lg. 1.6–7 (1925).
[9] Twenty-one years of the Linguistic Society, Lg. 22.1–3 (1946) [B67].
[10] Chapters 5–8 on phonemics, and chapters 10–16 on grammar (pp. 74–138, 158–280).

among the classics of American Indian research. Few anecdotes are more often told in support of the neo-grammarian hypothesis than Bloomfield's use of it to predict the discovery of a previously unattested consonant cluster in a Central Algonquian dialect.[11] The significance of his writings in this field has been fully explored elsewhere;[12] here it will be enough to point out the characteristic union of old and new in Bloomfield's work: the application of an established technique, developed in the comparison of Indo-European languages, to a linguistic family without written records —a family that many Indo-Europeanists have never heard of.

Bloomfield's profound influence on the development of our science was in some ways a paradox. He consistently discouraged would-be beginners in linguistics from entering the field, on the ground that they would find it impossible to make a living, yet the vogue that linguistics enjoys today is largely the result of his work in it. He had almost no students, yet most American descriptivists look up to him as their teacher. He despised all talk of schools and factions—'the blight of the odium theologicum',[13] yet many linguists regard themselves proudly as members of a school that bears his name. He avoided public discussion and only rarely engaged in controversy, yet his views on many controversial questions are well known and have become current doctrine. He kept himself as much as possible in the background, preferring his own work to the business of propaganda, yet no linguist of his generation had wider fame or was more universally revered.

His personality was not strongly magnetic. He was too unassuming to impose it on others, too withdrawn to enjoy the immediate satisfaction of dominating an audience. His influence, therefore, was not primarily a personal one. It is probable that many of those who count themselves his followers never saw him. That his teaching has nevertheless changed the course of linguistics in this country, that his approach and his method have come to be almost matters of orthodoxy to many students, is due to the tremendous impact of his book *Language* and of his other writings.[14] To appreciate that impact it is enough to recall the state of our linguistic methods before the appearance of *Language*. It was a shocking book: so far in advance of current theory and practice that many readers, even among the well-disposed, were outraged by what they thought a needless flouting of tradition; yet so obviously superior to all other treatments of the aspect that its unfamiliar plan could not be dismissed as mere eccen-

---

[11] A note on sound-change, Lg. 4.99–100 (1928) [B33].

[12] Charles F. Hockett, Implications of Bloomfield's Algonquian studies, Lg. 24.117–31 (1948) [68].

[13] Lg. 22.2 [B66].

[14] The following articles and reviews contain important general statements: . . . [B21, B28, B36, B37, B39, B42, B46, B61; the monograph *Linguistic Aspects of Science* (Chicago, 1939)].

tricity. Today, of course, the book no longer shocks anyone; more than any other work, it approaches the status of a standard text. Its innovations have become commonplace; some of its most novel features now seem slightly old-fashioned. The reason for this reversal is plain: not only did the book summarize and clarify the main results of our science up to the time of its publication, it also pointed the direction that linguistics was to take in the immediate future. It is not too much to say that every significant refinement of analytic method produced in this country since 1933 has come as a direct result of the impetus given to linguistic research by Bloomfield's book. If today our methods in descriptive analysis are in some ways better than his, if we see more clearly than he did himself certain aspects of the structure that he first revealed to us, it is because we stand upon his shoulders.

His own opinion of his book was characteristically modest. He thought of it as an elementary work, 'intended for the general reader and for the student who is entering upon linguistic work.'[15] In conversation he often referred to it as 'my high-school text', though surely no high-school student could read it through. Even professional linguists usually find it slow reading—not because it is obscurely written but because it so carefully says in every sentence exactly what it means, because every word is essential and every definition must be taken seriously. Bloomfield was regretfully aware that many readers found the book difficult, and acknowledged that the fault was his for not having written it more diffusely. He attributed his error to the lack of a popularizing tradition in linguistics. Only a series of better and better approximations to an ideal work, he used to say, would ultimately yield a satisfactory popularization. The object of such a work is admirably set forth in his own words, written six years before the appearance of his book:[16] 'Sound popularizing tries to lead the layman toward an understanding and appreciation of science, not to encourage his taste for the bizarre, irrelevant, and inaccurate.'

There can be no doubt that Bloomfield's greatest contribution to the study of language was to make a science of it. Others before him had worked scientifically in linguistics; but no one had so uncompromisingly rejected all prescientific methods, or had been so consistently careful, in writing about language, to use terms that would imply no tacit reliance on factors beyond the range of observation. To some readers, unaware of the danger that lies in a common-sense view of the world, Bloomfield's avoidance of everyday expressions may have sounded like pedantry, his rigorous definitions like jargon. But to the majority of linguists, the simple clarity of Bloomfield's diction first revealed in full the possibilities of

[15] Preface, p. vii.
[16] In a review of Lokotsch, *Etymologisches Wörterbuch der amerikanischen (indianischen) Wörter im Deutschen*, MPhil. 24.489 (1927) [B24].

scientific discourse about language. It was Bloomfield who taught us the necessity of speaking about language in the style that every scientist uses when he speaks about the object of his research: impersonally, precisely, and in terms that assume no more than actual observation discloses to him.

In his long campaign to make a science of linguistics, the chief enemy that Bloomfield met was that habit of thought which is called mentalism: the habit of appealing to mind and will as ready-made explanations of all possible problems. Most men regard this habit as obvious common sense; but in Bloomfield's view, as in that of other scientists, it is mere superstition, unfruitful as best and deadly when carried over into scientific research. In the opposite approach—known as positivism, determinism, or mechanism—Bloomfield saw the main hope of the world; for he was convinced that only the knowledge gained by a strictly objective study of human behavior, including language, would one day make it possible for men to live at peace with each other. The following statement is typical both of his confidence in the methods of science and of his hatred of superstition:[17]

> We have acquired understanding and the power of prediction and control and have reaped vast benefit in the domains where we have developed non-animistic and non-teleologic science. We remain ignorant and helpless in the domains where we have failed to develop that kind of science, namely, in human affairs, such as the correlation of incentive with the distribution of economic goods, or the disposal of conflicting national interests.
>
> The only exception here is our relatively good knowledge of the structure and history of languages, a body of knowledge which, against the predisposition and expectation of the discoverers, turned out to imply no animistic or teleological factors. Although this situation gives us no certainty, it offers a strong probability in favor of extending the methods that have been successful to replace those which have yielded no success. Mankind has always found such steps difficult and has resisted them with more than mere inertia. Obscurantism, the articulate vanguard of that resistance, has never employed rational argument, but only invective and, from the time of Galileo to our own, every degree of irrational sanction.

On May 27, 1946, at the summit of his career, Bloomfield suffered a stroke that put an end to his life as a productive scholar—to everything that gave satisfaction and purpose to his life as a man. For eight weeks he lay unconscious; then by slow degrees he began to regain his faculties— but never all of them. After many months he was able to walk again, supported by a cane and a companion's arm. After yet more months of creeping improvement, interrupted by a succession of minor strokes, he recovered so far as to be able to make short visits to his office in the Hall

---

[17] Lg. 20.55 (1944) [B62]. Although this article (Secondary and tertiary responses to language) began as a jeu d'esprit, its latter half contains an admirable and wholly serious defense of the mechanistic position; see pp. 51–5 (omitting the long quotation).

of Graduate Studies, where he would sit in a wheelchair at his littered desk and chat with friends. He could do no work. His eyes had been permanently affected by his illness, and his memory was impaired. When he received the first number of *Language* for 1948, with its dedication to him, he was deeply touched; but he could not read it. For a time there was hope that he might one day be well enough to resume his teaching; then the slow improvement ceased, and his paralysis began to grow more general. During the last year of his life he became steadily weaker, until, four months before his death, he was again confined to his bed. He died peacefully. To those who saw him during the three years of his empty survival, his death was not a new occasion for grief.

Throughout these years Bloomfield never complained. He rarely spoke of himself, and never to invite compassion or solicitude. That modesty which had prevented him from acknowledging his own true nature, and from taking seriously the tributes that he received from other scholars, now blinded him—perhaps mercifully—to the tragic significance of his uncompleted work. He gave the impression that his illness was a merely personal inconvenience, and therefore unimportant. In character he was unchanged. He lost none of his lively interest in the world about him, none of his warmth in human contacts, his fondness for conversation, his whimsical humor. But above all his other interests, what he liked best to talk about, then as always, was the study of language. Though he could no longer pursue it himself, he followed eagerly the work of his younger colleagues; and when they brought their problems to him, his criticism was no less trenchant, his advice no less clear-sighted than in the days of his own full vigor.

Leonard Bloomfield was unfailingly generous, a devoted worker in the cause of truth, an unrelenting fighter against reaction and stupidity. Above all, he was humane. We shall remember him with admiration for his greatness as a man of science, with love for his greatness as a human being.

## (2) Additional Facts and Anecdotes (CFH)

Here I supplement Bloch's obituary notice with all the information I have been able to collect. Some of it may be trivial, but I prefer to leave the judgment of that to the reader.

(a) (Information about high school and undergraduate days was made available, not merely kindly but with some enthusiasm, by Mr. Robert Shenton, Registrar of Harvard University, as soon as the cotrustee of the Bloomfield Estate, the Northern Trust Company of Chicago, gave the permission that is required by long-standing policy of the Harvard Faculty.)

Bloomfield's transcript from the Robert A. Waller High School of Chicago shows his home address of record as Hotel Schwarz, Elkhart Lake, Wisconsin. The transcript shows courses in English, Greek (elementary and advanced), Latin (ditto), German (ditto), French (ditto), History, Algebra, Geometry, Physics, and Chemistry. The grades show an average between B and C, with A's in German but D's in advanced French and in Physics. Grading must have been stiffer than it is now, since Harvard College viewed the record as acceptable. In fact, he was granted 'eight points' for 'extra studies' upon admission.

Moreover, upon entrance to Harvard College, examinations enabled him to start with what we would now call 'advanced placement' in Greek and Latin. His Harvard transcript shows: English Composition, two years; English Literature, two years (including Shakespeare, Chaucer, Beowulf); Greek, two years; Latin, three years; Mathematics, one year (trigonometry and plane analytic geometry); Zoology, one year; French, one year; Philosophy, one year (outline of the history of philosophy); German, two years. The grades are much better: nothing below a B, and mostly A's.

In 1904 he won a Detur prize, and chose to receive a copy of Furneaux's edition of the Annals of Tacitus (Clarendon Press).

It was in English A, during his first year, that his instructor was Charles Townsend Copeland (see Bloch's obituary notice). His course in Shakespeare was under Professor Kittredge, and the course in Beowulf may have been. Some of the Greek may have been under Professor Herbert Weir Smyth. In German, the professors were Francke and Walz, with assistants.

I have the binder of a notebook Bloomfield used at Harvard (it came to me enclosing sheets of notes on Menomini, all from a far later date), in which he inscribed his name followed by 'Harvard College, '07, 3 Foxcroft House'; the address is lined out and replaced (?) by '25 Hollis'.

But, with his head start, he had completed all the requirements by June, 1906. He was awarded the A. B. 'Magna cum Laude on February 27, 1907 as of the Class of 1906'; according to Mr. Shenton, the delay was entirely for financial reasons.

(b) (For the period at the University of Wisconsin, 1906–1908, I am indebted to Martin Joos, who consulted the files of the Department of German and also the University's Archives.)

Bloomfield was a teaching assistant. Joos writes that 'in each of his four semesters' he 'taught two sections of 2nd-year German, each 4 hours a week, section sizes running from 31 to 20; . . . In those days seemingly nearly every Wisconsin High School required German, 2 or more years, of all its pupils, and the University's College of Engineering assumed that its Freshmen had had those 2 years and proceeded to require two more college semesters of German of them, so that the German Department provided 3 sections for Freshman Engineers where they were segregated for 2nd-year German; LB did not teach any of those!'

The staff of the Department of German included: A. R. Hohlfeld, chairman; M. B. Evans, an assistant professor; Edwin C. Roedder, professor; C. M. Purin, a senior (undergraduate) assistant in 1906–1907; Eduard Prokosch, instructor; Bayard Quincy Morgan from 1907 on as instructor; Ernst Voss, professor; and a few others. Of these, Evans, Roedder, Prokosch, Purin, and Morgan were deeply concerned with pedagogy; Prokosch and Roedder also with linguistics. (For Roedder, see B48 fn. 2. For Prokosch, see Bloch's obituary notice, B4, and B49. For Evans, see the data on the Ohio State years, below.)

Bloomfield took ten one-semester courses in German and Germanic. The photographic copy of the original record is faded and cannot all be read, but the instructors for these courses included Hohlfeld, Voss, Prokosch, and Roedder. Two of the courses, clearly identifiable, were Prokosch's General Phonetics and his Gothic Grammar. Bloomfield also took Old Bulgarian, Lithuanian, and two semesters of Russian under Prokosch, and, from Professor A. F. Laird of the Department of Classics, a semester course in Latin Grammar, a semester course in Latin Syntax, and two years of Sanskrit.

Bloomfield was not a degree candidate at Wisconsin. At the end of 1907–1908, says Joos, 'he found that he had exhausted the whole University Catalog offerings in Indo-European studies: as good a reason as any for leaving.'

(c) (For 1908–1909, Miss Eileen Dockman, secretary to Professor Eric Hamp, kindly procured a copy of Bloomfield's transcript and arranged for me to consult the appropriate issue of the University of Chicago's *Annual Record*.)

Bloomfield attended the University of Chicago for four quarters, beginning with the summer quarter of 1908. Again he was a graduate assistant, doubtless teaching sections of elementary or intermediate German.

The Head of the Department of Germanic Languages and Literatures was S. W. Cutting. Francis Asbury Wood was Associate Professor of Germanic Philology; other members of the department were P. S. Allen, M. Schütze, A. C. von Noe, and C. Goettsch. Carl Darling Buck was Professor and Head of the Department of Sanskrit and Indo-European Comparative Philology.

In the summer of 1908 Bloomfield took Gothic, Old High German, and History of German Literature to 1700; Wood normally gave the first two of these, and Allen the third, but it is not clear that they were the ones teaching these courses in the summer quarter. Then he took Early New High German, Old Saxon, Middle Low German, and Old Frisian with Wood; Avestan and Old Persian (one course) and Problems in Indo-European Phonology and Morphology with Buck; and The German Romantic School with Schütze. For the spring quarter of 1909 he was registered for two of Buck's courses (Introduction to Indo-European Philology, and Greek Dialects), but the transcript shows no grades.

The French and German examinations were passed 10 October 1908. A few days later he was formally admitted to candidacy for the Ph. D. in Germanic Philology and in Comparative Indo-European Philology. The final examination for the Ph. D. was passed 15 March 1909, 'grade recommended—Magna cum Laude' (by S. W. Cutting). The degree was conferred 15 June 1909. The winter quarter record shows some incompletes, and the spring quarter does not show anything completed; presumably this reflects Bloomfield's period of concentration on his dissertation.

His marriage to Alice Sayers of St. Louis took place three days after his final examination for the doctorate; thus on 18 March 1909. The Bloomfields had no children of their own, but in time adopted two boys.

From the time of his marriage on, there are some indications of a family income independent of his relatively meager salary and royalties.

(d) In 1909–1910, at the University of Cincinnati, Bloomfield's colleagues (or superiors) in the Department of German included Max Poll and Claude M. Lotspeich. J. M. Burnham and George H. Allen were in Latin, and Joseph Edward Harry, a Professor of Greek, was Head of the Graduate School (all the preceding is from *Minerva*; I have found no other source). One published paper is marked as having been submitted from the University of Cincinnati: 'The *E*-Sounds in the Language of Hans Sachs', *Modern Philology* 9.489–509 (1912) is dated Cincinnati, Ohio, 30 December 1909.

(e) (Again largely from *Minerva*:) When Bloomfield went to the University of Illinois in 1910, the staff included: in German, Julius Goebel, Otto E. Lessing, George Henry Meyer, and Neil Connell Brooks; in Romance, Thomas E. Olivier and David H. Carnahan; in Greek, Charles Melville Moss; in Latin, Herbert Jewett Barton; in Scandinavian, George T. Flom; in Classical Philology, William A. Oldfather.

Bloomfield joined the American Philological Association in 1914, and attended the Annual Meetings in December 1914 and December 1916 (the former in Haverford, Pennsylvania, the latter in St. Louis, Missouri), delivering the two papers reprinted here as B8 and B9. There is no clear indication that he ever again attended any of the meetings of the APA, except in later years when it sometimes held a joint session with the Linguistic Society; but never after 1916 does he appear on the program in the printed *Transactions*.

It is hard for us today to realize how strong and deep was the tradition of German scholarship in American universities before the first World War, and how enormous a blow that tradition received at the time of the War. Of the situation at the University of Illinois I have no details, but see fn 3 of Hall's obituary notice (below); I suspect that there was a sharp diminution in the number of students in German courses, and that that may have been partly responsible in freeing Bloomfield's time for such enterprises as the Tagalog. Also, he received at Illinois no promotion subsequent to the 1913 move from Instructor in German to Assistant Professor of Comparative Philology and German. We know (see B49) that Prokosch lost his position at the University of Texas during the War. At the University of Wisconsin, at least one of the members of the Department of German quit his academic career and went into his family's business (a brewery); another left off teaching and became a dean; M. B. Evans's departure for Ohio State University in 1917 may well have been related.

(f) The last point is important, because Evans's presence as chairman of the Department of German at Ohio State must have played a part in Bloomfield's being invited there in 1921. He accepted, going to Columbus either just before or just after his second summer of field work with the Menomini. We know of no extended interruption of his stay in Columbus other than the five weeks spent in the summer of 1925 with the Cree of the Sweet Grass Reserve, Saskatchewan. For part, at least, of the Ohio State period, his address was 2061 Fairfax Road, Upper Arlington—at the time an upper middle-class or lower upper-class residential area, close to but not within walking distance of the campus. Apart from Evans, the most important people on the staff at Ohio State—ultimately more important to Bloomfield than was Evans—were George M. Bolling of Classics (Greek) and Albert P. Weiss of Psychology.

The *First German Book* that Bloomfield published in 1923 was probably largely worked out while he was still at Illinois; at least, certain remarks in his preface suggest this. The book was printed and distributed by R. G. Adams and Company, to be identified (except in a strict legal sense) with Long's Bookstore, located across North High Street from the main entrance to the Ohio State University campus. But it was copyrighted by Bloomfield. Five years later, after Bloomfield's move to Chicago, the book was reissued (with at most very minor changes) by The Century Company, New York and London, who copyrighted the new form. In his preface, Bloomfield speaks especially of Prokosch's *Introduction to German* (1911; see B4) as a source of inspiration. In turn, according to Martin Joos, the later elementary German texts of Prokosch and (B. Q.)

Morgan and of (M. B.) Evans and Röseler stemmed in part from Bloomfield's, with modifications in treatment in terms of the current market demands. I do not know how extensively Bloomfield's book was used. It was, as might be expected, beautifully organized from the learner's point of view, but contained some unorthodoxly simple treatments that probably disturbed the teachers who considered it for possible adoption. William G. Moulton knew it well and acknowledged its guidance in the text *Spoken German, Basic Course* (Henry Holt and Co.) that he and his wife prepared during the second World War.

Early in the Ohio State years, Bloomfield devised the nonsense syllables that E. A. Esper needed for the experiment later reported in the first of the *Monograph* series of the Linguistic Society (*A Technique for the Experimental Investigation of Associative Interference in Artificial Linguistic Material*, 1925). Recently, at my request, Professor Esper wrote to me recounting what he can recall of the events and atmosphere of the period, and with his kind permission I quote verbatim (and almost in full):

> I knew him [Bloomfield] through my teachers, Bolling and Weiss. I became Bolling's pupil in my sophomore year, 1914. There were not many true scholars at Ohio State at that time, and Bolling became my model, and I suspect still is. After we had got through the *Anabasis* and several of Plato's dialogues, the other members of the class disappeared, and for a number of years I was his only advanced pupil, sitting at his desk translating all of Homer, Euripides, etc. with no other interruption than Bolling's 'V-v-very good, go on.' After my graduation I became his assistant, and was allowed to teach the *Anabasis* and the *Apology*; my modelling had been so complete that in teaching I found it necessary to stutter. Bolling saw Thumb's article about association as related to *Analogiebildung*, in the *Indogermanische Forschungen*, and suggested that I take a course in experimental psychology. Thus I came under the influence of Weiss. As I indicated in the Preface to my *A History of Psychology*, both Bolling and Weiss were remarkable—especially in that environment—for their serious attitude toward scholarship, in the professional spirit of German scholarship. But both were also delightful persons. I wanted to continue in Greek, but Bolling was a one-man department, and thought I should go to Princeton for my doctorate. Dean West came to the campus and Bolling arranged a meeting; West said he would adopt me as a son, etc. but when he found out that I had married, the bottom fell out; I was disqualified for West's graduate hall, for which, as at Oxford, celibacy was requisite. Bolling was becoming very despondent about the future of classical studies (Bernard Bloch told me that Bloomfield was also pessimistic about linguistics; I had a letter from Bloomfield in about 1935 in which he said, sadly, 'things move so slowly'). So on his advice I took my Ph. D. in psychology, although I spent my last year taking examinations in Greek. My first 'publication' was a column of numbers in an article by Bolling; I had counted the abstract nouns in . . . in the 'older strata' of the Iliad vs. the Odyssey and thus supplied ammunition for Bolling's war against the Unitarians. Then my master's thesis was a replication of Thumb and Marbe's *Experimentelle Untersuchungen über die psychologischen Grundlagen der*

*sprachlichen Analogiebildung*; my thesis was published in the *Psychological Review* 1918, 468–487, after Miller had turned it down for the *American Journal of Philology*. (I think that the hostility between Bolling and Miller was one of the reasons for the founding of *Language*.) My doctoral thesis followed a suggestion of Thumb's; Bolling, Bloomfield, and Weiss took an interest in this and helped me with suggestions.

All this was by way of a perhaps irrelevantly reminiscent explanation of how I came to see and hear a good deal of Bloomfield, although I was never his pupil. I might have become such if I had had more sense and had been less preoccupied with my work with Bolling and Weiss; Bloomfield invited me to his house and showed me his numerous files of Menominee material; the effect on me should have been like that of Prokosch on Bloomfield, but Bloomfield was so modest and therefore tentative in his manner, and I was so overawed by this brilliant scholar that the occasion was rather aborted; when we had lunch together on his patio, his asking me my opinions on some linguistic matters (and he was particularly concerned at the time about function words) increased my shyness and awkwardness. I have always regretted that episode; I think that Bloomfield's aversion to imposing himself on others could make him seem formidable, because of the contrast between his modesty and his obvious status as a scholar. My wife and I had dinner several times at the Bloomfields' and often met Mrs. Bloomfield, who decidedly was part of the picture; she was enormously protective of Bloomfield and resentful of any possible slight, however unintended or non-existent; . . . .

I should mention that in the psychology department shop we had a sawbuck table at which our staff, together with friends from other departments, had a sort of smörgåsbord lunch every day. Bolling and Bloomfield were members of this group. I am sure that it was Bolling who was responsible for bringing Bloomfield to Ohio State from Illinois; I heard him say one day—I think probably to Evans, head of the German department—'Oldfather should be ashamed of himself!' I took this at the time to mean that he blamed Oldfather, professor of classics at Illinois and a power in the faculty, for Bloomfield's lack of promotion (he was an assistant prof. there and came to Ohio State as a professor). I think Bloomfield taught mostly German, including elementary German, at Ohio State; I doubt whether he had any advanced pupils who became linguists, although I haven't checked on that. At any rate, I don't think that either Bolling or Bloomfield were optimistic about the future of linguistics at Ohio State, and that was probably why he was ready to go to Chicago.

I think that Bloch was quite right about Prokosch having been Bloomfield's chief inspiration. At Chicago, he said, 'they were always wanting me to count something', and when he listened to Wood's lectures at the first hour after lunch, the writing with which Wood covered the board 'seemed first to turn red, then green, then blue . . .'

At that sawbuck table, much of the planning for the first issues of *Language* took place. It was there that I heard Bolling say something that has cheered me through the years: 'We can surely get a paper from [Maurice] Bloomfield; that old man must have many things in his drawers!'

Bloomfield and Weiss were intimate friends; they were similar in their simplicity, humor, and general attitude. They and their wives often went on picnics together; Mrs. Weiss was a very gracious and unassuming person in whose company Mrs. Bloomfield had no need for belligerency; the same, for that matter could be said of Weiss. Beginning in 1920 Weiss was an invalid, with heart trouble, so that the Bloomfields were frequent visitors at his home, where much of his work, including seminars, was done. Mrs. Weiss, in a letter, said that 'it is a pity that a record could not have been made of their discussions.' She said too that, 'About 1928 Albert and I spent the winter quarter in Washington, D. C., and that year Dr. Bloomfield was East and spent a day or so with Albert. They were so busy talking that I even ordered their meals at the restaurant.' I remember an occasion when Bloomfield and I were looking at a photograph of Max Meyer and Weiss; Bloomfield said, 'There are perhaps two of the most important men of their time.'

I think that the influence was just the opposite of what Fries claimed it to be in his paper on 'The Bloomfield School' [C. Mohrmann, A. Sommerfelt, and J. Whatmough, *Trends in European and American Linguistics 1930–1960*, Utrecht (1961), pp. 196–224]. . . . Also, I think that Bloomfield was wrong when he spoke of Weiss's 'great advance' over Meyer. I think that Weiss mostly amplified what he got from Meyer, and that so far as their writings go, Bloomfield's influence on Weiss was mostly limited to one paragraph in Weiss's two-page discussion of 'meaning' [*Theoretical Basis*[2] pp. 325–6]. Bloomfield, on the other hand, was strongly influenced by Weiss, because Bloomfield found Weiss's system such a welcome and sensible substitute for Wundt. But, of course, in a more general way, the association with Bloomfield was very stimulating for Weiss.

Esper's last paragraph is in reply to a specific question of mine, for I had always wondered whether Bloomfield's insistence that he learned from Weiss, rather than the other way around, was not simply another manifestation of his modesty. In addition to the specific point Esper makes about the handling of 'meaning', it is clear that Weiss was much taken by Bloomfield's view of mathematics as a specialization from language; see our quote from Weiss at the beginning of B47. In the main, however, Esper's testimony agrees with Bloomfield's own, and the issue must be viewed as settled.

(g) In 1927, Francis A. Wood retired, leaving vacant the Professorship of Germanic Philology at the University of Chicago; in the ensuing game of academic musical chairs, Bloomfield went to Chicago as his former teacher's successor, and Hans Kurath went from Northwestern to Ohio State as Bloomfield's.

Still at Chicago, from Bloomfield's student days, were Schütze, Allen, and Buck. In German there was now Archer Tayler, and, in anthropology, Edward Sapir, who had come in 1925 and was to leave for Yale in 1931. Walter Petersen had joined Buck. A number of brilliant students clustered around Sapir; most of them went on to Yale with Sapir, but Harry Hoijer stayed on, leaving only when Bloomfield left.

Charles F. Voegelin has told me of the relation between Bloomfield and Sapir as he observed it in the 1930's. Each had deep respect for the other, but with certain reservations. Sapir admired Bloomfield's ability patiently to excerpt data and to file and collate slips until the patterns of the language emerged, but spoke deprecatingly of Bloomfield's sophomoric psychology. Bloomfield was dazzled by Sapir's virtuosity and perhaps a bit jealous of it, but in matters outside language referred to Sapir as a 'medicine man'. One may profitably compare Sapir's 'The State of Linguistics as a Science', *Language* 5.207–214 (1929), a paper that had been read in December 1928 to a joint session of the Linguistic Society, the American Anthropological Association, and Sections H and L of the American Association for the Advancement of Science, in New York, with Bloomfield's 'Linguistics as a Science', delivered a year later (our B36).

At Chicago, if not before, Bloomfield had a chance to teach some linguistics, and perhaps no longer had to continue as a German language instructor. Most of the linguistics courses were surely on specific older Germanic languages. For instance, in the winter quarter of 1940 I took Old Icelandic from him. We read from Gordon's *Introduction to Old Norse* and were referred to Heusler; in lecture sessions, Bloomfield dictated a succinct but nearly complete descriptive and historical phonology and morphology; I do not remember whether the notes he drew on for this were old and yellowed, but it was obvious that he had given the same course many times earlier. He commented in passing on the extreme cruelty that had accompanied much of the spread of Christianity through Europe; and he tried to impress on us the importance of the surviving Old Icelandic literature as virtually the only extant European literature whose style had not been thoroughly reworked by the impact of Latin.

For a number of the later Chicago years (I do not know how early it began), the Bloomfields lived on the second floor of a converted coachhouse at 1030 E 49th Street; Swadesh, Voegelin, and I—doubtless also many others—visited them there.

(h) Bloomfield attended the First Annual Meeting of the Linguistic Society of America (New York, 1924: the organization meeting); the Second (Chicago, 1925), delivering his 'Set of Postulates' (B21); the Third (Cambridge, 1926), giving no paper; the Fourth (Cincinnati and Nashville, 1927), delivering in Cincinnati a paper 'The Pathology of Words,' never published, and in Nashville a paper 'A Reconstruction Confirmed' (Probably B33). He attended the Conference on a Linguistic Atlas held in New Haven, 2–3 August 1929. He was present at the Sixth Annual Meeting (Cleveland, 1929), delivering 'Linguistics as a Science' (B36). Then there was a hiatus. He attended the Twelfth Annual Meeting (New York, 1935), as president, delivering his Presidential Address 'Language or Ideas?' (B45); the Thirteenth (Chicago, 1936), with the never-published paper 'Infinite Classes'; the Fourteenth (Philadelphia, 1937), with 'Science Among the Humanities' (never published), delivered to a joint session with the Modern Language Association.

At the Linguistic Institute at the University of Michigan, summer 1938, summer meetings of the Linguistic Society were begun. At the first (Ann Arbor, 1938), Bloomfield presented 'Initial [k-] in German' (B48); at the second (Ann Arbor, 1939), 'Algonquian Word Formation' (never published separately, but doubtless incorporated into B64); at the third (Ann Arbor, 1940), 'The Phrase' (never published). He was on the staff of the Linguistic Institute all three of these summers. In 1938 he stayed in Ann Arbor, giving the introductory course (attended by virtually all the staff as well as by students), and working with an Ojibwa informant. In 1939 and 1940 he commuted from Chicago for one or two days a week. In 1939 he gave a series of lectures on Comparative Algonquian.

At some point during the 'Ann Arbor years', Bloomfield gave a talk treating of Central Algonquian tentatively in terms of Johannes Schmidt's wave hypothesis; this was never published. Several times during these years, I heard him repeat a one-hour talk (to varying audiences) into which he tried, with remarkable success, to pack everything 'of a general nature that we really know about language'.

(i) Here are anecdotes from the later 1930's and early 1940's, mainly from my own memory. The wording is not guaranteed to be verbatim in all cases.

J. M. Cowan has reminded me (I had forgotten it) that in the summer of 1938 or 1939, at Ann Arbor, during a public discussion, I said 'The trouble with you, Mr. Bloomfield, is that you don't believe in the phonemic principle'! This must have been virtually our first meeting; I tell the story, with some chagrin, only because his action in rising above the remark was so indicative of his stature.

Bloomfield: 'Can you read a grammar? I can't; I have to excerpt everything [and put it on slips filed in shoeboxes] or I don't learn anything about the language.'

Bloomfield: 'When I begin work on a language [in the field] I don't get anything down right on paper for the first month.'

I wrote a paper on Latin verb inflection, using various newfangled morphophonemic devices to try to make things seemingly more regular. Bloomfield's written comment at the top of the second page: 'This will get too complicated.' (Compare B64.) On an undergraduate student's term paper at Yale, later on (according to William J. Gedney's report), his sole inscription was 'You get things mixed up.'

In the winter of 1940, after Walter Petersen's death, his professional library was sold off; I bought two things by Meillet from it, one of them the *Altarmenisches Elementarbuch*. When I told Bloomfield of this, he said 'Don't spread yourself too thin.'

In the same vein, though not at the same time, he said, 'A linguist shouldn't marry. He should spend long summers in the field, and the rest of the year working up his data. That way, one could perhaps produce adequate descriptions of three languages in a lifetime.'

Bloomfield, Hoijer, and Hockett lunching together in Chicago. Hockett proposed that when it is impossible to hear word-boundary there is no justification for representing it by a space (or otherwise) in a phonemic transcription. Hoijer, with Bloomfield's obvious approval, says that that is just where the space is most needed. Subject changed.

Hockett touches on 'mental illness'. Bloomfield: 'No; there has to be something wrong chemically with the brain.'

Hockett boasting about the recent advances in linguistics. Bloomfield: 'I don't think we've learned anything of a fundamental sort that Leskien didn't know thirty years ago.'

Hockett asks if Bloomfield thinks psychology has made some progress beyond Weiss. Bloomfield says no: 'Weiss was way ahead of his time. Psychologists in general might catch up with him by about 1980.'

Bloomfield's characterization of American commercial white bread: Cotton batting wrapped in artificial leather and flavored with arsenic.

Bloomfield would not drink; he excused himself by saying 'My doctors won't let me.' If I remember correctly, he had or claimed to have gout. I do remember wondering if his delicate stomach was the result of the poor food he ate while living with the Menomini Indians in 1920 and 1921. But this may all be beside the point: Bloomfield's sense of humor at the time was usually too subtle for my immature wit to catch.

Bloomfield's fondly planned but (apparently) never executed practical jokes: (i) To dress in workman's clothing, board a Chicago streetcar, and put a nickel in the box (the fare was a dime at the time); then to respond to all the conductor's indignant protests with a continual broad smile, repeated indication that he had paid the fare, and a feigned inability to speak or understand any English. (ii) To write a letter to the Registrar or Bursar of the University, in an 'obviously Slavic' but actually faked language, clearly having to do with large sums of money that the University might get under undecipherable conditions.

In somewhat the vein of the latter, a few years later (I think at Yale), Bloomfield and I discussed the possibility of speaking in a sort of generalized Germanic, intelligible and yet not clearly identifiable as belonging to any of the attested branches. A day or so later he observed that this would not be possible unless one avoided all negative statements, since one's choice of a negative element would give the fake away as either North Germanic or West Germanic.

Bloomfield was not raised in any religious tradition, but his sense of morality, especially for his own comportment, was thoroughly Victorian. We were at lunch together at a South Shore Hotel (with Bloomfield as host). He pointed across the room discreetly and said 'That's Thomas Mann and his new wife. He's ninety years old and she's sixteen.'

William J. Gedney was at the University of Chicago for several summers before Bloomfield left for Yale, and reports Bloomfield saying on one occasion 'If you want to compare two languages, it helps to know one of them'.

(j) Bloomfield's call to Yale, in 1940, as successor to Prokosch (died 1938) and informally also as a successor to Sapir (died 1939), came during the Hutchins and Adler period at the University of Chicago. He asked me (!) if he should go, saying that Mrs. Bloomfield was happy in Chicago. I am sure that my affirmative answer had very little to do with his decision. The authorities at the University of Chicago made no effort whatsoever to keep him, despite strenuous efforts by H. Keniston.

At Yale, Bloomfield joined Sturtevant, Edgerton, and Goetze, Kennedy in Chinese, and, before long at least, a veritable host of bright young men, among them Cornyn, Dyen, Gedney, McDavid, Moulton, Trager, Wells. Bloch came from Brown in 1943, bringing with him the editorial office of the Linguistic Society.

From some of these younger men I have heard of a 'game' that Bloomfield often played with one or another of them, particularly to kill time during train rides, in the early 1940's. Bloomfield would be an informant, and the others would try to elicit and transcribe data. The elicitation was enormously slow: before he would tell how to say 'Good morning!' he would have to know whether it was a man or a woman speaking, to an addressee older or younger than the speaker, on the north or the south side of the street, and so on endlessly. In the course of an hour or so ten or twelve forms would be elicited. Forms with similar meanings would show the weirdest possible differences in shape. But no matter how many repetitions were called for, and no matter with what delay, there was complete consistency as to both sound and meaning.

With some people, Bloomfield developed a genuine joking-relationship. For example, the correspondence between him and J. M. Cowan, during the early War years when Cowan was working out of the American Council of Learned Societies in Washington, is full of fake insults, grossly amusing, and very largely unprintable.

In my case, however, the disparity of age was too great; any efforts on his part to establish such a relationship gave rise only to puzzlement. I corresponded with him during these years, first from Ann Arbor and then, after February 1942, from wherever the Army sent me; between 1942 and 1946 I was occasionally able to visit him at Yale. I was having all sorts of troubles, personal and professional, and wanted to use him as a sort of Father Confessor. He would have none of it. A single episode must serve to illustrate this; it is notable, I think, for the extremely simple way in which he phrased what he had to say. I told him, at Yale, first of the various cruel things others were doing to me, and then of what I was tempted to do by way of retaliation. He ignored the first altogether, and said 'Oh, you mustn't ever do that kind of thing. It just makes everybody unhappy.' At the time I was hurt; it took me many years to realize what a deep compliment he was paying me in thus focussing only on my own behavior, regarding all the rest as really irrelevant for a scholar.

The intent of the senior linguists at Yale in inviting Bloomfield had been clear: he was there to find a haven, surrounded by congenial colleagues, free from unpleasant duties, so that he could flourish as never before. One of the promises made him during the preliminary negotiations was that he would have time to work on his Menomini materials and that the result would be published in the William Dwight Whitney Linguistic Series of Yale University (as, indeed, it ultimately was). But two things interfered with these good intentions and high hopes. The first was Mrs. Bloomfield's recurring ill health. The Bloomfields never really got settled in Yale; for some years their address was the Taft Hotel, where they had a suite. The other was the entry of the United States into the second World War, which, in peculiar contrast to the impact of the first, turned all the linguistic talent in the country feverishly to work at practical language-analysis and language-teaching tasks. For the details of Bloomfield's part in this, see Bloch's obituary notice.

Bloomfield was on the staff of the Linguistic Institute at Chapel Hill in 1941, and at the Fourth Summer Meeting of the Linguistic Society, held in conjunction with the Institute, delivered 'Linguistic Aspects of Philosophy' (presumably B57). This was his last participation in either a linguistic institute or a meeting of the Linguistic Society of America.


(3) Edgar H. Sturtevant (Yale University), *The American Philosophical Society Yearbook 1949* (Philadelphia, 1950), pp 302–5.


When it became necessary to choose a successor to Eduard Prokosch as Sterling Professor of Germanic Languages at Yale, a committee of the faculties was appointed to consider the matter. Professor Karl Young of the Department of English was a member of the committee, and, when Leonard Bloomfield's name was suggested, he asked where he could get evidence about his qualifications. He was advised to read Bloomfield's most important book.[1] When Young had finished this volume, which many professional linguists have found slow and difficult reading, he gave

---

[1] *Language*, N.Y., Holt, 1933.

its author the highest praise he knew: 'The man is a poet.' The work of the committee might have ended right then, if there had not been grave doubt whether the officials of the university where Bloomfield was then situated would be so blind as to let him go.

It is too late to ask Young what he meant by *poet* in this connection. I imagine he referred to the marvelous clarity and incisiveness of Bloomfield's exposition, combined as it is with imaginative figures of speech that further illustrate his point of view. He was a poet in the same sense that Plato has been called a poet. Perhaps we may illustrate with the final paragraph of a review he published in *Language* 19: 168–170, 1943. In spite of much hearty praise, he blames the author for a few lapses 'into traditional philosophic jargon.' Then this:

> These 'philosophic' passages stand out darkly against the rational and humane illumination that pervades the treatise. They could serve as an instance of vestigial traits in culture: shreds of medieval speculation still hanging to the propellers of science and sometimes fouling them. The lesson of this contrast is brought home to the reader because the rest of the book speaks clearly with the voice of enlightenment. Philosophic and political meditations have no place in a scientific manual.

Unhappily such poetic passages as this can easily be warped into the most grotesque nonsense with the help of a little ill-will. Leo Spitzer has done just this in *Modern Language Quarterly* 4: 430, fn. 29, 1943.

The fact that Leonard Bloomfield was justly called a poet is of considerable interest, since he, as other linguists, has been widely held to be hostile to literature. This was a grave error; he was hostile only to those who objected to the findings of linguistic science; and some of these urged the claims of philosophy, poetry, or other kinds of literature, either as substitutes for linguistic studies, or as refutations of linguistic doctrine.

Bloomfield was rather widely known in his later years as an adherent of the American school of psychologists called Behaviorists. Certain it is that between the publication of *An Introduction to the Study of Language* in 1914 and the composition of *Language*, which was published in 1933, his views on psychology had undergone a profound change. The earlier book was frankly based upon the mentalistic psychology of Wilhelm Wundt, while the later adopts the behaviorist point of view as presented by Albert Paul Weiss.[2] It is significant that the two men were colleagues at Ohio State University from 1921 to 1927. It is important to note that Bloomfield has far less to say about psychology in the second book than in the first; he does not any longer base his treatment of language upon psychology of any particular school. One may even suspect that if he had

---

[2] Weiss, A. P., *A theoretical basis of human behavior*, 2nd ed., Columbus, Ohio, R. G. Adams, 1929.

treated the material a third time he might have declared the logical dependence of psychology upon linguistics.

His connection with this psychological school, at any rate, was scarcely more significant than his earlier dependence upon Wilhelm Wundt; both phases sprang from the obvious relationship of language with human psychology and Bloomfield's determination not to write about anything without mastering it to the best of his ability. In this case, however, he has acquired a position in the age-long conflict between the Church and Science. In at least one of the schools maintained by the Roman Catholic Church in the United States, the use of Bloomfield's *Language* as a textbook has, I am told, been forbidden, and the teacher in charge of the course has fallen back upon a much inferior book[3] of which Bloomfield disapproved as a work for the general reader.

. . .

The really important thing that one must say about Leonard Bloomfield is that during his later years he was the leader of American linguists. He never claimed such a position, and never even tried to attain it. He always, on principle, advised inquiring students to specialize in other subjects than linguistics, on the ground that paying positions in the latter field were very few. His classes were usually small, and he trained scarcely any candidates for the degree of Doctor of Philosophy.

As far as I know he had but one major triumph as a teacher. In the summer of 1938 his Introduction to Linguistic Science at the Linguistic Institute in Ann Arbor was attended throughout the eight-week session by nearly the entire membership of the Institute. We had always had introductory courses; in the early sessions of the Institute they were conducted by Professor Prokosch, and they were always relatively popular. In the summer of 1937 the introduction was given by Professor Edward Sapir before a regularly enrolled class of about thirty, including at least one member of the staff. This course of Sapir's was so remarkably effective that the director moved the next year's introduction to an evening hour, so that it could be more largely attended. But it was Bloomfield's handling of the course that made it the extraordinary success it was.

In general, however, he lectured to small classes; his great influence was largely exerted through his books and articles, although one must not forget his numerous conferences with individuals who sought him out. At any rate many descriptive linguists who got their training from Boas or Sapir have stoutly maintained that they learned their method from Bloomfield. In an important preface he is called the 'dean of American linguists.' When this was brought to his attention he said, 'So I'm a dean now!' (All college administrators were for Bloomfield a race apart.)

[3] Gray, Louis H., *Foundations of Language*, N.Y., Macmillan, 1939. Reviewed by L. Bloomfield, *Mod. Lang. Forum* 24:198 f., 1939 [B52].

Leonard Bloomfield died on April 18, 1949, at the age of sixty-two, after an illness of three years, during which time he had not been able to do any work. He left behind him in manuscript, a Menomini grammar, which is thought to be the most complete account of an Indian language ever written.

Much less ambitious but amply tested in the class rooms of a parochial school in Chicago is the manuscript of a textbook for teaching children to read English. By merely concentrating upon such groups as (*cat, hat, bat, sat*; *pad, had, bad, sad*; *can, man, ran, pan*) before any other value of the letter *a* is touched upon, then concentrating upon other values of single letters, he largely eliminates the handicap of the irregular spelling of English; he teaches children to read English almost as rapidly as Spanish or Finnish children are taught to read those languages. But educationists are convinced that all attention to specific letters delays children in learning to read rapidly; such a book as Bloomfield's is simply unorthodox; so far the educationists have prevented its publication.

Recently one of Bloomfield's colleagues procured a copy of the book and used it to teach his three-year-old daughter to read. Those who managed the child's other education advised that this should be stopped, for fear her other interests might be stunted, and that her eye-sight might suffer because by this amazingly efficient method she was learning to read so rapidly.

(4) Robert A. Hall, Jr. (Cornell University), *Lingua* 2.117–23 (1950).

[I delete one passage and some footnotes not needed in the context of this reprinting.—CFH]

Among modern American workers in linguistics, Leonard Bloomfield was one of those who were best known and who exercised the most influence on their contemporaries and on younger scholars. His book *Language* (1933) had given him literally world-wide fame; especially in the United States, it had served to train a whole generation of younger scholars, who followed its principles in their work and used Bloomfield as a point of departure for further advance. It was, therefore, a great loss to linguistics when Bloomfield was rendered intellectually inactive and incapable of further work by a severe stroke in May, 1946, followed by a long illness and finally by his death on April 18, 1949.

Bloomfield's academic career was that of a typical American professor.
. . .

But Bloomfield's intellectual life and scholarly production were more varied and ranged farther afield than those of most linguisticians. He did not merely choose a single field of endeavour and till it intensively;

he had several fields in which he had a specialist's knowledge, and also maintained from the outset of his career a deep interest in general linguistics. His initial field of specialization was Indo-European and Germanic philology, beginning with his Ph. D. thesis on *A semasiologic differentiation in Germanic secondary ablaut* (1909), and continuing throughout the rest of his life with a number of articles and reviews in the Germanic field; in addition, Bloomfield had a good knowledge of Greek, Slavic and Indic. From his thorough study of Panini, he derived an understanding—rare among Indo-Europeanists of his generation—of the nature of and need for synchronic analysis and description of linguistic structure. At the age of 27, Bloomfield published a book on general linguistics, *An introduction to the study of language* (1914), covering the whole field of language from the viewpoint of Wundt's *Völkerpsychologie*. This earlier work was replaced in 1933 by a new, completely rewritten book, *Language*, likewise covering the whole field, but abandoning Wundt's psychology for a behavioristic viewpoint, insisting on accurate description of linguistic events without adherence to any particular psychological theory.

After the publication of his *Introduction*, and while still at Illinois, Bloomfield began work with "unfamiliar" languages, applying the technique of recording texts from the lips of an informant and analyzing the material thus obtained; the first language he studied thus was Tagalog, treated in his *Tagalog texts with grammatical analysis* (1917). Thereafter, Bloomfield's main work of this type lay in the field of American Indian languages, primarily the Central Algonquian group (Cree, Menomini, Fox, Ojibwa). He recorded extensive texts in Menomini and in Cree, became a fluent speaker of Menomini and wrote an (as yet unpublished) descriptive grammar of that language, and initiated the comparative study of the Algonquian languages and the reconstruction of Proto-Central-Algonquian.

Nor was Bloomfield's activity limited to matters of theoretical linguistic analysis. He was keenly interested in the application of linguistics to practical matters, such as the teaching of reading and of foreign languages. For the initial stages of reading in the elementary grades—a subject which is, in general, badly mishandled in the English-speaking world and its schools—Bloomfield prepared an excellent text, which was tried with success in Chicago parochial schools in the early 1940's, but which has not yet found its way into print. His *First German book* (1923), a beginners' text, is one of the best works of its kind. When the Intensive Language Program of the American Council of Learned Societies got under way in 1942, as part of the nation's war effort, Bloomfield was one of its leading contributors, both in determining its theoretical bases and in writing texts for use in language teaching and learning: *Outline guide for the practical study of foreign languages* (1942); *Colloquial Dutch* (1944); *Spoken Dutch* (1944–5); *Spoken Russian* (1945; in collaboration with others).

Bloomfield's greatest contribution to linguistics as a science lay in the rigour of his method, which he applied to all aspects of the field. Before the appearance of Bloomfield's *Language*, linguistics was usually treated as an essentially humanistic discipline, often fruitful but not completely amenable to scientific method to procedure by postulates, hypotheses, and verification. The major advances of the nineteenth century in historical linguistics had, indeed, been made by virtue of scientific assumptions, but not explicitly stated, or else poorly stated, as in the famous *Junggrammatiker* slogan of "Ausnahmslosigkeit der Lautgesetze". Descriptive linguistics had, with few exceptions, remained on the level of our traditional West European normative grammar on the Graeco-Latin model; there had been scattered recognition of the need for improved methods of linguistic description (de Saussure, Boas, Sapir), but pre-Bloomfieldian efforts along this line had been relatively desultory and unsystematized. Bloomfield was the first to demonstrate the possibility and to exemplify the means of a unified scientific approach to all aspects of linguistic analysis: phonemic, morphological, syntactical; synchronic and diachronic. If a worker in linguistics, even in its more traditional branches (e.g. Romance, Indo-European), is today entitled to view himself as a social scientist, working in a branch of anthropology, and not (in Bloomfield's phrase) as a mere "crow-baited student of literature", this change in his status is largely due to Bloomfield's having placed the entire study of language on a truly scientific basis.

Of Bloomfield's *Language*, the first part is a manual for descriptive technique; the second, for historical study of language. The first part seemed more revolutionary (because it was more novel and unusual), aroused more discussion and controversy, served as a stimulus for more investigation and new formulation of discoveries, and in some respects seems more outdated today, than the second part. Those of us younger linguisticians who undertook descriptive work during the war years and after (whether in connection with the Intensive Language Program or not) found in the first part of Bloomfield's *Language* what we could find nowhere else—a reliable guide to synchronic analysis, which set us on the right track for further independent accomplishment. Naturally, work done in the fifteen years since 1933 has, in some respects, outdistanced or replaced Bloomfield's formulations in his *Language*. He rejoiced in this state of affairs, viewing science as a cooperative and cumulative effort; as he wrote in 1946[1]; "Nowadays the older worker in linguistics often learns from the younger, and has the supreme professional satisfaction of know-

---

[1] *Lang.* 22.3 (1946) [B67].

ext generation is going forward from the frontiers of what is
"

nd part of Bloomfield's *Language*, relatively conservative
seem in contrast with the first part, is nevertheless also a
capital importance. It is almost the only complete and well-
balanced discussion of historical linguistics available at the present time.
Bloomfield was one of the first to perceive that the phonemic principle
provided a firm scientific justification for the Neo-Grammarian hypothesis
of regular sound change, which he had tested and proved in a new field,
that of comparative Algonquian linguistics.[2] He therefore regarded current anti-Neo-Grammarian attitudes, such as the doctrines of Vosslerian
or Crocean "idealism", as anti-scientific and reactionary; in a number of
reviews in the journal *Language* and in Chapters 18 and 20 of his book
*Language*, he placed the principle of phonemic change on its proper basis
as a scientific hypothesis, and clarified its function as a productive assumption enabling us to classify and explain linguistic developments (as due to
sound-change, analogical replacement, or other types of borrowing).
Dialect geography received an understanding, sympathetic, but properly
proportioned explanation at Bloomfield's hands (in his Chapter 19), as a
branch of historical linguistics which serves to explain many divergent
and apparently "irregular" developments, but which is itself intelligible
only in the light of the assumption of regular sound-change. Here again,
recent studies which are altering somewhat the picture of historical linguistics that Bloomfield gives us (e.g. Haugen's work on Norwegian-
American and other cases of bilingualism and linguistic borrowing) use
Bloomfield as a point of departure, and build on his synthesis of preceding
accomplishments.

Bloomfield's work is still in the process of becoming known to the
general public, and of being discussed and often opposed, as it is gradually
assimilated into our corpus of general knowledge. To a certain extent,
some of its very virtues have stood in its way; this is especially true of two
aspects of his work: his simplicity of statement and style, and his scientific
principles. It has often been remarked that Bloomfield always said exactly
what he meant, no more and no less—a habit which has not made his
notions, especially in his book *Language*, easily accessible or interesting
to a reading public trained to expect verbosity and repetition. Not only
beginners, but even relatively advanced students have found *Language*
difficult going, because of Bloomfield's concise, closely-knit, unemotional,
quasi-mathematical reasoning and presentation, in which each sentence
must be thoroughly understood and remembered before proceeding to the

[2] Bloomfield's brief "Note on Sound Change", *Lang.* 5.99–100 (1928) [B33] has become
one of the best-known and most frequently cited items in the discussion of the Neo-Grammarian hypothesis. Cf. also C. F. Hockett, *Lang.* 24.125–7 (1948) [68].

next. Yet once the requisite effort has been made, and the reader has trained himself to follow Bloomfield, the resultant gain in economy and clarity is immense, and constitutes one of the major merits of Bloomfield's presentation, not dissimilar in ultimate effect—though of course conditioned by the exigencies of English prose—to the concision and precision which he so valued in Panini.

Likewise, Bloomfield's attitudes towards questions of psychology and the role of "mind" in language were so widely different from those which are normally held in our West European culture, that they have stood in the way of his being understood. Early in his career, he was a follower of Wundt, passing later to the "behaviorist" point of view best set forth by A. P. Weiss (*A Theoretical Basis of Human Behavior*). In *Language*, he argues strongly against the dualist, "mentalist" point of view which posits a special entity called "mind" or "spirit" to account for certain aspects of human life and actions; he often referred to his own attitude as "non-mentalist", in that he considered all phenomena of human behavior (including language) as explicable without the assumption of "mind". But this attitude—no different in its essentials from the "operationalist" philosophy underlying all scientific method[3]—clashes sharply with our traditional philosophical dualism, which is perhaps nowhere so deeply rooted and so endowed with social and intellectual prestige as in our ideas about language, both in academic teaching and in the folklore of our culture. Hence the naive reader, on first coming in contact with Bloomfield's uncompromisingly scientific attitude, is often shocked and repelled, and even with the best of will, finds considerable difficulty in adjusting to Bloomfield's frame of reference. In recent years, many critics of Bloomfield's ideas have assumed that he and other "non-mentalists" were deliberately neglecting a large segment of human behavior; the discussion has often been rendered needlessly acrimonious by ill will resulting from some critics' hostile emotional reactions and inability to separate scientific differences of opinion from attacks on the personal level.[4]

As a man, Bloomfield was wholly admirable: he was quiet, modest, kindly, friendly, and lovable. He was not aloof, but he was extremely shy in all contacts except those of family relationship or close personal acquaintance. He was always happier with humble, unassuming, ordinary folk than with the pompous "stuffed shirts" and "big shots" of academic life; the story is told (I do not know whether it is authentic or not) of his having once disappeared from a university President's reception, only to be found some time later engaged in quiet, friendly conversation with the janitor

---

[3] Cf. Charles F. Hockett, "Biophysics, Linguistics, and the Unity of Science", *American Scientist* 36. 558–72 (1948).

[4] Cf. the vicious and unprincipled attack on Bloomfield in *Encyclopaedia of Psychology* 838–70 (New York, 1946).

; room in the basement. He was reticent on matters involving
ition, and sometimes, to those who did not know him well,
s or unfeeling; yet he was in fact extremely sensitive, and
t his sympathy for what he considered misfortune or tragedy
_ his printed utterances.[5] In many respects, he stood apart
_.. our culture, observing it but not taking part in it; this was especially
true of his attitude towards traditionally venerated ideas and ideals in such
matters as religion and war.[6] This detachment gave Bloomfield an excellent vantage-point from which to analyze our society, particularly with
respect to language and our social attitudes towards language; at the same
time, however, it robbed him of the emotional participation which would
have given him a surer feeling for the blockings and hesitations which
stand in the way of the ordinary man's understanding of scientific linguistics.

Bloomfield had a keen sense of humor, quiet and often concealed, but
always present; it might perhaps best be defined as the humor of the quietly
outrageous. Once I heard him give, in a gathering of friends, a long haran-
gue on Yiddish—how it was nothing but a corruption of a vulgar Silesian
dialect, with only three hundred words, showing all the special tendencies
of the Jewish soul, utterly unanalyzable since it had no fixed sounds, etc.
etc.—which at the time surprised and shocked me, as it was so completely
in contradiction with his professed beliefs and scientific principles. It was
not until considerably later that I realized he had been indulging in his own
peculiar, dry humor, not devoid of a certain bitterness, and setting forth
this farrago of nonsense as a mockery of current "common-sense" and
folklore about language. This dry humor shows through on occasion even
in his serious writings, as when he remarks in *Language* (p. 149) a propos
of metaphor, that "*He married a lemon* forces us to the transferred meaning only because we know that men do not go through a marriage ceremony with a piece of fruit"! One particular form which his humor took
was the collecting of ignorant or stupid remarks about language (known
as *stankos* in the Bloomfield family dialect); this collection of "stankos"
served as the starting-point of one of his few polemic articles ("Secondary
and Tertiary Responses to Language", *Lang.* 20. 45–56 [1944]), which
exemplifies the bitter sarcasm of the scientist when badgered beyond en-
durance by misunderstanding and misrepresentation.

Like his great contemporary Edward Sapir, Bloomfield was cut off in
his prime, when he had already done great work but while there was still
promise of more to come. Those of us who follow in his footsteps must

---

[5] Cf. his moving words on the fate of the older Menomini culture, at . . . [B32].
[6] I have been told, by men who were colleagues of Bloomfield's at Illinois during the first
World War, of his detached attitude at that time of national crisis, and of the misunderstanding and difficulties that it engendered for him.

always regret, therefore, that we shall never have the fullest fruits of his mature genius—for instance, the completion of his work in Algonquian, or a revised edition of his *Language*. Nevertheless, his position in the history of our science is secure: by his original work in descriptive and historical linguistics, and by his codification and synthesis of our knowledge in the field as a whole, he undoubtedly made the greatest advance that linguistic science has yet seen in the twentieth century.